THE ROUTLE
HANDBOOK OF PHILOSOPHY
OF INFORMATION

Information and Communication Technology occupies a central place in the modern world, with society becoming increasingly dependent on it every day. It is therefore unsurprising that it has become a growing subject area in contemporary philosophy, which relies heavily on informational concepts. *The Routledge Handbook of Philosophy of Information* is an outstanding reference source to the key topics and debates in this exciting subject and is the first collection of its kind. Comprising over thirty chapters by a team of international contributors the Handbook is divided into four parts:

- Basic Ideas
- Quantitative and Formal Aspects
- Natural and Physical Aspects
- Human and Semantic Aspects

Within these sections central issues are examined, including probability, the logic of information, informational metaphysics, the philosophy of data and evidence, and the epistemic value of information.

The Routledge Handbook of Philosophy of Information is essential reading for students and researchers in philosophy, computer science and communication studies.

Luciano Floridi is Professor of Philosophy and Ethics of Information, Oxford Internet Institute, University of Oxford, UK.

Routledge Handbooks in Philosophy

Routledge Handbooks in Philosophy are state-of-the-art surveys of emerging, newly refreshed, and important fields in philosophy, providing accessible yet thorough assessments of key problems, themes, thinkers, and recent developments in research.

All chapters for each volume are specially commissioned, and written by leading scholars in the field. Carefully edited and organized, *Routledge Handbooks in Philosophy* provide indispensable reference tools for students and researchers seeking a comprehensive overview of new and exciting topics in philosophy. They are also valuable teaching resources as accompaniments to textbooks, anthologies, and research-orientated publications.

A full list of titles is available at: https://www.routledge.com/Routledge-Handbooks-in-Philosophy/book-series/RHP.

Recently published titles

The Routledge Handbook of the Philosophy of Paternalism
Edited by Kalle Grill and Jason Hanna

The Routledge Handbook of Social Epistemology
Edited by Miranda Fricker, Peter J. Graham, David Henderson, Nikolaj Pedersen and Jeremy Wyatt

The Routledge Handbook of Virtue Epistemology
Edited by Heather D. Battaly

The Routledge Handbook of Logical Empiricism
Edited by Thomas Uebel

The Routledge Handbook of Practical Reason
Edited by Ruth Chang and Kurt Sylvan

The Routledge Handbook of the Computational Mind
Edited by Matteo Colombo and Mark Sprevak

The Routledge Handbook of the Philosophy of Consciousness
Edited by Rocco J. Gennaro

The Routledge Handbook of Theories of Luck
Edited by Ian M. Church

The Routledge Handbook of Love in Philosophy
Edited by Adrienne M. Martin

The Routledge Handbook of Pacifism and Non-Violence
Edited by Andrew Fiala

The Routledge Handbook of Continental Aesthetics
Edited by Jorella Andrews

THE ROUTLEDGE HANDBOOK OF PHILOSOPHY OF INFORMATION

Edited by

Luciano Floridi

LONDON AND NEW YORK

First published 2016
by Routledge

2 Park Square, Milton Park, Abingdon, Oxfordshire OX14 4RN
52 Vanderbilt Avenue, New York, NY 10017

Routledge is an imprint of the Taylor & Francis Group, an informa business

First issued in paperback 2019

British Library Cataloguing in Publication Data
A catalogue record for this book is available from the British Library

Library of Congress Cataloging in Publication Data
A catalog record for this book has been requested

ISBN: 978-1-138-79693-5 (hbk)
ISBN: 978-0-367-37046-6 (pbk)

Typeset in Bembo
by HWA Text and Data Management, London

CONTENTS

Contents

FIGURES

TABLES

CONTRIBUTORS

Fred Adams is Professor of Linguistics and Cognitive Science and Professor of Philosophy at the University of Delaware. He has published over 100 articles on topics in philosophy of science, philosophy of mind, philosophy of language, theory of knowledge, cognitive science.

Patrick Allo joined the Oxford Internet Institute in 2015 as a Marie Sklodowska-Curie Fellow. He was previously a postdoctoral fellow of the Research Foundation Flanders (Belgium) at the Vrije Universiteit Brussel, and a guest professor of Ghent University. His main research interests include the relation between logic and information, the formal representation of information-flow, information visualization, and the use of logical methods in the philosophy of information and in the philosophy of mathematical practice. He is a founding member, and the current president of the Society for the Philosophy of Information.

William Bechtel is Professor of Philosophy and a faculty member in the Center for Circadian Biology, the Science Studies Program and the Interdisciplinary Program in Cognitive Science at the University of California, San Diego.

Selmer Bringsjord is Professor of Cognitive Science, Computer Science, and Logic and Philosophy, at Rensselaer Polytechnic Institute (RPI), in Troy, NY. He specializes in collaboratively building AIs (preferably ones with human-level powers), and in the philosophical and logico-mathematical questions that arise when such building is pursued.

Terrell Ward Bynum is Professor of Philosophy and Director of the Research Center on Computing and Society at Southern Connecticut State University; a pioneer in Computer and Information Ethics and in the Philosophy of Information; author and editor of numerous related books and articles; recipient of the Barwise Prize of the American Philosophical Association, the Covey Award of the International Association for Computing and Philosophy, and the Weizenbaum Award of the International Society for Ethics and Information Technology.

Sara Cannizzaro is a Research assistant at the Centre for Academic Practice Enhancement at Middlesex University. Her research interests are in biosemiotics, cybernetics and new media. Her publications include 'Transdisciplinarity for the 21st Century, or "Biosemiotics as Systems Theory"' and 'Where did Information Go? Reflections on the Logical Status of Information in a Cybernetic and Semiotic Perspective'.

Marcello D'Agostino is Professor of Logic at the Department of Philosophy, University of Milan, Italy. His main research interests lie in the areas of computational logic, philosophy of logic and philosophy of information. He received his PhD from the University of Oxford, with a thesis on the computational complexity of propositional calculi. He then became a Research Associate at the Department of Computing, Imperial College, London, Assistant Professor and Professor of Logic at the Department of Human Sciences, University of Ferrara, Italy.

Massimo Durante is Professor of Philosophy of Law and Legal Informatics in the Department of Law, University of Turin. He holds a PhD in Philosophy of Law (University of Turin), and a PhD in Moral Philosophy (Faculty of Philosophy, Paris IV Sorbonne). Author of several books, he has published articles in Italian, English and French. He is a Faculty Fellow at the Nexa Center for Internet and Society and a member of the Board of the International PhD program 'Law, Science, and Technology'.

Don Fallis is Professor of Information Resources and Adjunct Professor of Philosophy at the University of Arizona. His research areas are epistemology, philosophy of information, and philosophy of mathematics. His articles on lying and deception include 'What is Lying?' in the *Journal of Philosophy*.

Luciano Floridi is Professor of Philosophy and Ethics of Information, Oxford Internet Institute, University of Oxford.

Nir Fresco holds a PhD in Philosophy of Cognitive Science from the University of New South Wales, Australia. In 2013, he received the Brian M. Goldberg Award from the International Association for Computing and Philosophy for his research in the philosophy of computation. His postdoctoral studies thus far have been in philosophy of cognitive science and in philosophy of information. His main interest is to understand the role information theory plays in cognitive science.

Jan Kyrre Berg Friis is Associate Professor of Philosophy of Science and Technology at Department of Public Health Science and Deputy Director of MeST, Centre for Medical Science and Technology Studies, Copenhagen University. He has authored, edited and co-edited numerous books on philosophy of science and technology, among these: *A Companion to the Philosophy of Technology* and *New Waves in Philosophy of Technology*. He has published papers on topics such as hermeneutics, perception, science, and time.

Patrick Grim is Distinguished Teaching Professor of Philosophy at Stony Brook, author and editor of *The Incomplete Universe, The Philosophical Computer, Reflexivity: From Paradox to Consciousness, Beyond Sets, Mind and Consciousness*, and over 30 years of *The Philosopher's Annual*. His work spans ethics, philosophical logic, epistemology, philosophy of science, philosophy of law, philosophy of mind, philosophy of language, and philosophy of religion.

Beyond the borders of philosophy he has published in scholarly journals in theoretical biology, linguistics, decision and game theory, artificial intelligence, and computer science.

N.L. Harshman is an Associate Professor of Physics at American University, Washington D.C. where he studies mathematical physics and quantum information theory. His primary interest is the intersection of quantum information and control theory with symmetry, solvability and entanglement. His recent work focuses on how preferred or 'natural' observables are selected by the dynamics of few-body systems.

Vincent F. Hendricks is Professor of Formal Philosophy at the University of Copenhagen, Denmark. He is Director of the Center for Information and Bubble Studies (CIBS) sponsored by the Carlsberg Foundation and was awarded the Elite Research Prize by the Danish Ministry of Science, Technology and Innovation and the Roskilde Festival Elite Research Prize both in 2008. He was Editor-in-Chief of *Synthese: An International Journal for Epistemology, Methodology and Philosophy of Science* between 2005 and 2015.

Phyllis Illari is a Lecturer in Philosophy of Science in the Science and Technology Studies Department at University College London. Her current interests are mechanisms, causality, and information, and how they impact on evidence assessment in biomedical sciences. With Clarke, Gillies, Russo and Williamson, she is beginning an AHRC project 'Evaluating Evidence in Mechanisms', led by the University of Kent and UCL, and collaborating with NICE and IARC.

Sabina Leonelli is Associate Professor in the Philosophy and History of Science and Associate Director of the Centre for the Study of the Life Sciences (Egenis) at the University of Exeter. She uses empirical research to foster philosophical understandings of knowledge-making practices.

Olimpia Lombardi is Principal Researcher at the National Council of Scientific and Technical Research, Argentina, and Professor at the University of Buenos Aires, where she leads a research group devoted to the philosophy of physics and of chemistry. She has published several papers on matters such as time's arrow, information, quantum decoherence, interpretation of quantum mechanics and the physics-chemistry boundary. In 2013 she was awarded a substantial grant by the Foundational Questions Institute to study the concept of information.

George Medley will have completed his PhD in Philosophical Theology from King's College London, University of London, in early 2016. His primary research interests are in post-Kantian continental philosophy of religion and science and religion dialogue, with particular interest in the work of Wolfhart Pannenberg and Friedrich W. J. Schelling. He has taught modules in both philosophy and religion at colleges and universities in America, London, and Kenya.

Peter Milne is Professor of Philosophy at the University of Stirling, UK. He has published widely on topics in the philosophy of logic, formal logic, formal epistemology, the foundations of probability, and the history of modern logic and analytic philosophy.

Barton Moffatt is an associate professor in the Department of Philosophy and Religion at Mississippi State University. He works on issues in the philosophy of biology and in research ethics.

Ugo Pagallo is a former lawyer and current Professor of Jurisprudence at the Department of Law, University of Turin, Italy. He is also Faculty Fellow at the Center for Transnational Legal Studies in London, author of ten monographs, numerous essays in scholarly journals, and co-editor of the AICOL series by Springer. He was a member of the European RPAS Steering Group (2011–2012), and of the EU Onlife Initiative (2012–2013) and is currently is an expert for the evaluation of proposals in the EU robotics program (2015).

Martin Peterson is Professor of Philosophy and the Sue and Harry E. Bovary, Jr. Professor of the History and Ethics of Professional Engineering in the Department of Philosophy at Texas A&M University. He is the author of *An Introduction to Decision Theory* (Cambridge University Press, 2009) and *The Dimensions of Consequentialism* (Cambridge University Press, 2013).

Gualtiero Piccinini is Professor of Philosophy and Associate Director of the Center for Neurodynamics at the University of Missouri–St. Louis, USA. In 2014 he received the Herbert Simon award from the International Association for Computing and Philosophy. His book, *Physical Computation: A Mechanistic Account*, was published by Oxford University Press in 2015.

Giuseppe Primiero is Senior Lecturer in Computing Science at the Department of Computer Science, Middlesex University and Guest Professor at the Centre for Logic and Philosophy of Science, Ghent University. He is Vice-President of the DHST-DLMPST Commission on the History and Philosophy of Computing and a member of the Leadership Committees of the Society for the Philosophy of Information and the International Association for Computing and Philosophy. His research areas include logic, philosophy of information and computation.

Rasmus K. Rendsvig is a PhD candidate in theoretical philosophy at Lund University and member of the scientific division of the Center for Information and Bubble Studies, University of Copenhagen. His primary research interests relate to the interplay of epistemology and interaction in social contexts with a special focus on social influence and formal epistemology.

Federica Russo is Assistant Professor in Philosophy of Science at the University of Amsterdam. She is an expert on causation, causal inference, and scientific method. Among her recent publications: *Causality: Philosophical Theory Meets Scientific Practice* (co-authored with Phyllis Illari, Oxford University Press, 2014), *Causality and Causal Modelling in the Social Sciences. Measuring Variations* (Springer, 2009), and several articles in international journals and spanning various themes, such as causation and causal modelling, explanation, evidence, technology, and information.

Andrea Scarantino is Associate Professor of Philosophy at Georgia State University, USA. He has published more than 30 papers in both philosophical and scientific journals, including the *Australasian Journal of Philosophy*, *Philosophical Studies*, *Philosophy of Science*, *Emotion Review*,

Animal Behavior, Journal of Biological Physics and others. His primary research focus is on the nature and function of emotions, but he retains a strong interest in information theory and in non-linguistic communication. He is the editor of *Emotion Researcher, ISRE's Sourcebook for Research on Emotion and Affect.*

Alexander Shen is Research Director at the Laboratoire d'Informatique, de Robotique et de Microélectronique de Montpellier (LIRMM), France. He worked in the Institute of Information Transmission Problems (Russian Academy of Science, Moscow) from 1982–2005. He is the author of several textbooks and a monograph on algorithmic information theory.

Ulrich Stegmann is a Senior Lecturer in Philosophy at the University of Aberdeen (UK). His main area of research is the philosophy of biology. He is the editor of *Animal Communication Theory: Information and Influence* (Cambridge University Press, 2013).

John Symons is Chair and Professor of Philosophy at the University of Kansas, USA. He is the author of several books and numerous articles in philosophy of psychology, metaphysics and epistemology.

Mariarosaria Taddeo is a Researcher at the Oxford Internet Institute, University of Oxford, UK. Her area of expertise is information and computer ethics, although she has worked on issues concerning philosophy of information, epistemology, and philosophy of AI. She published several papers focusing on online trust, cyber security and cyber warfare. Dr Taddeo serves editor-in-chief of *Minds and Machines* (as of 2016) and is on the executive editorial board of *Philosophy & Technology*. Since 2013, she has been President of the International Association of Computing and Philosophy.

Katherine Thomson-Jones is Associate Professor of Philosophy at Oberlin College, USA. She is the author of *Aesthetics and Film* (2008), co-editor of *New Waves in Aesthetics* (2008), and she is currently writing a book on the philosophy of digital art.

Chris Timpson is Fellow and Tutor in Philosophy at Brasenose College, Oxford; and CUF Lecturer in the Faculty of Philosophy, University of Oxford. He did his undergraduate and graduate study at Oxford in philosophy of physics, and then taught at the University of Leeds in the Division of History and Philosophy of Science for three years, before returning to Oxford in 2007. His main interests are in the philosophy and foundations of quantum mechanics, with particular emphasis on quantum information theory.

Ioannis Votsis is Senior Lecturer at the New College of the Humanities, London, UK. His main research area is the philosophy of science but he also has active interests in the philosophy of logic, philosophy of artificial intelligence and meta-philosophy. Included in his publications are a number of papers on structural realism, observation and confirmation theory, the EPSA13 Conference Proceedings which he co-edited as well as several other co-edited special issues of journals on themes like underdetermination, novel predictions, theory-ladenness, unification and coherence.

Michael Wilde is a Research Fellow in Philosophy at the University of Kent, UK. He works mainly in epistemology and its application to medicine.

Jon Williamson is Professor of Reasoning, Inference and Scientific Method at the University of Kent, UK. He works on causality, probability, logics and reasoning, and their application in science and medicine. He is author of *Bayesian Nets and Causality* (Oxford University Press, 2005) and *In Defence of Objective Bayesianism* (Oxford University Press, 2010), co-author of *Probabilistic Logics and Probabilistic Networks* (Springer, 2011), and co-editor of several volumes, including *Causality in the Sciences* (Oxford University Press, 2011). He is also editor of the gazette *The Reasoner*.

Jason Winning is a PhD candidate in philosophy and cognitive science at the University of California, San Diego, USA. He completed a BS in computer science and an MA in philosophy at Northern Illinois University.

Marty J. Wolf is a Professor of Computer Science at Bemidji State University in Bemidji, Minnesota, USA. He holds a BA in chemistry and computer science from the University of Minnesota, Morris and a PhD in computer sciences from the University of Wisconsin, Madison. He has over 25 years of experience teaching undergraduate computer science and has published research in theoretical computer science, bioinformatics, graph theory and more recently in computer and information ethics and the philosophy of computation.

INTRODUCTION
Mapping the philosophy of information

Information is the Cinderella in the history of philosophy. Think of it for a moment. Understanding information is a necessary input for any philosophy of knowledge, no matter whether ordinary (epistemology) or scientific (philosophy of science). There is no ethics without choices, responsibilities, and moral evaluations, yet all these need a lot of relevant and reliable information and quite a good management of it. Logic was a matter of dialectics first, and then mathematical proofs, but today it is also if not mainly a question of information extraction, transmission, and dynamics. Ontology without informational patterns – real, virtual, possible, necessary, or even impossible – would be meaningless, and modal logic is a branch of information theory. The philosophy of mind needs informational states, and the philosophy of language without communication of information is pointless. Any philosophy of the logos is a philosophy of information and Christian philosophy of religion is inconceivable without the informational concept of revelation. The list could be extended and refined to aesthetics, hermeneutics, philosophy of biology, philosophy of physics, and so on. but the point is clear. To paraphrase Molière, Western philosophy has been speaking informationally without knowing it for twenty-five centuries. To use the initial analogy, we have always relied on Cinderella working hard in the house of philosophy. It is time to acknowledge her great and pervasive services.

It has taken the development of digital technologies, the information revolution, and the emergence of information societies to invite our Cinderella out of the kitchen and allow her to join the party with the other philosophical subjects. Today, the philosophy of information (Floridi 2010, 2011, 2013) is a growing area of research, and this Handbook clearly shows the many areas in which new, interesting, and vitally relevant ideas are being explored informationally. As with all good philosophy, the philosophy of information is not applied, yet it is highly applicable. Our Cinderella may be a princess, but she knows very well how to do the dishes, if necessary.

Of course, information 'can be said in many ways', just as being can (Aristotle, *Metaphysics* G.2), and the correlation is not accidental. Information, with its cognate concepts like computation, data, communication, and so on, plays an increasingly essential role in how we conceptualise ourselves, socialise among ourselves, understand our world, and interact with it. Turing is replacing Newton as the source of our deep metaphysics, that is, an informational rather than a mechanistic narrative has begun permeating everything we do and how we think about it on a daily basis.

Quite naturally, information has adapted to some of reality's complex contours. And so, because information is inevitably a multifaceted and polyvalent concept, the question 'what is information?' is misleadingly simple. As an instance of the Socratic question 'ti esti ...?', it poses a fundamental problem, intrinsically fascinating and no less challenging than 'what is truth?', 'what is right and wrong?', 'what is knowledge?', 'what is meaning?', and so forth. We know that these are not requests for dictionary consultations, but ideal roundabouts, points of intersection of philosophical investigations, which may diverge and take different directions from them also because of the approaches adopted. Such approaches to a Socratic question can usually be divided into three broad groups: reductionist, antireductionist, and non-reductionist. Philosophical theories of information are no exception.

Reductionist approaches to the philosophy of information support the feasibility of a 'unified theory of information' (UTI). This is supposed to be general enough to capture all major concepts of information that you will find playing a role in the following chapters – from Shannon's to Kolmogorov's, from Wiener's to Baudrillard's, from genetic to neural – but also sufficiently specific to discriminate between their nuances. The goal of reductionist analyses is to show that all kinds of information are ultimately reducible – conceptually, genetically or genealogically – to some *Ur*-concept, the mother of all instances. The ultimate UTI will be hierarchical, linear (even if probably branching), inclusive, and inevitably incompatible with any alternative model.

Reductionist strategies seem unlikely to succeed. Decades of research have shown no consensus or even convergence on a single, unified definition of information. This is hardly surprising. Information is such a powerful and flexible concept, and such a complex phenomenon that, as an *explicandum*, it can be associated with several explanations, depending on the level of abstraction adopted and the cluster of requirements and desiderata orientating a theory. Claude Shannon, for one, was very cautious: 'It is hardly to be expected that a single concept of information would satisfactorily account for the numerous possible applications of this general field [information theory]' (Shannon 1993, p. 180). He was probably right. For all these reasons, this Handbook does not endorse a reductionist approach or the possibility of a unified theory of information.

At the other extreme, we find antireductionist approaches to the philosophy of information. They stress the multifarious nature of the concept of information itself and of the corresponding phenomena. They defend the radical irreducibility of the different species to a single stem, objecting especially to reductionist attempts to identify Shannon's quantitative concept of information as the required *Ur*-concept, and to ground a UTI on a mathematical theory of information. Antireductionist strategies are essentially negative, and they can soon become an impasse rather than a solution. Admittedly, they allow specialised analyses of the various concepts of information to develop independently, thus avoiding the vague generalisations and mistaken confusions that may burden UTI strategies. But their fragmented nominalism remains unsatisfactory, insofar as it fails to account for the ostensible connections permeating and influencing the various ways in which information *qua* information 'can be said'.

Non-reductionists like myself seek to escape the previous dichotomy between reductionism and antireductionism by replacing the reductionist hierarchical model with a distributed network of connected concepts, linked by mutual and dynamic influences that are conceptual in nature, and not necessarily genetic or genealogical. This 'networked analysis' can be centralised in various ways or completely decentralised and perhaps multi-centred.

According to decentralised or multi-centred approaches, there is no key concept of information. More than one concept is equally important, and the 'periphery' plays a counterbalancing role. Depending on the orientation, information is seen as interpretation, power, narrative, message or medium, conversation, construction, a commodity, and so on. Thus, philosophers like Baudrillard, Derrida, Foucault, Lyotard, McLuhan, and Rorty are united by what they dismiss, if not challenge: the predominance of the factual. For them information is not *in*, *from*, or *about* reality. They downplay the aboutness of information and bend its referential thrust into a self-referential circle of hermeneutical communication. They focus only on the affordances, and miss the constraints. Their classic target is Cartesian foundationalism, seen as the clearest expression of a hierarchical and authoritarian approach to the genesis, justification, and flow of information. Disoriented, they mistake Cartesian foundationalism and its ultimate realism as the only alternative to their fully decentralised view.

Centralised approaches, on the other hand, interpret the various meanings, uses, applications and types of information as a system gravitating around a core notion that enjoys theoretical priority, like a nation state made of an archipelago of islands, yet with a single capital. The core notion works as a hermeneutical device that influences, interrelates, and helps to access other notions. In metaphysics, Aristotle held a similar view about being, and argued in favour of the primacy of the concept of *substance*. In the philosophy of information, this 'substantial' role has long been claimed by *factual* or *epistemically-oriented* semantic information. The basic idea is simple. In order to understand what information is, the best thing to do is to start by analysing it in terms of the knowledge it can yield about its reference. This epistemic approach is not without competitors. Weaver, for example, supported a tripartite analysis of information in terms of (1) technical problems concerning the quantification of information and dealt with by Shannon's theory; (2) semantic problems relating to meaning and truth, and (3) what he called 'influential' problems concerning the impact and effectiveness of information on human behaviour, which he thought had to play an equally important role (Weaver 1949). One of the tasks of the philosophy of information is to show how, in each case, the centrality of epistemically-oriented semantic information is presupposed rather than replaced.

This Handbook has been designed following the non-reductionist, yet centralised approach I just described. In order to avoid the excessive fragmentation of the philosophy of information into a myriad of unrelated theories and concepts, the following chapters have been written and edited on the basis of some short, accessible, and framing introductions to key ideas, presented in section A. The following, longer chapters have then been grouped into three sections, one on quantitative and formal aspects, one on natural and physical aspects, and one on human and semantic aspects. This is not the only way of structuring the vast and growing number of topics investigated by the philosophy of information, but it seems the best at this stage in the history of this new discipline. I hope it may provide a useful map, to be revised according to future needs. When exploring a new territory for the first time, a perfect map would be ideal and yet it is impossible by definition, for if we had it we would not be the first to explore it. At this stage, the best we can hope for is an approximate map. The bright side is that this is still much better than no map at all.

References

Floridi, Luciano. 2010. *Information – A Very Short Introduction*. Oxford: Oxford University Press.

Floridi, Luciano. 2011. *The Philosophy of Information*. Oxford: Oxford University Press.

Floridi, Luciano. 2013. *The Ethics of Information*. Oxford: Oxford University Press.

Shannon, Claude Elwood. 1993. *Collected Papers*, edited by N. J. A. Sloane and A. D. Wyner ed. New York: IEEE Press.

Weaver, W. 1949. 'The Mathematics of Communication'. *Scientific American* 181 (1):11–15.

PART I

Basic ideas

1

PHYSICS AND INFORMATION

N.L. Harshman

Introduction

Physicists use the concept of information in various senses: some notions of information are mathematical and precise, while others are qualitative and heuristic. As the history of physics and the technology of science have progressed, information as a concept and a tool has become more central to the discipline. However, no unified theory of information, data, and knowledge understood as physical phenomena has achieved consensus.

A practical way to frame inquiry into the physical nature of information is the following: What can information *do* for the working physicist? From this perspective, the definition and quantification of information is a legitimate mode of inquiry only in so much as it supports the methods and goals of physics as a science. Information in the form of measurement data and theoretical knowledge allows physicists to produce descriptions of the present, and more information means those descriptions are more thorough and more universal. More complete descriptions then lead to more accurate predictions of future events and retrodictions of past events, and eventually to better understanding, and possibly control, of the present. Explanation, the how and why of physical phenomena, may or may not be counted as information in this perspective, since some scientific positivists treat explanation as a kind of information that lies outside the scientific purview.

Generally physicists are realists: they are committed to the existence of mind-independent objects that provide a structure for reality. However, perspectives on information within physics can tend toward more epistemological or more ontological. On the epistemological side, an implicit assumption is that information is a property of the interaction of the system and the observer. Though the line between system and observer may be arbitrary, the separation is essential to the concept of information. Entropy, uncertainty, and computability are therefore properties of knowledge, not of objects or systems. In contrast, the ontological perspective is that information is a real thing. It is a property of a system with a physicality and truth-value that is independent of the observer – perhaps even independent of the existence of observers. Information, viewed from this perspective, is physically embodied in matter and energy and it obeys causal mechanisms. An even more extreme ontological view of information is that energy and matter may be only manifestations of the underlying informatic substratum, the shadows on the cave wall of reality cast by the true pure bits.

7

Viewed in this light, the observer is just a subsystem, an "information gathering and using system" or IGUS, obeying the same physical, fundamentally informational rules (see Gell-Mann 1995). In between these two extreme views of the physical nature information lies mainstream physics.

Information in classical mechanics

Classical mechanics refers to the deductive, dynamical framework originated by Isaac Newton. The spirit of classical mechanics and the role of information are perhaps best captured by the famous quote from mathematician and physicist Pierre-Simon Laplace:

> We may regard the present state of the universe as the effect of its past and the cause of its future. An intellect which at a certain moment would know all forces that set nature in motion, and all positions of all items of which nature is composed, if this intellect were also vast enough to submit these data to analysis, it would embrace in a single formula the movements of the greatest bodies of the universe and those of the tiniest atom; for such an intellect nothing would be uncertain and the future just like the past would be present before its eyes.
>
> *(Laplace, 1814; translation Truscott and Emory, 1951)*

In this statement of scientific determinism, information makes two appearances. First, it is the data that describes the present state of the universe and, second, it is the knowledge of the forces that propel the present into the future. The ideal of classical mechanics is that the quality of this physical information is infinitely improvable toward an ultimate, complete, deterministic description of the universe. In this context, the elegance of a theoretical description is the degree to which it allows information about physical states and laws to be compressed (see Chapter 5).

However, Laplace's quote also demonstrates the limits of the classical notion of information. To embody the "intellect" (sometimes called Laplace's demon) that knows and processes all information about the present state of the universe would, by some calculations, require more matter than the universe (Lloyd 2006). Further, chaos and complexity theory have shown that even simple systems can have exponential growth of uncertainty under dynamics, and generate long-range spatiotemporal correlations (Gleick 1987). Therefore even within classical mechanics deterministic prediction is always approximate. The finiteness of the observer guarantees the impossibility of total knowledge and the existence of ignorance, and this opens the door to probability (see Chapter 2) and randomness as useful concepts in physics.

Information in statistical mechanics

The nineteenth-century development of statistical mechanics by James Clark Maxwell, Ludwig Boltzmann, Josiah William Gibbs, and others made scientific progress by incorporating probability into physical models and quantifying the relationship between entropy and uncertainty. Inferring physical results from probabilistic methods met with resistance from classically-trained physicists, but it allowed the micro/macro connection to be established and heralded a golden age of reductionism (Von Bayer 1998).

The key step in statistical mechanics is realizing that to every macroscopic state (or macrostate) there are a huge number of possible microstates. For example, the macrostate of a quantity of nitrogen gas is well-modelled by three parameters: the volume, pressure and temperature, whereas the simplest microstate model requires on the order of 10^{24} parameters to specify the molecular states of the gas. Maxwell figured out how the probability distribution of microstates changed with variations of the ideal gas macrostate. Then Boltzmann recognized that entropy, originally defined macroscopically in terms of a differential ratio of heat transferred to temperature change in reversible processes, could also be interpreted as quantifying the uncertainty inherited from the probability distribution of the microstates. Mathematically the entropy S is expressed as

$$S = -k \sum_i p_i \log p_i$$

where the sum is over all possible microstates for a particular macrostate and p_i can be interpreted as the information content revealed if the macrosystem was determined to be in the ith microstate, and the entropy is the average information provided by the microstate description. A further assumption that there are W microstates which are all equally likely in equilibrium (so that $p_i = 1/W$) leads us to the simpler form of the equation found on Boltzmann's tombstone:

$$S = k \cdot \log W$$

The constant k (now called Boltzmann's constant) links the microscale energy to the macroscale temperature.

Systems placed in thermal contact tend toward an equilibrium in which the macrostate has a probability distribution of possible microstates with maximum entropy. Therefore, the Second Law of Thermodynamics emerges as a statement about the most likely dynamic evolution of probability distributions. Since this law of nature is inherently probabilistic, and seemingly a statement about our lack of information, it has a long history of generating apparent paradoxes. Perhaps most famous is Maxwell's Demon, a nimble creature who can intelligently manipulate microstates, disrupting the tendency toward equilibrium, and thereby challenge the Second Law. Throughout the twentieth century, every few decades has brought out another argument claiming to kill the demon and these thought experiments have probed thermodynamic cost of measuring, recording and erasing information (Von Bayer 1998).

Even though the underlying classical mechanics of the microsystems is symmetric under exchange of past and future, the probabilistic nature of large numbers imbues macrosystems with a tendency away from order in the past and toward disorder in the future. Ordered systems are easier to describe and predict, so in some sense they contain less information. However, when thermodynamic subsystems are allowed to interact, the uncertainty propagates and the entropy increases. Therefore the original state data about the subsystems are lost. Further, this thermal contact is unavoidable, so information about the past is inevitably lost to noise.

Physical communication

The nineteenth century also brought the development of electronic communication technologies. Energy and information transfer over long distances now became possible. Previously, communication required either a direct sense channel between source and destination (e.g. line of sight) or actual transfer of matter (a letter in a bottle). Electronic technologies allowed messages to be transformed into analog or digital signals and sent over wires or broadcast through the air. The new tools exploited the control of the electric and magnetic fields made possible by electromagnetic theory as discovered by Michael Faraday and Maxwell (among others). Strong electric fields could be generated at one location and conducted along wires across countries and under oceans. Oscillations of these fields could drive currents in antennas, creating radio waves that could bounce off the ionosphere and travel around the world.

The simplest and most basic electric device is the switch, which can be open or closed. The flow or absence of electric current in a conducting wire can carry a basic binary piece of information, a bit. The telegraph coded messages into timed sequences of open and closed circuits, and the logic that drives modern computers can also be reduced into the sequential and conditional operations of microscopic switches – the transistors in a computer chip. Much material science still focuses on making smaller, more stable and more controllable switches by creating new regular arrangements of atoms and molecules. As the size decreases, there is increasing possibility that computational power will be physically constrained by thermodynamics (Bennett 1982; Landauer 1991) or quantum mechanics (see below).

In computational devices, the information is digitized into discrete steps, but there are also analog electronic communication technologies where the signal is a continuous variation of electric field. For most of the twentieth century telephone and radio transmissions were analog, although in the last few decades most of these technologies are becoming digitized for practical reasons: digital signals can be optimized using the mathematical theory of information introduced by Claude Shannon (1948) (see Chapter 4). To send a message, it must be coded into a physical signal, a process that usually involves the transduction of energy from one form into another, like audio waves into pulses of light. The signal is then transmitted over a channel and some of the energy of the signal is inevitably dissipated by contact with thermal systems. Additionally, the signal becomes mixed with the disturbances caused by other transmitters. Therefore, the channel is inevitably noisy and lossy, so the transmission that arrives to the receiver and is decoded and passed on the destination will not carry the same information as the source intended.

This model of communication, developed by Shannon into a quantitative theory, applies whether we are shouting from mountaintops or shooting lasers through fiber optic cables. It gives physicists and engineers a practical guide to what is possible in such technologies. Shannon used the same entropy formula from statistical mechanics to quantify the entropy of the source and destination. The link between the two formulations is probability: the information of a message is related to the probability of that message being generated or received. A limitation of Shannon's theory is that it explicitly excludes the semantic content of information and only deals with the data. However, its success and generality inspired a shift to a more ontological view of information within the physics community, including the most extreme version called digital ontology, i.e. the universe is a discrete, digital algorithm. See (Floridi 2009) for a discussion (and rebuttal) of digital ontology from a perspective of informational structural realism.

Information and relativity

Relativity tells physicists how to compare physical quantities in different reference frames. Classical physics respects Galilean relativity, in which space and time are distinct, absolute and independent of the reference frame of the observer. The independence of physical phenomena from the choice of reference frame is a central tenet of physics, and reconciling Maxwell's electromagnetic theory with moving reference frames required a new form of relativity. Albert Einstein's work over the first few decades of the twentieth century on "special relativity" and then "general relativity" forced physicists to discard absolute space and absolute time as observer-independent quantities in favor of a unified, curved and dynamic spacetime that incorporates gravity as geometry.

Einsteinian relativity has consequences for the theory of information. Most importantly, it puts a universal speed limit on the transfer of information: the speed of light. For each instant in spacetime, there is a light cone, and influence cannot transmit outside that cone. The confidence in this limit is so strong that the majority of physicists will discard any theory that allows faster-than-light communication. On the practical side of physical communication, relativity explains dilations in time for which long-distance signal transmission must account. More generally, since information is embodied in matter and energy, and these must obey relativity, we can distinguish information that is discernable or verifiable in *any* reference frame from that information which is reference-frame dependent. For example, the temporal order of events is information that depends on the reference frame of the observer.

When the consequences of general relativity are extended to the cosmic scale, more exotic but potentially fundamental questions about information arise. Black holes were first discovered as a singular solution of Einstein's gravitational equation, and now we believe that most galaxies have many black holes, including supermassive black holes in most galactic centers. When matter and energy falls into a black hole, where does the information it contains go? It appears to leave an imprint on the event horizon of the black hole (Susskind and Lindesay 2005). There are even extreme solutions of Einstein's equations that allow spacetime to tie itself into knots, producing sticky situations where information from the future could be sent back to influence the past. There are theoretical consequences for computational complexity in these causally ambiguous topologies (Aaronson 2013). General relativity also enables us to study the large distance and time scale structure of the universe. If the Big Bang was the initial condition of our universe, did that initial boundary condition contain all the information of the universe? Is the time asymmetry we perceive, in which information about the past is lost as the current moment progresses to the future, an inevitable consequence of the laws of nature, or just a contingent consequence of our universe's peculiar initial condition?

Quantum information

In classical physics, the probabilistic nature of prediction and retrodiction is entirely due to ignorance about the mechanism or the initial conditions, whether employing Galilean or Einsteinian relativity. However, quantum mechanics and its extension to quantum field theories require the introduction of a new mathematical structure for probability. These rules accurately predict the most precise experiments ever conducted, such as particle properties or spectral properties, and they provide an accurate mechanism for reductionism. The price for this success is that quantum mechanics forces us to give up determinism. In the conventional interpretation, some (but not all) future predictions are truly random. There is no "hidden variable" that could ever be revealed that will allow better-than-quantum prediction.

The probability structure of quantum mechanics introduces a new kind of uncertainty that is irreducible from the measurement of experimental observables. Heisenberg's uncertainty principle is the most familiar example of this: the position x and the momentum p of a quantum particle are data that cannot be simultaneously refined by measurement to arbitrary precision. Their measurement uncertainties satisfy the inequality

$$\Delta x \Delta p \geq \hbar / 2$$

where Planck's constant $\hbar$ is a very small quantity compared to the macroscopic scale, but it sets the bar for action at the level of atoms, electrons, photons, and nuclei. The very act of measuring position disrupts momentum, and vice versa, and this is not a technological defect. It is a manifestation of a fundamental indeterminism at the quantum scale. Simultaneous precise information about both position and momentum does not exist; one precludes the other. Heisenberg's uncertainty principle is only one of many possible relations among incommensurate observables, and therefore unknowable physical data, implied by the rules of quantum mechanics (Griffiths 2005).

The quantum probability structure also introduces a notion of coherence. Coherence between different systems or different histories allows for the possibility of interference, with effects similar to classical wave mechanics. The double-slit experiment for matter waves is a famous example. See Feynman (1994) for an accessible discussion, but in brief, a beam of particles is directed at a wall with two slits or apertures cut out. As long as the information of which slit the particle passes through is unknown, then each particle transmits like a wave of probability and the combination of waves produces an inference pattern at the detector. However, if the slit through which the particle passes is observed, then coherence between the exclusive histories is destroyed and the interference pattern disappears. The information about which path the system took from the initial state to the final state is information that must remain unknown for the interference effect to be visible.

The foundations of what is now called quantum information theory were built in large part by the push-back against the end of determinism (Kaiser 2011). The Einstein-Podolosky-Rosen paradox (1935) and the work of J.S. Bell (1964, 1988) challenged the quantum probability structure with the criticism that it allows correlations among non-local measurements of systems, and these correlations are stronger than allowed by classical physics, even with hidden variables. This is explained by the possession of a coherent resource shared between the subsystems, now called entanglement following Schrödinger (1935). The non-classical correlations created by entanglement between spatially-separated observables and between sources and detectors have been convincingly demonstrated experimentally in multiple quantum systems (see for example, Aspect *et al.* 1982 and Weihs *et al.* 1998), although some quantum skeptics continue the search for loopholes.

Much of Shannon's mathematical theory of information can be carried over to the quantum probability structure. For example, Von Neumann entropy has a similar formula to Boltzmann's and Shannon's entropy. Von Neumann entropy quantifies the ignorance about a quantum state, as distinct from the intrinsic uncertainty in the manner of Heisenberg. One characterization of entanglement uses the Von Neumann entropy of the subsystems. For example, a "pure state" of a quantum system is a completely known state (even though some measurements may have intrinsic uncertainty) and it has no Von Neumann entropy. When the system in a pure state is partitioned (even theoretically) into subsystems that have non-zero Von Neumann entropy, then those subsystems are entangled (Plenio and Virmani 2007). That means that in quantum mechanics, there can be *missing information about the parts, even if the information about the whole is complete.* There are open questions about the implications of Von Neumann entropy and other aspects of quantum information for thermodynamics.

Many relationships among probability, information and computation developed over the course of the twentieth century by Andrey Kolmogorov, Shannon, Alan Turing, Gregory Chaitin and others can be updated for the new quantum rules. Quantum channels allow entanglement between the transmitter and the receiver to be used as a communication resource (Nielsen and Chuang 2000). These channels can then be used for novel information transfers called quantum encryption and quantum state teleportation. Coherence and entanglement can also be used as resources for quantum computation and quantum simulation, an observation often credited to Richard Feynman (1982). The advent, even theoretically, of quantum computers, impacts the categorization of computational complexity classes (Aaronson 2013). Practically, there are quantum algorithms that scale more efficiently than any known classical algorithm for the same problem. Most famously, a quantum computer could be able to run Shor's algorithm to factor large prime numbers in a time scale convenient enough to break RSA encryption, the main encryption scheme for internet commerce.

In quantum mechanics, the selective aspect of measurements creates a coupling between the system and observer, and this induces interpretational difficulties for quantum mechanics and the physics of information. Most famous is the *gendanken* experiment of Schrödinger's cat. When is the information of the cat's demise manifest? Only when someone looks inside the box? Who watches the watcher? One way to classify various interpretations of quantum mechanics is where the notion of information falls within the epistemological vs. ontological spectrum (Fuchs 2011; Pusey, Barrett and Rudolph 2012; Schlosshauer, Kofler and Zeilinger 2013). For example, is the mathematical structure that we call a quantum state a real physical object or a statement about our knowledge? Does, as Archibald Wheeler (1990) hypothesized, "it" (the totality of reality) emerge from "bit" (an underlying informational stratum)? Is reality at root an informational structure (Floridi 2008)?

Information and the physics of embodied minds

The mind is a complex physical object obeying mechanics at the border of classical and quantum. Although the mathematical theory of information does not require a mind to quantify data processes, without a description of mind it cannot speak about the semantic properties of information. The physical theory of mind has implications for information processes like decision making and learning. More generally, humans are information gathering and using systems, and our finiteness necessarily introduces a scale to "relevant" information (Gell-Mann 1995). This induces an informational hierarchy idiosyncratic to the human observer, one that we use to evaluate claims of reductionism, emergence and unification.

The physics of mind also asks whether digitized classical or quantum electronics (or some other constructed system) can perform the same information processing as human intelligence. Some argue that investigating the physical requirements for embodied logic and artificial intelligence reveals an intersection between intelligence and computability (Hofstadter 1979), and perhaps demonstrates the necessity of quantum mechanics for the existence of minds (Penrose 1989).

At the most general level, a physical theory of mind is necessary to have a scientific discussion of epistemological versus ontological theories of information, to determine whether semantic information is physical, and perhaps to answer the question "It from bit?"

References

Aaronson, S. (2013). *Quantum Computing Since Democritus*. Cambridge: Cambridge University Press.

Aspect, A., Grangier P., and Roger, G. (1982). "Experimental Realization of Einstein-Podolsky-Rosen-Bohm Gedankenexperiment: A New Violation of Bell's Inequalities." *Physical Review Letters* 49: 91–94.

Bell, J.S. (1964). "On the Einstein–Podolsky–Rosen paradox." *Physics* 1: 195–200.

Bell, J.S. (1988). *Speakable and Unspeakable in Quantum Mechanics*. Cambridge: Cambridge University Press.

Bennett, C.H. (1982). "The Thermodynamics of Computation – a Review." *International Journal of Theoretical Physics* 21, 905–940.

Einstein, A., Podolsky B., and Rosen, N. (1935). "Can Quantum-Mechanical Description of Physical Reality be Considered Complete?" *Physical Review* 47: 777–780.

Feynman, R. (1982). "Simulating Physics with Computers." *International Journal of Theoretical Physics* 21: 467–488.

Feynman, R. (1994). *Six Easy Pieces*. Reading, MA: Addison-Wesley, Chapter 6.

Floridi, L. (2008). "A defense of informational structural realism." *Synthese* 161: 219–253.

Floridi, L. (2009). "Against digital ontology." *Synthese* 168: 151–178.

Fuchs, Christopher (2011). *Coming of Age with Quantum Information: Notes on a Paulian Idea*. Cambridge: Cambridge University Press.

Gell-Mann, M. (1995). *The Quark and the Jaguar: Adventures in the Simple and Complex*. New York: Henry Holt and Company, LLC.

Gleick, J. (1987). *Chaos: Making a New Science*. New York: Viking Penguin.

Griffiths, D.J. (2005) *Introduction to Quantum Mechanics*. Second Edition. Upper Saddle River, NJ: Pearson Prentice Hall.

Hofstadter, D.R. (1979). *Gödel, Escher, Bach: An Eternal Golden Braid*. New York: Basic Books.

Kaiser, D. (2011). *How the Hippies Saved Physics: Science Counterculture and the Quantum Revival*. New York: W.W. Norton & Company.

Laplace, P.-S. (1814). *A Philosophical Essay on Probabilities*, translated into English from the original French sixth ed. by Truscott, F.W. and Emory, F.L. (1951). New York: Dover Publications.

Landauer, R. (1991). "Information is Physical." *Physics Today* 44: 23–29.

Lloyd, S. (2006). *Programming the Universe: A Quantum Computer Scientist Takes on the Cosmos*. New York: Alfred A. Knopf.

Nielsen, M. A. and Chuang, I.L. (2000). *Quantum Computation and Quantum Information*. Cambridge: Cambridge University Press.

Penrose, R. (1989). *The Emperor's New Mind: Concerning Computers, Minds, and the Laws of Physics*. Oxford: Oxford University Press.

Plenio, M.B. and Virmani, S. (2007). "An introduction to entanglement measures." *Quantum Information and Computation* 1: 1–51.

Pusey, M.F., Barrett, J., and Rudolph, T. (2012). "On the reality of the quantum state." *Nature Physics* 8, 475–478.

Schrödinger, E. (1935). "Discussion of Probability Relations Between Separated Systems." *Proceedings of the Cambridge Philosophical Society* 31: 555–563; 32 (1936): 446–451.

Shannon, C. (1948). "The Mathematical Theory of Communication." *Bell System Technical Journal* 27: 379–423.

Schlosshauer, M., Kofler J., and Zeilinger, A. (2013). "A Snapshot of Foundational Attitudes Toward Quantum Mechanics. On-line preprint: arXiv:1301.1069.

Susskind, L. and Lindesay, J. (2005). *An Introduction to Black Holes, Information and the String Theory Revolution: The Holographic Universe*. Singapore: World Scientific.

Von Bayer, H.C. (1998). *Maxwell's Demon*. (Alternate title for later editions: *Warmth Disperses and Time Passes*). New York: Random House.

Weihs, G., Jennewein, T., Simon, C., Weinfurter, H. and Zeilinger A. (1998). "Violation of Bell's inequality under strict Einstein locality conditions." *Physical Review Letters* 81, 5039–5043.

Wheeler, J.A. (1990). *A Journey Into Gravity and Spacetime*. Scientific American Library. New York: W.H. Freeman.

2

PROBABILITY AND INFORMATION

Peter Milne

Introduction

Serious thought about probability, both as degree of belief in the light of evidence and as reflecting the tendency to produce stable relative proportions of occurrence upon repetition (as with the ratio of heads to tails when a coin is tossed repeatedly), emerged in the middle of the seventeenth century (see Hacking 2006). While probability and the related notions of likelihood and chance are nowadays in part everyday notions, they have also been regimented or codified in the formal, mathematical theory of probability. This formal theory admits various interpretations, some but not all of which draw on the everyday notions. Here I shall sketch connections between information and some interpretations of the formal theory. I shall begin by introducing the bare bones of the mathematical theory, sufficient to the demands of this chapter.

Probability: the mathematical theory

Probabilities are assigned to events or, more exactly, *distributed over* a *family* or *field of events*. This field has the structure of a *Boolean algebra*; that is, it contains: (*i*) the certain event S which is sure to occur, and the impossible event $\emptyset$ which cannot occur; (*ii*) if it contains the event e, it contains the complementary event not-e which occurs just if e does not; (*iii*) if it contains the events e and f, it contains the event $e \& f$ of their joint occurrence and the event $e \lor f$ that occurs when at least one of e and f occurs ('$\lor$' from the Latin word 'vel' meaning 'or'). An assignment *prob* of numerical values to the members of the field of events is a *probability distribution* just in case it satisfies these *principles* or *axioms*:

1 for every event e, $0 \le prob(e) \le 1$;
2 $prob(S) = 1$; $prob(\emptyset) = 0$;
3 if the joint occurrence of e and f is impossible, i.e., if $e \& f = \emptyset$,
   $prob(e \lor f) = prob(e) + prob(f)$.

From these axioms it follows that $prob(e) + prob(\text{not-}e) = 1$, for e and not-e are jointly impossible and the event '$e \lor$ not-e' is certain.

To this we must add the definition of *conditional probability*. *prob*(*f* | *e*), read "the probability of *f* given *e*", is defined as follows when *prob*(*e*) > 0 (and is undefined otherwise):

$$prob\left(f\,|\,e\right)=\frac{prob(f\,\&\,e)}{prob(e)}$$

As the joint occurrence of *e* with itself is just the event of *e*'s occurrence, *prob*(*e* | *e*) = 1; since the joint occurrence of *e* and not-*e* is impossible, *prob*(not-*e* | *e*) = 0.

Some authors take the notion of conditional probability as basic. For each event *e*, they take the function *prob*(. | *e*) to assign numerical values to members of the field of events in accordance with the principles (1)–(3) above and add the extra constraint:

for any events *e*, *f* and *g*, *prob*(*f* & *g* | *e*) = *prob*(*g* | *e* & *f*) × *prob*(*f* | *e*).

This makes sense even when *prob*(*f* | *e*) = 0, for *prob*(*f* & *g* | *e*) = 0 too in this case.

Information and probability as subjective degree of belief

There is a very straightforward connection between probability and information: the more likely you think it is that an event will occur, the more strongly you expect it to occur, the less surprised you are when it does occur, to the point that if you are certain it will occur, its occurrence is "no news to anybody." The more convinced you are that it will occur, the less you feel you have learned when informed that it has occurred. A newspaper that reported only the obvious, platitudinous, and well known would be a newspaper in name only, it would contain no news.

There are immediately a number of things that can be said about this particular linking of probability and information. One is that the conception of *information* involved here is that of "news value" or "surprise value"; another is that, given how I have set it up, it involves an individual's evaluations of what is likely and to what extent. To speak very loosely, one's beliefs constitute one's map of how things are; like ancient maps of the world, it contains *terrae incognitae* where various possibilities come to mind but one is not certain which is the case; however, some are more likely, maybe much more likely, than others. To be (newly) informed that such-and-such is the case is to fill in some chunk of *terra incognita* in one's map – and to wipe out or close down some of the possibilities previously entertained. To speak *very* loosely, the larger the chunk of *terra incognita* filled in, the larger the swathe of possibilities closed down, the more you have learned, the more information you have gained – and probability, if it is anything, is a measure of possibilities. Thus we are led to the idea that probability and information go in opposite directions: the more probable, the less informative, and *vice versa*. And thus we are led to the idea that information as news value or surprise value should be measured by some decreasing function of probability. Since what is certain affords no surprise, we want *inf*(*e*) = 0 when *prob*(*e*) = 1. One very simple measure meeting this constraint is *inf*(*e*) = 1 – *prob*(*e*).

Digging deeper, one might hold that when events *e* and *f* are uncorrelated, the information that one gains when one learns that both have occurred is the sum of what one learns from learning each has occurred since, being uncorrelated, neither bears on the other. This quite natural thought gives us the constraint

inf(*e* & *f*) = *inf*(*e*) + *inf*(*f*) when *prob*(*e* & *f*) = *prob*(*e*) × *prob*(*f*),

prob(*e* & *f*) = *prob*(*e*) × *prob*(*f*) being the probabilist's way of capturing lack of correlation.[1] For this to hold generally, we *must* have *inf*(*e*) = –log(*prob*(*e*)) (where the base of the logarithms may be chosen arbitrarily).[2] Following a path laid out by the statistician and philosopher of science I. J. Good, we have arrived in a very straightforward way at one very common probability-based measure of information (Good 1950: 74–5).

We should look a little more closely at this. First, we started out from an individual's estimation of what is likely, what unlikely, and to what extent – from what, in the jargon, are known as *subjective probabilities*, *credences*, or *degrees of belief*. Much has been written on why a rational individual's degrees of belief ought to satisfy the standard mathematical framework of probability theory. Here we shall take for granted that they do. (Items in the further reading section present arguments for why this should be so.) What concerns us here is that different individuals may give different estimates of how likely an event is: our probability-based measures of information will inherit this subjectivity from degrees of belief. Moreover, an individual's estimate of how likely an event is may change over time, more particularly, with what the individual learns over time. Thus what we have here is a conception of information, and a measure to go with it, that may vary from individual to individual, and, for a single individual, may vary as what the individual takes herself to know changes over time.

The mere addition of new beliefs consistent with what one fully believed previously, i.e., with that to which one previously assigned maximum degree of belief, is most straightforwardly dealt with under the procedure known as *Bayesian conditionalization* (application of *Bayes' Rule*); much harder to model formally is the process of adding information that conflicts with what one previously believes – here belief revision theory tells part of the story but how to marry it with subjective probability is hardly a settled matter. *Subjective Bayesianism* adds to the subjective interpretation of probability as degree of belief updating of degree of belief by *Bayes' Rule*: upon learning that *e* and nothing more, the rational individual revises her degrees of belief according to the schema

$$prob_{new}(f) = prob_{old}(f|e),$$

provided that $prob_{old}(e) \neq 0$. $prob_{old}$ is commonly called the prior probability, $prob_{new}$ the posterior.

I have spoken of individuals' estimates of how likely events are. Mathematical probability theory assigns probabilities to events and gives to the field of events over which a probability distribution distributes probabilities in the structure of a Boolean algebra. Philosophers are most likely to think of propositions as the sort of thing one believes: if one believes that Dushanbe is the capital of Tajikistan then *that Dushanbe is the capital of Tajikistan* is the proposition believed. Degrees of belief too, then, are degrees of belief in propositions and, almost invariably, subjective probabilities are assigned to propositions, not events. The difference, however, is small, for, on the assumption that a rational individual's degrees of belief are governed by classical propositional logic and that she assigns the same probability to logically equivalent propositions, we can recover the Boolean algebraic structure of the domain of that to which probabilities are assigned.

Information and "logical probability"

All this inter- and intra-individual variability may lead one to think we are missing something important in the notion of information: we might think that how informative a message is has something to do with the content of the message, not how surprising (or not) its recipient finds it. In the 1950s this idea was tackled, still in probabilistic terms, in Yehoshua Bar-Hillel and Rudolf Carnap's notions of *content* and *semantic information* (Bar-Hillel and Carnap 1953) and Karl Popper's notion of *content* (Popper 1957, 1959, Appendix *IX). Both parties take probability as basic; both parties recognize 1 – *prob* and –log *prob* as possible measures. What is different here is the conception of probability. Here the probabilities in question are measures of logical strength, running from zero for logical contradictions such as '*e* & not-*e*' to 1 for logical tautologies, propositions such as '*e*   not-*e*' which cannot but be true. Carnap spent much of the later part of his career attempting to spell out the details of how to assign so-called *logical probabilities* to the sentences of formal languages in such a way as to accommodate a "logical" account of inductive reasoning. As the project progressed, more parameters entered the system so that what looks more and more like the variability from individual to individual of subjective probability becomes a part of the theory of supposedly logical probability. The widespread – but not universal – consensus among philosophers is that the project failed; and the current popularity of subjective probability (and Subjective Bayesianism) in the philosophical literature is in no small part due to this perceived failure.

Information and the classical conception of probability

Let's back-track a little. The idea of a logical conception of probability assigned to propositions first emerged – one source is Ludwig Wittgenstein's *Tractatus Logico-Philosophicus* – as a formal analogue of the *classical conception of probability* according to which the probability of an outcome just is the ratio of the number of cases favorable to the outcome to the number of all possible cases. One needs here a specification of the possible cases but in applications this is often just obvious – e.g., the six sides of a die or the 52 cards in a standard deck. (The aces of the four suits are the cases favorable to being dealt an ace so the probability of being dealt an ace is $4 \div 52 = \frac{1}{13}$.) The classical conception works wonderfully well for games of chance – dice, cards, roulette, for example – but is rather less useful if one wishes to bet on horses. For horse-racing one needs more information than just the number of runners: one needs to know the horses' recent form, the state of the ground, and something about the jockeys up that day – and maybe training regimes, the likelihood of each horse being doped, and goodness knows what else. It's all much simpler in the cases of dice, cards, and roulette wheels, or so it seems. If you have no special information to go on – and mostly you don't – you have no reason to expect one face of the die uppermost rather than another, one card rather than another, the ball to end up in one slot on the roulette wheel rather than another. One has one's possible cases to each of which – as the classical conception requires – one assigns equal probabilities ($\frac{1}{6}$, $\frac{1}{52}$, $\frac{1}{37}$ in Europe, $\frac{1}{38}$ in North America). In the absence of information pointing to one outcome rather than another, assigning equal probabilities to the basic possible cases seems the right, the reasonable, the rational thing to do. By assigning equal probabilities, one isn't building in information one hasn't got. And when you get the information as to which outcome occurred, each of the possible outcomes is equally – and maximally – informative. In advance, one expects to gain the same amount of information, whichever outcome occurs. Hold that thought!

Entropy

Now, take the measure of information –log *prob*. A *partition* is a set of mutually exclusive and jointly exhaustive events, such as the classical conceptions "possible cases": exactly one has to occur. Given a partition $\{e_1, e_2, ..., e_n\}$ of n events, let $X(e_i)$ be a quantity associated with each event, possibly but not necessarily varying from event to event in the partition. The (*mathematical*) *expectation* or *expected value* or *mean* of the quantity X with respect to the partition $\{e_1, e_2, ..., e_n\}$ is the sum

$$\Sigma_i^n =_1 X(e_i) \times prob(e_i).$$

Expectations are a bit like averages. To force through the analogy, think of $prob(e_i)$ as the proportion of cases yielding the value $X(e_i)$. The notion of expected value must be treated with care for the expected value of a quantity may not be a realisable value of that quantity; for example, with a fair die, one for which the probability of each face falling uppermost is $\frac{1}{6}$, the expected value of the number of spots on the uppermost face is 3.5 but no face has three and a half spots painted on it.

In the particular case in which the quantity of interest is information and we measure it by $-\log prob$, the sum in question is

$$-\Sigma_i^n =_1 (prob(e_i) \times \log prob(e_i))\,.^3$$

Due to a formal similarity with the physical quantity of the same name, this is called the *entropy* of the distribution *prob* with respect to the partition $\{e_1, e_2, \ldots, e_n\}$. Now, assigning different probabilities to the members of the partition may yield different values for the entropy and it is a mathematical fact of no little interest in the present context that the sum takes its maximum value when we assign the same probability to each of $e_1, e_2, \ldots, e_n$. We maximize entropy/expected information by assigning equal probabilities (as the classical conception says we ought).

Objective Bayesianism and the principle of maximum entropy

We'd like to say that we maximize the information we expect to get on learning the actual outcome by adopting the classical conception's uniform distribution, the assignment of probabilities that recommends itself by not "building in information we haven't got." Unfortunately, on closer inspection this thought may appear no more than a pun on different uses of the words "expect" and "expectation". It would take considerably more space than I have at my disposal here to defend the claim that it is not. Suffice it to say now that we have just encountered the basic result of the classical conception's closest modern descendant, *Objective Bayesianism*.

Objective Bayesianism, prominently championed by the physicist E. T. Jaynes among others, enjoins – at least in some of its guises – the rational individual to assign as degrees of belief that prior distribution of probabilities that maximizes entropy. (It merits the epithet "Bayesianism" because it accepts Bayes' Rule for updating degrees of belief.) Two comments are called for, one technical, one conceptual. First, the technical. There is no straightforward extension from "discrete" probabilities assigned to the members of a finite partition to continuous probability distributions, distributions such as the normal distribution, although there is a widely accepted work-around: the (relative) entropy of the assignment $prob_2$ to the members of the partition $\{e_1, e_2, \ldots, e_n\}$ relative to the "reference" distribution $prob_1$ is given by the sum

$$\Sigma_i^n =_1 prob_2(e_i) \times \log \frac{prob_2(e_i)}{prob_1(e_i)} \;;$$

this notion readily extends to the continuous case.[4] Second, the conceptual. Unlike the classical conception which mandates a uniform distribution, one can apply the rubric of maximizing entropy subject to constraints which do "point to one outcome rather than another"; from a long series of tosses of a die, one may learn that it is biased, giving a mean number of spots of 4.5, not the 3.5 obtained from the uniform distribution; one can maximize entropy subject to the constraint that the expectation be 4.5 and obtain a distribution skewed in favor of the faces with larger numbers of spots. One uses the information one has and still doesn't "build in information one hasn't got."

In a rather beautiful confluence of ideas, we have that the assignment of probabilities that minimizes (relative) entropy relative to the reference distribution $prob_{old}$ subject to the constraint that $prob(e) = 1$ is the distribution $prob_{new}$ obtained by Bayes' Rule (Williams 1980: 134–135). Here *minimization*, rather than maximization, is appropriate since we seek to make the least change consistent with the constraint.

Entropy in Shannon's approach

This far we have focused on probability as degree of belief, whether subjective or in some way objectively prescribed, taken information, or, perhaps better, informativeness to be a property of events, and arrived at entropy as the expected value of the latter quantity. While entirely natural given the Bayesian framework widely adopted in contemporary philosophy of science and formal epistemology, this is not at all how entropy entered into mathematical information theory. In Shannon's theory we deal with *statistical probabilities* – proportions of occurrence of signal items in a large sample of messages – and, quite generally, want a measure of the *uncertainty* associated with the assignment of probabilities to the members of a partition. Shannon lays down some desiderata that the measure should meet and proves that entropy, as defined above, is the unique measure meeting them (Shannon 1948, Appendix 2; Khinchin 1953). The important point here is that uncertainty is a property of the probability distribution as a whole. We do not start out from a quantity assigned to each of the members of the partition. This is not at all to deny that Shannon measures the information associated with a type of signal item e by $-\log prob(e)$ where $prob(e)$ is e's statitistical probability of occurrence.

A change of direction: from information to probability

All of the above has taken probability as basic and has measured information or entropy/ uncertainty in terms of it. Lastly, and very briefly, we look at an approach that reverses that direction. I. J. Good suggested "the possibility of deriving the axioms of probability from the concept of information instead of the other way round" and took some steps towards doing so (Good 1966); the project is developed further in (Milne 2012). Milne considers the amount of information e adds to f and lays down some intuitive constraints. $inf(e, e \& f) = 0$ and $inf(e, g) \leq inf(e \& f, g)$ are obvious ones. One, proposed by Good, which does a lot of work is this:

$inf(e \& f, g)$ is determined by $inf(e, g)$ and $inf(f, e \& g)$.

The information e and f jointly add to g is fixed by the amount of information e adds to g and the amount f adds over and above that once e has been "taken on board."

Milne distinguishes two conceptions of information: one, a "novelty value" conception, adds the constraint $inf(e, f \& g) \leq inf(e, f)$ for e can't be more novel with respect to a larger corpus of information than with respect to a smaller one; the other views $inf(e, f)$ as a measure of the proportion of possibilities left open by f that are closed down by e and holds that $inf(\text{not-}e, f)$ is determined by $inf(e, f)$ for possibilities not closed down by e are closed down by not-e and *vice versa*.[5] The former leads to a measure that rescales to a non-standard, probability-like function similar to those found in (Morgan and Mares 1995); the other leads to a measure that rescales as a conditional probability distribution along the lines laid out by R. T. Cox (Cox 1946; Cox 1961, Chapter 1).

For more on Bayesianism, see Chaper 16 of this handbook. For more on Shannon's work and the mathematical theory of information, see Chapter 4. For more on conceptions of semantic information, see Chapter 6.

Notes

1 $prob(e \& f) - (prob(e) \times prob(f))$ and $\dfrac{prob(e \& f)}{prob(e) \times prob(f)}$ have both been suggested as quantitative measures of correlation, one taking the value 0, the other 1, when e and f are uncorrelated. Although it may not be obvious, the first of these is equivalent to $(prob(e \& f) \times prob(\text{not-}e \& \text{not-}f)) - (prob(e \& \text{not-}f) \times prob(\text{not-}e \& f))$ and, under the name *the odds ratio*, the quantity $\dfrac{prob(e \& f) \times prob(\text{not-}e \& \text{not-}f)}{prob(e \& \text{not-}f) \times prob(\text{not-}e \& f)}$ is a widely used measure of correlation in medical statistics.

2 For $x > 0$, the logarithm to base 2 of x, written $\log_2 x$, is that number y such that $x = 2^y$; the logarithm to base 10 of x, written $\log_{10} x$, is that number z such that $x = 10^z$; y and z are related by the conditions $y = z \times \log_2 10$ and $z = y \times \log_{10} 2$. ($\log_2 10 \approx 3.322$; $\log_{10} 2 \approx 0.301$).

   Below we shall write $-\log prob(e)$ rather than $-\log(prob(e))$.

3 We stipulate that $prob(e_i) \times \log prob(e_i) = 0$ when $prob(e_i) = 0$.

4 The relative entropy is also called the *Kullback-Leibler divergence*. 'Divergence' because *in some respects* this quantity functions like a measure of how far apart the two distributions are – it is minimized when $prob_2$ is identical to $prob_1$.

5 We are thinking here of maximally specific possibilities so that in any possibility either e obtains or not-e obtains.

Further Reading

Childers, Timothy (2013) *Philosophy and Probability*, Oxford: Oxford University Press. A critical (and approachable) guide to conceptions of probability including Objective Bayesianism and the principle of maximum entropy.

Cox, R. T. (1961) *The Algebra of Probable Inference*, Baltimore, MD: Johns Hopkins University Press. A stimulating but idiosyncratic approach to the foundations of probability and to information-theoretic entropy.

Gigerenzer, G. *et al.* (1989) *The Empire of Chance: How Probability Changed Science and Everyday Life*, Cambridge: Cambridge University Press. A survey of how ideas of chance and statistical probability came to shape modern conceptions of nature, society, and the human mind.

Jaynes, E. T. (1968) "Prior Probabilities," *IEEE Transactions on Systems Science and Cybernetics* SSC-4: 227–241. Reprinted in R. D. Rosenkrantz (ed.), *E. T. Jaynes: Papers on Probability, Statistics and Statistical Physics*, Dordrecht: Reidel, 1983, pp. 114–130. A concise account of Jaynes's views on Objective Bayesianism and the principle of maximum entropy.

Jaynes, E. T. (2003) *Probability Theory: The Logic of Science*, Cambridge: Cambridge University Press. An encyclopedic summation of Jaynes's approach to Objective Bayesianism, data analysis, and the role of the principle of maximum entropy.

Jeffrey, R. C, (2004) *Subjective Probability: The Real Thing*, Cambridge: Cambridge University Press. A short, engaged and engaging elaboration and defense of the subjectivist interpretation of probability.

There are any number of textbooks, of greater or lesser mathematical sophistication, on probability theory, statistical inference, and information theory.

References

Bar-Hillel, Y. and R. Carnap (1953) "Semantic Information," *British Journal for the Philosophy of Science* 4: 147–157.

Cox, R. T. (1946) "Probability, Frequency and Reasonable Expectation," *American Journal of Physics* 14: 1–10.

Cox, R. T. (1961) *The Algebra of Probable Inference*, Baltimore, MD: Johns Hopkins University Press.

Good, I. J. (1950) *Probability and the Weighing of Evidence*, London: Charles Griffin.

Good, I. J. (1966) "A Derivation of the Probabilistic Explication of Information," *Journal of the Royal Statistical Society, Series B (Methodological)* 28: 578–581.

Hacking, Ian (2006) *The Emergence of Probability: A Philosophical Study of Early Ideas About Probability, Induction, and Statistical Inference* (second edition), Cambridge: Cambridge University Press.

Khinchin, A. I. (1953) "The Entropy Concept in Probability Theory" [Russian], *Uspekhi Mathematicheskikh Nauk* 8(3): 3–20. Translated in Khinchin, *Mathematical Foundations of Information Theory*, New York: Dover, 1957.

Milne, P. (2012) "Probability as a Measure of Information Added," *Journal of Logic, Language and Information* 21: 163–188.

Morgan, C. and E. Mares (1995) "Conditionals, Probability, and Non-triviality," *Journal of Philosophical Logic* 24: 455–467.

Popper, K. R. (1957) "A Second Note on Confirmation," *British Journal for the Philosophy of Science* 7: 350–353.

Popper, K. R. (1959) *The Logic of Scientific Discovery*, London: Hutchinson.

Shannon, C. E. (1948) "A Mathematical Theory of Communication," *Bell System Technical Journal* 27: 379–423, 623–656. Reprinted in C. E. Shannon and W. Weaver, *The Mathematical Theory of Communication*, Urbana, IL: University of Illinois Press, 1949.

Williams, P. M. (1980) "Bayesian Conditionalisation and the Principle of Minimum Information," *British Journal for the Philosophy of Science* 31: 131–144.

3

COMPUTATION AND INFORMATION

Gualtiero Piccinini and Andrea Scarantino

Computation and information are closely related. There are several notions of computation and several notions of information, so we need to be careful in sorting out their relations (Piccinini and Scarantino 2011).

Varieties of computation

The paradigmatic notion of computation is digital computation. Digital computation is the manipulation of discrete states, which we call "digits." For present purposes, digits are values of variables that can take one of finitely many different states, such as 1 or 0. A digit in this sense need not represent a number (or anything else); it is simply a state that a computer can distinguish reliably from other kinds of state. Digital computers manipulate sequences of digits according to a rule defined over the digits; the rule specifies a relationship that must hold between input digits and output digits; typically, the manipulation proceeds by means of a series of discrete steps that change the digits. Words made out of letters from the English alphabet are strings of digits in the present sense. A computation over such digits could be defined by the following rule: take English words in an arbitrary order as input and return them in alphabetical order as output.

Ordinary digital computers are not limited to performing one type of computation on their inputs. In other words, they are not limited to following one rule for processing digits. Rather, digital computers can follow any rule that can be given to them in the form of a computer program specifying the relevant steps to be performed. A computer program is a sequence of instructions, which are strings of digits that determine which step the computer is to perform at any given time based on the input it receives and the internal state it's in. In other words, a program spells out a rule for manipulating input digits in light of the computer's internal state.

By executing instructions, digital computers are sometimes said to process instructional information, which is defined in terms of the operations performed by the computer in response to their instructions (see Chapter 10). This sort of information should not be confused with the types of information we discuss below, which are not carried by computer instructions but rather by inputs or data stored in memory.

Programs are written in appropriate programming languages, and some programming languages are more powerful than others because they allow programmers to spell out a larger class of rules over strings of digits. In 1936, logicians Alonzo Church and Alan Turing argued that certain canonical programming languages (such as Turing machines, recursive functions, and the lambda calculus) are adequate for spelling out *any* rule for manipulating digits that can be spelled out at all. Such languages are all computationally equivalent to one another – any rule that can be spelled out within one of them can be spelled out within all of them. The resulting view is the Church-Turing thesis; it says that any digital computation that follows an algorithm can be performed in accordance with instructions spelled out within these canonical programming languages. It is a compelling view that has much evidence in its favor and no evidence against (Kleene 1952).

Turing also showed how to design a computing machine that can execute *any* program written within a canonical programming language. Given any arbitrary sequence of instructions written in a canonical programming language, such machines take one instruction at a time, execute the instruction on the relevant data, and then move on to the next instruction. Machines with this property are called *universal machines*. Since ordinary computers can execute any program on any input until they run out of memory or time, they are universal in Turing's sense.

Being a universal machine is sometimes confused with being able to perform *any* digital computation, or any computation whatsoever, or even with *being able to do anything*. Computers cannot perform arbitrary activities simply by computing; for example, they cannot create a sculpture or cook a meal simply by manipulating digits, although they might contribute to creating a sculpture or cooking a meal if their computations drive suitable machines for sculpting or cooking. More significantly, computers can only perform computations for which there are programs. By definition, the only computations for which there are programs are defined over a domain that has at most countably many entities – for instance, strings of letters from a finite alphabet. In addition, the vast majority of functions from strings of digits to strings of digits are such that there is no program for computing them. The best known example of a function for which there is no program is the halting function, i.e. the function that returns, for any program and any input, whether the program will return an output and stop computing or will simply continue to compute forever without ever returning an output. Therefore, universal machines, including ordinary computers, can only compute a small subset of all the functions from strings of digits to strings of digits.

Some authors have speculated that there might be physical systems that can compute something that universal machines cannot compute (e.g., Hogarth 1994). Such hypothetical physical systems are called hypercomputers. Somehow, hypercomputers would be able to compute at least one function for which there is no computer program, such as the halting function. As of yet, there is no compelling evidence that any hypercomputer can be built.

So far, we have focused on ordinary digital computers. There are other kinds of computing systems, such as quantum computers and analog computers. They perform, respectively, *quantum computation* and *analog computation*. Quantum computers manipulate qudits according to an appropriate rule defined over the qudits (plus, possibly, internal states of the quantum computer). Qudits are like digits in that they are defined in terms of finitely many possible states, but are unlike digits in that they can be in a superposition of the different states. (A superposition is a quantum state that is a mixture of two "basis" states; for example, a quantum state composed in part by a 1 and in part by a 0.) Analog computers manipulate continuous variables in accordance with an appropriate rule defined over the continuous variables (plus, possibly, internal states of the analog computer). Continuous variables can take any real value within a certain interval, and in this respect they differ from digits.

Quantum computers can compute the same functions as ordinary digital computers – they are computationally equivalent – but in some cases they can do it more efficiently. Analog computers compute a different sort of function from digital computers, but their computations can be approximated by digital computers by encoding analog inputs as strings of digits and performing digital computations on those.

Artificial neural networks are another important class of computing devices, and they perform many different kinds of computation. They are sets of connected units in which each unit processes a variable in accordance with a rule defined over the variable. Typically, artificial neural networks have units that receive inputs from the environment (input units), units that yield outputs to the environment (output units), and units that communicate only with other units in the system (hidden units). Each unit receives input signals and delivers output signals as a function of its input and current state. As a result of their units' activities and organization, artificial neural networks turn the input received by their input units into the output produced by their output units.

Some artificial neural networks have a fixed structure and process strings of digits in discrete steps. Such networks perform digital computations just like ordinary digital computers. In fact, ordinary digital computers are a special kind of artificial neural network of this kind – what is special about them is how large and well organized they are. Other artificial neural networks have a structure that changes over time and so is subject to learning; they may also process digits but not by means of discrete steps; rather, they manipulate digits by means of continuous internal processes. Yet other artificial networks manipulate continuous variables, like those manipulated by analog computers.

What of the neural networks to be found in real brains? They process trains of action potentials or spike trains, which are a special kind of signal transmitted from neuron to neuron. Some authors have argued that spike trains are neither strings of digits like those manipulated by digital computers nor continuous variables like those manipulated by analog computers; if this is correct, computation over spike trains is a different kind of computation than either digital or analog computation (Piccinini and Bahar 2013).

To capture all of these kinds of computation, it is useful to introduce a generic notion of computation. Computation in the generic sense is the manipulation of a vehicle according to a rule defined over the vehicle (plus, possibly, the internal states of the system). Depending on which kind of vehicle is manipulated, we obtain digital computation, analog computation, quantum computation, etc.

An important feature of computation is that it is defined solely in terms of specific degrees of freedom of the vehicles that are manipulated, without considering any further physical properties that are specific to the implementing medium. Because of this, the same computation can be implemented in any physical medium (mechanical, hydraulic, electronic, etc.) that possesses the relevant degrees of freedom. In this sense, computation is *medium-independent*. Medium independence entails multiple realizability – there are many ways of realizing the same computation. But multiple realizability does not entail medium-independence – many properties are multiply realizable but *medium-dependent*, because they are tied to specific physical effects. For example, there are many different ways of producing light, so light production is multiply realizable; but light production is *medium-dependent*, for it always depends on light being produced, which is a specific physical effect.

We now turn to information.

Varieties of information and their relations to computation

How are generic computation and information related? It depends on what sort of information we are talking about (see Chapter 10). In this chapter, we distinguish three notions of information: Claude Shannon's non-semantic notion of information, natural semantic information and non-natural semantic information.

Shannon (1948) was interested in solving the "fundamental problem of communication": reproducing at a receiver's end (e.g., an airplane) a sequence of symbols generated at a source (e.g., a control tower). Shannon showed that there is a way to talk about information transmission between source and receiver without making any assumptions about what the symbols mean, if anything.

The key insight here is that there is something we are informed about when a symbol is selected, namely that all symbols different from it have *not* been selected. Information in Shannon's sense is in effect the reduction of uncertainty generated by the occurrence of one of a set of alternative possible outcomes.

Let us suppose we have an experiment which involves the observation of a random variable X taking values a_1 and a_2 with probabilities $p_1=0.9999$ and $p_2=0.0001$ respectively. Before the random experiment takes place, symbol a_1 is almost certain to be selected, and symbol a_2 highly unlikely. The selection of both symbols generates information, since they both resolve the uncertainty characterizing the situation before the experiment takes place.

The selection of a_2 generates *more information* than the selection of a_1, because it is *less expectable*, or *more surprising*, in light of the prior probability distribution. Shannon information is measured in bits, where 1 bit is the information generated by the occurrence of an outcome that has a 50 percent probability of occurring. Any outcome with probability of less than 50 percent will generate *more* than 1 bit, any outcome with probability of more than 50 percent will generate *less* than 1 bit.

Shannon introduced two measures of information and applied them to study the efficient transmission of information across communication channels. The first is *entropy*, an objective measure of the uncertainty characterizing a source as a whole that tells us how surprising the selection of symbols at the source is on average. Zero entropy corresponds to the case in which the selection of a certain symbol has probability 1 and consequently is not surprising at all. Maximum entropy corresponds to the case in which the selection of each symbol is equally probable, in which cases there is maximal uncertainty as to which symbol will be selected.

The second measure Shannon introduced is called *mutual information*. Informally, mutual information is an objective measure of how much we can determine from a variable Y about another variable X. More precisely, mutual information tells us how much the uncertainty characterizing a source X is reduced on average by observing what symbol is selected at the receiver Y. If two variables are statistically independent, then nothing can be known about one by observing the other, and their mutual information is zero. Mutual information is maximal when knowing what symbol is selected at the receiver's end eliminates all uncertainty about what symbol was selected at the source.

Armed with the *non-semantic, objective,* and *quantifiable* notions of entropy and mutual information, Shannon proved a number of seminal theorems, which had a profound impact on the field of communication engineering (see Chapter 10). In the "fundamental theorem for a noisy channel," for example, Shannon proved that it was theoretically possible to make the error rate in the transmission of information across a randomly disturbed channel as low as desired up until the point in which the source information rate in bits per unit of time becomes larger than the channel capacity per unit of time.

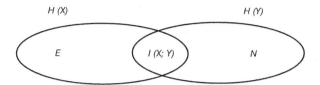

Figure 3.1 The mutual information *I(X;Y)* is the intersection between the entropy of the source *H(X)* and the entropy of the receiver *H(Y)*, in the sense that it represents their statistical dependency (it is equal to zero when *X* and *Y* are statistically independent). The portion of *H(X)* which does not lie within *I(X; Y)* is the equivocation *E*, the average amount of information generated at *X* but not received at *Y*. The portion of *H(Y)* which does not lie within *I(X; Y)* is the noise *N*, the average amount of information received at *Y* but not generated at *X*.

The first thing to note is that, strictly speaking, neither the selection of computational vehicles nor their transformation by means of rules needs to generate any Shannon information. This is because Shannon information requires uncertainty, whereas generic computation, in all of its varieties, is in principle compatible with deterministic variables and deterministic rules about their manipulation. In practice, real-world computers show noise at various junctures (e.g. in the communication between components and among computers). Noise is any random disturbance in signal transmission, which may lead to a difference between the received signal and the original signal transmitted by the source. Coding theory, a branch of communication theory focused on the efficient transformation of symbols into signals, can help us design ways of encoding information such that the intended message is retrievable in the presence of noise.

Cognitive scientists and computer scientists are most interested in the relation between computation and semantic information, i.e., information connected to the meaning of information bearers (rather than merely to how surprising they are). Following Grice's (1957) distinction between natural and non-natural meaning, we distinguish between natural (semantic) information and non-natural (semantic) information.

Natural information is the sort of information smoke carries about fire, whereas non-natural information is the sort of information words like "there is smoke" carry about smoke. Natural information has been accounted for in two main ways. Some have proposed that a signal carries natural information about anything it perfectly correlates with in accordance with a law of nature (Dretske 1981). This law-based theory of natural information guarantees that information is veridical: if the information carried by a signal is underwritten by a natural law, a signal carrying natural information that *P* entails that *P*. This is consistent with the view, defended by several authors, that information is always veridical (Grice 1957; Dretske 1981; Floridi 2005). One problem with the law-based proposal is that few of the relations between events that are of interest to information processing organisms and artifacts are law-like. For instance, there is no law of nature that guarantees that if a fire had not occurred, smoke would not have occurred, so on the law-based theory we would have to conclude that smoke does not carry information about fire.

Probabilistic theories of natural information replace the nomic requirement with the requirement that signals must reliably correlate with what signals are about (Shea 2007; Skyrms 2010; Scarantino, 2015). On this view, smoke carries natural information about fire because it reliably correlates with fire, in the sense that the presence of smoke significantly raises the probability of fire by virtue of the causal relation between them. An implication of probabilistic analyses of information is that smoke can carry information about the presence of fire, i.e. increase its probability, even when no fire is present. In this sense, natural information understood under a probabilistic theory is non-veridical (Scarantino and Piccinini 2010; but see Floridi 2005, 2010a).

Computational vehicles may or may not carry natural information about features of the external environment. Many ordinary computations operate on vehicles that carry no natural information about the external environment. For instance, ordinary mathematical calculations carried out on a computer are defined over numbers, regardless of what the digits being manipulated by the computer reliably correlate with. There are also many examples of natural information processing within computing systems. Any inputs to a computer that reliably correlate with some environmental variable carry natural semantic information. A computer may process such inputs to make the information more usable or accessible, to combine it with other information (either from memory or other sensors), or to perform control functions. For example, airplane computers use natural semantic information about the state of the airplane to regulate fuel injection, altitude, speed, and so on.

The processing of natural information must be carried out by means of computations, because natural information is a medium-independent notion. This is because whether natural information can be associated with a given vehicle does not depend on its specific physical properties, but on how it changes the probabilities of the state of affairs it is about (Scarantino, 2015). Since generic computation is just the processing of medium-independent vehicles, any processing of natural information amounts to a computation in the generic sense.

Bearers of non-natural information, unlike bearers of natural information, need not correlate reliably with what they are about. For instance, the words "there is smoke" non-naturally mean that there is smoke whether or not they correlate with the presence of smoke. Thus, there must be an alternative grounding process by which bearers of non-natural information come to bear non-natural information. A convention, as in the case of the meaning of English words, is a clear example of what may establish a non-natural informational link.

Non-natural information need not be based on convention. There may be other processes, such as biological evolution, through which non-natural informational links may be established. A paradigmatic example is offered by vervet monkey alarm calls, which "functionally refer" to different classes of predators despite the fact that no convention has associated the calls with the relevant predators (Seyfarth *et al.* 1980; Scarantino and Clay, 2014). What matters for something to bear non-natural information is simply that it comes to stand for something else relative to a signal recipient. Once this link is established, the bearer of information *represents* a certain state of affairs, and can do so successfully or unsuccessfully. The possibility of error is the key difference between natural information and non-natural information (or representation).

An important corollary of the distinction between natural and non-natural semantic information is that semantic information of the non-natural variety can be true or false. The statement "water is not transparent," for instance, contains false non-natural information to the effect that water is not transparent. Some authors take false non-natural information to be a genuine kind of information, even though it is epistemically inferior to true information. According to such authors, consumers of information value non-natural information insofar as it is true, but denying that false non-natural information is information too is not advisable, because it prevents us from capturing a large swath of information usages within the sciences (see Scarantino and Piccinini 2010, with response by Floridi 2010b).

Most generic computations process vehicles that carry non-natural information, which may be encoded in the inputs or memory states of a computer. A computer may process data carrying non-natural semantic information to make the information more usable or accessible, to combine it with other information (either from memory or other sensors), or to perform control functions. But a computer can also process vehicles that do not carry any non-natural information, as when computers put lists of meaningless words in alphabetical order. Although the words do not "represent" anything, the computation proceeds just the same. From this it follows that a generic computation may or may not involve the processing of non-natural information. The converse does not hold, in the sense that whenever non-natural information is processed, a generic computation takes place, because bearers of non-natural information carry the information they do by virtue of what they stand for and independently of the physical characteristics of their vehicles, and are in this sense medium-independent.

Computation and information processing are commonly used interchangeably, which presupposes that they are roughly synonymous terms with univocal meanings. As we have seen, this is not the case. There are multiple notions of computation and multiple notions of information, and the relations between them are complex. The claim that a system is processing information may mean nothing more than that the system can be analyzed in terms of its Shannon-information properties. Or it may mean that it processes semantic information, of either the natural or the non-natural variety. Furthermore, we have argued that computation does not presuppose information processing. Even though the computations performed by natural and artificial computing systems generally involve the processing of information, computations can at least in principle operate on vehicles that do not carry any type of information.

References

Dretske, F. (1981). *Knowledge and the Flow of Information*. Oxford, Blackwell.

Floridi, L. (2005). "Is Semantic Information Meaningful Data?," *Philosophy and Phenomenological Research,* 70.2, 351–370.

Floridi, L. (2010a). "Semantic Information and the Correctness Theory of Truth," *Erkenntnis*, 74.2, 147–175.

Floridi L. (2010b). "The Philosophy of Information: Ten Years Later," *Metaphilosophy*, 41.3, 402–419.

Grice, H.P. (1957). "Meaning," *Philosophical Review*, 66, 377–388.

Hogarth, M. L., (1994). "Non-Turing Computers and Non-Turing Computability," *PSA* 1994(1): 126–138.

Kleene, S. C. (1952). *Introduction to Metamathematics*. Princeton, NJ, Van Nostrand.

Piccinini, G. and S. Bahar (2013). "Neural Computation and the Computational Theory of Cognition," *Cognitive Science*, 34, 453–488.

Piccinini, G. and A. Scarantino (2011). "Information Processing, Computation, and Cognition," *Journal of Biological Physics, 37*(1), 1–38.

Scarantino, A. (2015). "Information as a Probabilistic Difference Maker," *Australasian Journal of Philosophy*, 93.3, 1-25

Scarantino A., and Clay Z. (2014). "Contextually variable signals can be functionally referential," *Animal Behaviour* 100:1–8, DOI 10.1016/j.anbehav.2014.08.017

Scarantino, A. and Piccinini, G. (2010). "Information without truth," *Metaphilosophy*, 41, 313–330.

Shannon, C.E. (1948). "A Mathematical Theory of Communication," *Bell System Technical Journal*, 379–423, 623–656.

Seyfarth, R.M., Cheney, D.L., and Marler, P. (1980). "Vervet Monkey Alarm Calls. Semantic Communication in a Free-ranging Primate," *Animal Behaviour*, 28, 1070–1094.

Shea, N. (2007). "Consumers Need Information: Supplementing Teleosemantics with an Input Condition," *Philosophy and Phenomenological Research, 75,* 404–435.

Skyrms, B. (2010). *Signals: Evolution, Learning, and Information*. New York: Oxford University Press.

4

MATHEMATICAL THEORY OF INFORMATION (SHANNON)

Olimpia Lombardi

Introduction

Information is everywhere, shaping our discourses and our thoughts. In everyday life, we know that the information spread by the media may trigger deep social, economic and political changes. In science, the concept of information has pervaded almost all scientific disciplines, from physics and chemistry to biology and psychology. For this reason, nowadays the understanding of the concept of information turns out to be particularly relevant (see Floridi 2010).

In general, information has content or meaning. Nevertheless, it can be quantified independently of its content. The mathematical theory of information, as developed by Claude Shannon in his classical article of 1948, supplies the formal tools to do that:

> Frequently the messages have meaning; that is they refer to or are correlated according to some system with certain physical or conceptual entities. These semantic aspects of communication are irrelevant to the engineering problem. The significant aspect is that the actual message is one selected from a set of possible messages.
>
> *(Shannon 1948: 379)*

That article was immediately followed by many works of application to communication fields such as radio, television and telephony. At present, Shannon's theory is a basic ingredient of the communication engineers' training.

Games and information

The Twenty Questions Game is well known: one player thinks of an object and the other player has twenty chances to guess what it is by asking yes-no questions. In order to simplify the game, let us suppose that the aim is to guess a number in a range between 1 and 8, say, 4. The best strategy is to ask if the number is in the lower half of the range (or in the upper half), until the range is just a single number. For example:

"Is it less than 5?" "Yes"
"Is it less than 3?" "No"
"Is it less than 4?" "No"
"So, it is 4!"

Of course, if the range is higher, more questions are needed. Therefore, it is easy to think that the number of questions necessary to find the number is a good measure of the information we get when we finally know the right answer.

But, how many questions do we need to guess a number? As we see, if we have 8 alternatives, the number N of questions is 3. If the range doubles, say from 8 to 16, one needs one more question to find the answer: N is 4. It is easy to realize that the number of questions N is such that 2^N is at least the number of alternatives n. Thus, guessing a number between 1 to n requires $N = \log_2 n$ questions. Therefore, $N = \log_2 n$ measures the amount of information contained in the fact that a particular number is selected in the range 1 to n, and, in a completely generic case, contained in the fact that a particular case is selected among n alternatives.

Ralph Hartley, in his 1928 paper called "Transmission of Information," was the first to use the word 'information' in a technical sense: for Hartley, it refers to a measurable quantity that expresses the resources needed to identify one among many equally likely alternatives, regardless of subjective or semantic aspects. But it was necessary to wait until 1948 to introduce non-equiprobable situations.

Probabilities and information

In the previous section we have considered cases in which all the alternatives are equally likely. However, the situations in which there are more likely and less likely cases are very common, and uneven distributions are particularly relevant to the amount of information.

Let us suppose that somebody tells us that the sun will rise tomorrow: we do not consider to have received much information, since the fact that the sun rises every day is almost certain. However, if one is told that he won the lottery, the amount of information received is very high, because winning is much less likely than losing. In both cases we are considering two alternatives (sun rising vs. sun not rising; winning vs. losing), but the alternatives are not equally likely. It seems clear that the more improbable an event is, the more information one gets from knowing that it happened. Then, the amount of information that an event contains is related to how easy or hard it is to guess it.

On the basis of Hartley's previous work, in his classical article Shannon (1948) introduced probabilities in the quantification of information. Since the amount of information must be higher when probability is lower, Shannon defined the information of an event a_i with probability $p(a_i)$ as $H(a_i) = \log_2\left(1/p(a_i)\right) = -\log_2 p(a_i)$, and called this magnitude "*entropy*" by analogy with thermodynamics. Shannon entropy of the event a_i becomes the information computed by Hartley when the n events a_i are equally likely; in fact, in the equiprobable case, the probability of any a_i is given by $1/n$; therefore, $H(a_i) = \log_2\left(1/p(a_i)\right) = \log_2 n$.

Although other units of measurement can be defined, the standard unit for information is called "*bit*," a contraction of *binary unit*. One bit measures the amount of information obtained when one of two equally likely alternatives is specified. One toss of a fair coin provides one bit of information, since before tossing the coin either heads or tails is equally likely to be the result.

Up to now we have considered the information provided by single events. However, communication engineering is not concerned with the occurrence of specific events, but with the communication process as a whole. Hence, Shannon focused on *average amounts of information and on the way in which such information can be reliably transmitted.*

Source, destination and average amounts of information

According to Shannon (1948, see also Shannon and Weaver 1949), a general communication system consists of five parts (see Figure 4.1):

- A *source S*, which generates the message to be received at the destination.
- A *transmitter T*, which turns the message generated at the source into a signal to be transmitted. When information is encoded, coding is also implemented by this system.
- A *channel CH*, that is, the medium used to transmit the signal from the transmitter to the receiver.
- A *receiver R*, which reconstructs the message from the signal.
- A *destination D*, which receives the message.

The source S is a system of n states s_i, each with its own probability $p(s_i)$; the sequences of states are called *messages*. Since the amount of information generated at S by the occurrence of s_i is $I(s_i) = -\log p(s_i)$ (from now on, log means $\log_2$), the *entropy of the source S* is defined as an average, that is, as the sum of the individual amounts of information weighted by the corresponding probability:

$$H(S) = -\sum_{i=1}^{n} p(s_i) \log p(s_i)$$

Analogously, the destination D is a system of m states d_j, each with its own probability $p(d_j)$. The amount of information received at D by the occurrence of d_j is $I(d_j) = -\log p(d_j)$, and the *entropy of the destination D* is the *average amount of information received at D*:

$$H(D) = -\sum_{j=1}^{m} p(d_j) \log p(d_j)$$

The relationship between $H(S)$ and $H(D)$ can be represented as in Figure 4.2, where:

- $H(S;D)$ is the *mutual information*: the average amount of information generated at S and received at D.
- E is the *equivocation*: the average amount of information generated at S but not received at D.
- N is the *noise*: the average amount of information received at D but not generated at S.

Equivocation E and noise N are measures of the dependence between source S and destination D:

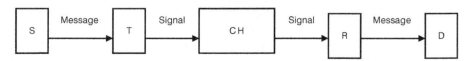

Figure 4.1 General communication system

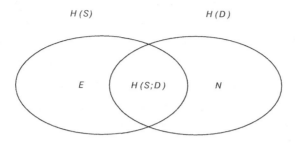

$$H (S ; D) = H (S) - E = H (D) - N$$

Figure 4.2 Relationship between the entropies of the source and the destination

- If S and D are completely independent, the values of E and N are maximum ($E=H(S)$ and $N=H(D)$), and the value of $H(S;D)$ is minimum ($H(S;D)=0$).
- If the dependence between S and D is maximum, the values of E and N are minimum ($E=N=0$), and the value of $H(S;D)$ is maximum ($H(S;D)=H(S)=H(D)$).

The values of E and N are functions not only of the source and the destination, but also of the communication channel CH, which introduces the possibility of errors during the transmission: CH is defined by the matrix $\left[p(d_j/s_i) \right]$, where $p(d/s_i)$ is the conditional probability of the occurrence of d_i in the destination D given that s_i occurred in the source S, and the elements in any row sum to 1 (see Figure 4.3).

As Shannon stresses, in communication "[t]he significant aspect is that the actual message is one selected from a set of possible messages." (1948: 379). Therefore, it is not necessary that the source S and the destination D be systems of the same kind: for instance, S may be a dice and D a dash of lights; or S may be a device that produces words in English and D a device that operates a machine. In Shannon's theory, the success criterion for communication is given by a mapping from the set of the states s_i of the source S to the set of the states d_i of the destination D. This mapping should be one-to-one (deterministic channel, Figure 4.4) or at least one-to-many (noisy channel, Figure 4.4b), since in these cases the occurrence of a given state at D makes possible to identify what state occurred at S. If the mapping is many-to-one, the occurrence of a state at D fails to identify the state occurred at S (channel with equivocation, Figure 4.4c).

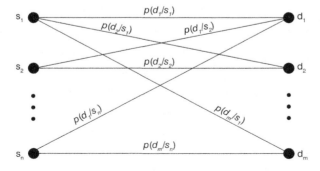

Figure 4.3 Channel $\left[p(d_j/s_i) \right]$

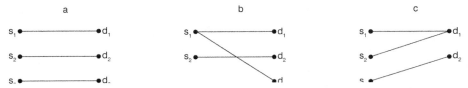

Figure 4.4 a) Example of deterministic channel; b) Example of noisy channel; c) Example of channel with equivocation

Information and coding

Once the message is produced by the source S, the transmitter T turns it into a signal that can be transmitted through the channel. In certain cases, the transmitter is a mere transducer; for instance, in classical telephony it changes sound pressure into an electrical current. However, at present almost always the transmitter encodes the message by turning each state of the source into a *code-word*, that is, a string of symbols, which usually are the *binary digits* 0 and 1.

Let us suppose that our source produces letters and that the messages are words in English. One strategy is to encode the letters with code-words of the same length. However, not all the letters are equally probable; for instance, the letter E occurs more frequently than X. Therefore, a better strategy is to code the most frequent letters with shorter code-words and the less frequent letters with longer code-words. Precisely this idea inspired Shannon to formulate the so-called *Noiseless-Channel Coding Theorem*, also known as *First Shannon Theorem*. According to this theorem, in the case of an ideal code, the minimum average length of the code-words is given precisely by the entropy of the source $H(S)$.

Let us consider an example given by Shannon himself: a source that produces a sequence of letters chosen from among A, B, C, D, with probabilities 1/2, 1/4, 1/8 and 1/8, respectively. If the four letters are encoded with code-words of the same length, for instance,

A 00
B 01
C 10
D 11

then the average length of the code-words is 2. But on the basis of the First Shannon theorem we know that there is a better coding. In fact, since the entropy of the source is:

$$H(S) = -\sum_{i=1}^{n} p(s_i) \log p(s_i) = -\left(\tfrac{1}{2} \log \tfrac{1}{2} + \tfrac{1}{4} \log \tfrac{1}{4} + \tfrac{1}{8} \log \tfrac{1}{8} + \tfrac{1}{8} \log \tfrac{1}{8}\right) = \tfrac{7}{4} \text{ bits}$$

there exists a coding for which the average length of the code-words is 7/4, for instance, this one:

A 0
B 10
C 110
D 111

where clearly the most probable letter is encoded with a shorter code-word and the less probable letters are encoded with longer code-words. The average length of these code-words is computed as:

$$\tfrac{1}{2}\times 1 + \tfrac{1}{4}\times 2 + \tfrac{1}{8}\times 3 + \tfrac{1}{8}\times 3 = \tfrac{7}{4}$$

and it is precisely the value of $H(S)$.

This example shows that, although defined as a statistical property of the source, the entropy $H(S)$ also measures how much the messages produced by the source can be compressed. It is quite clear that this result is highly relevant from a technical viewpoint, since it shows that the resources needed to transmit information reliably is less than what is pre-theoretically supposed.

Finally, it is worth mentioning the *Noisy-Channel Coding Theorem* or *Second Shannon Theorem*. This theorem shows that the probability of error in the transmission can be kept close to zero to the extent that the rate of information transmission over a channel is maintained below a property named *channel capacity*, which can be computed in terms of the mutual information $H(S;D)$.

Interpreting the concept of information

Despite its formal precision and its great many applications, Shannon's theory still offers an active terrain of debate about its interpretation.

The concept most usually connected with the notion of information is that of knowledge: information provides knowledge, modifies the state of knowledge of those who receive it (e.g. Dretske 1981; Dunn 2001; Floridi 2011). In general, this epistemic reading of information is adopted by authors who embrace a subjective interpretation of probabilities (Caves *et al.* 2002). A different view is that which considers information as a physical magnitude. This is the position of many physicists and most engineers, for whom the essential feature of information consists in its capacity to be generated at one place and transmitted to another, to be accumulated, stored and converted from one form to another (Landauer 1991, 1996). So, the link with knowledge is not a central issue, since the transmission of information can be used only for control purposes, such as operating a device at the destination end by controlling the source. In general, this view appears strongly linked with the *dictum* "no information without representation": the transmission of information necessarily requires an information-bearing signal, that is, a physical process propagating from one point of space to another. Therefore, information tends to be conceived as a physical entity with the same ontological status as energy (Stonier 1990, 1996).

The difference between the epistemic and the physical interpretations of information is not merely nominal, but may yield different conclusions in certain cases, such as the tradition that explains scientific observation in terms of information (e.g. Shapere 1982). This is particularly clear in the so-called "negative experiments," in which it is assumed that an event has been observed by noting the absence of another event. In this context, observation without direct physical interaction between the observed event and an appropriate destination is only admissible from an epistemic interpretation of information. According to a physical interpretation, by contrast, without interaction there is no observation: the event is only inferred (Lombardi 2004; Lombardi *et al.* 2014b).

According to a third position, information is a formal item. There are no sources, destinations or signals, but only random variables and probability distributions over their possible values: the word "information" does not belong to the language of factual sciences; Shannon's theory is a new chapter of the mathematical theory of probability (Khinchin 1957; Reza 1961). Not only messages have no semantic content, but the concept of information itself is purely mathematical. This syntactic nature is precisely what makes the concept a powerful tool for science. The relationship between the word 'information' and the different views about its meaning is the logical relationship between a formal term and its *interpretations*, each one of which endows it with a specific referential content (Lombardi *et al.* 2014a). The physical view is appropriate in communication, where information is transmitted by physical means. But this is not the only physical interpretation: *H*(*S*) may also represent the Boltzmann entropy of S. There are also non-traditional applications, as those based on the relation between Shannon entropy and gambling or investment in stock markets (Cover and Thomas 1991). In turn, the epistemic view may be applied in cognitive sciences, where the concept of information has been used to conceptualize the human abilities of acquiring knowledge (Hoel *et al.* 2013). This formal view resonates not only with the wide presence of the concept of information in all contemporary sciences, but also with Shannon's position when claiming:

> The word 'information' has been given different meanings by various writers in the general field of information theory. [...] *It is hardly to be expected that a single concept of information would satisfactorily account for the numerous possible applications of this general field.*
>
> *(Shannon 1993: 180)*

References

Caves, C. M., Fuchs, C. A., and Schack, R. (2002). "Unknown Quantum States: The Quantum de Finetti Representation." *Journal of Mathematical Physics*, **43**: 4537–4559.

Cover, T. and Thomas, J. A. (1991). *Elements of Information Theory*. New York: John Wiley & Sons.

Dretske, F. (1981). *Knowledge and the Flow of Information*. Cambridge, MA: MIT Press.

Dunn, J. M. (2001). "The Concept of Information and the Development of Modern Logic." pp. 423–427, in W. Stelzner (ed.), *Non-classical Approaches in the Transition from Traditional to Modern Logic*. Berlin: de Gruyter.

Floridi, L. (2010). *Information – A Very Short Introduction*. Oxford: Oxford University Press.

Floridi, L. (2011). *The Philosophy of Information*. Oxford: Oxford University Press.

Hartley, R. V. L. (1928). "Transmission of Information." *Bell System Technical Journal*, **7**: 535–563.

Hoel, E., Albantakis, L. and Tononi, G. (2013). "Quantifying Causal Emergence Shows that Macro Can Beat Micro." *Proceedings of the National Academy of Sciences*, **110**: 19790–19795.

Khinchin, A. (1957). *Mathematical Foundations of Information Theory*. New York: Dover.

Landauer, R. (1991). "Information is Physical." *Physics Today*, **44**: 23–29.

Landauer, R. (1996). "The Physical Nature of Information." *Physics Letters A*, **217**: 188–193.

Lombardi, O. (2004). "What is Information?" *Foundations of Science*, **9**: 105–134.

Lombardi, O., Fortin, S. and Vanni, L. (2014a). "A Pluralist View About Information." *Philosophy of Science*, **82**: 1248-1259.

Lombardi, O., Holik, F. and Vanni, L. (2014b). "What is Shannon Information?" *Synthese*.

Reza, F. (1961). *Introduction to Information Theory*. New York: McGraw-Hill.

Shannon, C. (1948). "The Mathematical Theory of Communication." *Bell System Technical Journal*, **27**: 379–423.

Shannon, C. (1993). *Collected Papers*, N. Sloane and A. Wyner (eds.). New York: IEEE Press.

Shannon, C. and Weaver, W. (1949). *The Mathematical Theory of Communication*. Urbana, IL and Chicago, IL: University of Illinois Press.

Shapere, D. (1982). "The Concept of Observation in Science and Philosophy." *Philosophy of Science*, **49**: 485–525.

Stonier, T. (1990). *Information and the Internal Structure of the Universe: An Exploration into Information Physics*. New York-London: Springer.

Stonier, T. (1996). "Information as a Basic Property of the Universe." *Biosystems*, **38**: 135–140.

5

ALGORITHMIC
INFORMATION THEORY

Alexander Shen

Algorithmic information theory uses the notion of algorithm to measure the amount of information in a finite object. The corresponding definition was suggested in 1960s by Ray Solomonoff, Andrei Kolmogorov, Gregory Chaitin and others: the amount of information in a finite object, or its *complexity*, was defined as the minimal length of a program that generates this object.

Informally, the amount of information in a finite object can be described as the number of bits (zeros and ones) needed to encode this object. For example, there are 26 letters in the Latin alphabet, so one can encode a letter by a combination of five bits (there are $2^5 = 32$ bit strings of length 5, and $32 \geq 26$). On the other hand, it is not possible to encode Latin letters by 4-bit strings, because we do not have enough 4-bit strings ($2^4 = 16 < 32$). So we can say that each Latin letter carries between 4 and 5 bits of information. In general, if there are N possible messages and we agree in advance on the list of all possible messages, then each message can be encoded by $\lceil \log_2 N \rceil$ bits.

A more complicated situation arises when we know in advance that some messages are more probable than others and want to minimize the expected number of bits per message. Then we can use shorter encodings for more popular messages, like in Morse code where short sequences of dots and dashes are used for some frequent letters. This approach leads to the notion of Shannon entropy of a random variable (see the chapter about Shannon information theory).

In both cases we assume that the set of possible messages (and a probability distribution on it, for the case of Shannon entropy) is fixed in advance. So we cannot measure the amount of information in an individual object (such as DNA sequence or a novel) in this way. Indeed, it is not clear what set of "possible DNA sequences" should we consider as an ensemble from which our sequence is taken. If we choose the set of all DNA sequences that existed on earth, the amount of information would be at most few hundred bits, a ridiculously small quantity; moreover, this set increases over time. Similarly, it is absurd to say that *The Brothers Karamazov* novel contains at most 4 bits of information on the grounds that Dostoevsky (its author) has written at most 16 novels.

Algorithmic information theory overcomes this problem in the following way. The amount of information in an individual finite object, or its *Kolmogorov complexity*, is defined as *the minimal length of a program without input that generates this object.* In this definition, programs and objects are binary strings. A programming language is specified by fixing an interpreter for it, i.e., an algorithm D such that $D(p)$ is the output generated by program p. We consider all algorithms whose inputs and outputs are binary strings, as interpreters. Then for a string x its *complexity with respect to D* is defined as $C_D(x) = \min\{l(p) \mid D(p) = x\}$ where $l(p)$ stands for the length of p, and the minimum of the empty set is $+\infty$.

The function C_D depends on the choice of D; better (more efficient) languages D may provide shorter programs and lower complexity than less efficient ones. One would like to find the optimal, i.e., most efficient, programming language in this sense. However, an obvious problem arises. It may happen that some D is very efficient for some class of objects, i.e., objects of this class have short programs, and at the same time D is less efficient for other objects. For each object x we can design a special programming language D_x where x has a very short program. For example, we may agree that a one-bit string 0 is a program for x: the interpreter D_x, seeing the input 0, interprets it as a command to produce x. So the complexity $C_D(x)$ is 1 if D_x is chosen as D. Moreover, having two arbitrary objects (strings) x and y, we may consider an interpreter D such that $D(0) = x$ and $D(1) = y$, thus making both complexities $C_D(x)$ and $C_D(y)$ equal to 1. However, we cannot assign short programs to many different objects, as there are not enough short programs for that. This argument shows that there is no interpreter that is better than every program of the form D_x.

So a weaker asymptotic notion of optimality is needed. We say that D *is better than* D' if $C_D(x) \le C_{D'}(x) + c$ for some c and for all x. The constant c in the definition means that we are ready to accept longer programs as soon as the overhead is bounded by some constant that depends only on the choice of D' and is independent of x. An interpreter is *optimal* if it is better than any other one. The *Kolmogorov–Solomonoff optimality theorem* says that optimal interpreters exist. We fix arbitrarily some optimal interpreter D. The value $C_D(x)$ is then called *Kolmogorov* complexity of x and denoted by $C(x)$. Using different optimal interpreters D_1 and D_2, we get different complexity functions C_{D_1} and C_{D_2}, but the optimality property guarantees that the difference is bounded: $|\,C_{D_1}(x) - C_{D_2}(x)| \le c$ for some constant c (depending on D_1 and D_2 but not on x) and for all x. So Kolmogorov complexity is defined up to a bounded additive term.

The Kolmogorov complexity of a string x is bounded by the length of x up to some bounded additive term: all n-bit strings have complexity at most $n + c$, where c is a constant not depending on n. Indeed, every n-bit string x can be generated by a program "output $XX\ldots$ $\ldots X$", where $XX\ldots X$ are the bits of x, and this program has length about n. So the complexity of a n-bit string cannot be much bigger than n (asymptotically, as n goes to infinity). But it may be much smaller than n; for example, the complexity of the string 0^n (n zeros) does not exceed $\log n + c$ for some c and for all n. Indeed, 0^n can also be generated by a shorter program "output $NN\ldots N$ zeros" where $NN\ldots N$ is n written in binary, and the length of this shorter program is about $\log n$. A counting argument shows that most strings of length n are *incompressible*, i.e., have complexity close to n. Indeed, compressible strings have programs whose length is significantly smaller than n. Using some $k < n$ as a threshold, we note that at most 2^k strings may have programs shorter than k: different strings have different programs, and the total number of all possible programs shorter than k is bounded by a total number of strings of lengths $0, 1, 2, \ldots, k-1$, i.e., is bounded by

$$1 + 2 + 2^2 + \ldots + 2^{k-1} = 2^k - 1 < 2^k.$$

We see that if k is significantly smaller than n, then the strings of complexity less than k form only a very small fraction ($1/2^{n-k}$) of all n-bit strings.

Tossing a fair coin n times and recording heads and tails, we get a n-bit string that is incompressible with high probability, i.e., with probability close to 1, according to the uniform distribution on n-bit strings usually associated with "fair coin tossing." So incompressible strings are also called *random*. Note, however, that there is no strict boundary between compressible (non-random) strings and incompressible (random) ones; the difference between the length and the complexity, called sometimes the *randomness deficiency*, is small for random strings and large for non-random ones, but there is no specific threshold that separates one collection from the other.

The notion of Kolmogorov complexity has some properties that are intuitively expected for a measure of information. Here is one example of such a property. Let A be some algorithm whose inputs and outputs are strings. One can easily show that the complexity of the string $A(x)$ may exceed the complexity of x at most by some constant c that depends on A but not on x. Interpreting the Kolmogorov complexity of a string as the "amount of information" in this string measured in bits, we may say that the algorithmic transformation of a string cannot create new information and increases the complexity only by some constant (depending on how much information was in the algorithm itself). This result allows us to define Kolmogorov complexity of arbitrary finite objects (like graphs, rational numbers, logical formulas, etc.) as the complexity of their binary encoding. The choice of a computable encoding changes the complexity defined in this way by at most an additive constant.

In saying that Kolmogorov complexity measures the amount of information in a given string, we do not mean that one can actually perform such a measurement. The exact value of complexity depends on the choice of an optimal interpreter, so the question like "which of the strings 000100010001001 and 10010000000 has higher complexity?" has no meaning, as the answer depends on the choice of the interpreter. Also one can prove that complexity function is non-computable: there is no algorithm that given x computes $C(x)$. Moreover, the complexity function has no non-trivial computable lower bounds; the proof imitates *Berry's paradox* about *the minimal natural number that cannot be described by twelve English words* (this description has exactly twelve words). Using this argument, Chaitin provided a proof of the Gödel incompleteness theorem based on Kolmogorov complexity; he showed that for large enough M one cannot prove any statement of the form "the complexity of x exceeds M" while these statements are true for all but finitely many x.

Kolmogorov complexity is sometimes called *descriptional complexity*. This should be distinguished from *computational complexity* where one studies the computational resources (processor steps, memory cells) needed to solve some problem. A string has small Kolmogorov complexity if there exists a short program that outputs it, even if this program needs a lot of time.

Information systems often store information in compressed form. A compressor program uses the regularities in the data, e.g., in some computer file, to compress this file and get a shorter one. This shorter file still contains all the information in the original file: one can restore the original file by applying a decompressor program to the compressed version. The size of the compressed version of a file is an upper bound for its Kolmogorov complexity (again up to some constant); such a bound depends on a specific method of compression and decompression used. Kolmogorov complexity, therefore, puts a limit to the possible compression of a file; no compressor can significantly compress a file whose Kolmogorov complexity is close to its length (such as a file that is a record of fair coin tossing).

When we say that Kolmogorov complexity measures the "amount of information" in a string, we do not distinguish between "useful" and "useless" information: a random noise has high Kolmogorov complexity but contains no "information" in the intuitive sense. Still we can define the amount of information in x about y for two binary strings x and y as the difference between the complexity of y and conditional complexity of y given x, the minimal length of a program that transforms x to y. To define the notion of conditional complexity in a more formal way, we consider algorithms $D(p, x)$ with two arguments as *conditional decompressors*. The first argument p is considered as a program, and the second argument x is considered as a condition. Then the function

$$C_D(y \mid x) = \min\{l(p) \mid D(p, x) = y\}$$

is defined. Again an optimal $D(p, x)$ exists that makes the function C_D minimal up to an additive constant. Some optimal $D(p, x)$ is fixed, and the corresponding function $C_D(y \mid x)$ is called *conditional complexity of y given x*.

Then the *amount of information in x about y* is defined as $C(y) - C(y \mid x)$. As shown by Kolmogorov and Leonid Levin, the notion of information defined in this way is almost symmetric: the amount of information in x about y and the amount of information in y about x differ at most by $c \log n$ for some c and for arbitrary n and arbitrary n-bit strings x and y. Both values are close to the *mutual information between x and y*, defined as $C(x) + C(y) - C(x, y)$. Here $C(x, y)$ stands for the complexity of a pair (x, y), i.e., the complexity of some of its computable encoding. Whereas the Kolmogorov complexity of a string x measures how many bits are needed to specify this string, there is a related notion, called *a priori probability* of a string x that measures how likely x appears as an output of a random process. Consider a randomized algorithm M without input that uses fair coin tosses, outputs some binary string (depending on the outcome of the coin tosses), and terminates. The algorithm M may also work infinitely long producing no output. By $p_M(x)$ we denote the probability of the event "the binary string x appears as the output of M". In this way for every M we get a real-valued function p_M defined on binary strings; these functions are called *lower semicomputable semimeasures*. Among all these function there exists a maximal one: there is some algorithm M such that for every algorithm M' the inequality $p_M(x) \geq \varepsilon \, p_{M'}(x)$ is true for some $\varepsilon > 0$ and for all x. We fix one of these maximal functions p_M and call it *discrete a priori probability of x*. As shown by Levin, it is closely related to Kolmogorov complexity: $\log_2(1/p_M(x))$ differs from $C(x)$ at most by $c \log l(x)$ for some constant c and for all x. Moreover, Levin suggested a different definition of complexity, called *prefix complexity*, that makes the difference between $\log_2(1/p_M(x))$ and the complexity of x bounded. Later this connection between a priori probability and complexity was rediscovered by Chaitin.

The algorithmic information theory may be considered as an extension of Shannon information theory to individual objects. The Shannon entropy provides an upper bound for Kolmogorov complexity in the following sense: the complexity of a N-bit string x does not exceed $NH + O(\log N)$, where H is the Shannon entropy of a random variable with two values whose probabilities p^0 and p^1 are frequencies of zeros and ones in x. Intuitively, Shannon entropy takes into account the statistical regularities while Kolmogorov complexity considers all algorithmically discoverable regularities, including the statistical ones, so Shannon entropy provides an upper bound for Kolmogorov complexity. One can show also that if a finite object is generated by a random process, then with probability close to 1 the Kolmogorov complexity of this object is close to the entropy of the random process.

Another, more recent result relates algorithmic information theory and classical information theory (by Andrei Romashchenko): the linear inequalities that are true for Shannon entropies of tuples of variables, and for Kolmogorov complexities of tuples of strings (with logarithmic precision in the latter case) are the same.

Switching from finite binary strings to infinite sequences of zeros and ones, one can draw a sharp dividing line between "random" and "non-random" sequences. The first attempts to provide such a definition were made in the beginning of the twentieth century by Richard von Mises who defined a *Kollektiv* as a sequence where zeros and ones appear with some limit frequencies that remains the same for every sub-sequence selected by some admissible rule. Mises did not give a precise definition; later Abraham Wald, Jean Ville, Alonzo Church, Donald Loveland, Kolmogorov and others studied different mathematical notions of randomness defined along these lines. It turned out that this notion is too broad; in the 1960s Per Martin-Löf suggested a stricter definition based on the ideas of constructive measure theory. A set X of binary sequences is *effectively null* if for every n one can effectively generate a sequence of intervals that covers X and has measure less than 2^{-n}. Martin-Löf proved that there exists a maximal effectively null set containing all others; *Martin-Löf random* sequences are sequences that do not belong to this maximal set. This notion is related to the notion of incompressibility: Claus-Peter Schnorr and Levin proved that a binary sequence is Martin-Löf random if and only if its finite prefixes are incompressible (have bounded randomness deficiency, where randomness deficiency is defined using special version of complexity called *monotone* complexity; prefix complexity can also be used). Martin-Löf's definition of randomness guarantees that most laws of probability theory hold for random sequences. For example, the *strong law of large numbers* says that with probability 1 a sequence of zeros and ones obtained by tossing a fair coin is *normal*, i.e., all combinations of n zeros and ones appear in the sequence with the same limit frequency 2^{-n}. The constructive version of this law guarantees that *every* Martin-Löf random sequence is normal. However, not every normal sequence is random: the *Champernowne sequence* 011011100101110 . . ., obtained by concatenation of all integers in binary (0, 1, 10, 11, 100, 101, 110,. . .), is normal but computable, and no computable sequence is Martin-Löf random.

There are interesting connections between computability (recursion) theory and algorithmic information theory, see [8, 9]. The notion of complexity is often used while discussing the methodology of natural sciences. The famous Occam's razor asks for the simplest possible explanation of some observations (sometimes one speaks also about the "economy of thought"), but does not say how we measure the 'simplicity'. With all disclaimers above (Kolmogov complexity is not uniquely defined and is not computable), we can use the algorithmic information theory to make this notion of "simplicity" more concrete. A more specific version of this approach is called the *minimal description principle*. Having some experimental data, presented as a binary string x, we look for a statistical model that treats this x as a typical example taken from some class S of strings. More formally, we consider a finite set of strings S that contains x, as a model for x. There could be several models for the same x; which is better? According to the minimal description length principle, a good model, called *sufficient statistic*, should have $C(S) + \log_2 \#S$ close to $C(x)$, where $\#S$ stands for the cardinality of S, and $C(S)$ is the complexity of S (defined as the complexity of the binary encoding of S; recall that S is a finite set of binary strings, so it can be encoded by a binary string). Each element of S has a two-part description. First we specify S using $C(S)$ bits. Then we specify the ordinal number of x in S, i.e., we specify that x is the n-th element of S in some fixed natural ordering. This second part n uses $\log_2 \#S$ bits. In total we use about $C(S) + \log_2 \#S$ bits for this two-part description, so $C(x)$ cannot exceed significantly $C(S) + \log_2 \#S$. The minimal description length principle says that for a good model these two values are close to each other. In this way we may hope to separate the regularities in x that force it to be in S, and random noise that determines which specific element of S was chosen. If there are several sufficient statistics, the *minimal sufficient statistic* where $C(S)$ is as small as possible, should be preferred.

The notions of complexity and randomness are important for the foundations of probability theory. A well-known paradox: seeing 1000 tails in a row while tossing a coin, we reject the hypothesis of a fair coin on the grounds that the probability of such an event is astronomically small, only 2^{-1000}. However, if the other day some other sequence y of 1000 heads and tails appears, the probability to see this sequence y is the same 2^{-1000}, yet we do not consider it as a reason to reject the fair coin hypothesis. What is the difference between the sequence x of 1000 tails and the sequence y? One can say that x was in our mind before the experiment while y was not; however, if a sequence with 1000 first binary digits of π appears, we also will suspect some cheating trick even if we never thought about this possibility before the experiment. Using the notion of complexity, we may explain the difference saying that x is simple while the complexity of y is close to its length.

There are many other philosophical questions related to the notion of complexity. For example, there is an experimental observation: tossing a fair coin many times and applying standard compression software to the resulting sequence, we never achieve a significant compression. Is this observation derivable from the laws of physics, or it is an additional law of nature? Does it happen because the coin tossing results have high Kolmogorov complexity, or just because our compressors are not clever enough? Can Kolmogorov complexity be applied somehow to the foundations of thermodynamics – in particular, can it be used to define entropy of a specific state of a dynamical system?

Though the notion of Kolmogorov complexity is purely theoretical, the ideas from algorithmic information theory can give insights for practical applications. Rudi Cilibrasi and Paul Vitanyi suggested to use compressed size as a first approximation to complexity, and defined a version of information distance: the distance between x and y is small if the concatenated string xy, being compressed, gives something much shorter than the concatenation of compressed versions of x and y. They applied this distance to the hierarchical clustering problems. They also tried another approach that used the number of appearences in a search engine as a way to estimate a priori probability.

Literature. Original papers: In [1] the notion of Kollektiv is introduced; [2, 3, 4] contain the definition of complexity (independently discovered); [5] describes the proof of Gödel incompleteness theorem using complexity; in [6] the definition of Martin-Löf random sequences is given. Textbooks and surveys: [7] covers a lot of material related to Kolmogorov complexity and algorithmic randomness, with historical account and references; [8, 9] also cover more recent results relating algorithmic information theory and recursion (computability) theory; [10] is a textbook that also contains some more recent results not covered by other books; [11] is a concise introduction to the subject (lecture notes of a course), and [12] is a survey describing philosophical aspects of algorithmic information theory.

References

[1]   von Mises, Richard. Grundlagen der Wahrscheinlichkeitsrechnung, *Mathematische Zeitschrift*, **5**, 52–99 (1919). Reprinted in Selected *Papers of Richard von Mises*. Volume 2. Probability and Statistics, General. American Mathematical Society, Providence, RI, 1964.

[2]   Solomonoff, Ray. A formal theory of inductive inference, *Information and Control*, **7**(1), 1–22 (1964), especially Section 3.1.2.

[3]   Kolmogorov, Andrei N. Three approaches to the quantitative definition of information. Russian original published in *Problemy peredachi informatsii* [Problems of Information Transmission], **1**(1),

3–11 (1965). Translation is reprinted in *International Journal of Computer Mathematics*, **2**, 157–168 (1968).

[4]   Chaitin, Gregory. On the length of programs for computing finite binary sequences: statistical considerations. *Journal of the ACM*, **16**(1), 145–159 (1969), especially Section 9.

[5]   Chaitin, Gregory. Computational complexity and Gödel's incompleteness theorem, ACM SIGACT News, 9 (April 1971), 11–12.

[6]   Martin-Löf, Per. The definition of random sequences, *Information and Control*, **9**, 602–619 (1966).

[7]   Li, Ming and Vitanyi, Paul M.B. *An Introduction to Kolmoghorov Complexity*, 3rd edition, Springer, 2008. XXIV, 792 p.

[8]   Downey, Rodney G. and Hirschfeldt, Denis R., *Algorithmic Randomness and Complexity*, Springer, 2010. XXIII, 855 p.

[9]   Nies, André. *Computability and Randomness*, Oxford University Press, 2012, 456 p.

[10] Vereshchagin, Nikolay K., Uspensky, Vladimir A. and Shen, Alexander, *Kolmorogov Complexity and Algorithmic Randomness*, Moscow, MCCME Publishers, 2012. [In Russian; for draft English translation see www.lirmm.fr/~ashen/kolmbook-eng.pdf]

[11] Shen, Alexander, *Algorithmic Information Theory and Kolmogov Complexity*, Technical Report TR2000-034, Uppsala University, 2000. Available at www.it.uu.se/research/publications/reports/2000-034/.

[12] Shen, Alexander, Algorithmic information theory and foundations of probability, *Reachability Problems, LNCS 5797*, Springer, 2009, 26–34. See also arxiv.org/abs/0906.4411.

6

SEMANTIC INFORMATION

Luciano Floridi

Introduction

This chapter introduces the concept of semantic information.[1] Suppose Alice and Bob exchange some messages about Bob's car. The mathematical theory of communication (MTC, see Chapter 4) provides a detailed analysis of how their data exchange works. However, as far as MTC is concerned, Alice and Bob might have been talking about the weather, their holidays, or indeed anything else, the analysis would not change. This is so because MTC studies information as a probabilistic phenomenon. Its central question is whether and how many interpretable data can be encoded and transmitted efficiently by means of a given alphabet and through a given channel. MTC is not interested in the meaning, reference, relevance, reliability, usefulness, interpretation, significance, or truthfulness of the information exchanged, but only in the level of detail and frequency in the uninterpreted data that constitute it. Thus, the difference between information in Shannon's sense and semantic information is comparable to the difference between a Newtonian description of the physical laws describing the dynamics of a car accident and the description of the same accident by the police. The two are certainly related, the question is how closely. In this chapter, we shall consider this issue, look at the definition of semantic information, and explore several approaches that have sought to provide a satisfactory account of what it means for something to be semantically informative. Then, by way of conclusion, we shall consider two significant problems affecting such approaches, the Bar-Hillel–Carnap Paradox and the Scandal of Deduction, and how they may be solved.

Factual semantic information

When data have a well-formed structure (syntax) and a meaning (semantics) they are more than just a string of gibberish; they amount to semantic content. Semantic content may be *instructional*. Suppose Bob's car has a flat battery. He calls the garage and Alice tells him over the phone *how* to use jumper cables to start his car's engine. Such instructional content cannot qualify as either true or false, in the same sense in which imperative (e.g., close the door!) cannot. We shall not purse this topic here because Chapter 9 is entirely devoted to it.

When semantic content can qualify as either true or false, then it is also called *factual*, because it is not *for* something but *about* something, as when Bob tells Alice that the battery is flat. This is the topic of the rest of this chapter.

The first question one may ask is what difference there is between some semantic *content* and some semantic *information*, when they are both factual. Suppose Bob lies to Alice: he tells her that his wife Claire forgot to switch off the car's lights, when in fact he forgot himself. Did Bob provide any information to Alice? Strictly speaking, he provided only a false "story", that is, some semantic content about a plausible situation. In fact, he failed to inform Alice because the semantic content was not true. Semantic content becomes semantic information only when it is veridical. In more formal terms, the definition (DEF) of semantic information is:

DEF   *p* qualifies as factual semantic information if and only if *p* is (constituted by) *well-formed*, *meaningful* and *veridical data*.

According to DEF, factual semantic information is, strictly speaking, inherently *truth-constituted* and not a contingent *truth-bearer*, exactly like knowledge but unlike propositions or beliefs, for example, which are what they are independently of their truth-values. Semantic information encapsulates truth, exactly as knowledge does: Alice fails to be informed and hence cannot know that Claire forgot to switch off the car's lights because it is not true that she did; but she is informed, and hence can know, that the battery of Bob's car is flat because it is true that it is. So the difference between factual semantic *content* and factual semantic *information* is that the latter needs to be true, whereas the former can also be false. Note that DEF speaks of *veridical* rather *true* data because strings or patterns of well-formed and meaningful data may constitute sentences in a natural language, but of course they can also generate formulae, maps, diagrams, videos or other semiotic constructs in a variety of physical codes, and in these cases "veridical" is to be preferred to "true".

DEF offers several advantages, three of which are worth highlighting in this chapter. First, it clarifies the fact that false information is not a genuine type of information. One speaks of false information not as one speaks of a false sentence, which is a genuine sentence that happens to be false, but in the same way as one qualifies someone as a false friend, i.e. not a friend at all. It follows that when semantic content is false, this is a case of *misinformation*. If the source of misinformation is aware of its nature, as when Bob intentionally lied to Alice, one speaks of *disinformation*. Disinformation and misinformation are ethically censurable but may be successful in achieving their purpose: in our example, Alice was still able to provide Bob with the right advice, despite being disinformed by him about the exact cause of the problem. Likewise, information may still fail to be successful; just imagine Bob telling Alice that his car is merely out of order, true but rather useless.

The second advantage is that DEF forges a robust and intuitive link between factual semantic information (henceforth I shall also speak simply of information whenever this does not generate confusion) and knowledge. Knowledge encapsulates truth because it encapsulates information, which, in turn, encapsulates truth, as in a three matryoshka dolls. Knowledge and information are members of the same conceptual family. What the former enjoys and the latter lacks, over and above their family resemblance, is the web of mutual relations that allow one part of it to account for another. Shatter that, and you are left with a pile of truths or a random list of bits of information that cannot help to make sense of the reality they seek to address. Build or reconstruct that network of relations, and information starts providing that overall view of the world that we associate with the best of our epistemic efforts. So once some information is available, knowledge can be built in terms of explanations or accounts that make sense of the available information. Bob knows that the battery is flat not by merely guessing rightly, but because he connects into a correct account the visual information that the red light of the low battery indicator is flashing, with the acoustic information that the engine is not making any noise, and with the overall impression that the car is not starting. It is exactly in this sense that information is the essential starting point of any epistemic and scientific investigation.

A third advantage will be appreciable towards the end of this chapter, where Def plays a crucial role in the solution of the so-called Bar-Hillel–Carnap Paradox. Before that, we need to understand what it means for something to convey the information that such and such is the case, that is, in what sense semantic information may be more or less informative, and whether this "more or less" may be amenable to rigorous quantification.

The analysis of informativeness

Approaches to the informativeness of semantic information differ from MTC in two main respects. First, they seek to give an account of information as *semantic* content, investigating questions such as "how can something count as information? and why?", "how can something carry information about something else?", "how can semantic information be generated and flow?", "how is information related to error, truth and knowledge?", "when is information useful?". Second, approaches to semantic information also seek to connect it to other relevant concepts of information and more complex forms of epistemic and mental phenomena, in order to understand what it means for something, such as a message, to be informative. For instance, we may attempt to ground factual semantic information in environmental information. This approach is also known as the *naturalization of information*.

Analyses of factual semantic information tend to rely on propositions, such as "Paris is the capital of France", "Water is H_2O" or "the car's battery is flat". How relevant is MTC to similar analyses? In the past, some research programmes tried to elaborate information theories *alternative* to MTC, with the aim of incorporating the semantic dimension (see Chapter 26). Nowadays, most researchers agree that MTC provides a rigorous constraint to any further theorizing on all the semantic and pragmatic aspects of information. The disagreement concerns the crucial issue of the *strength* of the constraint.

At one extreme of the spectrum, a theory of factual semantic information is supposed to be *very* constrained, perhaps even overdetermined, by MTC (see for example Dretske 1981), somewhat as mechanical engineering is by Newtonian physics. At the other extreme, a theory of factual semantic information is supposed to be *only weakly* constrained, perhaps even completely underdetermined, by MTC, somewhat as tennis is constrained by Newtonian physics, that is, in the most uninteresting, inconsequential and hence negligible sense. Most analytic epistemology seems to be based implicitly on this assumption.

The emergence of MTC in the 1950s generated some initial enthusiasm that gradually cooled down in the following decades. Historically, theories of factual semantic information have moved from "very strongly constrained" to "only weakly constrained". Recently, we find positions that appreciate MTC only for what it can provide in terms of a robust and well-developed statistical theory of correlations between states of different systems (the sender and the receiver) according to their probabilities.

Although the analysis of semantic information has become increasingly autonomous from MTC, two important connections have remained stable between MTC and even the most recent accounts: the communication model and the so-called "Inverse Relationship Principle" (IRP).

The communication model has remained virtually unchallenged, even if nowadays theoretical accounts are more likely to consider, as basic cases, multiagent and distributed systems interacting in parallel, rather than individual agents related by simple, sequential channels of communication. In this respect, our philosophy of information has become less Cartesian and more "social". I shall not dwell on it here because it is explained in Chapter 4.

IRP refers to the inverse relation between the probability of *p* – where *p* may be a proposition, a sentence of a given language, an event, a situation, or a possible world – and the amount of semantic information carried by *p*. IRP states that information goes hand in hand with unpredictability (Shannon's surprise factor). For example, a biased coin provides increasingly less information the more likely one of its outcomes is, to the point that if it had two identical sides, say heads, the probability of heads would be 1, while the informativeness of being told that it is heads would be 0. Karl Popper is often credited as the first to have advocated IRP explicitly (Popper 1935). However, systematic attempts to develop a formal calculus involving it were made only after Shannon's breakthrough. MTC defines information in terms of probability. Along similar lines, the *probabilistic approach* to semantic information defines the information in *p* in terms of the inverse relation between information and the probability of *p*. This approach was initially suggested by Yehoshua Bar-Hillel and Rudolf Carnap (Bar-Hillel and Carnap orig. 1953 rep. 1964). Several approaches have refined their work in various ways. However, they all share IRP as a basic tenet and for this reason they all encounter two classic problems, known as the "scandal of deduction" and the Bar-Hillel–Carnap Paradox.

The scandal of deduction

Following IRP, the more probable or possible *p* is, the less informative it becomes. So, if Alice tells Bob that a new battery will be available sometime in the future, this is less informative than if she tells him that it will be available in less than a month, since the latter message excludes more possibilities. This seems plausible, but consider what happens when the probability of *p* is highest, that is, when $P(p) = 1$. In this case, *p* is equivalent to a tautology, that is, something that is always true. Tautologies are well known for being non-informative. Bob would be receiving content but no semantic information if he were told that "a new battery will or will not become available in the future". Again, this analysis seems very reasonable. However, in classical logic, a conclusion Q is deducible from a finite set of premises $P_1,...,P_n$ if and only if the conditional [P_1 and P_2, and... P_n imply Q] is a tautology. Accordingly, since tautologies carry no information at all, no logical inference can yield an increase of information, so logical deductions, which can be analysed in terms of tautological processes, also fail to provide any information. Indeed, by identifying the semantic information carried by a sentence with the set of all possible worlds or circumstances it excludes, it can be recognized that, in any valid deduction, the information carried by the conclusion must be already contained in the information carried by the (conjunction of) the premises. This is what is often meant by saying that tautologies and inferences are "analytical". But then logic and mathematics would be utterly uninformative. This counterintuitive conclusion is known as "the scandal of deduction". Chapter 15 analyses it in detail so I shall not discuss it here any further.

The Bar-Hillel–Carnap paradox

Instead, let us return to IRP. The less probable or possible *p* is, the more informative it is. If Bob is told that the car's electric system is out of order, this is more informative than if he is told that either the battery is flat and/or the car's electric system is out of order, simply because the former case is satisfied by fewer circumstances. Once again, this analysis seems reasonable. But if we keep making *p* less and less likely, we reach a point when the probability of *p* is actually zero, that is, *p* is impossible or equivalent to a contradiction, but, according to IRP, this is when *p* should be maximally informative. We saw that the scandal of deduction is that tautologies, and hence basically mathematics and logic, cannot be informative. We are now faced by the opposite problem: contradictions are maximally informed. Bob would be receiving the highest amount of semantic information if he were told that the car's battery is and is not flat (at the same time and in the same sense). I called this other counterintuitive conclusion the Bar-Hillel–Carnap Paradox (Floridi 2005) because the two philosophers were among the first to make explicit the counterintuitive idea that contradictions are highly informative.

Since its formulation, the problem has been recognized as an unfortunate, yet perfectly correct and logically inevitable consequence of any quantitative *theory of weakly semantic information*. "Weakly" because truth-values play no role in it. As a consequence, the problem has often been either ignored or tolerated as the price of an otherwise valuable approach. A straightforward way of avoiding the paradox, however, is by adopting a semantically stronger approach, according to which factual semantic information encapsulates truth. This is the approach adopted in this chapter. Once again, the technicalities can be skipped in favour of the simple idea. The reader may recall that one of the advantages of DEF was that it could play a crucial role in the solution of the Bar-Hillel–Carnap Paradox. It is now easy to see why: if something qualifies as factual semantic information only when it satisfies the truthfulness condition, contradictions and indeed falsehoods are excluded a priori. The quantity of semantic information in *p* can then be calculated in terms of distance of *p* from the situation *w* that *p* is supposed to address. Imagine there will be exactly three guests for dinner tonight. This is our situation *w*. Imagine Bob is cooking the meal and Alice tells him that either

A there will or will not be some guests for dinner tonight; or
B there will be some guests tonight; or
C there will be three guests tonight; or
D there will and will not be some guests tonight.

The *degree of informativeness* of A is zero because, as a tautology, A applies both to *w* and to its negation. B performs better, while C has the maximum degree of informativeness because, as a fully accurate, precise and contingent truth, it "zeros in" on its target *w*. And since D is false (it is a contradiction), it does not qualify as semantic information at all, just mere semantic content, that is well-formed and meaningful data. Generally, the more distant the information is from its target, the larger the number of situations to which it applies, and the lower its degree of informativeness becomes. A tautology is an instance of true information that is most "distant" from the world. A contradiction is an instance of misinformation that is equally distant from the world. Of course, sometimes one may prefer an instance of misinformation – e.g. being told that there will be four guests, when in fact there will be only three – than an instance of semantic information that is too vacuous, e.g. being told that there will be fewer than 100 guests tonight.

Note

1 The chapter is based on (Floridi 2010, 2011), two books where the reader will find more details and advanced analyses.

References

Bar-Hillel, Y., and R. Carnap. orig. 1953 rep. 1964. "An Outline of a Theory of Semantic Information", In *Language and Information: Selected Essays on Their Theory and Application*, 221–74. Reading, MA and London: Addison-Wesley.

Dretske, F. I. 1981. *Knowledge and the flow of information*. Oxford: Blackwell.

Floridi, Luciano. 2005. "Is Semantic Information Meaningful Data?" *Philosophy and Phenomenological Research* 70 (2):351–370.

Floridi, Luciano. 2010. *Information: A Very Short Introduction*. Oxford: Oxford University Press.

Floridi, Luciano. 2011. *The Philosophy of Information*. Oxford: Oxford University Press.

Popper, Karl Raimund. 1935. *Logik der forschung: zur erkenntnistheorie der modernen naturwissenschaft, Schriften zur wissenschaftlichen weltauffassung, Bd. 9*. Vienna: J. Springer Eng. tr. The Logic of Scientific Discovery (London: Hutchinson, 1959).

7

THE METHOD OF ABSTRACTION

Luciano Floridi

Introduction

'In the development of our understanding of complex phenomena, the most powerful tool available to the human intellect is abstraction.' This citation come from *Notes on Data Structuring*, a very influential text written by one of the greatest computer scientists of our time, C. A. R. Hoare (Hoare 1972). Hoare is right. And philosophers should take notice, for we are in the business of conceptual design, a business that requires a very fine ability to handle abstractions. In this chapter, we shall look at what is probably the most important tool that can help us in such a business, the so-called method of levels of abstraction, or simply LoA.

In the first section, I shall illustrate what a LoA is intuitively. In the second section, I shall offer a definition of the basic concepts fundamental to the method. Although the definitions require some rigour, all the main concepts are introduced without assuming any previous knowledge. The definitions are illustrated by some simple examples, which are designed to familiarize the reader with the method. A comparison between levels of abstractions and interfaces is also developed in order to make the method more accessible and easily applicable in the following analyses. In the third section, I shall show how the choice of a LoA commits a theory ontologically. In the conclusion, I shall briefly summarize the results obtained. The reader interested in a more technical treatment and further applications may wish to consult Floridi (2008, 2010, 2011 and 2013).

On the very idea of levels of abstraction

Let us begin with a few examples. Imagine you ask the price of an item, let's say a second-hand car, and you receive the following answer: 5,000. The question concerned a *variable*, namely the price x of the car in question, and you received an exact numerical value for the variable, yet something is missing. You still have no idea about the price because you do not know the *type* of the variable: is it British pounds, US dollars, euros...? Of course, the context usually helps. If you are in England and you are asking a car dealer, your question should be understood as concerning the price in British pounds and so should the answer.

We can treat factual information of the kind illustrated above as a compound of question + answer. If some theoretical simplification is allowed, the question may be reduced to a Boolean one, followed by a yes or a no answer. In the original version of our example, the price of the second-hand car then becomes: [is the price of this car 5,000? + yes]. You see immediately that the problem lies not in the answer, but in the question: it contains no indication of the type of the variable being handled. The correct piece of information is of course: [is the price of this car £ 5,000? + yes]. We have just introduced the correct level of abstraction or LoA, represented by the symbol for British pounds, not, for example, by the symbol € for euros.

This is trivial, you may think. Grice's conversational rules obviously apply. It is, and they do. But this is also a crucial assumption, easily forgotten. In November 1999, NASA lost the $ 125m Mars Climate Orbiter (MCO) because the Lockheed Martin engineering team used English (also known as Imperial) units of measurement, while the agency's team used the metric system for a key spacecraft operation. As a result, the MCO crashed into Mars.[1] Assuming that contexts will always disambiguate the types of your variables paves the way to costly mistakes.

The idea of a 'level of abstraction' plays an absolutely crucial role in how we handle any information process, and so in how we negotiate our interactions with the world, and therefore in how we develop our philosophy and ethics of information. This is so even when a specific LoA is wrong or left implicit, as in the MCO example. So what is a LoA exactly?

The definition of a level of abstraction

The method of abstraction comes from modelling in science, where the variables in the model correspond to observables in reality, all others being abstracted. The terminology has been influenced by an area of computer science, called Formal Methods, in which discrete mathematics is used to specify and analyse the behaviour of information systems. Despite that heritage, the idea is not at all technical and, for the purposes of this chapter, no mathematics is required. Let us begin with another everyday example.

Suppose we join Alice, Bob, and Carol at a party. They are in the middle of a conversation. Alice is a collector and potential buyer; Bob tinkers in his spare time; and Carol is an economist. We do not know the subject of their conversation, but we are able to hear this much:

- Alice observes that it (whatever 'it' is) has an anti-theft device installed, is kept garaged when not in use, and has had only a single owner;
- Bob observes that its engine is not the original one, that its body has been recently re-painted but that all leather parts are very worn;
- Carol observes that the old engine consumed too much, that it has a stable market value, but that its spare parts are expensive.

The participants view the 'it' according to their own interests, which orient the choice of their conceptual interfaces or, more precisely, of their own levels of abstraction. We may guess that they are probably talking about the second-hand car we already met at the beginning of this chapter, but it could be a motorcycle or even an aeroplane, since any of these three artefacts would satisfy the descriptions provided by A, B, and C above. Whatever the reference is, it provides the source of information under discussion. We shall call this 'it' the *system*. A LoA consists of a collection of observables, each with a well-defined possible set of values or outcomes. For the sake of simplicity, let us assume that Alice's LoA matches that of an owner,

Bob's that of a mechanic, and Carol's that of an insurer. Each LoA (imagine a computer interface) makes possible a determinate analysis of the system. We shall call the result or output of such analysis a *model* of the system. Evidently, a system may be described at a range of LoAs and so can have a range of models. We are now ready for a more formal definition.

The term 'variable' is commonly used throughout science for a symbol that acts as a placeholder for an unknown or changeable referent. We saw that a 'typed variable' is understood as a variable qualified to hold only a declared kind of data. For example, if Bob asks Alice for her telephone number, whatever the latter is (variables), he expects natural numbers to be the TYPE of the variables she will provide. Since the system investigated may be entirely abstract or fictional the term 'observable' should not be confused here with 'empirically perceivable'. Historically, it might be an unfortunate terminological choice, but, theoretically, an *observable* is just an *interpreted typed variable*; that is, a typed variable together with a statement of what feature of the system under consideration it represents, for example a set of data could have NATURAL NUMBERS as a type and *telephone number* as a feature of the system. A level of abstraction (LoA) is a finite but non-empty set of observables, which are expected to be the building blocks in a theory characterized by their very choice. An 'interface' (called a 'gradient of abstractions') consists of a collection of LoAs and is used in analysing a system from varying points of view or at varying LoAs.

We saw that models are the outcome of the analysis of a system developed at some LoA(s). The *method of abstraction* consists in formalizing the model. In philosophy this often happens implicitly, and only in *qualitative* rather than quantitative terms, by using the concepts just introduced (and others relating to system behaviour which we do not need here). In the previous example, Alice's LoA might consist of observables for SECURITY, METHOD OF STORAGE, and OWNER HISTORY; Bob's might consist of observables for ENGINE CONDITION, EXTERNAL BODY CONDITION, and INTERNAL CONDITION; and Carol's might consist of observables for RUNNING COST, MARKET VALUE, and MAINTENANCE COST. For the purposes of discussion, the interface might consist of the set of all three LoAs. In this case, the LoAs happen to be disjoint, but in general they do not have to be. LoAs can be nested, disjoint, or overlapping and may, but do not have to be, hierarchically related or ordered in some scale of priority, or support some syntactic compositionality (the molecular is composed of atomic components). A particularly important case is that in which one LoA includes another. Suppose, for example, that Dave joins the discussion and analyses the system using a LoA that includes those of Alice and Bob. Dave's LoA might match that of a buyer. Then Dave's LoA is said to be more concrete, finely grained, or lower than Alice's or Bob's, each of which is said to be more abstract, more coarsely grained, or higher; for both Alice's and Bob's LoA abstracts some observables that are available at Dave's. Basically, Dave can obtain all the information about the system that Alice and Bob might have, for example the name of the previous owner, and that it is rather expensive to maintain, and so he can obtain some information that is, in principle, unavailable to one or the other of them, since Alice does not know about running costs and Bob has no clue about the ownership history.

A LoA qualifies the level at which a system is considered. One should rely on the method of abstraction in order to refer to the LoA at which the properties of the system under analysis can sensibly be discussed. In general, it seems that many uninteresting disagreements might be clarified, if the various interlocutors could make their LoAs explicit and precise. Yet a crucial clarification is in order. It must be stressed that a clear indication of the LoA at which a system is being analysed allows *pluralism* without endorsing *relativism*. One may refer to this middleground position as *relationism*. In philosophy, when one criticizes a position as *relativistic*, or when one objects to *relativism*, one should not equate such positions to non-absolutist, as if there were only two alternatives, e.g. as if either moral values were absolute or relative, or truths were either absolute or relative. The method of abstraction enables one to avoid exactly such a false dichotomy, by showing that a subjectivist position, for example, need not be relativistic, but only relational. To use a simple example: Alice may be tall when compared to Bob, but not when compared to someone in the basketball team. It does not mean that her height changes, but only that she is or is not tall depending on the frame of reference, that is, on the LoA. Relativism is really the equivalent of an 'anything goes' position. Now, it is a mistake to think that 'anything goes' as long as one makes explicit the LoA, because LoAs are mutually comparable and assessable. Consider again the example of Alice's telephone number. There might be some significant differences in the way in which Alice communicates it to Bob. She might add a plus and the relevant country code at the beginning, thus modifying the overall TYPE of the information provided. She might omit the plus, the country code, and the city code, if it is a local mobile phone. So there is quite a lot of 'relationism' ('it depends on . . .') but no 'relativism': it would be silly to conclude that any LoA would do. A string of letters would not work, nor would a mix of letters and numbers, or numbers and non-alphanumeric symbols, or an endless string. Using a different example, when we are asked to provide the number of our credit card, the type is (a finite number of) of natural numbers. This is why an interface can easily constrain the sort of input required. In general, only some LoAs are possible and, among those, some are better than others. Crucially, the assessment and corresponding preference is usually dictated by the purpose driving the original request for information. Introducing an explicit reference to the LoA clarifies that:

1 the model of a system is a function of the available observables;
2 different interfaces may be correctly ranked depending on how well they satisfy modelling specifications (e.g. informativeness, coherence, elegance, explanatory power, consistency with the data, etc.) and the purpose orienting the choice of the LoA (LoAs are teleologically oriented);
3 different analyses can be correctly compared provided that they share the same LoA.

Let us now agree that a system is characterized at a given LoA by the properties it satisfies at that LoA. We are interested in systems that change, which means that some of those properties change value. The evolution of a changing system is captured at a given LoA and at any instant by the values of its observables (the attributes of the system). Thus, a system can be thought of as having states, determined by the value of the properties that hold at any instant of its evolution, for then any change in the system corresponds to a state change and *vice versa*. Generalizing, this enables one to view any system as having states and transitions. The lower the LoA, the more detailed the observed changes and the greater the number of state components required to capture the change. Each change corresponds to a transition from one state to another. A transition may be non-deterministic. Indeed, it will typically be the case that the LoA under consideration abstracts the observables required to make the transition deterministic. As a result, the transition might lead from a given initial state to one of several possible subsequent states.

We have now moved from a static to a dynamic observation of a system, analysed as a transition system. The notion of a 'transition system' provides a convenient means to support the identification of the necessary and sufficient criteria for agency, being general enough to embrace the usual notions like automaton and process. In scientific investigations, it is frequently used to model interactive phenomena. Here we need only the idea; for a formal treatment of much more than is required in this context, the reader might wish to consult Arnold and Plaice (1994).

A *transition system* comprises a (non-empty) set S of states and a family of operations, called the *transitions* on S. Each transition may take input and may yield output, but, at any rate, it takes the system from one state to another and in that way forms a relation on S. If the transition does take input or yield output, then it models an interaction between the system and its environment and so is called an *external* transition; otherwise the transition lies beyond the influence of the environment (at the given LoA) and is called *internal*. It is to be emphasized that inputs and outputs are, like states, observed at a given LoA. Thus, the transitions that model a system are dependent on the chosen LoA. At a lower LoA, an internal transition may become external; at a higher LoA an external transition may become internal.

Returning to our example, the system being discussed by Alice might be further qualified by state components for LOCATION, WHETHER IN-USE, WHETHER TURNED-ON, WHETHER THE ANTI-THEFT DEVICE IS ENGAGED, HISTORY OF OWNERS, and ENERGY OUTPUT. The operation of garaging the system might take as input a driver, have the effect of placing the system in the garage with the engine off and the anti-theft device engaged, leaving the history of owners unchanged, and outputting a specific amount of energy. The 'in-use' state component could non-deterministically take either value, depending on the particular instantiation of the transition. Perhaps the system is not in use, being garaged for the night; or perhaps the driver is listening to a programme broadcast on its radio in the quiet solitude of the garage. The precise definition depends on the LoA. Alternatively, if speed were observed but time, accelerator position and petrol consumption abstracted, then accelerating to 60 miles per hour would appear as an internal transition.

Abstraction and ontological commitment

We can now use the method of abstraction and the concept of LoA to make explicit the ontological commitment of a theory, in the following way.

A theory comprises at least a LoA and a model. The LoA allows the theory to analyse a given system and to elaborate a model that identifies some properties of the system at the chosen LoA (see Figure 7.1).

The ontological commitment of a theory can be clearly understood by distinguishing between a *committing* and a *committed* component within the scheme. A theory commits itself ontologically by opting for a specific LoA. Compare this to the case in which one has chosen a specific kind of car (say a Volkswagen Polo) but has not bought one yet. On the other hand, a theory is ontologically committed in full by its model, which is therefore the bearer of the specific commitment. The analogy here is with the specific car one has actually bought (that blue, four-wheeled, etc., specific vehicle in the car park that one owns). To summarize, by adopting a LoA, a theory commits itself to the existence of some specific types of observables characterizing the system and constituting the LoA (by deciding to buy a Volkswagen Polo one shows one's commitment to the existence of that kind of car), while, by adopting the ensuing models, the theory commits itself to the corresponding tokens (by buying that particular vehicle, which is a physical token of the type Volkswagen Polo, one commits oneself to that token, e.g. one has to insure it). Figure 7.2 summarizes this distinction.

By making explicit the ontological commitment of a theory, it is clear that the method of abstraction plays an absolutely crucial role in philosophy, especially if the latter is understood as conceptual design.

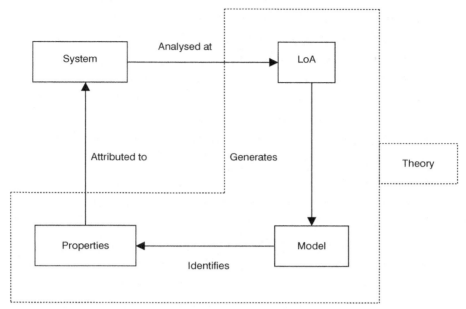

Figure 7.1 The scheme of a theory

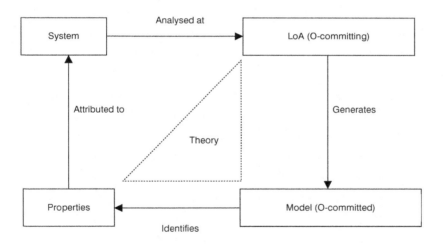

Figure 7.2 The SLMS (System-LoA-Model-Properties) scheme with ontological commitment

Conclusion

Quine once remarked that:

> The very notion of an object at all, concrete or abstract, is a human contribution,
> a feature of our inherited apparatus for organizing the amorphous welter of neural

input. […] Science ventures its tentative answers in man-made concepts, perforce, couched in man-made language, but we can ask no better. The very notion of object, or of one and many, is indeed as parochially human as the parts of speech; to ask what reality is really like, however, apart from human categories, is self-stultifying. It is like asking how long the Nile really is, apart from parochial matters of miles or meters.

(Quine (1992), pp. 6 and 9)

This chapter may be read as an attempt to clarify what 'human categories' in the first quotation above means, in terms of a less parochial method of levels of abstraction.

The method clarifies implicit assumptions, facilitates comparisons, enhances rigour, and hence promotes the resolution of possible conceptual confusions. If carefully applied, the method confers remarkable advantages in terms of consistency and clarity. Too often, philosophical debates seem to be caused by a misconception of the LoA at which the questions should be addressed. This is not to say that the method represents a panacea. Disagreement in philosophy is often not based on confusion. Indeed, informed and reasonable disagreement is precisely what characterizes philosophical questions, which remain intrinsically open to debate. But chances of resolving or overcoming it, or at least of identifying a disagreement as irreducible, may be enhanced if one is first of all careful about specifying what sort of observables are at stake and what goals are orienting their choice, and therefore what questions it is meaningful to ask in the first place.

Note

1 'Mars Climate Orbiter Mishap Investigation Board Phase I Report' (Press release). NASA: ftp:// ftp.hq.nasa.gov/pub/pao/reports/1999/MCO_report.pdf

References

Arnold, A. and Plaice, J. (1994), *Finite Transition Systems: Semantics of Communicating Systems* (Paris; Hemel Hempstead: Masson; Prentice Hall).

Floridi, L. (2008), 'The Method of Levels of Abstraction', *Minds and Machines,* 18 (3), 303–329.

Floridi, L. (2010), *Information – A Very Short Introduction* (Oxford: Oxford University Press).

Floridi, L. (2011), *The Philosophy of Information* (Oxford: Oxford University Press).

Floridi, L. (2013), *The Ethics of Information* (Oxford: Oxford University Press).

Hoare, C. A. R. (1972), 'Chapter Ii: Notes on Data Structuring', in Dahl, O. J., Dijkstra, E. W., and Hoare, C. A. R. (eds.), *Structured Programming* (Academic Press Ltd.), 83–174.

Quine, W. (1992), 'Structure and Nature', *The Journal of Philosophy,* 5–9.

PART II

Quantitative and formal aspects

8

THE LOGIC OF
INFORMATION

Patrick Allo

Introduction

The combination of *logic* and *information* is popular as well as controversial. It is, in fact, not even clear what their juxtaposition, for instance in the title of this chapter, should mean, and indeed different authors have a given a different interpretation to what *a* or *the logic* of information might be. Throughout this chapter, I will embrace the plurality of ways in which logic and information can be related and try to individuate a number of fruitful lines of research. In doing so, I want to explain why we should care about the combination, where the controversy comes from, and how certain common themes emerge in different settings.

Logic, in its most reductive sense, is the study of good and bad arguments. Here, the term "argument" has a rather narrow meaning: it is a relation between a set of expressions called "premises" and a single expression called the "conclusion." As a formal field of study, the aim of logic is to develop precise criteria for telling good and bad arguments apart. The class of good arguments is traditionally identified with the class of *deductively valid* arguments: arguments where the conclusion *follows from* the premises, or where the conclusion merely makes explicit what was already implicit in the premises.

In view of this informal description, it is natural to claim that good (or deductively valid) arguments are exactly those arguments where:

(CN) The content of the conclusion does not exceed the combined content of the premises.

And this establishes nothing short of a deep conceptual connection between the core task of logic and the notion of informational content.[1] In practice, however, the above principle does not play a major theoretical role in the development of logic. The idea that good arguments can be used to extract information from premises is not used to characterise the class of good arguments: the principle expressed by (CN) is the *explanandum* (what needs to be clarified) rather than the *explanans* (the clarification itself). As van Benthem and Martinez remark:

[Logic] has official definitions for its concepts of proof, computation, truth, or definability, but not of information!

(van Benthem and Martinez 2008)

The class of deductively valid arguments is standardly characterised by model-theoretic means, which (i) yields a formal explication of the idea that deductively valid arguments should preserve truth (if all the premises are true, then the conclusion must be true as well), that (ii) is provably equivalent to a characterisation that refers to the existence of a proof that starts with the premises and ends with the conclusion. It is thus no surprise that modern logic includes model-theory and proof-theory as two of its main pillars (computability or recursion-theory is often included as a third pillar), but not information theory.

While the mainstream approach in logic treats information as redundant for serious formal work, the suggestion that logic and information are intertwined is too deeply ingrained in the history of logic as well as in our informal talk about the subject to disappear altogether.

Hintikka, a major figure in twentieth-century logic, even went as far as claiming that the absence of a logical analysis of the notion of information was one of the scandals of the development of modern logic:

Logicians have apparently failed to relate their subject to the most pervasive and potentially most important concept of information.

(Hintikka 1973)

Two general principles underlie many natural connections between logic and information.

(LB) The logical is the lower-bound of the informative.

If, for instance, Alice tells Bob something he could have figured out for himself on the basis of what he already knew, she didn't tell him anything genuinely informative – Bob didn't have to ask additional questions to Nature to figure it out for himself.

(UB) The counter-logical (or absurd) is the upper-bound of the informative.

If Bob tells Alice something that he could not even in principle figure out by asking additional questions to Nature, Alice told him something that could not possibly be true. It is, to use a formulation from Carnap and Bar-Hillel (1952, 8), "too informative to be true".

In the fourth section we shall see how these two principles arise in specific formal settings, and relate to (CN).

The rise of the philosophy of information and the broadening of the scope of logic initiated by the dynamic and interactive turn in logic (see also Chapter 12) have led to a renewed interest in the conceptual connection between logic and information. And indeed, there are several theoretical reasons why the question deserves our attention as well.

The historical connection: In Medieval logic principles like (CN) are explicitly included as a necessary condition for valid consequence.[2] By extending information-theoretic views to modern logic, we can emphasise the continuity between modern and traditional conceptions of validity.

The deductive/inductive gap: A characterisation of valid arguments as truth-preserving arguments suggests a deep gap between deductive arguments and inductive arguments that merely make the conclusion more plausible. On an information-theoretic characterisation we have a natural progression: in deductive arguments the premises provide all the required information, whereas in inductive arguments they provide some but not all the information in favour of the conclusion.

Problems with truth-talk: The description of certain formal enterprises in logic in terms of the traditional concepts of truth and truth-preservation does not always do justice to what they try to achieve. Descriptions of non-classical logics, for instance, seem to imply radical changes to what we mean by truth. Informational descriptions of the same enterprises often lead to a more conservative picture, and overall facilitate a pluralistic outlook on logic (Allo and Mares 2012).

Attention for conceptual problems: Logic often clashes with the use of intensional idioms, and leads to unintuitive results when used within the scope of intensional operators like knowledge or belief. These issues surface in many different contexts, including the problems of logical omniscience and hyperintensionality in logics of knowledge and belief, and the problem of granularity in natural language semantics. The common trait of these problems is that logical equivalence is too coarse to be used as an account of sameness of meaning or sameness of content. To get a better grip on the general structure of these problems, it is advisable to study the relation between logic and information.

Overall, it seems that the connection between logic and information is not just intuitive, but that if we cannot conceive of logic as a means for (or as a model of) information manipulation, the study of logic itself loses much of its appeal.

A logical background

In this preliminary section, I give a brief overview of the basic building-blocks of formal logic, and make the claim that logic is the study of good deductive arguments more precise.

Logic is a formal discipline, but our use of the term "logic" itself is, even in scientific and scholarly contexts, often surprisingly sloppy. The description in the introduction is no exception to this rule. In particular, even though I related logic to a particular class of good arguments (the deductively valid ones), I did not for instance specify whether "good" was meant as a normative (how we should argue, reason, etc.) or as a descriptive (how we actually argue, reason, etc.) delimitation of this class of arguments. In addition, while I clearly distinguished between information and information theory, I did not draw a similar line between logic as a subject-matter and logic as a field of study. If we want to relate logic to information, we'd better be clear about this, for it is an entirely different question whether information (or information theory) plays a role in our best logical theories, or whether the facts of validity are just facts of information-containment. Clearly, the first question is empirical in the sense that we can just examine the existing theories and, as previously indicated, note that information theory is virtually absent. The second question, by contrast, cannot be addressed directly – we have no direct access to facts about validity – but is best recast in terms of how thinking about facts of validity as facts of information-containment can lead to better theories of validity.

Talking about logical theories requires a lot of care, but is overall easier than talking about logic. To do so, we first need to introduce the idea of a formal language.

Formal languages

By a formal language, we mean a schematic language that is introduced by, first, specifying what the logical and non-logical symbols of our language are, and, second, by listing formation-rules or ways in which symbols are combined in admissible expressions or well-formed formulae of our language. Logicians often study different types of languages, and it is easier to grasp the idea of a formal language by considering a specific example.

The language of propositional logic: In a propositional language, the non-logical symbols are called atomic expressions, denoted by the letters $p, q, r, \ldots$ The standard – so-called Boolean – operators: & (and), $\vee$ (or), $\supset$ (implies), and $\neg$ (not) are its logical symbols. Using these building-blocks, we say that:

1 All atomic expressions are well-formed formulae;
2 If "A" and "B" are well-formed formulae, then "$A \& B$", "$A \vee B$", and "$A \supset B$" are well-formed formulae as well;
3 If "A" is a well-formed formula, then "$\neg A$" is also a well-formed formula; and
4 Nothing else is a well-formed formula.

With these guidelines, we can always find out whether or not a given string of logical and non-logical symbols is a well-formed formula of the language of propositional logic.

Model-theory

Once we have a formal language, we can really start to develop the model and proof-theory of a given logical system.

In model-theory we develop an account of what it means for a *case* to support a formula, and use this to characterise the class of valid arguments. The former is done by exploiting the systematic structure of our formal language. Taking the language of propositional logic as an example, we stipulate that:[3]

1 a case c supports "$A \& B$" if and only if c supports "A" *and* supports "B",
2 a case c supports "$A \vee B$" if and only if c supports "A" *or* supports "B",
3 a case c supports "$A \supset B$" if and only if c supports "B" *whenever* it supports "A",
4 a case c supports "$\neg A$" if and only if c undermines "A".

An argument with $A_1, \ldots, A_n$ as premises and B as conclusion is valid if and only if every case that supports $A_1, \ldots, A_n$ is also a case that supports B.

What actually follows from what is then made entirely dependent on what *cases* are. When we require that cases are such that for every case c every atomic expression p is either supported or undermined by c (but never both supported and undermined!), and furthermore agree with the requirements 1–4 above, we have characterised the class of valid arguments of *classical propositional logic*: the logic based on the presuppositions that a formula A and its negation $\neg A$ are jointly exhaustive and mutually exclusive, and where as a consequence every formula of the form "$A \vee \neg A$" is supported by all cases (we call such formulae *tautological*), and every formula of the form "$A \& \neg A$" is undermined by all cases. We call such cases *complete* and *consistent*.

Different classes of good arguments can be characterised by weakening these requirements, but also by adding further structure to the nature of cases. This additional structure is typically coupled with the introduction of additional logical symbols, as in the case of first order classical logic, but also the modal logics of knowledge and belief we will encounter later on.

Amidst these alternatives, classical logic has a special status. This can be seen from the fact that (1) the uninterpreted "is supported by" relation can naturally be understood as "is true at", and given this assumption (2) the resulting class of valid arguments will coincide with the truth-preserving arguments. I elaborate further on this second point in the section on Soundness and Completeness. For the first point, it suffices to observe that if we only consider complete and consistent cases, the resulting identity between "not supporting" and "undermining", and between "supporting" and "not undermining", coincides with the orthodox identities between "absence of truth" and "falsity" (completeness), and between "truth" and "absence of falsity" (consistency). In other words, relative to complete and consistent cases, we can uncontroversially equate support with truth, and undermining with falsity.

Proof-theory

In many ways, the existence and construction of proofs form the focal point of logic. By a proof, we mean a set T of formulae $B_1, \ldots, B_n$ that (a) are organised in a list, tree, or other type of structure, where (b) a possibly empty subset *Prem* of T is taken to be given (the premises of the proof); (c) all other formulae in T are obtained by applying certain rules to the formulae that are also in that list; and (d) a single formula A in T is called the conclusion. One standard form for a proof is just an ordered list of formulae, where the first n formulae are the premises, all other formulae are obtained by applying rules to the formulae higher up in the list, and the final formula is the conclusion.

When we have such a list, we say that A can be deduced from *Prem*. Furthermore, when *Prem* is empty, we say that A is a theorem (it can be deduced from zero premises).

Completeness and truth-preservation

Good deductive arguments are standardly understood as truth-preserving arguments. Yet, so far we have only explicitly identified the class of valid arguments in terms of the preservation of support, and characterised a second class of good arguments in terms of what can be deduced. Using a simplified version of Kreisel's *Squeezing argument* (Kreisel 1967),[4] we can elucidate how these different notions hang together, and indeed agree on a single notion of consequence.

Consider the following two claims:

> *Claim 1:* Validity is a necessary condition for the preservation of truth.
> *Claim 2:* Deducibility is a sufficient condition for the preservation of truth.

Jointly, these amount to the thesis that at least all correct deductions are truth-preserving, and that at most all support-preserving arguments are truth-preserving. Given a set of sensible and intuitively correct rules of proof, we should be confident in the second claim (and indeed, we can examine each rule to confirm this). When it comes to the first claim, we just need to repeat our prior observation that the mutually exclusive and jointly exhaustive notions of support and undermining are just as fine-grained as the concepts of truth and falsity. Consequently, every truth-preserving argument will also preserve support. The support for the last insight is usually phrased in terms of the contrapositive claim: if an argument does not preserve support it will not preserve truth either. More exactly, we can easily transform a model that supports all the premises and undermines the conclusion into a description of how the world should be for the premises to be all true, and the conclusion to be false.

At this point, a formal result can be used to complete the argument. Since the notions of support and proof are entirely formally specified (proofs as well as models are mathematical structures), it can be rigorously proved that for every support-preserving argument there should also be a proof. Such results are called completeness-theorems. When added to our initial two claims, we thus extend our argument:

Proof: Validity is a sufficient condition for deducibility.
Conclusion: Validity and deducibility are necessary and sufficient conditions for truth-preservation.

In summary: given that truth-preservation lies between deducibility and validity, the completeness-theorem shows that truth-preservation is squeezed between the provably unique characterisations of good arguments in terms of deducibility and validity. These features of our formal concepts of validity and deducibility make the connection between logical consequence and truth-preservation particularly attractive.

Structural properties of consequence-relations

Logicians are not only interested in the equivalence of model and proof-theoretic characterisations of consequence-relations, but they also study the properties of the consequence-relations independently of how these are characterised. In particular, they investigate the so-called *structural* properties of (abstract) consequence-relations. If we use the turnstile ($\vdash$) to refer to the consequence relation of classical logic, we can say that it has the following structural properties:

Reflexivity: $\Gamma \vdash A$ whenever $A \in \Gamma$.
Cumulative transitivity: If $\Gamma \vdash A_i$ for all $A_i \in \Delta$, and $\Gamma \cup \Delta \vdash B$, then $\Gamma \vdash B$.
Monotony: If $\Gamma \vdash A$ and $\Gamma \subseteq \Delta$, then $\Delta \vdash A$.

Information as constraint, as resource, and as goal

The notion of information does not only appear to be redundant, but is also a source of further confusion. The latter arises because the notion of information can be used twice in our informal descriptions of what logic is about. It can be used as a constraint on what counts as a good argument – as in (CN) – but also to refer to the information we extract from our premises. As such, information is both the *goal* of logical reasoning and a *constraint* on good arguments. As has often been pointed out, these roles conflict. The so-called paradox of inference attributed to Cohen and Nagel is one among many examples of this tension:[5]

If in an inference the conclusion is not contained in the premises, it cannot be valid; and if the conclusion is not different from the premises, it is useless; but the conclusion cannot be contained in the premises and also possess novelty; hence inferences cannot be both valid and useful.

(Cohen and Nagel 1972, 173)

This is surely disconcerting, and only adds up to the initial impression that characterisations of logical consequence in terms of truth-preservation are not only technically convenient, but also philosophically more satisfactory. Truth serves as a constraint by ruling out arguments that would allow us to step from truth to falsity, and is also the aim of deductive inference: we want to derive new truths from previously accepted truths. Clearly, no conflict arises in this case, and this may suggest that we should not think of logic as something that regulates our use of cognitive resources like information. When we use logic to characterise the class of truth-preserving arguments, we choose our formal notions of support and undermining so that they are jointly exhaustive and mutually exclusive. Given these formal properties, the corresponding notion of information inevitably fudges the distinction between the absence of positive information and the presence of negative information. This obscures the partial nature of holding information, and makes it harder to use logic to reason about information as a cognitive resource.

Moving to a stronger notion of information doesn't help much here. If we adopt Floridi's suggestion that the informativeness of A is not only inversely proportional to the probability of A, but also proportional to how accurately and precisely A describes the truth (Floridi 2004), the problem remains. As illustrated by how scientists treat significant digits in calculations, no valid argument will ever increase the accuracy of our premises.

When two intuitively plausible principles are in conflict, this often indicates that they need to be formulated more precisely. The conflict exposed in Cohen and Nagel's paradox of inference (and many other similar insights) is the result of equivocation, and if we want to develop logic as a theory of how we should use cognitive resources like information, we need to refine the building-blocks of our theory, and pay more attention to the double role of information in logic.

One obvious way to deal with such conflicts is to look for potential equivocal uses of the technical terms that are involved. And since information is a notorious multifaceted concept, it is first in line for a closer examination. With our initial characterisation of deductive arguments we can easily resolve the conflict between the two uses of information. Deductions yield useful information because they make explicit what was already implicit in the premises, and valid because the only information that can be made explicit is the information that was already implicitly available from the premises. In loose terms: deduction transforms an available resource into a readily accessible resource.

The emphasis on the difference between implicit and explicit information is correct, but not entirely satisfactory. Our intuitive feel that information is both a constraint on and a goal of inference is merely transferred on the implicit/explicit divide, but the distinction itself remains to be explained. A good example of why the distinction is less clear than we might think is due to Gilbert Harman and Robert Stalnaker, who point out that it is regularly used to refer to two different distinctions.[6] Explicit information can mean information that has actually been derived, or it can mean information that is readily (or easily) accessible. Yet, since information can be explicit in one sense, but not in the other (think for instance of a complex formula that is listed somewhere in a very large unsorted list), logical deduction is not the only way to make explicit what was merely implicit (Harman 1986; Stalnaker 1991). Surely, crossing the border between implicit and explicit information requires computation, but not all computation is deduction.[7] Search and retrieval is just as much a computational process.

Logic and information systems

As an alternative to the refinement of the different senses of information, we could also explore different perspectives on the nature of logic, and the design of logical theories. My suggestion is that, on a narrow conception of logic, information can only act as a constraint because it fails to register the fine distinctions that are needed to reason about information as a partial and distributed cognitive resource.

The above insights can be made more precise by introducing a rudimentary notion of a system, and our means for describing and modelling such systems as information systems (see Figure 8.1).

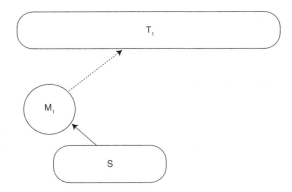

Figure 8.1 System, model, theory

By a *system* I mean any part of reality that can be the subject of further examination. On this account, any part of reality can be thought of as a system. This includes the whole universe, some well-defined spatiotemporal fragment of the universe like the state of a coin on the table, a multi-agent system (e.g. what different agents know and believe about the state of a coin on the table), or even a highly organised repository of information like an archive or a library.

A *theory* about a system S is a set of expressions that gives the best possible description of S given the language we use as well as (in a yet undefined sense) our knowledge of the system. A *formal theory* T is a theory that is formulated in a formal language, and a *logical theory* T' is a formal theory T that has been extended with all the logical consequences of T. We say that T' is the deductive closure of T,[8] and use it as a highly idealised description of our best knowledge of the system under consideration.

A *model* of a system is a set of observables (see Chapter 7 of this Handbook) that can be thought of as a set of facts about the system under consideration. A *formal model* is a mathematical construction (for instance based on set theory) that is used to determine which expressions of a formal language L are supported or undermined by a model.[9] A *total model* is maximally specific in the sense that it either supports or undermines every formula in L.

Formal languages like the propositional language described earlier in this chapter can be used to formulate theories about a given system, and the models of propositional logic (the *cases* from the second section) can be understood as formal models in the above sense. There are two important differences between total models and theories.

First, since models are mathematical structures, they are described in the language of mathematics, and this language is often richer than the formal languages we use to construct our theories. Consequently, it can happen that two distinct models M_1 and M_2 cannot be told apart with the limited resources of a certain formal language L. No theory that is formulated in L will be supported by M_1, but not by M_2. Put loosely: M_1 and M_2 contain more information than can be revealed with the limited resources of L. For the language and models of propositional logic, there is no such principled gap, but this is a rather exceptional situation. The study of the expressive limits of languages is an important field of formal study that is not without significance for the philosophy of information (van Benthem and Martinez 2008, 227–8), but lies outside the scope of this chapter.

Second, and more importantly, a theory T can be partial in the sense that (even when it is deductively closed) there can be formulae A such that neither A nor $\neg A$ is in T. For every sufficiently complex system there will be features of that system of which we are ignorant and (assuming that these features can be expressed in the formal language we use) our best

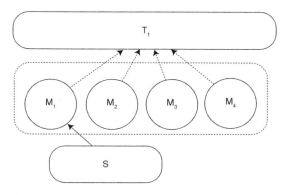

Figure 8.2 System, models, theory

knowledge of the system – our theories – will have gaps. To recapture this idea at the level of (total) models, we have to resort to the use of sets of models (as depicted in Figure 8.2), and stipulate that our theory T about a given system S is the set of all formulae of L that are supported by all models that, as far as we are concerned (this qualification is important: some of these models are in fact not models of S!), are equally good models of S. Conversely, we can say that the set of all equally good models of S are just those models that support all formulae in our theory T. The underlying idea that our ignorance about certain features of the system under consideration is reflected in the number of models that are equally good models of that system is further emphasised by calling these models *possibilities* (this can be compared to the sample space of possible outcomes in probability theory). Depending on how we conceptualise our information about the system, we shall call such possibilities epistemic (our knowledge of the system), doxastic (our beliefs about the system), or informational (our information about the system).

At the most basic level, we can distinguish between these by contrasting the two situations depicted in Figure 8.3. We consider two sets of models:

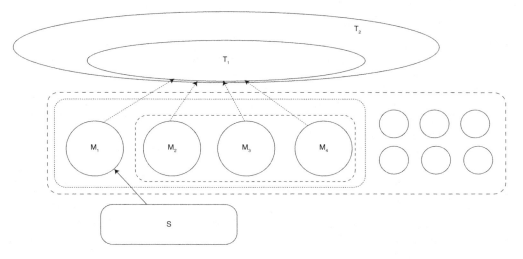

Figure 8.3 System, models, theory (2)

$$M_1 = \{M_1, M_2, M_3, M_4\} \qquad\qquad \text{(dotted line)}$$
$$M_2 = \{M_2, M_3, M_4\}, \qquad\qquad \text{(dashed line)}$$

and note that only M_1 is really a model of S.[10] As a consequence, since every formula in T_1 must be supported by each model enclosed in the dotted line, it must also be supported by M_1, and since M_1 is an actual model of S, every formula in T_1 is a correct claim about S. As such, we can think of the models $\mathbf{M}_1$ as a set of epistemic possibilities: the information in $\mathbf{M}_1$ is truthful. In the second case, however, the real model of S is not included in $\mathbf{M}_2$, and we have no guarantee that T_2 will be entirely correct. In this case, we can think of the models $\mathbf{M}_2$ as a set of doxastic possibilities. Finally, on a weak notion of semantic information (see Chapter 6), both $\mathbf{M}_1$ and $\mathbf{M}_2$ will count as sets of informational possibilities. On a stronger veridical account, only $\mathbf{M}_1$ will count as a set of informational possibilities. The weak notion is the standard in logical theorising, but the stronger notion has its place as well.

The above description of systems, models and theories gives rise to two equivalent notions of information about a system, which coincide with the qualitative approach that underlies the classical accounts of Carnap and Bar-Hillel (1952) and Kemeny (1953). Here, I presented it explicitly as a means of individuating the modeller's information about a system.

The first notion is related to the theory T about the system S, and identifies the informational content about the system with the subset of non-tautological formulae in T. The second notion is related to the set of (total) models of S.

If, as in Figure 8.3, we use $\mathbf{M}_1$ and $\mathbf{M}_2$ to denote two sets of models of S, and T_1 and T_2 to denote the two corresponding theories about S (A is in T if and only if A is supported by all models), we can say that:

- T_2 is at least as informative about S as T_1 if and only if T_1 is a subset of T_2.[11]
- $\mathbf{M}_2$ is at least as informative about S as $\mathbf{M}_1$ if and only if $\mathbf{M}_2$ is a subset of $\mathbf{M}_1$.

And this reveals a familiar inverse-relation between the size of theories and the size of sets of models: a larger theory means more information, but a larger set of models means less information. This is what van Benthem and Martinez (2008) call *information as range*.

[*Parenthetical remark*. The reference to the size of sets in the above principles should not be understood quantitatively (counting models or formulae), but qualitatively in terms of set-inclusion. This has two important consequences. First, it means that two sets of models or two theories (e.g. $\{M_1, M_2, M_3\}$ and $\{M_2, M_3, M_4\}$ in Figure 8.3) can be incomparable in the sense that each contains information that is not included in the other (figuratively speaking, they both could learn from each other). This qualitative aspect is what distinguishes logical approaches from probabilistic approaches. Second, it allows us to bypass the problem that, except in some borderline cases, sets of models as well as deductively closed theories are countably infinite and have thus the same cardinality. *End of parenthetical remark*.]

Using just the slightest bit of the language of set theory, this gives us:

$$\mathbf{M}_2 \subseteq \mathbf{M}_1 \text{ if and only if } T_1 \subseteq T_2$$

Which, if we talk about possibilities instead of models, expresses the idea that more information means fewer possibilities and *vice-versa* (Barwise 1997).

Statically, this inverse relationship principle identifies having information about a system with being able to exclude certain possible states of the system. From a dynamic perspective it identifies receiving or obtaining information about a system with the exclusion of possible states of the system.

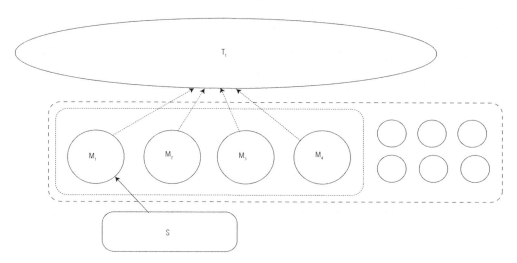

Figure 8.4 System, logical space, theory

While one's information about a system *S* can be identified with the set of possible states of *S* one can exclude, this account remains useless without an explicit account of the *total space of possibilities*. Given what has already been said, this space has to be identified with the set of all logical possibilities: new information is information that cannot be logically derived from one's prior information, but this also means that the only possibilities that can be excluded are logical possibilities.

The overall picture becomes even clearer if we look at the extremes, as expressed by the earlier suggestions that informativeness is bounded from below by the logical and from above by the counter-logical.

- If *A* is uninformative, it does not require the exclusion of any possibility, so the logical must be supported by any possibility.
- If *A* is over-informative, it requires the exclusion of every possibility, so the counter-logical must be undermined by every possibility (equivalently: supported by the empty set of possibilities).

More generally, we will then identify the content of T_1 with the logical possibilities that are excluded by T_1 (i.e. the logical possibilities that undermine some or all of the formulae in T_1). In Figure 8.4 this coincides with the possibilities outside the dotted area. If, in addition to T_1, one learns that some formula *A* is true as well, and *A* is supported by $\{M_1, M_2, M_3\}$, but not by M_4, the new information that is obtained is $\{M_4\}$, namely the one possibility that is excluded from $\mathbf{M_1}$ by learning that *A* is true.

Hence, we can see that if we take information about a system as our starting point, informativeness is constrained by logic: only logically contingent expressions can be non-trivially informative (if it can be true at all, then it is only informative if it is logically contingent). If, as we did in the previous section, we take valid arguments as our starting point, it is informativeness (or rather the lack thereof) that constrains logic.

When we reason about a system from an external perspective (the viewpoint of the modeller), logic is used in its constraint role. The idea is that we do not want to add anything to our theory that does not follow from that theory (and if theories are deductively closed, this means we do not want to change anything at all), for this comes down to excluding a possibility, and perhaps even the exclusion of the one possibility that is the actual model of the system under consideration. In other words: going beyond one's information – as would be the case if one would erroneously derive a formula that is included in T_2 but not in T_1 (see Figure 8.3) – is one way to step from truth to falsehood. Here, information acts as a constraint because it precludes erroneous or fallacious reasoning about the system.[12]

Sub-systems and distributed information

The description of systems in the previous section has two important features.

> *System*: the total information about the system is identified with the information in the correct model of the system. At the level of the model-theory this is the relative complement of the correct model in the total logical space; at the level of the formal language this is the set of formulae that are supported by the correct model.

> *Modeller*: there is one agent with partial information about the system. The agent's information can again be modelled as a set of formulae (a theory) or as a set of models.

In a more traditional setting we would identify the total information about a system with what is true *of* the system, or with the facts about the system. Here, we make it explicit that information is relative to the relevant level of abstraction (see Chapter 7). This means that what counts as a true claim about the system is mediated by the correct model of that system as well as by the language we use to describe that model. Apart from this relativisation, our thinking about the total information about a system is rather restrictive. The models of the system are unstructured repositories of total information, and the modeller is an unstructured repository of partial information.

These restrictions are quite useful to clarify the constraint role of information in a modeller's reasoning about a system, which is why I associated it with an external perspective on the system. In a sense, we adopted a relatively high level of abstraction: we ignored the deeper structure of the system, and only considered the information of a single modeller. From a formal point of view (and slightly simplifying matters), the adoption of an external perspective on logic and information is closely related to seeing consequence-relations (i.e. the "turnstile" ⊢) as informational or information-containment relations.

If we want to clarify the goal role of information in logic, we need to take into account the underlying structure of a system. Since almost anything can be a system, it can have many underlying structures as well. If we slightly abuse our terminology and provisionally ignore the distinction between a system and models of a system, we can just say that systems have sub-systems, and that the information about the system as a whole is distributed between its sub-systems. If a system is some mechanical artefact like a machine, then some piece of information about the state of that machine can be specifically located in one of its components (information is situated), while this component need not be the locus of all the information about the state of the machine (information is partial).[13]

The suggestion that information could be located in a physical object should not be taken literally. What we mean is that we can obtain information about a system by examining some of its sub-systems. To make this insight precise, we need to add structure to our models and speak of the information supported by a model and its sub-models. We then can say that a sub-model supports the information we can obtain by examining the sub-system it is a model of in exactly the same way – namely relative to a certain level of abstraction – as the correct model of a system supports the information we can obtain by reliably examining a system. The only relevant difference between a model and a sub-model is that sub-models do not satisfy the principle that allows us to infer the presence of negative information from the absence of positive information. The notions of support and undermining are not in general exclusive and exhaustive relative to sub-models.

From a formal point of view, the internal perspective on how logic and information are related is best approached by looking at how implication-relations and other conditional expressions are informational relations, and how the logic of these relations becomes a logic of information flow.

To see how partial and distributed information are deeply intertwined, we can look at a number of specific types of systems and their sub-systems.

Moments in time: A fairly intuitive type of system that can be modelled as a set of sub-models is a history that consists of a succession of different stages in time. Every time-stage contains all the information about itself (it's own "now"), but need not hold all (or even any) information about the past and the future. As a whole, the history contains all the information about every possible moment in time, but specific moments only hold information about moments that are informationally accessible. Thus, the past can be accessible thanks to all kinds of records (we have information about the past because we have informational technologies (Floridi 2014)), and the future can be accessible because some future events are entirely determined by the past and present (and we may know about these connections).

Moments in time can be seen as a variant or special case of the situations described below.

Situations: If the system we consider is a part or even the whole world, we can add structure by distinguishing the situations that are part of it. This is the approach from *situation theory*, one of the pioneering frameworks of the modern connection between logic and information (Barwise and Perry 1999; Devlin 1991; Israel and Perry 1990). On this account, a system is (or can be modelled as) a structure $(S, \leq\_)$, with S a set of situations, and $\leq\_$ a relation between three situations, say s, t, v, such that $s \leq_t v$ expresses that by combining information from s with information from t, we obtain information about v (Mares 2010; Allo and Mares 2012). This way of structuring systems allows us to model the following informational phenomena:[14]

1 If c is a situation that contains information about certain regularities in the world (Barwise (1993) calls such situation *channels*), then $s \leq_c t$ means that the information about regularities that is available in c, provides information that can be used to infer the presence of information in t from information that is available in s. That is, s carries information about t in virtue of c, and if an agent is attuned to the information in c, she will be able to exploit information in s to obtain information about t. Thus, X-rays carry information about such-and-so's bone being broken (Israel and Perry 1990), or smoke seen from the bottom of the mountain tells us that there must be a fire on the mountain (Barwise and Perry 1999).

2 If we posit the existence of a set of logical situations $\mathrm{Log} \subset S$, then we can define an information-inclusion relation $\leq$ between situations:

$s \leq t$ iff $s \leq_l t$ for some l in Log,

which holds if and only if all the information available in s is also available in t. It is, in other words, a relation that signals that – as an informational, but not necessarily as a concrete physical entity – one situation is part of another situation.

Such relations between situations can be used to model different types of implication-relations (Barwise 1993). For the general case, we have an implication relation $\rightarrow$ that can express informational connections between situations. Formally: the information that $A \rightarrow B$ will be available in a situation s if and only if for all situations t and u such that $t \leq_s u$ it is the case that if t has the information that A, then u has the information that B.

Other types of implication-relations can be seen as special cases. For instance, $\rightarrow$ can express connections between situations that are part of each other. Formally: the information that $A \rightarrow B$ will be available in a situation s if and only if for all situations t such that $s \leq t$ it is the case that if t has the information that A, then t has the information that B as well. In a sense, this *intuitionistic implication*, expresses connections between stages of information-accumulation. Finally, our implication relation from classical logic $\supset$ (see second section) expresses the most trivial kind of informational connection: the information that $A \supset B$ is available in a situation s if and only if it contains information that $\neg A$ (negative information that A) or that B.

Agents: If the system we are modelling is a multi-agent system with agents that can adopt various attitudes towards the current state of the system – such as knowing that A, believing that B, being ignorant with respect to C – different formal perspectives can be adopted.[15] We can model systems as so-called *interpreted systems* that treat global states of a system as the Cartesian product of the local states of the environments as well as of the agents (Fagin *et al.* 1995). Or, we can model systems as multi-modal Kripke-models where each possible state (including the actual state) of the system is included in this model, and a relation between these states models the information available to each agent. This can be seen as an elaboration of how we modelled the information available to the modeller of a system, and will receive a more detailed treatment in Chapter 12.

In either system, we can explicitly describe how the information in the system is distributed. We can for instance say that Alice knows that A, but that Bob does not know this.

$$K_a A \ \& \ \neg K_b A$$

By extending the language of propositional logic with modal operators for knowledge, we make room for partial information ($K_a A \lor K_a \neg A$ is not a logical truth) without having to invalidate $A \lor \neg A$.

Additionally, we can say that Bob knows that B, and that Alice knows that Bob knows whether B

$$K_b B \ \& \ K_a(K_b B \lor K_b \neg B),$$

but that Bob believes that Alice believes that he is ignorant with respect to B

$$B_b B_a(\neg K_b B \ \& \ \neg K_b \neg B).$$

This ability of expressing higher-order attitudes (one agent having information about the information of another agent) allows us to express a first type of informational connection between agents: knowing, believing or otherwise being informed of the state of other agents.

A second type of informational connections can be expressed by assigning information to groups rather than to individual agents. Thus, we can say that Alice and Bob both know that either A or B is true (with E for "everybody knows"):

$$E_{\{a,b\}} (A \lor B),$$

or that by pooling their knowledge they know $A \ \& \ B$ (with D for "distributed knowledge"):

$D_{\{a, b\}} (A \,\&\, B)$.

In either case, these connections bear on how (and how much) information is shared between agents.

A third type of informational connection does not only relate to how information *is* shared, but also to how it *can be* shared. That is, related to how agents can pass on information. This is the topic of dynamic epistemic logic (Baltag and Moss 2004; Baltag, van Ditmarsch and Moss 2008; Van Ditmarsch, van der Hoek and Kooi 2007), and one of the more active areas of development related to the dynamic and interactive turn in logic. Its primary concern is the individuation of several ways in which information can be communicated through public or private announcements, and how such announcements can modify the distribution of information. For instance, if neither Alice nor Bob knows which side of the coin lies face up, the public announcement that it lies *HEADS* up will lead to the common knowledge that it lies heads up, and hence make this information freely and transparently available to all agents in the system: the agents went from common ignorance to common knowledge. If, by contrast, it is privately announced to Alice that it lies *HEADS* up, she will come to know that it lies *HEADS* up, while Bob will remain ignorant, and will now falsely believe that they both are still ignorant: the agents went from common ignorance to unevenly distributed knowledge and even error. Not unlike the channels and constraints of situation semantics that express natural regularities, different types of announcements act as regularities of social interaction.

Conclusion: local changes versus global invariance

The place of information in logic is confusing because it serves two different and even opposed roles: it can serve as a constraint (the content of a valid argument should not exceed the combined content of its premises), and as a goal (we use logic to extract information from our premises, or more generally from our environment). This double role can be further clarified by looking at information systems. If we adopt an external perspective on such systems, the emphasis is on the fact that the total information in the system cannot increase,[16] and that our reasoning about the system should be constrained by the information we have about the system. Formally, this is associated with logic as a consequence relation: sets of premises are an unstructured repository of information, and all that can be extracted was already there from the start.

If, by contrast, we adopt an internal perspective on such systems by no longer treating them as unstructured information-repositories, we put more emphasis on how information is distributed within the system. While the total information in the system can still not increase, the distribution and thus the information available in certain sub-systems can indeed increase. Information, in this case, becomes the goal of logic, and logic becomes a logic of information flow. Formally, this is associated with various modal and conditional operators that allow us to describe features of informational connections and distributions of information.[17]

Notes

1 I here use the term "informational content" to speak of the semantic content or semantic information (as described in Chapter 6) we measure (quantitative) or individuate (qualitative).
2 See the principle "(Co) In a valid consequence, the conclusion is contained/understood in the premises." mentioned in Dutilh-Novaes (2012), and attributed to Abelard amongst others.

3 The terms "support" and "undermine" are non-standard, but perfectly suit our aims: we can be undecided between supporting and undermining a given proposition, and although it seems problematic to both support and undermine the same proposition, it is not entirely inconceivable either.

4 The full strength of Kreisel's argument surfaces only relative to full first-order logic, but the basic idea of looking at necessary and sufficient formal conditions for a precise though informal concept can be used for didactic purposes as well.

5 Chapter 15 deals explicitly with the question of how we should think about the information contained in logical and mathematical theorems, and how we can characterise the information obtained through deductive inference. Here, I only rely on these problems as a means to clarify the relation between logic and information.

6 Stalnaker and Harman focus on the concept of belief, but their diagnosis can be straightforwardly transferred to our thinking about information.

7 If we take complexity concerns into account, the converse is false as well: some deductions are not even feasible computations.

8 Given a theory T, we obtain the deductive closure of T by adding to T all the (and indeed, infinitely many) logical consequences of T. Analogously, we say that T' is deductively closed if and only if it already contains everything that follows from it.

9 Logicians often say that a model M is an interpretation of the language L. Here, we stick to our prior use of "support" and "undermine" instead of the more traditional notion of "truth in a model".

10 I leave aside the question of whether there can really be more than one genuine model of reality, or even whether there can ever be exactly one genuine model of reality. If one takes the method of abstraction seriously, it should already be clear that what counts as a real model of reality depends on the level of abstraction one adopts.

11 The subtraction of tautological formulae does not make a difference here.

12 Here too, what counts as an error is itself relative to the level of abstraction we adopt in our reasoning about the system. In particular, it depends on what can and cannot be said in and discerned with the formal language we use, and how we structure the logical space in which we situate our models of the system. These choices are themselves not constrained by logic.

13 This description still allows for information about a system that is not located in one of its strict sub-systems, but only in the total system.

14 When compared to moments in time or agents, situations have the peculiar feature that as sub-models or sub-systems they are of the same type as the system or model itself. The total system or model is just the largest situation.

15 The former is common in computer science, whereas the latter has become the standard in philosophical logic.

16 Abramsky (2008) relates this to Shannon's identification of information with negative entropy.

17 Similar features can also be recaptured by consequence relations, which then no longer satisfy all the structural rules of classical logic. This topic falls outside the scope of the current chapter.

Further reading

This chapter barely covers all of the pertinent ways in which logic and information can be related. In addition to the works cited in the text, the interested reader is invited to consult the following works:

1 The traditional connection between possibilities and content: Stalnaker (1984) and Rayo (2012).

2 The connection between non-classical logic, situation semantics, and information: Mares (1997, 2009, 2010); Restall (2005); Wansing (1993).

3 Informational semantics as a philosophical account of logical consequence: Allo and Mares (2012); Saguillo (2009)

4 The specificity of *being informed* in comparison with knowing and believing: Floridi (2006); Allo (2011).

5 The semantics of informative and inquisitive content as a common ground in conversations: Ciardelli *et al.* (2013).
6 An account of the role of logic within the philosophy of information: Chapter 12 of the e-Textbook *The Philosophy of Information: A Simple Introduction* available at http://www. socphilinfo.org/teaching/book-pi-intro.

References

Abramsky, Samson. 2008. Information, processes and games. In *Handbook on the Philosophy of Information*. Ed. Johan Van Benthem and Pieter Adriaans. Elsevier.

Allo, Patrick. 2011. The logic of 'being informed' revisited and revised. *Philosophical Studies* 153 (3): 417–434.

Allo, Patrick and Edwin Mares. 2012. Informational semantics as a third alternative? *Erkenntnis* 77 (2): 167–185.

Baltag, Alexandru, Hans P van Ditmarsch, and Lawrence S Moss. 2008. Epistemic logic and information update. In *Philosophy of Information (Handbook of the Philosophy of Science)*. Ed. Pieter Adriaans and Johan van Benthem. Amsterdam: North-Holland.

Baltag, Alexandru and Lawrence S Moss. 2004. Logics for epistemic programs. *Synthese* 139 (2): 165–224.

Barwise, Jon. 1993. Constraints, channels, and the flow of information. In *Situation Theory and Its Applications Vol. 3*. Ed. Peter Aczel, David Israel, Stanley Peters, and Yasuhiro Katagiri. Stanford, CA: CSLI.

Barwise, Jon. 1997. Information and impossibilities. *Notre Dame Journal of Formal Logic* 38 (4): 488–515.

Barwise, Jon and John Perry. 1999. *Situation and Attitudes*. Stanford, CA: CSLI Publications.

Carnap, Rudolf and Yehoshua Bar-Hillel. 1952. An outline of a theory of semantic information. In *Language and Information: Selected essays on their theory and application*. 221-74. Reading, Mass; London: Adidison-Wesley.

Ciardelli, Ivano, Jeroen Groenendijk, and Floris Roelofsen. 2013. Inquisitive semantics: A new notion of meaning. *Language and Linguistics Compass* 7 (9): 459–476.

Cohen, Morris R. and Ernest Nagel. 1972. *An Introduction to Logic and Scientific Method*. London: Routledge & Kegan Paul.

Devlin, Keith. 1991. *Logic and Information*. Cambridge: Cambridge University Press.

Dutilh-Novaes, Catarina. 2012. Medieval theories of consequence. In *The Stanford Encyclopedia of Philosophy*. Summer 2012 ed. Ed. Edward N Zalta.

Fagin, Ronald, Joseph Y Halpern, Yoram Moses, and Moshe Y Vardi. 1995. *Reasoning About Knowledge*. Cambridge, MA and London: MIT Press.

Floridi, Luciano. 2004. Outline of a theory of strongly semantic information. *Minds & Machines* 14 (2): 197–222.

Floridi, Luciano. 2006. The logic of 'being informed'. *Logique & Analyse* 49 (196): 433–460.

Floridi, Luciano. 2014. *The Fourth Revolution: How the Infosphere Is Reshaping Human Reality*. Oxford and New York: Oxford University Press.

Harman, Gilbert. 1986. *Change in View. Principles of Reasoning*. Cambridge, MA: MIT.

Hintikka, Jaakko. 1973. *Logic, Language-Games and Information. Kantian Themes in the Philosophy of Logic*. Oxford: Oxford University Press.

Israel, David and John Perry. 1990. What is information. In *Information, Language and Cognition*. Ed. Philip Hanson. Vancouver: University of British Columbia Press.

Kemeny, John G. 1953. A logical measure function. *The Journal of Symbolic Logic* 18 (4): 289–308.

Kreisel, Georg. 1967. Informal rigour and completeness proofs. *Studies in Logic and the Foundations of Mathematics* 47: 138–186.

Mares, Edwin. 1997. Relevant logic and the theory of information. *Synthese* 109 (3): 345–360.

Mares, Edwin. 2009. General information in relevant logic. *Synthese* 167 (2): 343–362.

Mares, Edwin. 2010. The nature of information: A relevant approach. *Synthese* 175 (1): 111–132.

Rayo, A. 2012. *The Construction of Logical Space*. Oxford: Oxford University Press.

Restall, Greg. 2005. Logics, situations and channels. *Journal of Cognitive Science* 6: 125–150.

Saguillo, José M. 2009. Methodological practice and complementary concepts of logical consequence: Tarski's model–theoretic consequence and Corcoran's information-theoretic consequence. *History and Philosophy of Logic* 30 (1): 21–48.

Stalnaker, Robert. 1984. *Inquiry.* Cambridge MA: MIT Press.

Stalnaker, Robert. 1991. The problem of logical omniscience, I. *Synthese* 89 (3): 425–440.

van Benthem, Johan and Maricarmen Martinez. 2008. The stories of logic and information. In *The Stories of Logic and Information.* Ed. Pieter Adriaans and Johan van Benthem. Amsterdam: North-Holland.

Van Ditmarsch, Hans, Wiebe van der Hoek, and Barteld Kooi. 2007. *Dynamic Epistemic Logic.* Dordrecht: Springer.

Wansing, H. 1993. *The Logic of Information Structures.* Berlin: Springer-Verlag.

9

INFORMATION PROCESSING AND INSTRUCTIONAL INFORMATION

Nir Fresco and Marty J. Wolf

Introduction

Humans use information in everyday activities, including reading, driving, learning, planning and decision-making. There is broad agreement that, in some sense, human cognition involves the processing of information, and, indeed, many psychological and neuroscientific theories explain cognitive phenomena in information-theoretic terms. However, it is not always clear which of the many concepts of 'information' is the one relevant to understanding the nature of human cognition. The particular concept of 'information' we choose also has implications for what qualifies as *information processing*. In this chapter, we take the basic information-processing model, roughly along the lines of Richard Atkinson and Richard Shiffrin's early Model of Human Memory (1971), to include (1) input, (2) processing, (3) storage, (4) retrieval and (5) output.

We might take information processing to be everything that our brain and perceptual apparatus engage in when negotiating with the environment (for more on information, cognition and knowledge see Chapter 27). Consider visual processing first. This may include seeing differences and similarities among things in the world, filling in missing details in pictures, visualizing things in one's head and remembering visual details to varying degrees of granularity. Similarly, auditory processing may include hearing differences between sounds, understanding a sentence even when some words are inaudible, remembering specific words and identifying and remembering general sound patterns. To take a different example, rational processing is information intensive, too. One accesses both short-term and long-term memory to retrieve important details for reasoning or decision-making and the same happens when you simply try to find the words you wish to say in a coherent conversation. Such tasks are constrained by the ease and speed of storing information to and retrieving information from both short- and long-term memory. To see that, just try to remember a funny experience from childhood but under time pressure (here long-term memory is accessed). This also suggests that information processing is measurable. For example, it can be measured for correctness and for speed.

Information processing is ubiquitous in biology, too. Communication and information flow can be traced at various levels of the biological organism: from organs and tissues through cells down to the level of genes and DNA bases. Inter-cell communication occurs in response to chemical signals outside the cells. Some cells have direct membrane-to-membrane contact for exchanging signals, whereas others engage in synaptic signalling whereby neuronal cells send electrical pulses along their axons. Information flow can also be traced at the system level in response to environmental stimuli. Take, for example, the *Bobtail* squid that has a mutually beneficial relationship with the *Vibrio fischeri* bacteria living on its underside.[1] The bacteria allow the squid to luminesce enabling the squid to escape from predators. The luminescence is a result of information flow among the bacteria about the local density of other bacteria. Another example is the information processing taking place in our bodies in the process of DNA repair. DNA is subject to many chemical alterations resulting from, among other things, exposure to chemicals in the environment and reactive oxygen radicals. To ensure that genetic information encoded in the DNA remains uncorrupted, any chemical changes must be corrected through the manipulation of information. (Biological information is discussed in detail in Chapter 23.)

Information processing is common in many other physical aspects of our lives (see the chapters in Part III for more on that), and, importantly, many identify information processing with computation. If they are right (see Chapter 3 for more details), then many of our cognitive activities (such as seeing and reasoning) are computational. Yet questions remain about whether there is a distinction between computation and information processing, and if so, what that distinction is. There is hardly any doubt that computers, which serve us daily in the office, school and home, are paradigmatic processors of information. You create a document, save it and later re-open it for further editing and modification. The document can even be deleted. This is both computation and information processing at their best. But what about other information processing systems?

The focus of this chapter will mainly be on the interrelation among *information processing*, *instructional information* and *digital computation*. In the second section, we elaborate on the basic information-processing model. What are its key operations? What is its relation to the Shannon-Weaver model of a general communication system (which is introduced in Chapter 4)? In the third section, we survey some classic and contemporary analyses of the relation between computation and information processing. We note from the outset that a key philosophical motivation for equating information processing with computation is that the latter provides a well-founded model for understanding cognition. If cognition, which engages in information processing, were accurately describable as computation, then this would lay the basis for a naturalistic explanation of cognition. The fourth section introduces an important, but usually neglected, type of semantic information: *instructional* (or procedural) *information*. In the fifth section, we show how digital computation can be described as a form of information processing, namely, the processing of data and instructional information. If that is correct, then digital computation is a type of information processing, but not vice versa. The sixth section summarizes this chapter.

The basic information-processing model

For introductory purposes, the model of information processing discussed here runs, to some extent, parallel to the Atkinson-Shiffrin model of human memory. According to the latter model, environmental stimuli are received through a sensory-motor apparatus and stored briefly in sensory memory – the first information-processing store. Short-term memory is used to retain information for several seconds to operate upon, facilitating attention, control and problem solving. Information learned for later use is retained in the third information-processing store – long-term memory.

The Atkinson-Shiffrin model, however, faces many problems and has been since widely criticized and revised (cf. Izawa 1999; Baddeley 2002). For example, one assumption of this model was that holding an informational item in short-term memory somehow guaranteed learning. But it has since been shown that much more important for learning is the processing that the item undergoes. Also, the simple unitary short-term memory assumed by this model is problematic and is actually a more complex system. Moreover, different types of information, such as factual information (see Chapter 6), instructional information and episodic information (e.g., specific memories associated with a person) are stored differently in long-term memory and encoding specificity plays an important role in long-term storage (Tulving & Thomson 1973).

Nevertheless, the Atkinson-Shiffrin model serves as a good starting point for examining the basic information-processing model, which consists of a few operations, some of which can be viewed as inverse operations. First, the model includes the input and output of information. Second, it includes the storage to and retrieval from memory. Third, it includes the processing of information that in turn may imply various operations, such as the encoding, decoding, production and manipulation of information. In this section, we examine these operations and the relation of this model to the Shannon-Weaver model of a general communication system.

Key operations of the model

The first operation of the information-processing model is the receipt or input of information. The information that the information-processing system (IPS) receives from the environment is the basis for further processing. The IPS, which, for now, should be construed broadly – be that a natural cognitive agent or an artificial computational system – engages with its environment through its input channels. (Input channels in the case of a cognitive agent include, for example, vision, hearing, smell, taste and touch, and in the case of a computer include a keyboard, camera, flash drive and network connection.) The IPS receives information about the current state of affairs in its environment, for example, that it is now cold or hot or that some key was pressed on a connected keyboard. The constant feed of environmental input allows the IPS to keep abreast of events in the world. If a person was intending to leave the house as she observed dark clouds approaching, she could decide to wear a raincoat or take along an umbrella.

The second, inverse, operation of this model is the sending – or output – of information. Based on the processing of information or actions performed by the IPS, it may produce some relevant information to the environment as output. The most conspicuous form of output in the case of animals is through the emission of sound, but hand waving or writing a note on a page can just as well convey information to others. In the case of a computer, sound, some display on the screen and signals sent through its networking interface qualify as output. The IPS' inputs and outputs are the basis for its communication with the environment. The IPS receives a message from its environment and based on this message and its current state (and possibly other factors), it responds to the message by (possibly) changing its state and sending a message.

The third operation of this model is the storage of information. Any information that needs to be processed by the IPS or used at a later stage must first be stored in some form of memory. Short-term memory is used to store information temporarily for immediate processing. Once the stored information has served its purpose, it is discarded and replaced with new information. When we try to recall our dreams or past experiences, we access our long-term memory where relevant information is stored for later use. In the case of a standard computer, consider the difference between Random Access Memory (RAM) and a hard drive. The former is volatile and a reboot of the computer or a power cut results in the loss of any stored information. The latter, on the other hand, allows long-term storage of information and unless overridden or deleted, stored information can, in principle, be accessed anytime in the future.

The fourth, inverse, operation of this model is the retrieval of information. Information stored by the IPS is of little use if it cannot be retrieved when needed. If we somehow stored some valuable information on the computer's hard drive (without any backup), but were unable to access that information later, by any means possible, that information would be as good as lost. The retrieval of information has an important speed constraint imposed on it. It is typically faster to retrieve information from short-term memory than from long-term memory. Try to recall the last word you have just read and compare it with remembering the last thing a particular colleague told you. The same goes for the computer's RAM compared with its hard drive (though significant improvements have been made with the rapid advance in computer technology).

The fifth operation of this model, and, perhaps, the trickiest to characterize, is the processing of information. 'Processing' could simply mean the encoding and decoding of information. Already Locke, in his theory of ideas, suggested that communication is fundamentally a matter of a speaker encoding her thoughts into words sent to a listener who decodes these words back into thoughts (1690). Taken literally, that would result in a narrow interpretation of 'processing' (we come back to this interpretation below in the discussion of the Shannon-Weaver model). Nevertheless, that is all that is required, in principle, for the communication of a message from a sender to a receiver. A message is first encoded in some manner and then sent to a receiver that decodes it. Absent noise on the communication channel, the message should be accurately reproduced by the receiver without any loss of information. Of course, in real world scenarios that is hardly ever the case. Information is lost or distorted as a result of noise and, thus, adverse effects of noise are minimized by means of introducing information redundancy and other error correction methods. (We return to this point below in relation to the Shannon-Weaver model.)

Other important aspects of information processing are the manipulation, deletion and production of information. The manipulation of *semantic* information implies a distinction between different informational contexts, for the syntactic manipulation of a string, for example, as information-bearer has semantic implications. Consider the sentence: 'A common predator of the mouse is the car.' This sentence does not make much sense. Yet, a single replacement of its last character with a 't' makes it very clear. Moreover, when semantic information is taken to include truth (see Chapter 6), the manipulation of information becomes even more sensitive to truth preservation. If the sentence 'All the guests at the reception are vegetarian' is true with respect to some state of affairs (the reception in question), then its simple negation ('At least one of the guests at the reception is not a vegetarian') ceases to be informational, since it is *false*.

The deletion of information is a peculiar operation in the context of information processing. People have a hard time explicitly and deliberately deleting information. You may try very hard to forget a bad experience you once had. In time, you might be able to repress it. But there is no guarantee that the information concerned has in fact been deleted. In a conventional computational system, on the other hand, information can be explicitly deleted, for example, by deleting a file from the hard drive. Yet, the underlying information may not be deleted permanently (that is, the file may still exist) even if the 'Trash' (in a Mac OS) or the 'Recycle Bin' (in a Windows OS) has been emptied. Only a displacement of the information-to-be-deleted with another piece of information in memory ensures the deletion of information. (Even that is not entirely accurate as computer hackers should know very well.)

Lastly, the production of new information raises some interesting questions. Suppose that you are informed that 'Socrates is a man' and you already know that 'All men are mortal', does the conclusion that 'Socrates is mortal' produce any new information? According to the so-called Paradox of (deductive) Inference (see Chapter 8), deductive derivations do not produce new information. The information contained in the conclusion of a valid derivation is already contained in its premises. If that is right, then conventional computational systems, which are typically founded on this fundamental principle of classical logic, tend to produce very little new information. Indeed, some have shown that deterministic computational systems have a limited capacity to produce new information (Adriaans & van Emde Boas 2011; Calude 2009). People, on the other hand, produce new information on a regular basis (just consider the advance of the natural sciences since the seventeenth century).

Information processing and the Shannon-Weaver model

The Shannon-Weaver model of a general communication system was introduced in the mathematical theory of communication. Shannon and Weaver analyzed the ways in which information could be transmitted efficiently across communication channels using messages. The model is analyzed in detail in Chapter 4. Here, you may recall that it consists of five essential components: an information source, a transmitter, a channel, a receiver and a destination (Shannon & Weaver 1949: 33–34). The information source has messages to be communicated to the destination. The transmitter operates on these messages to produce signals appropriate for transmission over the channel. The channel is simply the medium of signal(s) transmission. The receiver reconstructs the message(s) from the signal(s). Lastly, the destination is the person or system for which the message(s) is (are) intended. It is clear from the key operations of the IPS discussed above that these five components are essential to information processing.

As simple as the Shannon-Weaver model might appear, it is at the core of the computers and mobile phones we use everyday. Communication amounts to the transmitter producing a sequence of symbols (to be interpreted broadly) that is later reproduced (exactly or approximately) by the receiver. The message reproduction on the destination's end is performed only to some degree of accuracy as we often observe in phone conversations, text messaging and Internet surfing. You type and send a text message to your friend. Absent other interrupting factors (in either the cellular network or your friend's mobile phone which are typically referred to as noise on the communication channel), the message will (or at least should in principle) be accurately reproduced on her phone. And, under the right settings, the sent message will be stored on your phone: it can be retrieved and accessed again to be viewed, edited or even deleted.

This simple example leads to two important observations. First, the processing of information, on the Shannon-Weaver model, is primarily about the encoding, decoding and transmission of messages. Second, the Shannon-Weaver model is, at its core, memoryless: both the information source and the communication channel are memoryless (so the sent message cannot be stored on your phone, if it is memoryless). In the rest of this section, we briefly discuss these observations in turn.

Encoding/Decoding. The Shannon-Weaver model was aimed at quantifying the most efficient means of encoding and decoding messages, in order to maximize the amount of information that can be exchanged reliably between a sender and a receiver through a given channel in the presence of noise. In the mathematical theory of communication, and in information theory in general, the encoding/decoding process is a technical one. A code is some rule for converting an instance of information, which can be a word or any other communicatory element, such as a gesture, into another form or representation, which need not be of the same type. (That is, one set of signals is converted into another set.) Encoding is the process by which information from the source is converted into signals (specifically, symbols in the Shannon-Weaver case) to be transmitted. It is a set of exact and systematic regularities that can be built into the message constructed by the transmitter. Decoding is the inverse process where the receiver converts the signals received back into understandable information.

At the most fundamental level, the encoding/decoding mechanism allows the communication process between the transmitter and receiver to be both secure and noise-tolerant. Consider an exchange of information between Alice and Bob where they do not wish Carl, standing next to them, to understand that they are planning a surprise party for him. If they have a code that they both know, which Carl does not, they can encode the messages using this code and communicate freely without Carl understanding them.

Another important aspect of the encoding/decoding mechanism is building noise tolerance into the communication process. Noise is anything that interferes with the sending or receiving of signals. It makes the encoding and decoding messages more difficult to implement. For that reason, Shannon and Weaver introduced the notion of redundancy as any

> fraction of the message that is [...] redundant in something close to the ordinary sense [... being] unnecessary (and hence repetitive or redundant) in the sense that if it were missing the message would still be essentially complete, or at least could be completed.
>
> *(1949: 13)*

An extreme, but often wasteful, redundancy mechanism is sending each message twice: the message and its true copy. If the receiver receives two identical messages, it can be assumed to be correct. Whenever either message is lost or the two messages differ, the receiver cannot reproduce the original message, absent other (meta)information, and must request that the message be retransmitted.

Memoryless communication. The IPS discussed above presupposes a memory mechanism that allows the storage of information for a later retrieval. Yet, the Shannon-Weaver model is fundamentally memoryless (particularly, the information source and the channel). When the information source is memoryless, each message transmitted is independent of the previous ones sent. Consider the flip of a fair coin. Knowing that the outcome of the previous flip was *heads* gives no information about the next flip. Each flip is independent of the previous outcome. The probability of each coin flip landing on *tails* (or *heads*) is 0.5 and, thus, (as discussed in Chapter 4) we receive 1 bit of information with each flip.

In order to show that any translational machinery (called a transducer) involved in the encoding/decoding of messages cannot increase the entropy (a measure associated with uncertainty of a piece of information) of an information source, Shannon and Weaver assumed that the transducer has a finite internal memory (1949: 57). The input to the transducer is a sequence of input signals and its output a sequence of output signals. The transducer's internal memory allows its output to depend not only on the present input signal but also on its past history. This description should remind the reader of the Turing machine discussed in Chapter 3. The Turing machine is equipped with memory – which need not be finite, though – that makes its operations depend on the present symbol scanned and its current state. In physical systems, of course, the memory of the system is always finite (no matter how big your hard drive or cloud storage is). Nevertheless, the richness of operations performed by an IPS crucially depends on it having some finite memory. In Section 5, we show that the possession of memory divides computational systems into two classes making those in one class more computationally powerful than those in the other class.

Information processing and computation

In this section, we briefly survey some analyses of the relation between computation and information processing in the literature. Two of the earliest proponents of describing computation as information processing were Allen Newell and Herbert Simon. They advanced a substantive empirical hypothesis about how human cognition works: it is essentially a computational system of the specified sort. In their view, digital computational systems are physical symbol systems containing sets of interpretable and combinable entities (i.e., symbols and symbolic structures) and a set of processes that operate on these entities by producing, copying, modifying, combining and destroying them according to instructions (Newell & Simon, 1976: 116). These symbolic entities are physical patterns (i.e., tokens) that can occur as components of symbolic structures. A physical symbol system is situated in a world of objects that is wider than just these symbolic structures.

Newell and Simon's fundamental working assumption was that both a programmable computer and a thinking human being are information processors (1964). The smallest units of manipulable information in the computer's memory are symbol tokens and those symbols can be aggregated into lists and other more complex symbolic structures. The computer's program determines the transformation of input information into output information. One important class of information processes operating on symbolic structures is the *discrimination* processes that are used to compare symbols to determine whether they are identical. Other classes of operations include the *production, copying, deletion,* and *modification* processes of symbolic structures. Another class of operations is used to *find* information that is in structures stored in memory (ibid.: 291–292). '[A]ll past and present digital computers perform basically the same kinds of symbol manipulations' (ibid: 281). The manipulation of symbols and symbolic structures is equated with information processing on this view.

Another well-known and highly influential analysis of computational systems as information processors was offered by David Marr's study of human vision. 'Vision is a process that produces from images of the external world a description that is useful to the viewer and not cluttered with irrelevant information' (Marr 1982: 31). For Marr, much like Newell and Simon before him, computation involves the processing of information. Yet, it appears that he did not explicitly distinguish between computation and information processing. Computational (or information processing) systems (that is, either computers or cognitive systems) have three levels of description. The first/top level provides an extensional account of *what* is computed: what problem(s) does the system solve? This level characterizes the mathematical (or cognitive, in the context of cognitive systems) input/output function being computed. The objectives of an analysis at this level are (a) translating a general description of the cognitive phenomenon to be explained, such as vision or reasoning, into an account of a specific information-processing problem to be solved, and (b) singling out the constraints imposed on any solution to that problem.

While the top level deals with the abstract nature of computation, the remaining two levels add 'concreteness' to the physical computation in question. The second/middle level specifies *how* a function is computed: what algorithm(s)/program(s) does the system execute? At this level, a description of a detailed set of information-processing instructions for solving the information-processing problem is given. Any information-processing task is the transformation of a given input (e.g., a destination address or a physical object in your proximate environment) into a given output (e.g., directions on how to reach that destination or a three-dimensional representation of the visual object). The third/bottom level describes the actual implementation: how are the algorithms physically implemented? It specifies how the system works physically by identifying the physical structures for implementing the informational states over which the algorithm is defined. In essence, Marr's tripartite analysis emphasizes the intimate link between abstract and physical information processing.

There are more recent analyses of computation as information processing, but space only permits mentioning a few more examples here. Marcin Miłkowski, for one, argues that computation is information processing and that a mechanistic approach best accounts for the implementation of information processing in physical systems (2013: Chapter 2). The notion of information he has in mind is non-semantic, but not necessarily in the quantitative sense (ibid.: 43). Another recent account is offered by Mark Burgin and Gordana Dodig-Crnkovic (2013). On their view, computation is an information transformation process that is organized and controlled by an algorithm. An algorithm is a compressed informational/structural representation of a computational process. They allow that 'the computing device can be either a physical device, such as a computer, or an abstract device, such as a Turing machine' (ibid.), but in physical devices the algorithm is represented and embodied in some programming language. Importantly, '[c]omputation always works with data performing data transformations' (ibid.). While data as input come from the environment, their meaning and processing depend on the computational context and it remains an open question whether computers process only data or *information* as well (ibid.).

A recent detailed analysis attempting to disentangle the notions of 'computation' and 'information processing' has been offered by Gualtiero Piccinini and Andrea Scarantino (2011) (see also their chapter in this handbook). They defend several theses of which we mention just three. First, they argue that digital computation does not entail the processing of Shannon information (that is, quantitative information in the Shannon/Weaver sense of reducing uncertainty). Why so? Consider a digital computer. For its inputs to be considered carriers of Shannon information, they need to be selected in a probabilistic manner. However, the computer, in principle, works the same whether its inputs are selected either probabilistically or deterministically (Piccinini & Scarantino 2011: 27).

Conversely, they argue that the processing of Shannon information does not entail digital computation either. One reason they provide is that for Shannon information processing to be done by digital computational means, the information has to be produced and carried by strings of 'digits' (according to the mechanistic account, digital computation is performed on digits, which are, roughly, discrete stable states of a component in the computational system). Yet, Shannon information can also be produced and carried by continuous, rather than discrete, signals (ibid.: 28). Instead, so they argue, what the processing of Shannon information *does* entail is *generic* computation (which can be seen as the superclass of all types of computation, including digital, analog, quantum and molecular computation). According to the mathematical theory of communication, information is medium-independent, in the sense that whether information is associated with a specific vehicle does not depend on its specific physical features. Since generic computation is the functional manipulation of any medium-independent vehicle, if a vehicle carries Shannon information, its processing qualifies as *generic* computation (ibid.).

Piccinini and Scarantino also defend other theses concerning the relationship between computation and semantic information processing, but we now turn to the processing of a particular type of information as suggested by the title of this chapter. Digital computation could also be defined as the processing of discrete data (sometimes) in accordance with finite instructional information (possibly) through discrete state transitions (Fresco & Wolf 2014). The next two sections are devoted to unpacking this definition. But first we need to understand what instructional information is.

Instructional information in a nutshell[2]

In Chapter 6, Luciano Floridi defines one important type of semantic information that describes events, states of affairs, objects and properties of objects in the world. Instructional information is another type of semantic information – understood, for present purposes, as meaningful and well-formed data. Yet, rather than being descriptive, it is prescriptive. Instructional information prescribes an action to be performed by the receiver under the right conditions. When does semantic content give rise to instructional information rather than factual information? The latter is truth evaluable, whereas the former is not straightforwardly truth evaluable. Floridi argues that in order for semantic content to rise to the level of factual information it must also be true (this is known as the *Veridicality Thesis*, see Chapter 6). In the case of instructional information, there is no such requirement. Instead, to qualify as instructional information, semantic content needs to satisfy another condition that has to with its effectiveness in achieving a particular result in a given context.

Students of philosophy of language will recognize here the standard distinction between declarative sentences (which are correctly truth evaluable) and imperatives (which are not). At its core, symbolic, instructional information is intimately linked to imperatives (Fresco & Wolf 2014). 'An imperative [...] expresses an immediate demand for action but that does not describe a fact: an imperative is satisfied if we have the result of an agent's action' (Ross 1941: 54). '[T]he kernel [...] of the imperative [is] the action [...] that the imperative enjoins' (Hamblin 1987: 45). As such, instructional information cannot be straightforwardly evaluated alethically, but rather as *effective* or *ineffective* in achieving a particular result. Imperatives are evaluated relative to their utility in achieving some result.

> *The Sufficiency Condition for Instructional Information* (SCII). Semantic content is an instance of instructional information *if and only if* its satisfaction through action can systematically lead to a particular outcome in a given context.

Two important desiderata of instructional information (of particular importance for the analysis of computation) are (a) the lack of ambiguity of the action(s) prescribed, and (b) the executability of the action(s) prescribed (Fresco 2015). SCII can also be formulated as follows. Semantic content carries instructional information *i* for a system *S* *if and only if* when *S* acts in accordance with *i* under the right conditions, *S* systematically performs an action in a way that depends on the structure of *i*. At least, partial structuring of the underlying data is paramount to the prescription of action as is shown in the next section.

First, an ambiguous instruction (e.g., 'Break the note!') hinders *S*' capacity to systematically follow it. When the actions prescribed are specified ambiguously they *can* still lead to a particular outcome in a given context. An agent following an ambiguous instruction can repeatedly lead to the same outcome (e.g., breaking a banknote to smaller change). But when given to *different* agents it is less likely to be repeated by *all* agents to produce the *same* outcome. Since the requirement is for a systematic performance of action, ambiguity in the prescription of action hinders that systematicity.

Second, if an instruction cannot be executed in principle, for example, 'open and do not open the window', there is little point in instructing *S* to execute it. There is no right condition under which *S* can follow a contradictory instruction. Such a message still qualifies as instructional information (albeit *ineffective* as is discussed below), much like a logical contradiction still qualifies as semantic information.

Instructional information can be expressed either negatively or positively. In English, for example, the construction of a negative imperative typically differs from the positive one by the presence of some negative quantifier, e.g., 'Don't close the window!' In a general form, a negative imperative can be expressed as "prohibitive, prohibition" (Kaufmann 2012: 9). For our present purposes, a prohibitive that is satisfied through action can still lead to the particular outcome in a given context. It is occasionally used in computational systems and is referred to as NOP (short for no operation) (for example, an empty block statement '{}' in the C programming language is effectively a NOP).

Instructional information implies that at least two courses of action are possible in a given context, for example, 'turn right at the intersection when there is heavy traffic, otherwise turn left'. A selection between at least two alternatives has to be made by the instructed informee. Otherwise, some default action is taken irrespective of what action was prescribed by the instructional information. A particular action constitutes a way of bringing about a particular result in specific circumstances relative to a given level of abstraction (LoA) (see Chapter 7 for an analysis of the method of LoA). Thus characterized, it should be clear that instructional information presupposes that the instructed informee *is capable* of executing the prescribed action(s) under the appropriate conditions.

As a final clarification of the relation between instructional information and imperatives consider three (similar) messages sent to some receiver.

1   'Close the window!'
2   'To close the window, close the window!'
3   'To warm up the room, close the window!

Prima facie, it might seem that only the second and third messages qualify as instructional information. For only these two messages explicitly specify the particular outcome against which the effectiveness of the 'instructional information' can be evaluated. But a closer examination reveals the similarity between messages (1) and (2). They are both evaluated against the same condition being satisfied (the window being closed). The second is simply explicit about the specific outcome and, is, thus, more 'wasteful' in terms of the amount of information encoded.

Only the third message is an example of *effective* instructional information. The method of LoA is useful here. Relative to 'the window being closed' – the first two messages are *ineffective* instructional information. For they do not specify *how* to close the window. The third message, on the other hand, does not specify how to close the window, but, rather, how to warm up the room (provided that the result is achievable).

In short, imperatives *are* instructional information *in and of* themselves. But only when the particular outcome is known in context and obeying the imperative(s) systematically leads to the same outcome does the instructional information qualify as effective (Fresco 2015).

Computation and the processing of instructional information

The first important distinction that the instructional information processing (IIP) account draws is between *trivial* and *nontrivial* digital computation. Trivial computational systems process data, which need not be ordered, by way of exercising a single capacity the system has. Nontrivial computation is the processing of discrete data in accordance with finite instructional information possibly through discrete state transitions. (In the ensuing discussion, the 'possibly' qualification is clarified.) Nontrivial computational systems process instructional information under the right conditions by way of being capable of systematically processing at least two distinct imperative instructions (e.g., read input from the keyboard or reset the value of a variable) for their corresponding capacities.

The main distinction between trivial and nontrivial computational systems, on the IIP account, depends on the capacities of the system concerned. A nontrivial computational system has at least two capacities and it selects between them by processing instructional information in a way that systematically depends on the structure of that information. A trivial computational system, on the other hand, has only one capacity: it is capable of only one action, and, therefore, need not process instructional information.

For all genuine computational systems what matters to their data processing is the abstract form – that is, the type – of the processed data rather than the particular realization of the data – that is, the token data. The same data type can be realized in many different physical substrates, such as differing electrical voltages or differing water pressures. The same data transformation may take place in a variety of physical substrates in a way that does not affect the computation. This is the root of the multiple realizability of algorithms and data. An algorithm may be implemented in different programming languages and on different physical machine architectures.

Consider next some paradigmatic examples taken from computer science and computer engineering. First, take an AND gate and an OR gate, which are the fundamental building blocks of any digital computer. An AND gate performs a logical conjunction operation in hardware. A two-input, one-output AND gate takes two data as input and produces one datum as output. The input and output are typically treated as logical 0s and 1s. The AND gate produces 1 as output only when both inputs are 1; otherwise, it produces a 0. The OR gate, which performs logical disjunction, works similarly, only that it produces 0 as output only when both inputs are 0. These two gates perform *trivial* computation. They need not process instructional information, because each has only a single capacity (conjunction and disjunction). Moreover, no ordering of data is required: the order of the inputs does not matter, only the number of 0s and 1s received as input (whether the gate receives {0,1} or {1,0} as input, the output remains the same).

The AND and OR gates can also be used to draw another important distinction between *memoryless* and *memory-based* computational systems. Neither gate retains the previous state of its operation. Whenever the gate receives the two inputs to produce the single output, its operation is independent of any previous computation of the gate. Whether the gate produced a 0 or a 1 previously does not affect its present operation. The gate 'resets' itself, so to speak, with every operation. It is, thus, a memoryless system. This is the reason for the 'possibly' qualification above. On the IIP account, basic Boolean gates (such as the AND and OR gates) are classified as trivial computational systems that require no instructional information and no discrete state transitions.

Now consider a flip-flop – a basic memory cell – that stabilizes on one of two states (corresponding to low and high voltages, typically) based on its input. The flip-flop stays either 'low' (i.e., 0) or 'high' (i.e., 1) until it is triggered by the next input, and can, therefore, be used to store a single bit. A typical SET-RESET (SR) flip-flop, for example, has two inputs, S and R. When the inputs are both 0, the state remains unchanged. On the other hand, when one of the inputs is 0 and the other is 1, the flip-flop changes to the 1 state if S is 1, and to the 0 state if R is 1. Each of the input/state combinations of the SR flip-flop is instructional information that prescribes a transition to the next indicated state. When the flip-flop processes any of its instructions, it exercises a corresponding capacity to move from one memory state to another, thereby processing data through discrete state transitions in accordance with finite instructional information.

Nontrivial computation should not be equated with computation in memory-based systems. One useful example here is an Arithmetic Logic Unit (ALU), which is a fundamental building block of the central processing unit of standard digital computers. An ALU that is capable of two operations, say, conjunction and addition on two inputs consisting of *n* data each, can perform these two operations without any discrete state transitions. It can, therefore, be designed as a memoryless system. Despite being memoryless it, typically, requires instructional information to select between the conjunction and addition operations on the two inputs. That instructional information requires that the bit used to select between conjunction and addition (since a bit can have one of two values) be distinguished from the other 2*n* data inputs the ALU operates on. It, thus, requires some structuring of the underlying data.

In addition to physical systems, the IIP account classifies abstract systems according to their computational capacities. A paradigmatic example of an abstract memory-based model of computation is the Turing machine (see Chapters 3 and 10). While its memory is potentially infinite (which is not problematic, given that it is an *abstract* system), it processes data (symbols on the tape) according to instructional information (a combination of the input symbol read and its present state) through discrete state transitions (moving from one total memory state to another). As such, it is classified as a nontrivial memory-based computational system and is, thus, more computationally powerful than an AND gate or a flip-flop.

Conclusion

This chapter discusses some crucial intersections among computation, information and information processing. The information-processing model is not unique to computational systems only and it has been employed in many sciences that apply to basic organisms as well as to full-blown cognitive agents. We have seen what key operations an IPS (typically) performs. This holds for both cognitive agents and computational systems. All IPSs, at least to some degree, implement the Shannon-Weaver model of communication. There are many theories in the literature that equate information processing with computation of which we have briefly discussed some of the most important. Others insist that information processing should not be equated with computation. We have also introduced another important, yet often neglected type, of semantic information: instructional information. On the IIP account, we have shown that computation – or more specifically, digital computation – is only one form of information processing. There remain many open problems about the intricate relation between computation and information. For example, how are analog computation and information processing related? How are data implemented in analog systems where differences (recall the definition of data) are harder to discern? Do computers process other types of information essentially or just instructional information? Much more work awaits.

Notes

1 See http://www.nsf.gov/news/special_reports/science_nation/glowingsquid.jsp.
2 The fourth and fifth sections are largely based on (Fresco & Wolf 2014) and (Fresco 2014)

References

Adriaans, P., & van Emde Boas, P. (2011). Computation, Information, and the Arrow of Time. In *Computability In Context* (pp. 1–17). London: Imperial College Press.
Atkinson, R. C., & Shiffrin, R. M. (1971). The Control of Short-Term Memory. *Scientific American*, *225*(2), 82–90.

Baddeley, A. D. (2002). The psychology of memory. In A. D. Baddeley, M. D. Kopelman, & B. A. Wilson (Eds.), *The handbook of memory disorders* (2nd ed., pp. 3–16). New York: John Wiley & Sons, Inc.

Burgin, M. & Dodig-Crnkovic, G. (2013). The Nature of Computation and the Development of Computational Models. Computability in Europe 2013 conference (CiE 2013), The Nature Of Computation, University of Milano-Bicocca.

Calude, C. S. (2009). Information: The Algorithmic Paradigm. In G. Sommaruga (Ed.), *Formal theories of information* (vol. 5363, pp. 79–94). Berlin and Heidelberg: Springer-Verlag.

Fresco, N. (2014). Objective Computation versus Subjective Computation. *Erkenntnis*. doi: 10.1007/s10670-014-9696-8.

Fresco, N. (2015). Information-How. *Australasian Journal of Philosophy*, 1–21. doi: 10.1080/00048402.2015.1022561.

Fresco, N. & Wolf, M. J. (2014). The instructional information processing account of digital computation. *Synthese*, 191(7), 1469–1492.

Hamblin, C. L. (1987). *Imperatives*. Oxford: Blackwell.

Izawa, C. (Ed.). (1999). *On human memory: evolution, progress, and reflections on the 30th anniversary of the Atkinson-Shiffrin model*. Mahwah, NJ: Lawrence Erlbaum Associates.

Kaufmann, M. (2012). *Interpreting imperatives*. New York: Springer Science+Business Media B.V.

Locke, J. (1690). *An Essay Concerning Human Understanding: In Four Books*. London: Printed by Eliz. Holt for Thomas Basset.

Marr, D. (1982). *Vision: A computational investigation into the human representation and processing of visual information*. San Francisco: W.H. Freeman.

Miłkowski, M. (2013) *Explaining the computational mind*. Cambridge, MA: MIT Press.

Newell, A., & Simon, H. A. (1964). Information Processing in Computer and Man. *American Scientist*, 52(3), 281–300.

Newell, A., & Simon, H. A. (1976). Computer Science as Empirical Inquiry: Symbols and Search. *Communications of the ACM*, 19(3), 113–126.

Piccinini, G. & Scarantino, A. (2011). Information Processing, Computation, and Cognition. *Journal of Biological Physics*, 37(1), 1–38.

Ross, A. (1941). Imperatives and Logic. *Theoria* 7 (1): 46–71.

Shannon, C. E. and Weaver, W. (1949). *The Mathematical Theory of Communication*. Urbana, IL: University of Illinois Press.

Tulving, E., & Thomson, D. M. (1973). Encoding specificity and retrieval processes in episodic memory. *Psychological Review*, 80(5), 352–373. doi:10.1037/h0020071.

10

INFORMATION IN THE PHILOSOPHY OF COMPUTER SCIENCE

Giuseppe Primiero

Introduction

During the last decade, the philosophy of computer science has carved an important space within the landscape of philosophical investigations. The range of questions and problems it addresses is wide and varied: the methodology of design, the ontology and semantics of computational artefacts, abstraction and implementation, to name a few. This chapter focuses strictly on the philosophical interpretation of the notion of information within Computer Science.

The centrality of information in Computer Science is indisputable: the discipline is hardly comprehensible when abstracted from the conceptualization and use of this notion. Denning (1985) defined Computer Science as "the body of knowledge of information-transforming processes" and Hartmanis and Lin (1992) as "the study of information" in itself. Although the debate on the nature of this discipline is far from being settled, these two early definitions refer to information as an essential concept. *A fortiori,* information represents an optimal conceptual tool to explore the philosophy of computer science.

Given its ubiquity, information risks to become a misleading concept. A philosophical approach to the role of information in Computer Science requires, in the first place, articulating the actual configuration of the discipline. A list of the main research areas within academic departments and research institutions can be roughly given as follows:[1]

1 Algorithms and Data Structures
2 Programming Languages
3 Architecture
4 Operating Systems and Networks
5 Software Engineering
6 Databases and Information Retrieval
7 Artificial Intelligence and Robotics
8 Graphics
9 Human-Computer Interaction
10 Data Mining and Machine Learning
11 Bioinformatics

A quick overview of this list reveals the well-known methodology of the Level of Abstraction (LoA, see Chapter 7) at work, including all aspects from the very concrete to the formal, from the isolated act of computation to its complex environment: the formal structures underlying data and their algorithmic treatment (1); their implementation in language (2) and use for program design (5); the design and construction of (networks of) hardware to manipulate (3 and 4), visualize (8) and process data (6); data analytics and its use to lead automatic processes (10); the relation between machine and the user (9); the study of autonomous agents (7); the mechanical engineering of living systems (11).

This familiar way of representing the work of computer scientists tells us that the syntactic (see Chapter 4), the semantic (see Chapter 6) and the procedural (see Chapter 9) notions of information are all at work in different areas of Computer Science. Our task is to approach information focusing on the computational model, from the low-level processing of circuitry to the higher level of design, to sketch the philosophical issues that arise. For this reason, we will focus on the standard notion of digital computational system: we will show how the LoAs are structured, and will do so in terms of an *epistemology of control* and an *ontology of syntax and semantics* through the relation *abstraction-implementation,* i.e. the linking of a syntactic domain (abstraction, symbol manipulation) to a semantic one (domain of objects). This relation is considered at the core of the LoAs structure in Computer Science (see Rapaport 1999). In the second section we start from the lowest possible level of abstraction, where information is electric inputs running on wires; in the third section we consider how that level is controlled through syntax; in the fourth section we move to the semantics of programming languages and their control of algorithmic structures; in the fifth section we investigate the intentional stance behind the programming and algorithm design practice, and in the sixth section we summarize our analysis of the information flow within the computational system, analyzing briefly how programs are interpreted and checked.

Information inside the computing machine: structured data

In the long-standing philosophical debate about what Computer Science is, the mechanical formulation of the computational process is central. Newell *et al.* (1967) defined Computer Science as "the science of computers and related phenomena"; later Newell and Simon (1976) rephrased it as "the empirical study of computer related phenomena". Under this interpretation, the core business of Computer Science is the material execution and mechanical realization of those information-transforming processes referred to by Denning (1985). The physical core of a modern computer is the Central Processing Unit, roughly composed by:

- arithmetic and logic unit, for the data processing;
- registers, for their storage;
- program counter and instructions register, to store the machine state and current operation of the program;
- control unit, for the coordination of input/output devices.

While we are not strictly interested in the actual physical functioning of a CPU, we want to investigate which kind of information is at work at the physical level of the computing machine. The technical, well-known answer is that computing machinery at the physical level deals with *binary digits* (bits) expressing discrete, exclusive ON/OFF states of electrical-magnetic input. Philosophically, this description is still incomplete: the information flowing on wires is not simply 1s and 0s of bits randomly produced for the processing unit to operate on. These bits need to be structured and processed according to rules. Let us make an easy example. If we wire a switch to a LED (Light Emitting Diode) and connect it to a 5v supply on a breadboard, the effect is to turn the light on; if the switch is turned to OFF, so does the light. If we bypass first the wire through an *inverter* (a digital circuit which *inverts* the value passed to it, logically corresponding to a negation, see the diagram below), the effect is what we expect: when the switch is ON, the light will stay OFF; when the switch is OFF, the light will go ON (Figure 10.1).

If we combine two wires, each connected to a switch, through an OR gate with one bit output to a LED, then the output will be ON if at least one of the two switches is ON (see Figure 10.2).

With these simple cases in mind, we can already make some observations:

1   the input is given by a variable x (possibly composed by more than one bit) with value 0 or 1;
2   there is an output y whose value depends on x;
3   there is some rule establishing the dependency relation between x and y; for the *inverter* rule, such dependency is explained by saying that "if $x=0$ then $y=1$ and if $x=1$ then $y=0$"; for the OR rule, the dependency is explained by saying that "if $x1$ or $x2=1$ then $y=1$ and if both $x1$ and $x2=0$ then $y=0$".

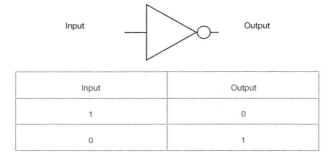

Input	Output
1	0
0	1

Figure 10.1 Inverter

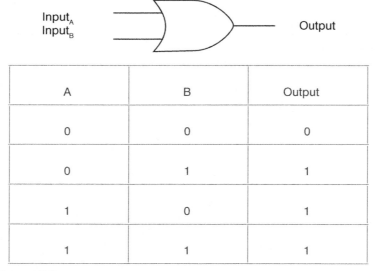

A	B	Output
0	0	0
0	1	1
1	0	1
1	1	1

Figure 10.2 2-input OR gate

The ontological domain of electrical inputs is an implementation; its structure is controlled in terms of value assignment, value dependency and rule execution.[2] A CPU and the board on which it is installed are just a more complex set of such structuring, including other essential Boolean circuits (implementing other logical operations, e.g. AND, XOR), further modified by the capacity to store values for future uses (memory), the ability to locate specific inputs (location assignment) and organize complex instructions (coordination). Hence, at this level, information corresponds to data as structured, physically evaluated variables, where structure control is meant to associate electrical charges to the realization of *actions* (Figure 10.3).

Look at Figure 10.3 below and let us unpack this definition. The pure syntactical, physical elements (electrical charge) create *distinction* or *difference* in the system, as the result of the evaluation of an empty element (value assignment function). The empty element in question, or variable, is an abstraction from the allocated memory space or physical wire taking a value (1,0). Its evaluation is the way difference is manifested. In Floridi (2011, pp.85–86), difference is specified as *de re* (lack of uniformity in the real world) or *de signo* (lack of uniformity between at least two signals). In the context of electrical values manifested in bits, one is dealing with a difference of the second kind (*de signo*), coupled with a physical effect that occurs in the real world (*de re*), be it simply a charged wire or a lightened up LED. In the context of physical computing systems, a difference *de re* allows to trace a difference *de signo*, while it is always the latter that causes the former. While data processing is most commonly interpreted by digital bits, there are examples of analog computers that essentially change the understanding of the data worked on, by forms of mechanical (like the physical movement of objects) or hydraulic (water droplets) quantities. If we stick to the digital realm, the essential nature of data at this level is that of tokens *physically realized* in an electrical charge, possibly manifested in an actually visible state of the system (e.g. by pixels on a display or a LED). At higher levels, the analysis of information in the context of Computer Science allows, and in fact requires, abstracting away from the physical expression of our inputs.

The structuring of physical data at the level of digital processing is given by a *spatial and temporally determined execution,* essential to their correct manipulation in terms of dependency relations. Typically, it will make a difference if the value of x is accessed at a memory slot before accessing a y from which it depends, or if the location is accessed after the relevant value is updated, or at which memory location one looks for a given value. The resulting structure can be taken either as an ontological or an epistemic property. In the former case (as argued in Fresco and Wolf 2013), data composed by logical operations and accessed by memory functions is structured in view of the capacity of the *abstract datum* to be so before any implementation. Under the epistemic interpretation (as argued by Floridi 2011), structure is determined by the knowledge process at stake at this specific LoA, i.e. when bits are taken as information. This means that structure is not inherited from abstract data as such, but only obtained in virtue of the operational view on data. While the epistemic reading makes the distinction between information and data essential, the ontological view reduces the possibility of structure to data themselves.

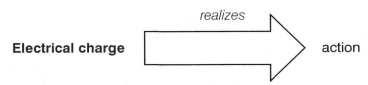

Figure 10.3 Structured physical data

In both cases, the explanation of *how* structure is obtained requires higher levels of abstraction. The epistemic account of data structure leads to the notion of low-level instructions that allow action-control. The ontological account will lead us through higher aspects of data representation and control, corresponding to different philosophical characterizations of the notion of information.

Operational information: controlling structured data

The philosophical analysis of low-level information requires explaining the process of data structuring. The ontological view on structure refers to essential properties of data and it requires expressing how these properties are actualized. The epistemic view on structure sees it as a necessary result of our knowing process and it immediately leads to a procedural account of actions. Both require explanation of how communication of data at the processor level is obtained. Technically, this is explained by low-level languages. Conceptually, it requires defining *actions* in terms of *operations,* so as to justify our *knowledge-that* in terms of *knowledge-how.*

A low-level language is a program that takes textual instructions and turns them into appropriate arithmetical and logical operations on numbers and bits, then correctly executed by the processor. Such a program is called an *assembler.* An assembly program is thus a series of *operations* on values to be performed on the physical locations known to the processor. Its syntax includes instructions such as *jump, loop, load*; values such as $0 \times FF$ (255 in decimal) and actual register numbers, e.g. *16* or ports, e.g. *DDRB* (to control specific pins on an Arduino board). As an easy example, the programmer who expects the machine to sum together any two positive inputs from registers will work with few lines of code, e.g. in the format for 16bit addition:

```
DATA SEGMENT
NUM DW 1234H, 0F234H
SUM DW 2 DUP(0)
DATA ENDS
CODE SEGMENT
ASSUME CS: CODE, DS:DATA
START: MOV AX,DATA
MOV DS,AX
MOV AX,NUM ; First number loaded into AX
MOV BX,0H ; For carry BX register is cleared
ADD AX,NUM+2 ; Second number added with AX
JNC DOWN ; Check for carry
INC BX ; If carry generated increment the BX
DOWN: MOV SUM,AX ; Storing the sum value
MOV SUM+2,BX ; Storing the carry value
MOV AH,4CH
INT 21H
CODE ENDS
END START
```

An assembly program has its own syntax and construction rules, which determine the correctness of the execution. It allows an agent to structure physical data, i.e. it permits control over the physical layer by defining what *operation* (at machine-code level) is to be performed in order to execute the required *action* (at digital data level)*:* for example, it allows assigning a value to an address or directing an output to a port.[3] We will say that machine code embeds a notion of **operational information** on structured, physical evaluated variables (Figure 10.4, see also Chapter 9).

Take a look at Figure 10.4, the essential element at this level is the use of a language to add structure to data. Such language is syntactically well-defined, hence structure is defined by correctness. Moreover, the language imports semantics as a way of denoting the physical entities that constitute the ontological domain of the relation language-objects. The semantics of data structuring, i.e. the range of available operations definable at machine-code level, is fixed by the physical layer information operates on: code 0xFF can only mean the decimal translation of 255; DDRB can only be used if the underlying hardware has a port that deals with a given set of pins; *jump* will correctly work if the specified address exists, and so on. Change the physical elements and the semantics changes accordingly. Here the semantic relation is not intended in terms of compositional rules and instructions that can be freely designed and modified by the agent, but is fixed by the ontological domain. This specific syntactic-semantic structure qualifies operational information as **well-formed performative data**.

The switch from information as structured data to operational information as its control device establishes therefore a semantic relation which maps ontology (of physical entities and physical actions) to a language (of operations). The corresponding satisfiability relation of operations by actions can be interpreted in terms of execution. The ontology and the epistemology of structuring assign different priorities to action and operation. If the relation of structuring performed by the language of machine code is intended as inherent to data (i.e. understood from an ontological viewpoint), it will not be *provided by* operations, but only *described by* them. This implies that abstract data (like a value jump to an address) enjoys a structuring property that exists independently of the contingent action actually performed (with a given value and at a given address). The action, in turn, is explained in terms of implementation of the abstract case, corresponding to a valid change generated by the action in the system. Hence, for the ontological view, structure is *a priori* and inherent to data. If, instead, one looks at the structure as the result of the operation obtained by execution of strings of machine-code language, the result is *a posteriori* in the domain of reference of the language and it is *assigned* by operations.

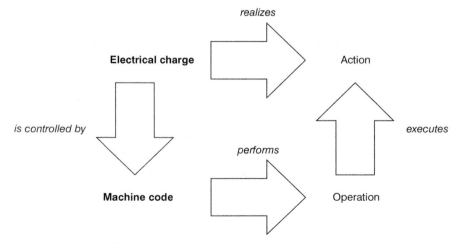

Figure 10.4 Operational information

Instructional information: programs and their semantics

Syntactic correctness and a denotational relation of satisfiability are the elements implemented at the level of actions-structuring by machine-code language operations. When data is abstracted from the physical layer, i.e. the specifics of the material execution and the ontology denoted by machine code are forgotten, a new control device is required to account for the meaning of computation. This time, the ontology of operations is understood as the reference domain of *instructions;* the latter, in turn, constitute a control device which corresponds, in the practice of Computer Science, to establishing the *interface* between the user and the machine language by means of a *programming language.*

A high-level program *denotes* the executable strings of low-level information of machine code. Each family of such languages interprets differently their linguistic constructs and the related semantics, here simplified in the following main distinction:

- *Declarative programming* refers to languages describing what computations (i.e. the low-level operations) should be performed. Functional languages (like Haskell, LISP, or JavaScript, although with relevant differences) are members of this family, with functions semantically defined by their input-output types (*signature*);
- *Imperative programming* refers to languages where the program is construed around states and actions telling *how* to change such states. Object oriented languages (like C or Java) are members of this family, with objects used to define every element and making use of various concepts and operations to re-use them.

A programming language offers a new control structure to be analyzed by properties of the program. While machine-code language provides a semantics for the execution (action), a programming language provides a semantics for the computation (operation). This is explained usually by referring to two main categories:

- *operational semantics:* it syntactically proves properties of the program in terms of rules from logical statements that formalize its states and procedures;
- *denotational semantics:* it compositionally expresses properties of the program in terms of formal statements that map to each syntactic object a mathematical one.

Each syntactic construct in a programming language expresses a functional executable procedure on the lower level of the machine language. This association of the high-level to the low-level language is nowadays mostly executed automatically through the processes of compiling, followed by the process of linking for the creation of an executable file. As a language, this novel control structure requires (again) correctness of its syntactic nature: the *compiler* is charged with the task of discovering syntactically incorrect code. But while the semantics of machine code was defined by the physical level, this new language instantiates a novel semantic relation with a domain of *abstract entities*. Let us extend the example from the previous section. To automatically produce and control the machine code to structure together the input values of two registers, the programmer will write some program, e.g. in C:

```
int main() {
int a, b, c;
printf("Enter two numbers to add\n");
scanf("%d%d",&a,&b);
```

```
c = a + b;
printf("Sum of entered numbers = %d\n",c);
return 0;
}
```

The C code above is syntactically well-formed, which guarantees control over operations at machine-code level (i.e. the code will compile correctly). Moreover, it *expresses* an instructional information of the form: "given positive integers *a,b,c* perform the operation *a+b=c* and print the result *c*." The elements denoted are no longer the implementable names for physical locations and circuit-closing operations, but abstract objects and their properties, such as *integer number* and *sum operation*. We will refer to this new level of abstraction as **instructional information** (Figure 10.5).

The information content of the machine language is now *denoted by* the language of the program in terms of instructions;[4] and the latter is *satisfied by* operational information in machine code. The new control device is represented by *syntactically correct* strings of programming code matching *appropriate* executable strings of machine code; the *meaning* of the former strings being given in terms of a domain of interpretation for the data as abstract objects and their properties, the new ontology of the language at hand. This syntactic-semantic structure qualifies instructional information as **well-formed, meaningful data**. Meaning is acquired at this stage by evaluating whether an operation (and in turn an action) is obtained at the implementation level. There is still no alethic assessment: like in the case of an order to a person, it makes no sense to ask of a piece of code in itself whether it is true or false.

But the programmer does not only want to know whether the produced code will execute some operation in a given domain of objects, making *something* happen at machine-

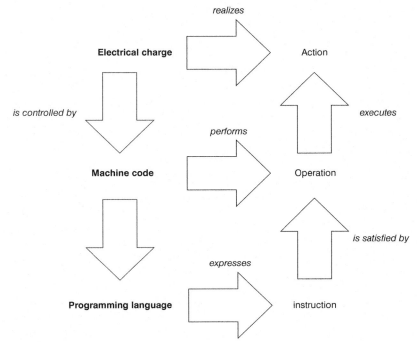

Figure 10.5 Instructional information

code level. The latter evaluates instructional information in view of the implementation. Instructions need to be evaluated also with respect to their *intended* meaning, i.e. the abstract objects and the operations defined on them. These reflect the *algorithm* implemented by the current program: the programmer wants to know whether the code written will make happen what she is expecting. In the following section, we consider this further abstraction level, to evaluate computation and its informational content in view of purpose and design, and to explore how further epistemic and alethic conditions are involved.

Abstract information: algorithm, design and purpose

The presence of a language at machine code and programming levels allows a mapping between symbols and meaning. When instructional information is not taken as an abstraction of the operational level, but as an implementation itself, the meaning of instructions is given by what *they are supposed* to make happen. This next level of interpretation for the notion of information within the computational paradigm is given by the purpose and design according to which a program implements (as efficiently and precisely as possible) an algorithm. This requires a further re-definition of information in view of its abstract content and epistemic value.

An algorithm is the abstract representation of a mathematical function required to fulfil a task. In our case, such task is represented by the *expected* machine behavior. Although it is debated how algorithms in Computer Science should be formally understood,[5] an abstract definition is in terms of a Turing computable or general recursive function implemented by a program, say for example one from natural numbers to natural numbers such as the sum of two integers.[6] A programmer who wants the machine to sum together any two positive inputs will write a program which implements a set of rules, for example as follows:

1 Read the Values of A and B
2 If A and B $\geq$ 0, SUM = A+B. Display SUM. Stop.
3 Otherwise, Return ERROR: 'No positive inputs'. Stop.

Besides the quantitative notion of algorithmic information,[7] the informational content of an implemented algorithm can be defined by abstraction and expressed in terms of the designer's intention to solve a formulated problem. For example, the designer might wish to know some physical quantity, for which she devises rules to perform a task, offering a corresponding solution, in our case the sum of two positive integers. The choice of which step to apply is crucial, because some solution will be *correct* to solve the problem at hand, others will not. It is in view of the designer's intention that the algorithm is considered a correct mathematical representation of the intended task and, in turn, the written program is deemed correct or not. Conversely, the program has to implement correctly the instructions expressed by the algorithm. Correspondence by implementation here is a relation of adequacy, not of mirroring. Accordingly, the content of an algorithm can be defined as **abstract, correctness-determining information** (see Figure 10.6).

As the informational content of the algorithm determines the correctness of all the lower level implementations, its semantic value cannot be dependent from those implementations. It has to be evaluated in terms of the ontology of the algorithm and the epistemology of its design. The former refers to the abstract representation of a function, akin to a mathematical model. The relation between mathematical and computational abstraction is not trivial. The algorithm is the mathematical description of the program's functional specification and as such it establishes correctness for the material artefact running the program. In this sense,

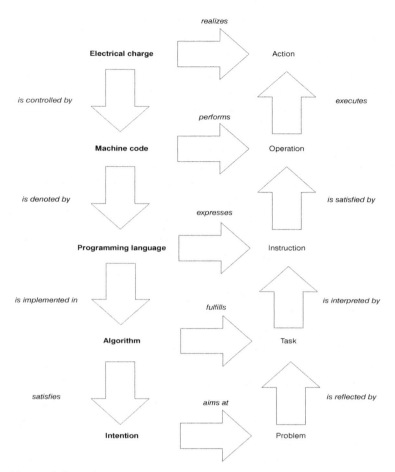

Figure 10.6 Abstract information

it represents a normative definition of the computational instrument (see Turner, 2011). In software engineering, the design of the specification of a system is a process that precedes the design of the algorithm that has to satisfy it. Such a process, performed with semi-formal or formal methods such as the Unified Modeling Language (Fowler 2003), State Transition Diagrams or flowcharts, is meant to offer a representation of the system as intended by the designer. The result is a representation that expresses the intended meaning of the system ("what is that the system should do?", "which problem should it solve?"). The algorithm then expresses the required instructional setting ("how is the system supposed to work?", "how should it solve the given problem?") in an *abstract* way, independent from any language-specific syntax.

From the point of view of our analysis of information in Figure 10.6, the specification and the algorithm together offer a definition of the computational system and an image of the artefact that has to implement it. Besides, this pair has to match the intention of the designer. Here the epistemic reading completes the picture. Correctness becomes not only an analytic definitional property, in the sense of being the correct decomposition of concepts required to define a function (and eventually its execution). It has to be designed correctly to satisfy the required function for the problem at hand, a synthetic composition of problem and solution.

The correctly designed algorithm acts now as an information-hiding device with respect to both implementation (the instructional information level) and the working device (the operational information level). When defining the algorithm, details essential to the implementation and execution level are ignored, but they can be reconstructed when required.[8] The designed algorithm immediately determines the correct implementations in any given algorithm and then in any language. From the point of view of the properties of the information, each construction made according to the rules defined by the algorithm represents a *true instance* of the abstract model defined by the specification and the algorithm. At this stage, the abstract nature of the informational content of an algorithm also defines *truthfulness* of its instances, and not just their correctness. The defining property of the informational content at the level of the algorithm is that every lower layer can be defined as a *true* and *correct instance* only in view of this one. Hence, the (full) informational content of an algorithm can be defined as **abstract, correctness- and truth-determining information.** To further qualify this claim we shall reconsider the full computational process in the next section.

The information flow of the computational process

The various notions of information from the literature in mathematics, epistemology and philosophy arise within the computational process. Each notion emerges naturally, defining the ontology and the epistemology of computation. The former is given in view of the relation of *abstraction-implementation* present at each level of the computational process, realizing *syntax* and *semantics*. The latter is instantiated in terms of the *control structure* that each abstraction level performs on the lower one(s).

Let us recall the abstraction-implementation relations. Structured physical data is the informational content where only quantitative on/off relations of bits are at stake. Electrical charges are the domain of reference of machine code, which represents its control structure. At this higher level, the only requirement is that assembly language is guaranteed syntactically well-formed by automatic compilation. This quantitative information has in itself no semantic, nor alethic value. This abstraction level sees action-control performed by operations of machine code in terms of signaling and communication, a task notoriously fulfilled by the Mathematical Theory of Communication, or Shannon's Information Theory (Shannon 1948), see Chapter 4. Next, programs are abstractions from machine code. The syntax of any given correct string of instructions can be different, depending on the specifics of the language, but it will denote the same operation to be performed at machine-code level. For the corresponding control structure, strings of instructions in a programming language range over operations of machine code. But programs are also implementations of algorithms. Any instruction interprets a task and as such it is loaded with the meaning defined by the designer's task. This requires that the *correct* syntactic string in the language expresses the *appropriate* instruction from the algorithm.

The implementation side of this relation is instantiated as follows:

bits – machine code – programming language – algorithm.

Its informational content is characterized by syntactic correctness (at the level of actions, instructions and operations) and a meaning relation (by interpretation of a task by instructions and their implementation by actions): a correct operation is evaluated in terms of the instructional information expressed in some programming language; and a correct language implementation is evaluated in terms of the abstract information expressed by the algorithm. Information is composed here by: physical data in the circuitry of the machine, taken as a relational entity that establishes ontological and epistemic difference; correctness as a property of controlled operations, which relate to the physical layer and can be interpreted independently from the actual operation of coding; finally, the proper meaning is given in the relation to instructions, evaluated in view of the task to be performed, fulfilling also a performative role.

This qualification of the information flow corresponds to *well-structured meaningful data*, which is usually given as the *standard definition of information* (SDI), see Israel and Perry (1990), Devlin (1991), Floridi (2005, 2014), see also Chapter 6. This notion of meaningful data satisfies all cardinal principles of SDI:

- *Typological Neutrality*: information cannot be dataless, and everything can be a datum;
- *Taxonomical Neutrality*: a datum is a relational entity, so is information;
- *Ontological Neutrality*: data implementing information are physical;
- *Genetical Neutrality*: data (and therefore information) can have a semantics independently of any informer;
- *Alethic Neutrality*: meaningful and well-formed data qualify as information, no matter whether they represent or convey a truth or a falsehood or have no alethic value at all.

It is thus clear that *meaning and correctness* are here the basic criteria of evaluation: is a given set of machine-code operations correct to perform some desired physical actions in a given physical environment? Does a given program express the correct instructions to obtain a certain output (functional correctness)? Finally, when the algorithm is taken operationally, is a given set of abstract rules the correct way to characterize the intention to obtain a result or resolve a problem?[9] No truth or falsity is conveyed, as it makes no sense to predicate truth of a list of instructions, be those expressed in common natural language or in the syntax of a given programming language.

The corresponding abstract relation is instantiated by the informational flow between

output – program – algorithm – intention.

This abstraction requires considering the output, the program and the algorithm as mathematical entities, realizing a definition of the specification. At this stage, an analysis in terms of correctness and meaning seems to remain unsatisfactory. As a mathematical model, the algorithm has instances that satisfy it, and some that do not, while each of those can be taken as correct on its own (when accounting for different tasks). This happens when the algorithm is interpreted as a recursive definition of a function in a specification (for example of the sum operation in terms of the successor function) defining the *model* of the task intended by the designer; such model will have (possibly many) abstract machine(s) as its instances and any implemented expression (for example in the C language, but also in natural language) of that algorithm will be a *true* realization of any such instance. This way of expressing the relation between abstract implementation, algorithm with its output and intention is akin to the definition of semantic satisfiability in a model, which does not define correctness, but *truth*. The informational content of such relation requires now for its definition reference to the semantic conception that encapsulates truth, see Floridi (2011) and Chapter 6. The information flow of the full computational process is thus based on meaningfulness, correctness and truth at different stages. We recall all these stages again in Figure 10.7. This description emphasizes the duality inherent to computation as an abstract process that is instantiated in a mechanical artefact, an issue that has affected crucially the idea of program verification, see Fetzer (1988).

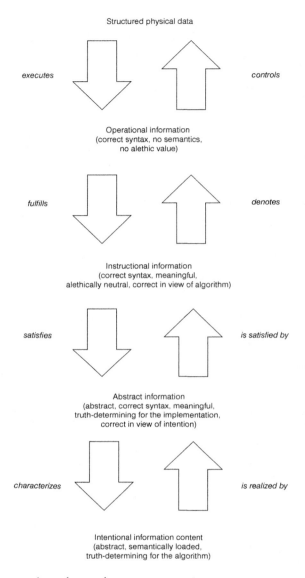

Structured physical data

executes   controls

Operational information
(correct syntax, no semantics,
no alethic value)

fulfills   denotes

Instructional information
(correct syntax, meaningful,
alethically neutral, correct in view of algorithm)

satisfies   is satisfied by

Abstract information
(abstract, correct syntax, meaningful,
truth-determining for the implementation,
correct in view of intention)

characterizes   is realized by

Intentional information content
(abstract, semantically loaded,
truth-determining for the algorithm)

Figure 10.7 Syntax, semantics and control

Verifying information

The informational view of digital computation presented here can be matched against formal verification as the reconstruction of the correct mapping between the instructional information level of the executable program and the abstract information level of the algorithm and its intended design. The practice of verification is the process of testing, which includes also empirical verification. It consists in checking whether the execution of a given program is error-free, in the sense of returning the expected behavior as by definition of its design and by realization of its purpose. Software testing is the general process of checking that the requirements guided by the design are met and is divided into various tasks:

1   check that the program responds to all valid inputs;
2   check that the computation is performing with respect to time;
3   check that the system is acceptable for a standard user;
4   check that the system runs well on the intended environment (physical and virtual).

These tasks describe a modular enterprise: from the verification of the functionality of a single piece of code, e.g. implementing a function or an object (unit testing); through checking the interface of different units (integration testing); to checking validity of data passing among interfaces (component interface testing); up to the verification of the fully integrated system (system testing).

Compilation and linking processes are nowadays mostly automatically generated; hence, the verification of the operational information results in a combination of testing the functionality of the automatic compiler software that generates the machine code, and of the various techniques comprising hardware testing. For the former, one is considering another piece of software on its own, hence the following steps from unit testing onwards apply. For the latter, it mainly consists of so called stress testing, to establish the limit of system's stability and performance, focusing on the physical execution. Unit testing is the basic verification of the correctness of instructional information (i.e. at program's level). It is in the first place an evaluation of the purely syntactic structure of the instruction and, in turn, of its execution as operation. The syntactic correctness check is required to establish whether the chosen procedures are implemented correctly according to basic syntactic rules of the language, e.g. by ensuring that C expressions terminate with a semi-colon, that opening brackets always have matching closing ones, and that operating on positive integers has the starting input defined using a failure on the $(n<=0)$ expression. To check the meaningfully loaded instructional information, one requires not only to know whether a specific function (or object) is correctly coded; one also requires to know whether the function (or object) is what it is needed in order to express the instruction for the desired operation. Integration testing can be seen as the checking of meaningful composition of elements of an analytic definition, and as such it is meant to verify truthfulness. For example, given the intended operation is the one of sum on integers, it requires using the appropriate input/output signature int->int (i.e. that the function takes integers as inputs and returns an integer as output) and the use of the sum = a + b function. For this purpose, a composition that uses an input/output signature real->int (i.e. from real numbers as input to integers as output) using the function a * b (i.e. by multiplication) would not satisfy the analytic definition of sum of integers. While correct in view of another algorithm, this implementation would not be a true instance of the model defined by the intended one. Component interface testing is then a similar analyticity test in the composition of different functions for the purposes of defining a more complex algorithm. Finally, testing the integrated system has to reflect the physical execution and its effectiveness at the implementation level, the correctness of the instruction and of the rules that define them at the abstraction level.

From the informational viewpoint, verification corresponds therefore to checking meaningfulness, correctness and truth at both the implementation level (*bits – machine code – programming language – algorithm*) and the abstraction level (*output – program – algorithm – intention*). The implementation level requires checking that physical execution restores downwards the valid reference domain for the program, going from instructions to operations to actions. The abstraction level moves upwards from the physical (operational) and syntactical (instructional) formulation of the computation to reconstruct the semantic information content at the level of algorithm, intention and purpose. This means also verifying that the defined computation can be subsumed as a true instance of the (intended) definition of the system.

Computing as science of information

Our view on information in the computational process touches on Computer Science and its philosophy, including aspects related to Computer Engineering, Information Systems, Information Technology and Software Engineering.[10] For this larger understanding of the discipline, the term Computing seems preferable. In this context, the view that Computing can be understood as a Science of Information is not new. Since the late 1960s, practitioners and philosophers have presented views based on a notion of information.[11] It is striking, though, that these views focus over largely distinct aspects of computing, fitting different notions of information to their tasks. In some cases, information refers to data processing; in other cases, physical, methodological or working principles on data structures are intended.[12] Our analysis has highlighted the need for conceptual precision in identifying what *information* means at each level of abstraction, hence for each of the different sub-disciplines in Computing. We examined information structures in view of a syntax-semantic relation between a domain of objects and a language at various LoAs. Object domains, in terms of implementations, represent the *ontologies* of Computing (from bits to algorithmic constructs, but also including their physical implementations, such as networks). Languages constitute control means (from machine-code strings, through representations such as FSMs, to designers' intentional states), expressing the *know-how* over ontologies; in this sense, they can be subsumed under the general heading of epistemology. Such a conceptual distinction is often blurred in practice, where a design task can be updated many times in view of insights coming directly from prototyping. A philosophical formulation of (digital) Computing can be presented then in terms of information as follows:[13]

> Computing is the systematic study of the ontologies and epistemology of information structures.

It is essential that the qualification of *systematic study* appealed by in this definition be understood in a broad methodological sense: it refers to designs, formal models, blueprints, testing, up to include those fragments of the discipline that deal with evaluation, behavioral and experimental methods, including e.g. Human-Computer Interaction and Computational Simulations.

Concluding remarks

The standard digital computational process includes all the various aspects of the notion of information: the quantitative definition of bits, the syntactic construction of operations, the meaning of instructions, the abstract format of algorithm and the epistemically loaded designer's intention. We have analyzed both its ontology through the syntax-semantics divide, and its epistemology, in terms of control structures. The information flow that results from them is based on the relation abstraction-implementation. At each level, important philosophical issues arise, in particular related to correctness, meaning and truth. The relational notion of correctness is clearly a common trait to evaluate information throughout the whole computational process. Meaning is a distinctive step to move from mechanical operations to their instructional counterparts. Truthfulness arises at the highest level of abstraction, when algorithms are accounted as mathematical structures defining models. Each such description defines a different, essential format of the notion of information within the philosophy of computer science and in turn offers a better definition of Computing as a Science of Information.

Acknowledgements

I wish to thanks Liesbeth De Mol, Matti Tedre and the participants at lectures given at IHPST, Paris and DSV, Stockholm University where preliminary versions of this work have been presented.

Notes

1 This list is essentially incomplete. A more systematic presentation is available through the Association for Computing Machinery Classification System, see www.acm.org/about/class/ccs98-html.
2 Under the general heading of *rule* and *dependency*, we subsume the whole fetch-decode-execute-check cycle of the program instructions performed by the CPU.
3 Under the general heading of *operation*, we subsume the whole set of arithmetical operations performed e.g. on the stack memory structure or on their simulation by CPU machine registers.
4 Under the general heading of *instruction*, we subsume the basic list of structures sufficient to program any algorithm in any language: assignment, sequencing, branching and iteration.
5 The two most known and alternative views see algorithms respectively as *abstract machines* or as *recursive definitions*, see e.g. Moschovakis (2001), Blass and Gurevich (2003).
6 For an easy introduction to the notion of Turing Machine and the computable functions in relation to information, see The Pi Network (2013), Chapter 12.
7 For Algorithmic Information Theory see Chapter 5.
8 For different views on this debate, see e.g. (Colburn, Shute 2007), (Turner 2011).
9 The algorithm *characterizes* the intention of the designer, in the same way as a characteristic function is a way of defining precisely a set by saying for any possible object whether it is a member of that set or not.
10 See e.g. https://www.acm.org/education/curricula-recommendations for the ACM Curricula Recommendations related to each sub-field.
11 A good selection of brief articles introducing different positions is available in Denning (2010).
12 For an overview of interpretations on the nature of Computing as a discipline, see Tedre (2014).
13 The present definition of Computing as a discipline dealing with information structures at ontological and epistemological levels is justified in the present chapter only in view of the digital computational model. It could be argued that paradigms such as bio-computing and analogue computing deal with a similar conceptual structuring of information in some format (e.g. referring to chemicals and water droplets as computational objects hiding more basic informational quantities). A further argument to restrict the present analysis to digital computing only is historical: certain older models of computing would struggle inside this definition, and so might be for future computational models. A more extensive analysis addressing these issues is outside the scope of the present contribution.

Further reading

For an overview of the topics and debates within the philosophy of Computer Science, see Rapaport (2005) and Turner (2014). For an advanced introduction to assembly for some common types of processors, see e.g. Dandamudi (2005). For a more extensive analysis of the semantics of programs, see Turner (2007) and White (2008). For an analysis of errors in information systems, see Primiero (2014); for one specifically devoted to computational systems, see Fresco and Primiero (2013). The Pi Network (2013) offers an overview of the philosophical issues related to information and Chapter 12 is specifically devoted to information and computation. For an overview of the information-hiding process by abstraction in terms of information, see Primiero (2009). Angius (2013) analyzes software verification in relation to the philosophical categories of abstraction and idealization.

References

Angius, N, 2013. Abstraction and Idealization in the formal verification of software systems. *Minds & Machines*, 23(2):211–226.

Blass, A. and Gurevich, Y. (2003). Algorithms: A Quest for Absolute Definitions, *Bulletin of the EATCS*, 8: 195–225.

Colburn, T. and Shute, G. (2007). Abstraction in Computer Science, *Minds and Machines*, 17(2): 169–184.

Dandamudi, S.P. (2005). *An Introduction to Assembly Language Programming,* Texts in Computer Science, New York: Springer.

Denning, P.J. (1985). What is Computer Science? *American Scientist*, 73: 16–19.

Denning, P.J. (2010). Ubiquity Symposium `What is Computation? (ed.), *Ubiquity,* vol. 2010, no. October (2010).

Devlin K. (1991). *Logic and Information*, Cambridge: Cambridge University Press.

Fetzer, J.H. (1988). Program Verification: The Very Idea, *Communications of the ACM*, 31(9): 1048–1063.

Floridi, L. (2005). Is Information Meaningful Data?, *Philosophy and Phenomenological Research*, 70(2): 351–370.

Floridi, L. (2011). *The Philosophy of Information*, Oxford: Oxford University Press.

Floridi, L. (2014). Semantic Conceptions of Information, *The Stanford Encyclopedia of Philosophy* (Spring 2014 Edition), Edward N. Zalta (ed.), http://plato.stanford.edu/archives/spr2014/entries/information-semantic/.

Fowler, M. (2003). *UML Distilled: A Brief Guide to the Standard Object Modeling Language*, Reading, MA: Addison-Wesley.

Fresco, N. and Primiero, G. (2013). Miscomputation, *Philosophy & Technology*, 26: 253–272. DOI: 10.1007/s13347-013-0112-0.

Fresco, N. and Wolff, M. (2013). Information Processing and the Structuring of Data, *The Israeli Society for History & Philosophy of Science Fourteenth Annual Conference.*

Hartmanis, J. and Lin, H. (1992). What is Computer Science and Engineering? In Hartmanis, J. and Lin, H., (eds), *Computing the Future: A Broader Agenda for Computer Science and Engineering*, Washington, DC: National Academy Press, pp. 163–216.

Israel D. and Perry J. (1990). What is Information? In Hanson, P. (ed.) *Information, Language and Cognition*, Vancouver, University of British Columbia Press, pp. 1–19.

Moschovakis, Y.N. (2001). What Is an Algorithm? In Engquist, B. and Schmid, W. (eds.) *Mathematics Unlimited – 2001 and Beyond*, New York: Springer, pp. 919–936.

Newell, A., Perlis, A. J. and Simon, H. A. (1967). Computer Science. *Science*, 157(3795): 1373–1374.

Newell, A. and Simon, H.A. (1976). Computer Science as Empirical Inquiry Symbols and Search. *Communications of the ACM*, 19(3): 113–126.

Primiero, G. (2009). Proceeding in Abstraction. From Concepts to Types and the Recent Perspective on Information, *History and Philosophy of Logic*, 30(3): 257–282.

Primiero, G. (2014). A Taxonomy of Errors for Information Systems, *Minds and Machine,* 24(3): 249–273.

Rapaport, W.J. (1999), Implementation Is Semantic Interpretation, *The Monist*, 82(1): 109–130.

Rapaport, W.J. (2005). Philosophy of Computer Science: An Introductory Course, *Teaching Philosophy* 28(4): 319–341.

Shannon, C.E. (1948). A Mathematical Theory of Communication, *Bell System Technical Journal*, 27: 379–423 and 623–656, July & October, 1948.

The Pi Network (2013). *The Philosophy of Information – A Simple Introduction*, Society for the Philosophy of Information, available at http://www.socphilinfo.org/teaching/book-pi-intro.

Tedre, M. (2014). *The Science of Computing: Shaping a Discipline*. Abingdon: CRC Press/Taylor & Francis.

Turner, R. (2007). Understanding Programming Languages, *Minds & Machines*, 17(2): pp. 203–216.

Turner, R. (2011). Specification, *Minds & Machines*, 21(2): 135–152.

Turner, R. (2014). The Philosophy of Computer Science. In Zalta, Edward N. (ed.), *The Stanford Encyclopedia of Philosophy* (Summer 2014 edition), http://plato.stanford.edu/archives/sum2014/entries/computer-science.

White, G. (2008). The Philosophy of Computer Languages. In Floridi, L. *The Blackwell Guide to the Philosophy of Computing and Information,* Oxford: Blackwell Publishing, pp. 237–247.

11

INFORMATION IN THE PHILOSOPHY OF AI AND THE SYMBOL GROUNDING PROBLEM

Selmer Bringsjord

Introduction, preview, plan

The field of artificial intelligence (AI) can be broadly characterized as the attempt to engineer an artifact that computes some set of functions that map information perceived in its environment (i.e., that map *percepts*) to *actions* performed in that environment. Such artifacts, in the authoritative nomenclature of the encyclopedic (Russell & Norvig 2009), are known as (artificial) *intelligent agents*, or as we shall hereafter sometimes simply call them: "IAs." The term "function" in this account can (without loss of generality) be understood as a function from the natural numbers ($\mathbb{N} = \{0, 1, 2, \ldots\}$) to the natural numbers that can be algorithmically computed (i.e., understood as a so-called *Turing-computable* function).[1] Addition over the natural numbers is for instance algorithmically computable; that is, there is an algorithm which, given any pair n, m of natural numbers as input, results in $n + m$ as output. Readers have of course been familiar with such an algorithm from their elementary-school days, when they passed from addition of pairs of single-digit numbers to such things as $339 + 17$.

Of course, humans routinely use information that is outside of natural numbers and the direct processing thereof. But the framework remains essentially the same if we are talking not of $\mathbb{N}$ but rather of an infinite set of strings that can be built from a finite alphabet. For instance, the alphabet could be the one that anchors the English language (let's call it E; it includes the letters a, A, b, B, . . . z, Z, and punctuation symbols like !, and the set LE – often called a *language* defined over a given alphabet – can denote sentences that can be built from E. Here's a sentence/string σ that's in LE:

```
Teddy, I have a lot of homework tonight.
```

Engineers might try to build an IA able to take such sentences in as precepts, and run algorithms that would produce such suitable actions as saying or writing the following pair of strings (σ_1 and σ_2, respectively) in sequence, each of which is also a member of L_E:

```
OK, then you can't play. But I can help you with your math
homework!
```

Given this account of AI, philosophy of AI can in turn be defined as the systematic attempt to answer a series of "big" questions that arise from not merely the conceptual *possibility* of IAs that compute some interesting percept-to-action functions, but rather from the brute fact that IAs are *already* managing to compute some functions of this type that are not merely interesting, but are directly and concretely constitutive of valuable human-level intelligent behavior. Two landmark examples of such now-with-us IAs are: Deep Blue, the chessplaying program from IBM that famously vanquished Gary Kasparov in 1997, at the time the best human chessplayer; and Watson, the IA that fairly recently beat the best human *Jeopardy!* players.[2] A third example of a kind of IA worthy of the attention of philosophers of AI is now maturing before our very eyes: viz., self-driving automobiles.[3] Such IAs aren't yet as widespread and as trustworthy as, say, a toaster, but most AI engineers and researchers regard it to be a forgone conclusion that self-driving cars and trucks (at least in fair weather; driving to a ski area in a blizzard to enjoy fresh powder may be a human-only activity for *quite* a while) will soon enough be routine.

I explain herein something that the previous paragraph has already made plain to alert readers: viz., that the concepts of *information* and *symbol* are central to both AI and philosophy of AI; and I specifically explain that the so-called *symbol grounding problem* (SGP) in philosophy of AI is probably the most important and difficult challenge facing ambitious AI researchers, period. Since, as will soon be seen, the symbols in SGP are of interest precisely because they are the bearers of information, it would be perfectly accurate to speak instead of the *information* grounding problem. But I will here dutifully follow common usage.

The plan for the remainder of the chapter is as follows. In the next section, I provide a short but more detailed account of IAs. Building on that account, I then provide a more detailed account of philosophy of AI, by pointing to a list L_h of the characteristic "big questions" alluded to above. Next, in the fourth section, SGP is defined – in a way that is sensitive to both how philosophers traditionally characterize SGP *and* to how the concrete commerce of AI will be forced to wrestle with this problem in the "real economy." With that definition in hand, I proceed in the next section to explain that SGP stands at the heart of philosophy of AI. The chapter is wrapped up with brief remarks about the future of AI, in connection with SGP.

AI and intelligent agents in more detail

The foregoing exposition defines IAs as computing percept-to-action functions. Let's make this a bit more precise, by first considering a simple IA we shall dub "FAC." FAC lives in an environment **A** in which humans and machines converse about basic arithmetic. What sorts of things can it perceive? It perceives symbols s_k^{ext} that denote natural numbers, where $k \in \mathbb{N}$. (By the superscript *ext* is indicated the fact that this is a symbol that has currency in the external environment.) The subscript k is often implicit. For instance, FAC might perceive the symbol four, or *the number that's one greater than three*, or just "4" and so on. These symbols carry information, of course. In particular, the specific symbols cited thus far all denote the natural number $4 \in \mathbb{N}$. But what function is it that FAC computes? It computes the factorial function, $n!$.[4] Hence when FAC perceives four, it decodes this as 4, arrives at $4! = 24$, and then – where this is the action it performs – prints out a symbol that denotes 24, for example 24.

Clearly, we here have two types of symbols in play: There are what we can call the *external* symbols, which are used in the environment in which IAs find themselves (e.g. four in the present example involving FAC), and there are as well *internal* symbols, the ones that are inside the IA, manipulated by computer programs. In the case of our IA FAC, there is an internal computer program P_{FAC} that computes the factorial function. The result of a run of this program, inside FAC, is of course a natural number n, represented by some internal symbol. That internal symbol is then translated into an external one (e.g., `four`), which is sent into the environment, where other agents, both artificial and natural, perceive it and act accordingly. Each of the remarkable "success-story" IAs cited at the outset (e.g., Watson) conform to the fundamental symbol-processing pipeline embodied by FAC.

While I will not fully construct it here, it should be clear to the reader that in a parallel with the IA FAC we could set out the basic structure of the IA Teddy that operates not over natural numbers, but instead over strings built from E; we of course saw three examples of such strings (sentences) above; they were labeled σ_1, σ_2, and σ_3. Teddy perceives the external symbols that, concatenated, compose σ_1, and then proceeds to emit the concatenated symbols that compose the sentences σ_2 and σ_3.

It may seem to the reader that the framework described in the previous two paragraphs is needlessly pedantic, but without a clear understanding of the concepts canvassed in those paragraphs, when we consider multi-faceted domains, there will be confusion as to what is happening in connection with SGP. It should be clear to the reader that Teddy could be an IA augmented with arithmetic capability. In particular, Teddy could be augmented to include the capability of FAC. But that is just the start, and points to bigger things. I have in mind here not just IAs seen in the past (e.g., Watson and Deep Blue), but IAs of the future. In a more extensive and more polemical essay on SGP (Bringsjord 2015), I consider future household robots intended by their creators to be able to shop, clean, do the laundry, and so on. In the present chapter, I soon ask the reader to consider the case of sophisticated toy robots for children. In the case of both the household robo-maids and such toy IAs, percepts will be much more nuanced than those in the case of Teddy and FAC combined (or for that matter in the case of Watson or Deep Blue), and the same will hold for the range of actions that the robots in question will be expected to perform. But the essential structure of what we have seen in the case of Teddy and FAC will carry over to these more robust cases. In particular, as we shall see, these IAs will still obey that essential pipeline: they will take in external symbols, translate these symbols into internal ones, and process those internal symbols (in conjunction with other pre-existing internal symbols) to produce new external symbols for "consumption" by the external environment.

Philosophy of AI in more detail

Without further ado, here is part of the promised list of questions by which philosophy of AI can be characterized. The idea is simply that philosophy of AI is the sub-field of philosophy devoted to answering them, and others like them.

$$\mathsf{L}_h$$

Q1 Will IAs eventually match (or perhaps even exceed) human intelligence?

Q1$_s$ Will the so-called "Singularity" (the time at which computing machines exceed human intelligence, and then quickly make ever smarter computing machines, leaving us in the dust see e.g. Chalmers (2010) for a defense) come to pass? If so, approximately when? Somewhere around 2050?

$Q1_{3Rs}$ Harkening back to elementary-school days, and thus dividing up human intelligence into the "three Rs" of reading, writing, and arithmetic, will IAs be able to reach human-level intelligence in one or more of these areas? If so, approximately when?

Q2 If the correct answer to Q1 ($Q1_s$) is a negative one, how close will IAs come? For example, it would certainly seem that while IAs might forever fail to have subjective awareness, or to have the sort of creativity that humans possess, there are nonetheless a host of human vocations and avocations that are clearly within the reach of IAs. Given that, will there be massive disemployment of humans?

Q3 Is the human brain ultimately a digital computer, in biological "clothing"? Is it weaker than such a thing? More computationally powerful than such a thing? Is the brain essentially what we have called an "IA," where the percept-to-action functions are simply embodied not in silicon, but carbon-based "neuro-flesh"?

Q4 Is the accumulating, cumulative, linked information on the internet what will give rise to the arrival of IAs that either approach human intelligence, match it, or exceed it?

A few remarks on L_h would seem to be in order.

First, there is of course a counterpart to this list that refers not to humans, but to mere animals. Let us leave this counterpart aside as beyond the scope of the present investigation.[5] Concretely, this means that variants of Q1 like

$Q1_{ac}$ Will IAs eventually match (or perhaps even exceed) canine intelligence?

will be ignored in the present discussion, despite the fact that such variants can be quite interesting to seriously ponder.[6]

Second, please consider for a moment question $Q1_{3Rs}$. This may strike readers as a strange question. Why do I specifically call out a question the relies on a triadic categorization of human intelligence used to refer to young students and their schooling, the "three Rs" of reading, writing, and arithmetic? Well, in reply, I would ask: What is the alternative? Thoughtful readers will promptly offer a reply:

> The alternative is to rely on a mature breakdown of human ability and accomplishment. After all, the particular sciences conform to a well-known breakdown (biology, physics, mathematics, etc.), and the same is true even for less precise pursuits (literature, drama, music, etc.); and human achievements under all these categories are easy to identify. Therefore instead of asking about the so-called "3 Rs," you could ask specifically if an IA could ever, say, write a belletristic novel, or prove a great theorem.

This is a sensible reply. But the route it describes isn't open to us in the span of one short chapter. Also, it wouldn't be appropriate to include here sub-questions under Q1 that refer to specialized knowledge outside the experience of nearly all readers, say to special relativity theory in physics. In addition, the so-called "three Rs," in connection with the IA Teddy, suffice quite nicely to convey the essence of the SGP, and its very concrete side – as we shall see momentarily.

A third point about the list: since some readers may be tempted to think that L_h is simply too small a list to convey a sense of what philosophy of AI is, I point out that expansion under questions in the list, in obvious ways, is easy to envisage and appreciate. For example, Q1, as we have already implicitly noted, is really an implicit reference to all the powers that constitute human intelligence, and to the sub-question corresponding to each such power as to whether a machine is up to the challenge of matching it. To give just one example, a rather important one in the history of philosophy of AI, consider

> $Q1_m$ Will IAs eventually match (or perhaps even exceed) the human power to make
> and prove new mathematical discoveries?

Since human intelligence is bound up inseparably with our ability to do mathematics, $Q1_m$ is clearly a sub-question under Q1.[7] In fact, slight narrowing of this question yields a question that falls under the third R in the three aforementioned Rs:

> $Q1_{m'}$ Will IAs eventually match (or perhaps even exceed) the human power to make
> and prove new mathematical discoveries *in the area of arithmetic* (and areas based on
> arithmetic)?

It turns out that this question has been at the center of one of the liveliest longstanding debates within philosophy of AI. One side in the debate answers $Q1_{m'}$ with a firm negative, citing for support Gödel's famous (first) incompleteness theorem that there are truths of standard arithmetic that are impossible for a standard computing machine to prove via standard techniques.[8] Those on this side are generally of the view that human persons can surmount this limitation, and hence cannot fundamentally be standard computing machines in biological "clothes"; such thinkers include Lucas (1964), Penrose (1994), and Bringsjord & Arkoudas (2004).[9] While Gödel's original work failed to produce concrete examples of truths that are beyond standard machines and standard techniques, we now have such examples. For instance, we now know that the eventual termination of a certain sequence of initially fast-growing numbers, the so-called Goodstein sequence, can be understood by some clever humans, but the proof of this termination must exceed standard proofs from standard arithmetic. So those on the humans-above-machines side may well have here what they are looking for.[10] Those on the other, opposing side include LaForte, Hayes and Ford (1998).

I shall return below to consideration of $Q1_{m'}$, and make a direct connection between it and SGP. The chief point at the moment is this broad one: that L_h is, when one thinks about it a bit, essentially an engine for producing additional questions that drive philosophy of AI.

The symbol grounding problem defined

SGP can be quickly defined in general terms by turning to the *locus classicus*, provided by Harnad (1990), wherein three examples of SGP are crisply and succinctly provided.[11] The first of these examples, and the only one I need herein, is John Searle's well-known Chinese Room Argument (CRA), which I have refined and defended at length (e.g., see Bringsjord 1992, Bringsjord & Noel 2002). It's possible that the reader is familiar with CRA; regardless, there's no need here to present CRA in its full and maximally powerful form. It suffices to report that CRA includes a thought-experiment in which a robot responds to squiggle-squoggles (Chinese, actually) by following a rulebook that pairs these squiggle-squoggles with other squiggle-squoggles (also Chinese) – the catch being that the robot's activity is based on an homunculus (= Searle himself) inside the robot who doesn't understand any Chinese, but who can deftly follow (in the manner of a computer program) the rulebook and thereby give outside observers the *impression* that the robot understands Chinese.

(The robot here is clearly an IA as characterized in the second section of this chapter.) As Harnad puts it when summarizing the CRA for purposes of presenting SGP:

> Searle's simple demonstration ... consists of imagining himself doing everything the computer does – receiving the Chinese input symbols, manipulating them purely on the basis of their shape . . ., and finally returning the Chinese output symbols. It is evident that Searle (who knows no Chinese) would not be understanding Chinese under those conditions – hence neither could the computer. The symbols and the symbol manipulation, being all based on shape rather than meaning, are systematically interpretable as having meaning – that, after all, is what it is to be a symbol system . . . . But the interpretation will not be intrinsic to the symbol system itself: It will be parasitic on the fact that the symbols have meaning for us, in exactly the same way that the meanings of the symbols in a book are not intrinsic, but derive from the meanings in our heads. Hence, if the meanings of symbols in a symbol system are extrinsic, rather than intrinsic like the meanings in our heads, then they are not a viable model for the meanings in our heads: Cognition cannot be just symbol manipulation.
>
> *(Harnad 1990, p. 337)*

Even a rapid reading of this quote reveals the absolute centrality of symbols and the meaning and understanding (or not) thereof. If CRA, when suitably rigorized and unpacked, is ultimately sound, given that IAs are by definition physicalized symbol systems (or Turing machines, etc.), it follows, forever and unshakably, that SGP is unsolvable. While my own view is indeed that CRA is sound, the present chapter is composed from the agnostic point of view. Some readers will be inclined to reject CRA,[12] others to accept it, and still others will be undecided; that's fine, and indeed is as desired for present purposes. The important point is to understand that, given the guidance provided by Harnad, SGP can be conveniently *identified* with the challenge that CRA poses to those of the opinion that IAs can genuinely understand the symbols they receive from the external world. The challenge is simply that if CRA is sound, it's impossible for present and future AI engineers to produce IAs that understand symbols. Put another way, if CRA is sound, the symbols used by IAs will never be "grounded."

Nonetheless, it must be admitted that CRA, for at least some readers, will be disturbingly abstract and farfetched. After all, it will not have escaped the reader's notice that the core thought-experiment in CRA is fanciful, since Searle must fit inside a robot. The force of CRA wouldn't be diminished if in the imaginary scenario Searle was instead tele-operating the robot in question from a distance (on the basis, still, of the rulebook's guidance for emitting strings in response to strings taken in), but in this variant we would still be dealing with an abstract gedanken-experiment. Fortunately, I can present SGP in a very straightforward and concrete way that harks back to the IAs FAC and Teddy, as follows.

Imagine that you own a young robotics company, SuperToys Inc., and that you are therefore rather keen on manufacturing and selling, specifically, sophisticated toy robots to children aged between five and twelve. You call these toys "supertoys."[13] What makes these toy robots super is that they are supposedly able to read, write, and do arithmetic, as prompted in interaction with the human children who own them and befriend them; and these IAs are able to do these "three Rs" at the level of a college-educated adult. Notice that I say, supposedly. There is some question as to whether the supertoys you will soon be selling really have the intelligence that your current marketing campaign says they have. Everything that you have seen, and everything that your firm's engineers have told you, tends to support that supertoys really and truly have the intelligence ascribed to them in the campaign devised by the Madison-Ave company you hired.

Your company's supertoys, *if* they can successfully tutor children, befriend and enlighten them, and so on, are likely to sell like hotcakes. You thus know that if your supertoys perform in stellar fashion, you could become quite rich; but you *also* know that if supertoys wreak havoc in the home of even one wealthy, well-connected family, the public-relations fallout could kill your dreams of becoming a modern-day Cornelius Vanderbilt. In short, supertoys had better understand their environment, and the symbols from that environment that they perceive. In this context, we can concretize SGP by considering the scenario shown in Figure 11.1 below.

In this scenario, nine-year-old Esther's parents have bought her, from your company, the supertoy Teddy2, and Esther utters the two sentences to it that are shown in the figure. The question is: Can Teddy2 truly understand the percept composed of these two strings? If Searle's CRA is sound, the answer, as we've noted, is "No." But we can think of the situation more pragmatically. We can note that if SGP is solvable, then whether or not Teddy2 can really understand Esther (including her rather deep and complex sarcasm regarding her very own mother), it follows that Teddy2 can certainly respond appropriately to Esther, in voice, and in physical behavior. For instance, Teddy2 might say:

> That's a double Yes, Esther. I do know you've mastered that, and I'm sorry your mother is skeptical. Sure, let's sit down together with her. I'll write out a couple of hard ones for you, and you can show your stuff. (We can practice a few now. Can you do 222 divided by 19 at your desk now?) After that, she'll be won over – but given her high expectations for you, I expect her to ask us to move on to fractions! So we'll need to work together on them!

Figure 11.1 A concretization of the SGP as the challenge of building supertoys

113

On the other hand, you don't want Teddy2 to respond in the following way, which would reflect a lack of understanding of the symbols it has received, and would be a potential public-relations nightmare for your company if the media obtained a transcript – or if they received copies of a complaint from Esther and a hundred other children irritated because of parallel failures of understanding.

> Esther, don't be foolish, girl. I do know you've mastered that, yes. And since, as you note, your mother knows that too, there is nothing to show her. Let's go outside and play together and have some fun. No kitchen table for me!

Note furthermore that when supertoys fail to genuinely understand the symbols they receive from their environments, the consequences could be rather more dire than those seen in the mild cases I have described so far. Imagine that Teddy2 observes Esther accidentally break a goblet at an elegant dinner party in her home, and then immediately thereafter perceives Esther's elder brother remark: "That's just great, Esther. Losing another Saint-Louis is sure to make mother positively ecstatic." Later that night the entire family is awakened by the sound of Teddy2 smashing goblet after goblet downstairs, under the intention to make Esther's mother all the more ecstatic. Since each of the family's Burgundy Botticelli glasses is a small fortune, a lack of understanding here proves rather costly.

At present, the brute fact is that a supertoy like a Teddy2 who understands sarcasm, irony, and the nuanced nature of tutoring young children is not only not on the market, but no such IA exists even in any cutting-edge AI laboratory on our planet. From this we can infer that there is currently no empirical confirmation of the claim that SGP, concretized in the way I have taken, is solvable even in the foreseeable future.

SGP is the heart of philosophy of AI

Now, according to the chapter's plan, let's see why SGP is the very heart of philosophy of AI. In order to see this, it suffices to return to the list L_h of questions with which philosophy of AI grapples, and give a short answer Ai in response to each question Qi. These answers make the centrality of SGP clear, in an efficient manner, because the answers in each case are seen to relate directly to SGP. (So that the answers are easy to find and read, I have in each case boxed their labels.) Here we go:

Q1 Will IAs eventually match (or perhaps even exceed) human intelligence?

$\boxed{\text{A1}}$ So far, IAs have proved and are proving their intelligence in structured non-linguistic environments (e.g., chess and various other games, transport), and in environments that, while linguistic in nature to a degree (e.g., *Jeopardy!*), are not in any way open-ended like the environment that Teddy2 must navigate. Hence, since navigation of an environment like that in which Teddy2 lives is entailed by solving SGP, the question Q1 appears to boil down to whether SGP is solvable, or at least to whether SGP is *apparently* solvable.

$Q1_s$ Will the so-called "Singularity" (again, the time at which computing machines exceed human intelligence, and then quickly make ever smarter computing machines, leaving us in the dust) come to pass? If so, approximately when? Somewhere around 2050?

$\boxed{\text{A1}_s}$ There seems to be little point in speculating about the timing of such an event as the Singularity, in light of the fact that this event, by definition, can occur only if the answer to Q1 is an affirmative – but as we have already noted, that affirmative entails that SGP is solvable, which in turn entails that a correctly functioning Teddy2 is feasible. Yet as we have just noted, Teddy2 doesn't exist, and isn't on the horizon either.[14]

$\text{Q1}_{3R}s$ Harkening back to elementary-school days, and thus dividing up human intelligence into "the three Rs" of reading, writing, and arithmetic, will IAs be able to reach human-level intelligence in one or more of these areas? If so, approximately when?

$\boxed{\text{A1}_{3R}}$ A well-functioning Teddy2 is by definition an IA that has reached human-level mastery of "the three Rs," and such a well-functioning IA is one that minimally behaves as if it truly grounds the symbols it perceives. But once again, a Teddy2 is minimally a long, long way off.

Q1_m. Will IAs eventually match (or perhaps even exceed) the human power to make and prove new mathematical discoveries *in the area of arithmetic* (and areas based on arithmetic)?

$\boxed{\text{A1}_m}$ This question ultimately distills to whether human persons can exploit an ability to understand symbolic expressions that standard computing machines can't (e.g., the aforementioned expression conveying that the Goodstein sequence terminates), and then harness their understanding to prove that these expressions hold, and thereby exceed the reach of standard computing machines. Hence, the question here clearly pivots around SGP.

Q2 If the correct answer to Q1 (Q1_s) is a negative one, how close will IAs come? For example, it would certainly seem that while IAs might forever fail to have subjective awareness, or to have the sort of creativity that humans possess, there are nonetheless a host of human vocations and avocations that are clearly within the reach of IAs. Given that, will there be massive disemployment of humans?

$\boxed{\text{A2}}$ Presumably any human vocation the "IA-ification" of which doesn't require the full gamut of human communication in a natural language (such as English, Chinese, Norwegian, etc.), or human creativity, will be within the reach of IAs, and hence will be a vocation that can be taken over by intelligent computing machines/robots. That said, the standard view in neoclassical economics is that there will be a net gain in human employment as a result of such IA-ification. I take no stand here on whether such optimism is justified.[15]

Q3 Is the human brain ultimately a digital computer, in biological "clothing"? Is it weaker than such a thing? More computationally powerful than such a thing? Is the brain essentially what we have called an "IA," where the percept-to-action functions are simply embodied not in silicon, but carbon-based "neuro-flesh"?

A3 Since our intellectual power, certainly for purposes of the present discussion, may be regarded to be coextensive with the power of our brains, this question is just another way of asking whether the brain is powerful enough to surmount SGP! Moreover, the principal source of arguments in favor of the proposition that the brain is, say, at least a Turing machine, would be our abilities in the realm of reading and writing and mathematics. This is so because the quickest way to demonstrate that our brains are at least as powerful as Turing machines (and their equivalents) is to simply show that literate humans can take as input a specification of a given Turing machine, and then, using paper, pencil, and an eraser, simulate that Turing machine step by step on any given input.

Q4 Is the accumulating, cumulative, linked information on the internet what will support the arrival of IAs that either approach human intelligence, match it, or exceed it?

A4 Given the foregoing discussion, it's easy to provide a brief, and generally negative, answer to this question. That answer can be quickly grasped by asking another question: Does allowing Teddy2 to have real-time access to all content on the internet give him the ability to function as the owner of SuperToys Inc. would want? The answer is: "Apparently not." And the rationale for this answer has already been appreciated, albeit implicitly. I say this because no doubt readers will have assumed that Teddy2 *does* have continuous wireless access to the internet. But the problem is that the internet only has data that is frozen, not data that is dynamic, novel, and needed on the spot. For example, the strings that, as shown in Figure 11.1, are perceived by Teddy2, are novel, and they demand an immediate answer from Teddy2 – but that answer, unlike the luxury that for instance Watson enjoyed in its playing of *Jeopardy!*, isn't to be found on the internet.[16]

The future of AI

Let us then take store of where the discussion has brought us.

There is no reason now to think that SGP will be surmounted in the foreseeable future. For if there was in place such reason now, then the likes of Teddy2 would be, from an engineering point of view, unproblematic. Yet to pose to an engineer the problem of building a well-functioning Teddy2, regardless of how much stock in a startup like SuperToys Inc. was provided to such an engineer, would be to pose to him/her an unsolvable problem.

Well-read readers may have some nagging doubts, because some of these readers may know that on some paradigms for AI engineering, there are no internal symbols – or at least no internal symbols designed to represent semantic information. So, are IAs built in by followers of such paradigms immune from SGP? No; and we have implicitly seen this negative in the course of the foregoing analysis, implicitly. For regardless of the technique used to try to build a smoothly working Teddy2, the AI engineers (let alone the customers who are supposed to buy supertoys) still have to be able to speak with the robots they produce, if for no other reason than quality assurance. Well, then we have an external symbol, undeniably: we after all have the symbols that are presented to the robot in question by quality-assurance engineers. And *then* what happens? What does the supertoy do with the external symbol? It must be translated into *something* symbolic, since after all the robot is *computing*. In addition, our supertoy must communicate back to the human some suitable external symbol, and we have SGP therefore rise up before us again. Since the supertoy in question is apparently just mindlessly manipulating internal symbols in order to map the perceived external symbols to the generated-for-human-consumption external ones, where is there any understanding, or grounding? Where is there any ultimate assurance that even if the supertoy sounds great when given a few test cases, it's not going to smash Saint-Louis crystal, idiotically but certainly not invidiously?

The brute fact is that at present there are no IAs that even give the *appearance* of understanding natural language in a conversation with humans. Will SGP *ever* be solved? I don't think so, and my attitude is to be expected, for I still believe that my own defense of an extended version of CRA is sound.[17] But most AI researchers and engineers, in my experience, are much more optimistic. If their sanguinity is well-founded, it follows that CRA is unsound. This chapter was not the place to try to ascertain whether or not CRA is sound. But we have seen that regardless of the ultimate status of CRA, one, SGP is at the heart of philosophy of AI and the fundamental questions that drive it, and that, two, SGP can be formulated as a concrete real-world problem readily understood independent of the fanciful CRA.

Acknowledgments

I'm indebted to Stevan Harnad for sustained and unforgettable discussions rather long ago both about SGP and Searle's Chinese Room Argument (CRA), and to Mariarosaria Taddeo and Luciano Floridi for their valiant, thought-provoking attempt to solve SGP. Reflection upon that attempt greatly deepened my understanding of both SGP and CRA. I'm also grateful to Floridi for pointing out that Gödelian arguments against ambitious AI relate directly to SGP.

Notes

1 A Turing machine is a simple idealization of a modern high-speed digital computer; a philosophically tuned introduction to Turing machines is provided in Boolos *et al.* (2003). There are many other equivalent idealizations; any of them will do to capture the essence of the functions in question. For instance, a bead-and-wire abacus, suitably neatened up and viewed as an input-output device, as Boolos *et al.* (2003) show, provides an alternative, and if this alternative is selected, we then would speak of the abacus-computable functions.

2 For an overview of Watson, see Ferrucci *et al.* (2010). For a discussion of Watson as a portal to reflection upon the history and future of AI, see Bringsjord and Govindarajulu (forthcoming). For such a discussion in the case of the earlier Deep Blue, see Bringsjord (1998).

3 At the moment, as I type this sentence, I'm at DARPA in Arlington, VA, in the United States, where I just saw a presentation that included synoptic coverage of some rather impressive self-driving technology from Google, Audi, Daimler, and General Motors.

4 Lest it be thought that this function is trivial, I point out that the program to compute this function was one of the first programs to be formally proved correct – by none other than Alan Turing (1949) – and the work was positively Herculean.

5 For consideration of a continuum of intelligence ranging from simple artificial animals to artificial persons, see Bringsjord *et al.* (2000).

6 Perhaps it's worth noting here for skeptics that dogs, by the lights of none other than Darwin (1997), have a level of reasoning ability not fundamentally different from that seen in the human case. Of course, as many readers will know or at least suspect, monkeys are traditionally the animals whose level of intelligence is analyzed and praised. This fact, combined with Darwin's views, makes Penn *et al.* (2008) required reading for anyone interested in the question of what it would take for a computing machine or robot to confirm an affirmative answer to Q1c.

7 For a negative answer to $Q1_m$, and a defense of that answer, see Bringsjord *et al.* (2006).

8 This theorem and its context is covered nicely in e.g. Smith "2013". Note carefully that I say "standard arithmetic," "standard computing machine" and "standard techniques." Often these provisos are perilously omitted. If one or more of these constraints are lifted, the Gödelian

theorem doesn't go through. For example, if the techniques include those allowing for non-standard computing machines capable of infinitary reasoning (e.g., reasoning over infinitely long expressions), the theorem doesn't hold.

9   What I say here should not be interpreted to imply that all on this side of the debate affirm all the arguments given by those on this side. For example, see Bringsjord and Xiao (2000); and the argument given in Bringsjord and Arkoudas (2004), while aligned in spirit with Lucas (1964), is of new, "modal" variety not seen or anticipated by earlier work.

10 For more, see Govindarajulu *et al.* (2013). For readable background on the sequence and termination of Goodstein's progression, in the context of Gödelian incompleteness theorems, see Smith (2013).

11 Before defining the symbol grounding problem I will give two examples of it. The first comes from Searle's (1980) celebrated "Chinese Room Argument," in which the symbol grounding problem is referred to as the problem of intrinsic meaning (or "intentionality"). Searle challenges the core assumption of symbolic AI that a symbol system able to generate behavior indistinguishable from that of a person must have a mind. More specifically, according to the symbolic theory of mind, if a computer could pass the Turing Test (Turing 1950) in Chinese – i.e., if it could respond to all Chinese symbol strings it receives as input with Chinese symbol strings that are indistinguishable from the replies a real Chinese speaker would make (even if we keep testing for a lifetime) – then the computer would understand the meaning of Chinese symbols in the same sense that I understand the meaning of English symbols (Harnad 1990, p. 337).

12 There are, it should be noted, philosophers and scientists who believe that they have solved at least the animal version of SGP – which presumably entails that they don't regard CRA to be extensible to the mere-animal case. See e.g. Taddeo & Floridi (2007). (This paper is reprinted in Floridi (2011) as Chapter 7; Chapter 6 is a sustained, stage-setting argument that other approaches fail to solve SGP, and is also derived directly from a journal paper; viz. Taddeo and Floridi (2005)). A distinction between the animal-level SGP versus the human-level SGP is made in Floridi (2014). In the present chapter, I'm (obviously) concerned with the human-level SGP. The claim that the animal-level SGP is solvable is perfectly consistent with Bringsjord's (2015) claim that the human-level SGP is unsolvable despite the ingenuity seen in Taddeo & Floridi (2007). Indeed, Bringsjord *et al.*'s (2000) framework for understanding AI in terms of a range of creatures from primitive animals to more intelligent mere animals to human persons is quite in line with (Floridi 2014).

13 My parable is related to Aldiss (2001), recommended reading for all students of AI, and the basis for the sci-fi film *A.I.*

14 Given this, suspicion on the part of the reader that the literature includes skepticism about the Singularity would be expected, and that skepticism isn't misplaced. For example, see Floridi (2015), Bringsjord *et al.* (2013).

15 For reasons largely mathematical, I don't think it's justified; but for a view of some of the standard optimism, see Hazlitt (1948).

16 For a more technical discussion, see Govindarajulu *et al.* (2014).

17 For this defense, see Bringsjord and Noel (2002), which builds on the earlier defense given in Bringsjord (1992).

References

Aldiss, B. (2001), *Supertoys Last All Summer Long: And Other Stories of Future Time*, Saint Martin's Griffin, New York, NY. The title story, the literary basis for the film *A.I.*, was originally published in 1969.

Boolos, G. S., Burgess, J. P. & Jeffrey, R. C. (2003), *Computability and Logic* (Fourth Edition), Cambridge University Press, Cambridge, UK.

Bringsjord, S. (1992), *What Robots Can and Can't Be*, Kluwer, Dordrecht, the Netherlands.

Bringsjord, S. (1998), Chess is Too Easy, *Technology Review* 101(2), 23–28.

Bringsjord, S. (2015), The Symbol Grounding Problem – Remains Unsolved, *Journal of Experimental & Theoretical Artificial Intelligence* 27(1). DOI: 10.1080/0952813X.2014.940139.

Bringsjord, S. & Arkoudas, K. (2004), The Modal Argument for Hypercomputing Minds, *Theoretical Computer Science* 317, 167–190.

Bringsjord, S., Bringsjord, A. & Bello, P. (2013), Belief in the Singularity is Fideistic, in A. Eden, J. Moor, J. Søraker & E. Steinhart, eds, 'The Singularity Hypothesis', Springer, New York, pp. 395–408.

Bringsjord, S. & Govindarajulu, N. S. (forthcoming), Leibnizs Art of Infallibility, Watson, and the Philosophy, Theory, & Future of AI, in V. Müller, ed., 'Synthese Library', Springer. URL: http://kryten. mm.rpi.edu/SB NSG Watson Leibniz PT-AI 061414.pdf

Bringsjord, S., Kellett, O., Shilliday, A., & Taylor, J., van Heuveln, B., Yang, Y., Baumes, J. & Ross, K. (2006), A New Gödelian Argument for Hypercomputing Minds Based on the Busy Beaver Problem, *Applied Mathematics and Computation* 176, 516–530.

Bringsjord, S. & Noel, R. (2002), Real Robots and the Missing Thought Experiment in the Chinese Room Dialectic, in J. Preston & M. Bishop, eds, Views into the Chinese Room: New Essays on Searle and Artificial Intelligence, Oxford University Press, Oxford, UK, pp. 144–166.

Bringsjord, S., Noel, R. & Caporale, C. (2000), Animals, Zombanimals, and the Total Turing Test: The Essence of Artificial Intelligence, *Journal of Logic, Language, and Information* 9, 397–418. URL: http://kryten.mm.rpi.edu/zombanimals.pdf

Bringsjord, S. & Xiao, H. (2000), A Refutation of Penrose's Gödelian Case Against Artificial Intelligence, *Journal of Experimental and Theoretical Artificial Intelligence* 12, 307–329.

Chalmers, D. (2010), The Singularity: A Philosophical Analysis, *Journal of Consciousness Studies* 17, 7–65.

Darwin, C. (1997), *The Descent of Man*, Prometheus, Amherst, MA. A reprint edition. The book was first published in 1871.

Ferrucci, D., Brown, E., Chu-Carroll, J., Fan, J., Gondek, D., Kalyanpur, A., Lally, A., Murdock, W., Nyberg, E., Prager, J., Schlaefer, N. & Welty, C. (2010), Building Watson: An Overview of the DeepQA Project, *AI Magazine,* 59–79. URL: http://www.stanford.edu/class/cs124/AIMagzine-DeepQA.pdf

Floridi, L. (2011), *The Philosophy of Information*, Oxford University Press, Oxford, UK.

Floridi, L. (2014), Perception and Testimony as Data Providers, *Logique et Analyse* 57(226), 151–179.

Floridi, L. (2015), Singularitarians, AItheists, and Why the Problem with Artificial Intelligence is H.A.L. (Humanity At Large), not HAL, *Philosophy and Computers* 14(2), 8–11. This is part of a newsletter published by the American Philosophical Association.

Govindarajulu, N., Licato, J. & Bringsjord, S. (2013), Small Steps Toward Hypercomputation via Infinitary Machine Proof Verification and Proof Generation, in M. Giancarlo, A. Dennuzio, L. Manzoni & A. Porreca, eds, *Unconventional Computation and Natural Computation; Lecture Notes in Computer Science*, Vol. 7956, Springer-Verlag, Berlin, Germany, pp. 102–112.

Govindarajulu, N., Licato, J. & Bringsjord, S. (2014), Toward a Formalization of QA Problem Classes, in B. Goertzel, L. Orseau & J. Snaider, eds, "Artificial General Intelligence; LNAI 8598", Springer, Switzerland, pp. 228–233. URL: http://kryten.mm.rpi.edu/NSG SB JL QA formalization 060214.pdf

Harnad, S. (1990), "The Symbol Grounding Problem", *Physica D* 42, 335–346.

Hazlitt, H. (1948), *Economics in One Lesson*, Pocket Books, New York, NY. This little classic can be obtained free of charge online in multiple places; e.g., see http://www.fee.org/pdf/books/Economics in one lesson.pdf.

LaForte, G., Hayes, P. & Ford, K. (1998), Why Gödel's Theorem Cannot Refute Computationslism, *Artificial Intelligence* 104, 265–286.

Lucas, J. R. (1964), Minds, Machines, and Gödel, in A.R. Anderson, ed., *Minds and Ma- chines*, Prentice-Hall, Englewood Cliffs, NJ, pp. 43–59. Lucas' paper is available online at http://users.ox.ac.uk/~jrlucas/mmg.html.

Penn, D., Holyoak, K. & Povinelli, D. (2008), Darwin's Mistake: Explaining the Discontinuity Between Human and Nonhuman Minds, *Behavioral and Brain Sciences* 31, 109–178.

Penrose, R. (1994), *Shadows of the Mind*, Oxford, Oxford, UK.

Russell, S. & Norvig, P. (2009), *Artificial Intelligence: A Modern Approach*, Prentice Hall, Upper Saddle River, NJ. Third edition.

Searle, J. (1980), Minds, Brains and Programs, *Behavioral and Brain Sciences* 3, 417–424.

Smith, P. (2013), *An Introduction to Gödel's Theorems*, Cambridge University Press, Cambridge, UK. This is the second edition of the book.

Taddeo, M. & Floridi, L. (2005), Solving the Symbol Grounding Problem: A Critical Review of Fifteen Years of Research, *Journal of Experimental and Theoretical Artificial Intelligence* 17(4), 419–445. This paper is reprinted in Floridi, L. (2011) *The Philosophy of Information*, Oxford University Press, Oxford, UK.

Taddeo, M. & Floridi, L. (2007), A Praxical Solution of the Symbol Grounding Problem, *Minds and Machines* 17(4), 369–389. This paper is reprinted in Floridi, L. (2011) *The Philosophy of Information*, Oxford University Press, Oxford, UK.

Turing, A. (1949), Checking a Large Routine, in "Report of a Conference on High Speed Automatic Calculating Machines," University Math Lab, Cambridge, UK, pp. 67–69.

Turing, A. (1950), "Computing Machinery and Intelligence," *Mind* LIX (59)(236), 433–460.

12

THE PHILOSOPHY OF DISTRIBUTED INFORMATION

Vincent F. Hendricks and Rasmus K. Rendsvig

Information in groups and social proof

As an individual you possess a lot of information or knowledge, but groups may be informed or knowledgeable as well. Sometimes information or knowledge in groups is more epistemically potent and conducive to deliberation, decision and action than individual possession – and then again sometimes not.

On June 5, 1989 a young student, later nicknamed the "Tank Man" or "Unknown protester," armed only with two plastic bags, was able to stop a column of Chinese tanks during the Tiananmen Square protests. How is that possible? During the Tiananmen Square protests, the Chinese regime was well aware of the threat which thousands of unarmed students and workers could present against a comprehensive political and military machine by merely sitting down in the public space. Thus, the regime sent soldiers and tanks into the square. Soon they had to realize that even a single man with two plastic bags in his hands can stop a column of tanks, as one cannot mow down an unarmed protester if *only everybody watches, and everyone knows that everyone is watching, everyone knows that everyone knows that everyone is watching and so on*. This sort of knowledge is formally referred to as *common knowledge* and may, as the example illustrates, be epistemically very commanding, but also quite important for explaining a wide range of other agent interactions, from bilateral trade to notions of communality and rational opinion aggregation.

Another type of group knowledge, distinct from common knowledge, is referred to as *distributed knowledge*. Knowledge may be unevenly distributed over the members in a group – Bob knows one thing, while Alice knows another, and together they know more, so distributed knowledge may roughly be characterized as the sum of all the knowledge that a collective has available for solving a problem, reaching a decision or performing an action to some desired end. Now, both distributed and common knowledge notions are tracking the truth for groups of agents. And while this tracking feature, individually or collectively, indeed characterizes knowledge, agents with mere information may ever so often get thrown off the truth track.

Agents acquire information from at least two sources: from their immediate environment and what their senses dictate, and from what other agents apparently decide to believe or do. In case of uncertainty as to what to believe or do, individual agents try to tap the immediate environment for more information to become wiser or facilitate qualified decision. But when the environment has no more information to offer or for some reason, bars additional tapping, agents may decide to consult or observe other agents. This latter source of information is known as *social proof* in social psychology (Cialdini, 2007) and may be an extremely influential vehicle for deliberation, decision and action individually and jointly (Hansen *et al.* 2013): *Single agents assume beliefs, norms or actions of other agents in an attempt to reflect the correct view, stance or behavior for a given situation.*

Sometimes social proof gives the right guidance, other times wrong guidance as to what to think or do among agents in a group. Social psychology and information theory have documented a number of socio-informational phenomena relying on social proof in which agents get more confused and off the truth track than rationally aligned by following the beliefs, norms of other agents (Hendricks and Hansen 2014, 2016). The socio-informational phenomena range from bystander effects, cascades and bandwagons, to belief polarization, all of which, together with common and distributed knowledge, may be formally characterized and their dynamics accounted for.

Informational attitudes in groups

Common knowledge is a *group notion*, in the sense that it pertains to the knowledge held not by individual agents, but a group of agents. Common knowledge is the strongest notion of group knowledge in the literature. Several weaker notions are useful and important. To describe more precisely these notions of group knowledge, what is needed is:

1   a set of agents capable of possessing knowledge about some set of ground facts;
2   assignments of knowledge to groups of agents;
3   the notion of *higher-order information.*

To denote agents let us use $a,b,c,...$, and let $K_a A$ be read "a knows that A," where A is a proposition that is either true or false (see Chapter 8), like "Alice's thesis defense is in Room 2-02."

Distributed knowledge

Let $G = \{a,b,c\}$ be a group of agents. What would make "the group G knows that A" true? One candidate could be that *somebody* in G must know A: either $K_a A$ or $K_b A$ or $K_c A$ must be true. At least if this is the case, then the group may make it to Alice's defense, as Alice may inform Bob and Carol about where to go. This is an instance of *distributed knowledge*: the knowledge that A is distributed across the members of the group, so that when the group pools its informational resources, it knows the proposition. Formally, G has distributed knowledge of A is written $D_G A$.

That Alice must *privately* know that A is not required for distributed knowledge. It could, for example, be the case that Bob knows that the defense is either in Room 2-02 or in Room 1-02, while Carol knows that it is in either 2-02 or 3-02, while Alice, being on the brink of a nervous collapse, has forgotten to check. In this case, it is still distributed knowledge in G that Alice's defense is in Room 2-02: if Bob and Carol were to pool their information, only one possibility would be left. Hence, a group may have distributed knowledge of propositions which none of its members privately know. Moreover, adding members to a group only increases the distributed knowledge: though A is in fact distributed knowledge already in $\{b,c\}$, adding Alice to obtain $G = \{a,b,c\}$ does not mean that the distributed knowledge is lost.

If G has distributed knowledge that A, does it then mean that they know where to go? Not necessarily. A group has distributed knowledge of A in the case that *if the group members were to share all their information with each other, then they would individually know A*. It is not part of the definition that Alice, Bob and Carol in fact communicate. In this sense, distributed knowledge is *potential knowledge* of the group.

The most celebrated instance of distributed knowledge is the *wisdom of crowds* in which the aggregated knowledge of a group is epistemically superior to the performance of the singular agents making up that group (Surowiecki 2004).

Everybody knows that

If "group G knows that A" is to have a stronger meaning than that A is "merely" distributed knowledge among G's members, then a natural candidate for a definition is that *everybody* in G knows A. This knowledge type is often formalized using the "Everybody in G knows that"-operator E_G, where the proposition $E_G A$ ("everybody in G knows that A") is true just in case $K_a A$ is true and $K_b A$ is true and so forth, for all members of G.

Clearly, if $E_G A$ is true, then $D_G A$ is true, i.e. if everybody in G knows that A, then A is also distributed knowledge in G. Hence "everybody knows that"-knowledge is stronger than distributed knowledge, but is it strong enough for Alice, Bob and Carol to make it to the right room? Each has the information to make it there, as it follows that they privately know the room number. Hence, finding the room is not contingent on information sharing and Alice is safe. But what if Bob and Carol will only go if they know that the other will go as well? Is "everybody knows that"-knowledge strong enough for Bob and Carol to *knowingly coordinate* on going to the right room? Here the answer is *No*. Though both know where the room is, both may be in doubt about *whether the other knows where the room is*, and hence about whether the other will show up. It is perfectly consistent with "everybody knows that"-knowledge of A that Bob lacks information about *what information Carol possesses*, for which reason he will not go. Hence everybody knowing is not necessarily sufficient for a coordinated effort of getting to the room in concert. Similarly, a broken-down car will not move an inch unless the participants coordinate the effort of pushing it all together at the same time. Not only do they have to know this fact each one of them, they also have to know that the others know that they know … . But that is *higher-order information* and quite different from everybody knowing whatever it is they all individually know.

Higher-order information

In one sense, both distributed knowledge and "everybody knows that"-knowledge are simple notions. Both "only" involve describing the knowledge agents and groups of agents have about ground facts, that is, facts that do not involve knowledge, belief or other propositional attitudes (desire, intention,…). Such propositions, like A about the room number of Alice's defense, are said to contain only *zero-order information*. Building from this, the proposition K_aA is said to be *first-order information*: in referring to Alice's *knowledge*, it contains information about *one level* of propositional attitudes towards a ground fact. Similarly, the propositions K_aK_aA and K_bK_aA are *second-order information*, as they contain two levels of propositional attitudes, $K_bK_aK_aA$ is *third-order*, etc. In short, *higher-order information* refers to second-order information and above. Characteristic of higher-order informational propositions is that they contain information about an agent's information about some (other or same) agent's information.

Common knowledge

If Bob will only show up if he knows that Carol will show up, and Carol will only show up if she knows that Bob will show up, and both of them know this about each other, then how many levels of higher-order information is needed before they show up to support Alice? The answer may be surprising: infinitely many. Let A be the proposition "Alice's thesis defense is in Room 2-02," and assume that K_bA. This is not enough for Bob to show up, as he will only go if Carol also goes. Assume that also K_bK_cA. Is this enough? Bob now knows that Carol can find her way, but does he know that she will show up? No, for the same reason that K_bA was not enough for Bob. But what if $K_bK_cK_bA$? Then Carol knows that Bob knows where the exam is, and Bob knows this! Surely they must coordinate! Under ordinary circumstances, it is most likely they would. But if one is strict about the setup, then there is still room for error. In particular, as K_bK_cA was not enough for Bob to go, then K_cK_bA is not enough for Carol either. As Bob tolerates no room for error, knowing K_cK_bA is therefore not enough. We may keep adding additional levels of knowledge, but it will not be sufficient: as long as we add only finitely many, then Bob will always consider it possible that Carol does not know enough about his intentions to go, and will hence not get on the bus. If this seems excessive, consider that the same logic applies to contexts in which there must be zero-tolerance for any coordination failure, such as potential nuclear conflicts.

The problem of coordination will be solved if Bob and Carol share the strongest form of group knowledge, namely *common knowledge*. A group G has common knowledge of a proposition A if everybody in G knows that everybody in G knows that … everybody in G knows that A, for *all* higher-order levels. That G has common knowledge that A is written in notation as C_GA, and may be defined using the E_G-operator: let E_G^1A denote E_GA and let $E_G^{k+1}A$ denote $E_GE_G^kA$. Then C_GA if, and only if, E_G^nA for all natural numbers n. As there are infinitely many natural numbers, common knowledge incorporates an infinite hierarchy of higher-order information.

Common knowledge suffices for resolving the coordination problem between Bob and Carol because Bob's doubt about Carol will vanish as the possibility of error has been replaced by infinite assurance on all higher-order levels. And that goes for Carol too, the same way it went for the "Unknown protester" and the driver of the tank in Tiananmen Square. It's common knowledge now.

Pluralistic ignorance

Did you ever go to a show because your friends seemingly wanted to? Did it ever turn out that you all would have preferred to stay at home? If so, then you may have been in a state of *pluralistic ignorance* when you made your decision. You collectively get to subscribe to a norm that you privately reject in part because you incorrectly believe that everybody else believes something although no one believes it as it were.

Pluralistic ignorance is an evil cousin of common knowledge. Where common knowledge is truth tracking and can make groups act as one, pluralistic ignorance uses the fact that groups are composed of individuals that seldom know each others' exact thoughts to create highly inefficient groups.

As common knowledge, pluralistic ignorance is also a higher-order notion, but defined using belief. A group is in a state of pluralistic ignorance with respect to proposition *A* if

1   all members of the group believe *not A*;
2   all members of the group mistakenly believes that everybody else believes *A.* (Krech and Cruthfield 1948), (Hansen *et al.* 2013), (Bjerring *et al.* 2014).

Pluralistic ignorance is unfortunately far easier to achieve than common knowledge, and it plays tricks on us regularly. In some cases, the result is harmless: in attempting to accommodate the preferences of the other, dating couples might go see movie *A*, where both would have preferred to see movie *B*. In other cases, the result may cause liver deficiency: if everybody on campus seemingly enjoys heavy alcohol consumption, new students may attempt to fit in by following suit (Prentice and Miller, 1993).

Social proof in action

Informational attitudes, like distributed knowledge, common knowledge and pluralistic ignorance describe *static* situations of knowledge and belief. Through observation and communication such static situations may change. Such changing situations are described by *information dynamics* (van Benthem 2014).

The bystander effect

One dynamic situation type in which pluralistic ignorance is the lead character is known as the *bystander effect*. The phenomenon covers the seemingly paradoxical inaction of witnesses in emergency situations where multiple witnesses are present. A paradigmatic example is the story of the murder of "Kitty" Genovese as referred by among others Latané and Darley (1970). In a case of much heated debate from New York City in the 1960s, the 28-year-old Catherine "Kitty" Genovese was assaulted and stabbed on the step to her front door. It happened despite scores of neighbors who witnessed large parts of this horrific chain of events, which lasted over half an hour. Subsequently the press reported that no less than 38 witnesses had admitted that they had omitted to act or call the police. In the public debate that followed, the common reader had no doubt as to what the explanation was. Like any other metropolis, New York City had made its citizens callous and indifferent towards fellow citizens. Looking closer at the press reconstruction of the neighbors' own explanations, it was however the fact that no one else seemed to have reacted, that had caused people to refrain from acting. The lack of reaction had instead made everyone believe that it wasn't a case of definite assault, but rather two lovers quarrelling. In other words, it was the ambiguity of the situation coupled with confusion over responsibility and pluralistic ignorance, which led to this tragic example of the bystander effect. That is, when others don't react, the individual views this information as a sign that a reaction is neither required nor socially demanded. The sad point at the end of the day *is that no one does anything, precisely because no one does anything.*

Bystander effects have frequently been reproduced in laboratory settings (see Latané and Nida (1981) for an overview), most notably by Darley and Latané (1968), and multiple explanations have been suggested. Among these are that bystanders believe that others are more qualified to aid than they themselves are, that bystanders feel averse to acting alone in comparison to acting in accordance with a majority, and that bystanders are in a state of pluralistic ignorance resulting in a wrong belief that no help is needed. Here, we focus on the latter explanation (see (Rendsvig 2014) for informational dynamics models; (Bicchieri and Fukui 1999) for game theoretical models).

Pluralistic ignorance in the bystander effect: structure

The structure generating this sort of bystander effect includes:

1   a state of nature that determines whether an emergency has occurred or not;
2   a set of agents that act concurrently in a number of rounds;
3   three possible actions in each round;
4   a preference order on the outcome of choices.

To illustrate the setup in the bystander effect, there may be a set of witnesses in an emergency situation, who act simultaneously in a number of rounds. They can choose to help, not to help, or to inquire or investigate further to obtain more information. All agents prefer to help if help is required, but not help otherwise; that is, their preference in choice depends on the true state of the world. The decision is performed under uncertainty: agents do not know whether the situation in fact calls for intervention. If an agent chooses to help or not to help, the agent cannot choose in later rounds. It is, however, cost-free to "skip a round" by inquiring further or surveying the situation. Hence, if agents are in doubt about what to do, surveying the situation may seem like a good choice, as it will allow the agent freely to gather additional information on which to base their decision.

There is no strategic interaction in the decision problem, so agents have no incentive to mislead others by choosing in contra to the best of their knowledge. Therefore the choices of other agents can be interpreted as conveying information regarding others' interpretation of the situation. Given this, agents may choose to base their action not only on their private information but also on the information extracted from their peers, i.e. on social proof.

The following epistemic assumptions are made pertaining to the information dynamical structure:

1   The structure above is known to all agents;
2   Common knowledge that each agent makes a rational decision in each round based on the available information, which consists of:
   a   A *public signal* indicating the true state of the world;
   b   A *public signal* consisting of the *actions performed* by the agents.

3   A belief among the agents that others:
    c   Given that they believe help is required, are more likely to help, than they are likely to either inquire or not help;
    d   Given that they believe help is not required, are more likely not to help than they are likely to either survey or help.

Pertaining to item 2, note three things: First, in *a*, agents are assumed to receive a *public* signal about the true state of affairs. This signal consists in the emergency event, for example, of a visual impression that an elderly lady falls. This signal is assumed to be common knowledge, as everybody can see that everybody else can see the event, and so on. It is not, however, known to other agents how each individual agent *interprets* this signal. Second, agents are not assumed to being made aware by the end of a round whether their actions were in accordance with the true state. That is, no external source of information is available between rounds to inform agents in later rounds. Third, notice the emphasis in *b*: it is only assumed that agents perceive the *performed output* of others' choice, not the choice itself. This is essential, as the choices to survey and not to help are *output equivalent*: a person inconspicuously looking around looks very much like someone not helping.

The assumption made in item 3 is that the group of agents already face pluralistic ignorance with regard to the *decision rules* used in the situation.

The assumption of pluralistic ignorance is crucial. Though the decision rules of all agents give them a propensity to survey the situation when in doubt, they simultaneously believe that others reason by a *different* choice rule, namely, that they would choose to help or not to help under the same circumstances. To illustrate how this assumption affects agents' interpretation of the public signal, let us go through the dynamics.

Not initiating a rescue

Consider three agents witnessing an event where an elderly woman trips in the street. Assume that the agents have two rounds in which to decide whether or not to help. The fact of the matter is that the lady needs help. The public signal sent by the event is, however, ambiguous: it may be interpreted as the lady tripping without being hurt or as the lady having badly twisted her ankle. Assume that all agents interpret the signal correctly, and therefore initially believe that the lady requires assistance.

Focus on a particular agent, *a*. Given that *a* believes that she is no better at interpreting the public signal than others, it will be reasonable for her to survey. By surveying, *a* can observe the actions of others, and thereby gather information regarding their interpretation of the public signal. Under the assumption that others are at least as good as herself in deducing the true state from the public signal, this further information will lead to a stronger basis upon which she can subsequently choose to either help or not help.

Notice how the reasoning for choosing to survey implicitly utilizes the assumption of pluralistic ignorance. For *a* to be able to infer information from other agents' actions in the first round, it must be assumed that these actions reflect the agents' private beliefs, even though the action chosen by *a* does not reflect her own beliefs to others.

To see how *a*'s action misrepresents her beliefs to others, recall the assumption in item 2b above, stating that agents perceived the *performed output* of the choices of other agents. In the presented case, the choice to survey and the choice not to help are *output equivalent*:

other agents cannot distinguish these two choices from each other, as both outcomes consists in standing still and witnessing the situation at hand. Following the assumption of pluralistic ignorance, all other agents now believe that *a* has chosen *not to help*.

Given that all agents have acted as *a* did in the first round, what new information is *a* left with, after she is done surveying the situation? She has seen two other witnesses not doing anything, and as she, due to pluralistic ignorance, believes that they follow a decision rule different from her own, she will infer that they all interpreted the public signal as showing that the true state is one in which no help is required. As this goes for all agents, a new situation of pluralistic ignorance arises: after surveying, all agents believe that an accident occurred and believe that everybody else believes that nothing requiring intervention happened!

As *a* takes the two other witnesses to be her epistemic peers, she will now have compelling reasons for revising her belief: she will change her mind, and conclude that her initial interpretation was wrong, and now believe that no intervention is required. Since the roles of all agents are symmetric, agent *a* is not a special case, though, and hence the second round will commence with all three agents believing that no help is required. As they can obtain nothing from surveying further (as this is the last round), the rational choice will be *not to help*.

In conclusion, a group of rational witnesses suffering under pluralistic ignorance regarding each other's decision rules may cause a bystander effect by social proof.

Acting in conformity

The outlined model for the bystander effect ignores the possibility of agents having *interactive* preferences. If the structure outlined above is conjoined with a preference to act in conformity with a majority, a model for the emergence and persistence of unpopular norms may be constructed (see Bicchieri and Fukui 1999). Though the bystander effect may occur on solely epistemic grounds, as illustrated above, conformity to group behavior plays an important role in situations with a similar structure (Miller and McFarland 1987).

A good example of how pluralistic ignorance incorporating a preference to conform in a bystander-effect-like setting may have negative consequences is in board decisions regarding strategic choices of organizations (Halbesleben and Buckley 2004). A round table discussion regarding a strategic choice may easily be seen to have a similar structure: a number of executives will all be witnessing a firm's poor business performance but will fear suggesting that the situation be remedied, due to adverse feelings about acting as a minority and a concern for maintaining the respect of their fellow board members, against a majority who believe that poor performance is due to outside factors, not a current poor strategic choice (Westphal and Bednar 2005). Bystander effects even occur in situations with big institutional agents, such as banks, credit institutions and private entrepreneurs. An example of this is the price increase of Danish corporate realty between 2003 and 2007 (Hendricks and Rasmussen 2012), (Hendricks and Hansen 2014, 2016).

Cascades

Did you ever go to see a movie because several friends had told you that they had heard it was good? Or buy a book because it was high on a best-seller list? Or choose one restaurant over another because it had more customers? If so, then you might have been part of a *cascade*.

A cascade may metaphorically be compared to a domino effect in a population: when all in an initial group make the same choice, others may choose to follow suit, reasoning that the initiators must each have had good reasons for their choice. Hence, the aggregated choices of the initiators send a public signal that their choice is a good one, worth following. Once more follow suit, and this signal only grows stronger.

There may be good reasons to trust such social proof: people do often make informed decisions, and when there is insufficient time to survey the available options, using social proof as an aggregation method may indeed prove fruitful. An example of a rational cascade, an *informational cascade*, stems from the seminal paper of Bikchandani *et al.* (1998). However, as in the case of the bystander effect, social proof may also lead to unfortunate outcomes, as we are warned against in the age-old retort "If all your friends jumped off a bridge, would you do it, too?"

The structure of cascades

In general terms, the structure underlying rational cascades consists of

1   a state of nature, determining a fact in relation to which one must act;
2   a set of rational agents that act sequentially;
3   a set of options between which the agents can choose;
4   a preference order on the outcome of each choice, in relation to the state of nature

Let us use the example of a restaurant choice (Banerjee 1992). The state of nature is such that, of two available restaurants, *Left* is better than *Right*. These two restaurants provide the options between which the agents must choose, and each agent prefers to go to *Left* if *Left* is the better restaurant, and each prefers to go to *Right* if *Right* is the better restaurant.

The decision is made under uncertainty, in the sense that no agent knows the state of nature, though it is common knowledge that everybody prefers to go to the better restaurant. Specifically, the following information is available:

1   The underlying structure, including the sequence in which agents make their choices, is common knowledge;
2   It is common knowledge that each agent makes a rational decision based on their available information, which consists of:
   a   a *private signal* about which action will lead to which outcome, which is known to be more often right than it is wrong;
   b   a *public signal* consisting of the string of actions performed by the previous agents.
3   Knowledge among the agents that their signals are equally likely to be correct.

In the example, agents may have read a review from home, indicating that *Left* is better than *Right*, or heard from a friend that *Right* is better than *Left*. The other agents do not have access to this private information: notice that in *b* it is only the *actions*, not the *signals*, of previous agents that can be observed. Notice furthermore the fact that the sequence of agents known to all is, in conjunction with *b*, taken to imply that any agent knows what public signal any previous agent received: everybody can see what everybody before them saw.

A *run* of such a model may be conceived as a line of agents, each waiting to make a decision between a (finite) set of choices. In runs where later agents choose to ignore their private information and act on the information conveyed by previous agents' actions, an *informational cascade* is said to be in effect.

Initiating a cascade

Let our set of agents, call them {*a,b,c,...*}, stand in line in alphabetic order, waiting to make their choice, each informed by their private signals. The choice for the first agent, *a*, is easy: say she received a signal, *left*, indicating that *Left* is the better restaurant. In that case, she will rationally choose the left restaurant.

The second agent, *b*, sees this choice, and from it, he may infer what signal *a* received: if *a* had received signal *right*, then she would have chosen *Right*. She didn't; hence she got signal *left*. Assume now that *b* also received signal *left*. His choice is as easy as *a*'s: he only has reason to choose *Left*.

The third agent, *c*, has seen the choices of both *a* and *b*, and may reason as *b* regarding *a*'s signal: *c* knows *a* received a *left* signal. What does *c* know about *b*'s signal? Does *c* consider it possible that *b* received a *right* signal, but chose *Left*? There is a subtlety here, that requires an assumption about the agents' *tie-breaking rule*. We make the additional assumption that it is common knowledge that if an agent has equally many signals indicating each restaurant, then the agent will choose in accordance with her own private signal. Under this assumption, *c* may conclude that *b* received a *left* signal – if *b* had received a *right* signal, then *b* would know of both a *left* and a *right* signal, and therefore follow his own private signal, *right*.

Hence *c* knows that two *left* signals have been given. If *c* also received a *left* signal, she should clearly chose *Left*. But what if she received a *right* signal? Well, all signals are known to be more likely to be correct than incorrect, so *c* can conclude that it is more likely that the *left* signal is correct, and the *right* signal incorrect. Hence, *c* will, completely rationally, choose *Left* – contrary to her private signal! Hence, *c* is in an information cascade.

The fourth agent, *d*, will also be in cascade. In fact, *d* will be in the same epistemic situation as *c*, as *d* cannot deduce *c*'s private signal. This is a corollary of *c* being in cascade: since *d* knows that *c* is rational and received the public signal (*left, left*), *d* can deduce that *c* would have chosen *Left no matter what private signal she received*. Hence, *d* will base his decision only on the choices of *a* and *b*, and will also be in cascade. Similar considerations apply to all subsequent agents: they will all be in the cascade, ignoring both their private information and the choices made by previous agents in the cascade.

Positive and negative cascades

In the example above, we arbitrarily specified which restaurant was the better one. Though all agents chose *Left*, the better restaurant could have been *Right*. It is less likely that the initial segment of private signals would have been *left, left* in that case, but not impossible. Moreover, the cascade would still have been rational.

This hints at the strength of cascades: even perfectly rational agents may be caught in a *negative cascade*, a cascade leading to the undesired outcome. It is more likely that agents benefit from using social proof, as *positive cascades* are more likely to occur. However, if the probability of a private signal is correct is 2/3, there is still a 1/9 probability that a negative cascade occurs due to the first two agents! Given that cascades can occur in investment situations and in relation to public opinion before elections, this is not negligible.

Cascades in the wild

The structure of cascades provided above makes very strong assumptions about the rationality of agents and their available information. In particular, the fact that agents are able to reason indefeasibly about the higher-order information of others – and thereby either deduce their private signals or that they are in a cascade – facilitates the occurrence of cascades but also ensures that such cascades are *fragile*: if agent *e* received *two* signals indicating *Right*, she would be able to break the cascade (as the signals from *c* and *d* cannot be deduced).

One striking assumption of the model is that the *social network* is common knowledge, and that it is furthermore known exactly how information travels through it. In real life, we seldom know that the action of *a* directly influenced *b* or that *c* was influenced only by *a* and *b*. More likely, we have no clue about the informational pathways. This entails that we cannot take a hyper-rational approach to social proof, but must rather rely on practical heuristics. Alas, the common heuristic applied is to assume that decisions are made on a *privately* informed basis, not on social proof. This is less than ideal, as it may facilitate stronger and more frequent cascades.

To illustrate the point, assume that Elise is to form an opinion about whether a new film is worthwhile. She has received no private signals, but seeks the advice of Alice, Bob, Carol and Dale, whom she trusts equally. Alice tells her that she heard the film was bad, while Bob, Carol and Dale tell her that they heard the film was good. If Elise assumes each is privately informed, the evidence to go to see the film is swaying. She would even have to read *two* bad reviews before she would be convinced that Bob, Carol and Dale were off the truth track. However, Bob, Carol and Dale may not be *independent information sources*: if Bob told Carol that the film was good, and Carol told Dale, then really these three should count as only *one piece of evidence* for the film being good. Hence, applying the heuristic from above puts Elise in a cascade that more information about her information sources would have prevented.

The example is fictitious, but the structure recurs in most of our institutionalized information aggregation systems: just consider that best-seller lists, online download counts, opinion polls, crowd-based opinion aggregators and even academic citations may all be the victims of such "infostorms" (Hendricks and Hansen 2014, 2016).

Group polarization

Shoppers on Amazon are prompted to buy additional items based on what they are currently viewing. On Facebook, the amount of interaction with friends determines their *edge rank* in relation to you, which in turn determines how frequently they appear in your news feed. Google by default uses your past 180 days' search history to provide Personalized Search for Everyone.[1]

A further common feature of modern web technologies is their being *social*. Most webpages offer a built-in button to "like," "share," or "comment on" the displayed item.

This provides the opportunity to show interest in, or discuss, the content easily on social sites and in the associated comment threads. This allows friends of yours who share your attitude toward a given issue to like the news item and be notified of comments so as to participate in the discussion and re-share it with their social network (Hendricks and Hansen 2014). Hereby, our private opinions are shaped by social deliberation.

In relation to social deliberation, an interesting phenomenon is *group polarization*. Group polarization refers to a reproducible product of group deliberation where each of the group members following a discussion ends up holding a more extreme position regarding some viewpoint than they did prior to deliberation (Sunstein 2009). The phenomenon can reliably be reproduced in lab settings (see Myers and Lamm (1976), Myers (1982) for reviews of experimental literature), using, among others, a setup like the following.

The structure of polarization

Group polarization may occur in situations in which there are:

1   a set of agents;
2   an issue on which agents' degree of agreement can vary on a scale with neutral midpoint and two extreme poles;
3   a division of agents into subgroups, which are homogeneous with respect to their degree of agreement relative to the midpoint;
4   a group deliberation process in which agents are free to discuss their opinions and arguments.

Given one such situation, a subgroup is said to *polarize* or *shift* in case the product of the group discussion has shifted further toward the pole initially favored. The shift is measured by comparing the average degree of individual pre-discussion expressions of agreement with a post-discussion expression. The latter may be given either by asking for post-discussion expressions from individual agents and finding the mean, or by requesting the group to reach consensus, or by requiring that the group determine this value by majority vote.

Based on homogeneous group experiments much akin to the above in setup, several studies have documented group polarization. Myers (1982) provides an overview of some of these studies. Two examples include racial attitudes among high-school seniors and responses to fictive international military crises involving the United States among US Army officers, ROTC cadets, and university students. In the former example regarding racial attitudes among high-school seniors, students were divided into high-, medium-, and low-prejudice groups, and following discussion it was seen that the high and low groups had polarized. The high group had moved from ~ 1.7 to ~ 3 on a scale from -4 to 4, with zero being neutral, -4 being low prejudice, and 4 being high prejudice. The low group moved from ~ -2.8 to ~ -3.5. In the latter study, groups consisting of, respectively, US Army officers, ROTC cadets, and university students were asked to choose among ten responses ranging from bilateral negotiations to nuclear force. Here, students initially favored the softer responses, whereas officers recommended the more militant solutions. After discussion, these two groups polarized, whereas the ROTC cadets where more neutral in both pre-discussion and post-discussion scores.

The black box of group discussion

The main task in explaining the general phenomenon of group polarization consists in unpacking the black box of group deliberation leading to an opinion shift (Myers 1982; Isenberg 1986). One suggested explanation focuses on *informational influence*. According to this theory, subjects in the deliberation processes receive and weigh information that affects their opinion on the issue at hand. It is assumed that the initial lean in direction influences the number of arguments for and against the given direction in favor of the leaned-to pole, and that more arguments in favor of the initial lean are therefore presented. Given that not all arguments have been considered by all agents, some agents will become more convinced of the leaned-to direction, thereby shifting the mean opinion of the group toward the given pole.

Several studies indicate that there is a certain structure to the arguments that provide a shift in opinion. Bishop and Myers (1974) have suggested and supported the view that the group shift is based on a number of parameters, namely, the direction of argument (which pole the group favors), the cogency or perceived validity of the argument, and the argument's novelty (the degree to which the argument was new to agents in the discussion).

By way of example, assume a homogeneous group of three agents initially agreeing on some stance to degree 2 on a scale from -4 to 4 because they each recall two arguments in favor of the positive direction. During discussion, they all advance their arguments, each hearing one novel argument from either of the other agents, one of which they find convincing. Assuming that each argument affects their degree of agreement by 1, each agent will, after the discussion, have changed their degree of agreement to 3, thereby producing a group attitude shift of 1.

It is argued (Myers 1982) that an additional element of *argument rehearsal* in group discussions amplifies the belief formation in groups, thereby creating a stronger polarization effect. This is supported by findings to the effect that being passively presented with arguments in favor of a direction does not produce as large a shift as active discussion does. Instead, arguments need to be rehearsed and internalized in order for an attitude change to have proper effect.

Bubble studies

Bubbles are typically associated with situations in finance in which assets trade at prices far exceeding their fundamental value (Vogel 2010). Stock and real-estate may get overheated but the same goes for opinions on the web, social status and a whole range of other phenomena in science and society. Now opinion, recognition or social capital is the liquidity to be invested in public viewpoints, fame or online-respect and "likes." One may accordingly consider opinion bubbles, political bubbles, bubbles of social capital, bullying bubbles, polarization bubbles, science bubbles, and so on (Hendricks 2014a).

It turns out, from an information theoretical perspective, that bubbles may essentially be viewed as *information control problems* (Hansen *et al.* 2013), (Hendricks and Hansen 2014) among deliberating agents who are collectively susceptible to robustly demonstrated socio-psychological features like boom-thinking, group-thinking and lemming effects. These, together with determinate market models and conditions, may make for bubble-hospitable environments over disparate ontologies ranging from cyber-bullying on social media (Hendricks 2014b), to research funding and science bubbles (Budtz Pedersen and Hendricks 2014), (Hendricks 2014c). Further bubble examples founded on social proof and particular market-conditions involve buying the same stock (Shiller 2004: 03); thinking the same thing; holding the same opinion online (Hendricks and Hansen 2014); subscribing to the same political program (McCarty *et al.* 2013); converging on the same enemies virtually or for real; all members thinking the same as the chairman of the board (Halbesleben and Buckley 2004); appreciating the same art; "liking" the same posts on social media (Centola 2010); taking the same medicine. Everybody is trending the same way dependent on the way in which the individual agent processes the available information about other agents' beliefs, norms and actions but independently of whether this mode of operation is necessarily tracking the truth or is the right thing to do – irrational group behavior or wrongful belief aggregation fuel bubbles (Ofek and Richardson 2003), (Hansen *et al.* 2013), (Hendricks and Hansen 2014, 2016).

That bubbles over different ontologies may be viewed as information control problems in networks subject to social proof is intrinsically connected to the current information-driven models of bubble emergence in economics. In particular (Abreu and Brunnermeier 2003; Brunnermeier 2008) isolate four main strands of bubble models including

1   Models in which all investors have rational expectations and symmetric information (Blanchard and Watson 1982).
2   Models for which investors are asymmetrically informed and the presence of a bubble is not common knowledge (Allen *et al.* 1993), (Brunnermeier 2013).
3   Models where bubbles persist due to limited arbitrage because rational and well-informed investors interact with noise traders psychologically biased in unfortunate ways (DeLong *et al.* 1990).
4   Models of bubbles in which different investors hold different beliefs about the fundamental value of the asset and agree to disagree accordingly (Harrison and Kreps 1978).

In all four model types, social information implicitly plays a key role but no over-arching information theory is *yet* present. Indeed problems of informational interaction, socio-psychological influence and information flows across networks of agents or investors are acknowledged by all parties and all models of bubble formation and so "while we have a much better idea of why rational traders are unable to eradicate the mispricing introduced by behavioral traders, our understanding of behavioral biases and belief distortions is less advanced" (Brunnermeier 2008: 14). This is where formal models of socio-informational phenomena like the ones presented here come in – they are part of uncovering and understanding the structure and dynamics of bubble formation.

Information may indeed be used for enlightenment, insight, education and qualified decision and deliberation, but may unfortunately also be used to manipulate people, opinions and markets. Sometimes the manipulation may be intentional – say for people to acquire certain consumer goods and financial products or subscribe to particular political or religious programs – and sometimes agents are the victims of manipulation as the unintentional result of wrongful collective information processing and erroneous group reasoning.

Thus, one information problem to address is to formulate *intervention strategies* for malignant bubbles like unjustified Twitter-storms (#marius or #voteman) where for instance a false tweet from Associated Press crashed the American stock markets in minutes or got the euro to plunge against the US dollar with a false rumor to the effect that the chairman of the German Bundesbank was about to resign (Hendricks 2014d). Another example relates to the strange bubble economics of selfies where social capital is used to overheat fame (Hendricks 2014e). Also polarization, radicalization and extremism may be considered as unfortunate and destabilizing bubble formation (Hendricks 2014f). Such "infostorms" (Hendricks and Hansen 2014, 2016) demonstrate how information technology and social media may amplify irrational group behavior. In this way, *bubbles refer to unfortunate (irrational) ways of collective aggregating behavior, opinions, preferences or actions based on social proof and marketplaces in science, society and elsewhere.*

But bubbles may not necessarily all be malignant if they mirror public conviction on correct information and social influence rails reason. In economics rational bubbles may exist in which it is reasonable for investors to continue their investment behavior all the way to bubble emergence. Could there be benign bubbles calling for crowd climate awareness, race and gender equality, health care benefits, anti-radicalization, anti-echo-chambering of ideologies or religious disagreement, and so on? How benign bubbles may be *stimulated and used to promote* good ideas and socially desirable initiatives is also a very important information control problem to be addressed.

Acknowledgements

This research was made possible by a generous grant from the Carlsberg Foundation to the Center for Information and Bubble Studies at the University of Copenhagen.

Note

1 Even when signed out; cf. http://googleblog.blogspot.dk/2009/12/personalized-search-for-everyone.html (accessed 4 April 2016).

References

Abreu, D. and Brunnermeier, M. K. (2003). "Bubbles and crashes," *Econometrica* 71: 173–204.
Allen, F., Morris, S. and Postlewaite, A. (1993). "Finite bubbles with short sale constraints and asymmetric information," *Journal of Economic Theory* 61, 206–29.
Banerjee, A. V. (1992). "A Simple Model of Herd Behavior," *The Quarterly Journal of Economics*, 107(3): 797–817.
Bicchieri, C. and Fukui, Y. (1999). "The great illusion: ignorance, informational cascades, and the persistence of unpopular norms," *Business Ethics Quarterly* 9(1): 127–155.
Bikhchandani, S., Hirshleifer, D. and Welch, I. (1998). "Learning from the behavior of others: conformity, fads, and informational cascades,"*Journal of Economic Perspectives* 12: 151–170.
Bishop, G. D. and Myers, D. G. (1974) "Informational influences in group discussion," *Organizational Behavior and Human Performance* 12: 92–104.
Bjerring, J. C., Hansen, J.U. and Pedersen, N. J. L. L. (2014). "On the rationality of pluralistic ignorance," *Synthese* 191(11): 2445–2470.
Blanchard, O. J. and Watson, M. W. (1982). "Bubbles, rational expectations, and financial markets." in *Crisis in the Economic and Financial Structure*, ed. P. Wachtel. Lexington, MA: Lexington.
Brunnermeier, M. K. (2008). "Bubbles," *The New Palgrave Dictionary of Economics*, Second Edition, S. N. Durlauf and L. E. Blume (eds.), London: Palgrave.
Brunnermeier, M. K. (2013). *Asset Pricing under Asymmetric Information*. Oxford: Oxford University Press, reprinted from 2001.

Budtz Pedersen, D. and Hendricks, V. F. (2014). "Science bubbles," *Philosophy and Technology* 27(2014): 503–518.

Centola, D., Willer, R. and Macy, M. (2005). "The emperor's dilemma: a computational model of self-enforcing norms," *American Journal of Sociology* 110(4): 1009–1040.

Cialdini, R. (2007). *Influence: The Psychology of Persuasion.* New York: HarperCollins Publishers.

Darley, J. M. & Latané, B. (1969). "Bystander 'apathy'", *American Scientist*, 57: 244–268.

DeLong, J. B., Shleifer, A., Summers, L. H. and Waldmann, R. J. (1990). "Noise trader risk in financial markets," *Journal of Political Economy* 98: 703–738.

Halbesleben, J. R. B. and Buckley, M. R. (2004). "Pluralistic ignorance: historical development and organizational applications," *Journal of Management History* 42(1): 126–138.

Hansen, P. G., Hendricks, V. F. and Rendsvig, R. K. (2013). "Infostorms," *Metaphilosophy*, 44(3): 301–326.

Harrison, J. M. and Kreps, D. (1978). "Speculative investor behavior in a stock market with heterogeneous expectations," *Quarterly Journal of Economics* 89: 323–336.

Hendricks, V. F. (2014a). "From the art world to fashion to Twitter, we're all living in bubbles," *Epoch Times*, 12 January 2014: http://www.theepochtimes.com/n3/445574-from-the-art-world-to-fashion-to-twitter-were-all-living-in-bubbles/

Hendricks, V. F. (2014b). "If you really want to help a troubled teen, don't like their YouTube video," *Business Insider*, 13 February 2014: http://www.businessinsider.com/if-you-really-want-to-help-a-troubled-teen-dont-like-their-youtube-video-2014-2?IR=T

Hendricks, V. F. (2014c). "Neuroscience risks being the next science research bubble," *Medicalxpress* 5 November 2014: http://medicalxpress.com/news/2014-11-neuroscience-science.html

Hendricks, V. F. (2014d). "When Twitter storms cause financial panic," *New Statesman*, 22 January 2014: http://www.newstatesman.com/business/2014/01/when-twitter-storms-cause-financial-panic

Hendricks, V. F. (2014e). "The strange bubble economics of selfies," Mashable, 15 May2014: http://mashable.com/2014/05/15/social-capital/

Hendricks, V. F. (2014f). "Denmark must not succumb to polarisation in the wake of Copenhagen attacks," *The Conversation*, 16 February 2015: https://theconversation.com/denmark-must-not-succumb-to-polarisation-in-the-wake-of-copenhagen-attacks-37083

Hendricks, V. F. and Hansen, P. G. (2014, Second revised and expanded edition 2016). *Infostorms: How to Take Information Punches and Save Democracy.* New York: Copernicus Books / Springer.

Hendricks, V. F. and Rasmussen, J. L. (2012). *Nedtur! Finanskrisen forstået filosofisk.* Copenhagen: Gyldendal Business.

Isenberg, D. J. (1986). "Group polarization: a critical review and meta-analysis," *Journal of Personality and Social Psychology* 50(6): 1141–1151.

Katz, D. and Allport, F. H. (1931). *Student Attitudes.* Syracuse, NY: Craftsman.

Krech, D. and Crutchfield, R. S. (1948). *Theories and Problems of Social Psychology.* New York: McGraw-Hill.

Latané, B. and Darley, J. M. (1970). *The Unresponsive Bystander: Why Doesn't He Help?* New York: Appleton-Century-Crofts.

Latané, B. and Nida, S. (1981). "Ten years of research on group size and helping," *Psychological Bulletin* 89(2): 308–324.

McCarty, N., Poole, K. T. and Rosenthal, H. (2013). *Political Bubbles.* Princeton, NJ: Princeton University Press.

Miller, D. T. and McFarland, C. (1987). "Pluralisitic ignorance: when similarity is Interpreted as dissimilarity," *Journal of Personality and Social Psychology* 53: 248–305.

Myers, D. G. (1982). "Polarizing effect of social interaction" in H. Brandstätter, J. H. Davis and G. Stocker-Kreichgauger (eds.) *Group Decision Making.* Sheffield: Academic Press.

Myers, D. G. and Lamm, H. (1976). "The group polarization phenomenon," *Psychological Bulletin* 83(4): 602–627.

Ofek, E. and Richardson, M. (2003). "DotCom mania: The rise and fall of Internet stocks." Working Paper No. FIN-01-037 58(3), 1113–38. New York University, Stern School.

Prentice, D. A. and Miller, D. T. (1993). "Pluralistic ignorance and alcohol use on campus: Some consequences of misperceiving the social norm," *Journal of Personality and Social Psychology* 64(2): 243–256.

Rendsvig, R. K. (2014). "Pluralistic ignorance in the bystander effect: informational dynamics of unresponsive witnesses in situations calling for intervention," *Synthese* 191(11): 2471–2498.

Shiller, R. (2004). *Irrational Exuberance.* Princeton, NJ: Princeton University Press.

Sunstein, C. R. (2009). *Going to Extremes: How Like Minds Unite and Divide*, Oxford: Oxford University Press.

Surowiecki, J. (2004). *The Wisdom of Crowds: Why the Many Are Smarter Than the Few and How Collective Wisdom Shapes Business, Economies, Societies and Nations*, New York: Doubleday.

van Benthem, J. (2014). *Logical Dynamics of Information and Interaction*, Cambridge: Cambridge University Press.

Vogel, H. L. (2010). *Financial Markets: Bubbles and Crashes*, New York: Cambridge University Press.

Westphal, J. D. and Bednar, M. K. (2005). "Pluralistic ignorance in corporate boards and firms' strategic persistence in response to low firm performance," *Administrative Science Quarterly* 50: 262–298.

13

MODELING
INFORMATION

Patrick Grim

The topics of modeling and information come together in at least two ways. Computational modeling and simulation play an increasingly important role in science, across disciplines from mathematics through physics to economics and political science. The philosophical questions at issue are questions as to what modeling and simulation are adding, altering, or amplifying in terms of scientific information. What changes with regard to information acquisition, theoretical development, or empirical confirmation with contemporary tools of computational modeling? In this sense the title of this chapter is read in the following way: What kind of information is modeling information? What kind of information does modeling give us?

Modeling and information also come together in a second way, however. The character of information transfer is one of the topics to which computational models have been quite successfully applied. Here the questions at issue are questions of informational dynamics. How can we expect information to flow across a network of agents? What characteristics of networks correlate with what aspects of that information flow – speed, for example, or accuracy? In this sense the title of this chapter is read in a different way: an outline of ongoing efforts to model information.

Because the topics come together in these two ways, this chapter will be divided into two parts.

The first will be an examination of the particular informational role of computational modeling and simulation. The second will survey some contemporary efforts to use computational tools in order to model information in general.

The first section, then, offers a philosophical outline of a basically descriptive question across a range of scientific disciplines: how do models produce information? The second section samples a range of modeling work exploring the flow of information in general. Intriguingly, one aspect of this second section is a return to the scientific procedure but from a distinctly prescriptive angle. How, for particular epistemic purposes, might we best optimize scientific information networks?

What kind of information do models give us?

Computational modeling and computer simulation represent a range of established techniques in the physical sciences (Gould *et al.* 2006; Hybertson 2009) and are growing as tools in economics, political science, and sociology (Schelling 1978; Axelrod 1997b; Kollman *et al.* 1997, 1999; Wilhite 2001; Macy & Willer 2002; Cedarman 2003; Lustick & Miodownik 2009).

The speed, breadth, and unfamiliarity of these developments have led some to claim that computer simulation represents a radical break from a traditional conception of science. Stephen Wolfram claims the result is "a new kind of science" (Wolfram 2002). Robert Axelrod (2005) follows Joshua Epstein and Robert Axtell (1996) in outlining agent-based simulation as a scientific technique beyond both deduction and induction.

It can be argued that each of these claims is an exaggeration; that computational modeling and simulation are new because computers are new, but that the general informational structures used in computational modeling and simulation have an extended and established pedigree in the long tradition of scientific modeling (Sterrett 2006; Grim *et al.* 2007, Grim *et al.* 2013a). What complicates the equation, however, is that modeling information is not all of one kind. Modeling and simulation, both before and within a computational guise, offer a range of informational techniques applicable at a number of levels for a variety of different scientific purposes.

Part of the problem of defining "models" is that there is no limitation on the kind of structure that can be put forward as a model, from physical structures to computational programs to abstract flow diagrams, algorithms or formulae. What qualifies any of these as a model is not what it is made of but a relevant similarity to some targeted aspect of reality. "Targeted" is clearly investigator-relative, as is "relevant similarity": to ask whether something is a model is to ask about its epistemic role in a pattern of exploration.

Not every intended model proves sufficient to its exploratory context: it may turn out that a proposed structure is not in fact a model for the proposed phenomenon. We may to our surprise discover that one phenomenon models another. Despite the objective overtones of these characterizations, however, the notion of a model is always contextualized to a specific epistemic target.

A model is a structure taken or intended to simulate some aspect of an actual or potential reality – some actual or possible course of events. In the context of computational, "simulation" as a count noun is commonly used to refer to a specific run of a computer program. But computational models are members of a wide and historically rich family, running from abstract models embedded in sets of equations to concrete physical models such as the Wright brothers' wind tunnel and hydraulic simulations of the effects of Hurricane Katrina (Interagency Performance Evaluation Task Force 2006). An intriguing agent-based model of disease infection, long before the advent of computational modeling, used herds of mice physically transported in patterns of "migration" by investigators (Greenwood *et al.* 1936).

Models can be abstract not merely in instantiation but in informational target. In some cases the attempt is to understand something as general as how complexity on a higher level can emerge from simple interactions on a lower level (Berlekamp *et. al* 1982; Wolfram 1983, 2002). In other cases the target is as specific as the effect of containment measures on an influenza pandemic in Southeast Asia (Ferguson *et al.* 2005) or even reconstruction of climate and cultural effects in the habitation patterns of the ancient Anasazi (Dean *et al.* 1999). Lustick and Miodownik track the range of information targets from "abstractions" through "ensembles" to concrete "virtualizations" (2009); Grimm and Railsback outline a roughly correlate classification in terms of "minimal," "synthetic" and "predictive" models (2005), though the last category confuses the specificity of target with the scientific purpose of the model. Different levels of abstraction are appropriate to different categories of scientific question, from "what caused the failure of the 17th street levee" to "how might life emerge?" The question of what level of abstraction a model represents, like the question of its target and its relative similarity – make sense only within the context of the epistemic goals of a particular exploration.

Whether abstract or concrete, in either instantiation or target, models track the effect of an independent variable on a dependent one. Typically, though not inevitably, that effect plays out as a causal sequence of events over time. With simulation of a course of events in mind, the central informational structure can be envisaged in terms of three simple parts: input conditions, mechanism, and output. The "input conditions" represent the configuration of simulation components or parameter values at the outset of a model run. The "mechanism" includes all inner workings of the model – all the means by which input is changed or transformed in the course of a simulation. In cases in which a simulation works in terms of a set of coupled equations, those equations constitute part of the mechanism. Where a simulation tracks population changes within an agent-based computational model, the mechanism includes the program-instantiated algorithm through which parameters of individual "agents" at one stage result in shifted parameters of agents at the next. The "output" of a simulation is its result: either an end-state of parameter values that result from the operation of mechanism on input, or a progressive history of states of the system over time. It should be emphasized that models are constructed for specific epistemic purposes, and that each of our three categories – input, mechanism, and output – are issues of interpretation relative to purpose. The purpose of any model is the investigator's purpose, and what is taken or read as input, output, or mechanism is relative to that purpose.

The various scientific purposes to which models are put can be outlined in terms of this basic three-part structure (Table 13.1). Here we will track four such purposes: prediction, retrodiction, explanation, and what might be termed "emergence explanation." Although the tripartite structure of models remains the same in each case, that structure is exploited in different ways for different informational purposes. Different aspects of the structure are interpreted as given information in each case, intended to correspond to ways we already know the world to be. Different aspects are taken as points of new information – those points at which the model is taken to tell us something new (Table 13.1).

Use of a model for *prediction* involves reading off new information from its *output*. For purposes of prediction we set up input conditions intended to correspond to the world at a particular point in time, while designing the mechanisms of our model to reflect how the world works. Output conditions are then read as a prediction of the state of the world at a later point. Weather prediction is a clear case: input conditions reflect barometric pressures, temperatures, and wind directions at noon today, the mechanism is a program instantiating equations that reflect what we take to be processes of weather change, and the output conditions represent a prediction of conditions tomorrow: heavy rain along the East Coast.

Table 13.1 Prediction, explanation, retrodiction and emergence explanation

	Prediction	Explanation	Retrodiction	Emergence explanation
Input	X	X	O	O
Mechanism	X	O	X	O
Output	O	X	X	X

Use of a model for purposes of *explanation*, though it exhibits the same tripartite structure, is importantly different. Here new information is read off the simulation's *mechanism*. Input conditions are set to correspond to conditions we know to obtain in the world at a particular time.

We are looking for output conditions which we know to correspond to conditions at a later time. If in the simulation our input conditions successfully generate those output conditions, we take the mechanism of the simulation to offer a potential explanation of how things in the world actually work. Consider, for example, a weather simulation that repeatedly and accurately transforms weather data on any given day over the last century into weather data for the following day. The fact that its input and output conditions match known weather data gives us reason to suspect that the simulational mechanism may also accurately represent the way real weather patterns work.

A *retrodictive* simulation uses the same tripartite structure in a third way: in order to yield new knowledge at the point of *input conditions*. In a retrodictive simulation, researchers know the state of the world at a particular point and take themselves to have a basic idea of how the world works. What they seek to determine is what the state of the world was at some prior point: what prior events may (or must) have been in order to produce the known result. Simulation input conditions that do produce that result are taken as candidates for how the past may indeed have been. Simulation input conditions that do not generate a realistic output can be ruled out. We may, for example, have no historical data on weather fronts prior to the great Natchez Tornado of 1840. We may, however, have a general model of tornado formation of which we are confident.

If input conditions instantiating a dry cold air mass from the west meeting a warm wet air mass from the Atlantic result in an output indicating tornado activity, while input conditions of a dry warm air mass from the west meeting a thunderstorm from the east do not, we have evidence that the tornado was preceded by the first weather pattern rather than the second.

We include as a fourth category ambitious attempts at very general explanation that might be termed "emergence explanations." Here the fact that simple rules operating on postulated inputs may generate certain patterns is offered as an explanation for those patterns in nature or reality.

Note that in such a case *both* mechanism and input are postulated: it is output alone of which we are fully confident. Steven Wolfram displays a pattern generated from random input according to a specific rule in one-dimensional cellular automata and compares the result to shell patterns in mollusks, with the clear implication that the pattern of mollusk shells may be formed precisely in terms of such a rule (Wolfram 2002). Both the structure and relative weakness of emergence explanation are evident from its tripartite representation. Here the attempt is to draw new information at not one but two points of the structure – as information regarding both mechanism (as in explanation) and input (as in retroduction) – on the basis only of a match at the point of output.

What kind of information do models give us? The answer appears to be that models do not offer merely one kind of information. Although the various applications of computational models, like their scientific predecessors, can be interpreted in terms of the same thee-part structure, one application of that structure offers predictive information, another retroductive information, and a third information in the form of explanation.

We have emphasized that models are constructed for specific epistemic purposes, and that each of our three categories – input, mechanism, and output – are issues of interpretation relative to purpose. It is given a specific epistemic purpose, a specific context and a specific interpretation that a model can be put forward for purposes of prediction, retrodiction, or explanation. It is embedded in such a context that the success or failure of a model will be judged as well.

The problem with simulations, Rodney Brooks has said, is that "simulations are doomed to succeed" (Brooks & Mataric 1993). Computational models have sometimes been impugned on the grounds that "you can prove anything with simulation" or that "you can produce any result you want by tweaking parameters." If simulational techniques were genuinely immune from failure, of course, they would be informationally useless. The claim that "you can prove anything by tweaking parameters," however, seems to assume that models are tied to the world only at output rather than open for various purposes to critique at input and mechanism as well.

Such an attack seems most legitimate only against "emergence explanation" as outlined above. What the tripartite structure seems to emphasize is that there are in fact many ways that models can fail. Lack of relevant correspondence is the mark of model failure, a failure that can appear at any of the outlined points of either assumed or "new" information.

A model is a general structure taken or intended to correspond to some general aspect of reality.

In that regard they are like theories, and can fail in all the ways that theories can fail. A "simulation" is generally used for a specific run of a model in terms of specific parameter settings. Simulations might be compared to specific experiments, and can fail in all the ways that experiments can fail. Far from being "doomed to succeed," modeling and simulation appear to have the full range of scientific failure as a very real option (Grim *et al.* 2013a).

Modeling information flow

Under various names, using various techniques, a range of attempts have been made, in different disciplines, to capture important aspects of information dynamics. Here we can only offer a sampling of attempts to model information flow. We will touch on cellular automata models starting with physics, moving on to game theory and networks, emphasizing current research trajectories and more recent philosophical development.

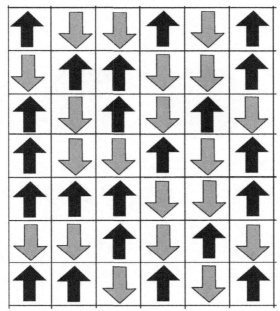

Figure 13.1 The Ising model

Some of the oldest models appear in analogies taken from physics. Figure 13.1 shows an Ising model for ferromagnetism. Directions of arrows represent spins of charged particles, each of which is pushed to align with its neighbors; magnetism is represented by the alignment of spins across the field. Reinterpretation takes the Ising model from physical to social application. If interpretation in terms of physical interaction between bordering particles is replaced with an interpretation in terms of cultural interaction between agents – in terms of social status, cultural traits, belief, opinion, or information states, for example – one has a first very simple model in which one might attempt to track patterns of cultural influence or information flow across a spatialized population (Galam *et al.* 1982; Galam & Moscovici 1991; Galam 1997; Castellano *et al.* 2009). "Sociodynamics" represents one class of physics-based models which operate in terms of equation-based transitions within a society as a whole (Helbing 1991; Wiedlich 1971, 1991, 2002). "Sociophysics" represents a closely related class which characteristically applies the tools of statistical mechanics to derive society-level results from probabilities at the individual level (Galam 2012).

A strong tradition of modeling information flow follows the general pattern anticipated in the Ising model. In a large class of cellular automata models, the social relations between individuals are envisaged in terms of neighborhood relations within a two-dimensional array. Each individual in such an array is thought of as having a particular cultural trait – a belief, perhaps, or a piece of information. In step-wise evolution of the array, individuals update their information in terms of the states of their immediate neighbors.

One simple version is the voter model, shown in Figure 13.2. At the beginning of a run, each agent in a two-dimensional array has some binary value of +1 or –1. At each time step, a single agent and one of its neighbors is chosen at random, and the agent adopts or "imitates" the value of its neighbor. Importantly, it is the local "information" of an immediate neighbor – rather than any social-level reflection of majority view, for example – that produces the effect. Concentrated information spreads, as in the top series in Figure 13.3. But social influence can also create polarized regions of opinion, as in the second array. The voter

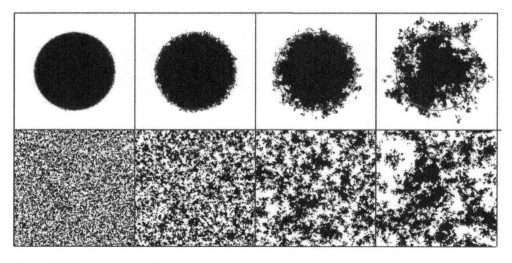

Figure 13.2 Evolution of a cellular automata 'voter' model, from an initial circular concentration of the like-minded (left) and a random array (right)

Source: Dornic, Chaté, Chave, and Hinrichsen (2001).

142

model has been studied extensively with the tools of statistical physics, as have variations in which there are a sprinkling of stubborn individuals (Mobilia 2003) and in which the range of states or opinions is expanded (Vásquez *et al.* 2003). Majority rule models consider variations in which majorities or structured minorities are required for conversion (Galam 2002). Social impact theory attempts to include persuasiveness of individuals and groups within cellular automata models as well (Latané 1981; Nowak *et al.* 1990).

Information also appears in the modeling tradition of game theory. An assumption of complete information is common in game theory, such that all players know the matrix of potential payoffs to each player from each possible combination of moves. On the other hand, game theory generally builds in imperfect information in the sense that each player does not know the history of all previous plays for all players.

With an eye to information, game theory can also be used as something more: as a model for how semantic information can develop in the first place. Here the seminal contribution is David Lewis's signaling games (1969). Developed in answer to Quine's critique of analytic truth by convention, Lewis develops a formal model of communicative coordination between players who share the same cooperative goals. Such a coordination, Lewis suggests, offers a way of understanding meaning, a suggestion carried further in work by Brian Skyrms (1996, 2010) and Hutteger *et al.* (2010).

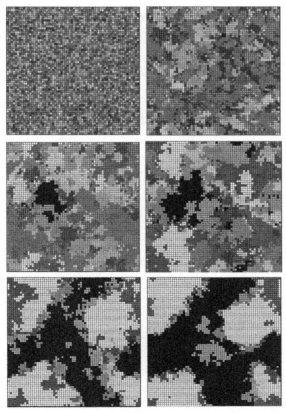

Figure 13.3 Emergence of communicative dialects in arrays of simple neural nets training up on behavior of successful neighbors in an environment of migraing food sources and predators
Source: Grim, Kokalis, Alai-Tafti, Kilb and St. Denis (2004).

Game theory joins cellular automata modeling in a range of work on the emergence of game-theoretic cooperation in iterated games (Nowak *et al.* 1994). Development of semantic information can then be modeled as the emergence of collaborative communicative strategies within arrays of mutually interactive agents (Floridi 2011). In Grim *et al.* (2004) the model is one in which individuals are stable in a cellular automata grid, but food items and predators wander in a random walk across the grid. Agents initially have one of a set of random communication strategies in terms of arbitrary sounds: perhaps making a sound s1 heard by themselves and neighbors when they are hit by a predator, for example, sound s2 when a food item comes their way. When agents pursuing purely their own interest update on the strategies of successful neighbors, Grim *et al.* (2004) show that a simple semantics in which particular sounds have particular meaning emerge. Figure 13.3, for example, shows the emergence of specific dialects by a mechanism of partial neural net training on the behavior of successful neighbors. In Grim (2011) the same mechanism is shown to be capable of producing pragmatic information transfer in the manner of Grice (1989).

These results emphasize the emergence of cooperation and communication across cellular automata arrays. The point is to show how semantic information, for example, can converge in the form of a uniform language across a population.

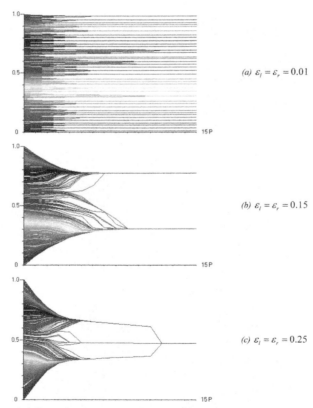

Figure 13.4 Images of different patterns of information convergence or polarization for individuals with random beliefs modeled as 0 through 1 and updating on neighbors with similar views within a threshold ε

Source: Hegselmann and Krause (2002).

In bounded confidence models agents may not trust the information received from all of those with whom they come in contact. The result can be a very different information dynamics. Often instantiated as a cellular automata, bounded confidence models have been used to show how information can fail to converge; how agents can come not to agree regarding a particular body of information but to disagree. In Deffuant models (Deffuant *et al.* 2000), agents embedded in an array have beliefs modeled as continuous values between 0 and 1. They update on the beliefs of their neighbors, approaching closer to those beliefs, but only if the neighbor's belief is within a threshold proximity to their own. Information from agents whose beliefs are "too far" away is distrusted or ignored. The result may be increasingly isolated opinion clusters, a configuration across which information can no longer flow. The Hegselmann Krause (2002) model of polarization is similar, though it drops the localized assumption: agents interact with all others in the population within the range of their bounded confidence. Different confidence levels turn out to be important for the formation of either informational convergence or informational polarization (Figure 13.4).

A final model worthy of note in the cellular automata tradition is Axelrod's cultural diffusion model (Axelrod 1997a). Most of the models discussed to this point can be thought of as modeling the flow of a single piece of information (Grim *et al.* 2004 is a marginal exception). Almost uniquely, Axelrod's model can be interpreted as modeling the dynamics of *sets* of pieces of information. Axelrod considers a 10×10 cellular automata array in which each agent has one of 10 "traits" on each of 5 "features" (Figure 13.5) Axelrod thinks of these as cultural options within categories: types of music or forms of marriage, for example. But they might also be thought as possible beliefs within particular information categories: beliefs as to the location of the treasure, for example, or when the next hurricane will hit.

The dynamics of information flow within the Axelrod model are driven by a pair of intuitions: that (a) agents tend to interact with those more like them, and (b) they come to be more like those with whom they interact. Both can be given an informational interpretation. In the evolution of the array, an agent chosen at random interacts with a randomly chosen neighbor with a probability correlate to the number of features on which they share the same trait. On interaction, that agent adopts one of the neighbor's traits on which the two disagree. The result is a dynamics driven by convergence of cultural information, but which for particular values – and in a manner amazingly fragile in terms of those values – also shows the emergence of polarized communities in the manner of the Deffuant and Hegselmann Krause models.

74741	87254	82330	17993	22978	82762	87476	26757	99313	32009
01948	09234	67730	89130	34210	85403	69411	81677	06789	24042
49447	46012	42628	86636	27405	39747	97450	71833	07192	87426
22781	85541	51585	84468	18122	60094	71819	51912	32095	11318
09581	89800	72031	19856	08071	97744	42533	33723	24659	03847
56352	34490	48416	55455	88600	78295	69896	96775	86714	02932
46238	38032	34235	45602	39891	84866	38456	78008	27136	50153
88136	21593	77404	17043	39238	81454	29464	74576	41924	43987
35682	19232	80173	81447	22884	58260	53436	13623	05729	43378
57816	55285	66329	30462	36729	13341	43986	45578	64585	47330

Figure 13.5 An Axelrod array of individuals with one of 10 traits on each of 5 features

Source: Axelrod (1997a).

Note: The underlined site and the site to its south share traits for two of the five cultural features, making a cultural similarity of 40%.

In original form, flow of information is envisaged in all the spatialized models above as flow across an Ising-like or cellular automata array. More recently the work has been extended to much wider classes of networks, allowing for questions regarding how information will flow differently across different types of social network (Newman 2003; Miller & Page 2007).

Information, after all, is characteristically social: socially instantiated and socially transferred. How can we expect information to flow across a social network? A strong research trajectory within contemporary computational uses resources from graph and network theory, representing individuals as nodes (or vertices) connected by communication links (or edges). Working with abstract rather than full social networks, how can we expect information to flow across networks of different structures such as those in Figure 13.6?

It has long been tempting to draw an analogy between information transfer and the dynamics of infection (Le Bon 1897; De Tarde 1903; Park 1904, Park & Burgess 1921; Blumer 1951, 1969). Douglas Hofstadter, Richard Dawkins, and Daniel Dennett all speak of information transfer in terms of memes spreading socially, competing for fitness and mutating on the model of viruses (Dawkins 1976, 1993; Hofstadter 1983; Dennett 1991). Gladwell 2000 makes the comparison explicit: "Ideas and products and messages and behaviors spread like viruses do." Lynch 1996, Blackmore 1999, and Brodie 2009 are all book-length elaborations of infection models of information flow. Network and complexity researchers have also followed this line. Gross *et al.* (2006) claim that work on disease propagation across networks has implications for "the spreading of information, opinions and beliefs in a population" because memes "can be described in a similar way."

Within such a model, only one link to a single "infected" node is required for transmission. The contagion dynamic that results produces a range of intriguing network effects, notable among which are the strength of weak ties (Granovetter 1973) and the small-world phenomenon (Watts & Strogatz 1998; Watts 1999). Replacement of a very few

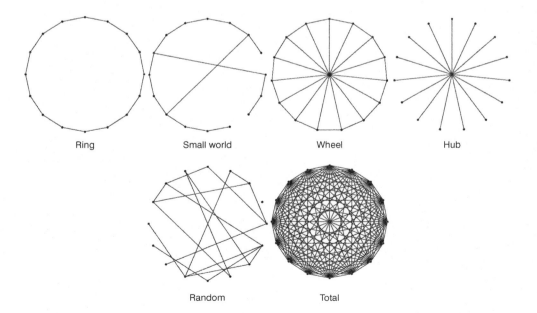

Figure 13.6 How will information flow across different abstract networks?

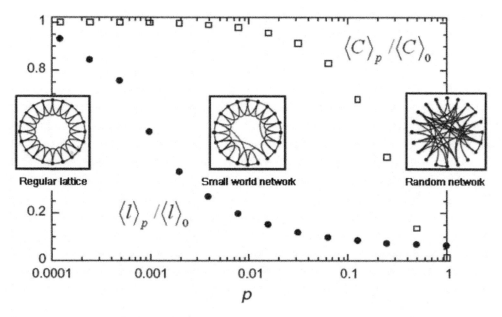

Figure 13.7 Rewiring of links in a regular ring network (left) with even a small probability p produces a small world network with a much higher speed to total infection

Source: Watts and Strogatz (1998).

short-range ties with a few long ones, as in the change from the ring to the small world in Figure 13.5, can speed up the rate of transfer across a network in which transmission would otherwise be local and slow. In the illustration from Watts and Strogatz (Figure 13.7), using a log plot for probability of rewiring, speed to total infection follows esssentially the descending curve of solid dots mapping shortest average path length between randomly chosen nodes. As Granovetter put it, "whatever is to be diffused can reach a larger number of people, and traverse a greater social distance," with the addition of a few weak long-range ties (Granovetter 1973, 1366).

In Figure 13.7, by mapping the flow of information there is reason to be suspicious of a simple infection model, however. Centola and Macy 2007 point out that information transfer often demands something more than the mere acquaintance suggested by an infection model. In many cases it requires the reinforcement effect of multiple information sources that Centola and Macy call "complex contagion." In cases of information that are best construed in terms of complex rather than simple contagion, it will be broad bands of influence rather than single strands that will be required for information to flow.

The emphasis on different dynamics for different sorts of information has been carried further in Grim 2009 and related work (Grim *et al.* 2010a, 2010b). This work uses a richer model of reinforcement in which the information at each node is modeled as a value between 0 and 1 and in which agents update in terms of an average of all of those with whom they are in contact. Concentration is also on linked sub-networks, reflecting a common feature of real social networks (Figure 13.8).

Within such a model, dramatic differences appear between infection dynamics on a given network and information transfer through reinforcement on the same network. For sub-networks with few links between them, infection dynamics measured in terms of time to

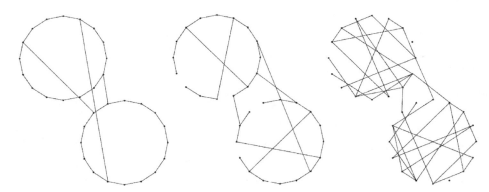

Figure 13.8 Linked ring, small world, and random sub-networks

full infection are particularly sensitive to the structure of the sub-networks involved. For infection, links between those sub-networks prove of relatively minor importance. In the case of information transfer, measured in terms of time to full information across the network, the situation is reversed. For information, it is the links between sub-networks that prove of primary importance. In later work, the dynamics of germs, genes, and memes are studied as distinct types of information with their own characteristic forms of transfer (Grim *et al.* 2015). There is, the authors conclude, no *one* way that information flows. In order to know how information will transfer across a network, the authors conclude, one must know not only the structure of the network involved but the specific type of information and characteristic forms of information transfer at issue.

Scientific information and scientific networks constitute a particular area of interest. A descriptive question in philosophy of science is how scientific information can be expected to flow across communication or information networks. An intriguing prescriptive question is close by: how might we optimize scientific networks in order to best facilitate the growth, spread, and application of scientific information?

Kevin Zollman (2007, 2010, 2013) considers simple networks in which each node is a scientific agent who uses Bayesian reasoning in a "bandit problem," updating beliefs about whether state s1 or state s2 holds in the world on the basis of observed results of action in both his own case and that of other agents to which he is connected in the network. In a central result for social epistemology, the probability of epistemic success – of discovering the truth – turns out to be higher in a ring network than a wheel, higher in a wheel than in a total network. Convergence to an agreed result is far quicker with total connectivity within a network, but accuracy of information within a community as a whole may be facilitated when information available to individual members of the community is limited by network structure. Grim *et al.* (2013b) explore a similar model in which agents hold hypotheses modeled on a full [0,1] spectrum, for a wider class of networks, and with an enriched notion of "epistemic landscapes" that represent problems of different degrees of difficulty. Results on epistemic success parallel Zollman's: the scientific community may learn more when individual scientists learn less.

Epistemic landscapes appear in a different sense in a model by Weisberg and Muldoon (2009). Here investigators are envisaged as agents traversing a landscape of scientific significance, following different strategies in the attempt to find the highest peaks. Information of their explorations is left "in the world," as it were – that a specific patch has been visited is left with a publication marker – but it is only through that information that agents are networked. Weisberg and Muldoon compare agents with three different strategies. "Hill climbers with experimentation" function alone, exploring for neighboring patches with a higher significance and continuing along that trajectory. "Followers" and "mavericks" both use the social information left in a landscape, but with different biases. Followers choose neighboring paths that have been explored, in search of higher significance. Mavericks deliberately choose neighboring paths that have been unexplored. Weisberg and Muldoon report that mavericks do the best of the three, but that a heterogeneous combination of followers with mavericks does better still, "making polymorphic populations of mavericks and followers ideal in many research domains" (225).

While a range of work supports claims for the epistemic benefit of diversity (Zollman 2007; Kitcher 1990, 2002; Strevens 2003), it turns out that Weisberg and Muldoon's model is seriously flawed. Alexander, Himmelreich and Thompson (2015) demonstrate significant programming errors in the implementation of the model. When re-run with corrections, success within a heterogeneous population of mavericks and followers appears to be due not to the combination of strategies but to the success of the mavericks alone. Alexander, Himmelreich and Thompson also introduce extremely successful populations of "swarm" agents which navigate an epistemic landscape in ways inspired by work in animal foraging (Couzin *et al.* 2002; Couzin *et al.* 2005).

So, at the end of this exploration, how does information flow? Just as there is not merely one kind of information offered in models, there is not merely one way that information flows. A range of different models have been constructed for information flow, probably best interpreted as capturing different aspects of the phenomenon: the way information can be expected to flow as a single piece of information across an imitative array, as a coordinated set of bits, in either convergence or polarization across a community, for example. The best available models, it can be suggested, show major characteristics of information to depend on at least two major factors: the social structure of information transfer and the specific dynamics characteristic of the particular type of information at issue.

References

Alexander, J. M., J. Himmelreich & C. J. Thompson (2015). Epistemic Landscapes, Optimal Search and the Division of Cognitive Labor. *Philosophy of Science* 82 (3), 424–453.

Axelrod, R. (1997a). The Dissemination of Culture: A Model with Local Convergence and Global Polarization. *Journal of Conflict Resolution*, 41, 203–226.

Axelrod, R. (1997b). *The Complexity of Cooperation: Agent-based Models of Competition and Cooperation*. Princeton, NJ: Princeton University Press.

Axelrod, R. (2005). Simulation in the social sciences. In J. Rennard (Ed.), *Handbook of research on Nature Inspired Computing for Economy and Management,* (pp. 90–100). Hershey: Idea Group.

Axtell, R. L., J. M. Epstein, J. S. Dean, G. J. Gumerman, A. C. Swedland, J. Harburger, S. Chakravarty, R. Hammond, J. Parker, & M. Parker. (2002). Population Growth and Collapse in a Multiagent Model of the Kayenta Anasazi in Long House Valley. In B. J. L. Berry, L. D. Kiel, & E. Eliott (Eds.), *Adaptive Agents, Intelligence, and Emergent Human Organization: Capturing Complexity through Agent-based Modeling,* Proceedings of the National Academy of Sciences of the USA 99, Suppl. 3 (pp. 7275–7279). Washington D.C.: National Academy of Sciences.

Berlekamp, E., J. Conway, & R. Guy (1982). *Winning Ways for your Mathematical Plays*. London: Academic Press.

Blackmore, S. (1999). *The Meme Machine*. Oxford: Oxford University Press.

Blumer, Herbert (1951). Collective Behavior. In A. M. Lee (Ed.), *Principles of Sociology* (pp. 67–121). New York: Barnes and Noble.

Blumer, Herbert (1969). Symbolic Interactionism: Perspsective and Method. New Jersey: Prentice-Hall.

Brodie, Richard (2009). *Virus of the Mind: The New Science of the Meme*. Carlsbad, CA: Hay House.

Brooks, Rodne, & Maja J. Mataric (1993). Real Robots, Real Learning Problems. In Jonathan H. Connell & Sridar Mahaderan (Eds.), *Robot Learning* (pp. 193–213). Dordrecht: Kluwer.

Castellano, C., S. Fortunato & V. Loreto (2009). Statistical Physics of Social Dynamics. *Review of Modern Physics*, 81, 591–641.

Cedarman, L. E. (2003). Modeling the Size of Wars. *American Political Science Review,* 97, 135–150

Centola, D. & M. Macy (2007). Complex Contagions and the Weakness of Long Ties. *American Journal of Sociology*, 113(3): 702–734.

Conway, J. R. G., & E. Berlekamp (1982). *Winning Ways for your Mathematical Plays,* vol. 4. London: Academic Press.

Couzin, I. D., J. Krause, R. James, G. D. Ruxton & N. R. Franks (2002). Collective Memory and Spatial Sorting in Animal Groups. *Journal of Theoretical Biology*, 218: 1–11.

Couzin, I. D., J. Krause, N. R. Franks & S. A. Levin (2005). Effective Leadership and Decision-Making in Animal Groups on the Move. *Nature*, 433, 513–536.

Dawkins, Richard (1976). *The Selfish Gene*. Oxford: Oxford University Press.

Dawkins, Richard (1993). Viruses of the Mind. In Bo Dalhbom (Ed.), *Dennett and His Critics: Demystifying Mind*. Oxford: Blackwell.

Dean, J. S., G. J. Gumerman, J. Epstein, R. L. Axtell, A. C. Swedland, M. T. Parker, & S. McCarrol. (1999). Understanding Anasazi Culture change through Agent-based Modeling. In T. A. Kohler & G. J. Gumerman (Eds.), *Dynamics in Human and Primate Societies: Agent Based Modeling of Social and Spatial Processes* (pp. 179–206). New York: Oxford University Press.

Deffuant, G., Neau, D., Amblard, F. & Weisbuch, G. (2000). Mixing Beliefs among Interacting Agents, *Advances in Complex Systems*, 3, 87–98.

Dennett, Daniel (1991) *Consciousness Explained*. Boston, MA: Little, Brown & Co.

De Tarde, Gabriel (1903). *The Laws of Imitation*. New York: Henry Holt and Co.

Dornic, I., H. Chaté, J. Chave & H. Hinrichsen (2001). Critical Coarsening Without Surface Tension: The Universality Class of the Voter Model. *Physical Review Letters* 87.

Epstein, J. M. & R. Axtell. (1996). *Growing Artificial Societies: Social Science from the Bottom Up*. Washington, D.C.: Brookings Institution Press, and Cambridge, MA: MIT Press.

Ferguson, N. M., Cummings, D. A., Cauchemez, S., Fraser, C., Riley, S., Meevai, A., Iamsirithaworn, S., & Burke, D. S. (2005). Strategies for Containing an Emerging Influenza Pandemic in Southeast Asia. *Nature*, 437, 209–214.

Floridi, L. (2011). *Philosophy of Information*. Oxford: Oxford University Press.

Galam, S., Y. Gefen & Y. Shapir (1982). Sociophysics: A Mean Behavior Model for the Process of Strike. *Journal of Mathematical Sociology*, 9, 1–13.

Galam, S. & S. Moscovici (1991). Towards a Theory of Collective Phenomena: Consensus and Attitude Changes in Groups. *European Journal of Social Psychology*, 21, 49–74.

Galam, S. (1997). Rational Group Decision Making: A Random Field Ising Model at $T=0$. *Physica A*, 238, 66–80.

Galam, S. (2002). Minority Opinion Spreading in Random Geometry. *European. Physical Journal B*, 25, 403.

Galam. S. (2012). *Sociophysics: A Physicist's Model of Psycho-Political Phenomena*. Berlin: Springer.

Gladwell, Malcolm (2000). *The Tipping Point: How Little Things Can Make a Big Difference*. New York: Little Brown & Co.

Gould, H., J. Tobochnik & W. Christian (2006). *An Introduction to Computer Simulation Methods: Applications to Physical Systems*. San Francisco, CA: Addison-Wesley.

Granovetter, Mark (1973). The Strength of Weak Ties. *American Journal of Sociology*, 78 (6), 1360–1380.

Greenwood, M., A. B. Hill, W. W. C. Topley & J. Wilson (1936). *Experimental Epidemiology*. Privy Council Medical Research Council, London: His Majesty's Stationery Office, 1936.

Grice, H. P. (1989). *Studies in the Ways of Words*. Cambridge, MA: Harvard University Press.

Grim, P. (2009). Threshold Phenomena in Epistemic Networks. *Proceedings, AAAI Fall Symposium on Complex Adaptive Systems and the Threshold Effect*.

Grim, P. (2011). Simulating Grice: Emergent Pragmatics in Spatialized Game Theory. In Anton Benz, Christian Ebert, & Robert van Rooij (Eds.), *Language, Games, and Evolution*, Berlin: Springer-Verlag.

Grim, P., T. Kokalis, A. Alai-Tafti, N. Kilb & P. St. Denis (2004). Making Meaning Happen. *Journal for Experimental and Theoretical Artificial Intelligence*, 16, 209–244.

Grim, P., R. E. Eason, E. Selinger, and R. Rosenberger (2007). What Kind of Science is Simulation? *Journal of Experimental and Theoretical Artificial Intelligence*, 19, 19–28.

Grim, P., C. Reade, D. J. Singer, S. Fisher, & S. Majewicz (2010a). Robustness Cross the Structure of Sub-Networks: The Contrast Between Infection and Information Dynamics. *Proceedings, AAAI Fall Symposium on Complex Adaptive systems: Resilience, Robustness and Evolvability*, FS-10-03.

Grim, P., C. Reade, D. J. Singer, S. Fisher & S. Majewicz (2010b). What You Believe Travels Differently: Information and Infection Dynamics Across Sub-Networks. *Connections*, 30, 50–63.

Grim, P., R. Rosenberger, A. Rosenfeld, B. Anderson, & R. E. Eason (2013a). How Simulations Fail. *Synthese*, 190: 2367–2390.

Grim, P., D. J. Singer, S. Fisher, A. Bramson, W. J. Berger, C. Reade, C. Flocken & A. Sales (2013b). Scientific Networks on Data Landscapes: Question Difficulty, Epistemic Success, and Convergence. *Episteme*, 10, 441–464.

Grim, P., D. J. Singer, C. Reade, & S. Fisher (2015). "Germs, Genes, and Memes: Function and Fitness Dynamics on Information Networks," *Philosophy of Science*, 82, 219–243.

Grimm, V. & S. F. Railsback (2005). *Individual-based Modeling and Ecology*. Princeton, NJ: Princeton University Press.

Gross, T., D'Lima, C. J. D. & Blasius, B. (2006). Epidemic Dynamics on an Adaptive Network. *Physical Review Letters*, 96(20).

Gumerman, G. J., A. C. Swedland, J. S. Dean, & J. M. Epstein (2003). The Evolution of Social Behavior in the Prehistoric American Southwest. *Artificial Life*, 9, 435–444.

Hegselmann, R. & U. Krause (2002). Opinion Dynamics and Bounded Confidence Models, Analysis, and Simulation. *Journal of Artificial Societies and Social Simulation*, 5(3).

Helbing D. (1991). A mathematical model for the behavior of pedestrians. *Behavioral Science*, 36, 298–310.

Hofstadter, Douglas R. (1983). Artificial Intelligence: Subcognition as Computation. In Fritz Machlup (Ed.), *The Study of Information: Interdisciplinary Messages*. Hoboken, NJ: John Wiley & Sons, Inc.

Huttegger, S. M., B. Skyrms, R. Smead & K. Zollman (2010). Evolutionary Dynamics of Lewis Signaling Games: Signaling Systems vs. Partial Pooling. *Synthese*, 172, 177–191.

Hybertson, Duane W. (2009). *Model-oriented Systems Engineering Science: A Unifying Framework for Traditional and Complex Systems*. New York: Auerbach Publications, CRC Press, Taylor & Francis.

Interagency Performance Evaluation Task Force (2006). *Performance Evaluation of the New Orleans and Southeast Louisiana Hurricane Protection System: Draft Final Report of the Interagency Performance Evaluation Task Force*, vol. 1. www.asce.org/files/pdf/executivesummary_v20i.pdf

Kitcher, P. (1990). The Division of Cognitive Labor. *The Journal of Philosophy*, 87, 5–22.

Kitcher, P. (2002). Social Psychology and the Theory of Science. In S. Stich and M. Siegal (Eds.), *The Cognitive Basis of Science*. Cambridge: Cambridge University Press.

Kollman, K., J. H. Miller & S. E. Page (1997). Political Institutions and Sorting in a Tiebout Model. *American Economic Review*, 87 (5), 971–992.

Kollman, K., J. H. Miller & S. E. Page (1999). A Simplified Framework for Analyzing the Behavior of Political Institutions. Working Paper.

Latané, B. (1981). The Psychology of Social Impact. *American Psychologist*, *36*, 343.

Le Bon, G. (1897). *The Crowd: A Study of the Popular Mind*. New York: Macmillan.

Lewis, D. (1969) *Convention*. Oxford: Blackwell.

Lustick, I. & D. Miodownik (2009). Abstractions, Ensembles, and Virtualizations: Simplicity and Complexity in Agent-Based Modeling. *Comparative Politics*, 41, 223–244.

Lynch, A. (1996). *Thought Contagion: How Belief Spreads through Society*. New York: Basic Books.

Macy, M. W. & R. Willer. (2002). From Factors to Actors: Computational Sociology and Agent-based Modeling. *Annual Review of Sociology*, 28, 143–166.

Miller, J. H. & S. E. Page (2007). Social Dynamics. In J. H. Miller & S. E. Page, *Complex Adaptive Systems* (pp. 141–177). Princeton, NJ: Princeton University Press.

Mobilia, M. (2003). Does a Single Zealot Affect an Infinite Group of Voters? *Physical Review Letters* 91.

Newman, M. J. (2003). The Structure and Function of Complex Networks. *SIAM Review*, 45, 167–256.

Nowak, A., J. Szamrej & B. Latané (1990). From Private Attitude to Public Opinion: A Dynamic Theory of Social Impact. *Pychological Review*, 97, 362–376.

Nowak, M., S. Bonhoeffer & R. M. May (1994). Spatial Games and the Maintenance of Cooperation. *Proceedings of the National Academy of Sciences USA*, 91, 4877–4881.

Park, Robert (1904). *Masse und Publikum*. Berlin: Lack & Grunau.

Park, Robert & Ernest Burgess (1921). Collective Behavior. In *Introduction to the Science of Sociology*. Chicago, IL: University of Chicago Press.

Schelling, T. C. (1978). *Micromotives and Macrobehavior*. New York: Norton.

Skyrms, B. (1996). *Evolution of the Social Contract*. Cambridge: Cambridge University Press.

Skyrms, B. (2010). *Signals: Evolution, Learning, and Information*. Oxford: Oxford University Press.

Sterrett, S. (2006). *Wittgenstein Flies a Kite: A Story of Models of Wings and Models of the World*. New York: Pi Press.

Strevens, M. (2003). The Role of the Priority Rule in Science. *Journal of Philosophy*, 100, 55–79.

Vázquez, F., P. L. Krapivsky & S. Redner (2003). Constrained Opinion Dynamics: Freezing and Slow Evolution. *Journal of Physics A. A* 36, L61.

Watts, D. J. (1999) Networks, Dynamics, and the Small-world Phenomenon. *American Journal of Sociology*, 105(2), 493–527.

Watts, D. J. & S. H. Strogatz (1998). Collective Dynamics of "Small-world" Networks. *Nature*, 393, 440–442.

Weisberg, M. & R. Muldoon (2007). Epistemic Landscapes and the Division of Cognitive Labor. *Philosophy of Science*, 76(2): 225–252.

Wiedlich, W. (1971). The Statistical Description of Polarization Phenomena in Society. *British Journal of Mathematical and Statistical Psychology*, 24, 251–266.

Wiedlich, W. (1991). Physics and Social Science – The Approach of Synergetics. *Physics Reports*, 204, 1–163.

Wiedlich, W. (2002). *Sociodynamics – A Systematic Approach to Mathematical Modeling in the Social Sciences*. Abingdon: Taylor & Francis.

Wilhite, A. (2001). Bilateral Trade and "Small-World" Networks. *Computational Economics,* 18, 49–64.

Wolfram, S. (1983). Cellular Automata. *Los Alamos Science,* 9, 2–21

Wolfram, S. (2002). *A New Kind of Science*. Champaign, IL: Wolfram Media.

Zollman, K. (2007). The Communication Structure of Epistemic Communities. *Philosophy of Science*, 74 (5), 574–587.

Zollman, K. (2010). The Epistemic Benefit of Transient Diversity. *Erkenntnis*, 72(1),17–35.

Zollman, K. (2013). Network Epistemology: Communication in Epistemic Communities. *Philosophy Compass*, 8(1), 15–27.

14

THE DECISIONAL VALUE OF INFORMATION

Martin Peterson

Introduction

Information is key to decision making. Everyone agrees that it is better to base decisions on more information rather than less, provided that the information is relevant and reliable. No one thinks that irrelevant or unreliable information is of any positive value. However, decision theorists disagree on how the notions of relevance and reliability should be understood. In this chapter we shall take a close look at the decisional value of information and discuss how the information available to the decision maker can guide deliberative processes.

A key assumption in decision theory is that decisions taken by human agents are triggered by the agent's *beliefs* and *desires*, as proposed by Hume (1739) and others. According to the Humean belief-desire model of rational decision making, your decision to buy a pair of warm gloves in preparation for your upcoming ski vacation in Switzerland was triggered by your belief that it will be cold in the Swiss Alps and your desire to stay warm. Information about beliefs and desires can be represented by propositions such as "I believe it will be cold in Switzerland next week" and "I prefer to pay $100 today to freezing in Switzerland next week." The decision matrix in Table 14.1 illustrates an example in which you are offered a choice between either buying a pair of gloves for $100 or go skiing without gloves. There are two states of the world that are relevant to this decision: "Cold and snowy weather" and "Warm and sunny weather."

Suppose that after having studied the latest weather reports you come to believe that the two states in Table 14.1 are equally probable (and that no other state is possible). This means that your subjective degree of belief in each state is ½. We can establish these probabilities by observing your preferences over a set of gambles and then reason backwards; we do not

Table 14.1 A decision matrix

	Cold and snowy weather	*Warm and sunny weather*
Buy gloves for $100	Warm fingers	No gloves needed, $100 lost
Ski without gloves	Cold fingers	No gloves needed, $100 left for Glühwein

have to ask you to explicitly state any numerical probabilities. We can figure out what your probabilities are based on the information you give to us. Here is how we do this. If you consider two events to be equi-probable rationality requires you to be indifferent between a gamble in which you win a prize you desire (say, $100) if the event occurs and nothing otherwise, and a gamble in which you win the same prize if the event does *not* occur and nothing if it does. Why? Well, if you had not been indifferent between these two gambles, you would have considered the preferred gamble to give you a higher probability of winning the prize, because your desire to win the prize ($100) is the same in both options. Therefore, the only explanation that is consistent with the Humean belief-desire model is that you considered the preferred gamble to give you a higher probability of winning $100. Note that we can also figure out what your desires are by using the same method, that is, by observing your preferences over some cleverly constructed gambles and then reason backwards.

One of the most important results in decision theory is the representation and uniqueness theorem originally stated by Ramsey (1926). What Ramsey showed, although he did not bother to include a formal proof of this in his original paper, is that *if* the decision maker's preferences over a large set of gambles fulfil a set of seemingly reasonable structural conditions, *then* it will always be possible to (i) construct a probability function that measures the agent's degrees of belief and a cardinal utility function that measures her desires, and then (ii) let the probability and utility functions represent the agent's preferences over all possible options open to her in a way that is consistent with the principle of maximizing expected utility. Moreover, this representation will be unique in the sense that there is no alternative representation that is incompatible with the principle of maximizing expected utility. This may all sound a bit technical and intimidating, but once we understand the technical concepts it will become evident that Ramsey's point is fairly simple. First, a *probability function* is a device that assigns a number between 0 and 1 to every proposition representing one of the decision maker's beliefs, which fulfils certain structural conditions which will not be discussed here. (For instance, the probability of a logical truth has to be 1, and the probability of some proposition p plus the probability of the negation of the same proposition p should also equal 1, and so on.) Second, a *cardinal utility function* is a device that assigns numbers to the propositions representing the decision maker's desires; that the function is cardinal just means that the numbers at least tell us something about the difference in value between each pair of desires, i.e. that the difference between a desire worth 50 units and another worth 40 units has to be larger than the difference between 10 and 5 units, because 50 minus 40 is more than 10 minus 5.

In order to explain the principle of maximizing expected utility consider Table 14.2. The numbers in parenthesis in Table 14.2 represent the agent's utility of each outcome on an interval scale. These numbers are established by analyzing information about the agent's preferences over various gambles along the lines explained above.

The expected utility of buying a pair of gloves for $100 is $1/2 \cdot 40 + 1/2 \cdot 80 = 60$ and the expected utility of skiing without gloves is $1/2 \cdot 0 + 1/2 \cdot 100 = 50$. This means that the expected utility of buying a pair of gloves exceeds that of skiing without gloves. Thus, a

Table 14.2 Utility is measured on an interval scale

	Cold and snowy weather (p=1/2)	*Warm and sunny weather (p=1/2)*
Buy gloves for $100	Warm fingers (40)	No gloves needed, $100 lost (80)
Ski without gloves	Cold fingers (0)	No gloves needs, $100 left for Glühwein (100)

rational agent will prefer to buy a pair of gloves for $100 over skiing without gloves. Similar but technically slightly different representation theorems were famously proven by von Neumann and Morgenstern (1947), Savage (1954), and Jeffrey (1983).

Bayes' theorem

Bayes' theorem is one of the most important mathematical result in the philosophy of information. For a general discussion of Bayes' theorem, see Chapter 16. In what follows we just discuss the importance of Bayes' theorem for decision making.

Somewhat generally put, decision theory is a theory about the structure of rational preferences. The theory cannot advise what you ought to prefer. It just tells you that all your preferences should be coherent in the sense that they have to fulfil a set of structural conditions identified by Ramsey (1926) and others. The upshot is that the only information that is *directly* relevant to the decision maker's deliberative process is information about the agent's preferences. If the decision maker's preference change, her decision may also change, but unless she altered her preference because it was incoherent with other preferences the change in preference cannot be explained by the theory.

Needless to say, the reason why a decision maker sometimes changes her preference can be that she receives new information she considers to be relevant to her preference. For example, information about the weather in your favorite Swiss ski resort can be indirectly relevant to your preference for warm gloves, because if you learn that the weather is likely to be cold and snowy during your visit it becomes more attractive to spend $100 on warm gloves.

The literature on how agents ought to update their beliefs in response to the information they receive is very large. The key result in this literature is known in probability theory as Bayes' theorem. In order to explain Bayes' theorem, imagine that you wish to calculate the conditional probability that your flight to your ski vacation in Switzerland will be delayed by more than one hour given that it is snowing at Zurich airport. Statistics show that, of all delays longer than one hour at Zurich airport, 80 percent occur when it is snowing. We can summarize this by writing $p(\text{snow}|\text{delay}) = .80$ (the | is read "given that"). You also know that 5 percent of all flights to Zurich are delayed by more than one hour irrespective of the weather conditions and that the probability that it will be snowing on your chosen day of travel is 10 percent. Again, we can summarize all this information by writing $p(\text{delay}) = .05$: and $p(\text{snow}) = .10$. By definition, the probability that A happens given that B happens is the probability that both happen divided by the probability that B happens, that is:

$$p(A|B) = \frac{p(A \wedge B)}{p(B)}. \text{ It follows that } p(B) \cdot p(A|B) = p(A \wedge B) = p(B \wedge A) = p(A) \cdot p(B|A).$$

This gives us the Inverse Probability Law:

$$p(B|A) = \frac{p(B) \cdot p(A|B)}{p(A)} \text{ given that } p(A) \neq 0 \tag{14.1}$$

By inserting the information given above into (14.1) it can be verified that the conditional probability that your flight to Switzerland will be delayed by more than one hour given that it is snowing in Zurich is 40 percent.

$$p(\text{delay}|\text{snow}) = \frac{.5 \cdot .80}{.10} = .40 \tag{14.2}$$

Although the Inverse Probability Law is useful in many situations, it is not unusual that the unconditional probabilities of events A and B are very difficult or impossible to determine. What is, for instance, the unconditional probability that it will be snowing in Zurich on March 1 next year? You could of course study historic meteorological data for that particular date, but that can also be deeply misleading. If next winter turns out to be very mild it is less likely that it will be snowing on any particular date, no matter what the weather was like in the past.

Bayes' theorem helps us to eliminate at least one of the two unconditional probabilities needed for applying the Inverse Probability Law. Bayes' theorem can be stated in many logically equivalent ways. The following is probably the most transparent formulation:

$$p(\text{B} \mid \text{A}) = \frac{p(\text{B}) \cdot p(\text{A} \mid \text{B})}{p(\text{B}) \cdot p(\text{A} \mid \text{B}) + p(\neg\text{B}) \cdot p(\text{A} \mid \neg\text{B})} \quad \text{given that } p(\text{A}) \neq 0 \tag{14.3}$$

This formula may look more complex than it is. The numerator in this ratio is the probability that B will occur multiplied by the probability that A will occur given that B occurs. Here is an example. Let A be the event "Martin is happy" and B the event "Martin is eating ice cream." The numerator is then the probability that Martin is eating ice cream times the probability that Martin is happy given that he is eating ice cream. Note that the left-hand part of the denominator is exactly the same as the numerator. However, to this number we then have to add the product of two other numbers: the probability that Martin is not eating ice cream times the probability that Martin is happy given that he is not eating ice cream. By calculating the ratio between the numerator and denominator (and we assume that the denominator is non-zero, to avoid division by zero) we can establish the probability that Martin is eating ice cream given that he is happy. Although our example may not be fully realistic, this method for manipulating data is surprisingly often of significant practical value.

In order to prove Bayes' theorem we use (14.1) as our starting point. All we have to show is that $p(\text{A}) = p(\text{B}) \cdot p(\text{A} \mid \text{B}) + p(\neg\text{B}) \cdot p(\text{A} \mid \neg\text{B})$. Note that the axioms of the probability calculus (see Kolmogorov 1956) guarantee that $p(\text{A}) = p(\text{A} \wedge \text{B}) + p(\text{A} \wedge \neg\text{B})$. Recall that

$$p(\text{A} \mid \text{B}) = \frac{p(\text{A} \wedge \text{B})}{p(\text{B})} ,$$

which entails that $p(\text{B}) \cdot p(\text{A} \mid \text{B}) = p(\text{A} \wedge \text{B})$. Therefore, $p(\text{A}) = p(\text{B}) \cdot p(\text{A} \mid \text{B}) + p(\neg\text{B}) \cdot p(a \mid \neg\text{B})$.

Let us now consider yet another flight you plan to make to Zurich. As before, we wish to calculate the conditional probability that your flight to Switzerland will be delayed by more than one hour given that it is snowing at Zurich airport. This time we assume that you do not know the unconditional probability that it will be snowing at Zurich airport on the date of your departure. As before, you know that $p(\text{delay}) = .05$ and that, of all delays longer than one hour at Zurich airport, 80 percent occur when it is snowing: $p(\text{snow}) = .80$. In order to apply Bayes' theorem we also need to know the conditional probability that it is snowing when there is no delay: $p(\text{snow} \mid \neg\text{delay})$. Suppose it is 0.30. Because $p(\text{delay}) = .05$ it follows that $p(\neg\text{delay}) = .95$, so:

$$p(\text{delay} \mid \text{snow}) = \frac{.05 \cdot .80}{[.05 \cdot .80] + [.95 \cdot .30]} = .12 \tag{14.4}$$

Decision making with unknown priors

Bayes' theorem enables the decision maker to adjust her beliefs about the world in ways that fit with the information available to her. However, the formulation of Bayes' theorem stated above requires that the decision maker knows the "prior" probability of an event (the starting point, so to speak), which in the example considered above entails that she needs to know the unconditional probability that it will be snowing in Zurich. Although the agent may sometimes happen to know the prior of some event, there are numerous decisions one can be confronted with in which the prior is unknown (including not knowable in time). Fortunately, there is a way around this problem.

In order to explain how Bayes' theorem can be applied in cases in which the prior is unknown it is helpful to discuss a familiar type of gambling example.[1] In American roulette the wheel has 38 numbered pockets and the house wins 2 times out of 38. Imagine that the first five times the croupier spins the wheel the house wins every single time. When you observe this highly unlikely sequence of events it seems natural to suspect that the wheel might have been manipulated (possibly by the owner of the casino), although it is of course *possible* that the house wins five times in a row even if that is not the case. So the question is: what is the probability that the roulette wheel in front of you is biased given that the house wins five times in a row?

We can solve this problem by applying Bayes' theorem *even if* we do not know the prior probability that the roulette wheel is biased. Let $p(B|5H)$ denote the probability that the wheel is biased given that the house wins five times in row. The outcome of all five spins of the wheel are independent of each other, so

$$p\left(5H \mid \neg B\right) = \left(\frac{1}{19}\right)^5.$$

Suppose you know that, if the wheel is biased, then the house wins with a probability of ½, meaning that

$$p\left(5H \mid \neg B\right) = \left(\frac{1}{2}\right)^5.$$

Note that this probability is *much* higher than the probability of $p(5H|\neg B)$, so your observations seem to fit better with the hypothesis that the wheel is biased. However, the problem is that you do not know the prior probability that the wheel is biased. That is, the unconditional probability $p(B)$ is unknown. All you know is that there is *some* non-zero unconditional probability that the wheel is biased. This means that if we try to apply Bayes' theorem we will face an equation with two unknown variables, $p(B|5H)$ and $p(B)$.

$$p(B \mid 5H) = \frac{p(B) \cdot \left(\frac{1}{2}\right)^5}{\left[p(B) \cdot \left(\frac{1}{2}\right)^5\right] + \left[(1 - p(B)) \cdot \left(\frac{1}{19}\right)^5\right]} \tag{14.5}$$

Although (14.5) may appear to be an unsolvable problem, it is not. The trick is to just randomly choose a non-zero value for $p(B)$. Suppose, for instance, that you randomly set the prior to .01. This is equivalent to saying that, before the croupier spins the wheel the first time, your unconditional probability that the wheel is biased is .01. By inserting this number into Bayes' theorem we find that $p(B|5H) = .9987$. Furthermore, we can easily calculate your conditional probability that the wheel is *not* biased given your observations, that is,

Table 14.3 An application of Bayes' Theorem

Before ("prior probability")	*After ("posterior probability")*
Wheel is biased: $p(B) = .01$	Wheel is biased:
Wheel is not biased: $p(\neg B) = .99$	Wheel is not biased: $= .0013$

$p(\neg B \mid 5H)$. It is .0013. So after having obtained information about the outcome of five spins, each being independent of the others, you have changed you view dramatically. By applying Bayes' theorem you have been able to *update* your initial probability according to the new information you have received. The new probability that the wheel is biased is called the *posterior* probability. Table 14.3 summarizes your information about the roulette wheel before and after having watched the house win five times in a row.

Look at Table 14.3 and recall that the prior probability you assigned to $p(B)$ was just an arbitrary guess. Would it have made a difference if you had instead guessed that $p(B) = .001$ or $p(B) = .5$? No, the final conclusion would have been almost (but not exactly) the same anyway. It can be easily verified that if $p(B) = .001$ then $p(B \mid 5H) = .9872$, and if $p(B) = .5$ then $p(B \mid 5H) = .9999$. The upshot is that the precise numerical value of the prior is not very important to the overall conclusion.

Needless to say, there are of course some possible priors that would yield a different conclusion. For instance, if $p(B) = .0001$ then the posterior probability that the wheel is biased is .8856, which is significantly lower than .9999. In order to overcome this problem we can ask the croupier to spin the wheel a couple of more times. This makes it possible to gather more information. This in turn makes it possible to update the probability by applying Bayes' theorem a second time to the extended data set. In this second calculation we use the "old" posterior probability of .8856 as the "new" prior. For instance, if we observe that the house wins five times in a row in the second experiment, we set the prior to .8856 (which was the posterior obtained in the first calculation) and then find that the new posterior probability is $p(B \mid 5H) = .9999$. So even if the initial prior is extremely low, we nevertheless come to believe that the wheel is biased. This is because we have to acquire new information about the roulette wheel that enables us to "wash out" incorrect prior probabilities. The upshot is that in many cases we do not *need* to know the prior. It will in the end make no or very little difference to the conclusion.

Games and information about other people's behavior

Needless to say, it is not just information about the probability of various events in the world that is relevant to rational decision makers. Another type of information that we often need to take into account is information about how other people behave. For instance, if you and I decide to meet up for dinner in a local restaurant tonight, but you call me one hour before to let me know that you are ill and cannot make it, then this piece of information may affect my decision to go to the restaurant. Perhaps I conclude that I prefer to have dinner at home if I know that you cannot make it to the restaurant.

If we define decision theory as the theory of rational decisions made by individual decision makers in which the outcome does not depend on how other people act, then game theory is the theory of rational decisions made by individuals in which the outcome partly depends on what other people do. A famous example of a type of situation that has been extensively studied by game theorists is the prisoner's dilemma. Let us discuss this well-known game in some detail.[2]

Imagine that two criminals, A and B, have been arrested by the sheriff. The sheriff believes that A and B have robbed a bank, but he cannot prove this unless at least one of them confesses. However, if they deny the bank robbery they can at least be convicted for stealing a car they used in the bank robbery. Theft is of course a less severe crime than robbery. The sheriff puts A and B in separate rooms and instructs them that they have to decide within one hour whether they wish to confess or deny the bank robbery. They have to make their decisions without knowing what the other prisoner decided to do. The sheriff tells the prisoners (see Table 14.4) that if both confess they will be sentenced to fifteen years in prison each, but if one confesses and the other does not, then the prisoner who confesses will get away with just one year while the other prisoner will be punished and sentenced to twenty-five years. If both prisoners deny the charges they will be sentenced to two years each.

The outcome –1, –25 in Table 14.4 is the outcome in which A has to serve one year in prison and B twenty-five. Just like all other prisoners, A and B wish to minimize the number of years in prison.

What makes this game interesting is that if both players (prisoners) are rational, and if both know that the other player is rational and has access to the same information, then both players will confess the bank robbery. This is surprising (unless you are an expert in game theory) because both prisoners would both have been better off if they had cooperated with each other and denied the charges. When each individual decision maker does what is best for her, the outcome gets worse for everyone.

Does it matter if the two prisoners get an opportunity to meet with each other before they tell the sheriff whether they confess or deny the charges? The answer is that as long as the numbers in the game matrix (see Table 14.4) represents everything the prisoners care about, it does not matter what they agree upon before they make their decision. Even if they promise each other to deny the charges, it will be rational for both A and B to break the promise and confess, no matter what they believe the other prisoner will do. It is impossible for rational players to cooperate in a prisoner's dilemma that is played only once and has the mathematical structure described above.

Many important problems in the real world have the same structure as the prisoner's dilemma, including many environmental problems. Global warming can, for instance, be analyzed as a prisoner's dilemma with n players in which it is optimal for each player (a country or an individual person) to emit more carbon dioxide than the planet can cope with, at the same time as we all know that when all n players do this, the outcome for all of us will be very bad.

It should be stressed that the analysis of the prisoner's dilemma depends on how many times the game is played. It can be played once, a finite number of times, or indefinitely many times.

In a one-shot prisoner's dilemma the conclusion is, as explained above, that when everybody does what is rational for him or her, the outcome for all of all players is worse than it would have been if the players had cooperated, but as long as all players are rational they will not cooperate.

Table 14.4 The Prisoner's dilemma

		B	
		Deny	*Confess*
	Deny	–2, –2	–25, –1
A	*Confess*	–1, –25	–15, –15

If the prisoner's dilemmas is repeated a finite number of times, and both players know already at the outset that this is the case, we can analyze this repeated prisoner's dilemma by reasoning backwards. Imagine, for instance, that you and I play the prisoner's dilemma once a day for seven days. We know already at the beginning of the week that we will not cooperate in the last round of the game on Sunday, because no matter what happens in the first six rounds we both benefit from not cooperating in the last round. Moreover, when we play the penultimate round on Saturday we know that we will not cooperate on Sunday, so we have no incentive to cooperate in the penultimate round. If we were to cooperate in the penultimate round that would not make cooperation in the last round more likely. This in turn entails, for the same reason, that it would be irrational to cooperate on Friday and in every round before that. The upshot is that rational and fully informed players who play a prisoner's dilemma that is repeated a finite number of times will not cooperate in any single round of the game.

However, the consensus view in the literature is that the most realistic and common type of repeated prisoner's dilemma are prisoner's dilemmas that are repeated an *indefinite* number of times. Note that an indefinitely repeated prisoner's dilemma need not be repeated an *infinite* number of times. All that is required is that there is no pre-determined and known last round of the game, meaning that, in every round, both players believe that there is some non-zero probability that the game will be played again. If this condition is fulfilled, it becomes important for both players to consider how the opponent will respond to the possible moves, because the backwards induction argument is no longer applicable. For instance, if player A decides to confess (not cooperate) there is a risk that B will punish him for that in the next round, but if A on the other hand denied the charges (cooperates) this may make B more willing to cooperate in the next round. Game theorists have shown that, under a wide range of assumptions about the information available to the players, it is often rational for them to cooperate in indefinitely repeated prisoner's dilemmas.

The game discussed in this section, the prisoner's dilemma, is of course just one of many different types of games. The prisoner's dilemma is not the only type of game that is worth attention by philosophers and others interested in rational decision making. Nash (1950), Luce and Raiffa (1957), Resnik (1993) as well as Peterson (2009) and (2015) provide extensive discussions of many other games.

Causal vs evidential information

So far we have assumed that the information considered to be relevant to an agent's decision is information about how the performance of an act casually influences its outcome. For instance, if you buy a pair of warm gloves (and wear them), this triggers a causal process in which your hands stay warm even when the temperature falls below freezing. However, one of the most prolific debates in decision theory concerns the role of information about causal processes for rational decision making. Much of this discussion has focused on a famous example known as Newcomb's problem.

Imagine that Alice is the team leader of a group of super-duper psychologists. The team, which we call the Prediction Team (PT), is extremely good at predicting people's choices. In fact, recent statistics show that 99 percent of all predictions made by PT are accurate. Now suppose that in front of you are two boxes, B_1 and B_2. Box B_1 is transparent and you can see that Alice has put $1,000 in it. If you decide to take only box B_1 you therefore know for sure that you will get $1,000. The second box, B_2, is not transparent, but you know that it either contains $1,000,000 or nothing.

Table 14.5 Newcomb's problem

	Second box contains $1M	*Second box is empty*
Take second box only	$1M (prob. .99)	$0 (prob. .01)
Take both boxes	$1M + $1,000 (prob. .01)	$1000 (prob. .99)

You are now offered the following choice. You either take just box B_2, or both B_1 and B_2. Just before you make your choice you are informed that just in case PT has predicted that you will take the second box only, Alice will put $1,000,000 in the second box. Moreover, just in case PT has predicted that you will take both boxes, then Alice has put nothing in the second box. You know for sure that the causal process in this situation is as follows: first PT makes its prediction, then Alice adjusts the content of the second box according to PT's prediction. A few minutes later you make your choice. Note that once Alice has put the money in the second box she cannot reverse her decision or do anything that affects its content. Whatever is in the boxes when you make your decision stays in the boxes until you open them. Alice cannot alter the past. The two alternatives open to you are thus as follows:

Alternative 1 Take box B_1 ($1,000) and box B_2 (either $0 or $1M).
Alternative 2 Take only box B_2 (either $0 or $1M).

The first philosopher to discuss this decision problem in print was Robert Nozick (1969), who attributes it to his friend William Newcomb. Nozick points out that one can look at Newcomb's problem in two fundamentally different ways. To start with, one can argue that the only option that is rationally permissible is to take both boxes. No matter whether Alice, the team leader of PT, has put $1,000,000 in the second box or not, you know that you get whatever is in the second box ($0 or $1,000,000) plus $1000 from box one if you take both boxes, depending on PT's prediction. Your choice does not causally influence PT's prediction, which was made before you made your choice. In light of this, it seems that the only rationally permissible option is to take both boxes, because if you do so you will always get $1000 more than if you take just one box. Taking two boxes dominates taking one box.

The crux with this argument is that its conclusion is incompatible with another argument which appears to be equally compelling. According to this alternative argument, you ought to take the second box only. In order to explain why, we can imagine that one thousand people have been confronted with the same decision problem before you. About half of them chose to take only the second box, and because PT's prediction is almost always correct, nearly all the people who took only one box became millionaires. The other half, who took both boxes, won just $1000 almost without exception.

It seems reasonable to require that a rational decision maker should take this information into account. Consider Table 14.5. By applying the principle of maximizing expected utility we find that the expected utility of taking only the second box is $.99 \cdot u(\$1M) + .01 \cdot u(\$0)$ = $.99 \cdot 1,000,000 + .01 \cdot 0$ = $990,000$, while the expected utility of taking both boxes is $.01 \cdot u(\$1M) + .99 \cdot u(\$0) = .01 \cdot 1,000,000 + .99 \cdot 0 = 10,000$. Because $990,000 > 10,000$ it follows that a rational agent will take the second box only.

At least one of the two arguments outlines above has to be wrong, because the conclusions are incompatible. For quite some time, the so-called *causal* analysis dominated the debate (Skyrms 1982). According to the casual analysis it is indeed rational to take both boxes, because a rational agent should only consider information that is causally relevant to her decision. The mistake people make if they take only one box is that they take causally irrelevant information into account. It is simply a mistake to think that you increase the probability of finding $1,000,000 in the second box by taking only that box. The money either is or is not in the box when you make your choice, so data about how other people have chosen in the past is irrelevant.

However, as is often the case with philosophical debates, people on the other side also have some good arguments to offer. According to the so-called *evidential* analysis, we are rationally permitted to take all evidence about a decision problem into account when making a decision, irrespective of its causal structure. Consider, for instance, the following seemingly simple decision problem proposed by Andy Egan. We are told that, before Paul is confronted with the scenario described below, he is informed by a reliable person that the number of psychopaths in the world is fairly low:

> Paul is debating whether to press the "kill all psychopaths" button. It would, he thinks, be much better to live in a world with no psychopaths. Unfortunately, Paul is quite confident that only a psychopath would press such a button. Paul very strongly prefers living in a world *with* psychopaths to dying. Should Paul press the button?
>
> *(Egan 2007: 97)*

Many people agree with Egan that Paul should not press the button, because if he does it seems likely that he will die himself. The crux is that Paul, if he were to press the button, would learn he is probably a psychopath himself. That is, Paul's own behavior seems in this case to be of *evidential* value for him, although the causal process is fixed once and for all. Paul already is a psychopath or not, no matter whether he decides to press the green button.

It seems that the only certain conclusion we can draw about the debate over causal and evidential decision theory at the moment is that the debate has not be settled yet. New and interesting arguments are likely to appear in the future.

Conclusions and some open problems

In this chapter we have considered the decisional value of information. The point of departure was the trivial idea that as the value of information increases the more reliable and relevant it is for the decision to be taken. A large part of the chapter was devoted to explaining the notions of "relevance" and "reliability" in probabilistic terms.

It is worth emphasizing that the focus on probabilistic reasoning in this chapter reflects the attention given in the academic literature to probability theory (not just by philosophers, but also by computer scientists, mathematicians, economists, psychologists, and others). That said, there are many open problems in the literature on which there is little consensus on how to solve.

There are, for instance, cases in which it is *in principle* possible to apply Bayes' theorem and other mathematical techniques, but in which it is unclear whether this is really the right approach. A good example of this is the debate in the 1990s about trichloroethylene. This is a clear non-flammable liquid commonly used as a solvent for a variety of organic materials. It was first introduced in the 1920s and widely used for a variety of purposes until the 1970s, when suspicions arose that trichloroethylene could be toxic. A number of scientific studies of trichloroethylene were initiated and in the 1990s researchers at the US National Cancer Institute showed that trichloroethylene is carcinogenic in animals, but there was no consensus on whether it was also a human carcinogen. A strict advocate of Bayesian reasoning would insist that the scientists participating in this debate should have updated their probability that trichloroethylene is a human carcinogen by applying Bayes' theorem. But this seems to have been a fairly *unrealistic ideal*, which we cannot demand that scientists actually use when human lives are at stake. On the contrary, there may be a need for non-technical models that are easier to apply to real-world problems.

There are also a number of open, more technical problems faced by advocates of probabilistic reasoning. Here is an example. Some events that actually occur in the real world have probability 0, but in the probability calculus the number 0 is reserved for events that are impossible, and therefore certain not to occur. Imagine, for instance, that you randomly throw a dart on the line of real numbers between 0 and 1. It is possible that the center of the dart hits the real line exactly on the ½ mark. But this event has probability 0, because there are infinitely many real numbers between 0 and 1 and all outcomes are equally probable. So if you assign some positive probability to all of them the sum will be infinite, which violates the laws of the probability calculus. One way of dealing with events that have probability 0 but may nevertheless occur is to represent their likelihood to occur with some other numerical structure, such as hyperreal numbers (hyperreal numbers are a special kind of very large or very small numbers discovered in the 1960s by Abraham Robinson), but there is no consensus on whether this solves the problem or not.

Notes

1 The following example comes from my textbook *An Introduction to Decision Theory*, pp. 127–129. Here I have shortened the explanations somewhat.
2 The literature on the prisoner's dilemma is very extensive. For an overview, see the introductory chapter to *The Prisoner's Dilemma* (ed. M. Peterson, CUP 2015). The discussion in this section is based on this chapter.

References

Egan, A. (2007) "Some Counterexamples to Causal Decision Theory," *The Philosophical Review*, 166: 93–114.

Hume, D. (1739/1888) *A Treatise of Human Nature*, ed. by L.A. Selby-Bigge.

Jeffrey R. (1983) *The Logic of Decision*, 2nd ed., Chicago, IL: University of Chicago Press.

Kolmogorov, A. N. (1956) *Foundations of the Theory of Probability*, transl. by N Morrison, New York: Chelsea Publishing Company.

Luce D. and H. Raiffa (1956) *Games and Decisions: Introduction and Critical Survey*, Hoboken, NJ: John Wiley & Sons, Inc.

Nash, J. (1950) "Non-Cooperative Games," unpublished diss., Princeton University.

Nozick, R. (1969) "Newcomb's Problem and Two Principles of Choice," in N. Rescher *et al.* (eds), *Essays in Honor of Carl G. Hempel*, Dordrecht: Reidel, pp. 114–146.

Peterson, M. (2009) *An Introduction to Decision Theory*, Cambridge: Cambridge University Press.

Peterson, M. (2015) *The Prisoner's Dilemma*, Cambridge: Cambridge University Press.

Ramsey F. P. (1926) "Truth and Probability," in F. P. Ramsey, 1931, *The Foundations of Mathematics and other Logical Essays*, Ch. VII, 156–198, edited by R. B. Braithwaite, London: Kegan, Paul, Trench, Trubner & Co., New York: Harcourt, Brace and Company.

Resnik, M. (1993) *Choices. An Introduction to Decision Theory*, Minneapolis, MN: University of Minnesota Press.

Robinson, A. (1996), *Non-standard Analysis*, Princeton, NJ: Princeton University Press.

Savage, L. J. (1954) *The Foundations of Statistics* (2nd edition 1972). Hoboken, NJ: John Wiley and Sons, Inc.

Skyrms, B. (1982) "Causal Decision Theory," *Journal of Philosophy* 79: 695–711.

von Neumann J., and O. Morgenstern (1947) *Theory of Games and Economic Behavior* (2nd ed.) 1947, Princeton, NJ: Princeton University Press. (1st ed. 1944, without utility theory).

15

THE PHILOSOPHY
OF MATHEMATICAL
INFORMATION

Marcello D'Agostino

Introduction: is there any content to this chapter?

It is somewhat ironical that, for some philosophically sophisticated readers, the very topic of this chapter, the concept of mathematical information, should be empty. Indeed, according to a time-honored philosophical tradition, there is no such thing as "mathematical information." This tradition, which started with the Vienna Circle and later became known as "logical neopositivism" or "logical empiricism" or also "logical positivism," maintained that the trademark of logical and mathematical statements, which separates them from all the other scientific statements, is that they are "tautological" and convey no information. This view was one of the basic tenets of the Vienna Circle, as clearly stated in the manifesto of logical neopositivism:

> The conception of mathematics as tautological in character, which is based on the investigations of Russell and Wittgenstein, is also held by the Vienna Circle. It is to be noted that this conception is opposed not only to apriorism and intuitionism, but also to the older empiricism (for instance of J.S. Mill), which tried to derive mathematics and logic in an experimental-inductive manner as it were.
>
> *(Hahn et al., 1973, p. 311)*

According to Rudolf Carnap, one of the most eminent members of the Vienna Circle, there is a fundamental distinction between the empirical sentences and the "mathematico-logical" ones. The former are "real sentences," they are "synthetic" and have content, while the latter are "analytic," have no content and are "merely formal auxiliaries" (Carnap, 1937, p. xiv). Unlike genuine informative sentences, mathematico-logical sentences cannot possibly be false, unless they are formally contradictory, simply because they "say nothing" about the world (Wittgenstein, 1961, 4.461). They are true or false in virtue of the rules of language that fix the meaning of the words, not in virtue of fact (Carnap, 1937, p. 116).

This position was intended to reconcile the basic tenet of empiricism – experience is the *only* source of knowledge – with the fundamental claim that logic and mathematics are infallible. In this way it appeared to provide a satisfactory explanation of logic and mathematics that avoided Kant's appeal to the creative power of "pure reason" as well as the excessive empiricism of John Stuart Mill, which was seen as undermining the necessity and certainty of mathematical truths. Despite its philosophical appeal, however, it is out of question that the idea that mathematics is utterly uninformative clashes with the layman's intuition and, as J.S. Mill would have put it, "a person must have made some advances in philosophy to believe it." [1]

Suppose that next week someone comes up with a proof that settles one of the six still unsolved millennium problems, such as the "$P = NP$?" question or the Riemann hypothesis. It would be very hard to say that a solution to one of them would not be informative: anyone will remain uncertain about the solution until a proof is obtained. So, recalling "the old important idea that information equals elimination of uncertainty" (Hintikka, 1973, pp. 228–229) we cannot help admitting that a positive or negative answer would provide us with genuinely new information, although it would not be a case of empirical discovery. Thus, the fundamental question we address in this chapter is: How can we vindicate the layman's intuition? In what sense, if any, is mathematics informative?

A minimal answer to a big question

We can already hear the more analytically oriented reader complain that, before starting our investigation, we should first clarify what we mean by "information." Unfortunately, taking this question seriously would amount to a show stopper. We cannot but agree with Floridi that "this is the hardest and most central problem in the philosophy of information," and that "information is still an elusive concept" (Floridi, 2011, p. 30). Although such a clarification is of paramount importance – and we hope that this Handbook will substantially contribute to it – we also maintain that a good deal of interesting problems can be fruitfully discussed independently of a fully satisfactory theory on the nature of information. Therefore, we shall adopt, as a working hypothesis, a *minimal* notion of information that is precise enough to support philosophical investigation and, at the same time, reasonably close to the layman's intuitive notion.

We take as our starting point the *operational* view that, whatever its nature may be, information manifests itself in an agent's disposition to *answer questions*. The fact that I hold information about Luciano Floridi's mobile number manifests itself in my disposition to answer the question "what is Luciano's mobile number?" Conversely, lack of information manifests itself in an agent's disposition to *abstain* from answering (or, equivalently, answering "I don't know"). It may well be that the answer is not immediately available to me, but that I have a *procedure* for obtaining it with relatively little effort and consumption of resources. For example, it may be that I can't remember Luciano's number, but I can quickly retrieve it from the contact list stored in my own mobile, in which case it would certainly sound bizarre to answer "I don't know." On the other hand, if I have no easy access to Luciano's number, I would answer "I don't know" even if there is an effective procedure that would allow me, *in principle*, to find it out, for example by dialing all the possible 10-digit numbers (assuming that 10 is the usual number of digits of a mobile number). What counts then is whether or not we possess not only an effective procedure that allows us to answer a question "effortlessly," but a *feasible* one that provides an answer within *bounded resources*. Reasonable bounds may then depend on (i) the resources available to us, (ii) the resources required to understand the question and, (iii) maybe also the "value" of the information in question. The existence of such a procedure ensures that the answer is always *practically* available for further use (including further question answering), and so is not informative, while its absence implies that the answer conveys genuinely new information.

Although admittedly vague, this notion appears to be firmly rooted in the ordinary usage of the word "information" and we can safely adopt it as a first approximation to an operational definition. Of course, there is no claim that this is the only reasonable operational notion of information, and not even that it does not require further analysis (it does), but only that it is a reasonable minimal notion that considerably overlaps with ordinary usage, complies with its operational connotations and is good enough for our philosophical task in this chapter.

Are the axioms of a mathematical theory really uninformative?

If we focus on axiomatized mathematical theories, like Euclidean Geometry or Peano Arithmetic, the claim that such theories are (not) "tautological" can be analyzed into two distinct components: (i) the axioms are (not) tautological; (ii) the inference process that leads from the axioms to the theorems is (not) tautological. (Typically, in mathematics the inference process is assumed to be some form of logical deduction.) In the context of this chapter by saying that a *sentence* is "tautological" we mean that it carries no information, while by saying that an *inference* is "tautological" we mean that its conclusion carries no *new* information with respect to its premises.[2]

According to J.S. Mill's radical empiricism, logical and mathematical axioms are not tautological for the simple reason that their nature is just as empirical as that of any other scientific truth:

> It remains to inquire, what is the ground of our belief in axioms – what is the evidence on which they rest? I answer, they are experimental truths; generalizations from observation.
>
> *(Mill, 1882, p. 286)*

As mentioned above, Carnap and the other members of the Vienna Circle found this view quite unpalatable. First, it appeared to derogate from the certainty of logic and mathematics. Second, as Carnap himself explains in his intellectual autobiography, the Viennese were strongly influenced by Frege and Russell's opposite view that "all mathematical concepts can be defined on the basis of the concepts of logic and that the theorems of mathematics can be deduced from the principles of logic" (Carnap, 1963, p. 46).[3] In Frege's view, the axioms of a mathematical theory are "self-evident," in the sense that they are "beyond a reasonable doubt by someone who fully understands the relevant propositions" (Burge, 1998, p. 312). Here "self-evident" does not mean "obvious" in a psychological sense, but something that justifies itself, i.e., requires no other grounds to be recognized as true. Occasionally, Frege conceded that correctly recognizing the self-evidence of some propositions may be somewhat demanding for a less-than-ideal agent.[4] From this point of view, a self-evident proposition may not be obvious, and can be perceived as informative by non-ideal agents. Conversely, some propositions may seem obvious to non-ideal agents without being self-evident or even true. These remarks were dramatically confirmed by the discovery of Russell's paradox (1901), which showed that Frege's Axiom V of his *Grundgesetze der Arhitmetik* (1893) was so far from being self-evident as to be inconsistent.

In any case, Frege's view suggested to the neopositivists what Imre Lakatos would have called "a progressive problem shift," from Kant's old question "how is pure mathematics possible" to the more accessible question "how is logical certainty possible"? They thought that the answer to this new question was to be found in Wittgenstein's view "that all logical truths are tautological, that is they hold necessarily in every possible case, therefore they do not exclude any case, and do not say anything about the facts of the world" (Carnap, 1963, p. 46). So, a typical logical truth such as "it rains or it does not rain" conveys no information: "I know nothing about the weather, when I know that it rains or does not rain" (Wittgenstein, *Tractatus*, 4.461). In this spirit, in the middle of the 20th century Bar-Hillel and Carnap's theory of "semantic information"[5] – which was meant to provide a semantic counterpart to Shannon and Weaver's purely syntactic theory of information – closed the circle, by providing what is, to date, the most comprehensive theoretical framework for Wittgenstein's thesis. Roughly speaking, this theory simply identifies the information conveyed by a sentence with the set of all "possible worlds" that are excluded by it. Bar-Hillel and Carnap showed also how this theory can be extended to first-order languages, i.e., to languages containing the usual quantifiers "for all" and "for some" as well as the standard Boolean operators. A straightforward consequence of Bar-Hillel and Carnap's theory is that all logical truths of the theory of quantification are equally uninformative (they exclude no possible world).[6]

Is deduction really uninformative?

Whatever position one may hold about the axioms of a mathematical theory, the problem of mathematical information remains at center-stage in the following form: is the information carried by a theorem really *contained* in the information (if any) carried by the axioms? Even if the axioms are regarded as informative, the conditional "If $A_1, \dots, A_n$, then T," where the axioms $A_1, \dots, A_n$ are incorporated as hypotheses in the antecedent, is itself a logical truth. Now, if logical truths are tautological, deductive reasoning "cannot lead to new knowledge but only to an explication or transformation of the knowledge contained in the premises" (Carnap, 1963, p. 46), which again clashes with the fact that many mathematical theorems do provide us with information that does not seem to be *available* just by grasping the axioms. Should we just dismiss this intuitive difficulty as philosophically naive, and content ourselves with claiming that the information carried by T was indeed already available, albeit implicitly, in the axioms? Or should we take it seriously and look into the possibility that deductive reasoning may, under certain conditions, generate information that is genuinely new?

The first position was strongly supported by most members of the Vienna Circle. Moritz Schlick, for example, in his *Allgemeine Erkenntnislehre* remarked that "exact inference is often credited with making a greater contribution than is within its power" (Schlick, 1974, p. 108). By contrast, he insisted that "the conclusion of a syllogism never contains knowledge that is not already assumed as valid in the major premiss or, perhaps, in both premises of the inference" and that the syllogism "is not an instrument by which new knowledge can be procured" (Schlick, 1974, p. 108). Indeed, a complex deduction may well have a great *psychological value*. "There may of course be cases where the conclusions of syllogistic procedures, say the results of some calculation, do astonish us and present us with unexpected findings." But this "shows merely that psychologically the final outcome was not conceived of along with the major premiss" and "does not mean that the end result is not contained logically in the major premiss" (Schlick, 1974, p. 111).

Despite being at odds with the layman intuitive judgment, this view that deductive reasoning is "objectively" uninformative caught on and became part of the logical folklore. In fact, it was not just a philosophical oddity of the neopositivists, but an idea firmly rooted in modern philosophy that can be found in such diverse authors as Bacon, Descartes, Kant and Mill. In his *Grundlagen*, Frege referred to it as to "the legend of the sterility of pure logic" (Frege, 1960, p. 24) and eighty years later Jaakko Hintikka still called it a true "scandal of deduction":

C.D. Broad has called the unsolved problems concerning induction a scandal of philosophy. It seems to me that in addition to this scandal of induction there is an equally disquieting scandal of deduction. Its urgency can be brought home to each of us by any clever freshman who asks, upon being told that deductive reasoning is "tautological" or "analytical" and that logical truths have no "empirical content" and cannot be used to make "factual assertions": in what other sense, then, does deductive reasoning give us new information? Is it not perfectly obvious there is some such sense, for what point would there otherwise be to logic and mathematics?

(Hintikka, 1973, p. 222)

This scandal has recently received renewed attention leading to a number of original contributions (e.g., Primiero 2008, Chapter 2; Sequoiah- Grayson 2008; Sillari 2008; D'Agostino & Floridi 2009; Duzí 2010; Jago 2013; Allo & Mares 2012). In the next three sections we shall illustrate the attempts made by distinguished philosophers such as Mill, Frege and Hintikka to account for an objective and non-purely psychological sense in which deductive reasoning, the only allowed kind of inference in mathematics, can indeed be informative.

Mill on the inductive nature of deductive reasoning

According to Mill a real inference is always "a progress from the known to the unknown: a means of coming to the knowledge of something we did not know before" (Mill, 1882, p. 227). Is then deductive reasoning ("ratiocination") a real inference? The answer, for Mill, is that what is usually called "deduction" is nothing but induction in disguise. The following inference:

All men are mortal
The Duke of Wellington is a man
The Duke of Wellington is mortal

is just a device to "decode" the inductive information, based on past experience, that had been previously encoded in the general statement "All men are mortal." The allegedly "deductive" step does nothing but extending this empirical knowledge to a new case (Mill, 1882, p. 224).

When, therefore, we conclude from the death of John and Thomas, and every other person we ever heard of in whose case the experiment had been fairly tried, that the Duke of Wellington is mortal like the rest; we may, indeed, pass through the generalization, All men are mortal, as an intermediate stage; but it is not in the latter half of the process, the descent from all men to the Duke of Wellington, that the inference resides. The inference is finished when we have asserted that all men are mortal. What remains to be performed afterward is merely deciphering our own notes.

(Mill, 1882, p. 232)

So, every mathematical inference is, in essence, inductive and "the general proposition on which it is said to depend, may, in certain cases, be altogether omitted, without impairing its probative force" (Mill, 1882, p. 237). A mathematical proof can always be described as a sequence of steps from particular truths to particular truths, each of which is grounded on experience. This is apparent in the ordinary process of proving a geometrical theorem by means of a diagram, where we reason on a *specific case*, by performing a thought-experiment, as it were, whereby we perceive that the same reasoning process could be indefinitely replicated in similar conditions (see Mill, 1882, p. 238). However, although each single step is ultimately based on experience, in mathematics this experience is so "superabundant" (Mill, 1882, p. 310) that the steps appear to be "obvious." Thus, the appeal to induction, by itself, fails to explain the apparent informativity of mathematical reasoning. Mill is aware of this difficulty:

> It might seem to follow, if all reasoning be induction, that the difficulties of philosophical investigation must lie in the inductions' exclusively, and that when these were easy, and susceptible of no doubt or hesitation, there could be no science, or, at least, no difficulties in science. The existence, for example, of an extensive Science of Mathematics, requiring the highest scientific genius in those who contributed to its creation, and calling for a most continued and vigorous exertion of intellect in order to appropriate it when created, may seem hard to be accounted for on the foregoing theory.
>
> *(Mill, 1882, p. 267–268)*

This brings us back to square one. What is, then, the source of mathematical information? According to Mill, an answer can be found by considering that, in most interesting cases, a reasoning process does not consist in a single chain of obvious inductive steps but in the combination of several such chains that converge to a conclusion. Hence, the mystery of mathematical information is dissipated simply by observing that "even when the inductions themselves are obvious, there may be much difficulty in finding whether the particular case which is the subject of inquiry comes within them; and ample room for scientific ingenuity in so combining various inductions, as, by means of one within which the case evidently falls, to bring it within others in which it cannot be directly seen to be included" (Mill, 1882, pp. 267–268). To use the working operational definition of Section 2, we might say that a mathematical theorem is informative when, because of the unforeseeable complexity of the reasoning process, we have no feasible procedure to obtain it within reasonably bounded cognitive/computational resources.

Frege on the ampliative power of deduction

As is well known, Frege totally rejected Mill's "preconception that all knowledge is empirical" and severely criticized Mill's inductivist view of logic and mathematics (see Frege, 1960, §§7–10). However, like Mill, he maintained that deductive reasoning is informative. Interestingly enough, his main argument for this claim was based on the very same premise – namely the thesis that arithmetic can be reduced to logic – that, later on, led the neopositivists to claim that mathematical statements have no information content. While the neopositivists used this premise together with Wittgenstein's idea that logic is tautological to conclude that arithmetic is also tautological, Frege used it together with the intuitive judgment that arithmetic is not tautological to conclude, by *modus tollens*, that logic is not tautological either. Given the reduction of arithmetic to logic, he believed that:

> the prodigious development of arithmetical studies, with their multitudinous applications, will suffice to put an end to the widespread contempt for analytic judgments and to the legend of the sterility of pure logic.
>
> *(Frege, 1960, p. 24)*

Notice that from this passage it is clear that Frege does not use the word "analytic" as synonymous with "tautological" in the sense of "uninformative" (on this point see also note 12 in the tenth section below), but in the foundational sense of being grounded on purely logical truths. Indeed, it is clear enough from §23 of the *Grundlagen* that Frege regarded arithmetical truth as informative albeit being "analytic" in this sense. Then, the same question keeps coming up: "Can the great tree of the science of number as we know it, towering, spreading and still continually growing, have its roots in bare identities? How do the empty forms of logic come to disgorge so rich a content?" (Frege, 1960, p. 22). Frege's answer is that the informativeness of deductive reasoning stems from a single source, namely the labor required to extract remote conclusions from the premises. In deductive reasoning the conclusions are contained in the premises "as plants are contained in their seeds, not as beams are contained in a house" (Frege, 1960, p. 101). The growth of a plant from seed to tree is indeed a resource-consuming process. As explained by Dummett (Dummett, 1991, Chapter 4), deduction is for Frege a creative process that cannot be reduced to a mechanical one. Its creative aspect lies in the discernment – by a process of dissection – of suitable patterns that are hidden in judgments and may be used to connect them in a deductive chain. When quantifiers are involved, this creativity is necessary even to carry out very basic steps, such as inferring the conclusion:

(1) There is a body such that, either Jupiter is larger than it and it is larger than Mars, or Mars is larger than it and it is larger than Jupiter.

from the premise

(2) Either Jupiter is larger than Neptune and Neptune is larger than Mars, or Mars is larger than Neptune and Neptune is larger than Jupiter.

This amounts to what we call an introduction of the existential quantifier, which is a primitive rule in Gentzen's "natural deduction." [7] The creative act here is that of discerning, in the premise (2) the complex predicate "either Jupiter is larger than x and x is larger than Mars, or Mars is larger than x and x is larger than Jupiter" as a pattern that allows one to see that the conclusion follows from the premise. As Dummett points out, this discernment is, in fact, preliminary to the formation of the quantified proposition that, in Frege's own language, represents (1), namely:

(3) For some x, either Jupiter is larger than x and x is larger than Mars, or Mars is larger than x and x is larger than Jupiter.

As Dummett puts it:

This predicate is not a component of the proposition it was extracted by dissection, in that we do not have to recognize its presence in order to grasp the content of the proposition; but it is a component of the quantified proposition.

(Dummett, 1991, p. 42)

Although, in some sense, the predicate "is there" to be discerned in (2), its discernment involves an act of pattern recognition, which is sometimes rendered complex by the fact that a single sentence may contain several such patterns, depending on how it is "dissected" into "functions" and "arguments." For example, consider the sentence "Cato killed Cato." Then:

If we here think of "Cato" as replaceable at its first occurrence, "to kill Cato" is the function; if we think of "Cato" as replaceable at its second occurrence, "to be killed by Cato" is the function; if, finally, we think of "Cato" as replaceable at both occurrences, "to kill oneself" is the function.

(Frege, 1967, p. 22)

Thus, for Frege constructing a deduction, unlike checking it for correctness, is not a mechanical process, but has "a creative component involving the apprehension of patterns within the thought expressed and relating them to one another, that are not required for a grasp of those thoughts themselves" (Dummett, 1991, p. 42). This is again in tune with our working definition of information given in the second section. The informativity of deduction stems from the fact that we don't have a practical procedure to construct a proof in a quantificational language, and that this activity requires considerable, and in general unpredictable, effort in order to recognize those patterns, among the many that can be discerned in the sentences that enter the proof, which are shared by other sentences and can therefore be fruitfully used to connect them. This seems to solve the paradox of deduction, namely the paradox of how deduction can, at the same time, be valid and fruitful:

Since [deduction] has this creative component, a knowledge of the premises of an inferential step does not entail a knowledge of the conclusion, even when we attend to them simultaneously; and so deductive reasoning can yield new knowledge. Since the relevant patterns need to be discerned, such reasoning is fruitful; but since they are there to be discerned, its validity is not called in question.

(Dummett, 1991, p. 42)

In conclusion of this section, we observe that (i) Frege's explanation of the source of deductive information applies only to reasoning in quantificational languages and does not apply at all to propositional logic; (ii) it, admittedly, applies to the process of "dissection" of sentences and concept-formation, which is preliminary to the specification of sentences in a formalized quantificational language; when the expressive resources are specified from the outset, it fails to capture the labor that is anyway needed to obtain the conclusion from the premises. This is now particularly evident in light of the then unknown undecidability of logical consequence in quantificational languages.

Hintikka on the informativity of quantification logic

In 1935–1936 we learned, as a result of independent investigations of Alan Turing and Alonzo Church, that the logic of quantification is undecidable, that is, there is no mechanical procedure that allows us to answer "yes" or "no" to all questions of the form "is φ a logical consequence of $\psi_1,\ldots, \psi_n$?" when $\varphi, \psi_1,\ldots, \psi_n$ are sentences of a fixed quantificational language containing at least one non-monadic predicate (e.g., a binary relation). The completeness theorem proved by Kurt Gödel (1929) ensured that there is, however, a semidecision procedure. Since there are proof systems (e.g., those based on the axioms and inference rules given by Whitehead and Russell in their *Principia Mathematica*) that allow us to prove all valid inferences, we do have a trivial procedure – namely that consisting of enumerating all possible proofs – that always allows us to answer "yes" after a finite number of steps (as soon as we hit a proof of the conclusion from the premises) whenever the answer is "yes." But there is no mechanical procedure that allows us to answer "no" whenever the answer is "no." If there were such a procedure we would be guaranteed to obtain always a yes-or-no answer after a finite number of steps, simply by running the two procedures simultaneously. But this is exactly what is ruled out by the undecidability theorem. Thus, if the answer is "no," it might be the case that we never come to know it, although in some cases we may be able to find a counterexample. But, even if the answer is "yes" there is no guarantee that we can obtain it within *bounded resources*, for there cannot be any general upper bound on the time required to obtain the answer as a function of the input question.[8] So, if we run our semidecision procedure on a supercomputer and the answer has not come after a long time, this does not allow us to conclude that the answer is "no," since there is still a chance that a positive answer will come up tomorrow. We must therefore admit that there are cases in which we do not *actually* possess the information carried by the conclusion of a valid inference, even if we possess the information carried by the premises. So, while "objectively" – according to the theory of semantic information – we already possess the information carried by the conclusion, "subjectively" we may not know that we possess it.

This has a strong paradoxical flavor. What kind of notion of information is one that does not allow us, in general, to know whether we possess information about something? This kind of information is not fully manifestable and has no clear *operational* value. Hintikka's positive proposal consists in distinguishing between two objective and non-psychological notions of information content: *surface information*, which may be increased by deductive reasoning, and *depth information* (equivalent to Bar-Hillel and Carnap's semantic information), which may not. While the latter justifies the traditional claim that logical reasoning is tautological, the former vindicates the intuition underlying the opposite claim. In Hintikka's view, quantificational deductive reasoning with polyadic predicates may increase surface information, although it never increases depth information. In the rest of this section we shall give the reader a flavor of Hintikka's distinction without even attempting to do proper justice to its technical content.[9]

According to Hintikka, in a quantificational language every quantifier, as well as every individual constant, "invites" us to consider a certain individual in relation with other individuals. For example:

- $(\exists x)$ *loves*$(x, Mary)$ ("someone loves Mary") invites us to consider an unspecified individual, call it a, such that *loves*$(a, Mary)$;
- $(\forall x)$ *loves*$(x, Mary)$ ("everyone loves Mary") invites us to consider *an arbitrary* individual in his relation to Mary, say an individual b that is somehow representative of all individuals in the domain and tells us that *loves*$(b, Mary)$

Despite the universally quantified sentence appearing to invite us to consider all the individuals that inhabit the domain in their relation to Mary, clearly we do not (and sometimes cannot, when the domain is unspecified or infinite) review in our intuition all these individuals and consider their relation to Mary, but just focus on a single, albeit generic, representative. (This is exactly what we do when we use figures to demonstrate a geometrical theorem.) Usually the depth of nesting of quantifiers in a sentence and the number of constants in their scope contribute to the difficulty of grasping the meaning of a sentence. For example, $(\forall x)(\exists y)$ (*loves*(x, y) and *loves*$(y, Mary)$) ("everyone loves someone who loves Mary") cannot be properly understood without imagining three individuals mutually related by the dyadic predicate "love"; an arbitrary one instantiating the variable x, a second one, which is also unspecified but depends on the first, instantiating y and the one denoted by "Mary."

To give an informal explanation of Hintikka's ideas, let us consider the geometrical example discussed by Kant in his *Critique of Pure Reason*, namely Euclid's Proposition 32 of the first book of the *Elements*:

(4) In any triangle the sum of the internal angles is equal to two right angles ($180°$).

This statement (Figure 15.1) invites us to consider an arbitrary triangle *ABC*, its internal angles and their sum. In proposition 29 Euclid had already proven (among other things) that

(5) if two straight lines are parallel, then a straight line that meets them makes the alternate angles equal.

In Figure 15.2, we are invited to consider two parallel lines, a third line that meets them and the alternate angles formed thereby.

We can safely claim that we understand the two propositions (4) and (5) taken separately and our understanding is helped by the exhibition of the two diagrams. However, simply understanding them is by no means sufficient to realize that (4) follows from (5). In order to "see" this we have to introduce a more complex diagram that results from an ingenious combination of the previous two (Figure 15.3).

After this construction has been carried out, we can indeed see that (4) is true. But to achieve this, we need to conceive an aggregate of objects in their mutual relations, in short a

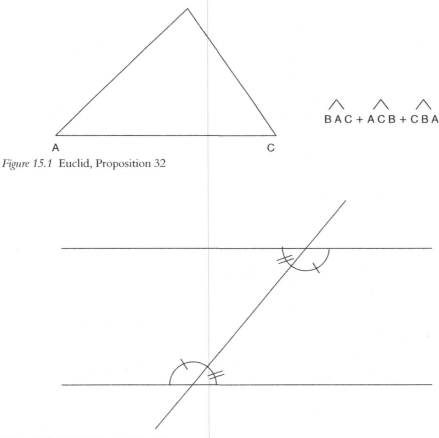

Figure 15.1 Euclid, Proposition 32

Figure 15.2 Euclid, Proposition 29

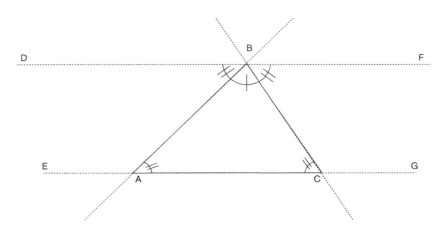

Figure 15.3 Proof of Proposition 32

configuration of objects, that is significantly more complex than the configurations that were needed to understand either the premise (5) or the conclusion (4).

Roughly speaking, Hintikka defines the surface information conveyed by a sentence ϕ as the set of types of "possible worlds" excluded by ϕ that can be described within bounded expressive resources, without increasing the complexity (number of distinct mutually related individuals) of the configurations that we have to master in order to understand any of the premises or the conclusion. Not surprisingly, given its essentially bounded nature, surface information is effectively computable and provides "an objective sense of information in which deduction can increase one's information – a sense that definitively confutes logical positivists on this point" (Hintikka, 1973, p. 230).

Without going into further details, we observe only that Hintikka's proposal classifies as non-tautological only some inferences of the polyadic predicate calculus, and so leaves the "scandal of deduction" unsettled in the domains of propositional logic and of the monadic predicate calculus.

The lesson from computational complexity

The theory of computational complexity can be considered a refinement of the traditional theory of computability taking into account the resources (time and space, that is, number of steps and amount of memory) used by algorithms. Its principal innovation consists in having replaced the concept of "effective procedure" with that of "feasible procedure."[10] An effective procedure or "algorithm" by and large consists in a "mechanical method," i.e. one executable in principle by a machine, to solve a given class of problems (answering a certain class of questions). An effective procedure is *feasible* when it can also be carried out in practice, and not only in principle. The expression "in practice" involves a certain degree of vagueness that computational complexity researchers have removed by agreeing to consider as feasible, executable in practice, algorithms that can answer the questions they are designed to answer within polynomial time. This means that there exists a fixed polynomial p such that, for any input of size n (i.e., that is encoded by a string of n occurrences of symbols), the algorithm yields an answer in a number of steps $\leq p(n)$.

The class P is the class of all *tractable* decision problems, i.e. those that can be solved by means of a polynomial time algorithm. On the other hand, if a problem is *intractable* – i.e., does not belong to P – then, even if decidable in principle, it is regarded as "undecidable in practice." The reason is readily explained: if the running time of an algorithm is not bounded above by a polynomial in the size of the input – for example, if it is expressed by an exponential function such as 2^n its execution may in some cases require a number of steps that grows fast beyond any practical limit as the input's size grows. In extreme cases, the time required could be longer than the life of the universe.

The bad news is that most interesting decidable problems that one encounters in many branches of mathematics do not belong to P. Among these there stands out the problem of establishing whether a certain proposition is a theorem of elementary Euclidean geometry, namely the geometry that can be expressed in a standard quantificational language. Although this problem was shown to be "algorithmically solvable" by Tarski in 1951, twenty-three years later Fischer and Rabin proved that it is, in fact, intractable.[11] According to our minimal notion of information in the second section, this implies that, in some cases, the information carried by a theorem in elementary geometry is not *actually* contained in the information carried by the axioms – although it is indeed *potentially* contained in it – because there is no feasible procedure to answer the question of whether an arbitrary sentence is true assuming that a yes-answer has been given for all the axioms.

Now, although there is no proof yet that propositional logic is intractable, a very general pessimistic result was obtained by Stephen Cook (1971), who showed that a large class of very difficult computational problems (the so-called *NP-complete problems*)[12] can be translated in polynomial time into the problem of deciding whether a given Boolean sentence is a tautology. Thus, a polynomial time algorithm for the tautology problem would automatically generate a polynomial time algorithm for each of the *NP*-complete problems. Since, despite all efforts, no polynomial time algorithm has ever been found for any of them, the dominant conjecture is that the tautology problem is intractable. If this conjecture is correct, we will never be able to guarantee that an answer to all questions concerning potential consequences of a set of assumptions can be actually obtained effortlessly, by means of a *feasible* mechanical procedure, even when these consequences follow by propositional logic only. This strongly suggests that both Frege's and Hintikka's solution of the "scandal of deduction" are not fully satisfactory, for the core of the problem seems to lie at the heart of propositional logic for which a mechanical decision procedure has been known since the 1920s.

Actual vs virtual information

This tension between the (presumptive) intractability of propositional logic and its alleged uninformativity is the motivation of a new approach put forward in (D'Agostino & Floridi, 2009) and further elaborated in subsequent papers (D'Agostino *et al.*, 2013; D'Agostino, 2014). In this approach there is a sense in which propositional logic is indeed informative. Here we shall only sketch the underlying ideas. Consider the following simple schematic inferences:

$$\varphi \rightarrow \psi$$

(Modus Ponens) $\qquad \varphi$

$$\underline{\qquad\qquad}$$

$$\psi$$

$$\varphi \lor \psi$$

(Disjunctive Syllogism) $\quad \underline{\neg\varphi \qquad\qquad}$

$$\psi$$

Here for each instance of the schematic letters, whenever we possess the information carried by the premises, we *immediately* infer the conclusion in virtue of the very meaning of the logical operators with no need for introducing and discharging assumptions (as in Gentzen's natural deduction). (D'Agostino & Floridi, 2009) presents a system of natural deduction consisting only of simple operational rules like these. Moreover, it can be shown that, whenever a conclusion follows from a set of premises by a chain of such simple inferences, there is a feasible procedure to construct such a chain. So, in accordance with our working notion of information of in the second section, we can say that we actually possess the information carried by the conclusion whenever we actually possess the information carried by the premises: the *marginal cost* of inferring the conclusion is negligible with respect to the cost of grasping the meaning of the sentences. All the information that can be extracted from the premises by means of these rules is *actual information*.

Now, not all arguments in propositional logic can be fully justified in this way. Consider the following inference:

(1)   If n is an integer, n is either even or odd

(2)   If n is an even integer, then there is an integer m such that $n = 2m$

(3)   If n is an integer, then $2n$ is an even integer

(4) n is even if and only if $n + 1$ is odd

(5) n is an integer
_____

$n^2 + 3n + 5$ is odd.

Here is a simple "proof by cases." By (5) n is an integer and so, by (1) n is either even or odd.

Case 1: n is even. Then, by (2) and Modus Ponens, $n = 2m$ for some integer m. So: $n^2 + 3n + 5 = (2m)^2 + 3(2m) + 5 = 2(2m^2 + 3m + 2) + 1$. Since by (3) and Modus Ponens $2(2m^2 + 3m + 2)$ is even, then by (4) and Modus Ponens $n^2 + 3n + 5$ is odd.

Case 2: n is not even. So, by Disjunctive Syllogism n is odd. Then, by (2), (4) and Modus Ponens $n = 2p + 1$ for some integer p. So, $n^2 + 3n + 5 = (2p + 1)^2 + 3(2p + 1) + 5 = 2(2p^2 + 5p + 4) + 1$. Since, by (3) and Modus Ponens $2(2p^2 + 5p + 4)$ is even, then $n^2 + 3n + 5$ is odd. Since either n is even or it is not, and in either case $n^2 + 3n + 5$ is odd, it follows that the conclusion is true independent of our being informed of whether n is even or not.

Here, in each case, we simulate information that we do not actually possess. This is what we call *virtual information*. We pretend we have an answer to the question of whether or not n is even and check what the consequences of each alternative are by means of simple inferences such as Modus Ponens or Disjunctive Syllogism. In each case we simulate an information state that is essentially richer than the actual one, containing information that is not even implicitly contained in it. Inference patterns of this kind, that essentially involve the manipulation of virtual information require, for each realistic agent, an *objective* effort that increases with the *depth* at which virtual information is introduced. In general, the propositional structure of an argument making use of virtual information is in Figure 15.4 where the conclusion θ occurs in all branches that are not explicitly inconsistent (marked with ×). Each branching increases the complexity of a logical inference from both the cognitive and the computational point of view and, therefore, also its informativity. In the papers cited above it is shown that if we fix an upper bound k on the depth at which virtual

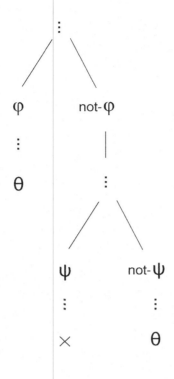

Figure 15.4 Inferential depth

information can be introduced, the relations of k-depth consequence are all tractable, albeit requiring increasing computational resources, and converge to classical propositional logic.

Conclusions: a Kantian view?

One of the trademarks of modern, or "logical," empiricism was the rejection of the possibility of "synthetic a priori" judgments in Kant's sense. While the precise sense attached by Kant to the opposition analytic/synthetic is not our concern here, there is very little doubt that in his view synthetic judgments – and by extension synthetic inferences – are capable of extending our knowledge, and are therefore informative, while analytic judgments and inferences are not.[13] Kant also thought that all analytic judgments or inferences are *a priori*, independent of experience, and that while synthetic judgments or inferences are usually *a posteriori*, in that they do depend on experience, in some important cases – such as those of mathematical statements – they may also be a priori.

The neopositivists' opposition to this Kantian view was clearly stated in the *manifesto* of the Vienna Circle as "the basic thesis of modern empiricism":

> The scientific world-conception knows no unconditionally valid knowledge derived from pure reason, no "synthetic judgments a priori" of the kind that lie at the basis of Kantian epistemology and even more of all pre- and post-Kantian ontology and metaphysics. [...] It is precisely in the rejection of the possibility of synthetic knowledge a priori that the basic thesis of modern empiricism lies. The

scientific world-conception knows only empirical statements about things of all kinds, and analytic statements of logic and mathematics.

(Hahn et al., 1973, p. 308)

In his (1973) Hintikka presented his view on the informativity of quantification logic, that we have briefly described in the seventh, as a vindication of Kant's old idea. Some laws or inferences of quantification logic are synthetic in that they cannot be obtained by simply analyzing the configurations of objects that are "given" with the very sentences by means of which they are expressed.

In the same vein, one could say that, in our discussion of propositional logic in the ninth section, analytical inferences are those that are recognized as sound via basic logical steps that process *actual* information, such as Modus Ponens and Disjunctive Syllogism, while synthetic ones involve the intuitive simulation of *virtual* information that is in no way "contained" in the premises. These two views can be seen as "orthogonal" in that they account for two different dimensions of mathematical information: in one of them, it stems from the complexity of the configurations needed to carry out an inference; in the other, it stems from the depth of the nested patterns of virtual information that are needed to obtain the conclusion. In either view, informativity is crucially linked to the cognitive and computational resources consumed in the inferential process: those needed to master a more complex configuration of individuals in their mutual relations, or to keep track of several sub-processes running in the tree-like structure of an argument by cases. Finally, both views allow for the definition of *degrees of informativity* of a logical inference depending on the maximum complexity of the configurations of objects required to carry it out (for the quantificational case) or on the maximum depth at which the use of virtual information is required (for the propositional case).

Notes

1 Sometimes "men fly to so paradoxical a belief to avoid, as they think, some even greater difficulty, which the vulgar do not see" (Mill, 1882, 315).

2 Thus, we do not use "tautological" in its technical sense of "being true in all possible worlds." The two senses coincide if Bar-Hillel and Carnap's notion of semantic information (see Chapter six of this Handbook) is adopted.

3 Indeed, this is not quite accurate a picture, since as Michael Dummett puts it: "Frege attempted to show that some mathematical propositions, those of number theory and analysis which he jointly classified as 'arithmetic', had the same character as, and in fact were, logical propositions; he never believed this to be true of the whole of mathematics" (Dummett, 1991, p. 10).

4 On this point see (Burge, 1998, §IV).

5 See Chapter 6 of this Handbook. See also (D'Agostino, 2013) for a discussion.

6 Another inevitable and undesirable consequence is that contradictions, like "it rains and it does not rain," carry the maximum amount of information, since they exclude all possible states. This is usually referred to as the "Bar-Hillell and Carnap Paradox." See Chapter 6 of this Handbook.

7 For an excellent exposition of natural deduction see (Tennant, 1990).

8 If there were such an upper bound, the logic of quantification would be decidable, since the answer would be "no" whenever no answer has been obtained within the upper time limit.

9 For Hintikka's own account, the reader is referred to (Hintikka, 1965, 1973). For a (very) critical exposition, see (Sequoiah-Grayson, 2008).

10 For an excellent exposition, still valid after thirty-five years, see (Garey & Johnson, 1979).

11 See (Rabin, 1977) for this and other intractability results.

12 See (Garey & Johnson, 1979) and (Stockmeyer, 1987) for an introduction to the theory of *NP*-completeness.

13 The reader is warned that the expressions "analytic" and "synthetic" have been used in several different meanings, albeit related by a "family resemblance," in the philosophical literature. See

(Hintikka, 1973) for a detailed discussion of a variety of different meanings. Here we only stress that, according to Frege's use of the term "analytic" in (Frege, 1967), analytic judgments may well be informative. See also the sixth section above and (Dummett, 1991).

References

Allo, P., & Mares, E. 2012. Informational semantics as a third alternative? *Erkenntnis*, 77(2), 167–185.

Burge, T. 1998. Frege on knowing the foundations. *Mind*, 107(426), 305–47.

Carnap, R. 1934. *Logische Syntax der Sprache*. Vienna: Springer.

Carnap, R. 1937. *The Logical Syntax of Language*. London: Routledge & Kegan Paul. English translation of Carnap (1934) by A. Smeaton.

Carnap, R. 1963. Intellectual autobiography, pp. 3–84 of: Schilpp, P. A (ed.), *The Philosophy of Rudolf Carnap*. La Salle, PA: Open Court.

Cook, S. A. 1971. The complexity of theorem-proving procedures, pp. 151–158 of: STOC '71: *Proceedings of the Third Annual ACM Symposium on Theory of Computing*. New York: ACM Press.

D'Agostino, M. 2013. Semantic information and the trivialization of logic. Floridi on the scandal of deduction. *Information*, 4, 33–59.

D'Agostino, M. 2014. Analytic inference and the informational meaning of the logical operators. *Logique et Analyse*, 227, 407–437.

D'Agostino, M. & Floridi, L. 2009. The enduring scandal of deduction. Is propositionally logic really uninformative? *Synthese*, 167, 271–315.

D'Agostino, M., Finger, M., & Gabbay, D. M. 2013. Semantics and proof theory of depth-bounded Boolean logics. *Theoretical Computer Science*, 480, 43–68.

Dummett, M. 1991. *Frege: Philosophy of Mathematics*. London: Duckworth.

Duzí, M. 2010. The paradox of inference and the non-triviality of analytic information. *Journal of Philosophical Logic*, 39, 473–510.

Floridi, L. 2011. *The Philosophy of Information*. Oxford: Oxford University Press.

Frege, G. 1960. *The Foundations of Arithmetic: A Logico-Mathematical Enquiry into the Concept of Number* (1884), 2nd edn. New York: Harper & Brothers.

Frege, G. 1967. *Begriffsschrift, A Formula Language, Modeled upon that of Arithmetic, for Pure Thought* (1879), pages 1–82 of: van Heijenoort, J. (ed.), *From Frege to Gödel. A Source Book in Mathematical Logic*, 1879–1931. Cambridge, MA: Harvard University Press.

Garey, M. R. & Johnson, D. S. 1979. *Computers and Intractability. A Guide to the theory of NP-Completeness*. San Francisco, CA: W.H. Freeman & Co.

Gödel, K.1929. "Über die Vollständigkeit des Logikkalküls". Doctoral dissertation. University Of Vienna.

Hahn, H., Neurath, O., & Carnap, R. 1973. The scientific conception of the world [1929]. In: Neurath, M., & Cohen, R.S. (eds), *Empiricism and Sociology*. Dordrecht: Reidel.

Hintikka, J. 1965. Are logical truths analytic? *The Philosophical Review*, 74(2), 178–203.

Hintikka, J. 1973. *Logic, Language Games and Information. Kantian Themes in the Philosophy of Logic*. Oxford: Clarendon Press.

Jago, M. 2013. The content of deduction. *The Journal of Philosophical Logic*, 42, 317–334.

Mill, J. S. 1882. *A System of Logic Ratiocinative and Inductive*, 8th edn. New York: Harper & Brothers.

Primiero, G. 2008. *Information and Knowledge. A Constructive Type- Theoretical Approach*. New York: Springer.

Rabin, M. O. 1977. Decidable Theories, pp. 595–630 of: Barwise, J. (ed.), *Handbook of Mathematical Logic*. Amsterdam: North-Holland.

Schlick, M. 1974. *General Theory of Knowledge*. New York: Springer-Verlag. Translation of the 2nd German edition of *Allgemeine Erkenntnislehre*, Berlin 1925.

Sequoiah-Grayson, S. 2008. The scandal of deduction. Hintikka on the information yield of deductive inferences. *The Journal of Philosophical Logic*, 37(1), 67–94.

Sillari, G. 2008. Quantified logic of awareness and impossible possible worlds. *Review of Symbolic Logic*, 1(4), 1–16.

Stockmeyer, Larry. 1987. Classifying the computational complexity of problems. *The Journal of Symbolic Logic*, 52, 1–43.

Tennant, N. 1990. *Natural Logic*. Edinburgh: Edinburgh University Press.

Wittgenstein, L. 1961. *Tractatus Logico-Philosophicus* (1921). New York: Routledge and Kegan Paul. Translated by D. F. Pears and B. F. McGuinness.

16

BAYESIANISM AND INFORMATION

Michael Wilde and Jon Williamson

Introduction

In epistemology, Bayesianism is a theory about rational degrees of belief that makes use of the mathematical theory of probability. There is disagreement among Bayesians, however, about which norms govern rational degrees of belief. In this chapter, we first provide an introduction to three varieties of Bayesianism: strictly subjective Bayesianism, empirically based subjective Bayesianism, and objective Bayesianism. Then we discuss how one might appeal to information theory in order to justify the norms of objective Bayesianism.

Bayesianism

Consider the following epistemological question. Given one's body of evidence, should one believe a particular proposition? For example, given that one's body of evidence includes the proposition that the outcome of the roll of the die is three, should one believe that the outcome is also odd? One theory says that one should believe all and only those propositions that follow from one's body of evidence. Call this the classical theory of rational belief. The classical theory maintains that one should believe that the outcome of the roll of the die is odd, if one's body of evidence includes that the roll of the die lands three. This is because it follows from one's body of evidence that the outcome of the roll of the die is odd, if one's body of evidence includes that the roll of the die lands three.

Formally speaking, let ω be an elementary outcome and Ω be a set of mutually exclusive and collectively exhaustive elementary outcomes. In the case of rolling a fair die, $\Omega = \{1, 2, 3, 4, 5, 6\}$. Then, propositions can be identified with subsets, $F \subseteq \Omega$, of elementary outcomes. For example, the proposition that the die lands odd is identified with the set of elementary outcomes at which the die lands odd, i.e., $odd = \{1, 3, 5\}$. One's body of evidence includes a proposition only if one's evidence rules out possible outcomes at which that proposition is false. For instance, if one's body of evidence includes the proposition that the outcome of the roll of the die is three, then one's evidence eliminates outcomes inconsistent with that proposition, i.e., $\{1, 2, 4, 5, 6\}$. Then, a proposition follows from one's body of evidence if and only if the set of elementary outcomes consistent with one's evidence is a subset of the proposition. To continue the example, if one's body of evidence includes the proposition that the outcome of the roll of the die is *three* = {3}, then it follows from one's body of evidence that the outcome is *odd*, since {3} ⊆ {1, 3, 5}.

There is another distinct epistemological question. Given one's body of evidence, *how strongly* should one believe a particular proposition? For example, given that one's body of evidence includes that the outcome of the roll of the die is odd, how strongly should one believe that the outcome is three?

The classical theory of rational belief is silent on questions about rational degrees of belief. Bayesianism, however, attempts to address such questions, by making use of the mathematical theory of probability. In particular, it introduces a function on propositions that satisfies the axioms of the probability calculus. (See Chapter 2 for more on the axioms of the probability calculus.) $P_{\mathcal{E}}$ is the probability function which gives the probability of each proposition on one's current body of evidence $\mathcal{E}$. It is called the *prior* probability function on one's evidence, since it gives the relevant probabilities before some novel piece of evidence has been learned. In the case of rolling a fair die, one natural prior probability function gives $P_{\mathcal{E}}(1) = P_{\mathcal{E}}(2) = P_{\mathcal{E}}(3) = P_{\mathcal{E}}(4) = P_{\mathcal{E}}(5) = P_{\mathcal{E}}(6) = 1/6$. Once again, one's body of evidence works to rule out certain basic outcomes, so that if one later learns the proposition that the die lands odd, so that one's new body of evidence is $\mathcal{E}'$ formed by adding *odd* to $\mathcal{E}$, then one would need to update the probability function to $P_{\mathcal{E}'}(1) = P_{\mathcal{E}'}(3) = P_{\mathcal{E}'}(5) = 1/3$. Bayesianism says that one's degree of belief in a proposition should match the probability of the proposition given one's evidence. In this case, given that one's body of evidence includes the proposition that the outcome of the die lands odd, one should believe that the die lands three to degree one-third.

Bayesianism is an attractive theory of rational belief. First, it is a simple and natural generalization of the classical theory of rational full belief. To begin to see this, note that Bayesianism preserves the classical theory: $P_{\mathcal{E}}(F) = 1$, if F follows from one's body of evidence; $P_{\mathcal{E}}(F) = 0$, if F is inconsistent with one's body of evidence. In addition, Bayesianism extends the classical theory by giving an account of the cases in between these two extremes. Having specified a probability function, a measure is provided of how close one's body of evidence comes to entailing or ruling out some proposition. Second, Bayesianism can help itself to all the many results in the mathematical theory of probability. Thus it has powerful resources to call upon in providing a theory of rational belief. Third, Bayesianism accommodates many of our intuitive judgements about rational degrees of belief. For instance, it accommodates the judgement that hypotheses are confirmed by their successful predictions, and that hypotheses are better confirmed if they make more surprising successful predictions. Bayesianism can account for all these intuitions and more (Howson and Urbach, 2006, pp. 91–130).

But why should one's degrees of belief be probabilities? The usual answer is to provide a Dutch book argument. Loosely speaking, if one is willing to bet the farm in exchange for a penny if some proposition is true, then it would seem that one has a high degree of belief in that proposition. On the other hand, if one is only willing to bet a penny in exchange for a farm if the proposition is true, then it seems that one has a low degree of belief in the proposition. This leads naturally to a betting interpretation of belief, according to which one's degree of belief in any given proposition is identified with one's willingness to bet on that proposition, i.e., with one's betting quotient for that proposition. The Dutch book argument then aims to show that betting quotients that are not probabilities are irrational in a certain sense. In particular, it is assumed that betting quotients susceptible to the possibility of sure loss are irrational. It is then shown that betting quotients are probabilities if and only if they are not susceptible to the possibility of sure loss. Thus one's betting quotients are rational only if they are probabilities. Given the betting interpretation of belief, one's degrees of belief are rational only if they are probabilities.

Thus the proponents of Bayesianism all tend to agree that degrees of belief should be representable by a probability function. That is, in order to be rational, one's degrees of belief must be probabilities. This is sometimes called the probability norm for degrees of belief. But is meeting the probability norm enough for one's degree of belief to be rational?

Strictly subjective Bayesians maintain that the probability norm is enough. They allow that any choice of prior degrees of belief is rational, as long as these degrees of belief are probabilities. One advocate of strict subjectivism is Bruno de Finetti (1937). However, other Bayesians have argued that certain probabilistic degrees of belief are more appropriate than others, given one's body of evidence. For instance, in the case of rolling a die, if one's evidence is only that the die is fair, then arguably one's degrees of belief are best represented by a probability function that gives $P_\mathcal{E}(1) = P_\mathcal{E}(2) = P_\mathcal{E}(3) = P_\mathcal{E}(4) = P_\mathcal{E}(5) = P_\mathcal{E}(6) = 1/6$. It looks like strictly subjective Bayesianism cannot account for the more or less objective nature of rational belief.

This has led some proponents of Bayesianism to advocate *empirically based subjective Bayesianism*. Richard Jeffrey (2004) and Colin Howson (2000) may be considered advocates of empirically based subjectivism.

Empirically based subjective Bayesians argue that meeting the probability norm is not sufficient for one's degrees of belief to be rational. Instead of allowing an arbitrary selection of a prior probability function, they argue that one's prior probability function should also be calibrated to evidence of physical probabilities. This is sometimes called the calibration norm. For instance, let P^* be the physical probability function. Then, if one's evidence includes that $P^*(1) = P^*(2) = P^*(3) = P^*(4) = P^*(5) = P^*(6) = 1/6$, one should choose as one's prior the probability function that gives $P_\mathcal{E}(1) = P_\mathcal{E}(2) = P_\mathcal{E}(3) = P_\mathcal{E}(4) = P_\mathcal{E}(5) = P_\mathcal{E}(6) = 1/6$. More generally, where $\mathbb{E}$ is the set of probability functions constrained in this way by the empirical evidence, one should choose $P_\mathcal{E} \in \mathbb{E}$. Empirical constraints such as this can also be justified by betting arguments (Williamson, 2010, pp. 39–42). But what if there is absolutely no empirical evidence? Then, the selection of a prior probability function is once again unconstrained, and which degrees of belief are rational again looks like a matter of personal choice.

In light of this, some proponents of Bayesianism advocate *objective Bayesianism*. One proponent of objective Bayesianism is Jon Williamson (2010). Objective Bayesians argue that one's prior degrees of belief are rational if and only if they are probabilities calibrated with the empirical evidence, that are otherwise sufficiently non-committal with regard to elementary outcomes. What does it mean for one's degrees of belief to be non-committal? The standard answer is that one's degrees of belief commit oneself to a particular elementary outcome over another to the extent that one believes the former to a greater degree than one believes the latter. This means that one's degrees of belief are *fully* non-committal between elementary outcomes when one believes all such outcomes to the same degree. Then one's degrees of belief are *sufficiently* non-committal only if they are as close to fully non-committal as meeting the probability and calibration norms permits. In the case of rolling a die when one has no evidence either way that the die is fair, the selection of a prior probability function is not a matter of personal choice according to objective Bayesianism. Instead, the sufficiently non-committal prior probability function gives

$$P_\mathcal{E}(1) = P_\mathcal{E}(2) = P_\mathcal{E}(3) = P_\mathcal{E}(4) = P_\mathcal{E}(5) = P_\mathcal{E}(6) = 1/6 \cdot$$

To sum up, there is no consensus among proponents of Bayesianism about which norms govern rational degrees of belief. In particular, there is disagreement regarding the following core norms:

Probability: Degrees of belief should be probabilities;
Calibration: Degrees of belief should be calibrated to evidence of physical probabilities;
Equivocation: Degrees of belief should be sufficiently non-committal.

There are three main lines of thought. Strict subjectivists advocate only the probability norm. They hold that one's prior degrees of belief are rational if and only if they satisfy the axioms of the probability calculus. For the strict subjectivist, then, one's prior degrees of belief are a matter of personal choice, so long as they are probabilities. Empirically based subjectivists go further by holding that one's prior degrees of belief are rational if and only if they are probabilities that are appropriately constrained by the empirical evidence; in particular, they hold that these degrees of belief should be calibrated to physical probabilities, insofar as one has evidence of them. That is, they advocate both the probability and the calibration norm, but not the equivocation norm. Objective Bayesians go further still, holding that one's prior degrees of belief are rational only if they are also sufficiently non-committal.

How is this disagreement to be settled? Some have looked to information theory to provide an answer.

Information theory and Bayesianism

The core norms of Bayesianism have been justified by appealing to information theory. In this section we provide an introduction to this line of research.

Information theory grew out of the pioneering work of Claude Shannon. Given finitely many elementary outcomes $\omega \in \Omega$, Shannon (1948, §6) argued that the uncertainty as to which outcome occurs is best measured by the entropy of the probabilities of the outcomes. The entropy of a probability function P is defined by:

$$H(P) = -\sum_{\omega \in \Omega} P(\omega) \log P(\omega)$$

Entropy increases the more evenly the probability is spread out over the possible outcomes; it is minimal when probability 1 is concentrated on one of the outcomes and maximal when each outcome has the same probability. Shannon argued that entropy is the only measure of uncertainty that (i) is continuous (small changes in probability lead to small changes in entropy), (ii) increases as the number of possible outcomes increases, and (iii) sums up in the right way when a problem is decomposed into two sub-problems.

Edwin Jaynes applied the information-theoretic notion of entropy to the problem of choosing a prior probability function (Jaynes, 1957). Jaynes suggested that one should choose a prior function that is maximally non-committal with respect to missing information, i.e., a function that is compatible with what information is available, but which is maximally uncertain with regard to questions about which no information is available. Applying Shannon's notion of entropy, this means that one should choose as one's prior, a probability function, from all those functions compatible with available evidence, that has maximum entropy. If $\mathbb{E}$ is the set of probability functions that are compatible with available evidence, Jaynes' maximum entropy principle says that one should choose $P_{\mathcal{E}} \in \text{maxent } \mathbb{E}$, where maxent $\mathbb{E} \overset{\text{df}}{=} \{P \in \mathbb{E} : H(P) \text{ is maximized}\}$.

The maximum entropy principle can be understood as an explication of the equivocation norm advocated by objective Bayesians.

The question remains as to why one's prior should be maximally non-committal. What advantage is there to adopting a non-committal prior?

Topsøe (1979) provided an interesting line of argument. Suppose the loss incurred by believing ω to degree $P_{\mathcal{E}}(\omega)$ when ω turns out to be the true outcome is logarithmic:

$$L(\omega, P_{\mathcal{E}}) = -\log P_{\mathcal{E}}(\omega).$$

Thus the loss is zero when ω is fully believed, but increases exponentially as degree of belief $P(\omega)$ decreases towards 0. Suppose P^* is the true chance function, so that one's expected loss is

$$\sum_{\omega \in \Omega} P^*(\omega) L(\omega, P_{\mathcal{E}}) = -\sum_{\omega \in \Omega} P^*(\omega) \log P_{\mathcal{E}}(\omega).$$

All one knows is that $P^* \in \mathbb{E}$. Thus one's worst-case expected loss is

$$\sup_{P^* \in \mathbb{E}} -\sum_{\omega \in \Omega} P^*(\omega) \log P_{\mathcal{E}}(\omega).$$

It turns out that, as long as $\mathbb{E}$ is non-pathological (e.g., if $\mathbb{E}$ is closed and convex), the prior probability function which minimizes worst-case expected loss is just the probability function in $\mathbb{E}$ that maximizes entropy. Thus the maximum entropy principle is justified on the grounds that the resulting prior minimizes worst-case expected loss. Note that the maximum entropy principle thus construed explicates the calibration norm as well as the equivocation norm, because it says that, when evidence determines just that the chance function $P^* \in \mathbb{E}$, one should take $P_{\mathcal{E}}$ to be *a function in* $\mathbb{E}$ – i.e., a calibrated probability function – that has maximum entropy.

One question immediately arises: why should loss be logarithmic? Topsøe, appealing to Shannon's work on communication and coding, suggested that loss is logarithmic if it is the cost incurred by transmitting the results of an observation. Grünwald and Dawid (2004) recognized that this limits the scope of the maximum entropy principle to certain communication problems. They generalized Topsøe's justification to cope with other loss functions, leading to a generalized notion of entropy which depends on the loss function in operation, and to a generalized maximum entropy principle which says that one should choose a prior probability function in $\mathbb{E}$ that maximizes generalized entropy.

This approach remains rather limited to the extent that one needs to know the true loss function in order to choose one's prior probability function, because one needs to know which generalized entropy function is to be maximized. Often, however, one wants to choose a prior in advance of knowing the uses to which one's beliefs will be put and the losses (or gains) which might result. Thus one needs to identify a *default* loss function – a loss function that encapsulates what one might presume about one's losses, in the absence of information about the true loss function. Williamson (2010, pp. 64–65) put forward four principles that constrain this default loss function:

L1: Fully believing the true outcome may be presumed to lead to zero loss.
L2: One can presume that loss strictly increases as $P_{\mathcal{E}}(\omega)$ decreases from 1 towards 0.
L3: The presumed loss $L(\omega, P_{\mathcal{E}})$ depends on $P_{\mathcal{E}}(\omega)$ but not on $P_{\mathcal{E}}(\omega')$, for other outcomes ω'.

L4: If one decomposes a problem into two sub-problems which are presumed to be unrelated, then the total loss can be presumed to be the sum of the losses incurred on each of the two sub-problems.

It turns out that the default loss function must be logarithmic if it is to satisfy these four principles. Thus one can apply Topsøe's original justification of the maximum entropy principle in the (rather typical) case in which one does not know the true loss function, and one can apply Grünwald and Dawid's generalization if one does happen to know the true loss function.

A second concern arises for this kind of justification of the maximum entropy principle. Recall that the probability norm is usually justified by means of the Dutch book argument: degrees of belief must be probabilities if one is to avoid exposing oneself to the possibility of sure loss, i.e., $L(\omega, P_{\mathcal{E}}) > 0$ for all ω. There are two respects in which this argument does not cohere well with the above argument for the maximum entropy principle. First, in the Dutch book argument the objective is to avoid sure loss, rather than minimize worst-case expected loss. Second, the notion of loss invoked by the Dutch book argument is not logarithmic loss. Instead,

$$L(\omega, P_{\mathcal{E}}) = (P_{\mathcal{E}}(\omega) - 1)S(\omega) + \sum_{\omega' \neq \omega} P_{\mathcal{E}}(\omega')S(\omega')$$

where the $S(\omega)$, $S(\omega')$ are stakes chosen by an adversary, which may be positive or negative and which may depend on one's belief function $P_{\mathcal{E}}$.

It is clearly less than satisfactory if the justification of one tenet of objective Bayesianism – the probability norm – is incompatible with the justification of the others, namely the calibration and equivocation norms, cashed out in terms of the maximum entropy principle. In view of this, Landes and Williamson (2013) attempted to reconcile the Bayesian norms, by extending the justification of the maximum entropy principle so as to justify the probability norm at the same time. The justification of the maximum entropy principle outlined above presumes the probability norm, since it shows that the *probability function* that minimizes worst-case expected loss is the probability function in $\mathbb{E}$ which maximizes entropy. What is needed is to show that the *belief function* that minimizes worst-case expected loss is the function in $\mathbb{E}$ with maximum entropy; that it is in $\mathbb{E}$ implies that the prior belief function is a probability function, i.e., it implies the probability norm.

Thus Landes and Williamson (2013) extend the concepts of loss and expected loss to handle losses incurred by an arbitrary belief function B, which is not necessarily a probability function, in order to show that belief functions which are not probability functions expose one to sub-optimal worst-case expected loss. The main issue is that in the original notion of expected loss,

$$\sum_{\omega \in \Omega} P^{\star}(\omega)L(\omega, P_{\mathcal{E}}) = -\sum_{\omega \in \Omega} P^{\star}(\omega)\log P_{\mathcal{E}}(\omega),$$

one considers a single partition of outcomes, namely the partition of elementary outcomes $\omega \in \Omega$. This is appropriate if one assumes the probability norm from the outset, as the probability of any proposition $F \subseteq \Omega$ is determined by the probability of the elementary outcomes,

$$P_{\mathcal{E}}(F) = \sum_{\omega \in F} P_{\mathcal{E}}(\omega),$$

i.e., the probabilities of the elementary outcomes tell us everything about the probability function. For example, if the elementary outcomes correspond to outcomes of a roll of a die, $\Omega = \{1, 2, 3, 4, 5, 6\}$, then $P(odd) = P_{\mathcal{E}}(\{1, 3, 5\}) = P_{\mathcal{E}}(1) + P_{\mathcal{E}}(3) + P_{\mathcal{E}}(5)$. However, it is no longer appropriate to consider only the partition of elementary outcomes when we do not assume the probability norm from the outset, because the degree of belief in F may be unrelated to the degrees of belief in the elementary outcomes that make up F. Thus we need to consider all partitions π of Ω when defining expected loss:

$$\sum_{\pi} g(\pi) \sum_{F \in \pi} P^{\star}(F) L(F, B) = -\sum_{\pi} g(\pi) \sum_{F \in \pi} P^{\star}(F) \log B(F).$$

Here g is a weighting function that provides each partition π with a weight that determines the extent to which that partition contributes to the expectation. Entropy may be defined similarly:

$$H_g(B) \overset{\mathrm{df}}{=} -\sum_{\pi} g(\pi) \sum_{F \in \pi} B(F) \log B(F).$$

This gives a generalized notion of entropy that depends on the weighting function. (Note that this generalization is different to the generalized entropies of Grünwald and Dawid (2004).) The case of standard entropy corresponds to the weighting g_Ω which gives weight 1 to the partition $\{\{\omega\} : \omega \in \Omega\}$ of elementary outcomes and weight 0 to every other partition. It turns out that, as long as the weighting function g is inclusive in the sense that for each proposition F, g gives positive weight to some partition that contains F, the belief function that minimizes worst-case expected loss is the probability function in $\mathbb{E}$ that maximizes entropy. This gives an integrated justification of the probability norm and the maximum entropy principle, albeit with respect to a generalized notion of entropy that is defined in terms of g. It is suggested in Landes and Williamson (2013) that the standard notion of entropy stands out as uniquely appropriate among the generalized entropies if we impose language invariance as a further desideratum: i.e., that one's prior belief function should not depend on the language in which the elementary outcomes are expressed.

Conclusion

In the first half of this chapter we introduced Bayesianism as a theory about rational degrees of belief. On the way, we noted some of the arguments in favor of Bayesianism, but we also noted a difficulty. If probabilities are given an interpretation in terms of rational degrees of belief, and rational degrees of belief are largely a matter of personal choice, it begins to look as if rational belief is a matter of personal opinion. However, this fails to do justice to the more or less objective nature of rational belief. To resolve this difficulty, the Bayesian usually attempts to reduce the element of personal choice by advocating further constraints on rational degrees of belief, namely the calibration and equivocation norms. The issue then becomes how to justify those norms. In the second half of this chapter we argued that one can appeal to information theory in order justify the Bayesian norms. The standard information-theoretic justification of the equivocation norm is incompatible with the standard Dutch book justification of the probability norm. However, recent results show that the norms of objective Bayesianism can receive a unified information-theoretic justification.

Acknowledgements

This research was supported by UK Arts and Humanities Research Council grants which fund the projects *From objective Bayesian epistemology to inductive logic* and *Evaluating evidence in medicine*.

Further reading

For more on the mathematical theory of probability see Chapter 2 of this volume. For an introduction to the philosophy of probability, see Gillies (2000). Gillies gives also a clear exposition of Dutch book arguments (2000, pp. 53–65). Bayesianism is named after the Reverend Thomas Bayes, who lived and preached in Kent (Bayes, 1764). One popular introduction and defense of Bayesianism is Howson and Urbach (2006). For a critical evaluation of Bayesianism see Earman (1992). Edwin Jaynes' magnum opus is Jaynes (2003). One recent defense of objective Bayesianism is Williamson (2010).

References

Bayes, T. (1764). An essay towards solving a problem in the doctrine of chances. *Philosophical Transactions of the Royal Society of London*, 53: 370–418.

de Finetti, B. (1937). Foresight: Its logical laws, its subjective sources. In Kyburg, H. and Smokler, H. (eds), *Studies in Subjective Probability*, pages 53–118.

Earman, J. (1992). *Bayes or Bust*. Cambridge, MA: MIT Press.

Gillies, D. (2000). *Philosophical Theories of Probability*. Abingdon: Routledge.

Grünwald, P. and Dawid, A. P. (2004). Game theory, maximum entropy, minimum discrepancy, and robust Bayesian decision theory. *Annals of Statistics*, 32(4): 1367–1433.

Howson, C. (2000). *Hume's Problem: Induction and the Justification of Belief*. Oxford: Oxford University Press.

Howson, C. and Urbach, P. (2006). *Scientific Reasoning: The Bayesian Approach*. Open Court, 3rd edition.

Jaynes, E. T. (1957). Information theory and statistical mechanics. *The Physical Review*, 106(4): 620–630.

Jaynes, E. T. (2003). *Probability Theory: The Logic of Science*. Cambridge: Cambridge University Press.

Jeffrey, R. (2004). *Subjective Probability: The Real Thing*. Cambridge: Cambridge University Press.

Landes, J. and Williamson, J. (2013). Objective Bayesianism and the maximum entropy principle. *Entropy*, 15(9): 3528–3591.

Shannon, C. (1948). A mathematical theory of communication. *The Bell System Technical Journal*, 27: 379–423 and 623–656.

Topsøe, F. (1979). Information theoretical optimization techniques. *Kybernetika*, 15: 1–27.

Williamson, J. (2010). *In Defence of Objective Bayesianism*. Oxford: Oxford University Press.

PART III

Natural and physical aspects

17

THE PHILOSOPHY OF DATA

Sabina Leonelli

Introduction

In contemporary scientific discussions of big data and data-intensive research, the term 'data' is sometimes used to indicate basic, incontrovertible facts on a given entity or process, which can therefore be assumed to provide reliable information about it. This chapter uses key literature in the Anglo-American philosophy of science to show that this conceptualization of data and their role as evidence is far too simplistic. Philosophers have long been aware of the context-dependent nature of data production and, more generally, the unreliability of sensory perception as grounds for knowledge of reality. A good instance of this is Wilfried Sellar's attack on the 'myth of the given', and particularly his claim that 'non-propositional items (such as sense data) are epistemically inefficacious and cannot serve as what is given' (Sellars reported in deVries 2014). This mistrust of data as empirical warrants does not, however, clarify the epistemic status of knowledge grounded on the production and analysis of data, such as, most notably, the knowledge generated through scientific methods. In considering this issue, this chapter reviews the work of philosophers who have considered the tensions and problems involved in using data as evidence for scientific claims, and the implications that this has for a broader conceptualization of the nature and function of data. There are of course many ways to think about data that do not pertain to the realm of science. Nevertheless, the production and use of data to produce scientific knowledge is a relatively well-demarcated domain of human activity, and thus constitutes a good starting point for reflections over the status and nature of data in a more general sense. Within the sciences, it is clear that data are deeply historical entities, which are generated (in the case of experimental data) or collected (in the case of data derived from fieldwork) under controlled circumstances to serve as evidence for knowledge claims. Thinking about scientific data can therefore encourage philosophers to avoid ahistorical, uncontextualized approaches to questions of evidence, and instead consider data as components of specific processes of knowledge-making.

Data in the philosophy of science

Data can be easily construed as a starting point for scientific reasoning about the world, its structure, and functioning. They are the facts from which reasoning proceeds, and the empirical basis for testing and validating any assertion made by scientists about the nature of reality. Within an experimental setting, data are commonly identified with the immediate traces left by measurement instruments and the manipulation of samples and, as such, they are taken to document features and attributes of the entities or processes under investigation. This is where the idea of 'raw data' comes from. Data are as close as a scientist gets to documenting specific aspects of a phenomenon of interest in a way that can inform further inquiry, without necessarily attempting to reproduce or represent the phenomenon itself. They are 'raw' because they have not yet been subjected to extensive research interventions, such as modelling and statistical analysis.

Interpreting the scientific meaning of data is left to the researchers who handle them, who decide whether to regard them as evidence for specific phenomena on the basis of their interests, background knowledge, and familiarity with the procedures through which the data were obtained. The importance of human agency in attributing meaning to scientific data provides a starting point for philosophical analysis. For centuries, philosophers have observed that despite their epistemic value as 'given', data are clearly made. They are the results of complex processes of interaction between researchers and the world, which typically happen with the help of complex interfaces such as observational techniques, registration and measurement devices, and the re-scaling and manipulation of objects of inquiry for the purposes of making them amenable to investigation. For example, data about an organism of interest to biologists are usually gathered through the use of instruments such as microscopes, mass spectrometers, genome sequencers; techniques such as control trials and mutant screens; and the modelling of the organism itself in a variety of ways, ranging from the standardization of its environment (from the field to a laboratory cage) to surgical interventions and the genetic manipulation of its offspring. These experimental processes embody specific interpretations of the world. For instance, genome sequencing machines incorporate assumptions about how a genetic sequence is assembled and what role it plays within the wider organism, while the ways in which laboratory organisms are kept and fed reflect researchers' ideas about what constitutes 'optimal' nutrition for 'normal' development.

Ronald Giere has discussed the large amount of conceptual and material scaffolding involved in scientific data production as exemplifying the perspectival nature of observation – that is, the extent to which what is perceived as a laboratory finding is actually the result of looking at the world through a specific theoretical perspective, honed through years of research, and steeped into well-entrenched assumptions and commitments about how the world works (Giere 2006; see also Gooding 1990). This means that experimental findings are never pristine, objective documents of a mind-independent reality ('raw' in the sense discussed above), but rather the results of situated attempts to interact with the world on the basis of a given worldview. The epistemic significance of data needs to be evaluated accordingly. As claimed by several philosophers and philosophically minded historians and sociologists, this is also the case for data generated outside the controlled environment of the laboratory, such as observations made during fieldwork (see for instance Hanson 1958; Latour and Woolgar 1979; Hacking 1983; Collins 1985; Franklin 1986; Galison 1987; Bogen and Woodward 1988). Building on this work, Hans Radder has argued that field observations are as context- and subject-dependent as experimental results (Radder 2006).

The tension between viewing data as instances of the world and emphasizing their man-made nature has acted as a thread for philosophical discussions of scientific methods at least since the scientific revolution. For the most part, philosophers have focused their efforts towards debunking the myth of data as given rather than made. Accordingly, almost every prominent philosopher in the Western tradition has been suspicious of the so-called 'method of induction', which is grounded on the idea that claims about the world may be generated through the accumulation of facts and the emergence of meaningful patterns from such facts. Many have viewed reliance on induction as equivalent to accepting that there can be a set of observations so reliable and fact-like that one can infer truthful generalizations about the world from them – and found this assumption wanting. In his seminal *Essay Concerning Human Understanding* (1690), John Locke noted that humans are far too conditioned by their own assumptions and interests to be able to observe the world objectively. Subsequent scholars have shown scientists to be no exception. Accordingly, scientific methods have been portrayed as efficient means to moderate, and where possible annihilate, such subjectivity – an achievement that presupposes the recognition that what one takes to be a fact about the world may well be a fallacious impression generated by the senses. Whatever fact science proceeds from, one must instead consider how belief in that fact was generated in the first place. In the case of data, this means questioning which instruments, procedures, materials and conceptual assumptions were made in order to produce a given dataset, and evaluate any possible interpretation of data against this background. A particularly vocal advocate of this view was Pierre Duhem, whose 1906 treaty on the structure of physical theory inspired later authors, such as Norwood Russell Hanson and Thomas Kuhn, to emphasize the inevitable influence of theoretical presuppositions on data collection, selection and interpretation, which they referred to as theory-ladenness (Duhem 1906; Bogen 2010; Schindler 2013).

The theory-laden, man-made nature of data caused much concern within twentieth-century philosophy of science, because it makes it difficult to think of data as providing objective evidence for given theories. Largely thanks to the influence of logical positivism and Karl Popper's falsificationism, most Anglo-American philosophers writing after World War II conceived of data chiefly as means to test theories. Within this tradition, data need to provide a benchmark as 'hard facts' that can confirm as well as disqualify researchers' theoretical hypotheses: they are the ground on which theories are validated, and thus need to be reliable and trustworthy. This requirement does not fit well with the realization that data are, at least in part, a reflection of scientists' specific interests, background knowledge, location, instruments, and research strategies. It also runs against the insight that 'publicly available data typically cannot be produced except through processes whose results reflect the influence of causal factors that are too numerous, too different in kind, and too irregular in behaviour for any single theory to account for them' (Bogen 2010, 18). Carl Hempel was one of many philosophers struggling to reconcile the local, idiosyncratic and theory-laden nature of data and their function as conformation for universal truths about nature. His solution was to rely on scientific methods to filter researchers' 'sensations, perceptions and similar phenomena of immediate experience' out of the process of inquiry, leaving only 'directly observable' and 'intersubjectively ascertainable' observations that can be taken as objective facts about the world and used to validate a given theory or explanation (Hempel 1970, 674).

Data in scientific practice

Philosophers' long struggle with the relation between theory and evidence contributed to establishing a view of scientific knowledge as a set of universally valid claims about the world. Within these accounts, the theory-ladeness of data is problematic because of the perceived tension between the context-dependent nature of data production and the use of data as evidence for supposedly objective, context-independent statements (often referred to as 'laws of nature'), the discovery of which is the ultimate goal of the science. Theories and explanations that abstract as much as possible from fallible human perception are conceived as the main product of research, and hence as the scientific elements that are most deserving of philosophical scrutiny. As a result, philosophers focused their attention on theoretical debates within the sciences, rather than on observational or experimental practices involving human subjectivity and experience. Following in this vein, the theory-ladenness of data, and hence their embeddedness in specific histories of inquiry, was presented as a threat to the legitimacy of scientific knowledge as a reliable source of insight about the world. It is no wonder that Hans Reichenbach (1938) characterized the messy and sometimes serendipitous processes of data handling as part of the 'context of discovery', which he carefully distinguished from the rational marshalling of data into evidence within neat arguments that is involved in the production of scientific claims about the world, a process which he dubbed the 'context of justification'. In Reichenbach's view, the value of research as a harbinger of truth is found by scrutinizing how scientists construe and present their conclusions, rather than through an examination of the conceptual and practical constraints that go into producing the data used as evidence for those claims.

This view of scientific knowledge has been challenged by the recent 'practice turn' within the philosophy of science. Starting from the 1970s, an increasing number of philosophers started to pay more attention to authors such as Francis Bacon (1994), William Whewell (1989) and John Stuart Mill (1843), who emphasized the fruitfulness of examining the actual features of processes of discovery, rather than their glorified *post facto* reconstruction. This interest has been primarily channelled in the study of the role of scientific models, whose epistemic role has been found to vary depending on their concrete features, ranging from mathematical formalizations to material objects, as well as the interests and values of their users – thus demonstrating the philosophical import of studying actual research practices in detail.[1] In response to this scholarship, some philosophers have become convinced that understanding the nature of knowledge and scientific reasoning meant studying the history and characteristics of research practices across different periods, locations and disciplines, including the specific constraints and the variety of worldviews underlying and shaping the production of data and its use as evidence for claims (Ankeny *et al.* 2011; Chang 2004). A parallel realization has been that science is an exceptionally diverse enterprise, which might be better investigated starting from the idiosyncrasies of specific cases rather than from an emphasis on common strategies and overarching theories (Kellert *et al.* 2006; Chang 2012).

In this context, many discussions of relevance to data have centred on 'models of data', i.e. manipulations of experimental data aimed at eliminating errors and producing statistical patterns, which can then be used to test theoretical predictions (Suppes 1962). The idea of models of data helps to understand how scientists transform a set of scattered data points into a smooth curve on a graph, which fits data points onto what scientists take to be a significant pattern. In Roman Frigg's and Stephen Hartmann's contemporary reformulation, models of data are a 'corrected, rectified, regimented and in many instances idealized version of the data we gain from immediate observation, the so-called raw data' (Frigg and Hartmann 2012). Focusing on these models is an excellent way to emphasize the complex processes through which data produced by a given set of instruments and/or procedures are marshalled into evidence for specific claims, and particularly the numerous assumptions and constrains underlying not only the production, but also the dissemination and use of data in scientific research.

Another set of discussions in which philosophical attention has turned to data in scientific practice is the philosophy of experiments. Within that realm, a central contribution is that of Ian Hacking, who coined a broad definition of experimental data as *marks* produced by human interactions with research instruments. By focusing on the material circumstances in which data are generated, Hacking's account remains agnostic about the epistemic role that data may play in scientific inquiry, and indeed does not even require data to function as evidence for claims about phenomena, though this is of course what data are typically used for in research. Hacking's objective is instead to stress the constraints and opportunities provided by the manifold of formats and shapes in which data are produced in the laboratory – comprising, in his words, 'uninterpreted inscriptions, graphs recording variation over time, photographs, tables, displays' (Hacking 1992, 48). Peter Galison has taken a similar position with respect to data obtained through experiments in particle physics, which has enabled him to study how data are exchanged across research communities in this area and how their scientific use is affected by their movements (Galison 1997).

Hacking's work inspired James Bogen's and James Woodward's seminal account of the relationship between data production and the development of claims about phenomena, according to which data cannot provide evidence for theories, but rather provide evidence for the identification and characterization of phenomena such as the melting point of lead or the existence of weak neutral currents. It is these phenomena, rather than data, that feature as evidence within theories. One of the key achievements of their approach, in which philosophical analysis is again tightly intertwined with an examination of research processes carried out in experimental physics, has been to resurrect a conception of data as things that can be straightforwardly observed. As they put it, 'we need to distinguish what theories explain (phenomena or facts about phenomena) from what is uncontroversially observable (data)' (1988, 314). Bogen and Woodward embrace the fact that data are 'typically the result of complex interactions among a large number of disparate causal factors which are idiosyncratic to a particular experimental situation', but do not view this as a threat to the potential value of data as evidence. To the contrary, they welcome the study of the messy context of discovery as a crucial starting point for understanding and evaluating how, when and why data can and do function as evidence for specific claims.

Another seminal figure to take inspiration from Hacking's work, as well as the oeuvre of French philosophers such as Gaston Bachelard and George Canguilhem, is Hans-Jörg Rheinberger. In his account, data are things that can be stored and retrieved, and are thus made durable – a very important characteristic, as data need to be passed around and scrutinized by peers in order to document the claims for which they are presented as evidence (2011). Despite their common emphasis on experimental data practices, Rheinberger's conclusions differ from Hacking's insofar as he does not view the marks produced by scientific instruments – which he calls 'traces' or 'signals' – as an example of data. Rather, he conceives of data as the result of further manipulations of the traces resulting from observation or experiments – manipulations that are performed with the purpose of storing those traces and making them available and intelligible to others. As an example, Rheinberger points to the first DNA sequence gel produced by Fred Sanger and collaborators in 1977. The gel helps to visualize the relatively simple molecular structure of the DNA sequence of bacteriophage PhiX174, by generating discrete stripes of varying lengths on a photosensitive plate. Each stripe is then made to correspond to one of the four nucleic acid bases of DNA (guanine, adenine, thymine and cytosine). Finally, the initial letters of these acid bases (GATC) are used as symbolic stand-bys for the stripes themselves – an important move, because these symbols can be digitalized and analysed much more easily than the cumbersome and idiosyncratic stripes initially generated by the DNA sequence gel. Rheinberger interprets those stripes as *traces* generated by this laboratory technique: the immediate products of experimentation, which however is difficult to move around in its 'raw' state. He contrasts these traces with the abstraction of these stripes into letters that can be easily moved around and used for further research, and refers to these letters as an example of the transformation of traces to *data* (ibid., 6–7). This account benefits from the extraordinary success of the use of letters as symbols for nucleobases, whose format has certainly facilitated the implementation of the molecular bandwagon in biology. Rheinberger also explicitly builds on Bruno Latour's work on scientific knowledge production, and particularly his analysis of chains of inference. As Latour demonstrates by following the stages through which data have been collected and mobilized to document the botanical and geological characteristics of a given area of the Amazon, the establishment of knowledge claims is grounded in the production and movement of objects that can serve as anchors for knowledge claims thanks to their stability across contexts – and which Latour calls, with characteristic flair, 'immutable mobiles' (Latour 1999).

Both Latour and Rheinberger recognize that the marks (or traces) produced in the course of research need to be processed in order to travel, and that travelling across labs and research contexts is crucial to their functioning as evidence. They also emphasize the epistemic importance of the mobility of data and the labour required to realize it. This shifts the philosophical focus from an analysis of the logical links between data and claims – an analysis can be performed without taking any contextual element into account and which was characteristic of traditional approaches within the philosophy of science – to a study of the relation between researchers' perceptions of what counts as data and the stages and contexts of investigation in which such perceptions emerge. In this latter sense, their account of data and their role as evidence is strongly influenced by their interest in how scientific practices actually unfold and generate knowledge claims.

Two conceptions of data: relational and representational

In (Leonelli 2009, 2014, 2016) one finds an investigation of how data are mobilized and manipulated in order to expand their evidential value, for instance when devising databases capable of making data usable as evidence for a variety of different claims. As a result, a *relational* account of data is advocated, where what counts as data depends on who uses them, how and for which purposes: 'any object can be considered as a datum as long as (1) it is treated as potential evidence for one or more claims about phenomena, and (2) it is possible to circulate it among individuals' (Leonelli, 2016). This account makes two key assumptions about data: that they are portable and that they consist of material objects. Portability is important because the establishment of scientific claims is widely recognized as a social activity that needs to involve more than one individual. Sharing data among individuals can therefore be viewed as a necessary, though not sufficient, condition for their prospective use as evidence. If data are not portable, it is not possible to pass them around a group of individuals who can review their significance and bear witness to their scientific value. Lorraine Daston and Peter Galison (1992) make the same point when describing data as quintessentially workable and 'communal', a point extended by Mary Morgan, who stressed the crucial importance of movement across contexts to assessing the value of data as evidence (2012). Materiality is then crucial to making data portable. As also emphasized by Hacking, whether we are dealing with symbols, numbers, photographs or specimens, all data types need a concrete medium in which they can be disseminated. This concrete medium can encompass both digital and analogue objects and processes, as long as it is physically possible to pass it around among individuals. The approach follows the lead of Orlin Vakarelov, who defines a medium as 'the concrete stuff. It is the system that gets pushed and pulled by the rest of the world […] in just the right way to support the patterns of interactions that constitute the information process' (Vakarelov 2012, 49).

According to the relational view, scientific data can thus be usefully characterized as objects that are explicitly collected and disseminated in order to provide evidence for claims about reality. This does not mean that whoever gathers data already knows how they might be used. Rather, what matters is that data are collected *with the expectation* that they may be used as evidence for one or more claims about the world at some point in the future. This implies that the same objects may or may not be functioning as data, depending on which role they are made to play in scientific inquiry. This accounts for the diversity of formats, media and context that data typically inhabit in scientific practice: within the relational account, the same objects can change some of their material features and yet be used as 'the same data' across a variety of contexts, as well as cease to function as data as soon as they are no longer regarded as sources of evidence for a claim.

The view contrasts sharply with those of philosophers and scientists who prefer a context-independent definition of what data actually are, a view that can be here broadly characterized as the *representational* account of data. Within this view, data can be identified regardless of the ways in which they are used at any point in time, and it is possible to evaluate objectively, without any reference to the relevant research context, what information a given dataset contains, and whether this is being interpreted correctly or incorrectly. In a recent report, for instance, the Royal Society proposed to define data as 'numbers, characters or images that designate an attribute of a phenomenon' (Royal Society 2012, 12). This definition can easily be interpreted to depict data as representations of a given entity or process, in the sense of providing access to one or more of its characteristics. This reflects the common intuition that data, especially when they come in the form of images like photographs, somehow mirror the phenomena that they are created to document, providing a snapshot of those phenomena that is amenable to study under the controlled conditions of research. It also reflects the idea of data as 'raw' products of research, which are as close as it gets to unmediated knowledge of reality. This is a useful view insofar as it makes sense of the truth-value sometimes assigned to data as irrefutable sources of evidence – the Popperian idea that if data are found to support a given claim, then that claim is corroborated as true at least as long as no other data are found to disprove it. As soon as a Popperian view of scientific progress is abandoned, however, the representational view of data runs into problems.

One problem is that this view makes it difficult to accommodate the wide variety of uses and media for data found in scientific practice. In particular, it restricts any given dataset to the role of representing one (and only one) phenomenon, while, as amply demonstrated by the recent emphasis on re-purposing existing data through making them widely accessible, the same dataset may well be interpreted as representing a variety of phenomena, depending on the expertise and interests of the researchers involved and the level of abstraction (see Chapter 7). Another problem with this account is that it makes it hard to account for situations where scientists produce data without knowing exactly what it is that those data are documenting – *which* attribute of *which* phenomenon is being represented. Such a situation may emerge, for instance, in the research approach that Friedrich Steinle (1997), Richard Burian (2007) and Maureen O'Malley (2008) have described as *exploratory experimentation*, where data production is driven by the availability of specific instruments or procedures (such as a genome sequencer that makes it easy to produce sequencing data from any organic sample), and by the hope that data generated through those means will inspire new observations, questions or insights on as yet unknown phenomena. Researchers do not typically start their inquiries with a clear idea of what their data may represent; and even by the end of their study, they may have diverging interpretations of exactly which phenomena are being captured by the data. Perhaps the most famous example of such a situation consists of the photographs of DNA structure made by Rosalind Franklin in the early 1950s. Franklin, a crystallographer by training, was producing those images to explore the arrangement of nucleic acids in chromosomes. James Watson and Francis Crick, with backgrounds in biology and biochemistry, interpreted the same photographs as evidence for how DNA coding works – a discovery that eventually earned them the Nobel Prize. Rosalind's interpretation of the significance of her data was not wrong nor uninteresting, indeed it foreshadowed other developments in biology, such as the discovery of copying mechanisms for DNA. Nevertheless, Watson's and Crick's interpretation was widely regarded as much more important, and this was in part due to their own ambitious quest of finding the mechanism for inheritance (the 'code of life'): when they saw the data, they were immediately able to use them as evidence for their hypothesis (in James Watson's words, 'everything fell into place', Watson 1968).

The relational view on data can make sense of cases like this, but it is not without its problems either. For example, the representational view of data makes better sense of the idea that a specific dataset remains the same even when it is copied in multiple versions or when it changes format, e.g. from a .jpeg to a .pdf file or from one inscription to another (as in the case of the abstraction of stripes into symbols used by Rheinberger, discussed above). In those cases, it is the representational value of the data that defines their identify and continuity in time and space, rather than the specific embodiment of the data at any given moment. Another problem with the relational approach concerns how portability itself is defined, and whether it always requires that data are conceptualized as material entities. Would a sighting of an object by witnesses count as making that object portable, because the witnesses carry the image of the object in their head? So, when a scientist sees an event that no one else witnesses, which leaves a trace in her memory and which she then tells others about, does this count as data? Such a case is not typically regarded as an instance of data production by today's scientific institutions (see Steve Shapin's 1994 history of witnessing in science), and yet this question becomes highly relevant when going beyond the scientific domain and thinking about data in other knowledge domains, such as legal cases.

Data as sources of information

This chapter has focused on data as artefacts that are taken to carry information about the world, and on the processes through which the attribution of information content to data can be made, from the point of view of the philosophy of science. These issues have strong bearing on the philosophy of information. Despite his insistence on a mathematical interpretation of information, Claude Shannon himself recognized the polymorphic nature of the notion of information and its inter-dependence with fields of application: 'It is hardly to be expected that a single concept of information would satisfactorily account for the numerous possible applications of this general field' (Shannon 1993, 180). Few philosophers, however, have ventured to examine how data and information are treated within scientific practices, and with which implications. Luciano Floridi has paved the way towards such investigations by providing a framework that places the study of data at the heart of the philosophy of information (see Chapters 6 and 7 of this book). In his view, 'there can be no information without data representation' (or 'physical implementation', Floridi 2005). Data thus function both as *sources* from which information can be obtained and as *media* in which information can be inscripted. Indeed, Floridi defines information itself as 'data + meaning', and a datum consists of 'x being different from y, where the x and the y are two uninterpreted variables and the domain is left open to further interpretation'

(Floridi 2011: 85; Chapter 6). Floridi calls this latter characteristic an 'uninterpreted difference', thus stressing the materiality of data in ways that resonate with Ian Hacking's views on 'marks' and more generally with the relational account. This is particularly evident in Floridi's definition of data as 'relata' and *'diaphora de re*, that is, as lack of uniformity in the real world out there' (ibid., 85–87). Moreover, he provides a taxonomy of data types which is extremely useful when analysing the status and role of data in scientific practice. For instance, he distinguishes between primary data, in which information is encoded, and secondary data, which provide information through their absence, and meta-data, which provide information about the ways in which data came to be, which is highly relevant to interpreting their significance.

One crucial issue raised by Floridi's interpretation concerns the relation between data and truth-value. Floridi maintains that the truthfulness of data needs to be evaluated in relation to the context in which they are produced, and specifically the goal and level of abstraction for which data are taken to carry information. Thus, truthfulness is not an intrinsic property of data themselves, but rather is determined by the situation in which data are generated. Thus, data are *relata* with respect to the context in which they have been produced, but their significance does not change in relation to the contexts in which they are used as evidence – researchers need to uncover the truth-value of data by identifying what they were originally taken to indicate. This position places Floridi's account beyond accusations of relativism. However, it also moves him away from a more radically relational view, within which the significance of data – the information that they are taken to carry – can vary depending on the context in which they are adopted and used. In this latter approach, the conditions under which truth is established are dependent on the theoretical, material and social commitments of the group(s) involved in interpreting data – a position that can more easily be interpreted as a form of relativism, or 'perspectivalism' in Giere's words. Data are functional components of a process of inquiry, defined by their role as evidence. It is therefore not by looking at data in isolation that questions of truth-value can be addressed; rather, it is by exploring the ways in which data are situated in specific contexts of inquiry.

An advantage of latter approach is its ability to reconcile the *prima facie* contradictory perceptions of data as 'given' and 'made' which, as noted at the start of this chapter, have long plagued philosophical and scientific discussions of data processing and interpretation. Data do not need to be conceptualized as objective and context-independent units in order to make sense of their value as evidence towards scientific claims. Acknowledging the subjective, context-dependent nature of data is a fruitful starting point when fostering their adoption as evidence for a variety of different claims. This framework also helps to understand the link between data and scientific knowledge production. Data are not, by themselves, a form of knowledge. Rather, data need to be interpreted in order to yield knowledge; and interpretation, in whichever form and through whichever process it is achieved, involves using data as evidence for one or more claims about phenomena. It is those claims, rather than the data, which express knowledge about reality, and are therefore often referred to as 'knowledge claims' or *propositional knowledge*. This form of knowledge is also what scientists typically refer to as expressing the scientific significance of data.

In closing, a few words about the notion of evidence used in this chapter. A feature that all the above accounts of data have in common is an understanding of evidence as the grounds on which specific claims about reality acquire credibility. In more general terms, evidence is here assumed to consist in whatever makes a given assertion believable, or anyhow increases its intelligibility and/or plausibility to a given audience. The definition is necessarily broad, as there are several ways in which evidence may be provided, not all of which are in the form of data. For example, a logically constructed argument may function as evidence, by increasing the plausibility of a given claim (as when I tell my toddler son that 'lying is dangerous', and provide evidence by arguing that 'it is very hard to hide the truth, and if you are found out, you may be punished'). Specific actions, such as pointing to an object or staging a demonstration, can also function as evidence for assertions (e.g. supporting the claim 'the leaves have fallen from the trees' by pointing to a nearby forest, or the claim 'it is possible for adult humans to jump over this fence' by successfully doing it).[2] This definition of evidence restricts the notion to a relation with a propositional statement, which may be overly restrictive when considering situations where evidence is accrued to demonstrate a state of affairs not easily captured by language. Whether the epistemic role of data as evidence is always in relation to a proposition is a question worth asking, though existing accounts of the epistemic status of data tend to give this for granted.

Notes

1 Notable contributions to this scholarship include Nancy Cartwright (1983), Mary Morgan and Margaret Morrison (1999) and Ronald Giere (2006), among many others.
2 An overall review of philosophical debates around the notion of evidence is provided by Thomas Kelly (2014).

References

Ankeny, R.A., Chang, H., Boumans, M. and Boon, M. (2011). 'Introduction: philosophy of science in practice'. *European Journal for Philosophy of Science* 1 (3): 303–307.

Bacon, F. (1994). *The Novum Organum: With Other Parts of the Great Instauration*. Edited and translated by Peter Urbach and John Gibson. La Salle, IL: Open Court.

Bogen, James. "Noise in the World." *Philosophy of Science* 77 (2010): 778–791

Bogen, J. (2013). 'Theory and Observation in Science'. In *The Stanford Encyclopedia of Philosophy* (Spring 2013 Edition). Edited by Edward N. Zalta. URL http://plato.stanford.edu/archives/spr2013/entries/science-theory-observation/. Accessed February 20, 2014.

Bogen, J. and Woodward J. (1988). 'Saving the Phenomena'. *The Philosophical Review* 97(3): 303–352.

Burian, R. (1997). 'Exploratory Experimentation and the Role of Histochemical Techniques in the Work of Jean Brachet, 1938–1952'. *History and Philosophy of the Life Sciences* 19: 27–45.

Cartwright, N. (1983). *How the Laws of Physics Lie*. Oxford: Oxford University Press.

Chang, H. (2004). *Inventing Temperature: Measurement and Scientific Progress*. New York: Oxford University Press.

Chang, H. (2012). *Is Water H₂O? Evidence, Realism and Pluralism*. Dordrecht: Springer.

Collins, H.M. (1985). *Changing Order: Replication and Induction in Scientific Practice*. Chicago, IL: The University of Chicago Press.

Daston, L. and Galison, P. (1992). 'The Image of Objectivity'. *Representations* 40: 81–128.

DeVries, W. (2014). 'Wilfrid Sellars'. *The Stanford Encyclopedia of Philosophy* (Fall 2014 Edition), Edward N. Zalta (ed.), URL http://plato.stanford.edu/entries/sellars/. Accessed April 2015.

Duhem, P. (1906). *La théorie physique. Son objet, sa structure*. Paris: Chevalier & Rivière (Vrin, 2007).

Edwards, P.N. (2010). *A Vast Machine: Computer Models, Climate Data, and the Politics of Global Warming*. Cambridge, MA: MIT Press.

Floridi, L. (2005). 'Is Information Meaningful Data?' *Philosophy and Phenomenological Research*, 70(2): 351–370.

Floridi, L. (2011). *The Philosophy of Information*. Oxford: Oxford University Press.

Franklin, Allan. *The Neglect of Experiment*. Cambridge, UK: Cambridge University Press, 1986.

Frigg, R. and Hartmann, S. (2012). 'Models in Science'. In Edward N. Zalta (ed.) *Stanford Encyclopedia of Philosophy*. Accessed October 20, 2014.

Galison, P. (1997). *Image and Logic: A Material Culture of Microphysics*. Chicago, IL: University of Chicago Press.

Giere, R.N. (2006). *Scientific Perspectivism*. Chicago, IL: University of Chicago Press.

Gooding, D.C. (1990). *Experiment and the Making of Meaning*. Dordrecht & Boston: Kluwer.

Griesemer, J.R. (2006). 'Theoretical Integration, Cooperation, and Theories as Tracking Devices'. *Biological Theory*, 1(1): 4–7.

Hacking, I. (1983). *Representing and Intervening: Introductory Topics in the Philosophy of Natural Science*. Cambridge: Cambridge University Press.

Hacking, I. (1992). 'The Self-Vindication of the Laboratory Sciences'. In *Science as Practice and Culture*, edited by Andrew Pickering, 29–64. Chicago, IL: The University of Chicago Press.

Hanson, N.R. (1958). *Patterns of Discovery*. Cambridge: Cambridge University Press.

Hempel, C.G. (1970). 'Fundamentals of Concept Formation in Empirical Science'. In *Foundations of the Unity of Science, Volume 2*, edited by Otto Neurath, Rudolf Carnap, and C. Morris, 651–746. Chicago, IL: University of Chicago Press. Originally published as Carl G. Hempel, *Fundamentals of Concept Formation in Empirical Science*. Chicago, IL: The University of Chicago Press, 1952.

Kellert, S.H., Longino, H.E. and Kenneth Waters, C. (2006). *Scientific Pluralism*. Minneapolis, MN: University of Minnesota Press.

Kelly, T. (2014). 'Evidence', *The Stanford Encyclopedia of Philosophy* (Fall 2014 Edition), Edward N. Zalta (ed.), URL http://plato.stanford.edu/archives/fall2014/entries/evidence/. Accessed October 20, 2014.

Kuhn, T.S. (1962). *The Structure of Scientific Revolutions*. Chicago, IL: University of Chicago Press.

Lakatos, I. (1968). 'Criticism and the Methodology of Scientific Research Programmes'. *Proceedings of the Aristotelian Society*, 69: 149–186.

Latour, B. (1999). 'Circulating Reference': Sampling the Soil in the Amazon Forest.2 In *Pandora's Hope: Essays on the Reality of Science Studies*, by Bruno Latour, 24–79. Cambridge, MA: Harvard University Press.

Latour, B. and Woolgar, S. (1979). *Laboratory Life: The Construction of Scientific Facts*. Princeton, NJ: Princeton University Press.

Leonelli, S. (2009) 'On the Locality of Data and Claims About Phenomena'. *Philosophy of Science,* 76(5): 737–749.

Leonelli, S. (2014) 'Data Interpretation in the Digital Age'. *Perspectives on Science*, 22(3): 397–417.

Leonelli, S. (2016) *Data-Centric Biology: A Philosophical Study*. Chicago, IL: Chicago University Press.

Mill, J.S. (1843). *A System of Logic, Ratiocinative and Inductive, Being a Connected View of the Principles of Evidence, and the Methods of Scientific Investigation*. London: John W. Parker.

Morgan, M.S. (2012). *The World in the Model: How Economists Work and Think*. Cambridge: Cambridge University Press.

Morgan, M.S. and Morrison, M. (1999). *Models as Mediators: Perspectives on Natural and Social Science*. Cambridge: Cambridge University Press.

O'Malley, M.A. (2008). 'Exploratory Experimentation and Scientific Practice: Metagenomics and the Proteorhodopsin Case'. *History and Philosophy of the Life Sciences*, 29(3): 337–358.

Radder, H. (2006). *The World Observed/The World Conceived*. Pittsburgh, PA: University of Pittsburgh Press.

Radder, H. (2009). 'The philosophy of scientific experimentation: a review'. *Automated Experimentation*, 1: 2.

Reichenbach, H. (1938). *Experience and Prediction: An Analysis of the Foundations and the Structure of Knowledge*. Chicago, IL: University of Chicago Press.

Rheinberger, H. (2011). 'Infra-experimentality: From Traces to Data, From Data to Patterning Facts'. *History of Science*, 49(3): 337–348.

Royal Society. (2012). 'Science as an Open Enterprise'. Accessed January 14, 2014. URL http://royalsociety.org/policy/projects/science-public-enterprise/report/.

Schindler, S. (2013). 'Theory-laden Experimentation'. *Studies in History and Philosophy of Science* 44 (1): 89–101.

Shannon, C.E. (1993). *Claude E. Shannon: Collected Papers*. Edited by Neil J. A. Sloane, and Aaron D. Wyner. Piscataway, NJ: IEEE Press.

Shapin, S. (1994). *A Social History of Truth*, Chicago, IL: University of Chicago Press.

Steinle, F. (1997). 'Entering New Fields: Exploratory Uses of Experimentation'. *Philosophy of Science*, 64: S65–S74.

Suppes, P. (1962). 'Models of Data', in Ernest Nagel, Patrick Suppes and Alfred Tarski (eds.), *Logic, Methodology and Philosophy of Science: Proceedings of the 1960 International Congress*. Stanford, CA: Stanford University Press, 252–261. Reprinted in Patrick Suppes: *Studies in the Methodology and Foundations of Science. Selected Papers from 1951 to 1969*. Dordrecht: Reidel 1969, 24–35.

Vakarelov, O.K. (2012). 'The Information Medium'. *Philosophy and Technology* 25(1): 47–65.

Watson, J. (1968). *The Double Helix*. Athenaeum.

Whewell, W. (1989). 'Novum Organon Renovatum, Book II', In *William Whewell's Theory of Scientific Method*, edited by Robert E. Butts, 103–249. Indianapolis, IN: Hackett Publishing Company. Originally published in William Whewell, *Novum Organon Renovatum, Book II*. London, UK: John W. Parker and Son, 1858.

18

INFORMATIONAL METAPHYSICS

The informational nature of reality

Terrell Ward Bynum

> Information is information, not matter or energy.
> No materialism which does not admit this can
> survive at the present day.
>
> *Norbert Wiener*

Introduction

The present chapter provides a brief introduction to one important topic in the burgeoning new field of *informational metaphysics* – a field which, in turn, is part of the broader "Philosophy of Information" movement to which the present volume is dedicated. Specifically, this chapter focuses upon *physical information* – also called "environmental information" – and explores some metaphysical ideas intended to explain the nature of physical information and to provide a theory or model of its role in ultimate reality. The first section briefly describes the historical context in which the physical nature of information was first recognized and scientifically analyzed by Norbert Wiener. Then the second section explores the implications of Wiener's discovery for our understanding of the nature of the universe. At the end of that section, the "Wienerian" conception of the universe is briefly compared to that of today's physics. The remaining sections of this chapter provide a few examples of metaphysical ideas regarding the nature of reality and the role of physical information in the universe.

Physical information and the birth of the information age

As early as 1944, MIT mathematician/philosopher Norbert Wiener came to believe that he and other pioneering information researchers were laying the foundations of a new age – Wiener called it "the automatic age" or "the new industrial revolution" – which would have staggering implications for the future of science, philosophy and, even, civilization:

> In 1944 and 1945, Wiener was already thinking about a scientific model involving communication, information, self-control – an all-embracing way of looking at

nature that would include explanations for computers and brains, biology and electronics, logic and purpose. He later wrote: "It became clear to me almost at the very beginning that these new concepts of communication and control involved a new interpretation of man, of man's knowledge of the universe, and of society."
(Rheingold 2000, p. 110; quoting from Wiener 1966, p. 325)

Near the end of the Second World War, Wiener had a crucial new insight: he realized that *information is physical* since it is governed by the second law of thermodynamics. Information, he saw, plays a significant role in every physical entity and process. Delighted by this discovery, he walked the halls of his building at MIT, in one of his famous "Wiener walks" (Conway and Siegelman, 2005), telling everyone he met that "information is entropy" (Rheingold 1985, p. 112). This was an important new addition to the foundations that he and others were building of the new age that he envisioned. By that time, Alan Turing already had published his groundbreaking theory of computation, and Wiener himself already had created the new science of communication and control, which he would later call "cybernetics."

In autumn of 1946, Wiener gave a keynote speech at the New York Academy of Sciences in which he declared that

Entropy here appears as the *negative* of the amount of information contained in the message. . . In fact, it is not surprising that entropy and information are negatives of one another. Information measures order and entropy measures disorder.
(Wiener 1946, quoted in Conway and Siegelman, 2005, p. 164)

A short time after Wiener's speech, Warren McCulloch, a friend and colleague of Wiener's, sent prepublication copies to forty prominent scientists in America and around the world, including, for example, Claude Shannon at Bell Labs, quantum physicist Erwin Schrödinger in Austria, and (very likely) probability theorist Andrey Kolmogorov at the Soviet Academy of Science. (Conway and Siegelman, 2005, p. 166)

In 1948, Wiener's book, *Cybernetics: Or Control and Communication in the Animal and the Machine*, was published and it became an immediate scientific best seller. "The book flew off the shelves. *Cybernetics* went through five printings in the first six months and became the talk of international publishing circles." It was "the Big Bang that launched the Information Age" and "put science and societies worldwide on a new trajectory" (Conway and Siegelman, 2005, p. 181). Influential publications, such as *Scientific American, Newsweek, Business Week, Time Magazine,* and *The New York Times* – to name only a few examples – published major articles about Wiener and his new science. In that same year, Claude Shannon published two important papers on information theory (Shannon 1948a and 1948b), with an acknowledgement to Wiener for his helpful advice.

In summary, by the end of the 1940s, the "Information Revolution" had been launched – through the work of pioneers, such as Turing, Wiener, Shannon, Zuse, von Neumann, and others. Especially important to the success of that revolution were Wiener's science of cybernetics and his discovery that information is physical.

The importance of physical information – Wiener's universe and today's physics

Philosophically, Wiener was a materialist, and his realization that entropy measures lost information provided a new way to understand the nature of physical objects and processes. Indeed, it was a new way to understand the ultimate nature of the universe. To use today's language, Wiener's discovery revealed that all physical entities in the world are "informational objects" or "informational processes" – an account of the nature of the universe that is worthy of today's "Information Age"! The very nature of the universe, then, explains why the so-called "Information Revolution" has enabled humanity to change the world more quickly, and more profoundly, than any previous technological revolution: The Information Revolution provided scientific theories and tools for analyzing, manipulating, creating and altering physical entities at, what could turn out to be (see below), the deepest level of their being.

The second law of thermodynamics applies to every physical change in the universe, and Wiener realized that an increase of "entropy" amounts to *a loss of physical information*. All physical objects and processes, then, can be viewed as patterns of information (data structures) encoded/embodied within an ever-changing flux of matter-energy. Every physical object or process is part of a creative coming-to-be and a destructive fading-away, as current information patterns – data structures – erode and new ones emerge. This "Wienerian" view of the nature of the universe makes every physical entity a combination of matter-energy and physical information. As science writer Charles Seife noted, in his book *Decoding the Universe*,

> Every particle in the universe, every electron, every atom, every particle not yet discovered, is packed with information […] that can be transferred, processed, and dissipated. Each star in the universe, each one of the countless galaxies in the heavens, is packed full of information, information that can escape and travel. That information is always flowing, moving from place to place, spreading throughout the cosmos.
>
> *(Seife 2006, p. 3)*

Even living things, according to Wiener, are informational objects. They store and process physical information in their genes and use that information to create the building blocks of life, such as amino acids, proteins and genes. Indeed, they even use stored information to create new living things; namely, their own offspring. Animals' nervous systems store and process physical information, thereby making their activities, perceptions, and emotions possible. And, like every other physical entity in Wiener's universe, *even human beings can be viewed as informational entities*. Thus, humans are essentially *patterns* of information that persist through an ongoing exchange of matter-energy. So according to Wiener,

> We are but whirlpools in a river of ever-flowing water. We are not stuff that abides, but patterns that perpetuate themselves.
>
> *(Wiener 1954, p. 96)*

. . .

> The individuality of the body is that of a flame […] of a form rather than of a bit of substance.
>
> *(Wiener 1954, p. 102)*

Through metabolic processes like breathing, digesting, perspiring, and so on, the matter-energy that makes up a person's body is constantly changing. In spite of this continuous exchange of matter-energy with the outside world, *the pattern of information encoded in a person's body remains very similar over time*, changing only very gradually. This preserves, for an extended period, a person's life, functionality and personal identity. So a human being can be understood as an "informational object" whose personal identity is constituted by a persisting pattern of physical information, rather than the particular atoms, molecules, and energy that happen, incidentally, to make up one's body at any given moment. Eventually, of course, the information pattern that constitutes a person's identity, and accounts for his or her ability to live and function, will have changed significantly. The inevitable result is aging, increasing disability and death – that is, the destruction of the physical information pattern that constitutes the essence of one's physical being.

Significant developments in physics since Wiener's time have deepened and extended this "Wienerian" view of physical reality. Some important physicists have argued that even matter-energy owes its very existence to information. For example, in 1990, an influential paper by physicist John Wheeler introduced his famous phrase "it from bit" (Wheeler 1990), and thereby gave significant impetus to the development of informational physics. In that paper, Wheeler declared that "all things physical are information theoretic in origin" – that "every physical entity, every it, derives from bits" – that "every particle, every field of force, even the spacetime continuum itself . . . derives its function, its meaning, its very existence" from bits. He predicted that "Tomorrow we will have learned to understand and express *all* of physics in the language of information" (emphasis in the original). In addition, since 1990 a number of physicists – some of them inspired by Wheeler – have made significant strides toward fulfilling his "it-from-bit" prediction. In 2006, for example, in his book *Programming the Universe*, Seth Lloyd presented evidence supporting the view that the universe is not only a vast sea of quantum information ("qubits"), it is actually a gigantic quantum computer:

> The conventional view is that the universe is nothing but elementary particles. That is true, but it is equally true that the universe is nothing but bits – or rather, nothing but qubits. Mindful that if it walks like a duck and it quacks like a duck then it's a duck . . . since the universe registers and processes information like a quantum computer, and is observationally indistinguishable from a quantum computer, then it *is* a quantum computer.
>
> *(p. 154, italics in the original)*

Five years later, in 2011, three physicists used axioms from information processing to derive the mathematical framework of quantum mechanics (Chiribella *et al.* 2011). These are only two of a growing number of achievements that have begun to fulfill Wheeler's "it from bit" prediction, and at the same time deepen and extend a Wienerian view of the nature of the universe (see the *Bynum's quantum informational structural realism* section).

What is physical information?

Physical information consists of *physical data*, and it is *syntactic*, not semantic. But what is *a datum*? A datum is essentially a difference, so a *physical* datum is a difference "embodied in," "carried by" – some would say "encoded in" or "registered by" – the matter-energy of a physical being. All the differences embodied within a physical entity, right down to the subatomic quantum differences, constitute the *physical structure* of that entity; so *physical beings are data structures*, some of them enormously complex. Some differences are perceivable at the "macro-level," while others are non-perceivable ones at various "micro-levels." Removing differences – "erasing *data*" – embodied within a physical being erodes the physical structure of that being; and if there is enough erosion, or the right sort of erosion, the being may be significantly altered, damaged, or even destroyed. *Physical beings are data structures*, but the data they encode are not *made of* matter-energy – the data are *relations, not material objects*. As Luciano Floridi explains, a datum is ultimately reducible to *a lack of uniformity*. More formally, according to the *diaphoric interpretation* (*diaphora* is the Greek word for 'difference'), the general definition of a datum is:

Dd datum $=_{\text{def.}}$ *x* being distinct from *y*

where the *x* and the *y* are two uninterpreted variables and the domain is left open to further interpretation.

(Floridi 2011, p. 85)

Consider the *relata* that make a house a house. A house builder may begin with a pile of lumber and a pile of bricks and a pile of metal pipes, and so on. However, piles of building supplies do not constitute a house, because *they do not have the form of a house* – that is, *they do not embody/carry/encode the appropriate relata*. If a house builder removes lumber, bricks, pipes, and so on, from the piles, and uses those supplies to build a house (thereby *changing the space-time relationships* among the various building supplies), that same matter, which initially comprised piles of lumber, bricks, and so on, would then comprise a house. So, it is the *form of the house, the pattern of relata, the data structure,* not the matter in the building supplies that make the house a house. The form of the house is *physical*, in the sense that it exists in space-time, and it can be observed, measured and scientifically studied. *The informational pattern encoded in the house is a physical phenomenon, but it is not matter or energy.* So Wiener's statement that "information is information, not matter or energy" is fully consistent with his materialistic view of the ultimate nature of the universe.

Plato on the nature of matter – informationally analyzed

Plato lived more than two millennia before today's Information Revolution, and so he did not couch his metaphysical descriptions and explanations in informational terms. Nevertheless it may be of interest here to discuss, briefly, Plato's account of the nature of matter from the point of view of an informational metaphysician. Plato accepted, from the philosopher Empedocles, the view that there are four basic elements (Empedocles called them "roots") that comprise all of matter: earth, air, fire and water. In addition, Plato accepted the hypothesis of the atomists, Leucippus and Democritus, that matter consists of very tiny, separate *invisible* units (atoms). In the second division of his *Timaeus* (47E–69B), Plato presented a description of the "deep structure" of matter, which was imposed, he said, upon inchoate matter by a totally rational god, the Demiurge (the "Craftsman" or "Artist"). As Gregory Vlastos explains, in his book, *Plato's Universe*,

> The matter which confronts the Demiurge in its primordial state is inchoate. The four primary kinds of matter, earth, water, air and fire, are present here in a blurred, indefinite form; their motion is disorderly. The Demiurge changes all this. He transforms matter from chaos to cosmos by impressing on it regular stereometric form. When he has done his job, all of the fire, air, and water in existence will consist of tetrahedra, octahedra, and icosahedra respectively, that is to say of solids whose faces are invariably equilateral triangles. And earth will be found to consist of minute cubes [hexahedra].

(Vlastos 1975, 2005, pp. 69–70)

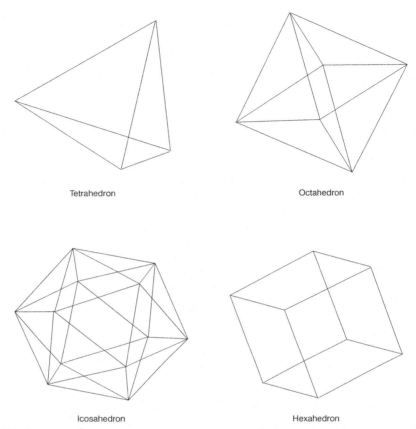

Tetrahedron   Octahedron

Icosahedron   Hexahedron

Figure 18.1 Geometric figures

The Demiurge did not create inchoate matter. It was present before he imposed order and structure on it – thereby "impressing" information onto the matter – or "encoding" information in the matter – essentially creating "beautiful" data structures. The structures that carry physical information in Plato's physical realm (beneath the moon), therefore, are tetrahedra (fire), octahedra (air), icosahedra (water), and cubes (earth); but since these are all constructed from two kinds of triangles, it is the triangles that constitute a "deeper microstructure" which encodes physical information within earth, air, fire, and water. And since the triangles, in turn, could be constructed from straight lines and angles, perhaps the lines and angles comprise the deepest microstructure that carries physical information in Plato's physical realm.

The geometric figures that comprise earth, air, fire and water, according to Plato, are mere *imperfect copies* of the perfect, unchanging geometric forms which a rational mind could access in the realm of Platonic forms. Those perfect forms are *not part* of the physical earth, air, fire and water corpuscles; but they can help a rational being better understand the nature of those corpuscles.

Dipert's "world as pure structure"

Randall Dipert's model of physical reality, "World as Pure Structure" (Dipert 2002, pp. 147–149) has much in common with Plato's account of matter. Both philosophers assume that, at the deepest level of physical reality, all existing entities are discrete; and both use structures from pure mathematics to describe and understand physical structures. Plato uses mathematically "beautiful" 3-dimentional tetrahedra, octahedra, icosahedra, and cubes, all of which could be constructed from simpler structures; namely, two specific triangles. Similarly, Dipert uses *a very large set* of "undirected graphs," all of which could be constructed using one symmetric relation that he calls "the World Relation":

> An ideal description of the structure of the world, what physics and cosmology aim for, is necessarily a mathematical structure. Mathematical structures require at least one relation in order to be nontrivial. In fact, it is possible to describe any structure at all in terms of structures using only one symmetric relation, which I dub the "World Relation." I argue that a subset of these [undirected] graphs is maximally simple, in terms of the numbers of properties and relations needed to describe a structure, any structure. The structures induced by one symmetric relation are precisely those that [Undirected] Graph Theory describes.
>
> *(Dipert 2002, p. 147)*

An important difference between Plato's account of physical reality and Dipert's is that Plato's is, presumably, a version of realism – that is, Plato took his account to be *a true description* of physical reality. Dipert, on the other hand, offers his account as *a model* of physical reality, employing mathematical structures that constitute

> the only minimal and perfect characterization of entities that convey information. They "are" not themselves pure informational entities, but they are an ideal, or an almost ideal, representation of information-carrying entities of all sorts.
>
> *(Dipert 2002, pp.148–149)*

According to this model, the discrete entities of which the physical universe is composed are combinatorially "horrendously complex, although ultimately finite." They can all be constructed using just connecting lines and points (called "nodes" and "arcs"), where the length of the line is irrelevant. Even small such structures – for example, with seven to forty nodes – "carry enormous amounts of information because of the phenomenon of combinatorially explosive nonisomorphic graphs. With only nine nodes, [for example,] there are 308,708 distinct, that is nonisomorphic, graphs." To reduce the number of undirected graphs to the fewest possible, while retaining the ability to describe "any structure" in a digital universe, Dipert employs Leibniz's principle of "no distinction without a difference" to eliminate automorphic graphs. Nevertheless,

> [even] with this limitation, the number of distinct . . . graphs, and thus "simplest" information-carrying entities, rises suprapolynomially. Such a feature is necessary if we guess that the universe is, information-theoretically, enormously complex and has a colossal number of other such possible structures, that is, possible worlds.
>
> *(Dipert 2002, p. 147)*

Dipert's model of the structure of reality is remarkably powerful and flexible, enabling him to cast light upon a vast variety of contemporary scientific facts and theories, as illustrated by the following extended passage from his article "The Mathematical Structure of the World: the World as Graph":

I need to sketch how structuralism could plausibly analyze physical (and phenomenal) objects, their structure (what we might call physical structure), including redescribing space, time, fields and forces, and quanta. In short, how would my "theory of everything" (TOE) link up with theories of everything (TOEs) in contemporary physics? My speculations are these. Physical objects, even the finest subatomic particles, certainly do not correspond to vertices. Instead, they themselves are composite entities, subgraphs of the world graph. Physical microstructure is graph-theoretic macrostructure. Space and time are frameworks or grids that may conveniently, if sometimes imperfectly, be laid on the world graph. If there is something that is an aspect of things or experience called "time," and if it is asymmetric, this is ultimately because there are asymmetric paths connecting certain subgraphs that are the entities and their states. Forces, fields, and causal chains are also such paths among the subgraphs we identify as physical objects/states, and each is distinguished (if at all) by its structure. Some of the stranger physical phenomena are, I believe, accommodated without too much difficulty: the two electrons in the double slit experiment [in quantum mechanics] are not, for example, the fully distinct entities that we imagine them to be (or location and momentum are not independent properties). They graph-theoretically overlap.

(Dipert 1997, pp. 355–356)

Steinhart's digital metaphysics

A different kind of informational model is Eric Steinhart's "Digital Metaphysics" (Steinhart 1998), which was inspired by the theory of *cellular automata*, first developed in the 1940s by John von Neumann and Stanisław Ulam, and later made better known in the 1970s by Conway's simulation game, *The Game of Life*. To understand Steinhart's model, one could begin by imagining all of space-time – it is colossal, but not infinite – then dividing space-time into very, very tiny units, "perhaps 10^{30} across a single atomic nucleus." Steinhart's model assumes that each of these very tiny space-time units is actually a computer – a unit of "computational space-time (CST)":

> Honoring Leibniz, we refer to the units of CST as *monads*. . . . Each monad in CST has a finite number of states, computes a finitely specifiable algorithm, and is linked to a finite number of neighbors. . . . Every physically possible world is a causally closed and spatio-temporally maximal (but finite) totality of [such] monads arranged to form a *massively parallel dynamical system*.
>
> *(Steinhart 1998, p. 119)*

Rather than modeling information-carrying *structures*, like Dipert, Steinhart aims to model *"what nature is actually doing"* when it generates physical structures:

> The claim that space-time computes has nothing at all to do with symbol manipulation or numerical calculation; it says that physical processes are ultimately effective procedures (i.e. programs) functionally composed of primitive natural operations. . . . Think of how the Jacquard loom, the player piano, and even fertilized eggs and seeds are programmed. Programs [in my sense] are not recipes; they are dynamic rational patterns. . . . Their executions are series of concrete transformations of states of affairs, that is *histories*.
>
> *(Steinhart 1998, p. 119)*

For Steinhart, the deepest level of physical reality consists of his "monads," that is, very tiny computers forming "a massively dynamical system." Everything else in the world is "an appearance supervening on monads":

> Monads alone are *real*; everything else is some appearance distributed over and supervening on monads. . . . Thus quarks, electrons, atoms, molecules, organisms, humans, characters, brains, minds, languages, ethical norms, religions, economies, nations, planets, stars, etc. are all equally patterns over sets of monads.
>
> *(Steinhart 1998, p. 123)*

The "laws of nature" in any particular universe – including ours – result from the specific programs and patterns of programs running on the tiny monads that constitute the universe. Changing the programs that run on the monads would create a different possible world. And, according to Steinhart, all possible worlds must be finite and digital. Steinhart rejects the idea that any possible universe could be infinitely complex, because infinities generate paradoxes and contradictions. Since continuities entail infinities, nature cannot contain continuities. Therefore, all logically possible universes (including ours) must be digital and finitely extended.

Floridi's informational structural realism

In his book, *The Philosophy of Information* (Floridi 2011), Luciano Floridi presents his theory of Informational Structural Realism. Before doing so, however, he felt the need to argue against digital ontology because some people may, *mistakenly*, assume that it is Floridi's own theory. As a result, his book contains a chapter refuting digital ontology (Chapter 14) before he presents his own theory (Chapter 15).

Floridi's refutation of digital ontology

In Chapter 14, Floridi's refutation focuses especially upon versions of digital ontology that presuppose the "Zuse Thesis" advocated by the German computer scientist Konrad Zuse:

> The universe is being deterministically computed on some sort of giant but discrete computer.
>
> *(Zuse 1967, 1969) [quoted in Floridi 2011, p. 319]*

Such theories are summarized by Edward Fredkin as theories which are

> based upon two concepts: bits, like the binary digits in a computer, correspond to the most microscopic representation of state information; and the temporal evolution of state is a digital informational process similar to what goes on in the circuitry of a computer processor.
>
> *(Fredkin 2003, p. 189) [quoted in Floridi 2011, p.318]*

To begin his refutation of this kind of digital ontology, Floridi provides the following summary:

> The overall perspective, emerging from digital ontology, is one of a metaphysical monism: ultimately, the physical universe is a gigantic digital computer. It is

fundamentally composed of digits, instead of matter or energy, with material objects as a complex secondary manifestation, while dynamic processes are some kind of computational states transitions. There are no digitally irreducible infinities, infinitesimals, continuities, or locally determined random variables. In short, the ultimate nature of reality is not smooth and random but grainy and deterministic.

(Floridi 2011, p. 319)

Most versions of digital ontology typically presuppose that the entire physical universe is an enormous computer (pancomputationalism). Nevertheless, digital ontology *can* be separated from pancomputationalism; and, indeed, some versions of pancomputationalism (for example, Laplace's) are analogue rather than digital. Floridi makes it clear that his Informational Structural Realism is *neither digital nor analogue*; and he also notes that it is *not* committed, one way or the other, to pancomputationalism.

It is my view that Floridi's case against digital ontology, as defined above, is strong. Readers interested in the step-by-step details are referred to Chapter 14 of *The Philosophy of Information*. Here, I want to summarize some of Floridi's key points against digital ontology in order to set the stage for discussions below about his Informational Structural Realism, and about my suggested quantum variant of it, which is not subject to any of the objections listed here:

Criticism (i), digital ontology requires more digital memory than is possible: If one assumes (like Fredkin, quoted above, for example) that ultimate reality consists of classical bits being processed like those in a traditional computer, our current scientific understanding of the universe would lead us to conclude that *the evolution of the universe since the Big Bang could not have occurred* because there would not have been enough digital memory. Floridi explains (2011, p. 323):

> Here is a very simple illustration: Lloyd (2002) estimates that the physical universe, understood as a computational system, could have performed 10^{120} operations on 10^{90} bits [. . .] since the Big Bang. The problem is that if this were true, the universe would 'run out of memory':

> To simulate the Universe in every detail since time began, the computer would have to have 10^{90} bits – binary digits, or devices capable of storing a 1 or a 0 – and it would have to perform 10^{120} manipulations of those bits. Unfortunately, there are probably only around 10^{80} elementary particles in the Universe.
>
> *(Ball (2002, 3 June)) [quoted in Floridi 2011, p. 323]*

It is important to note that the "bits" of digital ontology, as defined here, are *traditional binary bits* that can be *either 1 or 0 but not both*. Therefore, criticism (i) would *not* apply to quantum bits (qubits), which can be *both* 1 and 0 at the same time, as well as an infinite number of states between 1 and 0 (see the *Bynum's quantum informational structural realism* section below).

Criticism (ii), digital ontology requires a radical change in current scientific practice: A second criticism of digital ontology (Floridi 2011, p. 324) is the fact that "its success would represent a profound change in our scientific practices and outlook." Since a significant amount of current science is based upon powerful analogue ideas like force fields, waves, continuous functions, differential equations, Fourier transforms, and so on, this places a heavy burden of proof upon advocates of digital ontology, who would have to show that the powerful analogue ideas of contemporary science can be successfully reinterpreted digitally.

Criticism (iii), digital ontology misapplies the concepts "digital" and "analogue": Even if defenders of digital ontology could – somehow – reinterpret the powerful analogue concepts of contemporary science, Floridi argues that "it is not so much that reality in itself is not digital, but rather that, in a metaphysical context, the digital vs analogue dichotomy is not applicable." He introduces a thought experiment to demonstrate that the concepts "digital" and "analogue" apply only within our models of reality. They are features of our models "adopted to analyze reality, not features of reality in itself." Some models are analogue and some are digital, and we are unable to know whether reality itself is either of these or something to which neither concept can be applied. To overcome this impasse, Floridi "seeks to reconcile digital and analogue ontology by identifying the minimal denominator shared by both." Thus, Floridi adopts the following strategy:

> What remains invariant [in ultimate reality, given our model-building perspective] cannot be its digital or its analogue nature, but rather the structural properties that give rise to a digital or analogue reality. These invariant, structural properties are those in which science is mainly interested. So it seems reasonable to move from an ontology of things – to which it is difficult not to apply the digital/discrete vs analogue/continuous alternative – to an ontology of structural relations, to which it is immediately obvious that the previous dichotomy is irrelevant.
>
> *(2011, p. 334)*

Floridi's case against digital ontology is intended to clear the way for his positive defense of Informational Structural Realism in Chapter 15 of *The Philosophy of Information*. His move "to an ontology of structural relations" is central to that defense, which is discussed in the next section.

Floridi's informational structural realism

In presenting his positive case for Informational Structural Realism, Floridi agrees with Putnam's "No-Miracles Argument":

> (Some form of) realism 'is the only philosophy that does not make [the predictive success of] science a miracle'.
>
> *(Putnam 1975, p. 73) [quoted by Floridi on p. 345]*

Like every version of realism, Floridi's presupposes that there exists "a mind-independent reality addressed by, and constraining, knowledge." In addition, his theory supports the adoption of models which "carry a minimal ontological commitment in favour of the structural properties of reality and a reflective, equally minimal, ontological commitment in favour of structural objects." (2011, p. 339) Unlike other versions of structural realism, though, Floridi's theory

> supports *an informational interpretation of these structural objects*. This second commitment [. . .] is justified by epistemic reasons. We are allowed to commit ourselves ontologically to whatever minimal conception of objects is useful to make sense of our first commitment in favour of structures. The first commitment answers the question 'what can we know?'; and the second commitment answers the question 'what can we justifiably assume to be in the external world?'.
>
> *(2011, p. 339) [my emphasis added here]*

The "structural objects" that Floridi presupposes – the primordial "*Ur*-relations" of the universe – are what he calls *dedomena*: "mind-independent points of lack of uniformity in the fabric of Being" – "mere *differentiae de re*" (he also refers to them, metaphorically, as "data in the wild"). These cannot be directly perceived, and they cannot be detected by any kind of scientific instrument. Instead, Floridi infers their existence by a transcendental argument according to which *dedomena must exist to make it possible for any structured entities at all to exist.*

> Dedomena are not to be confused with environmental data. They are pure data or proto-epistemic data, that is, data before they are epistemically interpreted. As 'fractures in the fabric of Being', they can only be posited as an external anchor of our information, for dedomena are never accessed or elaborated independently of [an epistemic model of reality]. They can be reconstructed as ontological requirements, like Kant's *noumena* or Locke's *substance*: they are not epistemically experienced, but their presence is empirically inferred from, and required by, experience. Of course, no example can be provided, but dedomena are whatever lack of uniformity in the world is the source of (what looks to informational organisms like us as) data [. . .].
>
> *(2011, Chapter 4, pp. 85–86)*

Floridi makes a case for the view that the ultimate nature of any possible universe must include at least some dedomena, because the relation of difference is a precondition for any other relation:

> Let us consider what a completely undifferentiable entity x might be. It would be one unobservable and unidentifiable at any possible [level of abstraction]. Modally, this means that there would be no possible world in which x would exist. And this simply means that there is no such x. [. . .] Imagine a toy universe constituted by a two-dimensional, boundless, white surface. Anything like this toy universe is a paradoxical fiction that only a sloppy use of logic can generate. For example, where is the observer in this universe? Would the toy universe include (at least distinguishable) points? Would there be distances between these points? The answers should be in the negative, for this is a universe without relations.
>
> *(2011, Chapter 15, p. 354)*

Thus, there can be no possible universe without relations; and since dedomena are preconditions for *any* relations, it follows that every possible universe must be made of at least some dedomena. (Note that there might also be other things which, for us, are forever unknowable.) There is much more to Floridi's defense of Informational Structural Realism, including his replies to ten possible objections, and I leave it to interested readers to find the details in Chapter 15 of *The Philosophy of Information.*

Floridi views the fact that his ontology applies to every possible world as a very positive feature. It means, for example, that Informational Structural Realism has maximum "portability," "scalability," and "interoperability."

Regarding *portability*, Floridi notes that:

> The most portable ontology would be one that could be made to 'run' in any possible world. This is what Aristotle meant by a general metaphysics of Being *qua* Being. The portability of an ontology is a function of its importability and exportability between theories even when they are disjointed ([their models] have

no observables in common). Imagine an ontology that successfully accounts for the natural numbers and for natural kinds.

(p. 357)

Scalability, according to Floridi, is the capacity of a theory to work well even when "the complexity or magnitude of the problem increases."

> Imagine an ontology that successfully accounts not only for Schrödinger's cat but also for the atomic particles dangerously decaying in its proximity.

(p. 357)

The *interoperability* of an ontology is "a function of its capacity of allowing interactions between different [scientific or common-sense] theories." Floridi illustrates this by inviting us to

> Imagine an ontology that successfully accounts for a system modeled as a brain and as a mind.

(p. 358)

Using these three notions – portability, scalability, and interoperability – Floridi introduces the concept of "a specific metaphysics," which he defines as "an ontology with fixed degrees of portability, scalability, and interoperability" (p. 358). It is possible to criticize a specific metaphysics if it is "too local," in the sense that its degrees of portability or scalability or interoperability are limited. Thus, he notes:

> For example, a Cartesian metaphysics is notoriously undermined by its poor degree of interoperability: the mind/body dualism generates a mechanistic physics and a non-materialist philosophy of mind that do not interact very well. Leibniz's metaphysics of monads is not easily scalable (it is hard to account for physical macro-objects in its terms).

(p. 358)

The most "local" kind of ontology would be naïve realism, because it assumes that a model is a direct and accurate representation of the modeled entity. At a given moment in the history of science, this could make naïve realism appear to be very strong; but, as Floridi points out, it is "dreadfully brittle" and "easily shattered by any epistemic change," even by a simple counter example or by a skeptical argument, rather than a whole scientific revolution.

In my view, Floridi has successfully argued for Informational Structural Realism, including his transcendentally inferred assumption that every possible world must include dedomena within its underlying fabric of reality. As explained in the next section, however, I also believe – and I think that Floridi would agree – that metaphysical theories which do not apply to every possible world can nevertheless be philosophically rewarding and worthy of consideration in appropriate circumstances.

As an example of a "more local" metaphysics, which nevertheless is worthy of one's consideration, I suggest adding quantum properties to Floridi's dedomena to generate an ontology that would apply to our own world (and any other world that happens to include quantum structures). Such a metaphysics would not attempt to explain Being *qua* Being, like Aristotle's or Floridi's; but perhaps it could aid our philosophical understanding – and maybe even our scientific understanding – of *this particular world*. In the section below, therefore, I will explore the idea of trying to develop a *quantum variant* of Floridi's Informational Structural Realism.

Bynum's quantum informational structural realism

To begin, I adopt an epistemological justification modeled upon that of Floridi (see previous sub-section):

> For epistemic reasons, we are allowed to commit ourselves ontologically to whatever minimal conception of objects is useful to make sense of our first commitment in favor of *quantum structures*. The first commitment answers the question 'what can we know?'; and the second commitment answers the question 'what can we justifiably assume to be in the external world, *given the existence of quantum structures?*' [my changes are in italics]

In Floridi's case, the required primordial entities are "dedomena" – "mind-independent points of lack of uniformity" – "mere *differentiae de re*" – primordial data. These must be part of the ultimate fabric of any world (including our own) where at least one structure, no matter how minimal, exists. In *my* case, the primordial data that are needed must account for the existence of quantum information – *qubits* – physical entities in our universe which can represent, simultaneously, *0 and 1 and an infinite set of numbers between 0 and 1*. Prerequisites of such entities would be mind-independent dedomena-"packets" containing an infinite number of dedomena for each qubit in our universe. If we assume the existence of such "packets" – let us call them "primordial qubits" (PQs) or "primordial quantum data" – we can provide an opportunity for creative philosophers to develop metaphysical explanations of quantum phenomena and, perhaps, even eliminate some of the alleged "weirdness" or "spookiness" of such phenomena.

The key move is to "think outside of the box" – or, as I prefer to say, *think outside of the "quantum-foam bubble" which is our universe* (see below). Imagine, for want of a better metaphor, a vast primordial PQ "ocean" or source. Conceivably, such a source could contain many other things besides PQs; but, for our purposes, we need only assume that the primordial "ocean" is a vast source of PQs. Given this assumption, the birth of our universe (the Big Bang) can be interpreted as the sudden appearance of a constantly expanding "bubble" immersed in the primordial PQ ocean. Instead of air, the bubble is filled with *quantum foam*, a "medium" which consists of an enormous number of "virtual quantum particles":

Quantum foam: In our universe, totally empty space does not exist. Thus, even if all of the usual matter and electromagnetic radiation were removed from a given region of outer space, leaving only what is sometimes called "the quantum vacuum," there would remain what physicist John Wheeler called "quantum foam" – "virtual quantum particles" that are constantly coming into existence, interacting with each other, and disappearing within a tiny fraction of a second. As physicist Frank Close explains, in his book *Nothing: A Very Short Introduction*, "When viewed at atomic scales, the Void is seething with activity, energy and particles" (Close 2009, p. 94). He went on to note, later in that same book, that

> There is general agreement [among physicists] that the quantum vacuum [i.e., quantum foam] is where everything that we know came from, even the matrix of space and time. . . . the seething vacuum offers profound implications for comprehending the nature of Creation from the Void [i.e., creation from quantum foam].
>
> *(p. 106)*

And also,

> the multitude of disparate phenomena that occur at macroscopic distances, such as our daily experiences, are controlled by the quantum vacuum [i.e., the quantum foam] within which we exist.
>
> *(p. 122)*

These ideas from contemporary quantum physics suggest the following account of the birth and nature of our universe:

> In the beginning was the primordial qubit source (the "PQ ocean"). The birth of our universe (the Big Bang) was the formation and very rapid expansion of a quantum-foam bubble (our universe) within the PQ ocean. Initially, the PQs in the ocean interacted with the bubble very rapidly, generating additional quantum foam and an explosive expansion of the bubble (called "inflation" by physicists). During the Big Bang, quantum laws together with quantum foam generated elementary particles and the spacetime matrix. As the rapidly expanding bubble began to cool, the various kinds of "standard-model" quantum particles came into existence, including – eventually – the Higgs boson. With the arrival of the Higgs boson, the rate of expansion dramatically decreased but was not entirely eliminated. Our universe continues to expand at an accelerating rate as the PQ ocean generates more and more quantum foam within it. (Perhaps the increasing quantum foam is the "dark energy" that is accelerating the expansion of our universe.)

A key assumption of this metaphysical "thought experiment" is that quantum phenomena, such as *superpositions, decoherence, entanglement, "spooky action at a distance,"* and *teleportation*, should be viewed, not as weird and inexplicable phenomena, but rather as scientific evidence that casts light upon the nature of the primordial quantum data source and upon quantum foam. I have expanded upon this idea elsewhere, in Bynum (2013).

Concluding comment

This chapter is intended to provide some examples of philosophical ideas and theories from the new and rapidly growing field of *informational metaphysics*. This new "field" is actually a "subfield" of the much broader Philosophy of Information Movement, which recently has captured the imagination and enthusiasm of a number of philosophers across the globe. The present volume provides a broad introduction to that important new area of philosophical research.

References

Ball, P. (2002). "The Universe is a Computer." *Nature News*, doi: 10.1038/ news020527-16.

Bynum, T. W. (2013). "On the Possibility of Quantum Informational Structural Realism," *Minds and Machines*, 23, DOI 10.1007/s11023-013-9323-5.

Chiribella, G., G. D'Ariano, and P. Perinotti (2011). "Informational Derivation of Quantum Theory." *Physical Review A*, 84, 012311.

Close, F. (2009). *Nothing: A Very Short Introduction*. Oxford: Oxford University Press.

Conway, F. and J. Siegelman (2005). *Dark Hero of the Information Age: In Search of Norbert Wiener the Father of Cybernetics*. New York: Basic Books.

Dipert, R. R. (1997). "The Mathematical Structure of the World: The World as Graph." *Journal of Philosophy*, 94, 328–358.

Dipert, R. R. (2002). "The Subjective Impact of Computers on Philosophy: Prolegomena to a Computational and Information-Theoretic Metaphysics," in J. H. Moor and T. W. Bynum, Eds., *Cyberphilosophy: The Intersection of Philosophy and Computing*. A Metaphilosophy Anthology. Oxford: Blackwell, pp. 139–150.

Floridi, L. (2011). *The Philosophy of Information*. Oxford: Oxford University Press.

Fredkin, E. (2003). "An Introduction to Digital Philosophy." *International Journal of Theoretical Physics*, 42, 189–247.

Lloyd, S. (2002). "Computational Capacity of the Universe." *Physical Review Letters*, 88, 237901–237904.

Lloyd, S. (2006). *Programming the Universe: A Quantum Computer Scientist Takes on the Cosmos*. New York: Alfred A. Knopf.

Putnam, H. (1975). "What Is Mathematical Truth?" in H. Putnam (Ed.), *Mathematics, Matter and Method: Philosophical Papers*. Cambridge: Cambridge University Press, pp. 60–78.

Rheingold, H. (2000). *Tools for Thought: The History and Future of Mind-Expanding Technology*. Revised Edition 2000, Cambridge, MA: MIT Press. Originally published in 1985 by Simon and Schuster, New York.

Seife, Charles (2006). *Decoding the Universe: How the New Science of Information is Explaining Everything in the Cosmos, from Our Brains to Black Holes*, New York: Viking Penguin.

Shannon, C. E. (1948a) "A Mathematical Theory of Communication," Parts I and II. *The Bell System Technical Journal* XXVII, 379–423.

Shannon, C. E. (1948b) "A Mathematical Theory of Communication," Parts I and II. *The Bell System Technical Journal* XXVII, 623–656.

Steinhart, E. (1998). "Digital Metaphysics," in T. W. Bynum and J. H. Moor, Eds., *The Digital Phoenix: How Computers are Changing Philosophy*. A Metaphilosophy Anthology. Oxford: Blackwell, 1998, pp. 117–134. Revised edition 2000.

Vlastos, G. (2005). *Plato's Universe*. Parmenides. Originally published in 1975 by University of Washington Press, Seattle, WA.

Wheeler, John A. (1990). "Information, Physics, Quantum: The Search for Links," in W. H. Zureck, Ed., *Complexity, Entropy, and the Physics of Information*, Redwood City, CA: Addison Wesley.

Wiener, N. (1948). *Cybernetics: or Control and Communication in the Animal and the Machine*. Boston, MA: Technology Press.

Wiener, N. (1950/1954). *The Human Use of Human Beings: Cybernetics and Society*. Houghton Mifflin, 1950. (Second Edition Revised, Doubleday Anchor, 1954).

Wiener, N. (1966). *I Am a Mathematician: The Later Life of a Prodigy*. Cambridge, MA: MIT Press.

Zuse, K. (1967). "Rechnender Raum." *Elektronische Datenverarbeitung*, 8, 336–344.

Zuse, K. (1969). *Rechnender Raum*, Wiesbaden: Vieweg. English translation: *Calculating Space*, MIT Technical Translation AZT-70-164-GEMIT, Project MAC, 1970. Cambridge, MA: Massachusetts Institute of Technology.

19

THE PHILOSOPHY
OF QUANTUM
INFORMATION

Chris Timpson

Quantum information theory is an exciting and still youthfully vigorous area of research which lies at the intersection of quantum physics, communication theory, and the theory of computation. Its point of departure is to seize upon the very marked and peculiar ways in which the quantum world differs from our classical conceptions of physics, and to see in these differences *opportunities* for new forms of communication and computation. The oddity of the quantum world, in this approach, is not seen as a potentially troublesome conundrum, best avoided or treated in as classical-like a way as possible, but rather as something which we may be able to harness to our advantage, to do things which we would not otherwise be able to do, or to do things in ways in which we would not otherwise be able to do them. The defining, strikingly non-classical, and conceptually puzzling quantum features such as *superposition*, *entanglement*, and *non-commutativity* (we shall see more of each of these notions in due course) are positively embraced, and put to concrete work.

The field primarily began to emerge in the early- to mid-1980s, with the work of Deutsch and others (Benioff 1980; Feynman 1982; Deutsch 1985) on the concept of quantum computers – a distinctively *quantum* approach to information-processing. In the 1990s, the concept of quantum information proper was introduced by Schumacher (1995) in his development and extension to the quantum realm of Shannon's paradigm of information theory [see Chapter 2] (this was Schumacher's *quantum noiseless coding theorem*, see also Barnum *et al.* 1996). In addition, the first protocols were developed which unequivocally involved the transmission of quantum information proper (Bennett *et al.* 1993), whilst Shor (1994) showed that there exists an efficient quantum algorithm for an important computational problem – factoring large numbers – for which it is universally believed that there is no efficient classical algorithm: thus the claim that quantum computers are 'exponentially more powerful' than classical ones. By 2000 and the publication of the canonical textbook of Nielsen and Chuang, quantum information theory had reached a mature stage. (Nielsen and Chuang is now in its second edition (2010) and is still canonical.) Even so, however, the general view is that in some ways, quantum information scientists have only scratched the surface so far. There is still much to be done to reach a general understanding of the ways in which the quantum world differs from the classical world, to understand how these differences might be harnessed for interesting information-processing and communication ends, and to settle how these quantum-classical differences should be understood at the fundamental conceptual level.

The *philosophy* of quantum information – the topic of this chapter – has three main components or tasks. The first task is that of seeking to understand the nature and content of quantum information theory as it currently stands, and of seeking to highlight or to resolve any conceptual puzzles internal to the theory. The second task is that of reflecting on how the existence and striking success of quantum information theory affects our understanding of information – or *theories* of information – more generally: what does the advent of quantum information mean for the concept of information? The third task is that of exploring whether and how developments in quantum information theory affect the traditional, well-worn, conceptual problems in the foundations of quantum theory itself, for many have seen suggestive avenues here.

In this chapter I shall focus on the first two of these questions (for the third, see Timpson 2013). But first we need to begin by getting some grip on the characteristic features of quantum theory which have such an important role to play.

Features of quantum theory

The starting place is with the concept of *superposition*. In classical physics it is always the case that, for whatever physical property one considers, a given system either determinately does, or determinately does not, have a particular value of that property. We might think of energy, position, momentum, angular momentum, and so on: the *dynamical* variables – those that are susceptible to change over time – as opposed to the fixed properties such as charge or mass. We can put this in terms of the features of the *states* of the system: the state of a system at a given time fixes *numerically exact* and *ontologically determinate* values for all the physical properties of the system at that time. Conversely, a specification of all of the values of the physical properties uniquely determines the state. We might be *ignorant* of what true state a system is in, in which case we might work with a probability distribution over the possible states, but there is always a fact about what the true state of a system is, and this true state is one in which all the physical values are determinate. In quantum physics, by contrast, this is not so.

Let us imagine a single particle for which there are only two possibilities of where it can be located. Either in a box located at the origin of some coordinate system set-up in the lab (call it 'Box 0' for 0 on the x-axis), or in a box one unit of length away along the x-axis (call it 'Box 1' for 1 on the x-axis). (Suppose the boxes to be of relatively small extent compared to the distance separating them.) Then in classical physics – and, one might be inclined to add, in common sense – at any time, the particle will either determinately be in Box 0, or it will determinately be in Box 1 – it has definite value 0 or definite value 1 for position on the x-axis. Certainly, whenever we open a box to look (whenever we 'perform a position measurement') we will find the particle to be in one or other location. But classical physics (and common sense) in addition insists that when we open a box we are merely revealing a position which was already determinate. If there was to begin with some probability of the particle being in Box 0 and some probability of it being in Box 1, then that was just down to our ignorance. Really, it was (must!) be in one or the other.

In quantum mechanics, however, as well as the two possibilities of the particle's determinately being in Box 0 and its determinately being in Box 1, it is also perfectly possible that it should be *neither* determinately in 0, *nor* determinately in 1: there can simply be no fact of the matter either way. (This is the example of Schrödinger's cat, where the cat is neither alive nor dead, but in some sense both.) Yet even so, if we look, we will only ever find the particle to be in one or other box, so it's not as if the particle might actually be determinately in some third box instead, or that it might have split in two. We need more states in the theory, to correspond to these kinds of cases. Label the state corresponding to definitely being in Box 0, $|0\rangle$, and label the state corresponding to definitely being in Box 1, $|1\rangle$. Then there is a further family of states which correspond to not having either position determinately, and in these circumstances, the system is said to be in a *superposition* with respect to spatial location. States of this kind are given by a linear combination of the two definite position states, of the form:

$a|0\rangle + b|1\rangle$.

The coefficients a and b are complex numbers, whose moduli squared sum to one ($|a|^2 + |b|^2 = 1$). The number $|a|^2$ gives the probability that the particle will be found in Box 0 when we look, the number $|b|^2$ gives the probability that the particle will be found in Box 1 when we look. With probability one, therefore, the particle will be found to be in one or other box when we look. Crucially, however, for states of this kind, these probabilities are not understood as stemming from ignorance of a pre-determined fact of where the particle was located: in these states, there are no such facts, according to quantum mechanics.

Now imagine that we introduce a further pair of boxes: Box 2 sitting at two units along the x-axis, and Box 3 sitting at three units along the x-axis. Suppose that our first particle remains constrained only to be found in Box 0 or 1, and that we introduce a second particle, which will only be found in Box 2 or Box 3. We can now think about correlations between the positions of our two particles. Suppose that our boxes are prepared in such a way that whenever the first particle is found to have x-position 0, the second particle is found to have x-position 2; and that whenever the first particle is found to have x-position 1, the second particle is found to have x-position 3. In other words, the two particles are always found two units of position apart. There are two importantly different scenarios in which correlations such as this might arise.

In the first scenario, there is a definite value for x-position for particle 1 (it is either definitely in Box 0 or definitely in Box 1) and there is a definite x-position for particle 2 (it is either definitely in Box 2 or definitely in Box 3): the correlations arise simply because these definite values have been arranged to coincide in a particular manner. Either the true state of the pair of particles is $|0\rangle|2\rangle$, i.e., the first particle is sitting in Box 0 and the second particle is sitting in Box 2; or the true state of the pair is $|1\rangle|3\rangle$, i.e., the first particle is sitting in Box 1 and the second in Box 3. We may not know which particle is where, in which case we will introduce a probability distribution over the two states, but each particle is somewhere, and wherever it is, it is two units away from the other particle.

Much more interesting is the scenario in which there is no definite value for x-position for either particle: each is in a superposition with respect to position. Remarkably, it is still possible in this case for the stated correlations to exist. In a state like

$a|0\rangle|2\rangle + b|1\rangle|3\rangle$

we have superposed the two states considered in the previous paragraph. (Take neither a nor b to be zero.) Now there is no fact about where particle 1 is, and no fact about where particle 2 is, yet *it is still the case* – it is a fact – *that the particles are a distance of two units apart!* This is an extraordinary state of affairs. The two particles can definitely be two units apart, without either even *having* a position themselves. States of this kind are called *entangled* states, and they all possess this striking feature of holism. When one's systems of interest are in an entangled state, there are facts about the properties of the whole joint system which are not reducible to facts about properties possessed by the individual systems making up the whole.

So far we have only considered the simplest form of measurement procedure on our particles, namely, opening a box to see whether a particle is inside. There also exist more sophisticated possibilities. First, notice a very important feature of the two states we started with, $|0\rangle$ and $|1\rangle$. It is possible to distinguish between these two states perfectly in a single-shot measurement. That is, if a particle is definitely in one or other state to begin with, but we don't know which, then we have a measurement procedure (opening one or other box, or both) which, in one go, will allow us to tell what that state was. Compare this with the pair of states $|0\rangle$ and $a|0\rangle + b|1\rangle$. If our particle was definitely prepared in one or other of *these* states to begin with, then there is no measurement procedure which applied on a single occasion is guaranteed to determine which state the particle was actually prepared in. For example, if we opened Box 0 and found the particle there, then this could have arisen either because the initial state was $|0\rangle$, or because it was $a|0\rangle + b|1\rangle$. Both options give a non-zero probability to this measurement outcome, so we cannot distinguish between the two possibilities from this piece of data. If we had opened Box 0 and found instead that the particle *wasn't* there, then this would tell us that the initial state was certainly $a|0\rangle + b|1\rangle$ and not $|0\rangle$, but we are not guaranteed, when we perform the measurement once, that this will be the outcome we see: it only occurs with some probability less than one.

States, like $|0\rangle$ and $|1\rangle$, between which it is possible to distinguish perfectly (i.e., with probability 1) in a single-shot measurement are called *orthogonal*. States like $|0\rangle$ and $a|0\rangle + b|1\rangle$, where this is not possible, are called *non-orthogonal*.

It turns out that whilst superposition states of the form $a|0\rangle + b|1\rangle$ are (for a, b non-zero) not orthogonal to $|0\rangle$, nor indeed to $|1\rangle$, there is, for each of them, *some other* superposition state to which it *is* orthogonal. In other words, there is some measurement scheme which will perfectly distinguish between suitably chosen pairs of these superposition states (such schemes will need to be more sophisticated than just opening a box and looking). Sets of mutually orthogonal states are said to correspond to *observable quantities* in quantum mechanics. (*Position on the x-axis* is the observable quantity which goes with $|0\rangle$ and $|1\rangle$, of course.) Two observable quantities are said to *commute* when each member of the set of orthogonal states associated with one quantity is either identical with or orthogonal to any member of the set of orthogonal states associated with the other quantity. If two quantities do not commute, then when a system is in a state which gives it a definite value of one quantity, it will be in a superposition with respect to, and thus lack a definite value for, the other quantity. Furthermore, when two quantities do not commute, they cannot both be measured at the same time.

The summary is that the space of possible states in quantum theory is much richer than the space of states in a classical theory. In a classical theory of our particle in a box, the only states we have available are 'position is 0', 'position is 1' and statistical mixtures of the two (probability distributions representing our ignorance of what the actual state is). In a quantum theory for our particle in a box, we not only have the two definite position states, but all the superposition states as well – and statistical mixtures of all these too if we are ignorant of what actual state may have been prepared – whilst to all orthogonal pairs of states there corresponds an observable quantity, which quantities cannot all take definite values at the same time. Finally, when we imagine combining two systems, quantum theory, unlike a classical theory, allows there to be states of the whole which are not just products of the states of the parts. In other words, there are properties of the whole which are not determined by (do not supervene on) the properties of the parts.

Before moving on we should say something briefly about dynamics – the rules for evolution over time of the states of the system. In quantum mechanics there are (or there are apparently!) two rules for evolution over time. For closed systems, the evolution of the state is given by the so-called *unitary* evolution derived from the Schrödinger equation: it is deterministic and continuous. For systems when they are observed – when measurements are made – the evolution is indeterministic and discontinuous. When you open a box, the system jumps from $a|0\rangle + b|1\rangle$ to either $|0\rangle$ or $|1\rangle$, with corresponding probabilities $|a|^2$ and $|b|^2$, respectively. How these two apparently incompatible rules for time-evolution are to be reconciled – or if they can be – is perhaps (once we have got used to the idea of superposition) the deepest of the traditional conceptual problems of quantum mechanics.[1]

Quantum information theory

At least one way of thinking about what an information theory in general is, is as a theory describing what kinds of transformations – what processes, or what protocols – are possible given a certain defined range of resources.

Quantum information theory is a development of classical Shannon information theory which introduces new communication primitives – the quantum bit or *qubit*, and shared entanglement; which explores what can be done with these new primitives; and which generalises Shannon's notions of information source and information channel to the quantum realm.

A *classical* bit is any two-state (classical) physical system, such as a classical ball placed in one or other of our boxes 0 or 1, or two distinct voltage levels in an electric circuit. Generically we label the two possible states of a bit with the Boolean logical values 0 or 1. We also use talk of bits to characterise the *quantity* of Shannon information produced by a (classical) source: the amount of (Shannon) information produced by a source is defined to be the number of bits that would be required to encode the output of the source optimally (Shannon 1948). The maximum amount of information that one physical bit can contain is therefore one bit's worth. The reason we are interested in a count in bits is because we are interested in the number of distinct possible messages that a Shannon information source will (over a suitably long run) produce with non-negligible probability, and we are therefore interested in the number of distinct states of some encoding medium or some transmission medium that would be required in order to allow us to differentiate between which of these possible messages was actually produced by the source on a given occasion. Suppose there are m such distinct messages for a given source, then m distinguishable states of the transmission or encoding medium will be required. If $m = 2^n$ (or approximately so) then we can readily count the number of states in terms of the number of some standard physical resources: the number of two-state systems. The number required in this example is of course n bits.[2]

A *quantum* bit – a *qubit* – is, in perfect parallel with the case of the classical bit, any two-state *quantum* system, i.e., any system possessing two distinguishable (i.e., orthogonal) quantum states. For example – a quantum particle in our boxes 0 and 1 from earlier, or an atom with two particular energy states of interest, or a photon with horizontal or vertical polarisation. The two states are conventionally labelled (as earlier) $|0\rangle$ and $|1\rangle$, and are often termed the *computational basis states.* They are chosen to be states of the system which can readily be prepared (it is relatively easy to put the system controllably into one or other of the states) and which can readily be measured. However, in marked contrast to the case of the classical bit, there will of course be *very many more* distinct states that a qubit could be in than just $|0\rangle$ or $|1\rangle$. All of the superposition states $a|0\rangle + b|1\rangle$ are available too. Since the coefficients a and b can vary continuously, there are in fact, even for the humble qubit, the simplest possible instance of a quantum system, an infinite number of states which it can occupy.

An infinite number of distinct states in the humble qubit! This might seem to give us straight away an astonishing advantage over the classical case, information-theoretically.

Cannot we now encode an infinite amount of information into a single one of these simplest of systems, if we want to? Well, no: this is too quick. For although a qubit possesses an infinite number of *distinct* states, it only ever has at most *two* states which can be *distinguished* from one another at a given time, as we have already seen.[3] True, I could prepare a qubit in any one of its possible states, choosing one at random from the infinite set, but this would not count as encoding an infinite amount of (classical) information into the qubit, for there is no way of *decoding* that information: finding out what the state prepared was. This is an instance of an extremely important principle, which we can call the *Inaccessibility of Unknown State Identity*, or perhaps the *Hiddenness of Quantum Information*:

> Given a single copy of a system prepared in an unknown quantum state, it is impossible to determine the identity of that state by measurement on, or interaction with, the system alone.

Only if the state of a system has been selected as one from a known *orthogonal set* of states is it possible to determine the identity of the state otherwise than just by asking whomever prepared it what its state is.

These facts force us to recognise an important conceptual distinction which is easy to miss in the classical case. This is the distinction between *specification information* – the amount of (classical) information required to specify the state of a given system; and *accessible information* (Schumacher 1995) – the amount of (classical) information which can successfully be encoded into a given system. (Encoding only counts as successful if *decoding* is in principle possible.) These two quantities coincide in the classical case, but differ in the quantum, as we have just seen: the specification information for the unknown state of a qubit may be infinite (two continuous parameters required), but the accessible information – the most that can be encoded – is just one bit, since by definition a qubit has only two states in any mutually orthogonal set of its states. An important result known as the *Holevo bound* (Holevo 1973) shows quite generally that the maximum accessible information for a quantum system with d mutually orthogonal states available to it is $\log_2 d$.

There is no particular advantage, then, in straightforwardly encoding *classical* information into qubits: the main interest of quantum information theory therefore lies elsewhere, particularly when one begins to focus on quantum states themselves being the items of information-theoretic interest, and when one looks at the distinctive possibilities that arise when entanglement is used as a resource.

Quantum information proper

In the Shannon paradigm, the aim of a communication protocol is the reproduction at some location of a message – a sequence of distinguishable states – selected elsewhere. The apparatus of Shannon's theory is then used to characterise the resources required to achieve this, particularly in the presence of noise. But the theory is largely silent on any particular reason why one might want to reproduce a given sequence of states: ultimately this will be down to the interests of whomever is seeking to design and build the communication system in question. (Very often, reproducing a sequence at a destination will enable the user to achieve something else that they are interested in.)

It was Schumacher's (1995) insight that the general framework which Shannon developed for thinking about information sources could be applied also in the case of quantum mechanics. Instead of thinking of an information source as producing a sequence of distinct and distinguishable (i.e., classical) states as its messages, each state appearing in the sequence with some fixed probability, we can think of a source as producing a sequence of systems being in particular *quantum* states, where a given quantum state will occur with a fixed probability in the sequence (call this a *quantum information source*). So considering, for example, a set $\{|a_i\rangle\}$ of non-orthogonal quantum states, we can contemplate a source which would produce a sequence of quantum systems, one after the other, where the probability that a given system in the sequence will be in the particular state $|a_i\rangle$ is $p(a_i)$. Then the message produced from a particular run of the source might be a sequence like $|a_2\rangle|a_5\rangle|a_1\rangle|a_4\rangle|a_4\rangle|a_4\rangle|a_7\rangle$...., and so on: a specific sequence of non-orthogonal states. The task of communication, following the Shannon paradigm, would then be to reproduce this sequence of states at the destination. Alternatively, it might be that one's source produces a sequence of quantum systems each of which is entangled in some way with some *other* quantum systems. Then the task of communication will be that of producing at the destination a new sequence of systems which are entangled in *exactly the same way* to this other set of systems as those in the sequence initially produced by the source were. Either way, Schumacher observed that the resources required to achieve these tasks could be quantified. He derived, using an extension of Shannon's techniques, the minimum number of qubits that would be required to encode the output of a quantum information source in such a way that the output sequence of states could be reproduced at the intended destination as required, including any entanglement which might have existed between systems in the output sequence and other systems. This was Schumacher's quantum noiseless coding theorem. In perfect parallel to the classical case, the minimum number of *qubits* required to encode the output of a *quantum* information source defines the notion of the *amount of quantum information* that a given quantum source produces. Again in parallel to the classical case, the maximum amount of quantum information that a qubit can contain is simply one qubit's worth.[4]

A moment ago we noted that Shannon's theory had little to say on the general question of what *purpose* there might be in trying to reproduce elsewhere a sequence of states generated by some source. This question clearly also arises in the quantum case: why should we wish to be able to reproduce at location B a sequence of quantum states, or a pattern of entanglement, produced at location A? Well, the specific reasons could be many and various, but as before, the most general and fundamental answer is that this will ultimately just come down to the interests of whomever is setting-up the communication protocol. But given the introduction of the notion of a quantum information source, there is a further specific question which we might now press, and to which we can give some substantive answers, namely: why would anyone be interested in reproducing at a destination a sequence of quantum states *as opposed to* a sequence of distinguishable – classical – states?

One immediate very important example is given by the case of quantum computation. A useful way to think about quantum computation is in terms of the so-called *quantum circuit* architecture. Here we imagine a (possibly large, but finite) register of qubits, each of which can be acted on individually and jointly by various *quantum logic gates*, where each quantum gate implements some unitary quantum dynamics on the qubits it acts on. The register begins with each qubit in the standard $|0\rangle$ computational basis state, then, analogously to a sequence of logic gates in a classical logic circuit, some particular sequence of quantum gates is applied to the register, corresponding to a particular quantum computation being performed. This will typically leave the register in an entangled state. Readout is then performed by measurement in the computational basis – the 0 or 1 boxes for each qubit are opened – leaving one with a string of classical bit values as the result of the computation. It turns out that a relatively small set of one- and two- qubit quantum gates are sufficient, when suitably combined, to produce the result of any possible unitary dynamics on the qubits in the register, so we can think of a (suitably sized) quantum computer as a good model of any quantum-mechanical system whatsoever; and moreover, we recover the feature of computational universality familiar from the classical Turing machine model. Any possible quantum computation can be performed (given enough time, and given a large enough register) by a machine of finite specification, i.e., one which is able to apply each of the gates in the small 'universal set' of gates to its register of qubits, as needed.

Now, whilst the set of functions which a quantum computer can compute is in fact the same as the set of functions a classical Turing machine can compute, the important point is that quantum computers can perform some computations much more quickly than any classical computer. However, in order to achieve this, we will need to ensure that a computation 'remains quantum' from beginning to end. There is a very strong tendency for noise – unwanted interaction with uncontrolled or external degrees of freedom – to make quantum superposition states such as $a|0\rangle + b|1\rangle$ start behaving as if they were just an ordinary classical statistical mixture of definite classical bit values 0 and 1, with a probability $|a|^2$ of the definite value being 0 and a probability $|b|^2$ of the definite value being 1. If this occurs on too wide a scale in our quantum computer, it will just start behaving exactly as a classical computer does, and the quantum speed-up will be lost. Therefore it is important when designing practical quantum computers – which will typically involve various components located in various different spatial locations – that the quantum states involved in the computation can reliably be stored, and also reliably and accurately moved from one location to another, whilst preserving any necessary entanglement structure. In other words, it will be necessary that sequences of quantum states produced in one location can be *reproduced* at another location, accurately, and preserving any necessary entanglement to other systems. Moreover, we will be interested in the minimum resources required to achieve such transmission, in order to build the optimum computer. Thus we require the notions of quantum information source, of quantum compression (coding), and of successful message reproduction that Schumacher introduced, in order to design and construct practical quantum computers.

Speaking more generally, one will be interested in reproducing quantum states at a destination whenever having a system, or systems, with a well-defined (even if perhaps unknown) quantum state in one's possession will confer an advantage in some task one is trying to achieve.

A further example of gaining an advantage is provided by the special kind of non-classical, holistic, correlations that obtain between systems in entangled states. Entanglement proves to be an extremely important non-classical communication resource. When two spatially separated parties – traditionally called Alice and Bob – share some entanglement, each possessing one half of a pair of qubits in an entangled state, say, they can do remarkable new things that they would not otherwise be able to do. The two paradigm cases of such *entanglement-assisted communication* are *superdense coding* (Bennett and Weisner 1982) and *quantum teleportation* (Bennett *et al.* 1993).

In superdense coding, shared entanglement is deployed to improve classical information transfer. When Alice and Bob share a state like: $1/\sqrt{2}\,(|0\rangle|2\rangle + |1\rangle|3\rangle)$, i.e., Alice has boxes 0 and 1 close by her (her qubit), and Bob – far away – has boxes 2 and 3 close by him (his qubit), Alice can manage to transmit to Bob two bits of classical information whilst only sending him a single qubit. At first sight this looks like a violation of the Holevo bound – Alice has somehow managed to stuff two classical bits into one qubit! She pulls the trick off by, first, applying one of four unitary gates to her qubit, corresponding to a choice of two classical bit values on her part, then, second, sending her qubit to Bob. When Bob receives it, he performs a measurement on both qubits taken together (this is called performing a joint measurement), and he can infer what gate Alice applied, thus infer the bit values she wishes to transmit. Formally, therefore, there is no violation of the Holevo bound, since two qubits are involved in the protocol. But what is remarkable is the time-ordering in the procedure: Alice is able to encode two classical bit values into these two qubits *when she only has access to one of them*. At the time Alice chooses her bit values, Bob *already has* his qubit – his half of the entangled pair! Since we are ruling out superluminal information transmission (quantum theory enforces the impossibility of signalling faster than light, which is healthy, for consistency with special relativity) it is remarkable that she can manage this.

By contrast with superdense coding, quantum teleportation uses shared entanglement to transmit *quantum information* in a remarkable way. In fact, it was the very first protocol explicitly to involve the transmission of quantum information properly speaking: the reproduction at one location of a quantum state produced at another location.

Again, we begin with Alice and Bob widely separated, but sharing the entangled state $1/\sqrt{2}$ $(|0\rangle|2\rangle + |1\rangle|3\rangle)$. Alice is presented with a qubit in some unknown (to her) quantum state $|\psi\rangle$. As we know, $|\psi\rangle$ could be any one of an infinite number of (non-orthogonal) states. We can think of this state as the output of some quantum information source. Alice's task is now to bring it about that Bob should come to have a copy of the state $|\psi\rangle$, whatever it is. How could she do this? We stipulate that she is not allowed simply to package up the qubit which is in the state $|\psi\rangle$ and send it to Bob, and we stipulate more strongly that she is not allowed to send *any* quantum systems *at all* to Bob (to stop her swapping the state $|\psi\rangle$ onto some other qubit and sending that to Bob instead). However, she is permitted to send him a small number of classical bits if she wishes. Can she achieve the task?

The answer is *yes*, but only by making use of the shared entanglement. The procedure is as follows. Alice begins by making a particular fixed joint measurement on the qubit in the state $|\psi\rangle$ and her half of the entangled pair. (Which measurement she performs is, and must be, independent of the identity of the state $|\psi\rangle$, not least since Alice has no idea what the state is, and cannot find out.) This measurement will have one of four outcomes, each with equal probability, and thus independent of the identity of $|\psi\rangle$. Alice records the outcome in two classical bits, and then sends these to Bob. Conditional on these bit values, Bob should then perform one from a previously chosen set of four unitary gates on his half of the entangled pair. The result is that his half of the entangled pair will now be guaranteed to be in the state $|\psi\rangle$, whilst following Alice's measurement, the states of her qubits were both completely scrambled – they have no definite value for any observable quantity. Thus the state $|\psi\rangle$ has disappeared from Alice's location, and reappeared at Bob's location, whilst nothing that bears any relation to the identity of $|\psi\rangle$ has passed between them! This is a truly remarkable phenomenon, and warrants the 'teleportation' label.

Dwelling on this point a little further: it is true that it is not *matter* – colloquially speaking, 'the stuff of Alice's initial qubit' – that has been transported in this protocol. Rather, there is a physical system at A and there is a distinct physical system at B, and the latter has been made to have the state which the former used to have, but has no longer.[5] Moreover, the process is not instantaneous, it can only be completed when the classical message Alice sends reaches Bob. But even so, the manner in which the result is achieved is striking. The information characterising Alice's initial qubit has in some sense been completely disembodied during the protocol: to repeat, *nothing that bears any relation to the identity of* $|\psi\rangle$ *passes between Alice and Bob*. The information seems to disappear from Alice's location and to reappear at Bob's, without having been anywhere in between during the process. Furthermore, this process seems to be extraordinarily efficient: it takes an infinite number of bits to specify the state of Alice's initial qubit, yet she has managed to transport it to Bob whilst only sending him a measly two bits!

Quantum teleportation is both conceptually and information-theoretically striking, whilst it brings together in one package a number of *characteristic* features of quantum information. First, the impossibility of determining an unknown state, the *hiddenness* of quantum information – Alice can't find out what $|\psi\rangle$ is and then hope to send a classical description of it to Bob; second, the fact that shared entanglement can be used as a resource; and third, the *impossibility of cloning quantum information*.

The significance of this last is as follows. A key feature of the teleportation protocol is that Alice's copy of $|\psi\rangle$ disappears, and a new copy appears with Bob. The important *no-cloning theorem* (Dieks 1982; Wootters and Zurek 1983) tells us that this couldn't have been otherwise. The theorem states that given only a single instance of a quantum system in an unknown state $|\psi\rangle$, it is impossible to generate any further systems in the same state, i.e., it is impossible start with a qubit in the state $|\psi\rangle$ and a register of n qubits each in some standard state, say $|0\rangle$, and to end up with more than one system in the state $|\psi\rangle$. Thus if Bob is to end up with a copy of (i.e., a system in) $|\psi\rangle$, Alice cannot be left with a copy, and this is indeed what we see in teleportation.

No-cloning represents an extremely important difference between quantum and classical information, for classical information can of course be cloned – for example, we can readily measure a classical bit, and then prepare many, many new bits with the same value as the measured one. Clearly we could not do the same thing with quantum states, for measurement cannot tell us what unknown state we have before us. It follows that unknown quantum states will be very precious: if you start with only one copy of $|\psi\rangle$, you had better look after it, for you will not be able to generate more.

In teleportation and superdense coding, shared entanglement is used as a communication resource. It is also *used up* in the course of these protocols. That is, Alice and Bob start with some shared entanglement, but finish without any. Since entanglement is useful, and is used up, it becomes natural to seek to quantify the *amount* of entanglement one has when one has a group of systems in some entangled state. An *ebit* is the term for a basic unit of entanglement, and this is the amount of entanglement used in the teleportation or in the superdense coding protocols above. It turns out that one ebit is the *maximum* amount of entanglement there can be in a pair of qubits. If one has a large number of less entangled systems, it proves to be possible to distil their entanglement into a smaller number of maximally entangled systems, leaving-over a number of unentangled systems. The maximally entangled systems would then be useful for teleportation, or what have you. The cornerstone of the quantitative theory of entanglement is the proposition that it is not possible for two separated parties, Alice and Bob, to increase the amount of entanglement (if any) that they share by anything that either could do locally to the systems in their possession, nor by any classical communication between them, nor by any combination of the two: in other words, no increase of entanglement by local operations and classical communication. Strikingly, it is possible to teleport entanglement: suppose Cynthia hands Alice a qubit to teleport to Bob, which Alice obliges by doing. If the qubit Cynthia initially gave Alice was in fact half of an entangled pair, the other half of which Cynthia is still holding, then Bob's qubit will now be entangled with Cynthia's. This is called *entanglement swapping*: there was entanglement between C and A and between A and B, but this is turned into entanglement between C and B. Two quantum systems which were initially independent of one another, and have never directly interacted with one another, can nevertheless be made to enter into these special quantum-correlated states.

Internal puzzles of the theory

Quantum information theory presents a number of fairly immediate conceptual puzzles internal to the theory. For example, an important question to ask is – just what is it that powers quantum computation? Where does the speed-up come from?

An immediate attractive thought is that it just comes from the possibility of superposition. Suppose I have some quantum gate that, when I prepare my n-qubit register in the computational basis in some sequence of $|0\rangle$s and $|1\rangle$s, evaluates some particular function of the string of 0s and 1s. If I now prepare, as I can, each qubit in the register in an equal superposition of $|0\rangle$ and $|1\rangle$, I will have as my input to the quantum gate, a state in which all 2^n strings of 0s and 1s are equally superposed. After the quantum gate operates on this superposed input, the output will be a superposition of each value of the function for all 2^n inputs. In other words, in one computational step, all possible values of the function have been computed. And this looks like a massive parallelism speed-up.

Unfortunately, things aren't so simple. In order to read any result out, we need to do a measurement of the register in the computational basis, to get a sequence of 0s and 1s which we can actually read. Thus we cannot access all 2^n values of the function: in fact we will get one of them, at random. So this is no better than classical, in terms of what we have epistemic access to. Indeed, one might argue more strongly that a computation doesn't count as being performed at all, properly speaking, unless it is in principle possible to read its outputs out. In which case, in the example just given, it wasn't even the case that the 2^n values of the function were really evaluated in the first place.

Another reason to think that it cannot be superposition, or just superposition, which is at the heart of things, is that it is not only quantum systems which can be in superpositions: classical waves, such as waves on a string, for example, can be superposed too. But there is no computational speed-up available here.

A more plausible thought is therefore that it must be *entanglement* which is responsible, for no classical system, even one which supports superposition, can support entanglement; and indeed, in those quantum algorithms, such as Shor's (1994), which give a speed-up there seems to be both parallelism *and* entanglement at play. Yet this suggestion is not entirely straightforward either. The Gottesman-Knill theorem (Gottesman 1998) implies that if you restrict the gates available to your quantum computer to a particular sub-set of gates, but one which includes the possibility of making as much entanglement as you like, your computer cannot be more powerful than a classical one. Thus entanglement on its own is not enough. The question therefore remains open exactly what needs to be added, or exactly what is responsible for the speed-up (Jozsa and Linden 2003; Aaronson 2013; Cuffaro 2015). Significant questions have also been asked (Steane 2003) about the role of parallelism in quantum computational speed-up given that an important alternative architecture for quantum computation – *measurement-based* or *one-way* computation (Raussendorf and Briegel 2001) – does not have anything that looks like the parallel-processing of the circuit model in it. Here there is no unitary, superposition-supporting, evolution over time, instead there are only sequences of *measurements* made on a network of pre-entangled quantum systems. A final thought might be, following Bub (2007), that the key to speed-up is not that the quantum computer evaluates *all* the values of a function at the same time, but rather that it manages to produce the result of a computation without actually evaluating *any* of the values in the intermediary steps. This perhaps suggests a re-orientation of the question: rather than ask why quantum computers are so quick for some tasks, perhaps we should be asking why classical computers are so slow (Timpson 2009).

Another set of puzzles cluster around the question of what exactly is going on in teleportation. The key questions here are 1) How does *so much* information get from Alice to Bob in teleportation, when she only sends him two bits? And 2) Just *how exactly* does the information *get* from Alice to Bob? Perhaps the view which has been most tempting for many in regard to (2) is that the answer is: backwards in time! (Jozsa 2004; Penrose 1998) The thought is that there must be some physical, spatiotemporally continuous, route by which the information characterising |ψ⟩ gets to Bob, yet it cannot be via the two classical bits that Alice sends him, since a) there is not enough room in these bits to carry all the information, and anyway, b) their values are simply independent of the identity of the teleported state. On the other hand, in order for Alice and Bob to share an entangled pair, it must have been created at some point in the past, and then split into two parts, one which was sent to Alice and one which was sent to Bob. Thus there is another spatiotemporally continuous path connecting Alice and Bob apart from the path of the two classical bits: there is the path that goes from Alice's measurement at the beginning of the protocol, backwards in time to the event of the creation of the entangled pair, and then forward in time along the path of the half of the pair which is sent to Bob. So the conclusion reached is that it must be through *this* path that the information characterising |ψ⟩ reached Bob, there is no other alternative. We have reached the startling implication that quantum information is a *new kind of information* which can travel backwards in time!

For some, understandably, this is too much. Deutsch and Hayden (2000) view the conclusion as untenable and instead develop an alternative approach to quantum theory which allows them to find, after all, an always-forward-in-time route for the quantum information travelling between Alice and Bob. They argue that the information is, after all, actually carried by the two classical bits: it was just hidden away in them in such a way that it couldn't be revealed by looking at them. Yet a further response, however, is to reject both the backwards-in-time and the Deutsch-Hayden answers to the puzzle as being predicated on a mistaken picture of how we should conceive of quantum information and questions of its location and travel in protocols such as these (Timpson 2013), of which more in a moment.

This brings us to perhaps the key question of all: Just what *is* quantum information?

Quantum information theory and the nature of information

There are two aspects to the question 'what is quantum information?', the first conceptual, the second, ontological. Both shed light on how we should think about information theory and its relation to physics and to the physical world.

On the conceptual side, the core questions are i) is the concept of quantum information *primitive* or *defined* and ii) if defined, what relation does it bear to the concept of Shannon information? On the ontological side, the core questions are iii) what kind of existence or being does quantum information have (if any), and iv) what is the relation between quantum information and our traditional conception of the physical world as being constituted by material particles and fields?

The prevailing view on the conceptual side seems to be that quantum information is *sui generis* and a primitive concept, for example:

> Quantum information, though *not precisely defined*, is a fundamental concept of quantum information theory.
>
> *(Horodecki et al. 2006)*

> |ψ⟩ may be viewed as a carrier of "quantum information" which…we leave … *undefined in more fundamental terms*. Quantum information is a new concept *with no classical analogue.*
>
> *(Jozsa 2004)*

However, claims to this effect seem to be based on an erroneous, or at least, an unnecessary, conception of the content of the classical Shannon theory of information. If an appropriate view is taken of the Shannon theory then it is possible to see quantum and Shannon information as species of a single genus (Timpson 2013). If one approaches the Shannon theory as fundamentally concerning inference and the reduction of uncertainty then it will be impossible to set the quantum and the classical theories together, for uncertainty and inference give us no model to understand what quantum information could be. We can't find out what an unknown state $|\psi\rangle$ is; and if we could, and did, then we would no longer be dealing with some quantum information that a system instantiates, but rather with some classical information *about* a system, and these are very different things. But we need not and, arguably, *should not* think of the Shannon theory this way. The core content of the theory is not about uncertainty and inference (epistemic notions) but is rather about the (mechanical) production and reproduction of messages of a certain type, and the resources required to achieve this. When put like this we can now see quantum and classical information as different species of a single genus, falling within a general paradigm that Shannon introduced; for just the same is true of the quantum theory. All that differs between the two is the nature of the message which is produced and which is required to be reproduced. In the classical case it is a sequence of distinguishable states produced by a classical source; in the quantum case it is a sequence of potentially non-orthogonal quantum states produced by a quantum source, including any entanglement correlations.

On the ontological side of the question, it is tempting to conceive of quantum information as something new which is *postulated* by quantum information theory. (This thought naturally goes along with *sui generis* primitivism on the conceptual side.) Quantum information then constitutes the subject matter of the theory – the thing which the theory is about – and the theory goes on to formulate various laws about how this subject matter behaves: how it may be produced, compressed, lost, exploited, transported from A to B, changed from one form to another, and so on. This mind-set tends to force the concept of quantum information into being that of some sort of novel substance (particular) or stuff. According to temperament one might then be inclined to think of this as some novel material – or perhaps quasi-material – substance or stuff; or one might be inclined to think of it as some sort of immaterial substance or stuff. Once conceived on the "substance or stuff" model it will then be natural to ask questions such as whether quantum information is something which exists above and beyond, in addition to, the familiar material notions of particles and fields, or whether it is perhaps more fundamental than these familiar notions, and if so, whether these latter familiar items might be reducible to quantum information. Might the world be made of (quantum) information? Some notable physicists think so:

> An alternative view is gaining popularity: a view in which *information* is regarded as the primary entity from which physical reality is built.
>
> *(Davies 2010)*

> The universe is the biggest thing there is and the bit is the smallest possible chunk of information. The universe is made from bits.
>
> *(Lloyd 2006)*

> What is the message of the quantum? .. .I suggest that ... the distinction between reality and our knowledge of reality, between reality and information cannot be made.
>
> *(Zeilinger 2005)*

It from bit symbolizes the idea that every item of the physical world has at bottom … an immaterial source and explanation;…all things physical are information-theoretic in origin.

(Wheeler 1990)

But it is quite wrong to think of quantum information as something which is postulated by quantum information theory (Timpson 2013). Quantum information theory is not that kind of theory: it is not in the business of postulating any *thing*, whether material, quasi-material, immaterial, substance, or stuff. Rather it is in the business of uncovering and describing *what can be done* with the various things and stuffs already postulated in the world by our familiar (quantum) physical theory. Moreover, when we recognise this, we release a great deal of tension which we felt about understanding quantum teleportation. It is only on the "substance or stuff" model that one will feel forced to think of information as something which always must have a spatiotemporal location and for which a spatiotemporal path must be traced from A to B. It was this pressure which gave rise to the backwards-in-time model and the "hidden in the classical bits" model for the information flow. But we do not need to trace a path for the information in teleportation, because there is no thing "the information" to trace a path for. The only job to do is to describe the processes which are involved in completing the teleportation protocol, and in the quantum case, when entanglement is involved, there need be no locally defined properties which have a dependence on the identity of the unknown state instantiated between A and B in order for the state to be transmitted from A to B.[6]

Returning to our main question: What, then, is the ontological status of quantum information? We must distinguish two cases. In the first case we say that quantum information is what is produced by a quantum information source that is required to be reproduced at the destination. What is produced? A sequence of quantum states. What is a sequence of quantum states? In the helpful philosophers' jargon of the type/token distinction, it is a type – a particular pattern of properties and relations – of which there can be various tokens, located in various places. The tokens are the *concrete* things which instantiate the type, an *abstract* thing. A group of qubits, each being in the appropriate quantum state, will be the concrete physical objects which constitute the token of a particular type. This type which they instantiate – the abstract thing – will be the piece of quantum information – the message – that the quantum source produced.

In the second case we say that quantum information is a property of a source: 'the quantum information of a source', i.e., its compressibility. As with any property, quantum information so conceived will be abstract rather than concrete. It will be a *physical property* since it is a property formulated in a physical theory and defined on the basis of various other physical properties; but just as with any property, physical or no, it will not be part of the spatiotemporal contents of the world.

In either case, therefore, quantum information is ontologically abstract, rather than concrete.

Conclusion

A prominent and enticing slogan of quantum information theory is that "Information is Physical" (Landauer 1996). From what we have seen, this slogan cannot be taken to express a substantive ontological claim. If we take it to refer to pieces of quantum information – what is produced by the source that needs to be reproduced at the destination – then it is a category mistake. It is the tokens which instantiate the type which are physical, not the type itself. If we take it to refer to the information of the source – the amount of quantum information the source produces – then it is trivial. For it is trivial that a physically defined quantity is physical. The correct interpretation of this slogan, I submit, is as a misleadingly-stated *methodological* claim, not *ontological* one. It is the claim that it is a very productive and salutary business to try to discover what information-processing capacities or opportunities may be hidden away in our most fundamental physical theories. *Qua* methodological claim, this is exactly right, and important, as evidenced by the impressively rude health, richness, and interest of quantum information theory. But it is unfortunate that this key methodological commitment of the discipline is sometimes given a misleading ontological cast.

We may adopt the following useful mnemonic: rather than think of quantum information theory as a theory of some enticingly new stuff – *quantum information* – we should think of it as a *quantum* information theory. A theory of what one can do by way of computation and communication with the distinctively non-classical features of quantum theory. Thus it is all a question of bracketing:

Not: (quantum information) theory, but: quantum (information theory).

Since quantum information theory is itself therefore completely neutral on the question of the nature of the physical world – it is about what can be done with quantum physical resources – we can see that no novel information-based immaterialism or other reductionism regarding the physical world can gain the least support from the rich successes of quantum information theory.

Notes

1 This problem is usually called the *Measurement Problem*. For an up-to-date framing of the issue, and review of approaches to it, see Wallace (2009).

2 Nothing important really hangs on the choice of two-state systems, as opposed to three or four, or *d*–state systems. One is really just interested in counting the number of distinguishable states that one's medium will need to have, and there are many ways in which one can do that.

3 Although a qubit may have many *pairs* of orthogonal states (for any a and b, given a state $a|0\rangle + b|1\rangle$ there is some other state of the qubit orthogonal to it), no set of *mutually* orthogonal states of the qubit has more than two members. The states of a quantum system in fact form a *vector space*. The states $|0\rangle$, $|1\rangle$ of a qubit form a *basis* for the vector space of its states, which is therefore a two-dimensional vector space. Any other pair of mutually orthogonal states of the qubit can just be thought of as *rotation* of the $|0\rangle$, $|1\rangle$ basis states, and thus amount to another choice of basis for the space.

4 Whether a given qubit does in fact contain a qubit's worth of quantum information will depend on whether it has been used to encode the output of a quantum source, and on how much (quantum) information that source actually produces, if so.

5 From the perspective of quantum field theory however – our current fundamental theory of matter and forces – there isn't a very strong notion of 'physical system located at a particular position'. Rather, there are just various quantum fields which permeate all of space and evolve over time. Particular features in a particular region of space will then be determined by what quantum state the field(s) local to that region have. In which case teleporting the state might amount to teleporting the matter, in so far as the latter is a well-defined or interesting notion.

6 However, the detailed story one will tell about the exact physical process involved will depend on one's interpretation of quantum mechanics. See Timpson (2013: Chapter 4) for details.

References

Aaronson, S. 2013, *Quantum Computing Since Democritus*, Cambridge: Cambridge University Press.

Benioff, P. 1980, 'The computer as a physical system: A microscopic quantum-mechanical Hamiltonian model of computers as represented by Turing machines', *Journal of Statistical Physics*, 22(5), 563–591.

Bennett, C., Brassard, G., Crépeau C., Jozsa, R., Peres, A., and Wootters, W. 1993, 'Teleporting an unknown state via dual classical and EPR channels', *Physical Review Letters*, 70, 1895–1899.

Bennett, C. and Weisner, S. 1982, 'Communication via one- and two-particle operators on Einstein-Podolsky-Rosen states', *Physical Review Letters*, 69(20), 2881–2884.

Bub, J. 2007, 'Quantum computation from a quantum logical perspective', *Quantum Information and Computation*, 7(4), 281–296.

Cuffaro, M. 2015, 'On the significance of the Gottesman-Knill Theorem' arxiv:quant-ph/1310.0938. Forthcoming in the *British Journal for the Philosophy of Science*.

Davies, P. 2010, 'Universe from bit', in Davies and Gregersen (eds.), *Information and the Nature of Reality*, pp. 65–88.

Deutsch, D. 1985, 'Quantum theory, the Church-Turing Principle and the universal quantum computer', *Proceedings of the Royal Society of London A*, 400, 97–117.

Deutsch, D. and Hayden, P. 2000, 'Information flow in entangled quantum systems', *Proceedings of the Royal Society of London A*, 456, 1759–1774.

Dieks, D. 1982, 'Communication by EPR devices', *Physics Letters A*, 92(6), 271–272.

Feynman, R. 1982, 'Simulating physics with computers', *International Journal of Theoretical Physics*, 21(6/7), 467–488.

Gottesman, D. 1998, 'The Heisenberg representation of quantum computers', arxiv:quant-ph/9807006.

Holevo, A. 1973, 'Information theoretical aspects of quantum measurement', *Problems of Information Transmission (USSR)*, 9, 177–183.

Horodecki, M., Horodecki, P., Horodecki, R., and Piani, M (2006). 'Quantumness of ensemble from no-broadcasting principle', *International Journal of Quantum Information*, 4(1), 105–118.

Jozsa, R. 2004, 'Illustrating the concept of quantum information', *IBM Journal of Research and Development*, 4(1), 79–85.

Jozsa, R. and Linden, N. 2003, 'On the role of entanglement in quantum-computational speed-up', *Proceedings of the Royal Society of London A*, 459(2036), 2011–2032.

Landauer, R. 1996, 'The physical nature of information', *Physics Letters A*, 217, 188–193.

Lloyd, S. 2006 *Programming the Universe*, New York: Vintage.

Nielsen, M. and Chuang, I. 2010, *Quantum Computation and Quantum Information*. Cambridge: Cambridge University Press.

Penrose, R. 1998, 'Quantum computation, entanglement and state reduction', *Philosophical Transactions of the Royal Society of London A*, 356, 1927–1939.

Raussendorf, R. and Briegel, H. 2001, 'A one-way quantum computer', *Physical Review Letters* 86, 5188.

Schumacher, B. 1995, 'Quantum coding', *Physical Review A*, 51(4), 2738.

Shannon, C. 1948, 'The mathematical theory of communication', *Bell Systems Technical Journal*, 27, 379–423, 623–656.

Shor, P. 1994, 'Algorithms for quantum computation: Discrete logarithms and factoring', *Proceedings of the 35th Annual IEEE Symposium on Foundations of Computer Science*, pp. 124–134.

Steane, A. 2003, 'A quantum computer only needs one universe', *Studies in History and Philosophy of Modern Physics*, 34(3), 469–478.

Timpson, C. 2009, 'Philosophical aspects of quantum information theory', in D. Rickles (ed.), *The Ashgate Companion to Contemporary Philosophy of Physics*, pp. 197–261. Farnham: Ashgate.

Timpson, C. 2013, *Quantum Information Theory and the Foundations of Quantum Mechanics*, Oxford: Oxford University Press.

Wheeler, J. 1990, 'Information, physics, quantum: The search for links', in W. Zurek, ed., *Complexity, Entropy and the Physics of Information*, pp. 3–28, Reading: Addison-Wesley.

Wootters, W. and Zurek, W. 1983, 'A single quantum cannot be cloned', *Nature*, 299, 802–803.

Zeilinger, A. 2005, 'The message of the quantum', *Nature*, 438, 743.

20

INFORMATION AND CAUSALITY

Phyllis Illari and Federica Russo

Philosophy of causality meets information

Philosophical theorizing has been concerned at least since ancient Greek thinkers with the problem of connecting events as causes and effects. For Aristotle causes are first principles that explain the 'why of things', but they are also 'efficient' in that they are the 'source of change or rest'. In this sense Aristotelian efficient causation is very close to the attempts made by contemporary philosophy of science to give an account of how something gives rise to something else.

Recent debates in philosophy of causality have highlighted that it is one thing to establish *that* C causes E and another thing to establish *how* C causes E. This derives from the work of Hall (2004), who distinguishes two concepts of causation – dependence (that) and production (how) – and is followed up by philosophers interested in analysing the different evidential components (dependence or association (that) and production or mechanisms (how)) which enter into causal assessment (Russo and Williamson, 2007; Illari, 2011a; Clarke *et al.*, 2014). Recent philosophical literature exploring how C causes E has focused on examining the ways in which mechanisms explain such connections. Here, we will focus on understanding production, which is broader in scope, as will become clear.

Concerning *how* C and E are connected, so far we have two dominant accounts. One is in terms of physical processes, characterized using concepts from physics such as conserved quantities. For instance, there is a physical process explaining how hitting a billiard ball makes it move on the table, involving conservation of momentum. Another account is in terms of mechanisms such as: there is a complex biochemical mechanism that explains how proteins are synthesized, or there are complex socio-economic mechanisms explaining how education affects wealth and vice-versa. In brief, mechanistic explanation of the link between C and E involves finding the parts and their activities by which C brings about E.[1] While these approaches certainly have merits, there are many situations in which we would look for a *productive relation* between cause and effect and yet we wouldn't characterize it as either a physical process using quantities from physics, or a mechanism in the sense just sketched.

Suppose you just installed your new smart TV, together with the Blu-ray and the home theatre system. You then try out a DVD, and the image appears, but there is no sound. This *absence* suggests that something went wrong with plugging in the cables between the Blu-ray player and the loudspeakers. But it is not clear how a physical process or a mechanism can connect this cause to the *absence* of sound.

Consider a different case. Doctors fighting an epidemic might reason in a similar way to decide whether they have two separate outbreaks, or a single virus or bacterium that has spread to a distinct population. Epidemiologist John Snow famously stopped the cholera epidemic in London in 1854, arguably by figuring out the 'channels' through which the disease was spreading. To stop an epidemic it is important to understand the mode of communication of the disease. This means understanding how a bacterium (or other agent) spreads, and also how the disease is transmitted from person to person. Snow's innovation was to realize that cholera was being transmitted by water, at a time when the dominant medical theories suggested only two transmission mechanisms, one by touch (contagion) and one by transmission through the air (miasmas). Snow hypothesized poor hygiene in behaviour and living conditions were the main channels for the spread of the disease. He managed to plot cholera deaths and contaminated water by comparing cholera deaths in different parts of London; it turned out that different water suppliers were active in these neighbourhoods. He managed to convince the authorities to block a suspected water pump and the epidemic gradually stopped (Paneth, 2004). In other words, Snow managed to block what was *linking* different cholera deaths. But this link is not clearly either a physical process or a mechanism.

Snow's question, and the question about the Blu-ray player, are questions about what can cause what; more precisely, these are questions about how C and E are connected, i.e. *causal linking*. As we will show in this chapter, this is reasoning about linking, it is about how cause and effect can – or cannot – be connected, and it seems to be distinct from reasoning about difference-making, which is broadly about plotting variations in one variable against variations in another variable, in abstraction from the explanation for that variation.[2] This reasoning is important in daily life, and in science. We will show how current work has turned to giving an account of this in terms of informational linking.

Towards an informational account of causality

Hans Reichenbach (1956) and Wesley Salmon (1984) were the first to try to express the idea of tracing linking for causality, giving an account of causality as mark-transmission. A main goal, at least of Salmon's approach, was to distinguish causal processes from pseudo-processes, in the context of physics. Reichenbach and Salmon's core claim can be expressed in simple terms: a process is causal when, if you mark it at an earlier point, the mark is transmitted to later points in the process. So, for example, a moving car is a causal process because, if you mark or dent the side of the car at an early point in the process, the dent will be carried along with the moving car, and will be detectable later on. On the other hand, the car's shadow is a pseudo-process because, if you mark or interrupt the shadow, that kind of mark will not be transmitted, and will not be detectable later.

However, the problem with this approach is that some causal processes cannot be marked without changing the process itself, such as those involving fundamental particles, as any change would profoundly alter the process. Some less delicate processes, such as transmission of bacteria, might be altered by introducing a dye or other marker. So causal processes are not those which actually transmit marks, but those which *would* transmit a mark, if only a mark could be introduced.

The counterfactual characterization of mark-transmission, presented in detail in Salmon (1984) was criticized by Dowe (1992), which led Salmon to reformulate his theory. In Salmon's revised theory, processes are world lines of objects, and causal processes are those that transmit conserved quantities when they interact. These are any quantities that are universally conserved, as described by physical theory (e.g., mass-energy, linear momentum, or charge). Causal interactions happen when causal processes intersect, exchanging conserved quantities, so changing each other. When pseudo-processes meet, such as car shadows falling on each other, no quantity is transmitted, and nothing is changed by such apparent 'interactions'. See Salmon (1994) and Illari and Russo (2014a, Chapter 11).

This change solves the original problem, but the new account, often called the 'Salmon-Dowe' account, now lacks the very general applicability of the idea of mark-transmission. On the mark-transmission view, causal linking is beautifully general, because we can think of so many different kinds of processes as being marked. We try to alter the signal we think might be interfering with the loudspeakers, and see if the sound they emit changes. We could put floats, or a dye, into a river, and watch to see where the currents take them, to see if the route matches the outbreaks of cholera. The idea of mark-transmission applies across many different scientific fields. Indeed, the idea also matches some of the ways we might reason about linking, and try to establish routes of linking. In contrast, the Salmon-Dowe view is set up using the terms of physical theory, and using examples from physics, but such physical quantities do not seem to be relevant to understanding causality in other sciences or everyday cases.

Nonetheless, it might be possible to redeploy the Salmon-Dowe view of process tracing, making the notion of process more general, applying also outside physics, while still avoiding the key problem for the mark-transmission account. In order to reclaim that generality, we need to introduce *information*. Some little-noticed remarks of Salmon actually give us this hint. For example, in his 1994 paper, Salmon (1994, p. 303) comments on his *own* earlier work:

> It has always been clear that a process is causal if it is capable of transmitting a mark, whether or not it is actually transmitting one. The fact that it has the capacity to transmit a mark is merely a symptom of the fact that it is actually transmitting something else. That other something I described as information, structure, and causal influence.
>
> *(Salmon, 1984 pp. 154–7)*

In trying to give an account of causal linking, a major problem is that there is an enormous number of links that we might want to trace, that are of very different types. The examples of causal links that we used above lead us to formulate the question: what do bacteria and signals in cables have in common? The diversity of worldly causal links is recognized by Elizabeth Anscombe (1975), who draws our attention to the richness of the causal language we use to describe different kinds of linking, such as pulling, pushing, breaking, binding, and so on.

It is a real problem to understand what features are shared by cases of causal linking, given how diverse they are. But information theory gives us a very general formal framework that can be used to represent and assess *any* kind of process. Anything can be described informationally, from a person to a supernova to a tsunami. The formal framework of information theory ensures that the description, in spite of its unprecedented generality, is not empty or vacuous. Information theory itself is part of mathematics (see Chapter 4), but the maths gives us new ideas, new ways of thinking we did not have before. The views of this chapter all, in one way or another, hold that the idea of information helps us understand linking. The crude idea is that all these diverse kinds of causal links, energy, radio waves, electrons, bacteria, and bits, are all forms of information. Put this way, all these scientists are asking a version of the same very general question: Can information be transmitted between C and E? And how? We will also examine how thinking about information *alongside* thinking about mechanisms can help us understand causal linking.

John Collier was probably the first philosopher who explicitly gave an informational account of causality: "The basic idea is that causation is the transfer of a particular token of a quantity of information from one state of a system to another" (Collier, 1999, p. 215).

Collier fills this out by offering an account of what information is and an account of information transfer. The account of information is given using algorithmic information theory (AIT), deriving from the work of Kolmogorov (see Chapter 5), to define formally the information in anything, and formalizing ideas of complexity and compressibility (Kolmogorov, 1965; Kolmogorov, 1983). The idea is that something, say a car, is more 'complex' than something else, such as a rock, the longer its description *needs* to be: a complete description of a car that cannot be shortened – compressed – without loss of information will be longer than an incompressible complete description of a rock.

The next step for Collier is to give an account of information transfer, to describe a flow of information, which happens over time, such as a moving car. Collier initially describes this in terms of identity of at least some part of the information at the beginning and at the end of the process (Collier, 1999, p. 222). This is refined in more recent work, where Collier says that an information channel is a family of infomorphisms (Collier, 2011). The idea of an 'infomorphism' derives from work by Barwise and Seligman (1997), subsequently refined by Dretske (1999) and Floridi (2010). The covariance model of an infomorphism states that if two systems a and b are coupled in such a way that a's being (of type, or in state) F is correlated to b being (of type, or in state) G, then such a correlation carries for the observer of a the information that b is G. For example, the dishwasher's yellow light (a) flashing (F) is triggered by, and hence is informative about, the dishwasher (b) running out of salt (G) for an observer O, like Alice, informed about the correlation. Collier's use of infomorphism can be understood in a very similar way, by supposing you have two systems, each consisting of a set of objects, where each object has a set of attributes. For example, a switch has possible attributes on or off, and a bulb also has attributes on or off. If knowing the attributes of the switch tells you about the attributes of the bulb, there is an infomorphism. So in a torch, with the main working components being bulb, battery, switch and case, the information channel is a series of infomorphisms, connecting switch to bulb via battery and case. Of course, knowing the attributes of the switch might not tell you everything about the state of the bulb, as information might be lost.

Collier's final view is:

> *P* is a causal connection in a system from time *t0* to *t1* if and only if there is a channel between *s0* and *s1* from *t0* to *t1* that preserves some part of the information in the first state.
>
> *(Collier, 2011, pp. 10–11)*

On this view, information flow is characterized in terms of the identity of information at various stages in the information channel (Collier, 2011, pp. 11–12). Consider Salmon's example of the dented car. The car is a real causal process, and that is why it transmits marks, like dents. Collier, though, doesn't have to think in terms of marks that are introduced, like the dent. For Collier, the car itself is an informational structure, and as it moves, that identical item of information exists at each moment of the process. Information, however, can be lost in an information channel, and this is important to thinking about the transmission of cholera by water. We don't need to introduce a mark, as we can think of the bacteria itself in the sewage system as informational. In this kind of case there will be information loss inherent to the system, as not all of the bacteria will be transmitted from the source to a particular downstream town. Some will die, perhaps be eaten, or be diverted; others will reach different towns. Nevertheless, some part will be transmitted, and so we can construe the sewage system as an information channel. Note that when engaged in causal inference, we will usually think in terms of being able to *detect* the relevant informational structure – the bacterium or the car – only at various points in the route of transmission. However, this is about how we gather evidence of transmission. Collier's idea is that there is an informational structure at every point in the process, and part of the information will exist at least at multiple points in the process. This has a great deal in common with Reichenbach's 'at-at' theory of mark-transmission, which was also developed by Wesley Salmon (Salmon, 1977; Salmon, 1984; Reichenbach, 1956). According to the 'at-at' theory, a mark is transmitted from *A* to *B* if the mark appears at each point between *A* and *B*. When two processes intersect and undergo modifications that persist after the interaction, that interaction is causal and the processes are also causal, rather than pseudo-processes.

Collier says that a major virtue of his theory is its generality. He has given a view that 'applies to all forms of causation, but requires a specific interpretation of information for each category of substance (assuming there is more than one)' (Collier, 1999, pp. 215–6). Collier also claims that his view subsumes other theories of causality, most notably the Salmon-Dowe conserved quantities view, simply by interpreting the conserved quantities view as limiting the kind of informational connection we find in its domain of application.

What problems can an informational account of causality solve?

Recall that the purpose of an account of production is to help us conceptualize causal linking, and understand how it functions in our causal reasoning. This means this chapter focuses on production accounts of causality, which can be seen as complementary to difference-making or variation accounts of causality. The philosophical literature pointed to two problems that beset production accounts: applicability and absences (Schaffer, 2000; Dowe, 2008). Below, we briefly present each and explain how an informational account can help address each of these problems, so deepening our understanding of causal linking.

Applicability is the prime virtue of the informational account, as might be expected as this is what it has been designed to achieve. Previous accounts that bear on causal linking have been the Salmon-Dowe theory, focusing on the exchange of conserved quantities, Reichenbach-Salmon mark-transmission, and the idea of Glennan (1996) that there are causes where there are mechanisms. The informational account is more widely applicable than all three. It does not require the presence of conserved quantities, or the introduction of a mark. It can merge usefully with the mechanistic approach, deepening that account, as we will see shortly. The informational account conceives of the causal linking in a way that can be formally defined in terms of computational information theory. But we do not always have to *specify* the information-theoretic structure of a phenomenon. Much of our causal language provides an informal, but meaningful, account for an informational description. This description gives the 'bones' of the causal linking, in a way that is applicable to phenomena studied in physics, as well as psychology, or economics. So information is a general enough concept to express what diverse kinds of causal links in the sciences have in common.

The second problem, the problem of causation by absences, has undermined several production accounts. Everyday language, as well as scientific language, allows absences to be causes or effects. Someone apologizing for missing a meeting might say 'I'm so sorry I wasn't there, my bus didn't turn up.' This intends to claim that the *absence* of the bus caused the person to miss the meeting. Similarly, cerebral hypoxia – i.e., lack of oxygen in the brain

– causes brain damage and even death. But how can absences, like missing buses or lack of oxygen, be connected to something else by conserved quantities, or mark-transmission, or anything? Absences seem to introduce *gaps* in any causal connection, gaps that traditional production concepts were unable to account for. Schaffer (2004), for instance, argues that causation by absences shows that causation does not always involve a persisting line, or a physical connection. The problem of absences bothered scholars to the point that Dowe (2001) conceptualized them not as cases of genuine causes, but of *quasi*-causation.

The solution to this problem that informational accounts offer is entirely novel. Notice, first, that whether or not you think a gap exists depends on what you think the gap is in. There seem to be no gaps in a table, but if you are considering it at an atomic level, well, then there are gaps. This is what our most advanced physical theories tell us. If you happen to visit CERN in Geneva, stop by the shop; one thing you can buy is a bracelet with the following printed sentence: 'The silicon in this bracelet contains 99.9% of empty space.' That we always need to be careful about which features of the world we are prioritizing, and for what purposes, is a lesson of the Method of Levels of Abstraction (see Chapter 7). For the purposes of dining, we consider the table at the level of abstraction where it exhibits properties such as solidity and stability, and we do not think there are any gaps in it. For the purposes of physical theorizing, we consider the world at a very different level of abstraction, paying attention to much smaller constituents of the world, and so to many features of atoms, including their non-continuous nature, which then does imply that there are gaps in the table.

Now, information can be transmitted across what, from a purely physical point of view, might be considered gaps. Suppose the person missing the meeting leaves a message for her boss: 'If I'm not there, it's because my bus didn't turn up.' Then her boss knows about the absence of the bus from her absence at the meeting. Information channels can also involve absences. Recall that a binary string is just a series of 1s and 0s, such as 11010010000001, which can be conveyed as a series of positive signals, and *absences* of a positive signal. Gaps in information-transmission will not be the same as gaps in continuous spacetime. Floridi (2011, p. 31) argues that a peculiar aspect of information is that absence may also be *informative*.

However, it is worth noting that this potential is not fulfilled either by the 'at-at' theory of causal transmission of Salmon (1977), nor yet by the closely allied persistence of the identical item of information through multiple places in a process view of Collier (1999). Since they both rely on something persisting at least at some points in a process, merely physical gaps may still interrupt the process, and so seem to break the causal linking, as it is difficult to see how either a mark or an item of information can be continuously transmitted between, say, an absent bus and being late for a meeting. This is in need of future work.

From considering absences, we can see both that information-transmission offers a possible novel account of causal connection, causal linking, and also that a novel account is needed. The persistence of the problem of absences indicates that we have not yet fully understood causal linking. An informational account allows greater flexibility, offering the possibility that the kinds of connections that exist in different domains is an empirical discovery, that can be understood as further constraints on kinds of information transmission discovered there.

The final problem that then arises for the informational account is the problem of vacuity. There are so many different ways to describe information. The field of mathematical information theory has flourished since Shannon, so there are even multiple formal measures of information. This is important because it yields the applicability that has eluded previous accounts of causal linking. But it might be a weakness if the account is vacuous, if it does not seem to say anything. This might be thought to be the case if there is no one concept of information that is always applied, that can be understood as meaning something substantive.

Alternatively, the rich variety of informational concepts available can be seen as a huge advantage of the informational approach. There are two points worth noting. First, the formal measures of information available, whatever they apply to, however general, are not vacuous. They are also increasingly connected to information-theoretic methods for causal inference. Second, what is *needed* to make any account of causal linking work is something like a light-touch generality. To illuminate our reasoning about linking, we need to be able to see causal linking, in a way that does not obscure the important differences between kinds of causal linking. The informational account offers this, the opportunity to describe – perhaps formally describe – patterns that cannot be described in other ways. Ultimately, the problem of saying something general enough to be widely applicable, while still saying something substantive enough to be meaningful, is going to be a problem for *any* account of production that aims for generality. The challenge that has to be met is precisely to find a concept that covers the many diverse kinds of causal linking in the world, one that nevertheless says something substantive about causality.

In sum, we seem to reason about possible causal linking, and attempt to trace causal links, in many important causal inference tasks in the sciences. Informational approaches to causal production offer a novel approach to conceptualizing causal linking in a way that assists in this task.

How to integrate an informational account into a mechanistic approach

An informational account of causality can be useful to help us reconstruct how science builds up understanding of the causal structure of the world, assisting with the questions of linking we have described. We have seen that traditional accounts of production such as the Salmon-Dowe account do not focus their attention explicitly on *linking*. The core of the mechanisms literature focuses on causal explanation, examining how we (causally) explain natural and social phenomena by identifying the mechanisms underlying them, i.e. identifying their key entities, activities, and organization. The question arises whether such mechanistic approaches, which have been very fruitful in understanding mechanistic explanation, are complementary, or in opposition, to an informational account of linking.

Illari (2011b) and Illari and Russo (2014b) do not attempt to give an account of causality *tout court*. Instead, they seek to give an account only of a part of causality – of production, or causal linking. Ultimately, their guiding idea is that this account will be complementary to difference-making, in that evidence of linking provides further support to evidence such as joint variation between variables. They also argue that an informational account is complementary to mechanistic accounts, helping illuminate the scientific practice and conceptualization of causal linking in the emerging field of exposome research, for example (see below). Broadly, we find mechanisms that help us grasp causal linking in a coarse-grained way. Then we can think in terms of causal linking in a more fine-grained way by thinking informationally. An informational account of causality may also give us the prospect of saying what causality *is*, in a way that is not tailored to the description of reality provided by a given discipline. And it carries the advantage, over other causal metaphysics, that it fares well with the applicability problem for other accounts of production (processes and mechanism).

Illari (2011b) is interested in how an informational account of causality can be combined with our recent better understanding of mechanisms to solve two problems. The first problem is that the informational account has undeniable generality due to its formal properties. Yet, how can a formal informational account give us understanding of the richness of causal links like 'binding', 'growing', 'preying' or 'repressing' in specific domains like biology or psychology (Machamer *et al.*, 2000), or the social sciences (Russo, 2009)? Describing these links informationally allows a very general account, but at the cost of losing rich details that are far too useful to discard.

The second problem is this: when scientists look for a causal link, they often speak of looking for a 'mechanism' for the effect. For example, finding mechanisms of disease transmission, which spell out how diseases spread, has been very important. But this raises the question of how we understand mechanisms as causal links. It is widely agreed that mechanisms are activities and entities organized to produce some phenomenon (Illari and Williamson, 2012; Glennan, 2008). But this looks like taking a whole, the mechanism, and breaking it up into parts, rather than linking anything. How should we understand such arrangements of parts as linking cause and effect? Harold Kincaid explains the problem using the terminology of 'vertical' and 'horizontal' mechanisms (Kincaid, 2011, p. 73). Vertical or constitutive explanations consider a system and explain it by invoking the properties that constitute it and their organization. An etiological or horizontal explanation, instead, considers a system and explains it by invoking the intervening causes (entities and activities) that lead up to some phenomenon. So it is not clear how finding a 'vertical' mechanism helps us with causal linking that happens in the 'horizontal' mechanism.

The problem of how to understand information substantively enough for it to become meaningful in the special sciences, and the opposite problem of how to understand causal linking in mechanisms are entangled, and it can be difficult to see any solution to both. Illari (2011b) argues that mechanisms (as characterized by the mechanists discussed in Illari and Russo (2014a, Chapter 12)) are the channels through which the information flows. On the one hand, this allows us to integrate causality as information flow in the style of Collier with the rich detail of causal relationships we understand from mechanisms. The functional organization of mechanisms structures, or channels, where information can and cannot flow in many sciences. On the other hand, connecting informational causality to mechanisms can allow us to trace the 'horizontal link' – information – across the more familiar 'vertical' or constitutive mechanism. This allows us to ally the resources of our understanding of mechanisms to an information-transmission approach to causality. Note that this is in accord with Collier's view (Collier, 2011, p. 8).

Broadly, mechanisms are what connect C and E. We can find, study and describe them in science. But we study them so assiduously because they hold together the conditions for certain kinds of information transmission. So building up our understanding of mechanisms builds up understanding of information channels – possible, impossible, probable and improbable causal links. This is what we know of the causal structure of the world. We have come to understand many different specific kinds of linking, from radio waves, to hormone signalling in the human brain, to protein receptors on the surface of cancer cells that can be used to signal to the damaged cell to kill itself. We can think of all these very generally, as forms of informational linking, but we can also categorize the different kinds of information transmission we find. In some cases we can even measure them, although much of the time they will be described more informally, as are the many activities in mechanisms.

Illari and Russo (2014b) try to develop these ideas and pull together other strands of the causality literature, using exposome research (the science of exposure) as an example. Exposome research is an emerging field of research within the health sciences, aiming to push back the frontiers of what we know about the causal role of environmental factors for a number of diseases, for instance cancer or allergies. While traditional epidemiology (notably environmental epidemiology) managed to find stable correlations (or joint variations) between categories of determinants (e.g. certain health conditions, socio-economic status, dietary and various life habits) and categories of disease, molecular epidemiology seeks to find correlations at the *molecular* level. The goal is then to measure levels of chemicals and hazards in water or air *and then* changes in our bodies at different 'omics' levels (proteomics, genomics, metabolomics, etc.). This way, scientists try to reconstruct *linking* between exposure and disease, reconstructing how disease evolves, from exposure to early clinical changes to proper disease manifestation. But such linking has to be reconstructed from the biological and statistical interpretation of very complex data analyses. In addition, exposome research provides useful insights about how reasoning about mechanisms, processes, and difference-making complement each other. This has been examined by Russo and Williamson (2012), and Illari and Russo (2014b) build on this work. Illari and Russo examine how ideas of causal linking are used in cutting-edge science, particularly when the science is exploring an area with great uncertainty, due to the existence of both known unknowns, and unknown unknowns. Illari and Russo argue that, in this case, while known mechanisms are used in study design, too little is known for the possible causal links to be sufficiently illuminated using known mechanisms. Mechanisms can give some coarse-grained connections, but what is sought is considerably more fine-grained linking. Instead of reasoning about mechanisms, the scientists reach for the language of chasing signals in a vast, highly interactive search space. Here, the level of unknowns means that linking mechanisms are generally unavailable. In the discovery phase, and possibly beyond it, scientists also need to conceptualize the linking they are attempting to discover in terms of something that can link profoundly inhomogenous causal factors.

Finally, understanding the relationship between mechanisms and information helps us see why one mechanism supports multiple causes, in both the discovery phase and when much more is known. A single mechanism may have more than one function, producing a certain cause effectively, and if the mechanism malfunctions, it may produce one or a few alternative causes reliably, or cease to produce anything reliably at all.

Connected debates

A great deal of the history of theorizing about causality is structured by Hume's work. Hume famously denied that we see any 'secret connection' between causes and their effects – we can only observe effects regularly following their causes in time. Much work in philosophy of science is still in the broadly Humean tradition (Psillos, 2002), although others have sought to find what Mackie (1974) dubbed the 'cement of the universe'. An attempt to give an account of causal linking in terms of information could very well be construed as an attempt to describe the cement of the universe informationally. If construed in this way, it would appear to be a poor attempt.

However, within the Philosophy of Information (PI), giving an account of causality should not be construed in Humean terms, as a search for some elusive causal link. Instead, an informational account of causality, possibly combined with a theory of mechanisms, is very much a *post*-Humean project. Indeed, it can be seen as an attempt to give an account of causality in the spirit of the timely philosophy advocated by Floridi (2011), and apply that account to particular scientific cases such as exposome science above. Understood as a post-Humean project, an informational account of causality has three aims:

1 Metaphysical: say what causality itself is, starting from interesting cases in science;
2 Epistemological: provide a concept of productive causality that can answer needs that have been recognized in the causality literature;
3 Methodological: provide a concept of productive causality that can answer the needs of scientific cases that present interesting challenges, such as exposome science.

The boundaries between these aims are permeable and the choice of the labels themselves is also idiosyncratic, as it depends on one's objective (for a discussion, see Illari and Russo (2014a, Chapter 22)). In particular, there is a very thin line between the epistemological and methodological aims; in this context, the emphasis is on the contribution to philosophical theorizing (whence the label 'epistemological') and to scientific method (whence the label 'methodological'). Any of these aims is individually worth achieving. For instance, Illari and Russo (2014b) lay out in detail how they take themselves to meet aim three with regard to exposomics science. Here, we explain the project more broadly within the context of PI.

One important aspect of that context is the consideration of philosophy of technology alongside philosophy of science. To begin with, there are two – somewhat artificial – distinctions that are worth considering as they illuminate current thinking. One distinction places science on one side and technology on the other side; the other distinguishes between the epistemic agent (or knowing subject) and the object of study.

This distinction between science and technology has a lengthy pedigree, with the famous view that science (*epistêmê*, i.e. pure theory) is epistemically superior, while technology (*technê*, i.e. art) is merely a means to 'make crafts' – a view that, by and large, we inherit from Greek philosophy. However, today the situation is quite different. Arguably, without science it would be impossible to build any complex experimental apparatus to examine bio-specimens in exposome research or to accelerate particles at CERN. *At the same time*, without technology science would not progress at all (Russo, 2012). So the interesting question is not 'what comes first' or 'what is more essential', but how *techno-science* deeply changes epistemological, metaphysical, and methodological questions, as well as our relation with the world, with ourselves, and among ourselves. In other words, the interesting questions on techno-science are asked from a PI perspective, notably one that takes the fourth revolution as a starting point (Floridi, 2011).

This perspective makes the second distinction – between epistemic agent and object – crumble away. The reason is that scientists are no longer (if they ever were) 'just' passive observers of a Nature that stands in front of them. At least since the scientific revolution the scientist, now a *techno*-scientist, is increasingly a *maker*. The techno-scientist makes artefacts, such as computers, software for the analysis of data, particle accelerators, and of course experiments under specific and controlled conditions, etc., but the techno-scientist also makes *knowledge* – i.e. the techno-scientist is a *homo poieticus* (Floridi and Sanders, 2003). We are not passive observers but active learners and creators. This does not necessarily lead to a constructivist position in the manner of Bruno Latour (Latour and Woolgar, 1986) or Isabelle Stengers (Stengers, 1993), but instead leads to a *constructionist* position, according to which we 'shape' the objects of inquiring by studying them, *and* the objects of inquiry constrain knowledge construction (Floridi, 2011). So this is not a traditional realist position, but it is not an antirealist position either, as it does *not* deny reality. What it undermines is the view that reality is totally other, detached from us, and in this sense the position is neo-Kantian in spirit (Floridi, 2011).

The relation between science and technology, and between the epistemic agent and reality, have a bearing on questions about causality. In fact, this very active process of construction and reconstruction is an accurate representation of exposome science as it is practiced. Exposome scientists go to great lengths to construct the links between exposure and disease. On the one hand, they need to find the right 'intermediate' biomarkers, the ones that are linked to exposure and to disease. On the other hand, they need to place this reconstructed link into a plausible network of relations. Whether scientists hit upon the right intermediate biomarker will be theoretically justified to the extent that the complex (internal) biochemical mechanisms also include that biomarker. This means that linking cannot be seen with the naked eye, nor using experimental set-ups, and not even with found correlations. Instead, linking is *reconstructed* by putting together the many pieces of the evidential puzzle. And it is scientists who carry out this work of reconstruction. This requires much empirical evidence and a great deal of interpretation of the evidence using the right concepts. The thought is that information is precisely one concept needed to do that. It is worth noting that this problem is not specific to exposome science. It is shared by experimental and observational methods alike. In fact, any scientific conclusion is the result of a reconstruction and interpretation of evidence.

So, more generally, any causal claim derived from techno-scientific research will be the scientists' interpretation of very many pieces of the 'evidential' puzzle. It will be a reconstruction of information coming from experimental analyses, plus statistics, plus biological or physical theories, for example. It will be an a posteriori reconstruction of data- or technology-driven research. In this context, informational thinking helps with conceptualizing production (the linking) as the evolution of biomarkers, from exposure to early clinical changes, to disease.

Against this background, giving an account of causal linking in terms of information is not to give an account of the cement of the universe, as Mackie originally construed it, nor is it an attempt to present the hidden nature of causality. Indeed, the project that Reichenbach and Salmon engaged in was already different from this, as in various ways they attempted to spell out what we were learning from science about causality. But these earlier production accounts did not explicitly include any epistemic agent in the process of finding, conceptualizing, or using linking. They still saw Nature as separate from the techno-scientist or any other person. However, from a PI perspective, the epistemic agent is an integral part of the process of finding and conceptualizing causal linking, and the 'poietic' practices of the scientific community craft our knowledge, builds the technology we need to test it against reality, and then crafts the artefacts our enhanced knowledge allows us to make, testing that knowledge again in changing our lives.

It is in this context that Illari and Russo (2014b) argue that information is the most general possible characterization of causal production or linking. It provides a very general concept of causal linking, and a "lite" metaphysics of causal production which can be widely applicable. If informational linking helps in these complex poietic practices, then informational linking is as real as it needs to be. The informational structural realist approach (see Chapter 18), in so far as it is also embarked on a project of understanding the world informationally, is in the same spirit. Informational structural realists share the wish to identify generalities in the post Stanford School age of pluralism (Cartwright, 1999; Dupré, 1995), where general concepts are unfashionable.

Structural realism is a view in the scientific realism debate that says that what is real, what science ultimately tracks through time, is the fundamental structure of the world. It is this structure that is described, for example, in the mathematical expressions that are so important to physical theory. In their theory, Ladyman and Ross (2007) set out an extended attempt to explain how structural realist ideas, originally developed in the philosophy of physics, can actually be extended into the – prima facie very different – special sciences. They are explicit about their reasons for using informational language, and about their influences:

> As we noted at the top of the chapter [chapter 4], special sciences are incorrigibly committed to dynamic propagation of temporally asymmetric influences – or, a stronger version of this idea endorsed by many philosophers, to real causal processes. Reference to transfer of some (in principle) quantitatively measurable

information is a highly general way of describing any process. More specifically, it is more general than describing something as a causal process or as an instantiation of a lawlike one: if there are causal processes, then each such process must involve the transfer of information between cause and effect (Reichenbach, 1956, Salmon, 1984, Collier, 1999); and if there are lawlike processes, then each such process must involve the transfer of information between instantiations of the types of processes governed by the law.

(Ladyman and Ross, 2007 pp. 210–11)

So they are clear that generality is an important reason for using informational language. For Ladyman and Ross, as for Collier, the idea of compressibility is important to their theory, which they call 'information-theoretic structural realism'.

As of today, the only other major informational structural realist is Luciano Floridi (2011), who of course situates his work explicitly within the Philosophy of Information. Floridi's motivations are in some ways quite different from those of Ladyman and Ross. He uses informational language in a neo-Kantian effort to describe what we know of the world, with the minimal metaphysical commitments possible. Again, though, it is the generality of informational language, in this case allied to its minimal commitments, that is so attractive.

Neither Floridi, nor Ladyman and Ross, are trying to address the issue of causal linking. Nevertheless, they are trying to argue for a view about the nature of the world, and in that sense they are offering a metaphysics, as well as a conceptualization, using informational concepts. But the driving aim is generality, to describe different things in a way that illuminates what they have in common, in a minimal way. This is not to deny the differences, but to describe things at a level of abstraction (see Chapter 7) that is appropriate for some purposes. The description will only be useful if it does capture some features of the world – what Ladyman and Ross call 'real patterns'. So this informational metaphysics, and the informational account of causality, is minimally realist. Thinking of causality informationally captures useful generalities, generalities that can illuminate our causal reasoning. It does not describe the hidden nature of causality, or the 'cement of the universe'. Rather, it makes the process of knowledge construction explicit, showing how general concepts such as a concept of informational linking function in this process. If, in cases like exposome research, thinking of the link informationally is the best way to describe what is sought – and found – then we have the best possible reason to think that link is real, and is informational.

Notes

1 In philosophy of science there is a lively debate on the concept of mechanism. Here, we adopt the proposed consensus definition of Illari and Williamson (2012), 'A mechanism for a phenomenon is composed of entities and activities organized so that they are responsible for the phenomenon.' The debate on mechanisms rapidly expanded from biology to many other disciplines, including psychology and neuroscience and the social sciences (Illari and Russo, 2014a, Chapter 12).
2 For a detailed discussion of variational reasoning in causal methodology see Russo (2009) and Illari and Russo (2014a, Chapter 16).

Related topics

Related chapters include:

18. Informational Metaphysics (the informational nature of reality), Terry Bynum
21. Philosophy of Science and Information, Ioannis Votsis
23. The Philosophy of Biological Information, Barton Moffatt

Further reading

Salmon (1994) provides Salmon's own reassessment of his earlier mark-transmission theory, and his shift to the conserved quantities view. Collier (1999) is a good introduction to his approach to informational causality. Illari (2011b) explores the aims of an informational account of productive causality, while Illari and Russo (2014b) apply such an approach in detail to the emerging scientific field of exposome research.

References

Anscombe, G. E. M. 1975. Causality and determination. *In:* Sosa, E. (ed.) *Causation and Conditionals.* Oxford: Oxford University Press.

Barwise, J. and Seligman, J. 1997. *Information Flow: The Logic of Distributed Systems.* Cambridge, Cambridge University Press.

Cartwright, N. 1999. *The Dappled World: A Study of the Boundaries of Science.* Cambridge, Cambridge University Press.

Clarke, B., Gillies, D., Illari, P., Russo, F. and Williamson, J. 2014. Mechanisms and the evidence hierarchy. *Topoi,* online first.

Collier, J. 1999. Causation is the transfer of information. *In:* Sankey, H. (ed.) *Causation, natural laws, and explanation.* Dordrecht: Kluwer.

Collier, J. 2011. Information, causation and computation. *In:* Crnkovic, G. D. and Burgin, M. (eds.) *Information and Computation: Essays on Scientific and Philosophical Understanding of Foundations of Information and Computation.* Singapore, World Scientific.

Dowe, P. 1992. Wesley Salmon's process theory of causality and the conserved quantity theory. *Philosophy of Science,* 59, 195–216.

Dowe, P. 2001. A counterfactual theory of prevention and 'causation' by omission. *Australasian Journal of Philosophy,* 79, 216–226.

Dowe, P. 2008. Causal processes. *In:* Zalta, E. N. (ed.) *The Stanford Encyclopedia of Philosophy.*

Dretske, F. 1999. *Knowledge and the Flow of Information.* Cambridge, Cambridge University Press.

Dupré, J. (ed.) 1995. *The Disorder of Things.* Cambridge, MA, Harvard University Press.

Floridi, L. 2010. Semantic information and the correctness theory of truth. *Erkenntnis* 74, 147–175.

Floridi, L. 2011. *The Philosophy of Information.* Oxford, Oxford University Press.

Floridi, L. and Sanders, J. W. 2003. Internet ethics: the constructionist values of *Homo Poieticus. In:* Cavalier, R. (ed.) *The Impact of the Internet on Our Moral Lives.* New York, SUNY.

Glennan, S. 1996. Mechanisms and the nature of causation. *Erkenntnis,* 44, 49–71.

Glennan, S. 2008. Mechanisms. *In:* Psillos, S. and Curd, M. (eds.) *Routledge Companion to the Philosophy of Science.* Abingdon, Routledge.

Hall, N. 2004. Two concepts of causation. *In:* Paul, L. A., Hall, E. J. and Collins, J. (eds.) *Causation and Counterfactuals.* Cambridge, MA, MIT Press.

Illari, P. 2011a. Mechanistic evidence: disambiguating the Russo–Williamson Thesis. *International Studies in the Philosophy of Science,* 25, 139–157.

Illari, P. 2011b. Why theories of causality need production: an information-transmission account. *Philosophy and Technology,* 24, 95–114.

Illari, P. and Russo, F. 2014a. *Causality: philosophical theory meets scientific practice.* Oxford, Oxford University Press.

Illari, P. and Russo, F. 2014b. Information channels and biomarkers of disease. *Topoi,* Online first.

Illari, P. and Williamson, J. 2012. What is a mechanism?: Thinking about mechanisms across the sciences. *European Journal of the Philosophy of Science,* 2, 119–135.

Kincaid, H. 2011. Causal modeling, mechanism, and probability in epidemiology. *In:* Illari, P. M., Russo, F. and Williamson, J. (eds.) *Causality in the Sciences.* Oxford, Oxford University Press.

Kolmogorov, A. N. 1965. Three approaches to the quantitative definition of information. *Problems of Information and Transmission,* 1, 1–7.

Kolmogorov, A. N. 1983. Combinatorial foundations of information theory and the calculus of probabilities. *Russian Mathematical Surveys,* 38, 27–36.

Ladyman, J. and Ross, D. 2007. *Every thing must go,* Oxford, Oxford University Press.

Latour, B. and Woolgar, S. 1986. *Laboratory Life: The Construction of Scientific Facts.* Princeton, NJ, Princeton University Press.

Machamer, P., Darden, L. and Craver, C. 2000. Thinking about mechanisms. *Philosophy of Science,* 67, 1–25.

Mackie, J. L. 1974. *The Cement of the Universe. A Study on Causation.* Oxford, Oxford University Press.

Paneth, N. 2004. Assessing the contributions of John Snow to epidemiology. 150 years after removal of the Broad Street pump handle. *Epidemiology,* 15, 514–516.

Psillos, S. 2002. *Causation and Explanation.* Abingdon, Acumen Publishing.

Reichenbach, H. 1956. *The Direction of Time.* Berkeley and Los Angeles, CA, University of California Press.

Russo, F. 2009. *Causality and Causal Modelling in the Social Sciences. Measuring Variations,* New York, Springer.

Russo, F. 2012. The *Homo Poieticus* and the bridge between *Physis* and *Techne. In:* Demir, H. (ed.) *Luciano Floridi's Philosophy of Technology: Critical reflections.* Dordrecht, Springer.

Russo, F. and Williamson, J. 2007. Interpreting causality in the health sciences. *International Studies in Philosophy of Science,* 21, 157–170.

Russo, F. and Williamson, J. 2012. EnviroGenomarkers. The interplay between difference-making and mechanisms. *Medicine Studies,* 3, 249–262.

Salmon, W. C. 1977. An "At-At" theory of causal influence. *Philosophy of Science,* 44, 215–224.

Salmon, W. C. 1984. *Scientific Explanation and the Causal Structure of the World.* Princeton, NJ, Princeton University Press.

Salmon, W. C. 1994. Causality without counterfactuals. *Philosophy of Science,* 61, 297–312.

Schaffer, J. 2000. Causation by disconnection. *Philosophy of Science,* 67, 285–300.

Schaffer, J. 2004. Causes need not be physically connected to their effects: the case for negative causation. *In:* Hitchcock, C. (ed.) *Contemporary Debates in Philosophy of Science.* Oxford, Blackwell.

Stengers, I. 1993. *L'invention des sciences modernes.* Paris, La Découverte.

21

PHILOSOPHY OF SCIENCE AND INFORMATION

Ioannis Votsis

Introduction

Of all the sub-disciplines of philosophy, the philosophy of science has perhaps the most privileged relationship to information theory. This relationship has been forged through a common interest in themes like induction, probability, confirmation, simplicity, non-ad hoc-ness, unification and, more generally, ontology. It also has historical roots. One of the founders of algorithmic information theory (AIT), Ray Solomonoff, produced his seminal work on inductive inference as a direct result of grappling with problems first encountered as a student of the influential philosopher of science Rudolf Carnap. There are other such historical connections between the two fields. Alas, there is no space to explore them here. Instead this chapter will restrict its attention to a broad and accessible overview of the aforementioned common themes, which, by their very nature, mandate an (almost exclusive) emphasis on AIT as opposed to general information theory.

Induction, probability and confirmation

David Hume is widely known for having noted that there is something unsettling about the trust we put in inductive inferences. Roughly speaking, these are inferences where the truth of each and every premise does not guarantee, but nonetheless is meant to suggest, the truth of a conclusion. The most paradigmatic of such inferences, abundant in science and everyday life, project past observations into the future. But what underwrites their 'validity'? Hume reasoned that nothing can play that role as neither a deductive nor an inductive approach gets us anywhere. Take the latter. We may, for example, argue that inductive inferences have often produced true or at least largely accurate conclusions in the past hence they will continue to do so in the future. Alas, *that* inference is inductive thereby rendering this approach circular. Indeed, that's even putting aside additional difficulties, an evident one being that numerous *prima facie* reasonable inductive inferences yield false or highly inaccurate conclusions. Bertrand Russell's chicken story is instructive. A chicken, fed daily for a number of weeks, formulates the inductive inference that it will be fed every day. The day comes when its neck is wrung instead, thereby making that inference unreasonable.

Now consider the deductive approach. We may attempt to find deductive support for a principle of induction. Such a principle would presumably be a contingent and very general truth, something to the effect that nature is uniform in such and such a way. Notice that deduction guarantees the truth of a conclusion so long as the premises employed are true and their content is *at least as general* as that of the conclusion. That's why deduction is sometimes characterized as 'content-preserving'. But we know, recall the poor chicken, that the future need not resemble the past. Hence, if the premises are made up of contingent truths about the past – as it seems they should if they are to be evidential in content – they would not be sufficiently general to guarantee the truth of a conclusion about the future.[1] The deductive approach to propping up induction then appears hopeless.

At least among philosophers, there is a consensus that the problem of induction is insoluble. One of the leading dissenting voices in modern times is Karl Popper. It's not so much that he believes that the problem of induction can be solved as that he deems that induction and its problem should be shunned. In its stead, Popper argues that scientific (and presumably everyday) reasoning proceeds, and ought to proceed, first conjecturally and then deductively. The conjectural stage, also known as the context of discovery, is not, according to him, guided by logic but by creativity and imagination. The stage that follows, also known as the context of justification, is guided by deductive logic. We deduce consequences from conjectures and test them against observations. A contradiction spells the end of the conjecture. Agreement, Popper holds, merely postpones a conjecture's demise. Scientific conjectures cannot be verified but only falsified in such a framework. The problem of induction in Popper's so-called falsificationist framework simply fades away.

Despite Popper's hostility toward verification, his account of goings-on in the context of justification shares much with what we would today call the study of confirmation. This is the study of the conditions under which evidence supports, or ought to support, a hypothesis and sometimes even the level of that support. An influential figure in this study as well as in the related studies of induction and probability is Carnap. Let us begin with his take on probability.

The axioms are the least controversial part of the theory of probability. What is highly controversial is the interpretation of the emerging notion of probability, which is meant to conform to those axioms. Carnap thought that two interpretations stand out and give rise to two distinct notions of probability. One interpretation conceives of probability in terms of relative frequencies (in the long run). This is what Carnap called 'probability$_2$'. It is the interpretation we most commonly encounter in statistics and applied science and can be expressed as follows: The probability of an event type E in a class of events types C is the relative frequency of instances of E in (the limit of) a long (potentially infinite) series of a random experiment whose outcomes are event types C. More simply, the probability is given by counting how many times E occurs, e.g. drawing spades, in a repeated test, e.g. always drawing from a randomly shuffled full deck of cards, as opposed to alternatives in C, e.g. drawing clubs, hearts or diamonds. The other interpretation championed by Carnap conceives of probability in logical terms. This is what he calls 'probability$_1$'. The so-called 'logical' interpretation is an attempt to show that there exists an inductive relation between statements analogous to the relation of entailment in deductive logic. The analogy is facilitated by the notion of confirmation or support. We say that in cases where a statement B deductively follows from a statement A the latter statement fully supports the former. If we accept the claim that some support relations are only partial then it seems only reasonable to suppose that there are partial entailment relations, and hence, that there is a real need for a *logic* of induction.

To elucidate his notion of a partial entailment or inductive support relation, Carnap asks us to construct an artificial language that contains names for objects and properties as well as some basic logical machinery, e.g. the conjunction & and negation ~ operators. In such a language we can describe a possible state of the world in terms of combinations of conjunctions of atomic statements or their negated counterparts. Suppose there are two objects, denoted by letters a and b, and one property, denoted by letter P, we want to model with our language. A complete description of a *possible* state of this world is given by a statement that states for any given object whether or not it has that property. In our little example this gives rise to exactly four such complete descriptions, also known as 'state descriptions':

   1. $Pa \& Pb$ 2. $\sim Pa \& Pb$ 3. $Pa \& \sim Pb$ 4. $\sim Pa \& \sim Pb$

One upside of this approach is that the state descriptions can faithfully encode the content of any statements about the world. For example, the statement that there exists at least one thing with the property denoted by P, $(\exists x)Px$, is representable in terms of the disjunction of state descriptions 1, 2 and 3. Another upside is that we can use the state descriptions to determine inference relations. On the assumption that Pb, we can infer $(\exists x)Px$ by appealing to an inclusion relation between the corresponding representations. To be precise, Pb corresponds to the disjunction of state descriptions 1 and 2 and this is included in the disjunction of the state descriptions corresponding to $(\exists x)Px$. In short, this enables us to model deductive inference, i.e. the relation of full support, in terms of the inclusion relation.

What about inductive inferences? Well, we may express such partial support via an overlap relation. Suppose we want to find out whether Pb partially supports the statement that every object has property P, i.e. $(\forall x)Px$. Whenever we ask of a given statement whether it supports another statement we assume that the first is true. On that assumption, certain state descriptions are ruled out, namely those where the statement does not hold. Thus, Pb rules out state descriptions 3 and 4 since they assert $\sim Pb$. Carnap suggests that the support Pb confers to $(\forall x)Px$ is given by the number of state description(s) that correspond to $(\forall x)Px$ but also correspond to Pb, i.e. the number of overlapping state description(s) between those statements, divided by the number of state description(s) that correspond to Pb. Since $(\forall x)Px$ is represented by state description 1 and Pb by state descriptions 1 and 2, the overlap is state description 1. The support relation is thus determined at 1/2. Thus, assuming that each and every state description has an equal weight, the degree of confirmation conferred by Pb onto $(\forall x)Px$ is 0.5.

As it turns out that assumption leads to some undesirable consequences. Suppose we get Pa as evidence and we want to figure out how much support this statement lends to Pb. We know that Pb holds in two state descriptions: 1 and 2. Thus, its original confirmation level stands at 0.5 since it holds in two out of four possible state descriptions. Now we acquire evidence Pa, which also holds in two state descriptions: 1 and 3. The overlap between Pa and Pb is state description 1. But notice that the ratio of this overlap to the number of state descriptions corresponding to Pa is also 0.5. It seems that the confirmation level has remained unchanged even in light of new evidence. This contradicts the intuitive idea that the confirmation of a proposition should increase when we learn something new about, and hence have in some sense additional evidence for, that proposition.

Aware of this difficulty, Carnap proposed a novel way of assigning weights to descriptions. In his view, weight should be equally distributed between structural descriptions, not state descriptions. A structural description is a coarsening of the notion of a state description where what matters is, unsurprisingly, structure. In our example, state descriptions 2 and 3 share structure in that they both posit that one object possesses the property denoted by P and one object lacks it. State descriptions 1 and 4 each have a structure that's unlike no other, namely all objects possess the property denoted by P and none of them do, respectively. We thus end up with three different structural descriptions. Each is assigned a 1/3 weight. If we maintain indifference with respect to the weight of state descriptions *within* a given structural description, state descriptions 2 and 3 each gets assigned a weight of 1/6 whereas state descriptions 1 and 4 each gets 2/6.

The revised account of confirmation given by Carnap can be captured by the following function c:

> **Carnap's confirmation function:** $c\ (h,\ e)\ =\ w(h$ overlap $e)/w(e)$ where h is a hypothesis, e is a piece of evidence and w the structural weight function.

This then is Carnap's proposed logic of induction that serves also as a theory of confirmation. It is not offered as a solution to the problem of induction but rather as a means through which we can make sense of the level of support premises grant to a conclusion.

Unfortunately, this is not the end of the story for Carnap's theory as it is afflicted by additional difficulties. One major difficulty concerns the largely arbitrary decision of weight assignment. Carnap was well aware that alternative assignments are possible, each giving rise to different confirmation functions. Moreover, the choice of confirmation function has dramatic consequences on which hypothesis, from a number of rivals, is best supported by a body of evidence. As will become obvious below, this is a problem that appears in many guises and plagues various accounts of confirmation and simplicity.

Having glanced at the philosophical discussions surrounding induction, confirmation and probability, it is now time to turn to the corresponding information-theoretic ones. We begin with Solomonoff (1964a, b), who picks up on the theme of induction. Solomonoff, like Carnap, is not interested in providing a solution to the problem of induction, as some have suggested.[2] As he clearly indicates: 'In general, it is impossible to prove that any proposed inductive inference method is "correct"' (1964a, p. 4). Rather he is interested, again like Carnap, in the practical problem of figuring out which hypotheses are best equipped to handle future cases on the basis of some existing evidence. Unlike Carnap, he places this problem in an AIT framework. Indeed, Solomonoff thinks that all problems concerning inductive inferences can be restated in such a framework. Here we focus on those problems that concern inductive inferences from evidence to hypotheses. The restatement of such problems in an AIT framework rests on the largely undisputed assumption that languages, whether natural or artificial, encode information in terms of sequences of symbols. Since evidence and hypotheses carry information, it is not unreasonable to suggest that they can also be encoded thus. Now take a body of evidence formulated as a sequence of symbols. Any extension of this sequence can be thought of as a hypothesis that predicts how the existing sequence of symbols develops. Thus, the question 'What is the probability of a hypothesis given certain evidence?' now reduces to the question 'What is the probability that a given extension turns out true?'[3]

Solomoff's proposed answer to this question involves a theorem that is derivable from the axioms of probability:

> **Bayes' theorem**: $P(H/E) = P(E/H) \times P(H) / P(E)$ where $P(H/E)$ is the posterior probability of a hypothesis H given a piece of evidence E, $P(H)$ is the prior probability of H, $P(E/H)$ is the likelihood of E given H and $P(E)$ is the prior probability of E.

The theorem is a central cog in an influential theory of confirmation that is known as Bayesian confirmation theory. Intuitively, the prior probabilities are the probabilities we take

H and *E* to possess *before* any calculation is made and the likelihood of the evidence is how likely the evidence is made by the hypothesis. How do we determine these probabilities? Bayes' theorem itself does not offer any guidance. Indeed, strongly subjective Bayesians deem that that's how things should be. Probabilities in their view should express degrees of belief, roughly, a subjective measure of confidence in a given proposition. This puts them directly at odds with Carnap's account which deems probabilities to be purely objective.

Having said this, subjective Bayesians do not claim that we are entirely in the dark when attempting to determine initial probabilities. First of all, there are the trivial, least controversial assignments. Tautologies, for example, are thought of as being certainly true and hence assigned probability 1. By contrast, contradictions are thought of as being certainly false and therefore assigned probability 0. Similarly, when a hypothesis deductively entails the evidence, the likelihood is assigned probability 1. Other rules of thumb include the assignment of non-extreme values when there is no a-priori reason to have too little or too much confidence in a proposition and the assignment of low probabilities to surprising evidence and, conversely, high probabilities to evidence that is to be expected. A natural question to ask at this point is 'Why should we take this approach seriously if different subjects have the freedom to choose different priors?' An answer that goes a long way in allaying concerns, though admittedly not all the way, is that once the evidence begins to trickle in and Bayes' theorem is repeatedly put to use, if certain rather reasonable conditions are met, any initial differences in the priors fade away as the values of the posterior probabilities converge. This effect is known as 'the washing out of the priors'.

Solomonoff's contribution comes in the form of a method that removes subjectivity from the choice of priors. His method appeals, among other things, to the intuitions underlying Occam's razor.[4] Simpler hypotheses, Solomonoff reasons, are more likely to be predictively accurate than more complex ones. In AIT terms, the role of simpler hypotheses is played by shorter input strings, i.e. programs, in a Universal Turing Machine (UTM) whose output is the desired sequence extensions. That is to say, shorter input strings are claimed to be better predictors of a given output string than longer ones. A UTM is the highly abstracted notion of a machine that can emulate all other Turing machines, themselves abstractions, and therefore capable of implementing any computable function. On the assumption that simplicity is a virtue – more on this in the section below – simpler hypotheses are rewarded with higher prior probabilities.

In his bid to dodge the arbitrariness problem that afflicted Carnap's weight assignment, Solomonoff constructs what has since been called the 'universal distribution'. A distribution is a statistical notion that signifies the assignment of probabilities to each member of a set of alternative hypotheses about a given domain.[5] By a universal distribution, Solomonoff means an assignment of probabilities that concerns *all* the alternative hypotheses to *any* given domain. In AIT terms, it is the distribution that assigns probabilities to all output sequences in a UTM that has been fed with a random input sequence. Take a string *a* expressed as a binary sequence, e.g. 01011101... Various input strings, also expressed as binary sequences, produce *a* as an output. Suppose σ_i is one such input string. Let us denote its length with $L(\sigma_i)$. The probability that *a* is produced by σ_i is given by $2^{-L(\sigma_i)}$. This means that the shorter the input string the higher the probability.[6]

Let us take stock of what the notion of a universal distribution is meant to accomplish. By targeting such a distribution, Solomonoff mirrors Carnap's attempts to determine the probabilities of each and every hypothesis formulable in an artificial language. The only difference is that the language chosen is that of a UTM. That's supposed to be a key strength of the approach, for UTM, qua the most general-purpose type of machine, is uniquely positioned to arbitrate between competing hypotheses and hence, the intuition goes, the resulting distribution is likewise unique. To its supporters, it represents the most promising method of assigning prior probabilities to rival hypotheses.

Although it might not seem like it at first, the said universality also turns out to be a shortcoming of sorts. Under Solomonoff's proposal, the input strings, also known as 'descriptions', are meant to be fed into an ideal abstract machine. But clearly, our worldly dealings are with concrete machines. The push to develop a more practicable version of the aforementioned ideas has resulted in what is nowadays called the 'minimum description length' (MDL) approach. The approach dates back to Jorma Rissanen's pioneering work – see Rissanen (1978). This 'practical turn' facilitates the application of the central ideas of AIT to a number of fields, including data compression, machine learning, and model selection. Take the last field as an illustration. A model, crudely speaking, is a set of alternative hypotheses, functions or probability distributions that share the same form. For example, all polynomials of degree n, where $n > 0$, have the same form and therefore can be said to fall under the same model.[7] Model selection employs rules that determine which of a number of different models best accounts for a set of data. MDL's rules capitalize on the idea that the more a data set exhibits regularity, the shorter the formulable descriptions whose output is that data set. Following AIT norms, such rules then urge us to pick the model with the shorter description.

An interesting facet that is sometimes neglected in reconstructions of Solomonoff's arguments is that higher priors are not only reserved for shorter descriptions but also for multiple descriptions of the same sequence. The rationale behind this second condition is that 'if an occurrence has many possible causes, then it is more likely' (1964a, p. 8). Note, however, that the calculation of priors now becomes more complicated as the two conditions sometimes pull in opposite directions. A natural solution to this problem is the assignment of weights, which Solomonoff duly proposes. Though such a move is clearly necessary, it makes philosophers of science twitchy for much the same reasons as those given above concerning Carnap's weight assignment. Unless a clear justification can be found for those weight assignments, it seems always possible to come up with an alternative assignment that inverts the rankings of what counts as the most simple and therefore, in some sense, most desirable hypothesis.

As already noted, Solomonoff was not alone in laying the foundations for AIT. Two other figures played an equally pivotal role: Andrey Kolmogorov (see, for example his 1965) and Gregory Chaitin (see, for example, his 1966). The central ideas found in AIT seem to have been independently produced by all three theorists. Interestingly, though Solomonoff seems to have got there first, the idea of measuring complexity in terms of the shortest program that can produce a certain output is now widely known as 'Kolmogorov complexity', also sometimes called 'Kolmogorov-Chaitin complexity'.

Earlier in this section we noted Solomonoff's interest in devising a practical solution to the problem of drawing reasonable inductive inferences. As it turns out, his solution is quite impractical. This is not only because the machines at issue are abstract but also because the approach is un-computable, i.e. no Turing machine can compute some of its algorithms in a finite number of steps. Having said this, as with any ideal solution to a problem, its strength lies not in its practicability but rather in its ability to play a regulative role in our search to find solutions that approximate the ideal. That's where MDL and other AIT-inspired approaches come in handy.

Simplicity

William of Occam (also spelled 'Ockham') is one of few notable philosophers to have emerged in the middle ages. His name has become synonymous with the idea that simplicity is a virtue of hypotheses. This is sometimes understood as the claim that 'the simplest hypothesis is the most likely to be true'. Yet Occam's own pronouncements, typified in what has come to be known as 'Occam's razor', do not quite say this. For example, in *Summa Logicae*, he states: 'Pluralitas non est ponenda sine necessitate' (1974, p. 185). This translates, roughly, as 'plurality is not to be posited without necessity'. The plurality at issue here seems to be an ontological one. That is to say, the emphasis is on reducing ontological complexity. There is no direct mention of simpler hypotheses in this or other quotations.[8] Having said this, it is natural to interpret the positing of fewer entities in terms of simpler, or as they are sometimes called 'more parsimonious', hypotheses, for, if anything, hypotheses are at least hotbeds of entity postulation.

One worry that philosophers express about AIT is that its formal treatment of simplicity is too hastily connected to intuitive formulations of simplicity principles, including Occam's razor. For example, it is not clear why a shorter input string *invariably* translates to a more frugal ontology and vice-versa. The philosopher of science Elliott Sober complains that syntactic approaches to simplicity like those deployed in AIT fall afoul of 'the problem of measurement': 'Since a proposition can be encoded in many different ways, depending on the language one adopts, measuring simplicity in terms of code features will fail to be linguistically invariant' (2002, p. 16). Sober uses a *version* of the well-known grue paradox to demonstrate this problem. I here present the gist of his argument, omitting certain details. Compare the following hypotheses:

H_1: All emeralds are green.
H_2: All emeralds are green until a fixed future date d, thereupon they are blue.

If our simplicity judgments rely on the syntactic length of a hypothesis, then it appears that H_1 is simpler than H_2. Suppose, however, that we start out with a different language, one that contains the predicates grue and bleen instead of green and blue. An object is grue if and only if it is green prior to d or blue thereafter. An object is bleen if and only if it is blue prior to d or green thereafter. Utilizing these predicates, we can formulate the following two hypotheses:

H_1': All emeralds are grue until a fixed future date d, thereupon they are bleen.
H_2': All emeralds are grue.

In this language, H_2' is simpler than H_1'. Note, however, and this is the crucial point, that H_1 is logically equivalent to H_1' and H_2 is logically equivalent to H_2'. That, in effect, means that H_1 and H_1' express the same hypothesis. Ditto for the pair H_2 and H_2'. So, depending on the language we start out with, we end up making inverse determinations of the simplicity of two hypotheses. That surely can't be right. Sober concludes: 'Stipulating which language should be used resolves this ambiguity, but a further question needs to be answered. Why should we adopt one language, rather than another, as the representational system within which simplicity is measured?' (2002, p. 16).

Pertinent to this type of objection is an *invariance theorem* that Solomonoff and others proved. According to this theorem, for any two general-purpose machine languages and a sufficiently long output string, the length of the shortest description yielding that output in the one language will not exceed a constant c when compared to the length of the shortest description yielding the same output in the other. This is taken to mean that even though some languages are more economical than others it (virtually) does not matter anymore what language we choose. That doesn't seem right. The theorem suggests that the extent to which the lengths of shortest descriptions vary from language to language is limited. That definitely reduces the impact of objections such as the above but it does not eliminate them. After all, two general-purpose languages may still yield inverted simplicity judgments even though any differences in length will, following the invariance theorem, be comparatively small. It appears then that to banish grue-like objections altogether, AIT theorists need to prove a stronger theorem, e.g. one that establishes the existence of a uniquely privileged machine language.

Returning to Occam's dictum, what the clause 'without necessity' is meant to range over becomes a significant interpretational issue. Among the various candidates, two are worth mentioning and relate to a well-known distinction in the philosophy of science, namely explaining versus saving a class of phenomena. The phrase 'to save the phenomena' goes back to Andreas Osiander who wrote the preface to Copernicus' *De Revolutionibus Orbium Coelestium*. Probably eager to avoid the wrath of the church, Osiander argued that Copernicus' radical model of the universe with the Sun, not the Earth, at its centre, was merely aimed at saving, i.e. accounting, for the phenomena in what we would nowadays call an *instrumentalist* manner. There is thus no question of the truth or even probable truth of this model. This contrasts with what we might call a *realist* view, according to which (adequate) explanations don't just save phenomena but also reveal the truth about the underlying structure of the world.

Such matters are not only important for scholarship or history. They are also matters about which disagreement can lead to radically distinct conceptions of how hypotheses ought to be chosen. Indeed, the said disagreement can be found both within philosophical discussions as well as AIT ones. As already hinted, there are philosophers who insist on instrumentalist, also known as pragmatic, readings of simplicity principles, e.g. Bas van Fraassen (1980), and those who plunge for more realist-oriented interpretations, e.g. Kevin T. Kelly (2008). Similarly, there are AIT theorists who claim that their fondness for simplicity has nothing to do with truth, e.g. Peter Grünwald (2007), and those who unabashedly flirt with truth, e.g. Samuel Rathmanner and Marcus Hutter (2011).[9]

How exactly does this dispute matter? Well, the pragmatists are not perturbed much by the existence of conflicting simplicity judgments. Take two competing hypotheses that are expressible as programs in two separate computer languages, say C and PASCAL.[10] One program may be shorter in C and the other program shorter in PASCAL. Thus, depending on the language we start out with, each hypothesis is deemed simpler and hence to be preferred. For a pragmatist this is not as pressing a concern. That's because there is no overarching aim to find the one true hypothesis. The aim is rather to find hypotheses that make life easier for us by, for example, allowing us to make the same, or more or less the same, predictions faster, more efficiently, and so on. By contrast, it is plain that those whose goal is the truth have to reject the claim that one hypothesis is both closer to the truth and at the same time further away from it in relation to another.

In addition to MDL, there are other information-theoretic methods on offer. Sober, for example, is a fan of the Akaike Information Criterion (AIC). Named after its creator, the statistician Hirotugu Akaike, this is also a model selection method. AIC balances considerations of simplicity and goodness of fit to the data. The latter is calculated using well-known statistical methods like maximum-likelihood estimation. The former is measured via the number of free parameters, i.e. those whose values are adjustable, present in a model. The idea, roughly, is that models with fewer free parameters are simpler because they require less ad hoc intervention to produce a higher goodness of fit. In short, AIC rewards goodness of fit but penalizes complexity. In doing so, it guards against the well-known problem of over-fitting, which can be explained as follows. Most data sets contain noise. This means that a model that fits the data perfectly is guaranteed to be false and is an imperfect predictor of new data. One straightforward way to avoid this consequence is to opt for simpler models that do not hug the data as closely and hence have at least a chance of being true or perfect predictors. Thus, there seems to be a good rationale for penalizing complexity both through AIC but also through other approaches that counsel against over-fitting.

The last method to be briefly explored here is the Bayesian Information Criterion (BIC) due to Schwarz (1978). This is remarkably similar to AIC in that both approaches trade off simplicity and goodness of fit via an almost identical mathematical expression. In fact, the only difference between them seems to be that BIC takes into account the size of the data set in its estimation of the simplicity term. The consequence is that BIC tends to penalize complexity more than AIC, especially as the size of the data set increases.

These and other methods all vie to capture the idea that simplicity is a virtue and a powerful criterion in model selection. If there is no way to decide between the available methods, does this mean, as some philosophers have suggested, that simplicity is merely an aesthetic criterion? This question overlooks some important details in the debate over the right way to measure simplicity. First of all, it has already been made clear that, on account of the presence of noise in data sets, some (at least minimal) bias toward simpler models is required. Second, the aforementioned and other methods have been shown, either by mathematical proof or by simulation, that they are, under certain (arguably natural) conditions, quite good at finding and even finding fast the (by stipulation) true hypothesis or at least the one that best predicts the data (Gerda Claeskens and Nils Lid Hjort 2008). Third, though these methods do not produce identical judgments, they do, once again under certain (arguably natural) conditions, exhibit strong convergences (see, for example, Jun Shao 1997). And, fourth, even if the world is in fact rather complex and hence demands rather complex models to faithfully describe it, it is obviously not maximally complex and therefore imparts upon us the tenet that complexity should at least sometimes be penalized. These four considerations transform the original inquiry from one where the virtue of simplicity as a non-merely-aesthetic criterion is doubted to one where what is being doubted is only how much of an objective role simplicity should play in determining our selections of models and hypotheses.

Two notions intimately related to simplicity are non-ad hoc-ness and unification. Both are considered virtues and are employed by practising scientists as informal criteria in deciding between competing models and hypotheses. Although we do not have the space to explore them at length here, it is important to at least make some cursory remarks regarding the role they play in AIT and the philosophy of science. In both disciplines, simplicity and non-ad hoc-ness are often mentioned in the same breath (e.g. Grünwald 2007 and Kelly 2008). The semantic proximity of the two notions becomes obvious when one considers, for instance, that the request to reduce the number of free parameters in a model also has the direct effect of suppressing ad hoc-ness. After all, the fewer parameters we can adjust means that there are fewer opportunities to fit the data in a quick-gains, short-sighted, fashion.

The unifying power of a hypothesis is perhaps not as easy to connect to its level of simplicity and non-ad hoc-ness. Alas, no serious attempts to articulate the notion of unification seem to exist within the AIT literature, though this author suspects that it will be an area of growth in the future. The same is not true of the philosophical literature. The *locus classicus* here is Friedman (1974), who argues that the fewer independently acceptable law-like premises required in the derivation of an explanation the more unified that explanation.[11] Though Friedman does not specifically address the connection between simplicity and unification or ad hoc-ness, it doesn't take much cognitive ability to identify the common emphasis on fewer postulates. Other philosophers have taken a more direct approach to connecting the aforementioned themes, e.g. Kelly (2008) and Votsis (2015).

The latter account builds on Friedman's insights to argue that the more confirmationally connected the content parts of a hypothesis, the higher its degree of unification. Highly unified hypotheses in this sense are invariably non-ad hoc, and hence in some respect quite simple, in that they are not composed of confirmationally unrelated parts that are forcibly contrived to fit together.

Scientific realism

An inveterate family of debates in philosophy is that between the realists and the anti-realists. The realists advance an ontological claim that some category of things is real plus an epistemological claim that we have knowledge of this category. Anti-realists deny at least the second claim, sometimes also the first. The debate manifests itself in distinct ways depending on the sub-field of philosophy within which it is conducted. That includes meta-ethics, the philosophy of language and the philosophy of mathematics. Here we are interested in the philosophy of science manifestation, widely known as 'the scientific realism debate'. Scientific realists argue that our best scientific theories, i.e. those that enjoy substantial predictive and explanatory success, reveal real objects and their properties to us, e.g. that DNA molecules are helical in structure or that neutrinos possess a half-integer spin. Moreover, they argue that historically consecutive theories become increasingly successful and, in so doing, move closer to a true description of the world. Scientific anti-realists deny that any such knowledge can be had or progress toward it can be made. To be exact, nowadays the central point of contention is whether unobservables, i.e. objects and properties that are not verifiable via our unaided senses, are knowable. While scientific anti-realists are at most willing to concede that observables are knowable, scientific realists grant the knowability of both observables and unobservables.

There are various connections between the scientific realism debate and information theory. The first of these has already been touched upon in our discussion of simplicity. Scientific realists typically cite simplicity as a truth-apt criterion for choosing between rival hypotheses. By contrast, their anti-realist counterparts claim that it is at best a pragmatic consideration in such matters, at worst a merely aesthetic one. That the scientific realists are keen on recruiting simplicity and other so-called 'theoretical virtues' like unifying power becomes all the more evident when the hypotheses in question are empirically equivalent, i.e. they possess identical empirical consequences, but are otherwise theoretically inequivalent. In such cases, deciding between rival hypotheses on purely empirical grounds becomes impossible. Faced with such an impasse, scientific realists employ simplicity as a tiebreaker criterion in the hope that it is indeed capable of leading us to the truth.

The second connection we also already touched upon. Whether or not a scientific realist or anti-realist view of science is more warranted presumably depends on whether or not the claims about which we can be realists or anti-realists can be, and indeed are, confirmable. For example, were it to turn out, as some have argued, that the support a piece of evidence provides can spread to different parts of a hypothesis and indeed to parts that make claims about unobservable entities, then scientific realism would gain the upper hand in the debate. Note that the issue of how far support spreads is central to the study of confirmation. Otherwise put, it is the issue of which of a competing number of inductive inferences (that take a piece of evidence as input and yield one or more parts of a hypothesis as output) is most warranted. And that's precisely a topic that AIT theorists also obsess about, one of their counsels being that we should choose those inferences that maintain a certain kind of balance between simplicity and goodness of fit.

The third and final connection is one that we are to freshly address in the remainder of this section. It concerns the source of our ontology. According to the majority of scientific realists, that ontology is best sourced from the wells of successful science and finds its most paradigmatic form in the entities and properties posited by physics. Indeed, some scientific realists advocate an even stronger claim, namely that the only things that can truly be said to exist are those posited by fundamental physics. Thus, pianos, proteins, governments and pulsar stars are nothing more than a bunch of fundamental particles that behave in accord with the laws of physics. How does information theory bear on this issue? Well, a view has recently been put forth that the fundamental ontology of the world is informational. Seeing as this view builds on another, namely structural realism, it is sensible to consider the latter first.

Structural realism is undoubtedly the most influential realist view in the last fifteen years. Its central tenet is that we should be realists only about structure.[12] Though controversy clouds how exactly structure is to be understood, every party in the debate agrees that some abstract logico-mathematical notion is required. One such notion, for example, is set-theoretical. A structure S in this sense is denoted by a pair $<U, R>$, where U is a non-empty set of objects and R a non-empty set of relations, i.e. ordered n-tuples, defined over those objects. What's so special about such structures? Well, they allow us to obviate the specific character or nature of the objects and relations under consideration and focus instead on their structural features (see Chapter 7 Levels of Abstraction). For example, the objects may be human beings, particles or mountains and the relations may be x is meaner than y, x is in a higher energy state than y, and x has a higher elevation than y. For a number of reasons, one of which being that the history of science seems to show a continuity only of structures across scientific revolutions, structural realists argue that the *posited* specific character or nature of (unobservable) objects and relations becomes irrelevant. All that seems to matter are general logico-mathematical properties of such relations, e.g. that a relation between the target objects is irreflexive, anti-symmetric and transitive. That's why structural realists find the set-theoretical and/or other such notions of structure valuable.

There have traditionally been two kinds of structural realism. Crudely put, epistemic structural realism (ESR) holds that we cannot know more about unobservable objects other than the logico-mathematical properties of the relations they instantiate. Equally crudely, ontic structural realism (OSR) holds that such objects are at best weak relatives of traditionally conceived ones and at worst fictions that need to be conceptualized away. In the last few years, Luciano Floridi (2011) has developed a brand of information-theoretic realism that is a close relative of structural realism, especially OSR, which he calls 'informational structural realism' (ISR). *Qua* realism, ISR is ontically committed to the existence of a mind-independent reality and epistemically committed to some knowledge of that reality in both its observable and potentially its unobservable guises.[13] *Qua* structural, ISR is committed to a structural conception of reality. *Qua* informational, ISR is committed to an understanding of reality that is purely informational. In more detail, Floridi defines ISR as follows:

> Explanatorily, instrumentally and predictively successful models (especially, but not only, those propounded by scientific theories) at a given LoA can be, in the best circumstances, increasingly informative about the relations that obtain between the (possibly sub-observable) informational objects that constitute the system under investigation (through the observable phenomena).
>
> *(2011, p. 361)*

Four parts of the quote are worth highlighting. The first concerns the reference to successful models. This reference is in step with the realist idea that *success* is a key motivator for the view that we may potentially possess some knowledge of unobservables, or sub-observables as Floridi calls them. The second part concerns the LoA, i.e. level of abstraction, concept. In rough terms, a *level of abstraction* is that component of a theory that 'make[s] explicit and clarif[ies] its ontological commitment... [by] determin[ing] the range of available observables' (p. 348). This is presumably required to provide an analysis of the system under study through a model that identifies the system's structure. Naturally, different levels of abstraction are possible. Floridi argues that the levels of abstraction required by his version of structuralism concurrently entail a first-order ontological commitment to the structural properties of the system and a second-order ontological commitment to the structural character of the system's *relata*. The third part, i.e. the part about such models being increasingly informative, is also borrowed from realism. It relays the idea that there is *progress* in getting to know the systems under study. The fourth part concerns the ontology, which, as already noted, consists not of garden-variety physical things but of *informational* things that are structurally conceived.

Why would we want to replace a physical with an informational ontology? Floridi's argument is, in effect, that it would offer a much more general and unified ontological platform. To better understand this argument, we need to make a small detour into three interdependent notions from computer science, namely *portability*, *interoperability* and *scalability*. Roughly speaking, we say of a piece of software that it is portable when, for example, it can be run on more than one type of microprocessor. Equally roughly, we say of a piece of software or hardware that it is interoperable when, for example, it can communicate and interact with other pieces of software and hardware of different types. Finally, we say that a software or hardware solution is scalable when, for example, it remains a solution to a problem even if the size of the problem varies. Floridi's suggestion is that an informational ontology is much more portable, interoperable and scalable than a traditionally conceived physical ontology. As an illustration take portability. OSR, Floridi notes, is already quite portable in that it conceives of its ontology in such a way that it is exchangeable between physical and mathematical theories. This is a consequence of the fact that the ontology in OSR is described through highly abstract mathematical structures. ISR takes a step further, he then argues, by making its ontology 'portable to computer science as well' (p. 359). Similar remarks are made in relation to the virtues of interoperability and especially scalability.

Although an interesting idea, it is quite difficult to fathom how the world itself is somehow informational. We certainly represent the world through information. No contention there. But to call the ontology of this world informational is something that opponents of this view would perhaps deem to be a category mistake. Not unless, of course, what is meant by an informational ontology is something much more akin to what is generally understood by a physical ontology. Such an interpretation would run the risk of turning the dispute into a terminological squabble. Interestingly, Floridi's characterization of the operative notion of information in terms of 'differences *de re*' seems to have that effect as an unintended by-product (p. 356). For he appears to be telling us that all that matters are the differences in and between ontological units.[14] But if that's the case, asserting that these units are informational or indeed physical adds nothing of essence to the story. This is not an invitation to conflate informational and physical ontologies but, rather, a reminder that the notion of a physical ontology can be construed in a minimalist way, i.e. without making strong metaphysical assumptions about what it takes for something to be physical.

Let us end this section by saying that the jury is still out on whether ISR will, and more importantly whether it justifiably ought to, develop into a major force within the scientific realism debate. But even if ISR fails on both accounts, it should be clear that there may yet be space in that debate for an informational ontology, perhaps not in terms of replacing a physical ontology but rather in a pluralistic framework where informational and physical 'entities' live side-by-side.

Some concluding remarks

In spite of the numerous connections between the fields of information theory and philosophy of science, the interaction between the fields' practitioners remains disappointingly slender. At least part of the reason why philosophers of science have not engaged with the literature on information, and particularly, on AIT (as much as this author and others would have hoped for) seems to be that, more often than desirable, the formal results in that literature are hastily and haphazardly linked to existing philosophical problems.[15] On the other side of the divide, at least part of the reason why information theorists and in particular AIT theorists have not engaged as much with the philosophical literature seems to be that philosophers tend to pursue more 'arcane' aspects of the foregoing themes and certainly less clearly practicable ones. As a result, philosophers sometimes lose touch with reality, in spite of their best intentions. These obstacles notwithstanding, I would like to end on a more positive and constructive note. It is this author's hope that entries like the present will assist in fostering greater interaction between philosophers and information theorists. After all, both groups are keen on making progress toward solving some of the world's most daunting problems.

Notes

1 Hume's own objections to the deductive approach differ from that just given. One of his objections is that deduction is inapplicable in such cases, for in his view deductive arguments involve only necessary truths as premises. Today this view is considered antiquated.

2 Hutter (2007) claims that Solomonoff's theory effectively solves the problem of induction. Solomonoff himself is more guarded.

3 Solomonoff makes these connections explicit when he asserts: 'In the language of Carnap (1950), we want $c(a, T)$, the degree of confirmation of the hypothesis that a [the sequence extension] will follow, given the evidence that T [the original sequence] has just occurred. This corresponds to Carnap's probability$_1$,' (1964a, p. 2).

4 It is widely thought that Solomonoff's approach is motivated solely or mostly by Occam's razor. Solomonoff certainly didn't think so. In his mind, the approach stands on much firmer ground via successful applications to a diverse number of specific problems where we have 'strong intuitive ideas about what the solutions are' (1964a, p. 5).

5 For example, suppose we want to find out the probability of which side a coin lands on when it is tossed. On the assumption that the coin and tossing mechanism are unbiased (and that the coin cannot land sideways) the distribution assigns equal probability to heads and to tails.

6 Note that the shortest input string has length 1 and yields probability 0.5. The longer the input string, the closer the associated value gets to zero.

7 Thus, second degree polynomials fall under the same model; third degree polynomials fall under another model, and so on.

8 Here are some further quotations from Occam: 'Si duae res sufficiunt ad eius veritatem, superfluum est ponere aliam (tertiam) rem' and 'Frustra fit per plura, quod potest fieri per pauciora' (quoted in Charlesworth 1956, p. 105). The first translates roughly as 'If two entities are sufficient for truth, it is superfluous to posit a third' and the second roughly as 'It is in vain to attempt to do with more what can be done with fewer.'

9 Grünwald, for example, says that 'there is no place for a "true distribution" or a "true state of nature" in this view' (p. 27). Rathmanner and Hutter, by contrast, assert that 'we are interested in finding the true governing process behind our entire reality' (p. 1089).

10 Since no UTM is at hand, AIT theorists employ the next best thing, namely general-purpose computer languages like C and Pascal.

11 Friedman's view is flawed but fruitful as has been repeatedly pointed out in the literature. Interestingly, it chimes well with a passage found in Aristotle, who asserts in *Posterior Analytics*: 'Let one demonstration be better than another if, other things being equal, it depends on fewer postulates or suppositions or propositions' (Barnes, 2002, p. 39).

12 For an in-depth critical survey of the varieties of structural realism, readers may consult Frigg and Votsis (2011).

13 The qualification that ISR is 'potentially' but not strictly committed to our ability to know unobservable reality actually raises doubts about its credentials as a realist view.

14 In information-theoretic terms, we might express such differences as distinct symbols, e.g. 0s as opposed to 1s. In physical-theory terms, we might express such differences as distinct states, e.g. spin up or spin down.

15 Solomonoff stands out in having valiantly toiled to make his formal work intuitively comprehensible.

References

Akaike, H. (1973) 'Theory and an Extension of the Maximum Likelihood Principle' in B. N. Petrov and F. Csaki (Eds.), *Second International Symposium on Information Theory*, Budapest: Akademiai Kiado, pp. 267–81.

Barnes, J. (2002) *Aristotle: Posterior Analytics*, reprinted second edition, translated with commentary, Oxford: Oxford University Press.

Carnap, R. (1950) *Logical Foundations of Probability*, Chicago, IL: University of Chicago Press.

Chaitin, G. (1966) 'On the Length of Programs for Computing Finite Binary Sequences', *Journal of the ACM*, vol. 13: 547–569.

Charlesworth, M. J. (1956) 'Aristotle's Razor', *Philosophical Studies*, vol. 6: 105–112.

Claeskens, G. and N. L. Hjort (2008) *Model Selection and Model Averaging*, Cambridge: Cambridge University Press.

Floridi, L. (2011) *The Philosophy of Information*, Oxford: Oxford University Press.

Frigg, R. and I. Votsis (2011) 'Everything You Always Wanted to Know about Structural Realism but Were Afraid to Ask', *European Journal for the Philosophy of Science*, vol. 1(2): 227–276.

Friedman, M. (1974) 'Explanation and Scientific Understanding', *Journal of Philosophy*, vol. 71(1): 5–19.

Grünwald, P. (2007) *The Minimum Description Length Principle*, Cambridge, MA: MIT Press.

Hume, D. ([1739] 1975) *A Treatise of Human Nature*, L. A. Selby-Bigge & P. H. Nidditch (Eds.), Oxford: Clarendon Press.

Hutter, M. (2007) 'On Universal Prediction and Bayesian Confirmation', *Theoretical Computer Science*, vol. 384: 33–48.

Kelly, K. (2008) 'Ockham's Razor, Truth, and Information' in *Handbook of the Philosophy of Information*, J. van Behthem and P. Adriaans (Eds.), Dordrecht: Elsevier.

Kolmogorov, A. (1965) 'Three Approaches to the Quantitative Definition of Information', *Problems of Information Transmission*, vol. 1(1): 1–7.

Ockham, W. (1974) *Summa Logicae*, P. Boehner, G. Gál and S. Brown (Eds.), New York: The Franciscan Institute.

Popper, K. R. (1959) *The Logic of Scientific Discovery*, New York: Basic Books.

Rathmanner, S. and M. Hutter (2011) 'A Philosophical Treatise of Universal Induction', *Entropy*, vol. 13: 1076–1136.

Rissanen, J. J. (1978) 'Modeling by Shortest Data Description', *Automatica*, vol. 14(5): 465–471.

Schwarz, G. (1978) 'Estimating the Dimension of a Model', *Annals of Statistics*, vol. 6(2): 461–464.

Shao, J. (1997) 'An Asymptotic Theory for Linear Model Selection', *Statistica Sinica*, vol. 7: 221–264.

Solomonoff, R. J. (1964a) 'A Formal Theory of Inductive Inference. Part I', *Information and Control*, vol. 7(1): 1–22.

Solomonoff, R. J. (1964b) 'A Formal Theory of Inductive Inference. Part II', *Information and Control*, vol. 7(2): 224–254.

Sober, E. (2002) 'The Problem of Simplicity', in *Simplicity, Inference and Modelling: Keeping it Sophisticatedly Simple*, A. Zellner, H. A. Keuzenkamp and M. McAleer (Eds.), Cambridge: Cambridge University Press.

Van Fraassen, B. C. (1980) *The Scientific Image*, Oxford: Clarendon Press.

Votsis, I. (2015) 'Unification: Not Just a Thing of Beauty', *Theoria*, vol. 30(1): 97–114.

22

TELEOSEMANTICS AND NATURAL INFORMATION

John Symons

Introduction

We human beings tend, rightly or wrongly, to explain the intelligent behavior we observe among our fellow organisms by reference to their mental states: their thoughts, feelings, and the like. Our understanding of the bear's desire for honey, for example, allows us to loosely predict what he would do in its presence and to explain to one another why he investigates holes in trees.

Generally speaking, when we think about mental states like belief and desire we assume that they are *directed towards*, or that they are *about* things. Philosophers call this *aboutness* relation "intentionality." Alexius Meinong (1899) and others noted that those things towards which beliefs and desires are directed are not always physically present to the organism and in some cases might not even exist at all. My desire to own a regular, seven-sided polyhedron, for example, has no object because the kind of polyhedron that I covet is mathematically impossible. Here, mental states have a puzzling relationship to their objects. In the case of the absent honey, for example, many philosophers would argue that the bear's desire is at least partly composed of or directed towards something like a mental representation of the honey. To use philosophers' jargon the bear's representation of honey forms the content of this particular desire. The content of my desire for an impossible object is a little harder to pin down.

The enterprise of explaining intelligent behavior is generally thought to call on a range of philosophically problematic notions. Most philosophers will assume that the concepts of intentionality, representation, and content force themselves on us as soon as we reflect on the nature of intelligent behavior.

In addition to the intentionality of mental states, philosophers have also been concerned with the ways in which representations track aspects of the organism's environment. When we see intelligent behavior we often have good reasons to believe that the organism's mental representations are related to aspects of its environment in a regular manner. Bears want honey because it is tasty and its tastiness is the body's way of indicating that it is a good source of carbohydrate for hungry bears. Similarly, my belief that Motan is on the mat tracks the state of affairs in front of me at this instant and allows me to navigate my room in ways that are good both for me and for my cat. Reflecting on this tracking relationship, some philosophers (e.g. Daniel Dennett 1987, 75) take it as obvious that natural selection would favor organisms with true representations of the world. Building on this apparently straightforward observation, other philosophers, (like Nicholas Shea 2007, 404) argue that any adequate theory of mind must account for the truth of representations underlying successful behavior.[1]

For many philosophers and scientists the best way to make sense of the tracking relationship between mental representations of objects and the objects themselves (for example, the bear's representation of honey and honey itself) is in terms of information. The idea is that representations somehow carry information about the objects in the world in ways that make them useful for organisms. On this account, an organism that exhibits intelligent behavior does so via its sensitivity to the information about its environment that is contained in its representations. Sensitivity, along with the ability to manipulate useful information, allows an organism to adapt its behavior in intelligent ways and to thrive thereby.[2]

Fred Dretske's *Knowledge and the Flow of Information* (1981) provided the most influential early theory of how this might work. Dretske's informational semantics was inspired by the mathematical theory of information and builds on the idea that representations are best understood as causally related in some way to their objects.[3] For other scientists and philosophers, non-informational accounts of signaling, communication, and perception can suffice to explain intelligent behavior. The debate over whether to understand representation and intelligent behavior in informational terms or in some other way is lively and ongoing.[4] This chapter explores part of this debate, specifically, the relationship between teleosemantic theories of mental content and the concept of information.

Teleosemantics is a prominent and influential theory that was largely developed in the 1980s and 1990s by Ruth Millikan and David Papineau.[5] Very roughly, teleosemantics explains the meaningfulness of representation in terms of biological functions. The role of information in biologically oriented theories like teleosemantics is a topic of great controversy.[6] Reading the literature on these questions is complicated by diversity of jargon and by differing uses of the same terms. However, a much deeper obstacle is the presence of competing conceptions of explanation in the philosophical literature. Philosophers differ sharply with respect to what counts as a good explanation of notions like normativity, meaning, and representation. The initial challenge for readers is to determine what the various interlocutors take to be the demands, standards, and commitments that we ought to adopt with respect to explanations in the philosophy and science of mind. In addition to determining the kinds of explanations that philosophers are after, the second challenge involves comparing and evaluating these differing views of what is required for an explanation to count as a good explanation. Part of the purpose of this chapter is to help readers determine for themselves which style of explanation most closely matches their own.

The role of information in these debates is generally determined by the explanatory demands that the philosopher assumes are in play. If, for example, like Fodor and Pylyshyn, we regard properties like systematicity as crucial for any acceptable theory of mind we will have a different view of the role information plays in explanation than if, for example, we see mind in behaviorist, or dynamicist terms.[7] Similarly, if, for example, like Shea or Dennett we see true representations as playing a central role in intelligent behavior, we will have a very different view of the role of information than might be the case for philosophers like Stephen Stich (1983) or Christopher Stephens (2001). Stich and Stephens have defended ways of thinking about the mind that do not assume a direct relationship between intelligent behavior and true belief.

While this chapter focuses on teleosemantics and its critics, this debate is an instance of a broader set of questions concerning competing conceptions of explanations. The chapter describes the landscape of problems that teleosemantics was intended to solve before going on to present Ruth Millikan's central arguments. From there, criticisms of her position are described and some responses are sketched. Nicholas Shea's criticisms of Millikan takes center stage. He argues for the importance of information (an input condition) in any theory of representation and contends that Millikan's emphasis on the role of selection in the appearance of the agent's capacities (the output conditions) leaves her theory vulnerable to objections. I will examine the success of Millikan's response to critics below and will describe her view of information as it appears in her more recent work. I argue that Millikan's emphasis on the properties of the consumer of representations can be reconciled in a relatively straightforward manner with the importance of information so as to preserve the theoretical virtues of her approach while acknowledging the intuitive appeal of information-based theories.

The purpose of teleosemantics

The tendency to explain behavior in terms of conscious mental states is difficult for most of us to resist. Even in cases where we are aware that no mental state is in play, or where we understand that mental states have no relevant causal relationships to the behaviors or phenomena of interest, we find ourselves ascribing thought and feeling to the organisms and other intelligent systems we encounter. It is our deeply engrained habit to engage not only with the natural world but with artifacts and with the worlds of fiction as though they are filled with meaning, purpose, and thought.

Daniel Dennett offered an explanation of how we got into this situation. Specifically, Dennett explains how this interpretive strategy – what he calls the *intentional stance* – emerged in our species over the course of natural history.[8] Dennett's approach is intended to show how we became natural mind readers. However, even given a naturalistic explanation of the *ability* to read the world as filled with minds, questions remain. We can still ask, for example, how the success of the intentional stance can be reconciled with the widely held view of the physical world as devoid of purposes, meanings, and the like? Why should adopting the intentional stance provide an advantage to a species in a world without meaningful mental states? More deeply, we can also ask what it means for our thoughts to represent reality correctly or incorrectly. What does it mean to apply the normative judgment of rightness or wrongness to the representational aspects of mental life? When we say that an animal or a person made a mistake, that they have a false belief, or are in error in some other way, how do we reconcile our normative claim with the non-normative facts of science?

Millikan's theory specifically addresses the problem of normativity. The view was articulated in detail in her book *Language, Thought, and Other Biological Categories* (1984) and elaborated upon in her (1993) and (2004). While teleosemantics appears in the context of traditional philosophical debates concerning mind and language, and must be understood in those terms, it approaches the question of mental representation from a distinctively biological perspective.

The biological orientation of Millikan's methodology owes much to Dennett's philosophy of mind. However, there are significant differences. As with Dennett, the action of natural selection on agents and systems plays a central explanatory role in her view. Unlike Dennett, she rejects the view that we use something like the intentional stance to *predict* the behaviors of others arguing instead that standard folk psychology provides explanations of intelligent behavior in retrospect. (2004, 21–24) Another difference between Dennett and Millikan is her focus on explaining the normative aspect of mental representation.[9] As discussed below, the possibility that mental representations can misrepresent the world is essential, she argues, to the nature of representation. Thus, at its heart, the goal of teleosemantics is to provide an explanation of how a system's use of representations can be correct or incorrect.

From a certain perspective, it appears fundamentally misguided to say that a simple organism or even a non-cognitive system can misuse a representation, or that it can objectively fail to achieve a purpose. The critic's concern here is simple – we might project rightness or wrongness onto the use of representations in non-human contexts, but to claim that there is some non-human dependent sense, in which an animal can be wrong about its representations, is confusedly anthropomorphic.

Millikan sees the normative aspect of representation as natural and objective and she aims to explain it in terms of the biological notion of function. Her theory assumes that the emergence of mental representation is a process that takes place over the course of natural history and that it can be explained in scientifically respectable terms. According to its proponents, teleosemantics explains the normative aspect of mental states biologically, in the same way an evolutionary biologist would explain the function of the heart or the shape of a finch's beak.

On her view, representational systems (like most other biological systems) should be explained as products of natural selection. The function that these systems were selected for; their so-called *proper function*, is to allow the animal to relate representationally to particular aspects of the environment. An animal's representation of berries, for example, is part of (or the product of) a system that allows the animal to detect food in its environment. This system exists insofar as it provided an evolutionary advantage to that animal's ancestors. She argues that this advantage serves to explain why the representational system does what it does. Essentially, the core of teleosemantics is the simple contention that an animal's representation of, say, berries, is meaningfully related to berries because of the evolutionary history that gave rise to the process or mechanism in the animal's brain that produces that representation.

In very broad terms, Millikan's view is that a representation of a berry can serve a representational role in virtue of being produced by a mechanism that has the right kind of proper function. In general, the function of the mechanism that produces the representation is the detection of specific aspect of the environment for the agent. A great deal rests on the idea of proper functions in her theory and I will discuss this idea in detail below. *Going wrong*, in this context, means *failing to perform the function*. To use her example, a representation can fail to perform its function while still being a representation in the same way that a can opener can fail to perform its function without ceasing to be a can opener. Knowing that a can opener is failing requires knowledge of the purpose for which it was made. Similarly, determining rightness and wrongness in the context of representations requires knowledge of their purposes.

As we shall see, Millikan's theory of representation is non-informational in the sense of not being what had counted as a standard informational theory of mind prior to her work. Specifically, her theory differs in important ways from Fred Dretske's informational theory of mind as articulated in his (1981). In particular, when readers call her view non-informational, what they mean is that the theory is built around the selective pressures governing the users or consumers of representations rather than on the transmission and reception of information from the environment to the organism or system. An explanation that starts from the characteristics of users, rather than from the flow of information, has some strategic and theoretical advantages, as we shall see, but it also makes her version of teleosemantics vulnerable to non-trivial criticisms.

Meaning and representation

Even a very minimal level of meaningfulness; the semantic property of thoughts, for example, poses a conceptual challenge. When I think of San Francisco, my thought is meaningful insofar as it is about San Francisco. But what is it for my thought of San Francisco to be *about* a city? How does a physical structure or process in a brain relate to a city in a way that somehow carries meaning?

Conceptual problems concerning meaning and reference occupied analytic philosophers of language for much of the twentieth century and this tradition has had considerable influence on the neighboring sub-disciplines of philosophy of mind and philosophy of psychology. Philosophers of language created theories of reference in order to provide a set of necessary and sufficient conditions for characterizing the referential relationship between terms in a language and objects in the world. Attempts to provide a naturalistic account of mental representations were shaped by the powerful influence of philosophy of language.

Continuing the tradition of philosophy of mind and language, Millikan keeps the focus on the strangeness of the representational relation. However, unlike traditional philosophers she crafted biological explanations that target the most conceptually problematic aspect of this strangeness, namely the normativity of representation. This section describes (in simplified terms) the traditional answers to the problem of representation so as to understand the purpose and character of Millikan's view.

Conditions for folk psychological explanations

Let's begin with our commonsense view of psychological explanation before considering the normative aspects of representation. Any of us, reading a novel or watching a cartoon will slip into interpreting the characters as intentional agents with inner lives that explain their actions: Roadrunner saw that Wiley Coyote was approaching, believed that he was dangerous, and wanted to escape. Referring to Roadrunner's beliefs, his desires, what he sees, or what he fears in order to explain behavior exemplifies what Dennett called "folk psychology." Folk psychological explanation is generally reliable (by some standards), but it is also thoroughly anthropomorphic (by any standard).

Folk psychological explanatory strategies depend on our confidence that the patterns we mention in our explanations are real enough to help us predict the behavior of reasonably intelligent organisms. In addition to assuming that complex organisms have the kind of inner system of beliefs, desires, and actions that we find in ourselves, we also assume that the organism must, in some sense, get the world right in order to thrive. In this respect, folk psychological explanations incorporate normative judgments essentially.

As we saw above, when we consider an animal getting the world right and thriving as a result, it is natural to think in informational terms. Intuitively, we assume that organisms are sensitive to information in their environments and that they manipulate and respond to environmental information for their purposes. This assumption that intelligent systems can be right or wrong about aspects of their environment is at the heart of folk psychological practice.

These two facets of our folk psychological theorizing, namely the belief-desire-action model of the organism's inner life on the one hand and the idea that it is sensitive to environmental information on the other, are not as tightly coupled as one might assume. One very important feature of Millikan's view, for example is that the consumers of representation need not be cognitive systems in the traditional sense. So how does one distinguish between the representational or informational features of an organism and its cognitive capacities?

One could, for example, imagine an organism whose behavior is tightly coupled to environmental information in a reliable and adaptive manner without that organism having a complex cognitive mechanism involving the interplay of beliefs and desires. A simple system might make use of the position of a light source or the distribution of some chemical in the environment in a way that is adaptive without having beliefs about the light or desires to approach the light.[10]

On the other hand, one can also imagine agents with complex cognitive inner lives being systematically mistaken with respect to environmental information. It is likely, for example, that much of our own interplay of adult human beliefs, desires, and actions is epiphenomenal with respect to the actual mechanisms guiding our behavior. We think our actions are motivated by beliefs and desires of a particular kind when in fact they are sometimes caused by mechanisms to which we do not have conscious access. If this is the case, even occasionally, then complex cognition and environmental information could also be uncoupled along these lines.

The possibility that these two aspects of folk psychological explanation can be uncoupled will be important when we assess criticisms of teleosemantics below.[11]

Explaining representation

A natural starting point for any effort to explain representation in naturalistic terms is to assume that there is an isomorphism between the representation and what is being represented. A representation of the coyote is about the coyote, one might think, in virtue of sharing the relevant kind of structure or form with it. On reflection, we soon recognize that the fact of simply sharing some features in common with some object is not sufficient for something to be a representation of that object. After all, we could discover countless isomorphisms between some brain process and objects in the world. The representation of the coyote may be isomorphic with the coyote, but it is also, from another perspective, isomorphic with a dog, a horse, a cat, etc. Isomorphism alone is not enough for a satisfying theory of representation.

Another way we might link representation and the thing represented is via a causal connection between the two. In that way, the intentional content of a representation would be explicable in virtue of a causal chain connecting the thing represented and the representation; the representation of the coyote is about the coyote because it was caused by the coyote. It is natural, from this perspective, to think that the causal connection between the representation and the represented object can somehow provide a respectable explanation of the intentional content of the representation. Unfortunately, causal relations alone are not sufficient for characterizing the representational relationship. The reason is as follows: many things contribute to causing a representation that have nothing to do with what it is that the representation is about. Roadrunner's being delayed by a train causes him to see Coyote's trap. But the content of the visual representation is the trap, not the myriad causal factors, including the train, his parent's romance, the presence of oxygen in his immediate environment, etc., that contributed to Roadrunner having the representation he does.

So, the causal relationship has to be elaborated somewhat in order for us to have an explanation of why it is that Roadrunner's representation of the trap is a representation of the trap. The usual way of elaborating this relationship is in terms of the notion of information. Specifically, the idea is that the representation carries information about its cause. The most influential early proponent of this way of thinking about representations was Fred Dretske. He argued that representation is a causal-informational relation.

Information, on Dretske's view, is "an objective commodity" (1981 vii) prior to, and in some sense serving as the condition for intelligent behavior. Information is not (as is often argued) the result of an interpretive process of some sort. Treating information as an objective feature of the natural world was an improvement over thinking of representation in terms of isomorphism or causal relations alone. However, other philosophers soon pointed out that Dretske's account is still insufficient. The reason is simple: many things that are not representations are causally related to other things in ways that can be understood to carry information. For an experienced hunter, battered vegetation, or a trough in the soil on the forest floor, carry information about his prey. But a causal-informational connection alone does not make marks on the forest floor representations of the prey. So, what, in addition to causal-informational connection makes a representation a representation and not merely an indicator of some other connected feature of the natural world?

At this point, in the effort to understand the difference between indicators and representations, we see the appearance of teleological theories of content. As mentioned above, Millikan and others recognized that the challenging feature of this problem involves normativity. Of course, in one sense this recognition was not novel. Understanding how representations can fail to represent (or can represent non-existent objects) has long posed a difficulty. However, teleosemantics focuses sharply on cases of error, arguing that philosophical theories should have the resources to explain the occasions where Roadrunner is mistaken about his representations. Roadrunner swerves to avoid the black circle on the road ahead thinking that it is a hole when it is in fact a piece of paper. This is the kind of misrepresentation that teleosemantic theorists take to be the most puzzling and philosophically distinctive feature of representation. They hope to account for the normative features of intentional content while simultaneously providing a naturalistic explanation of that content.

Proper functions

How is it that we can categorize a physical process in an animal's nervous system using normative notions like truth or falsity? As we saw above, teleosemantic explanations make reference to the evolutionary history of organisms that use mental representations. They explain content in terms of biological purposes. For Millikan, the relevant purposes are the proper functions of the organism's representational systems. The proper function of a system is simply what it ought to do by virtue of what it is – it's *raison d'* **être**. Any one system can serve a variety of functions, not all of these functions will count as the system's proper function. So, for example, one of the functions of the heart is to serve as a symbol of love in some cultures. This would *not* count as a proper function of the heart, neither would the sound it makes, its weight, what it tastes like in a stew, etc. Instead, we would ordinarily say that the proper function of the heart is to help circulate blood in the organism's body. Other functions are accidental by-products of the function for which it was selected.

Millikan's strategy then is straightforward: first, she recasts intentionality in terms of purposes. Then, she provides a biological account of purposes. Not all purposes will be relevant. On Milikan's view, representational relations are established via the functional properties of some mechanism in the animal. Those functions are selected via learning or via the evolutionary history of the species. What specifically gets selected are the functions of the representation producing mechanisms in the animal. The selected function of a representation of a berry is to represent berries for the user of the representation. In cases where the user mistakes something else for a berry, the representation is not functioning correctly. Her argument for the idea of false representation as failed representation works by analogy. There are other perfectly natural ways in which we talk about failure of function that have a similar conceptual flavor, most notably in cases involving artifacts. The following is an example of how her argument by analogy works:

> False representations are representations, yet they fail to represent. How can that be? It can be in the same way that something can be a can opener but be too dull and hence fail to open cans [...] They are "representations" in the sense that the biological functions of the cognitive systems that made them was to make them represent things. Falsehood is the thus explained by the fact that purposes often go unfulfilled.
>
> *(2004, 64–5)*

The analogy with failure in artifacts is unconvincing without further elaboration. [12] The first challenge is to make sense of the idea of purposes playing any role in an ostensibly naturalistic theory? In her book, *Varieties of Meaning*, Millikan acknowledges that talk of biological or sub-personal purposes is likely to be interpreted as a kind of metaphorical extension of ordinary person-level purposes and meanings. The success of her project requires that she respond to this criticism.

Her view is that sub-personal or biological purposes are not fundamentally different in kind from the intentions or purposes that we find in the personal level. Instead, she argues that the purposes of the whole adult human person emerge from sub-personal level processes and mechanisms. Thus, she contends, when we say that the eye is "*meant* to close automatically" in the presence of some foreign object that comes too close, this sense of *meant to* is not fundamentally different from what we mean when we say "I didn't *mean to* blink" (2004, 3).

She can argue for the continuity between these two examples by first arguing that the lack of awareness of a purpose does not entail that some action is not purposive. This is a plausible contention. We can, after all, imagine cultivating a pattern of behavior for some purpose such that it becomes habitual, or perhaps we come to forget the original purpose. Alternatively, we could imagine tricking someone into performing some action for some purpose through behaviorist-style reinforcement along the lines of Millikan's examples (2004, 10). The fact that some purpose is hidden from introspective view does not make it any less of a purpose. She presents reasons that are intended to undermine the assumption that there is a principled distinction between so-called *real* purposes (associated with conscious agency) and the kinds of purposes that we might ascribe to parts of an agent or to some other non-cognitive system.

Blurring the distinction between purposes at the level of the whole person and purposes of parts of the person is only one component of her argument. For teleosemantics to serve as a naturalistic theory of the normative aspects of representation, it must provide a naturalistic theory of purposes. For philosophers like Millikan and Dennett such an account is already available and widely accepted, namely the theory of natural selection. The challenges of circularity, regress, and anthropomorphism are solved simultaneously by recourse to the biological explanation of the origin of purposive systems.

Skepticism concerning naturalization derives from the concern that explanations of purpose will beg the question; assuming the higher-level purposes that they seek to explain in the explanans by ascribing purposes to pre-purposive nature. To avoid circularity, question-begging, and regress, the Darwinian must demonstrate that natural selection is the source of purposes without itself being purposive.

Arguing that proper functions are the source of the normative features of representation and are the basis upon which higher-level features of human cognition can emerge faces a basic challenge. The worry is that we interpreters ascribe functions to biological systems and, moreover, that an indeterminate variety of interpretations are compatible with the facts. As Mark Rowlands explains (1997) grounding content in terms of function is open to criticism insofar as any particular biological function is not, by itself, sufficient to fix a single interpretation of the semantic content it is understood to ground.

According to advocates of teleosemantics, when the coyote detects the roadrunner in its environment, his properly functioning neural system is in a state that can be understood as being associated with the content "roadrunner." This is because, on Millikan's view, the proper function of this system is to detect roadrunners. However, as Fodor (1996) and others have noted, there will always be alternative interpretations of the function of this system that are consistent with what we observe. The content of the system might be the pattern of the roadrunner's tailfeathers, roadrunner-like movement, food here now, etc. Millikan is not especially concerned with the logical possibility that there are interpretations of any representation's content that are coextensive with the one that we assume is in play. The fact that the "roadrunner" is virtually always co-present with "roadrunner-like movement" is not a problem for teleosemantics insofar as it assumes that the content should be grounded in the causal history of the representation. "Roadrunners" played a causally relevant role in the appearance of the representation on this view while "roadrunner-like movements" were caused by roadrunners and are, at best, causally secondary or irrelevant to the selection pressure that gave rise to the representation.

Neander (2012) points out another aspect of the indeterminacy problem when she notes that contributions to fitness that support a proper function can include a multitude of factors that we would ordinarily regard as irrelevant to the content of the representation. It is difficult for Millikan's account of content to screen off such contributions in a non-question-begging manner. So, for example, Coyote's representation could consistently be interpreted as "roadrunner in the presence of oxygen." Following Peitroski (1992) Neander points out that teleosemantic theories are in trouble if they force us to say that an animal's representation is something that the animal could know nothing about. Coyote is in no position to have views about oxygen, but oxygen is certainly some part of the function of his representational system.

Pietroski objects to teleosemantics insofar as it requires us to deny the existence of the very thing that we had hoped to explain. Whereas we assumed that the animal's representation had some content, and that this was the target of our explanation, in fact we were wrong, the real content is the set of conditions that led to selection of the function of that representation. If, for example, the content of an animal's representation is fixed by some disposition that increased fitness, this disposition might have only an accidental relationship to what we would ordinarily say the representation is about. This means that teleosemantics is at least partially a revisionary account of mental life.

The next section examines the manner in which the indeterminacy challenge relates to the problem of determining what constitutes a good explanation of content.

Information and the explanation of content

As we have seen, Millikan's view is shaped by reflection on the characteristics of the so-called consumers of representation. The content of representations, on this view, is to be understood in terms of the historical conditions under which the relevant function of the organism or system was selected. Those conditions are partly determined by the sources or the producers of the representation, but only insofar as the producers are relevant to the selective pressures on consumers. In some cases, matters are complicated by the producers and consumers having a co-adaptive relationship, but for the most part her view is that representational content is grounded in the biological functions of the consumer.

Critics have argued that thinking about content in this way simply fails to capture the fact that referring to the truth of the representation is often the most straightforward and natural way of explaining why the consumer's behavior succeeded rather than failed. Why did Roadrunner reject the booby-trapped birthday cake from Coyote? Because, his belief that the cake was a trap was true. Roadrunner's successful avoidance of danger is easiest to explain in terms of the truth of his beliefs.

Godfrey-Smith (1996) and Nicholas Shea (2007) both make the point that while the teleosemantic approach denies that the principal function of representation is to carry information it still seems to assume that a true representation is one that depicts the world in a way that captures the conditions that have historically caused a certain kind of success. The notions of success and truth are thoroughly entangled according to these critics such that success over the course of natural history simply cannot explain truth in a non-question-begging manner.

Shea's criticism assumes that Godfrey-Smith's slogan "truth is a fuel for success," is intuitively obvious, at least in the explanation of intelligent behavior in adult humans. He also argues that it can be extended to the explanation of simple representational systems in biology, well beyond its home in folk psychological explanation. He is also committed to the idea that scientists will explain the success of a piece of behavior by reference to the behaviors having been caused by a true representation. (2007, 417) These assumptions are all weaker than they first appear. Stephen Stitch for example has long argued against the view that psychological explanations should follow the standard belief-desire model. Alternatives to treating beliefs as simply true or false have been proposed by other philosophers for example by Chris Stephens in his 2001 paper. In Stephens's view, the correct approach is to understand the functional utility of belief and desire forming mechanisms. On his account natural selection is not always going to favor reliable inference methods. Allowing for the possibility that behavior can be successful in spite of the possession of false beliefs runs counter to the intuitions underlying folk psychology, but it should not be surprising if the science of simple representational systems provides revisionary results.

Even in the case of adult human cognition, it seems intuitively obvious that certain behaviors might be motivated by false beliefs while still being evolutionarily advantageous. So for example positive self-deception (unrealistically optimistic beliefs, or overestimation of one's own virtues) is a commonly recognized feature of adult psychology and is also regarded as conducive to reproductive success (Taylor and Brown 1988).

While we might admit the possibility of a revisionary account of the relationship between truth and success, the evolutionary accounts provided by teleosemantics do seem to rely on something like reliable correlations between representations and states of the world. Nevertheless, carrying information is simply not the proper function of representation on their view. Neither, according to teleosemantics is it the purpose of the producer system to produce patterns or entities that carry correlation information. However, Shea argues that it is simply implausible to explain simple representation without reference to correlational information. Millikan responds by pointing out that the success of the behaviors of humans and animals may depend on any number of different kinds of representations for example maps, beliefs, perceptions, or no representations at all. There may be cases where an informational account is required, but the argument from success to truth does not entail that an explanation of the truthfulness of representations is universally required of all explanations of behavioral success. Recall our discussion in Section 3.1 of the ways that different aspects of folk psychological explanation can be decoupled from one another.

In fact, Millikan does present an account of what she calls "locally recurrent natural information" in her book *Varieties of Meaning*. On first glance, including information in this way might be regarded as a concession to criticisms from Shea and Godfrey-Smith. However, her view of information plays a different explanatory role in her theory from the role Shea sees for correlational information.

What she means by the notion of locally recurrent natural information (henceforth LRNI) is illustrated by examples of coinciding features of the natural world, like, for example the motion of dark clouds and the coming of rain: She writes: "that there is a black cloud at a certain time, *t*, moving towards a place, *p*, is a sign that it will rain at *p* shortly after *t*" (2004, 47–8). In her view, these natural signs are useful to an organism insofar as the variables (in simple cases they often represent times and places) allow the organism to apply the understanding of the regular coinciding of black clouds and rain to novel circumstances. The coinciding of the two structures in the natural world is an example of the kind of LRNI that an animal can use to generate some successful behavior. In her response to Shea (Millikan 2007, 453) she clarifies the sense in LRNI are local. What she means by local is not a geographic region, rather what she has in mind is something like the domain of a mathematical function. The generality LRNI is restricted to "the set of all actual instances falling under that locally recurring sign type." In her view, an animal can use LRNI to successfully guide behavior in case the places that they live happen to be such that LRNI are statistically reliable.

> Sometimes organisms just happen to live and die within areas where the statistics on a certain recurrent sign are good or good enough. Other times they may develop crude or less crude ways of tracking locally recurrent signs in domains well enough to be useful – ways of tracking that work, at least, in the areas in which they live.
>
> *(2007, 454)*

Shea had argued that correlational information is needed in order to explain how simple representational systems are connected to reality. By contrast Millikan argues that LRNI suffices to address those cases where reference to the truth of a representation needs to be included in an explanation. Nevertheless, as argued above, the fact that an organism can make use of LRNI does not entail that the proper function of the representation is to carry information in the traditional sense advocated by Dretske.

On one level, Shea and Godfrey-Smith argue convincingly that teleosemantic accounts fail to provide a deeper explanation of the kind of truth supporting correlations that obtain between representations and states of the world. However, teleosemantic accounts are, in some sense, orthogonal to that particular explanatory project. Insofar as teleosemantics might seem question begging – assuming the truth of representations rather than explaining it – Millikan suggests in response that reference to history removes the question-begging feature of the explanation.

Shea argues that there is something Panglossian in the teleosemantic approach. Dr. Pangloss, we recall from *The Imaginary Invalid,* explained the power of sleeping pills to cause his patients to sleep by adverting to their possession of dormitive virtue. Similarly, tokens of representations coincide with their contents because they contributed to the successful behavior that led to their being adaptive. This strikes many readers as question begging.

Millikan responds by pointing out that Dr. Pangloss' explanation can be somewhat more satisfying once we take into account the history of sleeping pills. If we assumed "that a sleeping pill is something that by definition has in its history that it was selected for manufacture owing to containing something capable of causing sleep." (2007, 437) then it would make perfect sense to say that the pills put John to sleep because they were sleeping pills. The issue between Millikan and Shea concerns the differing kinds of explanations that philosophers seek, or more specifically, the differing standards for what counts as an acceptable explanation of intentional content.

Conclusion

The claim that content can be grounded in historical events and that a theory of representation can be based solely on the properties of consumers is controversial insofar as it leaves so many questions unanswered. Some of those questions might seem less urgent or interesting given a commitment to teleosemantics. However, it is important to recognize that many of the criticisms of teleosemantics derive from explanatory goals that Millikan simply doesn't share. Millikan acknowledges that there is a range of distinct explanatory demands that her account will not address for reasons explained above.

Responses to Millikan tend to emphasize the distinction between explanations that are based on the properties of the organism and those that derive from properties of environmental information. While this is a natural reading of the debate over her work, her most significant theoretical contributions are targeted at the normative aspect of representation and they leave ample space for information-based theories to play a role in explaining other aspects of the problem of representation. Furthermore, in reading Millikan and her critics one must be attentive to the kinds of explanations that are at stake. Sometimes, critics see her work as failing to satisfy explanatory demands that they incorrectly assume she is aiming to meet. It is common to see Millikan and her critics operating on what we might think of as different explanatory registers.

While there is disagreement over the explanatory role of information in theories of representation, there are some obvious commonalities in all viable contemporary theories. To begin with, philosophers agree that organisms have adapted, via natural selection, to respond to their environments in ways that are conducive to their reproductive success. Teleosemantic theorists like Millikan regard such adaptations as continuous with the features that we associate with adult human cognitive capacities. Explanations of the latter will arise out of our understanding of the former. As we have seen, for Millikan the kinds of purposes we find in higher-level human agency – conscious awareness of one's purposes for example – are not fundamentally different in kind from the kinds of biological purposes that a reflex or some other automatic biological process might have. Those natural purposes are the foundation upon which her account of representation stands.

Acknowledgments

Thanks to Polo Camacho, Luciano Floridi, and Armin Schulz for insightful comments and criticism of an earlier draft of this chapter.

Notes

1 Alvin Plantinga has taken the opposite position with respect to the relationship between the truth of beliefs and their evolutionary history, arguing that if evolutionary explanations are correct then the function of evolved capacities (like the capacity to believe) is survival and not the production of true beliefs (1993, 218).

2 See Adams 2003 for a discussion of what he calls the informational turn in philosophy of mind. He helpfully describes the difference between non-naturalistic theories of information in Bar-Hillel and Carnap (1952) from naturalistic accounts of information as applied to philosophy of mind in the 1980s.

3 Causal theories of representation in their modern form were first defended in Stampe (1977). The appeal of causal theories is straightforward. Since at least some mental representations should track events and objects outside the mind then presumably there should exist some causal connection representations and non-mental states of affairs. For an introductory discussion of causal theories of representation see Adams and Aizawa (2010).

4 See Stegmann (2013, 1–35) for a comprehensive introduction to the role of information in animal communication and signaling.

5 While David Papineau is also responsible for a prominent version of teleosemantics (see for example Papineau 1984, 1987, 1997), in this chapter I concentrate on Millikan's version of the view for the purpose of examining the debate about the role of information in any theory of content. Criticisms of Millikan's view and her responses to those criticisms provide a better venue for thinking about information in this context. Papineau's views differ from Millikan's in ways that are described by Karen Neander in her excellent Stanford Encyclopedia of Philosophy article "Teleological Theories of Mental Content" (2012).

6 See Neander (2012) for a complete overview of the controversies surrounding teleological theories.

7 See Symons (2001) for my account of differing views of explanation in the study of representation. See also Calvo and Symons (2014) for our discussion of the role of systematicity arguments in these debates.

8 See Dennett (1988). See also Symons On Dennett (2002) for an explanation of the relationship of the intentional stance to traditional questions in philosophy of mind.

9 Dennett largely follows Millikan in her account of the normative aspects of representation. In his criticisms of the notion of intrinsic intentionality he takes Millikan to have correctly addressed the issue via an appeal to natural selection (Dennett 1988, 200).

10 Think, for example of Braitenberg's vehicles.

11 In fact, there are a variety of different ways that this decoupling can be articulated that have bearing on the relationship between content and information. Luciano Floridi has recently argued for a constructionist account of how meaningful representation results from repurposing what he calls "natural data" generated by the senses (forthcoming).

12 Artifacts and biological systems will have different individuating characteristics by virtue of the kinds of functions that are proper to them. For an alternative approach to the individuation of biological entities in virtue of functions see Symons (2010).

Bibliography

Adams, F. (2003) "The Informational Turn in Philosophy," *Minds and Machines*, 13: 471–501.

Adams, F. and K. Aizawa (2010) "Causal Theories of Mental Content," *The Stanford Encyclopedia of Philosophy* (Spring 2010 Edition), Edward N. Zalta (ed.), URL http://plato.stanford.edu/archives/spr2010/entries/content-causal/.

Bar-Hillel, Y. and R. Carnap. (Orig: 1953 rep. 1964) "An Outline of a Theory of Semantic Information". In *Language and Information: Selected Essays on Their Theory and Application*, 221-74. Reading, MA; London: Addison-Wesley.

Calvo, P. and Symons, J. (2014) *The Architecture of Cognition: Rethinking Fodor and Pylyshyn's Systematicity Challenge*. Cambridge, MA: MIT Press.

Carnap, R. and Bar-Hillel, Y. (1952) *An Outline of a Theory of Semantic Information*. Research Laboratory of Electronics. Cambridge, MA: MIT.

Dennett, D. (1987) *The Intentional Stance*. Cambridge, MA: MIT Press.

Dennett, D. (1988) "Evolution, Error and Intentionality," in Y. Wilks and D. Partridge, eds, *Sourcebook on the Foundations of Artificial Intelligence*, Albuquerque, NM: New Mexico University Press 1988.

Dretske, F. (1981) *Knowledge and the Flow of Information*, Cambridge, MA: MIT/Bradford Press.

Floridi, L. (forthcoming) "Perception and Testimony as Data Providers," *Logique et Analyse*.

Fodor, J. (1996) "Deconstructing Dennett's Darwin," *Mind and Language* 11: 246–262.

Godfrey-Smith, P. (1996) *Complexity and the Function of Mind in Nature*. Cambridge: Cambridge University Press

Meinong, A. (1899) "Über Gegenstände höherer Ordnung und deren Verhältniss zur inneren Wahrnehmung," *Zeitschrift für Psychologie und Physiologie der Sinnesorgane*, 21, pp. 187–272.

Millikan, R. (1984) *Language, Thought and Other Biological Categories*, Cambridge, MA: MIT Press.

Millikan, R. (1989) "In Defense of Proper Functions", *Philosophy of Science*, 56(2), 288–302.

Millikan, R. (1993) *White Queen Psychology and Other Essays for Alice*, Cambridge, MA: MIT Press.

Millikan, R. (2004) *Varieties of Meaning*, Cambridge, MA: MIT Press.

Millikan, R. (2007) "An Input Condition for Teleosemantics? Reply to Shea (and Godfrey Smith)," *Philosophy and Phenomenological Research*, 75(2), 436–455.

Neander, K. (2012) "Teleological Theories of Mental Content," *The Stanford Encyclopedia of Philosophy* (Spring 2012 Edition), Edward N. Zalta (ed.), URL http://plato.stanford.edu/archives/spr2012/entries/content-teleological/.

Papineau, D. (1984) "Representation and Explanation," *Philosophy of Science*, 51, 550–572.

Papineau, D. (1987) *Reality and Representation*, Oxford: Blackwell.

Papineau, D. (1997) "Teleosemantics and Indeterminacy," *Australasian Journal of Philosophy*, 76, 1–14.

Pietroski, P. (1992) "Intentional and Teleological Error," *Pacific Philosophical Quarterly*, 73, 267–281.

Plantinga, A. (1993) *Warrant and Proper Function.* Oxford: Oxford University Press

Rowlands M. (1997) "Teleological Semantics," *Mind*, 106(422), 279–303.

Shea, N. (2007) "Consumers Need Information: Supplementing Teleosemantics with an Input Condition," *Philosophy and Phenomenological Research*, 75(2), 404–435.

Stampe, D. (1977) "Toward a Causal Theory of Linguistic Representation," in P. French, H. K. Wettstein, and T. E. Uehling (eds.), *Midwest Studies in Philosophy*, vol. 2, Minneapolis, MN: University of Minnesota Press, pp. 42–63.

Stegmann, U. (2013) *Animal Communication Theory: Information and Influence*, Cambridge: Cambridge University Press.

Stephens, C. (2001) "When is it Selectively Advantageous to Have True Beliefs? Sandwiching the Better-Safe-than-Sorry Argument," *Philosophical* 105(2), 161–189.

Stich, S. (1983) *From Folk Psychology to Cognitive Science: The Case Against Belief*, Cambridge, MA: MIT Press.

Symons, J. (2001) "Explanation, Representation and the Dynamical Hypothesis," *Minds and Machines*, 11(4), 521–541.

Symons, J. (2002) *On Dennett*, Belmont, CA: Wadsworth.

Symons, J. (2010) "The Individuality of Artifacts and Organisms," *History and Philosophy of the Life Sciences*, 233–246.

Taylor, S.E. and Brown, J. (1988). "Illusion and well-being: A social psychological perspective on mental health," *Psychological Bulletin*, 103(2), 193–210.

23

THE PHILOSOPHY OF BIOLOGICAL INFORMATION

Barton Moffatt

Introduction

Information talk is everywhere in the biological sciences. Use of the term information and related concepts like code, program and signal are put to a wide range of uses in the scientific description of natural phenomena. Philosophers of biology are keen to understand what biologists mean by information and related concepts, what work these concepts do, and how they are interrelated. This chapter focuses on a few select arguments, briefly setting out some of the best known philosophical arguments on this topic. Hopefully this will give the reader both a taste of the specific argumentation employed by philosophers of biology and some exposure to the type of interests that motivate their projects. The chapter begins by briefly describing some of the typical ways informational concepts are used in biology. There follows a detailed look at Griffiths' Parity argument and then a discussion of two semantic accounts of information developed by John Maynard Smith and Eva Jablonka. Next, the chapter reviews Sarkar's argument about the epistemic role played by information and Godfrey-Smith's argument exploring the connections between informational concepts. The chapter ends with a discussion of some other noteworthy work in the area and a brief look at where the field is headed.

"Information talk" in biology

Biological information is entrenched in biology: genes carry information, cells signal each other and some biologists claim that biology is an informational science (Ideker *et al.* 2001). This section briefly sets out examples of information talk in biology. An illustrative case of a standard usage of information talk is provided by the US Department of Energy's widely distributed primer on molecular genetics. This primer frequently invokes informational concepts. It defines a gene as

> a specific sequence of nucleotide bases, whose sequences carry the information required for constructing proteins, which provide the structural components of cells and tissues as well as enzymes for essential biochemical reactions.
>
> *(Casey 1992, p. 7)*

Informational terms are central to the primer's description of gene expression. It states

> The protein-coding instructions from the genes are transmitted indirectly through messenger ribonucleic acid (mRNA), a transient intermediary molecule similar to a single strand of DNA. For the information within a gene to be expressed, a complementary RNA strand is produced (a process called transcription) from the DNA template in the nucleus.
>
> *(Casey 1992, p. 7)*

This passage is typical of one way information talk appears in biology. Genes carry the information expressed in protein synthesis.

Other informational terms like code are also prominently featured in the primer. The information carried by genes is encoded in the sequence of nucleotides. The primer states,

> If unwound and tied together, the strands of DNA would stretch more than 5 feet but would be only 50 trillionths of an inch wide. For each organism, the components of these slender threads encode all the information necessary for building and maintaining life, from simple bacteria to remarkably complex human beings.
>
> *(Casey 1992, p. 6)*

DNA is represented as carrying encoded information. Interestingly, this passage also highlights an aspect of information talk that has garnered significant philosophical attention. DNA is described as carrying all of the information necessary for development. This claim is widely challenged by philosophers and much of the philosophical interest in biological information stems from disagreement with this position.

Information talk is invariably found in biology textbooks as well (Godfrey-Smith 1999). Genetics textbooks routinely describe genes as carrying information in a code which gets converted, by transcription, into RNA, which is then translated into proteins. This depiction of gene expression relies heavily on the notion of information and related terms: *code*, *transcription*, and *translation*. The central dogma of molecular biology claims that genetic information, in the form of the genetic code, is transcribed into RNA and then translated into proteins (Crick 1958). Clearly, gene expression is described in informational terms in standard biology textbooks. Additionally, textbooks describe certain cellular functions as proofreading and editing, further extending the informational description of cell function (Godfrey-Smith 2000a). The fact that information talk is embedded in the description of cell machinery makes it inescapable.

Nobel Laureate Walter Gilbert's work illustrates another kind of information talk in biology. In "A Vision of the Grail," Gilbert says, "The information carried on the DNA, that genetic information passed down from our parents, is the most fundamental property of the body...[and] there is no more basic or more fundamental information that could be available" (Gilbert 1993, p. 83). Gilbert claims that information is a fundamental property of our biology that will revolutionize our conception of ourselves. He writes

> I think that there will also be a change in our philosophical understanding of ourselves. Even though the human sequence is as long as a thousand thousand-page telephone books, which sounds like a great deal of information, in computer terms it is actually very little. ... To recognize that we are determined, in a certain sense, by a finite collection of information that is knowable will change our view

of ourselves. It is the closing of an intellectual frontier, with which we will have to come to terms. ...We will understand *deeply* how we are assembled, dictated by our genetic information.

(Gilbert 1993, p. 96 italics in original)

This passage is an excellent example of a second common usage of 'information' in a biological context. In this view, genetic information is a fundamental, defining feature of our biology; it assembles and dictates our development.

Although commonplace, information talk is not limited to textbooks and general proclamations by biologists; current research in biology often uses informational concepts in still different ways. Concepts like *signal* and *network* are common in molecular and cellular biology and are yet another instantiation of information talk in biology.

The ubiquity of information talk in biology introduces two related philosophical problems. The first problem is that it is unclear what biologists mean by information in these contexts. There is no philosophical consensus on what biologist mean by information and the meaning of the concept of biological information is unclear. In addition, there is a related problem about the justification of biologists' usage of information. Given the disagreement about the meaning of the concept of information in biology, it is also unclear what justifies the role this concept and related concepts play in the development of biological thought. Is information talk a principled, necessary part of modern biological knowledge, a merely colorful description that is of no philosophical significance, or something entirely different?

Informational parity

Much of the philosophical interest in information talk grew out of a concern that informational concepts were used to support genetic determinism. The determinists argued that genes were special because they and only they carried developmental information. Other developmental resources necessarily played a lesser role because they do not carry information. This view is thought to prioritize genetic aspects of development and support genetic determinism – the idea that genes determine development (Keller 1993). Paul Griffiths and his co-authors are probably most closely associated with the rejection of this view, developing the parity thesis in response – the idea that information cannot be used to make a principled distinction between the role of genes and environments in development. In Griffiths' (2001) "Genetic Information: A Metaphor in Search of a Theory," the argument has the following form:

1 Accounts of information come in roughly causal or intentional versions;
2 If we apply the causal version to biological phenomena in development, it applies equally to genetic and environmental factors;
3 If we apply the intentional version to biological phenomena in development, it also applies equally to genetic and environmental factors;
4 Therefore, information talk applies to both genetic and environmental features in development;
5 Therefore, there is no principled way to use information to distinguish between the roles genes and environments play in development.

This argument has the form of a constructive dilemma. Information is either causal or intentional. Parity between the roles that both genes and environments play in development is a consequence of each type of information. Therefore information cannot be used to assert that genes play a special role in development. The core of this argument consists in the claims that information is either causal or intentional and that parity follows from each. Premise one claims that there are two distinct, respectable accounts of information – causal and intentional. The second premise asserts that the causal account of information applies equally as well to genes and environments (see Chapter 4). It is just as easy to understand environmental features as reducing uncertainty over a communication channel as it is to understand genes as doing the same. Griffiths uses the example of a TV test card to illustrate this point. Ordinarily, the image one sees on a TV screen consists of the broadcast signal and environmental interference. The broadcast image constantly varies, but when technicians want to learn about the environmental conditions interfering with the broadcast, they hold the broadcast constant by broadcasting the familiar image of the test card. This procedure allows them to see the environmental interference in the TV image. The key point is that both the signal and the interference are connected to the broadcast. Either one can be considered a source of information. For Griffiths, the situation in biological development is the same. While biologists might sometimes regard genes as the source and environments as the interference, this conception can always be inverted, as in the TV test card case, by conceptualizing the environment as the signal and the genes as the interference. The upshot is that this account of information cannot differentiate between the role of genes and environments in a principled way.

The third premise mirrors the second in that it claims that the semantic or intentional account of information equally applies to both genes and environments (see Chapter 6). Griffiths uses a discussion of a wide range of cases of non-genetic inheritance to fill out this claim. He sets out several examples of non-genetic developmental factors that are inherited and that qualify as semantic information because evolution has shaped their form. In particular, niche construction (where organisms alter their environment) offers a clear case in which environmental resources are inherited and have had their form shaped by evolution, which means that they count as a carrier of semantic information. Since niche construction and other similar examples are clear cases of non-genetic phenomena carrying semantic information, Griffiths concludes that semantic information does not license a principled distinction between the role of genes and environments in development. Griffiths' work has been influential as an antidote to determinism and as a spur to clarify what biologists mean by information.

Maynard Smith's semantic biological information

For many, the central question in the philosophy of biological information concerns what information means in this context. Many biologists and philosophers have proposed accounts of biological information to answer this question. In this section, I will set out two similar accounts of semantic information. In "The Concept of Information in Biology" (2000), late biologist John Maynard Smith argues that biologists conceptualize information semantically because evolution has shaped its form. For Maynard Smith, genes are meaningful in the same way that words are in a language (see Chapter 6). In addition, he thinks that there is an important "arbitrariness" in the relevant chemical processes involved in gene expression that make them symbolic. The combination of the intentional and the symbolic aspects of gene action suggests that genes carry information in a meaningful way. Finally, he argues that the functional similarity with evolved and intentional programs justifies the description of particular evolutionary effects as intentional.

We can reconstruct his reasoning thus:

1 Information talk is a ubiquitous and successful feature of biological practice;
2 Biologists use informational concepts only to describe what genes do;
3 Biologists say that genes and only genes carry information because evolution shapes gene form and this form is symbolic;
4 The form of a gene is symbolic because there is an important "arbitrary" element between its chemistry and the role it plays;
5 The indistinguishability of evolved programs and intentional ones means that biologists are justified in attributing intentionality to genes;
6 Therefore, biologists are justified in describing gene action as symbolic because evolution has shaped the form of genes in an arbitrary way.

This argument justifies the biological practice of characterizing only genes as carrying information by developing a semantic account of information as evolved form, outlining an important symbolic feature of the chemistry of gene action and by justifying this usage with a thought experiment. With respect to the first premise, Maynard Smith reviews the varied ways that biologists use information. He observes that a high number of informational terms are commonly used in molecular biology. He remarks that "transcription, translation, code, redundancy, synonymous, messenger, editing, proofreading, library" are all technical terms in biology (Maynard Smith 2000: p. 178). Their presence indicates that researchers had the information analogy in mind and that it was useful during this period. Some usages, like the concept of code, are so clear and successful that Maynard Smith thinks that they require no justification. In other cases, biologists need to clarify what they mean. The case of genetic information is one of these cases.

The second premise outlines Maynard Smith's project as a defense of the current usage of information as only applying to genes. He considers explicating the meaning of information talk with Shannon information (see Chapter 4), but rejects this attempt because, although it can make sense of genes carrying information, it also licenses the idea that environments carry information in the same way. He develops his semantic account of information as meaningfulness so he can save a special informational role for genes.

The third premise sets out Maynard Smith's version of genetic information as meaningfulness due to evolved form. The central idea is that genes are meaningful because evolution shapes their form. Genes are semantic in the same way that words are semantic because the intentionality inherent in evolution shaped their form. He writes

> In biology, the statement A carries information about B implies that A has the form that it does because it carries that information. A DNA molecule has a particular sequence because it specifies a particular protein. But a cloud is not black because it predicts rain. This element of intentionality comes from natural selection.
>
> *(Maynard Smith 2000: pp. 189–90)*

The key point is that genes mean something because evolution shaped their form to carry out a particular function. Additionally, there is an important symbolic aspect in this account. Information does not merely come from evolution shaping the form of something to carry out a function. There also has to be something symbolic about the way the form carries out the function. Although Maynard Smith does not explicitly link these two points, arguably the best reading of his position suggests that the arbitrariness of genetic chemistry is a necessary part of why genes carry information. Premise 4 explicates what it is for an interaction to be symbolic in terms of arbitrariness. Specifically, a chemical interaction is symbolic if there is no necessary connection between the form of the molecule and its meaning. This arbitrariness marks symbolic systems.

This account allows him to claim that environmental interactions are not informational. Clouds are not black because they carry the information that they bring rain. The form of the rain cloud is not shaped by the information it carries. As such, it does not qualify as semantic information. For Maynard Smith, the blackness of a rain cloud is informational in the Shannon usage, but not semantically informational, in that the form of the cloud is not shaped by the information it carries. To drive this point home, Maynard Smith compares the information gained by seeing a black rain cloud and hearing a weather forecast of impending rain. Both reveal that rain is due, but only the forecast can be said to be meaningful. Maynard Smith identifies the relevant difference in this case as a difference in intentionality. The forecast has the form that it does because it carries information about the impending rainstorm. This is not the case with the storm cloud; its form is not shaped by the information it carries.

Maynard Smith ends his argument with a thought experiment to justify biologists' use of information talk. He considers two ways to devise a program to play a game, Fox and Geese, in which four geese try to corner a fox on a checkerboard. In one instance, an engineer creates a program by a process of selection. He invents rules for the geese and a way of varying both the parameters for these rules and the weightings for determining which rule should be used next. Then the engineer creates a population using random parameters and next rule weightings. He runs the game against a competent fox, saving the most successful players. Next, he randomly varies the program of the successful geese, again playing those geese against a fox. The engineer continues this process until he has created a group of geese that can defeat any fox. Maynard Smith contrasts this approach with that of a second engineer. This engineer simply figures out the optimal geese strategy and programs the geese to do the appropriate things at the appropriate times. Maynard Smith points out that no one could have a problem with saying that the second engineer's program contained information or instructions embodying his or her intentions. He argues that since the two programs are indistinguishable in the sense that you could not tell them apart if given a description of their moves in a game, then we are as justified in attributing intentionality in the form of information or instructions to the first selective program as to the second. Premise five sets out Maynard Smith's claim that this symmetry justifies the description of evolved form as intentional. The five premises together support the conclusion that biologists use information talk semantically when they describe genes and that this usage is justified.

Jablonka's semantic biological information

Manyard Smith's is not the only semantic account of biological information. In "Information: Its Interpretation, Its Inheritance, and Its Sharing" (2002), Eva Jablonka offers her own account of semantic information. Although Jablonka does not present her account explicitly as an argument, we can reconstruct her reasoning as follows:

1 Cases of "information" involve an interaction between a source and a receiver that affects the actual or potential action of the receiver;
2 In "information" cases, the interaction outlined in (1) involves a reaction to the organization of a source (as opposed to its physical or chemical properties);
3 In "information" cases, the interactions outlined in (1) and (2) are evolutionarily advantageous;

4   In "information" cases, the interactions outlined in (1), (2) and (3) are systematic, where variations in the organization of the source reliably lead to variations in the functional responses of the receiver;

5   Therefore, "a source – an entity or a process – can be said to have information when a receiver system reacts to this source in a special way. The reaction of the receiver to a source has to be such that the reaction of the receiver can actually or potentially change the state of the receiver in a (usually) functional manner. Moreover, there must be a consistent relation between variations in the form of the source and the corresponding changes in the receiver." (Jablonka 2002: p. 582)

The basic form of Jablonka's argument consists in an enumeration of common features in "information" cases and the conclusion that these features define semantic information. The strength of this analysis rests on the accuracy and appropriateness of these features. Jablonka's first feature sets the structure of her account. A source must have an actual or potential effect on a receiver. This premise defines the basic components of an informational account utilizing Shannon's well-known framework (see Chapter 4). An informational system has a source, a receiver and a communication channel connecting the two.

The second premise characterizes the kind of interaction between the source and receiver as mediated by the organization or form of the source. A source's organization affects the receiver. For example, it is not the physical or chemical make-up of a train schedule but its organization that provides information. The source could be made of printed paper, electronic screens, sound waves, etc. and still carry the same information because they have the same organization.

The third premise is that the reaction that the source has on the receiver must be adaptive in the sense that it provides some sort of evolutionary advantage over time. Jablonka explicates evolutionary advantage as having a function in the Wright (1973) sense, where the function of something, say the heart, is explained by the fact that ancestors with hearts were better able to produce viable offspring. However, Jablonka also wants to include functions in the Cummins (1975) sense, where to have a function is to contribute to the production of a behavior in a system. In a Cummins function, the function of the heart is to pump blood in the circulatory system. Jablonka links the two by suggesting that in biological systems anything that has a Cummins style function is the product of natural selection and thereby has a Wright style function as well. Jablonka takes this general functionality as a key feature of biological information. She does qualify this criterion or feature of biological information by backing away from the claim that the response in a receiver due to the source must be directly adaptive. It is enough if the response is part of a larger, more general adaptive system. She illustrates this point with an example about black clouds carrying information about the weather for apes. Jablonka does not require a directly adaptive cloud reading module in the brain of the ape for this to count as information. The fact that the ape's perceptual system is generally adapted to respond to environmental stimuli is adaptive enough to count as informational.

The fourth premise articulates the idea that informational systems exhibit consistency between differences in organization and differences in function. There is a systematic relationship between variations in form and adaptive responses. Systems without variation in organization are not informational. In the ape example, variations in the appearance of the sky consistently lead to different adaptive behaviors. Jablonka identifies this consistency as an important common denominator in "informational" cases.

These considerations lead to Jablonka's proposed definition of semantic information as the conclusion of the argument that combines these common denominators into a generalized account. The definition of semantic information as set out by Jablonka is that an interaction is informational if the interpreting system of the receiver has evolved a consistent reaction to variations in organization or form of a source. This definition generalizes the common denominators articulated in the premises and offers a clear account of biological information that applies equally to genetic and environmental factors. Genes and environments carry semantic information if and only if they are interpreted as such.

The key difference between Jablonka's account and Maynard Smith's account of semantic information centers on the object of evolution. For Maynard Smith, semantic information is created when evolution shapes the form of the source; DNA carries information because evolution has shaped its form. For Jablonka, the interpreting system of the receiver creates semantic information when evolution shapes its response to the form of the source. The case of black storm clouds carrying information illustrates this difference. Maynard Smith argues that black clouds are not meaningful and do not carry semantic information about impending rain because evolution did not shape their form. Jablonka disagrees; black clouds can be meaningful if there are organisms that have evolved adaptive responses in variations in their form. The form of the source does not have to be the product of evolution, although it can be in the case of an evolved "signal."

Epistemic role of information in biology

Much of the above debate about the meaning of biological information deals in possible meanings of information in the sense that it attempts to capture what biologists could mean by information and not a historical sense of what biologists did in fact mean by information. Some philosophers of biology are equally interested in understanding the epistemic impact that the concept of information has had on the development of biological knowledge. One notable argument is Sahotra Sarkar's "Information Talk Plays No Explanatory Role" argument. He defends the position that information talk plays no explanatory role in current biology. His general target is the so called Central Dogma of molecular biology, already encountered above: information resides in the DNA and is carried by RNA to proteins in a one-way process (the flow of information only goes from DNA to RNA to proteins and never from proteins to RNA or from RNA to DNA). Specifically, his view is that information talk, as expressed in the Central Dogma, is

> little more than a metaphor that masquerades as a theoretical concept and ... leads
> to a misleading picture of the nature of possible explanations in molecular biology.
> *(Sarkar 1996: p. 187)*

Sarkar's view offers the sharpest contrast with those who think that informational concepts are epistemically important in biology (Ideker *et al.* 2001). At issue are substantive disagreements about both basic biological facts and relevant interpretations of information talk.

The basic argument in Sarkar (1996) goes as follows:

1 A significant scientific explanation must both "codify a body of knowledge" and "answer new questions that are recognized to be important" (Sarkar 1996: p. 188);
2 'Information' in the sense of sequence information related to the concept of coding does little or nothing to codify a body of biological knowledge;
3 "Information" in the sense of feedback from cybernetics cannot codify a body of knowledge about eukaryotic gene regulation;

4 "Information" in the sense of the reduction of uncertainty or entropy from information theory (Shannon information) only applies to sets of sequences and as a result cannot capture what biologists usually mean by information in the Central Dogma;

5 Existing technical accounts of information in biology do not capture the sense of information in the Central Dogma;

6 Therefore, "there is no clear technical notion of 'information' at work as an explication of the Central Dogma in molecular biology" (Sarkar 1996: p. 187);

7 Therefore, information talk in the sense outlined in the Central Dogma plays little or no role as a significant explanation in molecular biology.

The structure of the argument is clear; Sarkar sets out a criterion for explanatory significance, reviews the technical accounts of information and concludes that none of them captures the meaning of information as used in the Central Dogma (Crick 1958). Additionally, Sarkar notes that some current usages of information talk use information in significant explanations, but that these explanations have nothing to do with the way information is commonly used in the Central Dogma. For example, Sarkar discusses other examples of informational applications like Kimura's work on molecular clocks (Kimura 1968), but these kinds of applications do not cover the Central Dogma usage.

The first premise sets out Sarkar's criterion for explanatory relevance. A significant explanation must both unify a body of knowledge – revealing a general pattern – and address a problem of current biological interest. Sarkar proposes this as an uncontroversial criterion of explanatory relevance, although he does not explain why revealing a pattern or addressing a current problem is necessary as a criterion of explanatory relevance.

The second premise asserts that the concept of sequence information does not codify a body of knowledge (in the sense of revealing a general pattern) because of the complexity of eukaryote genetics. By sequence information, Sarkar means information that is carried by the genetic code and which specifies the ordering of amino acids in proteins. This account does not codify knowledge because, for Sarkar, explanations of it are of little predictive utility. Specifically, since biologists need to know a number of things about the machinery of gene expression, like which version of the code is being used, where transcription starts and the intron/exon boundaries, among others, to understand how sequence information determines the structure of proteins, sequence information on its own does not explain the structure of proteins. The fact that biologists cannot predict protein structure directly from sequence information means that, for Sarkar, this kind of information does not codify existing knowledge.

The third premise extends the same kind of reasoning to the concept of cybernetic information. Cybernetic information is not as clearly defined in the biological literature as sequence information, but Sarkar identifies information involved in or responsible for the phenomenon of feedback as the relevant idea. Sarkar introduces Monod's operon model of gene regulation as an example of cybernetic information (Monod 1971). Sarkar argues that explanations based on this version of information also fail to codify an existing body of knowledge because they fail to generalize to cover all eukaryotic gene regulation; again, for Sarkar, this account fails to explain because it fails to generalize a pattern. Premise four asserts that Shannon information also fails to count as explanatorily relevant because it is not currently applied to biological questions of interest. Quastler and others applied Shannon information to biological phenomena in the 1950s and 1960s, but the research program was ultimately unproductive (Kay 2000). Sarkar argues that the fact that this research is no longer active is grounds for dismissing it as explanatorily irrelevant.

The fifth premise discusses examples of the use of the concept of information in explanatorily relevant work in biology, but claims that these applications have nothing to do with the Central Dogma. In particular, Sarkar reviews Kimura's work on using information as a measure of the tempo of evolution (Kimura 1968). This work, according to Sarkar, might become explanatorily relevant, but the fact that under this approach any two sequences of the same length have the same information strongly suggests that this cannot capture what is meant by information in the Central Dogma. Sarkar concludes from these premises that there is no clear technical idea of information behind the central dogma. This absence allows Sarkar to conclude that the concept of information as found in the Central Dogma plays no explanatory role in current molecular biology.

Connection between information and other "informational" concepts

Even if we were to understand what biological information is and what it does perfectly, there would still be a remaining puzzle of how it relates to other informational concepts in biology. Many biologists think of information as a unifying concept in biology linking seemingly distinct usages of information talk (Ideker *et al.* 2001). Griffiths (2001) describes a "very bad argument" which concludes in the absence of evidence that all instances of information talk are identical. Of course, it is an equally bad argument to claim in the absence of evidence that all instances of information talk in biology are unrelated. But, does the existence of the genetic code, signaling systems, etc. mean that biology is necessarily informational? In "On Genetic Information and Genetic Coding" (2002), Peter Godfrey-Smith outlines a strategy for accounting for the broadly informational representation of genes. He acknowledges that loosely semantic descriptions of gene action are very common in molecular biology but worries that some of these descriptions and representations support genetic determinism. Since there is the potential for harm, Godfrey-Smith argues that we need to do two things to deal with information talk. First, we need to examine and clarify carefully the theoretical role that information talk plays in biological investigations. Second, we need to identify explicitly what kind of information talk is justified by this role and, more importantly, what kind of talk is not justified and is merely unwarranted inflation. For Godfrey-Smith, we understand information talk (specifically the use of the concept of "code") by situating it in its theoretical context and warning against unjustified expansions of information talk outside of these particular contexts.

In detail, Godfrey-Smith's argument is as follows:

1 The concept of information as derived from information theory does not play a theoretical role in current biology;
2 The concept of coding does play a specific, current theoretical role in molecular biology as shorthand for "the idea of a template as an ordering mechanism for proteins, and this solution features a relation between nucleic acid bases and proteins which can be described as a combinatorial, chemically arbitrary rule of causal specificity" (Godfrey-Smith 2002: p. 394);
3 Therefore, of the large set of semantic representational practices, the use of the concepts of "code" and "coding" are justified in these contexts;
4 Therefore, all other examples of information talk are inflationary and are as such unjustified by theoretical necessity.

The aim of the argument is to differentiate clearly between the representations that are theoretically motivated and those that are not. The first premise asserts that the sense of information derived from information theory cannot capture the distinctive semantic role attributed to genes. Godfrey-Smith argues that Shannon information can be applied to the roles of both genes and environments in development. In addition, Shannon information is bi-directional; gene products have information about genes in the same way that genes have information about gene products. These cases show that this account of information cannot capture the special semantic representation of genes. The second premise outlines the key finding of his paper: a theoretical role for coding. Specifically, Godfrey-Smith argues that the concept of "coding" plays an important theoretical role in explaining the relationship between the order of nucleic acids in DNA and the structure of amino acids. According to Godfrey-Smith, this template role is unique to genes and captures why biologists attribute semantic significance to genes. The application of the concept of coding offers a solution for a biological question: how does the cell construct proteins? Godfrey-Smith's approach to coming to terms with information talk is to focus solely on the theoretical role of coding as an example of a case in which biologists are justified in using a semantic description of gene action.

Godfrey-Smith's conclusion is that biologists are justified in using the concept of "code" in this theoretical context. This follows from the fact that it plays a useful theoretical role in solving a biological problem and the assumption that anything that plays a useful theoretical role is justified. A second conclusion is equally important: this use of coding in no way justifies inflationary uses of code, in which genes code for complex traits or act as a blueprint for development. Godfrey-Smith goes to great pains to delineate the limits of justified code talk by explicitly restricting it to this investigative context. Genes can only code for the ordering of amino acids in proteins. Godfrey-Smith outlines a strategy for getting at what biologists mean when they use informational concepts to describe what genes do: 1) identify the specific job done by the semantic or representational concept and 2) restrict the usage to just this role.

Conclusion

The aim of this chapter has been to introduce readers to some key arguments that have shaped the debate on the nature and utility of biological concepts of information. The literature on information in the philosophy of biology can be thought of in terms of three broad projects: 1) what is information; 2) what role does it play in biology; and 3) how is it related to other seemingly informational notions? The chapter sets out a few selected arguments in detail because it is important to see exactly which aspects of the biological world are deemed information bearing. The devil is in the biological details. It should be noted that there is a great deal of diversity in the motivations behind differing projects. As mentioned, the question of genetic privilege (the idea that genes direct development) runs through much of the debate, but it is hardly the only motivation. Many scholars are interested in the structure of biological knowledge; others seek to justify explicitly the legitimacy of current biological descriptions of the natural world. Still others are keen to check what is seen as inflationary rhetoric about the utility of informational concepts in biology.

While it is important to stress the diversity of types of arguments about biological information, it is also important to acknowledge the many excellent alternative accounts of biological information not set out in detail here. This chapter is not intended to be an exhaustive review of every account of biological information, but interested readers would be advised to explore the growing literature in the philosophy of biology on information and related concepts. For instance, Winnie (2000) sets outs an account of biological information as Kolmogorov information using an algorithmic measure of information (Chapter 5). The well-developed biosemiotic research program understands biological information in terms of a three-part relationship between a sign, an object and an interpretant (see Queiroz *et al.* (2011) and Chapter 24). In addition, Sarkar (2003) sets out his own semiotic account of biological information and Stegmann (2005) offers an account of biological information as instructional content. The collection *Information and Living Systems: Philosophical and Scientific Perspectives*, edited by George Terzis and Robert Arp (2011), contains the biosemiotic paper in addition to a number of other well-drawn accounts of biological information. Bergstrom and Rosvall (2011) object to the association of causal information with Shannon information and develop a transmission account of biological information that is truer in nature to Shannon's account (Chapter 4).

In addition, there is a good deal of commentary and critique of existing accounts of information that would be helpful to those interested in exploring these issues more. The Maynard Smith paper in particular has generated a number of excellent critiques, and interested readers could use these commentaries as an entry point into the details of the debates about biological information. Sterelney (2000), Godfrey-Smith (2000b) and Sarkar (2000) respond to Maynard Smith in the same *Philosophy of Science* volume. Other commentaries in *Biology and Philosophy* present critiques of Bergstrom and Rosvall's transmission information (Shea 2011; Maclaurin 2011; Stegmann 2013).

If we take a step back and take a broader view on these issues an interesting question arises. What is it for a particular account of biological information to be successful? There is very little explicit agreement about what counts as success in this area. Is it enough if an account is conceptually coherent? Or does it also need to capture the standard ways in which biologists use the term? Many proposals pitch themselves as a principled reformation of typical usages, striking a middle ground between slavish adherence to actual usage in biology and purely principled philosophical account. Answers to these questions in part depend on the details of the particular project each philosopher is working on. If, like Griffiths, for example, you argue that concepts of information cannot justify a principled distinction between the role of genes and environments in development, then you need to articulate accounts of information that are both principled and match biological usages as much as possible. However, if your interest lies simply in considering the possible ways in which information could be carried by a natural system, you would have a very different criterion for success. Future research could focus on further exploring these criteria of success (see Stegmann (2005) for a discussion of desiderata).

Additionally, there is plenty of room for new accounts of biological information. There are few constraints on what can count as biological information and many interesting possible applications. It is still a productive area of the philosophy of biology for students looking for projects. There is plenty of excellent work on biological information in the philosophy of biology, but it is fair to say that there is a good deal of open conceptual space in this area – that is, there is an opportunity for new conceptually possible accounts of information in this domain. One nice feature of the debate in this area is that new accounts of biological information allow us to reexamine some of the earliest arguments, like the parity thesis argument.

Possibly the greatest arena for exciting new work revolves around understanding our concept of signal. There is an opportunity for more work that addresses philosophical aspects of biological signaling systems. Signal has become ubiquitous in biology in a way that surpasses the way that information is used. Fortunately, the same issues remain open: what is a signal; how does signal relate to other similar concepts used throughout biology; and what is the epistemic contribution of signal? Brian Skyrms' (2010) *Signals: Evolution, Learning and Information* is an excellent starting place for students interested in using the concept of signal to understand biological phenomena.

References

Bergstrom, C.T. and Rosvall, M. (2011) "The Transmission Sense of Information." *Biology and Philosophy* 26 (2):159–176.

Casey, D. (1992) "Primer on Molecular Genetics." *June 1992 DOE Human Genome 1991–92 Program Report.*

Crick, F.H.C. (1958) "On Protein Synthesis," *Symp Soc Exp Biol* XII: 139–163.

Cummins, R. (1975) "Functional Analysis," *Journal of Philosophy* 72: 741–765.

Gilbert, W. (1993) "A Vision of the Grail," in D. Kevles and L. Hood (eds) *The Code of Codes: Scientific and Social Issues in the Human Genome Project.* (Cambridge, MA: Harvard University Press).

Godfrey-Smith, P. (1999), "Genes and Codes: Lessons from the Philosophy of Mind?" in Valerie G. Hardcastle (ed.). *Biology Meets Psychology: Constraints, Conjectures, Connections.* Cambridge, MA: MIT Press, 305–331.

Godfrey-Smith, P. (2000a) "On the Theoretical Role of 'Genetic Coding,'" *Philosophy of Science* 67: 26–44.

Godfrey-Smith, P. (2000b). "Information, Arbitrariness, and Selection: Comments on Maynard Smith." *Philosophy of Science* 67, 202–207.

Godfrey-Smith, P. (2002) "On Genetic Information and Genetic Coding," in P. Gardenfors, J. Wolenski and K. Kajania-Placek (eds) *In the Scope of Logic, Methodology, and the Philosophy of Science* (Dordrecht, Kluwer). Vol. II, pp. 387–400

Griffiths, P. (2001) "Genetic Information: A Metaphor in Search of a Theory," *Philosophy of Science* 68: 394–412.

Ideker, T., Galitski, T. and Hood, L. (2001) "A New Approach To Decoding Life," *Annu. Rev. Genomics Hum. Genet.* 2: 343–72.

Jablonka, E. (2002) "Information: Its Interpretation, Its Inheritance and Its Sharing," *Philosophy of Science* 69: 578–605.

Kay, L.E. (2000) *Who Wrote the Book of Life? A History of the Genetic Code,* Stanford, CA: Stanford University Press.

Keller, E.F. (1993) "Rethinking the Meaning of Genetic Determinism," The Tanner Lectures on Human Values, Salt Lake City, Utah, February 18, 1993.

Kimura, Motoo (1968) "Evolutionary Rate at the Molecular Level," *Nature* 217 (5129): 624–626.

Maclaurin, J. (2011) "Commentary on 'The Transmission Sense of Information' by Carl T. Bergstrom and Martin Rosvall," *Biology and Philosophy* 26: 191–194.

Maynard Smith, J. (2000) "The Concept of Information in Biology," *Philosophy of Science* 67: 177–194.

Monod, J. (1971) *Chance and Necessity: An Essay on the Natural Philosophy of Modern Biology,* New York: Alfred A. Knopf.

Queiroz, J., Emmeche, C., Kull, K. and El-Hani, C. (2011) "The Biosemiotic Approach in Biology: Theoretical Bases and Applied Models" in George Terzis and Robert Arp (eds) *Information and Living Systems: Philosophical and Scientific Perspectives.* Cambridge, MA: MIT Press.

Sarkar, S. (1996) "Biological Information: A Skeptical Look at Some Central Dogmas of Molecular Biology," in Sahotra Sarkar (ed.), *The Philosophy and History of Molecular Biology: New Perspectives.* Dordrecht: Kluwer.

Sarkar, S. (2000), "Information in Genetics and Development: Comments on Maynard Smith." *Philosophy of Science* 67: 208–213.

Sarkar, S. (2003) "Genes Encode Information for Phenotypic Traits," in Christopher Hitchcock (ed.) *Contemporary Debates in Philosophy of Science.* Oxford: Blackwell.

Shea, N. (2011) "What's Transmitted? Inherited Information," *Biology & Philosophy* 26: 183–189.

Skyrms, B. (2010) *Signals: Evolution, Learning and Information,* New York: Oxford University Press.

Stegmann, U. (2005) "Genetic Information as Instructional Content," *Philosophy of Science* 72: 425–443.

Stegmann, U. (2013) "On the 'Transmission Sense of Information'," *Biology & Philosophy* 28: 141–144.

Sterelny, K. (2000) "The 'Genetic Program' Program: A Commentary on Maynard Smith on Information in Biology," *Philosophy of Science* 67: 195–201.

Terzis, G. and Arp, R. (eds) (2011) *Information and Living Systems: Philosophical and Scientific Perspectives,* Cambridge, MA: MIT Press.

Winnie, J. (2000). "Information and Structure in Molecular Biology: Comments on Maynard Smith." *Philosophy of Science* 67: 517–526.

Wright, L. (1973) "Functions," *Philosophical Review* 82: 139–168.

24

THE PHILOSOPHY
OF SEMIOTIC
INFORMATION

Sara Cannizzaro

Introduction

This chapter presents the debate on the philosophical nature of information that can be found in contemporary semiotics, particularly in a number of developments broadly grouped within the umbrella field 'biosemiotics'. As an international and interdisciplinary research field, biosemiotics has continued to flourish over the past 50 years and, as its prefix shows, biosemiotics is indebted to *semiotics* in respect to its conception of communication as *sign processes*. Biosemiotics, however, currently extends the remit of much semiotics in that it does not limit its object of research to the investigation of human communications alone (i.e. anthroposemiotics), but encompasses all types of communications in the biosphere, that is, cells', plants' and animals' communications, including of course, those communication processes pertaining to the human animal. It is crucial to note early on that the very term 'information' is a controversial one in biosemiotics due to its affinity to sciences close to the development of technology and computing methods (for example, information theory and cybernetics) and thus, to its possible mechanistic connotations which are rejected by much of contemporary biosemiotics. Biosemiotics in fact champions largely qualitative approaches to quantitative approaches, and by adhering to the *semiotic paradigm* rather than the strictly Shannon information paradigm (see Chapter 4), it uses analytical terms as 'meaning' and 'signs' rather than 'information'. However, since 'information is an implicitly semiotic term' (Kull *et al.* 2009: 169), then a discussion of information within the broad remit of biosemiotics should not be dismissed on the premise of disciplinary stereotypes (e.g. semiotics as being a purely humanist-indeterminist field with no space for any form of determinism). Hence, this chapter presents an overview of the general approaches and types of informational concepts that are implicitly or explicitly present in biosemiotics, including associated disciplines and schools of semiotics as Tartu-Moscow semiotics, zoosemiotics, and cybersemiotics.

Broadly speaking, biosemiotic accounts of information often swing between two approaches: those which emphasize the *determinacy* of information (Sebeok 1978, 1981, 1991; Sharov 1992, 2010) and those who emphasize its *indeterminacy* (Hediger 1981; Sebeok 1978, 1991; Hoffmeyer 1996a, 2008; Brier 2003, 2008). However, in the context of biosemiotics, both the 'determinacy' position and the 'indeterminacy' position should not be understood in the typical sense i.e. determinacy as being framed by linear-cause effect relationships, devoid of subjectivity, while indeterminacy as being grounded in non-linear complex relationships, rich in subjectivity. In biosemiotics, these positions do not adhere to extreme determinacy or indeterminacy[1] and should both be taken as variants of the common interest the field bears for meaning-rich communications.

Biosemiotic 'determinacy' – on functional information

Those who have taken sides with the 'determinacy' aspect of information include Sebeok (1978, 1981, 1991) and Sharov (1992, 2010). In a strikingly cybernetic fashion, Sebeok explicitly links communication with its capability to reduce entropy and favour adaptation and survival with regard to living entities. In his 1991 essay on 'Communication' Sebeok claimed that communication is a criterial attribute of life as it reduces the disorganizing effects of the Second Law of Thermodynamics (1991: 22). He argues that communication effectively canalizes energy, decreases *entropy*, favours the emergence of order, and establishes bonds and creates the conditions for the emergence and evolution of life. In short, Sebeok's claim that communication decreases entropy and favours the emergence of life and evolution, suggests a degree of functionalism that is much in line with cybernetics' understanding of communication and information. That is, communication, when successful, plays a role in 'controlling' the development and evolution of living beings.

A good example of how communications exercise 'control' onto an ecosystem is brought by Wilden (1980). Take a red and brown species of moth in a red-coloured environment that is preyed upon by a predator who can distinguish colours. The communication in question takes place between the moths and the predator. When a sufficient number of moths manage to camouflage themselves in a red environment by turning red, then the communication is successful (for the moth species, and in the long term, for the predator too, see below). Now, posit that the predator becomes more skilled in recognizing colours and is capable of recognizing subtle nuances of red. If the moth species does not develop more complex colours for camouflage (in other words, if it does not perform effective communication strategies for self-preservation), the predators will quickly eliminate the moths and, once these are extinct, the predators will starve and hence eliminate their own species too, hence the control function that communication bears on the survival of species.

It is important to note here that 'control' needs not be construed with the ideological and instrumental notion of 'technocratic management' and technological oppression, but as the active effort of a living system to attain and maintain a state of organization or, in other words, as goal-seeking. This claim, a cornerstone of Sebeokean semiotics, demonstrates Sebeok's fundamental adherence to a first order cybernetic view of organisms as control systems regulated by communications and functional information. However, Sleigh notes that (2007: 173) 'despite using the language of cybernetics, Sebeok did not cite Wiener or Shannon in his 1968 collection [on animal communication]'. Still, one can deduce that his concept of thermodynamic entropy is strictly related to the concept of information if one (briefly) considers the history of the term, illustrated as follows.

Classical thermodynamics (lead by the study of steam engines in the nineteenth century) explained that when a mechanical system performs activity (or work) part of the useful energy that it possesses is transformed (or dissipated) in heat energy through friction. This irreversible process of the transformation of usable energy into unusable energy was expressed by the Second Law of Thermodynamics according to which, with time, systems end up in an unproductive, disorderly state. Such a state is described as entropy. When entropy reaches its maximum level and then remains constant, the system terminates its spontaneous activity. It is therefore understandable how the concept of entropy became popular beyond the discipline of physics in which it originated. As Thompson (cited in Clarke 2002: 21) explains, it became a synonym for melancholy reflections on the devolution of the biological and the human. Entropy in fact became widely deployed both in its intuitive and counter-intuitive mathematical sense in arts and literatures as well as chemistry, information theory and, of course, cybernetics. The development of entropy within information theory and cybernetics was aided by the work of Austrian physicist Ludwig Boltzmann who integrated into statistics the concept of thermal entropy. He thus framed entropy as a statistical measure of disorder. Concentrating on reflections on probable or improbable states of the systems in question, Boltzmann postulated an extension of the concept of entropy (on the basis of probability) to systems that have nothing to do with heat engines (Clarke 2002: 24), as for example information systems. Notably, information theory was the first discipline that came to dominate the mathematical conception of thermal entropy to express information as a measure of one's freedom of choice when one selects a message (Shannon and Weaver 1949: 10). In fact, when, in a communication process, the message is selected, entropy decreases and the communication can finally proceed, thus reducing the indeterminacy of the system. Therefore, the alignment of entropy *to* information *in* information theory *seems* to contradict the negative value that entropy bears in thermodynamics and seems rather to hint at the generative, order-creating potential of information. One in fact can note that if, in a thermodynamic system, entropy increases and favours disorganization, in an information system entropy decreases and the result is the strengthening of the organization of the system, or, when the argument is transposed onto cybernetics, the very emergence of it. In fact, this new concept of 'emergence of a system following a decrease of entropy' was appropriated by first order cyberneticians such as Wiener (1951) and implicitly, as it should now be clear, by Sebeok too.

According to Sebeok, communication was broadly conceived upon cybernetics' functional conception of information (grounded in Shannon information): that is, an initial selection of information is necessary for a decrease of entropy and the beginning of life. Following this view, Sebeok (1991) claims that, in light of its capability of decreasing entropy, biological semiosis was the very first form of communication that gave origin to life. Sebeok indeed argued that the evolution of living beings was brought by the development of symbiotic, dynamic and self-regulatory communication systems, and that the Earth's Biosphere is a structure held together by these communication processes. Sleigh (2007: 173) agrees with this view when stating that, in the context of biology, Sebeok's approach was functionalist since he was concerned more with whether communications did the job rather than the form they took. Similarly, cybernetician Erich Jantsch (1980) holds that evolution 'kicked off' through the advent of changes in modes of communication, or 'inventions of life' such as *respiration, sexuality* and *heterotrophy* in the prokaryotes. Jantsch argued that these communicative processes (information-transfer events, as he called them in an information theory fashion) favoured the evolution of life from simple unicellular organisms into larger multicellular organisms. In other words, according to Jantsch, the evolution of life occurred through the optimization of goal-oriented, functional or pragmatic information (1980: 134). Similarly to Jantsch, Sebeok's conception of information is also a fundamentally pragmatic one. Additionally, Sebeok's argument which sees the whole Earth as a unitary system being regulated by communications, is particularly close to cybernetician James Lovelock's Gaia Theory, which holds that the whole biosphere is a giant control system regulated by communications (1979). Thus, if one looks at Sebeok as a cybernetician, one may notice how he interrogates the effectiveness of a communication process, in other words, its teleological nature: for what purposes in fact do sources formulate messages? Sebeok's answer is that messages are needed to travel because they contain information that is biologically and socially important for the organism (1991: 26), and thus necessary for survival. Thus, Sebeok's formulation of 'information' in his early version of biosemiotics is one that stresses its control function and is intended as a goal-oriented or teleological, adaptive strategy.

Similarly to Sebeok, Sharov (1992, 2010) proposes a version of functional information. In Sharov's view, sign systems have a control function, not just for the human, but also for the animal and vegetative world. He argues that the object of research of biosemiotics should not be limited to organisms but should encompass all agents, including artificial ones. This is because agents, whether learning or non-learning, have 'goal-directed programmed behavior' (2010: 1052). Sharov, perhaps provocatively, also explains that agents are always 'subjective beings' because non-learning agents (e.g. technology) are always produced by agents capable of learning (human beings). He adds that agents often outsource their functions to server agents which thus become (as also argued by McLuhan 1964) the *extensions of man*, that is, entities that have a degree of 'control' over humans, but that, since they are part (extensions) of humans, humans can in turn control. For example, take an invasive technology such as smartphones. It can be considered invasive as its compulsive use in the classroom, in the workplace, in domestic and social situations, might interfere with various aspects of life. One can argue that the smartphone technology exercises control over us, but if considering that the compulsive smartphone behaviour has been programmed into the technology itself by other human beings, then one can see how the control is effectively exercised by other human enterprises through the phone. In this sense the mobile phone would be a 'subjective being' or non-human agent.

The functions that agents possess vary according to level of organization. At a cellular level they include resource-capturing, growth, and metabolism; at an organismic level, they include eating, digestion, excretion, sensing, movement, mating, reproduction; and at a super-organism level (e.g. colonies, families, societies) they include dance, construction of nests, defence. To preserve themselves and disseminate their functions, the ensemble which Sharov calls the *pragmasphere* (2010: 1055), agents use signs or *functional information*. Sharov defines functional information as the 'set of signs that encode and *control* the functions of organisms' (2010: 1050, my italics). Sharov's mentioning of the controlling function of signs recalls an early Tartu-Moscow semiotics' conception that 'the sign systems for the collective as a whole and for the individual person serve not only as a means of communication but also as a means of control' (Ivanov 1965: 33). There is an obvious difference between Sharov's and Ivanov's conception of sign systems, in that as a semiotician associated to linguistics, Ivanov conceived signs only within the world of the human animal, whereas as a contemporary biosemiotician, Sharov conceives of signs across both human and non-human animals, in addition to technological agents. However, beyond this difference, the fundamental common point to these views is the control function of signs. This commonality underlines a view of information that emphasizes *constraints* as a means to semiotic affordances i.e. the emergence of meaningful communications. This view is even more evident in Sharov's original definition of functional information as the 'micro-state [of a system] which controls the choice of system trajectories at bifurcation points' (1992: 348). More specifically, functional information furnishes a set of limitations on the trajectories that a system can follow (through meaning), but also contributes to the safety of self-maintenance and self-reproduction of the system (1992: 361). Sharov's argument takes a firm stand on the 'affecting', framing or constraining capacity that information has in orienting and thus benefiting, the development of natural and artificial agents. Sharov's functional information inserts in biosemiotics a strong argument on the side of developmental constraints or determinacy, an argument which, as the next section shows, stands in opposition to other accounts of information that instead emphasize freedom.

Biosemiotic 'indeterminacy' – on abduction …

There are biosemioticians who, in explicitly addressing the notion of information, emphasize its indeterminacy, or its subjective aspect. These include (again) Sebeok (1978, 1991) but also Hoffmeyer and Emmeche (1991), Queiroz, Emmeche and El-Hani (2005), Hoffmeyer (1996a, 2008) and Brier (2003, 2008). Arguably, Sebeok is the only scholar in biosemiotics whose conception of communication (and information) includes, in almost equal parts, both determinacy and indeterminacy. Though Sebeok must have certainly appreciated cybernetics' firm stand on constraints and the determinacy of information, he also contends in the same essay on communication (1991) that information can be indeterminate since one can never be entirely sure about what has been originally communicated from the source and, generally, what (where) is the exact meaning of a communication. Sebeok argues that a message can yet be defined as a *selection* out of a code by a source for the purpose of communication (and thus communication bears a degree of determinism). Notwithstanding, he explains that if in an engineering system the mechanisms of selection are usually given, in biological communication many of the rules governing this act of selection are unknown (Sebeok 1991: 25). For example, compare the act of selection involved in getting the computer to display a string of text as hyperlinked, and that involved in distinguishing important sounds from non-important ones. In the first case, i.e. when writing the HTML code for creating hyperlinks, one ought to use the <a> tag as in

<a href="http://www.frogsandtoads.com">frogs and toads</a>

The computer's operating system will decipher the <a> tag in the web page as a code carrying the message 'create a hyperlink connected to the word in between the <a> tags', which in the above case is 'frogs and toads'. Hence the information present on a webpage i.e. the hyperlinked words, constitutes a selection out of a code, the HTML code.

On the other hand, in the second case, consider how the human hearing organ 'decides' which one amongst the several noises that we hear in a single instant, is a sound worthy of attention. When crossing the street, for example, we are more likely to pay attention to the noise of a car approaching rather than to the sound of the wind (which we perceive as a background noise). It is easy to see that the unconscious 'decision' to pay attention to a certain sound rather than another, is an act of selection whose rules are much fuzzier than those dictated by a code. Surely, the context of hearing (e.g. crossing the street) will play a key part in the noise-selection i.e. deciding to focus on the noise of an approaching car rather than on the noise of the wind. But how exactly context helps us to select relevant information (distinguishing the important noise from the less important one) is a fuzzy business. That is why, as Sebeok states, in living systems, the rules of selection of information are unknown. From here also comes the challenge that the hearing aid engineers face when they build appliances (the hearing aids) that mimic the complex act of selection (discrimination of sound information) that the human hearing organ is capable of performing. In fact, the hearing organ needs time to learn to discriminate relevant sounds from non-relevant ones. Hence when the hearing-impaired person wears a hearing aid for the first time, s/he will find it difficult to discriminate sounds and distinguish background noise from important sounds, as all sounds will sound important!

Hence, as Sebeok makes us notice, in living beings the definition of information as an act of selection does not involve an element of strict determinism but also a degree of indeterminacy. Sebeok's view is that information is functional (tends towards a goal), but it also rests on trust and feelings rather than conceived truth; in other words, communication is oriented by a goal which is fuzzy and only broadly definable.

Sebeok's position on indeterminacy is a zoosemiotic one because it owes much to the studies on interspecific (e.g. human and non-human animal) communications carried out by the ethologist Heini Hediger (1908–1992). Hediger is known for having investigated what he called the *Clever Hans phenomenon*. Clever Hans was a uniquely 'intelligent' horse who was believed to be capable of counting and telling the time by both his trainer and the independent commission of scientists who assessed his case in 1904 (Favareau 2010: 240). Yet the horse was later proved to simply respond to the subtle nonverbal cues transmitted to him unwittingly by his trainer. Proof of this was that the animal could not perform any of his intelligent actions in the absence of his trainer. Hediger recognized the role of nonverbal communications played out in this case and 'justified' the trainer and the committee's deception by explaining that nonverbal communication travels along a profusion of channels and is therefore often invisible. Hediger proposed the following general implication of the story of Clever Hans: that animal communication cannot be understood in isolation and must be taken in its context. This context would include the trainer's skills in training the animal, as well as his uttermost desire to be successful at giving training (since this desire would very likely reinforce the unwitting cues that are communicated to the animal), and the past experiences of both trainer and animal. This means that 'in experiments involving animals one does not work with pure unaltered animal behaviour, but always with the behaviour of the animal plus the influence of the human observer' (Hediger 1981: 244–245). This conclusion illustrates the fundamental uncertainty that delineates human-non-human animal communication, since one does not know 'how much, through the catalytic effect of man, has been manipulated into the animal' (Hediger 1981: 244). In other words, the Clever Hans effect teaches us that it is hard to tell who is 'responsible' for the message given out by a communication system, whether observed or observer, or whether sender or receiver, and whose fault it is in case of failed communication.[2] Following Hediger, one can see how the influence of the observer is one of those factors that make the information that emerges in a communicational exchange difficult to determine.

The indeterminacy of information was of course noticed by Sebeok in his essay brilliantly titled 'Looking in the destination for what should have been sought in the source' (1978). While Hediger categorizes the Clever Hans effect as a peculiar feature of interspecific communication e.g. between human and non-human animals, Sebeok instead recognized that the Clever Hans effect and, by implication, the indeterminacy of information, is a universal feature of all types of communication. Sebeok in fact affirms that the Clever Hans effect 'infects all dyadic interactions' (1979 [1978]: 87), whether human-human, human-non-human animal, or animal-computer.

Therefore, one can notice that admitting the indeterminacy of information raises questions about its reliability. How can communication be correctly interpreted so as to result in successful functionality, i.e. survival or even simple message exchange, if information is indeterminate and one can never be sure about what has been communicated from the source? Sebeok provides an answer to this question by stating that to understand communications, one has to reflect 'on the best guessing strategy' (Diaconis cited in Sebeok 1979 [1978]: 93) or, in other words, what the modern founding father of semiotics, C. S Peirce, would call *abduction*. The semiotic process of abduction has often been referred to as right-guessing (Sebeok 1983; Sebeok and Umiker-Sebeok 1981; Eco 1983, Bonfantini and Proni 1983) but, on the other hand, Peirce himself held that it would be impossible to guess the causes of a phenomenon by pure chance (i.e. by simply guessing at random). In Peirce's words guessing refers to 'an act of *insight*' (Peirce cited in Sebeok 1988 [1983]: 18]). A famous example of abduction is illustrated in an anecdote recollected by Sebeok and Umiker-Sebeok (1981: 11–16), in which Peirce himself rightly guesses without any apparent proof, which one of the waiters on the Bristol boat stole his Tiffany lever watch and overcoat. The story goes that after having asked the waiters to line up on the deck, Peirce (1929 in Sebeok and Umiker-Sebeok 1988: 11–16) examined them one by one looking for cues that might help him identify the thief. As he recollected:

> I went from one end of the row to the other, and talked a little to each one [...] about whatever he could talk about with interest, but would least expect me to bring forward, hoping that I might seem such a fool that I should be able to detect some symptom of his being the thief. When I had gone through the row I turned and walked from them, though not away, and said to myself, "Not the least scintilla of light have I got to go upon." But thereupon my other self [...] said to me, "But you simply must put your finger on the man. No Matter I have no reason, you must say whom you will think to be the thief." I made a little loop in my walk, which had not taken a minute, and as I turned toward them, all shadow of doubt had vanished.

After the abductive leap had taken place, and Peirce had gained a feeling about who the thief might have been, he had the following conversation with the detective he had hired to help him solve the case:

> Detective: What makes you think he has stolen your watch?
> Peirce: Why? [...] I have no reason whatever for thinking so; but I am entirely confident that it is so.

Hence, contrary to his detective advice (according to which the thief was another man) Peirce went to the suspect's private lodging and observed

> I saw no place in that room where the chain was likely to be, and walked through into another room. Little furniture was there beyond a double bed and a wooden trunk on the further side of the bed. I said, "now my chain is at the bottom of that trunk under the clothes: and I am going to take it..." I knelt down and fortunately found the trunk unlocked. Having thrown out all the clothes... I came upon... my chain.

This anecdote not only illustrate that a semiotician can make a great detective, but it also shows that in semiotics abduction amounts to the process of deriving strong intimations of truth without consciously knowing how these intimations occur.[3]

According to Peirce, abduction works because man has developed as part of the universe. On the other hand, in light of his studies of 'observership' in zoosemiotics, Sebeok gives a more articulated justification for abduction. In his framework, the unconscious intimations of truth that come to humans through abduction appear to be simply suggested by iconic nonverbal communications, which are captured unconsciously by a communication's destination. Thus, through the notion of abduction (and of 'observership' which comes with it – see Cobley 2011), information is yet indeterminate, but because of the presence of nonverbal communication and the human's (or even animal's) capability of guessing it correctly, such informational indeterminacy is decreased, hence the reason why Sebeok's notion of indeterminacy does not exclude a degree of determinacy.

...and on semiotic freedom and the cybersemiotic star

Among the biosemioticians who have also held an indeterminacy position on information, albeit in a more forceful manner than Sebeok, are Hoffmeyer (1996, 2008) and Brier (2008). While Sebeok approached the problem of information from the perspective of a humanist (albeit a biologically and cybernetically-informed humanist), Hoffmeyer and Brier have approached the issue of subjective information within the field of biology as a response to mechanicism and genetic reductionism. Hoffmeyer proposes the term *semiotic freedom* (1996a) as a solution to conceptions of information found in the natural sciences which typically conceive information as a discrete unit to be transferred from sender to receiver.[4] He claims that the physicalist account of information that refers to information as 'isolated facts' or 'chunks of knowledge' (Hoffmeyer 1996b: 63) and as objective, is vitiated by a logical error. For example, let us consider the analogy of receiving a receipt in the supermarket that describes the total that one has to pay for shopping: the bill certainly contains information about the individual prices of the purchased items, but it is mainly the total, that is, the *processed* information, that becomes information *relevant to us* and that we take on (Hoffmeyer 1996b: 63). This example shows that there is no such thing as objective or neutral information, since the very notion of information already presupposes its filtering, thus a pre-existing degree of meaningfulness to someone.

In this respect, Hoffmeyer clearly conceptualizes information in terms of Bateson's view of information as a 'difference which makes a difference' (2000a [1970]). Citing Immanuel Kant's statement that 'in a piece of chalk there are an infinite number of potential facts', Bateson argues that a potential fact becomes an actual fact only when this is perceived as making a difference to a living organism. For example, imagine a beach covered in pebbles and surrounded by high, muddy cliffs as is typical of the UK. To many passers-by, all the similarly-shaped pebbles on the beach will be just 'pebbles', but those aware of the geological age of the surrounding cliffs, and that the presence of mud in the cliffs indicates the presence, in ancient times, of deep sea, the beach of pebbles will turn into a beach of fossils. The 'pebble' that is slightly hollow on the inside will turn out to be a worn Ichthyosaurus vertebra whereas the 'pebble' surmounted by ribs will turn out to be a fragment of the internal cast of an Ammonite shell. That is to say that, like Kant's piece of chalk, a beach of pebbles yields an infinite amount of potential facts. But when the beach of pebbles enters the sphere of perception of the fossil-hunter, then a potential fact becomes an actual fact, and the 'pebble' becomes effectively a fossil and it turns into a reptile's bones or a mollusc's remains: that is how a potential fact has become information.

This example shows how Bateson's conceptualization implies that information does not exist in isolation, but only *in relation* to a perceiving organization. In other words, Bateson proposes to consider information in terms of the *meaningful* (and in so doing he initiates a 'semiotic turn' in cybernetics, his methodological field). Since for Hoffmeyer and Bateson, the conceptualization of information must contain a degree of meaningfulness, then it must also account for the subject for which it is itself relevant. Hoffmeyer claims that 'the unfortunate thing about the physicists' concept of 'information' is that it no longer refers to a person or to any other subject. The 'information' of the physics world is not something that 'someone' has; it is there, in the world, quite regardless of whether 'someone' is also there' (Hoffmeyer 1996b: 63). This conception is so very different from a typical semiotic formulation in which 'a sign is something which stands *to somebody* for something in some respect or capacity' (Peirce 1955a: 99, my italics). In semiotics the presence of the interpreter is the precondition for meaningful communications to occur, hence for information to emerge.

Thus, Hoffmeyer proposes a *relational* view of information because, as he argues, relation is a fundamental principle of life. He explains that phenomena such as contrast, frequency, symmetry, correspondence, relation, congruence and conformity are not easily described in terms of discrete elements or quantities if at all. They are, as Bateson noted, variables of zero dimensions and cannot be located (Bateson 2000c [1967]: 408) and yet all communicative processes in nature depend upon discontinuities of this kind (Hoffmeyer 2008c: 29). Thus Hoffmeyer's fundamental argument is that in biosemiotics (or, the semiotics of the living), it is not feasible to embrace a discrete notion of information, but rather a relational one that can account for the connectedness of natural phenomena, like, for examples, perceptions and their relation to a subject. This is why he proposes to use the expression 'semiotic freedom' instead of information, since the former term suggests more forcefully the relational or 'indeterminacy' aspect of information, or, in other words, the richness or depth of meaning that the concept can communicate. 'Logical depth', a term borrowed by Charles Bennett from IBM, expresses the number of steps in an inferential process or chain of cause and effect linking something with its probable source (Hoffmeyer 1996b: 64). Hoffmeyer states that he opted for the expression 'semiotic freedom' rather than 'depth' to save giving the (false) impression that one is dealing with a quantitative term on a par with logical depth (1996b: 66), and he concludes that information is based on *interpretation*.

However, 'interpretation' is arguably a tricky terminological choice because of its potential to be read as total indeterminacy of meaning, a conception which is understandably unwelcome in the sciences but also incorrect from a strictly semiotic point of view in the humanities. This point is elucidated in Umberto Eco's *The Limits of Interpretation* (1992), where the author explains that one should distinguish between interpretation as hermetic drift and Derrida's infinite deferral of meaning, and interpretation as Peirce's *unlimited semiosis*. Eco clarifies that in Derrida's framework, the truth can never be reached because meaning is deferred *ad infinitum*. On the other hand and in an opposing fashion, Peirce's notion of unlimited semiosis is an inferential but speculative process (e.g. based on abduction) which brings one closer to a 'true' or, at least, workable, state of knowledge. Hence it is fundamental to clarify that Hoffmeyer's notion of 'depth of meaning' should be aligned to Peirce's unlimited semiosis rather than Derrida's infinite deferral. This is to be expected, simply because Hoffmeyer regularly cites Peirce rather than poststructuralists such as Derrida with reference to the issue of interpretation. Yet, the point about the different connotations of 'interpretation' remains important. Hoffmeyer in fact does not discount that steps of semiosis could be described through principles similar to those of logical depth. Indeed, this may eventually turn out to be a necessary step because it would give 'interpretation' a more scientific valence and prevent Hoffmeyer's view of information from falling into the loophole of 'infinite deferral'. Thus a view on information based on interpretation would surely account for indeterminacy, but it would also account for a degree of determination, that is, the realistic stance inherited from Peirce's unlimited semiosis.

Similarly to Hoffmeyer (1996a), Brier develops the indeterminacy aspect of information, and takes the debate on a subject *versus* object level. In his yet insufficiently acknowledged masterpiece *Cybersemiotics: why information is not enough!* (2008) Brier argues that the objective conception of information underwriting the sciences is undermined by its inability to account for the inherently subjective aspect of information. He criticizes the 'objectivist' overtone of the concept of information as found in information theory (Shannon and Weaver 1949) and in Norbert Wiener's First Order Cybernetics (1951), but also in Bateson's more 'subjective' view of information because it is still predicated on Wiener's statistical information and because one cannot determine to whom 'the difference makes a difference' (Brier 2008: 179). In other words, Brier affirms that Bateson does not develop a theory of the observer. Brier explains how, instead, Maturana and Varela's second order cybernetic theory of autopoiesis (1980) does provide a theory of the observer and, in so doing, they reveal something important about the relativity of social concepts (2008: 182). Maturana and Varela in fact claimed that living systems do not have a purpose (e.g. survival) but 'it is the observer who puts the [living systems considered as] machines to some use' (1980: 85). In other words, in second order cybernetics, information (about the purpose of a system) is not in the observed systems, but in the observing system – for example, that the purpose of the conspicuous colouring of frog species is to discourage predators from attacking, would be a property assigned to the frogs by the herpetologists. It is in this sense that information (in this case, about the purpose of the frogs' colouring) is *constructed* by a system's observer (the observing scientists).

But according to Brier, this important revelation aside, Maturana and Varela's constructivist view of information does not explain the rigid constraints that physical things place on our construction of 'objects' in the world. The conclusions to be drawn from Brier's critique of information are that the concept of information should not be simply objectivist or discrete as in First Order Cybernetics, nor entirely constructionist as in second order cybernetics, but must be somewhere in between naïve objectivism and radical subjectivism, along the line of Peirce's semiotics. Also, Brier contends that social systems theorist Luhmann, who extended cybernetics to the study of human social systems, also failed to account for qualities and emotions in his communication theory (Brier 2008: 240).

In light of this critique, Brier proposes a model of communications and information, illustrated in the shape of a 'cybersemiotic star' (2003). The star is a diagram illustrating how human beings' knowledge systems can be mapped over four ontological aspects: life, consciousness, meaning and energy (2008: 361) developed from a general area of social semiotic interaction. In this perspective, human communication is embodied and biologically situated (life); it also has a conscious experiential and intentional aspect (first-person consciousness); the subject's consciousness is situated in cultural practice (meaning) through a shared language; lastly, it is environmentally situated (energy) in a universe that is partly independent of our perception of it. Many human diseases can be used to illustrate the workings of the semiotic star, for instance, alcoholism. In fact, alcoholism has a pure physical-chemical aspect about metabolism (energy); it rests on a biological aspect (life) as most living beings are attracted to the state of being drunk (monkeys and birds are attracted to overripe fruit); it bears a psychological experiential aspect of relief from stress, duties and ethics (consciousness); finally, the condition of alcoholism is culturally situated in society, which dictates how one ought to behave when drunk (meaning) but which also regulates drunken behaviour in private (for example, in Muslim culture where the consumption of alcohol is not allowed).

In this context, information is a concept that stands its grounds only when complemented by other levels of knowledge and experience such as *firstness* (qualia), *secondness* (causality), *information* (or quasi-semiotics), *biological communication* (pertains to all living beings) and *cultural paradigms* (that pertain to humans only). The innovative aspect of Brier's synthesis is certainly the insertion of *qualities* – e.g. *qualia* or qualisigns such as the sense or redness or sweetness – in a scientific communicational framework and thus the elevation of *qualia* to a status of reality ontologically at the same level of atoms, energy, statistical information and human language, though they are not researchable (quantifiable) in the same way.

Conclusion

Within the broad field of contemporary semiotics, particularly in biosemiotics, accounts of information swing between *determinacy* and *indeterminacy*. Those who have emphasized the determinacy of information include Sebeok (1978, 1981, 1991) and Sharov (1992, 2010). Sebeok explicitly links communication with its capability to reduce entropy and favour adaptation and survival with regard to living entities. Sharov, similarly, declares that information regulates the vital functions of living beings. An emphasis on 'functional information' which provides affordances-through-*constraints* is Sebeok's and Sharov's main insight here. On the other hand, those who have emphasized the indeterminacy aspect of information include Sebeok (1978, 1991) Hoffmeyer (1996a, 2008) and Brier (2003, 2008). Sebeok claims that the content of a communication is always a best guess inference due to the abductive nature of information. Hoffmeyer criticizes the physicalist notion of information in favour of Bateson's milder view of information as 'a difference which makes a difference' (2000b [1970]: 459), and proposes to substitute the term 'information' with the expression 'semiotic freedom' and 'depth of meaning'. Brier affirms that the overly objectivist notion of cybernetic information is not enough to account for first-person experience, and proposes a cybernetic and semiotic (cybersemiotic) framework for information that includes Peirce's qualisigns, or feelings. These approaches bear a common point: they make Peircean *concepts* central (Sebeok refers to Peirce's *abduction*, Hoffmeyer, through Bateson, refers to *relation*, and Brier refers to *qualia*) to an *agentive* conception of communication and information. Indeed, in light of the fact that information can only be conceived in relation to a perceiving organization hence in relation to agency, and within a specific functional-pragmatic context, the expression 'semiotic information' nearly comes out as an oxymoron.

It might be worth noting how Cobley argues that there is a general tendency to over-emphasize 'agency' in biosemiotics, a move that needs to be approached with caution (2010: 225) due to the consequences that the term may cause when translated across the sciences and the humanities. In fact, whereas the sciences struggle to achieve a conceptualization of 'agency', the study of culture in the humanities 'already has agency in bucketloads – indeed, it has more than it knows what to do with' (Cobley 2010: 241). One may argue that the obsession with agency will constitute a problem for the humanities only if agency continues to be intended as a strictly human phenomenon. For example, the core feminist proposition according to which gender is entirely divorced from biological sex appears to be based on a mechanistic (hence reductive) understanding of biological agency, one which fails to account for semiotic freedom. Hoffmeyer and Brier instead teach us that agency is a precondition of living nature, before becoming the province of the human animal, while Sharov teaches us that it may include not just natural but also artificial agents (in light of the fact that non-learning artificial agents are always created by a learning human agent). With his understanding of information which equally sits on both side of determinacy and inderminacy, Sebeok has taught us that information, and by extension, agency, should be carefully considered within the remits of both ecological constraints and semiotic affordances. As Cobley (2010: 227) puts it, biosemiotics should really try to steer 'a path between over-interpretation and reductionism'. That is the reason why, perhaps, biosemiotics should not get rid of the concept of information just yet.

Notes

1 Exception has to be made for a version of biosemiotics known as code biology which appears to be closer to a fuller 'determinacy' of information. According to its key exponent, Barbieri (2010: 756) code biology is concerned with 'the study of codes in living systems' because organic codes (e.g. the genetic code) have shaped the history of life on Earth. Indeed, for Barbieri life is based on the two fundamental processes of copying and coding – copying generates organic information, whereas coding generates organic meaning (Barbieri 2013). As Marcoš and Cvrčková (2013) explain, for Barbieri, semiotics is completely decipherable in scientific terms provided that the codes are known. However 'to model life as a hierarchy of codes [...] is a very catchy and respectful idea yet we feel that modelling living processes as a deterministic program-run machine (like a computer) belongs to physiology rather than to semiotics – and physiology can do without the concept of meaning' (Marcoš and Cvrčková 2013). Hence they observe that the view of meaning put forth by code biology is a reduction and is comparable to Shannon's treatment of information (see Chapter 4). The strict affiliation of code biology to unmediated information theory rather than semiotics is the reason why code biology is not being treated in the body of the current chapter.
2 For example, the common reaction to the misunderstandings which can occur while communicating with hard of hearing people who use hearing aids, is 'You misunderstood – are you not wearing your hearing aids at the moment?' This insensitive yet unfortunately common reaction stems from the naïve assumption that the responsibility for successful communication (i.e. understanding of speech) rests solely with the destination of the communication (the hard of hearing person). But as the Clever Hans effect shows, the whole communicational context, including the communicative skills and intentions of the person starting the conversation, is responsible for any occurred misunderstanding.
3 In semiotics, the concept of abduction has been explored in the light of right-guessing (Sebeok 1983; Sebeok and Umiker-Sebeok 1981; Eco 1983; Bonfantini and Proni 1983). Peirce himself defines abduction as a 'singular guessing instinct or theory of why it is that people so often guess right' (Sebeok and Umiker-Sebeok 1981: 16) and speaks of abduction as 'a process which I am utterly unable to control and consequently unable to criticize' (1955b: 303). However, abduction is not to be understood as some sort of magic intuition, as Peirce himself said, it would be impossible to guess the causes of a phenomenon by pure chance. In his philosophical framework, abduction is a type of inference, along the line of deduction or induction, but while deduction and induction-based enquiry pursues objective truth, abduction-based inquiry pursues possible or hypothetical truths. In fact, in abduction, one notes a resemblance between two different classes of objects and speculates on the reason why such similarity is the case (e.g. if the beans on the table are white, and a bag in the corner of the room contains white beans, then it is hypothetically inferred that the beans on the table most likely come from the bag in the corner). In general, abduction is about inferring the circumstances that have caused such resemblance, or more generally, about finding the cause of an effect. It should not be surprising that a field where abductive reasoning is a common method of enquiry is that of crime investigation. However, because of the hypothetical nature of abductive inference (guessing the circumstances of an event that is now past and cannot be directly observed), abduction can also be 'wrong' and therefore fallible. That is why, in a strictly philosophical fashion, in crime investigation one ought to speak of abduction, rather than deduction, when guessing the circumstances of a crime, at least up to the point at which evidence is verified (e.g. when the culprit confesses the crime).
4 An example of biological view based on a Shannonian understanding of biological information is Dawkins' theory of memes (1976), but see also Chapter 24.

Further reading

S. Brier and C. Joslyn edited a useful special issue on information in the *Journal of Biosemiotics* (*Biosemiotics*, 6(1), 2013) which covers different and contrasting approaches to information in biology and semiotics. S. Cannizzaro, 'Where did Information go? Reflections on the Logical Status of Information in a Cybernetic and Semiotic Perspective', (*Biosemiotics*, 6(1):

105–123, 2013) is an article in this special issue which investigates information from the perspective of semiotic philosophy, cybernetics and systems theory. T. Deacon, 'Information' in D. Favareau, P. Cobley and K. Kull (eds.) *A more developed sign: interpreting the work of Jesper Hoffmeyer* (Tartu: Tartu University Press, 2012) develops the notion of information proposed by leading biosemiotician Jesper Hoffmeyer.

References

Barbieri, M. (2010 [2008]) 'Biosemiotics: a new understanding of life', in D. Favareau (ed.) *Essential readings in biosemiotics*, Dordrecht, London and New York: Springer, pp. 751 – 795.

Barbieri, M. (2013) 'The paradigms of biology', *Biosemiotics* 6(1): 35–59.

Bateson, G. (2000a [1972]) *Steps to an ecology of mind,* Chicago and London: University of Chicago Press.

Bateson, G. (2000b [1970]) 'Form, substance, and difference', in *Steps to an ecology of mind*, New York: Ballantine, pp 454–471.

Bateson, G. (2000c [1967]) 'Cybernetic explanation', in *Steps to an ecology of mind*, New York: Ballantine, pp. 405–416.

Bonfantini, M. and Proni, P. (1988 [1983]) 'To guess or not to guess?' in T. A. Sebeok and U. Eco (eds.) *The sign of Three: Dupin, Holmes and Peirce*, Bloomington, IN: Indiana University Press, pp. 119–134.

Brier, S. (2003) 'The cybersemiotic model of communication: an evolutionary view on the threshold between semiosis and informational exchange', *TripleC* 1(1): 71–94.

Brier, S. (2008) *Cybersemiotics: why information is not enough!* Toronto: University of Toronto Press.

Clarke, B. (2002) 'From thermodynamics to virtuality', in B. Clarke and L. Henderson (eds.) *From energy to information: representation in science and technology, art and literature.* Stanford, CA: Stanford University Press, pp. 17–34.

Cobley, P. (2010) 'The cultural implications of biosemiotics', *Biosemiotics* 3 (2): 225–244.

Cobley, P. (2011) 'Observership: the view from semiotics', in T. Thellefsen, B. Sørensen, P. Cobley (eds.) *From first to third via cybersemiotics. A Festschrift honouring Professor Søren Brier on the occasion of his 60th Birthday.* Available at http://samples.pubhub.dk/9788770719964.pdf [accessed on 02/07/2012].

Dawkins, Richard (2006 [1976]) 'Memes: the new replicators', in *The selfish gene*. Oxford, New York: Oxford University Press, pp. 189–201.

Eco, U. (1988 [1983]) 'Horns, hooves, insteps: some hypotheses on the three types of abduction', in T. A. Sebeok and U. Eco (eds.) *The sign of three: Dupin, Holmes and Peirce*. Bloomington, IN: Indiana University Press, 198–220.

Eco, U. (1992) 'Unlimited semiosis and drift', in *The Limits of Interpretation*. Bloomington, IN: Indiana University Press, pp. 23–43.

Favareau, D. (2010) 'Introduction and commentary: Heine K. P. Hediger', in D. Favareau (ed.) *Essential readings in biosemiotics*. Dordrecht, London and New York: Springer, pp. 237–240.

Hediger, H. K. P. (2010 [1981]) 'The Clever Hans phenomenon from an animal psychologist's point of view', in D. Favareau (ed.) *Essential readings in biosemiotics*, Dordrecht, London and New York: Springer.

Hoffmeyer, J. (1996a) *Signs of meaning in the universe*, Bloomington, IN: Indiana University Press.

Hoffmeyer, J. (1996b) 'On the sensory universe of creatures: the liberation of the semiosphere', in *Signs of meaning in the universe*, Bloomington and Indianapolis, IN: Indiana University Press, pp. 52–67.

Hoffmeyer, J. (2008) 'From thing to relation. On Bateson's bioanthropology', in J. Hoffmeyer (ed.) *A legacy for living systems: Gregory Bateson as precursor to biosemiotics. Series biosemiotics*, Vol. 2. Dordrecht and London: Springer.

Hoffmeyer J. and Emmeche C. (1991) 'Code-duality and the semiotics of nature', in M. Anderson and F. Merrell (eds.) *On semiotic modelling*, Berlin: Mouton de Gruyter.

Ivanov, V. V. (1977 [1965]) 'The role of semiotics in the cybernetic study of man and collective', in D. P. Lucid (ed.) *soviet Semiotics: an anthology*, Baltimore, MD and London: Johns Hopkins University Press.

Jantsch, E. (1980) 'The inventions of the microevolution of life', in *The self-organising universe: scientific and human implications of the emerging paradigm of evolution*, New York: Pergamon Press.

Kull, K., Deacon, T., Emmeche, C., Hoffmeyer, J., Stjernfelt, F. (2009). Theses on Biosemiotics: prolegomena to a theoretical biology. *Biological theory,* 4(2): 167–173.

Lovelock, J. (1979) 'Cybernetics', in *Gaia: a new look at life on Earth*. New York: Oxford University Press, pp. 48–63.

McLuhan, M. 1964. *Understanding Media. The extensions of man*. London : Routledge & Kegan Paul.

Marcoš, A. and Cvrčková, F. (2013) 'The meaning of information, code… and meaning', *Biosemiotics* 6(1): 61–75.

Maturana, H. and Varela, F. (1980) *Autopoiesis and cognition: the realisation of the living*, Boston, MA: Riedel, pp. 73–95.

Peirce, C. S. (1955a [1897–1903]) 'Logic as semiotic: The theory of signs', in J. Buchler (ed.) *Philosophical writings of Peirce*. New York: Dover, pp. 98–119.

Peirce, C. S. (1955b [1891–1902]) 'Perceptual judgments', in J. Buchler (ed.) *Philosophical writings of Peirce*. New York: Dover, pp. 302–305.

Peirce, C. S. (1992 [1867–1893]) Deduction, induction and hypothesis', in N. Houser and C. J. W. Kloesel (eds.) *The essential Peirce, selected philosophical writings, Vol. 1*. Bloomington and Indianapolis, IN: Indiana University Press.

Queiroz, J., Emmeche, C., and El-Hani, C. N. (2005) 'Information and semiosis in living systems: a semiotic approach', available at http://www.library.utoronto.ca/see/SEED/Vol5-1/Queiroz_Emmeche_El-Hani.htm [accessed on 11/07/2014].

Sebeok. T. A. (1979 [1978]) 'Looking in the destination for what should have been sought in the source', in *The sign and its masters*, Austin, TX: University of Texas Press.

Sebeok, T. A. (1981) 'The ultimate enigma of 'Clever Hans': the union of nature and culture', in T. A. Sebeok and R. Rosenthal (eds.) *The Clever Hans phenomenon: communication with horses, whales, dolphins, apes and people*. New York: New York Academy of Sciences.

Sebeok, T. A. (1988 [1983]) 'One, two, three Spells U B E R T Y', in U. Eco and T. A. Sebeok (eds.) *The sign of three: Dupin, Holmes, Peirce*. Bloomington, IN: Indiana University Press.

Sebeok T. A. (1991) 'Communication', in *A sign is just a sign. Advances in semiotics*, Bloomington, IN: Indiana University Press.

Sebeok, T. A. and Umiker-Sebeok, J. (1981) ''You know my method': a juxtaposition of Charles S. Peirce and Sherlock Holmes', in T. A. Sebeok (ed.) *The play of musement*, Bloomington, IN: Indiana University Press, pp. 11–54. Also available at http://www.visual-memory.co.uk/b_resources/abduction.html [accessed on 11/07/2014].

Shannon, C. and Weaver, W. (1949) 'Recent contributions to the mathematical theory of communication', in *The mathematical theory of communication*, Urbana, IL: University of Illinois Press, pp. 3–28.

Sharov, A. A. (1992) 'Biosemiotics: functional-evolutionary approach to the analysis of the sense of information', in T. A. Sebeok and J. Umiker-Sebeok (eds). *Biosemiotics. The semiotic web 1991*. New York: Mouton de Gruyter.

Sharov, A.A. (2010) 'Functional information: towards synthesis of biosemiotics and cybernetics', *Entropy* 12(5): 1050–1070.

Sleigh, C. (2007) 'The Macy meanings of meaning', in *Six legs better: a cultural history of myrmecology*, Baltimore, MD and London: Johns Hopkins University Press, pp. 167–189.

Wiener, N. (1951) *The human use of human beings*, London: Free Association, pp. 1–20.

Wilden, A. (1980) 'Epistemology and ecology', in *System and structure: essays in communication and exchange*. London: Tavistock Publications, pp. 202–229.

25

THE PHILOSOPHY OF COMMUNICATION AND INFORMATION

Ulrich Stegmann

Introduction

What is the relation between communication and information? At first glance, the answer seems straightforward. Communication occurs when a sender conveys information to a receiver. And information is what is being conveyed by a sender to a receiver. This is how human language, a paradigmatic communication system, appears to work. You ask your friend for the time and are told that it is 4 pm. It is natural to think that this is an instance of communication *because* your friend conveyed to you the information that it is 4 pm. The natural answer carries a long way, but not all the way.

This chapter discusses four issues that are central to our current understanding of communication and its relation to information. The first issue concerns the nature of communication. What is communication? The second issue is communication as a possibly distinguishing feature of humans. What, if anything, is communication in non-human animals? The third topic concerns the dynamics of communication. How can communication systems arise and how can they be maintained? The last issue is the relation between information and communication. How important is information to communication?

What is communication?

Some of the most influential views about the nature of communication originated from thinking about one particular communication system, human language. Philosophers of language are particularly active in attempting to determine the nature and mechanisms of linguistic communication. They commonly distinguish between the code model and the inferential model of communication. Some authors add two further accounts of communication, the signaling model and the extended senses model.

According to the code model, physical signals (lines on paper, sounds, and so on) are associated with distinct thoughts. A group of signals and their associated thoughts constitute a code. The code is shared between speakers and hearers. When a speaker intends to communicate her thought to a hearer, she first determines which physical signal is associated with her thought (encoding) and then sends that signal to the hearer. The hearer perceives

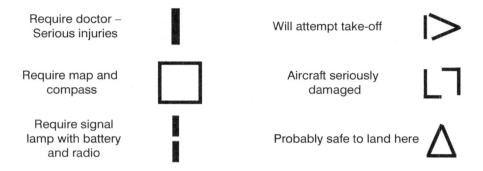

Figure 25.1 Some signals from the international ground/air emergency code

only the physical signal. But he can retrieve the speaker's thought by determining which thought the code assigns to the signal he receives (decoding). The gist of the code model can be illustrated with conventional codes.

Suppose the captain of a stranded ship wants to communicate to a rescue aircraft that *it is probably safe to land here*. Luckily she remembers the international ground/air emergency code. The code has a symbol with precisely that meaning (Δ, Figure 25.1). So she and her crew dig a Δ-shaped system of ditches in the sand. The aircraft pilot perceives only the shape in the sand. Yet, in virtue of consulting the same code, he retrieves the captain's belief that *it is probably safe to land here*. Communication has occurred.

The code model has informed much theorizing about human verbal communication. Until well into the twentieth century, many scholars regarded spoken and written words as signals that are associated with specific thoughts. Speakers convey their thoughts by putting them into words and hearers apply a shared code to the speakers' utterances in order to retrieve the thoughts. The model is therefore very close to the intuitive view of communication sketched at the beginning. Communication occurs when a sender conveys a piece of information (meaning or thought) to a sender, and information is what is being conveyed. The code model adds to this view a claim about *how* the information is conveyed. Information is conveyed by means of a correspondence rule that assigns discrete meanings to physical signals (the code). Semioticians like Ferdinand Saussure (1916) sought to establish this account as a general theory of communication. The code model also underpinned important strands within modern philosophy of language (compositional theories of meaning) and linguistics (generative semantics).

The code model has a noteworthy consequence. It implies that language comprehension involves no more than recovering the linguistic meaning of a sentence (Bach and Harnish 1979; Sperber and Wilson 1995). This implication, however, is untenable. Consider the sentence

[1] "You will be here tomorrow"

The sentence has a linguistic meaning. It means, roughly, that the hearer will be where the speaker is now, at the time of utterance, the day after the speaker utters the sentence. Nevertheless, the sentence is referentially ambiguous. If Kate utters [1] to John in his office on 4 April, then the sentence conveys the thought that John will be in his office on 5 April. But if John phones Kate from his home on 30 April, then the same sentence conveys the thought that Kate will be at John's home on 1 May. So, in order to comprehend precisely which thought

[1] conveys, the hearer must do more than merely determine (decode) its linguistic meaning. What is conveyed in these exchanges is more than what is linguistically encoded.

Moreover, suppose Kate utters [1] as John's line manager, intending to convey that John *ought* to be there. In this context, Kate takes the attitude of requesting or ordering towards [1]; uttering [1] is said to carry "illocutionary force." It is important to both John and Kate that her attitude is conveyed to John. But John will not understand that he has been given an order if all he does is to decode the sentence's linguistic meaning.

Finally, a sentence may not express the intended thought explicitly. When Kate says "Mary is always right" in an ironic tone, then that sentence implies Kate's belief that Mary is not always right (the implied thought is an "implicature"). Again, determining the sentence's linguistic meaning will not be enough for the hearer to grasp what the sentence conveys.

Many philosophers of language agree that these limitations render the simple code model inadequate as an account of human verbal communication. In response, many pragmatists seek to add a separate, pragmatic level of decoding. It remains controversial, however, whether rules of pragmatic interpretation can save the code model (Sperber and Wilson 1995). Let us now turn to the inferential account of communication.

According to the inferential model, the crucial elements in communication are intentions and inferences. The speaker has a thought she wants to convey and intends the hearer to figure it out. In human verbal communication, she provides evidence for her thought by uttering a sentence. The hearer tries to infer the speaker's thought by attending to her utterance, its contexts, and certain rules of conversation. Communication has occurred if he succeeds in inferring the speaker's thought.

Inferential models originated with a seminal paper by Grice (1957). Grice focused on the speaker's intention to convey something by uttering a sentence. He asked: under what conditions does the speaker "mean" something by making an utterance? According to Grice, a speaker S means something by uttering x if and only if S intends

a x to produce a certain response in a certain audience A,
b A to recognize S's intention (a)
c A's recognition of S's intention (a) to function as at least part of A's reason for A's response r.[1]

Suppose Kate wants to convey to John her belief that birds can fly and so she says "birds can fly." Kate intends (a) the sounds of "birds can fly" to produce in John the belief that birds can fly, (b) John to recognize her intention, and (c) John's recognition of her intention to be part of John's reasons for believing that birds can fly. Here the speaker-meaning of the sentence "birds can fly" matches its linguistic meaning. But the two can come apart. If Kate says ironically to John "Mary is always right," then she intends John to believe the opposite of the sentence's linguistic meaning.

For our purposes the main point of Grice's account of speaker-meaning is twofold. First, his account is widely taken as an account of communication. It is concerned with utterances, which are paradigmatic vehicles of human communication. Crucially, the account specifies the conditions under which utterances manage the feat of getting the hearer to entertain the speaker's thought. Second, grasping the speaker's thought relies on the hearer's inferential abilities. It relies in particular on the hearer's ability to infer the speaker's intention to convey a thought by employing her utterance as a piece of evidence.

Shortcomings of Grice's original analysis prompted many revisions (e.g. Bach and Harnish 1979; Avramides 1989). An influential account indebted to, but clearly distinct from, Grice's analysis is relevance theory (Sperber and Wilson 1995; Carston 2002). Relevance theory seeks to address the worry that understanding is often rapid and does not require a self-conscious process of inferential reasoning. Relevance theorists argue that understanding utterances is a sub-personal, computational process, rather than a high-level cognitive activity.

Human linguistic communication is now often construed along broadly Gricean lines. Contemporary pragmatists regard human verbal communication as involving features of both the code and the inferential model. There is, however, a third view of the nature of communication.

The code and inferential models can be seen as focusing too much on the speaker's mental states (Green 2007). On the inferential model, for instance, the route to entertaining Kate's thought that birds can fly goes through John's inferring that Kate *wants* him to believe that birds can fly. On the code model, John determines which *thoughts* are associated with Kate's utterance. Some philosophers emphasize that communication is less about gaining access to the speaker's mental states and more about gaining access to the speaker's perceptions of the world (McDowell 1980; Millikan 2004). If Kate phones John to tell him that an important letter has arrived, John learns something about Kate's intentions or her attitude towards the letter's arrival. But more importantly, he also gains access to a state of the world he presently cannot perceive himself. The primary goal of communication is therefore to "widen each other's perceptual reach" (Green 2007, p. 10). Green characterizes this view as a third model of communication, referring to it as the "extended senses" model. It is unclear, however, whether this view constitutes a distinct account of communication or whether it merely represents a shift of emphasis (from speaker's mental states to states of the world).

Some philosophers distinguish a fourth account of communication, the signaling model (Bennett 1976; Green 2007). Since the signaling model aims to capture the ostensibly communicative interactions in non-human animals, it will be discussed in the next section.

Before turning to communication in non-human animals, it is worth noting that so far we assumed receivers to acquire the *same* thoughts as the senders. This is indeed a widely held view, although one generally accepted without much argument. Several philosophers endorse a less demanding view (e.g. Sperber and Wilson 1995; Carston 2002). On that view successful communication requires only some degree of similarity between the contents of speakers and hearers: for *A* to understand what *B* said is for *A* to grasp a proposition *similar* to the one expressed by *B*. There are several difficulties with the weaker view, however. For instance, it becomes difficult to make sense of the standard distinction between, on the one hand, saying or understanding exactly what someone said and, on the other hand, saying or understanding something similar but not identical (Cappelen and Lepore 2006).

Communication in non-human animals

This section explores the sense in which communication occurs in non-human animals. After introducing two ways of crediting animals with communicative abilities, the focus will be on the relation between animal communication and human language.

Human language takes pride of place in philosophical work on communication. Yet communication is arguably a much broader phenomenon. Biologists of all stripes agree that non-human animals can communicate. They point to the roaring contests of rival stags, the waggle dance of honey bees, and a panoply of other interactions in a wide range of species. An instance of animal communication that has attracted much attention is the alarm call system of vervet monkeys. Vervets can emit three acoustically distinct types of alarm calls in response to perceiving three classes of predators (snakes, leopards, eagles). Monkeys that have not perceived the threat but hear an alarm call respond as they would to the predator itself, e.g. run up a tree when hearing the leopard-specific alarm call. Vervets thus seem to warn one another about the presence of snakes and other predators. However, animal senders lack *intentions* to inform receivers. Even ardent defenders of the reality of animal communication admit that while senders emit signals that are meaningful and informative to receivers, there is no evidence that senders are in a psychological state of intending to inform others (e.g. Seyfarth and Cheney 2003). The lack of such intentions is problematic because it threatens to undermine the very idea of communication in animals. Recall that communication is often conceived in broadly Gricean terms, as involving a set of complex mental states, e.g. intentions to inform others and intentions for others to recognize one's intention. How can this tension be resolved?

One answer is inspired by an instrumentalist approach towards propositional attitudes. The instrumentalist approach is exemplified by Daniel Dennett's (1983) intentional stance. One takes an intentional stance towards a system if one explains and predicts its behavior by attributing to it mental states. Attributing mental states to a system can be justified simply on the basis of increasing explanatory and predictive power. Importantly, this practice is justifiable even if the system lacks the attributed mental states in any psychologically realistic sense. So, in the present context the crucial question is whether or not attributing complex Gricean intentions yields a significant epistemic pay-off. If it does, then it is reasonable to construe animals as engaging in strong, Gricean communication. Whether or not the intentions are psychologically real is irrelevant.

Another answer is to allow that communication comes in different forms and that, furthermore, animals instantiate a comparatively unsophisticated variant. Several philosophers distinguish more or less explicitly between communication in a strong, Gricean sense and communication in a weak sense, as information transfer. Animals are then regarded as engaging in the latter but not the former (Bennett 1976; McDowell 1980).

Information transfer is the core of the fourth account of communication, the signaling model. On the signaling model, animals do not need to entertain communicative intentions, nor do they need to encode thoughts or extend each other's perceptual reach. They only need behaviors that have the evolutionary function to convey information (Bennett 1976). Bennett's version of the signaling model was broadened by Green (2007). For Green signals are structures designed for transferring information, where the design may be due to evolution *or* deliberate planning. Systems communicate with one another as long as they exhibit structures designed to convey information, whether the design is a due to a natural process or human deliberation.

The signaling model of communication resonates well with the sciences. In animal behavior studies, communication is normally understood as information transfer by means of signals (Bradbury and Vehrencamp 2011). Signals are structures or behaviors that evolved in order to convey information. The roaring of stags during the mating season, for example, is taken to have evolved in order to convey information to his rivals about the sender's fighting prowess. Signals are distinguished from cues. Cues convey information without having evolved for this purpose. The amount of time a starling spends foraging on a patch informs other flock mates about how much food is left. Yet foraging time has not evolved in order to convey information about how much food is left; it is simply a function of how readily the starling finds food.

However, the signaling model is much less straightforward than the slogan "information transfer" suggests. We will look in more detail at the role of information in communication below. As we will see, the status of information is unclear and partly contentious. Here I bracket these complexities and, instead, focus on the relation between human *language* and animal communication. This topic is important because even if one accepts that animals can communicate in some sense, there are significant differences between human and animal communication. Indeed, linguistic communication was for a long time seen as the distinctive mark of humans.

Philosophers like John McDowell, Robert Brandom, and Donald Davidson stand in this tradition. They see the differences between human language and animal communication as symptomatic of a fundamental discontinuity. The discontinuity has two aspects (Bar-On 2013a). One aspect is the gulf in communication systems among humans and current animal species ("synchronic discontinuity"); another is the impossibility of a philosophically illuminating account of the emergence of human language from non-linguistic precursors ("diachronic discontinuity"). The three philosophers do not deny that, since humans evolved from animals, our linguistic abilities have precursors in the sense of there being certain stages in language evolution that differ from our present state. Human language is not a miracle, appearing fully-formed out of nowhere. But attempting to trace those precursors is to stay within the descriptive realm of the natural sciences. And such descriptions cannot do justice to our linguistic practices, which are thoroughly normative. Their normativity surfaces in the rules that render the application of words to things correct and incorrect. McDowell (1980) therefore insists that our linguistic practices figure in "the logical space of reason," which is distinct from the logical space of the natural sciences. No list of human language precursors will bridge these two spaces. Human verbal communication is not an elaboration of animal communication.

Davidson (2001) and Brandom (2009) emphasize the (purported) inability of animals to form concepts. Davidson concedes that animals respond differently to the presence and absence of external objects and to the behaviors of others. Animals can also respond to another individual's behavior as they would respond to the object itself, as seen in vervets. There is even a possibility of error. A vervet, say, might run up the tree in response to a leopard-specific alarm call, although the sender has emitted the call by mistake (what looked like a leopard from the distance turned out to be an antelope). Yet these abilities are no more than the manifestations of dispositions and habits. Animals lack concepts of phenomena like truth and belief. They consequently do not treat the sender as a subject with its own point of view about the world, a view that may be true or false. Such an ability already requires possessing a language (Davidson 2001). There is then no intelligible intermediate stage between the non-linguistic, concept-free communication of animals and linguistic communication in humans. Again, the latter is not a more elaborate version of the former. Bar-On (2013a) calls the approach of these authors "continuity skepticism."

Continuity skepticism comes under pressure from two directions. One source of pressure are certain conceptual advances in economics and evolutionary biology. Evolutionary game theory, for instance, raises the prospect of naturalizing the origin of communication systems. We will return to this topic in the next section. First we will look at the second source of pressure, i.e. the spectrum of empirical findings from linguistics and psychology.

Scientifically inclined theorists of language evolution tend to advocate a multi-component view of human language. "Human language" here refers to the internal (neural and psychological) faculty that allows humans to learn and employ culturally specific communication systems, such as Chinese or English. On the multi-component view, the human language faculty is composed of several partly independent subsystems. Each subsystem has its own neural implementation and function (e.g. Christiansen and Kirby 2003; Fitch 2010). Now, some components of the human language faculty are found in animal species, whereas others are not. We already encountered one of the missing components: the intentions on the part of senders to inform receivers (e.g. Seyfarth and Cheney 2003). Two other missing features are the possession of a large vocabulary (e.g. Fitch 2010) and, more controversially, "discrete infinity" (Hauser *et al.* 2002). Discrete infinity is the ability to construct and understand an infinite number of linguistic expressions, where the expressions are composed of a finite set of components. While animals lack these components of the human language faculty, others are present in at least some animal communication systems. One example is the ability to employ signals or expressions in order to refer to states in the environment. This is what the vervets appear to do when emitting a leopard-specific alarm call in response to a leopard (Cheney and Seyfarth 2007). Furthermore, animal receivers engage in inferences on the basis of perceiving a signal and their background knowledge (e.g. Fitch 2010). So, according to the multi-component view, there is not so great a gap between human language and the communication system that existed in the hominid lineage descending from our last common ancestor with chimpanzees. The gap was closed by piecemeal acquisition of the components that now make up the human language faculty.

Contemporary theorists of language evolution focus on the precise order in which our "proto-language" evolved from our ancestors. Some theorists argue that the evolution of sophisticated mental abilities preceded the evolution of linguistic expressions. These theorists maintain that a crucial first step was the evolution of the ability to form communicative intentions and the ability to attribute mental states to others (e.g. Fitch 2010). Recently, some philosophers have revived the hypothesis that language evolved from innate affective expressions, such as screams or sighs. On this account, fully-fledged communicative intentions were not preconditions for language evolution (Bar-On 2013b).

In conclusion, there is a remarkable overlap between animal and human communication, alongside the undeniable differences. Characterizing this overlap, and tracing possible precursors of human linguistic communication, can illuminate the nature of human language itself. This undermines radical continuity skepticism. As indicated above, the continuity skeptic comes under pressure also from theoretical advances. The next section sketches some of these advances and explores their significance for our understanding of communication.

The emergence and persistence of communication systems

Suppose you want to establish a communication system. You start performing some actions in order to convey a thought, e.g. blow a whistle to convey "come over here!" You must get the prospective receiver to interpret your action as a signal. This is easy if you can tell him what the signal is supposed to mean, because you can then rely on a pre-existing and shared communication system. But it is hard to see how you could achieve this without telling him, or without employing some alternative means of communication. So, how can a system of signs emerge in the first instance? David Lewis (1969) answered this question by appeal to rational choice theory. More recently, philosophers have turned to evolutionary games theory. Both approaches suggest that communication systems can emerge, and be maintained, without prior and explicit agreement among their users.

Consider, first, the rational choice approach. Two biologists, Nelly and Steve, aim to prove the presence of otters along a river. They first have to find footprints or other evidence at several locations and then document the evidence by taking pictures and producing some casts. Nimble Nelly searches down at the river bank whereas stout Steve remains with the bulky equipment up on the main road, delivering it to Nelly if and when needed. Since Nelly cannot document the evidence without the equipment and Steve does not know when and where to

Table 25.1 A sender-receiver game. Each of the players can choose between two strategies

Nelly's strategy Ne_1	If there is evidence, then whistle If there is no evidence, then remain silent
Nelly's strategy Ne_2	If there is evidence, then remain silent If there is no evidence, then whistle
Steve's strategy St_1	If Nelly whistles, bring her the equipment If Nelly remains silent, stay with equipment in truck
Steve's strategy St_2	If Nelly whistles, stay with equipment in truck If Nelly remains silent, bring her the equipment

deliver it, they need to coordinate their actions. Coordination is achieved by a system whereby Nelly whistles just in case she finds evidence and Steve brings the equipment just in case Nelly whistles. That is, Nelly follows strategy Ne_1 and Steve implements strategy St_1 (Table 25.1).

The combination of strategies $<Ne_1, St_1>$ benefits both participants equally: If Nelly whistles when finding evidence and Steve fetches the equipment, they can document the evidence; and if she remains silent in the absence of evidence and Steve stays away, then they keep the equipment in good shape for later use. Let us represent the positive outcome as a pay-off with the value "1" (top left cell in Table 25.2). Both suffer, however, if one of them departs from this combination of strategies. For example, if Nelly whistles when finding evidence (Ne_1), but Steve reacts by staying away with the equipment (St_2), then they cannot document the evidence. The pay-off for implementing combination $<Ne_1, St_2>$ is "0" (bottom left cell in Table 25.2). Note that the combination $<Ne_2, St_2>$ is beneficial.

Nelly and Steve implement a system in which each action always matches a state of the world, e.g. a whistle matches the presence of evidence. Moreover, the pay-off is optimal in the sense that neither participant could increase her/his pay-off by deviating from the system. The system is said to be in a so-called Nash equilibrium. Finally, it is natural to describe the whistles as having a meaning, perhaps something like "Bring the equipment over here!" Lewis called an optimal system of interactions of this kind a "signaling system." Signaling systems belong to a larger class of communicative interactions, which are known as "sender-receiver games" in rational choice theory.

Let us now ask how such a system of interactions can arise in the first place. Lewis assumed that in coordination tasks agents are instrumentally rational and choose whichever action is most beneficial to them. So Nelly and Steve might simply discuss the various combinations, discard those with zero pay-off, and choose $<Ne_1, St_1>$ because it requires whistling only occasionally (unlike $<Ne_2, St_2>$). In this case the task is solved by explicit agreement and prior communication. However, Lewis saw that prior communication is in fact unnecessary. Choosing a particular coordination equilibrium, like $<Ne_1, St_1>$, may also be down to salience, precedent, or chance. Suppose Nelly and Steve quarrel and eventually

Table 25.2 A pay-off matrix for the sender-receiver game

		Nelly's strategies	
		Ne_1	Ne_2
Steve's strategies	St_1	1	0
	St_2	0	1

Nelly storms off while Steve retreats to the equipment. Since resentful Nelly is inclined to whistle only when she finds it necessary in order to draw Steve's attention, she implements Ne_1 by habit (chance). Steve expects Nelly to let him know when to fetch the equipment and therefore decides to stay with the equipment until he hears from her (St_1). Assuming that his expectation results from previous experience with fieldwork, he implements St_1 mostly due to precedent. Consequently, our team can solve their coordination problem without first agreeing on how to coordinate their actions. Nonetheless, they still need to act in an instrumentally rational way. They must still choose actions that they believe to be in their common interest.

The key lesson to be drawn from Lewis' (1969) rational choice approach is that communication systems can arise spontaneously. Communicators do not need prior agreement about which particular signaling convention to adopt (see Chapter 12). Lewis argued, in addition, that explicit agreement is unnecessary for *maintaining* a communication system. While eliminating explicit agreement as a precondition, Lewis' solution still relies on conscious agents and rational decision-making. Some philosophers have gone further, purging rational agents from the explanation of communication. They employ evolutionary games theory to argue that communication systems can arise and be maintained through purely natural, biological processes (e.g. Huttegger 2007; Skyrms 2010). That is, the dynamics of communication systems can be fully "naturalized." The following paragraphs introduce the evolutionary games theory approach (see Chapter 13).

Suppose there are two cognitively unsophisticated organisms with innate behavioral dispositions. Senders perceive certain states of affairs and react by behaving in distinct ways. Receivers can perceive the senders' behaviors and respond with some further behavior that has equal consequences for both. In the simplest case there are two states of the world, two organisms, and two types of behavior for each organism (Table 25.3).

Suppose some senders follow strategy S_1. That is, they emit chemical substance F if they locate food but substance N as long as they do not. Other senders simply swap the substances they emit in response to the presence and absence of food (S_2). Receivers also have two choices. Some move towards the sender when perceiving F but continue searching for food as long as they perceive N (R_1). Others respond in the opposite way to the two substances (R_2). We assume that an individual's genes determine which strategy it follows.

The receiver's behavior will generate pay-offs for both the receiver and the sender (Table 25.4). We also assume that the pay-offs are always the same for both. For instance, both sender and receiver benefit from the combination of strategies S_1 and R_1. The sender emits substance F when locating food. The receiver's response, moving towards the sender, allows

Table 25.3 Sender and receiver strategies for responding to food

Sender strategy S_1	If there is food, then emit substance F If there is no food, then emit substance N
Sender strategy S_2	If there is food, then emit substance N If there is no food, then emit substance F
Receiver strategy R_1	If perceiving F, move towards sender If perceiving N, continue searching for food
Receiver strategy R_2	If perceiving F, continue searching for food If perceiving N, move towards sender

Table 25.4 A pay-off matrix for food-searching organisms

		Sender strategies	
		S_1	S_2
Receiver strategies	R_1	1	0
	R_2	0	1

them to jointly process the food for consumption (pay-off = 1, top left cell in Table 25.4). If the receiver does not approach the sender (R_2), they waste the food.

Strategy combinations $< S_1, R_1 >$ and $< S_2, R_2 >$ show how a receiver can respond appropriately to world states even if it cannot perceive that state itself and relies, instead, on the sender's behavior. Given that senders and receivers successfully coordinate their behaviors in response to states of the world, it is natural to gloss their coordination as an instance of communication by means of signals (e.g. with compound *F* meaning something like "There is food").

Let us now ask how such a system can emerge and how it can be maintained. In order to address this question we need to shift our focus from individuals to *populations*. Recall that the strategy an individual organism pursues is genetically determined. So they cannot change their strategies within their lifetime. But populations can drop or adopt strategies in the sense of decreasing or increasing the relative numbers of individuals pursuing any given strategy. The change of numbers is a consequence of how many offspring an individual with a given strategy has (we assume that individuals simply pass on their own strategy to their offspring). We assume two populations, one composed of senders and the other of receivers. Senders pursue either strategy S_1 or S_2 and receivers either R_1 or R_2.

The emergence and maintenance of communication strategies at population level are illustrated in Figure 25.2. The vertical axis represents the proportion of senders implementing strategy S_2 ("S_2-senders") as opposed to strategy S_1 ("S_1-senders"). The horizontal axis represents the proportion of receivers implementing strategy R_2 ("R_2-receivers") as opposed to strategy R_1 ("R_1-receivers"). Thus, any point in the square represents a pair of populations with a certain combination of S_1- and S_2-senders as well as R_1- and R_2-receivers. The arrows indicate the directions in which natural selection will change a given combination over evolutionary time. Suppose the population starts from somewhere near the lower right hand corner of the square, which represents a population in which most senders are S_1 and most receivers are R_2. The pay-offs for most senders and receivers are then 0 (bottom left cell in Table 25.4). Natural selection will therefore drive the two populations away from this composition on one of many possible trajectories. For illustration, consider the following two trajectories:

4 Most senders remain S_1, so that R_1-receivers will produce more offspring than R_2-receivers. In the next generation the process repeats itself. Over a few generations R_1-receivers will therefore become more frequent in the population. This process will move the system along the bottom of the horizontal axis to the left, towards $< S_1, R_1 >$. The combination of strategies $< S_1, R_1 >$ is evolutionarily stable. A combination of strategies is evolutionarily stable if natural selection drives the system towards it (starting from other combinations) and if natural selection allows the system to persist in this state.

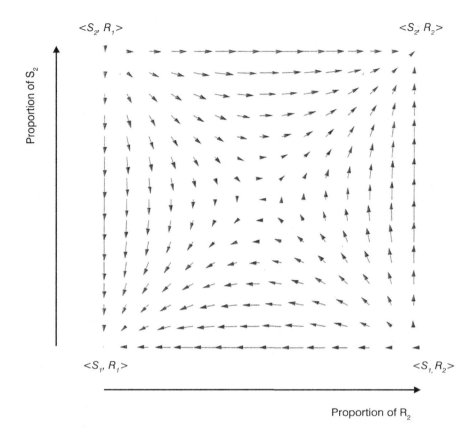

$<S_2, R_1>$ $<S_2, R_2>$

Proportion of S_2

$<S_1, R_1>$ $<S_1, R_2>$

Proportion of R_2

Figure 25.2 The evolutionary dynamics of two populations, one composed of senders and the other of receivers. Senders pursue either strategy S_1 or S_2, receivers either R_1 or R_2 (see tab. 25.3). Vertical axis: proportion of S_2-senders; horizontal axis: proportion of R_2-receivers

Source: *Signals: Evolution, Learning, & Information* by Skyrms (2010) Fig.1.1 p.11 (adapted). By permission of Oxford University Press

5 The proportion of both S_2-senders and R_1-receivers increase more or less simultaneously; this will drive the system diagonally towards the middle of the square, where half the sender population are S_1 and the other half are S_2 (likewise for receivers). Populations with these compositions are evolutionarily unstable, and selection will eventually drive them to either $< S_1, R_1 >$ or $< S_2, R_2 >$. Which of the two equilibria will eventually be reached depends on both the starting point and the initial trajectory, and both factors can have random causes.

The upshot is that communication systems can arise and persist without organisms exercising rational choice or entertaining intentions to communicate. Their signals have a kind of meaning, a meaning that is sufficient to coordinate their behaviors in response to environmental circumstances. An obvious concern is the large gap between the very simple system described here and real-world communication systems, especially human natural languages. Much formal work goes into narrowing this gap by complicating the conditions in various ways, e.g. by introducing more players or allowing for fewer signals than there are world states.

Information and communication

In exploring various aspects of communication, we helped ourselves to the notion of information whenever convenient. It is time to have a more careful look at the relation between these two phenomena. The section starts with a sketch of three notions of information pertinent to communication. The remainder of the section considers information in the signaling model, where it is meant to play a particularly central role.

According to the intuitive view of communication sketched at the beginning of this chapter, "information" denotes whatever is communicated. A large number of things have been proposed as the content of communication. The list includes propositions, thoughts, linguistic meaning, emotions, beliefs, and attitudes among others. On this view the relation between information and communication is very close. Any communication process involves a transfer of information because there is always something that is being communicated.

Pragmatists tend to use a stricter notion of information. According to Sperber and Wilson (1995), for instance, information is any thought (conceptual representation) that is presented as factual. Information excludes emotions and attitudes but is not restricted to facts or truths. This notion of information has two important consequences. First, communication does not require, and is not limited to, the transfer of information. Emotions and attitudes can also be communicated (Bach and Harnish 1979). Recall the situation in which Kate is John's line manager and she requests John to be there by uttering "You will be here tomorrow." Kate communicates not only the thought that John will be there but, in addition, the attitude she takes towards her thought. Second, to the extent that information is transferred, both truths and falsities can be communicated (Sperber and Wilson 1995). If John comes to believe that the Earth is flat on the basis of Kate's uttering "The Earth is flat," then Kate has conveyed information to John. It does not matter that the thought is false.

A third, mathematically based notion of information is employed when using evolutionary games theory to investigate the origin and maintenance of communication systems (Skyrms 2010). Suppose a signal's occurrence makes some state more probable than it would be otherwise. For instance, dark clouds in the sky make rain more probable than a cloudless sky. The dark clouds are then informative in the sense that someone who knows about the general relation between clouds and rain can learn something from the current presence of dark clouds. They can infer that rain is more likely now. Skyrms suggests that a signal carries information about some state of the world to the extent it changes (increases or decreases) the state's probability. The more the signal changes the probability, the more information it carries. And if it does not change the probability it carries no information. Skyrms's notion of information is a particular version of probabilistic theories of natural information (Stegmann 2015).

Finally, recall that information plays a dominant role in the signaling model. Communication *consists* in evolved signals transferring information from senders to receivers. The remainder of this section therefore explores more closely the status of information within the signaling model. For this purpose we will focus on animal communication, because it is the model's primary home. In what follows I make two main points. The first is that, on closer inspection, "information transfer" turns out to be an ambiguous notion because there is no generally accepted definition of information in animal communication studies. The second point is that even within animal communication studies it is controversial whether communication amounts to information transfer at all (see Chapter 23 for information in other areas of biology).

Within animal communication studies the information concept is employed in at least four different ways (Stegmann 2013). In some contexts, carrying information is simply a matter of correlation. An example is the "waggle dance" of honey bees. Karl von Frisch discovered that certain features of the waggle dance correlate with the location of valuable resources. He also claimed that worker bees use these features in order to find the resources. In the 1970s some ethologists suggested that the recruits use the dancer's odors instead. This gave rise to a protracted and bitter dispute known as the "bee language controversy." It was fiercely contested whether or not bee recruits use the dancer's movements in order to find food. However, all sides accepted that the movements correlate with the location of resources, and all appear to have agreed that the movements carry spatial information (Munz 2005). It is therefore likely that participants of the bee language controversy understood information merely in terms of correlation. That is, a signal carries information about a state S if it correlates with S. This sense of information may be captured by probabilistic theories of natural information.

In other contexts, carrying information is construed as a receiver-dependent feature. Many authors use "information" interchangeably with what receivers come to know, what they infer, or what they predict when perceiving a signal (e.g. Seyfarth *et al.* 2010; Bradbury and Vehrencamp 2011). A signal's information content is thus equated with what receivers predict, infer, or learn from it and is therefore a receiver-dependent property. "Predictions" and "inferences" are here used in a broad sense that does not presuppose significant cognitive abilities. As a corollary, carrying information, too, becomes a receiver-dependent property. A signal carries information relative to, say, members of the same species that can predict something from it. But it does not carry information relative to a different species whose members cannot use it for predictions. In short, a signal carries information about a state S just in case a receiver can infer S from it.

Furthermore, a signal's "carrying information" is sometimes construed as being dependent not only on the presence of a receiver, but also on the way in which the receiver processes the signal. Some ethologists distinguish informational from non-informational interactions on the basis of whether or not the signal evokes in the receiver a mental representation or a "mental image" of the referent. Some referential signals, like the vervet monkey's alarm calls, are said to carry information just in case receivers infer or predict something from them by means of these internal states. Correspondingly, the term "information" is used to denote whatever a receiver's mental representations encode (e.g. Maynard Smith and Harper 2003; Seyfarth and Cheney 2003). In these contexts, a signal carries information about a state S just in case it elicits in the receiver a mental representation of S.

Finally, the idea that signals enable receivers to make predictions or acquire knowledge is often put in terms reducing the receiver's uncertainty about a state of the world (Seyfarth *et al.* 2010; Wheeler *et al.* 2011). It is natural to interpret "reduction of uncertainty" psychologically, i.e. as referring to a receiver becoming more confident or certain that a state obtains. But uncertainty is also often understood in terms of the quantities of Shannon's mathematical theory of communication. Two such quantities are "Shannon entropy" and "mutual information" (see Chapter 4). This suggests a fourth way of understanding information: a signal's information is identical with, or measured by, the value of the signal's entropy/mutual information. Correspondingly, a signal carries information about a state S just in case it has non-zero Shannon entropy/mutual information with respect to S (Halliday 1983).

In conclusion, the term "information" is used in many different ways in animal communication studies and there is no information concept that is both robust and widely accepted. Critics have seized on this fact. They argue that "information" is often ill-defined and appeals to something more abstract and elusive than notions like mechanism and function (e.g. Rendall *et al.* 2009). It has also been objected that construing communication as information transfer has troublesome methodological consequences. On the informational construal of communication, we are tempted to approach all kinds of communicative processes from the viewpoint of just one particular instance of communication, i.e. human language. Since human language is highly exceptional and sophisticated, it is not a suitable starting point (Owings and Morton 1997).

For these and other reasons some ethologists recommend abandoning the information concept (e.g. Dawkins and Krebs 1978; Owings and Morton 1997; Rendall *et al.* 2009). Signals do not convey information; they rather persuade or manipulate receivers to respond in certain ways. Information-free communication revolves around the idea that a signal can elicit a receiver response by a variety of non-informational mechanisms. For example, some primate squeaks and screams have acoustic properties that "directly" evoke attention and arousal (Rendall *et al.* 2009). Similarly, the territorial songs of birds can impact on the receiver's hormone levels and make aggressive responses more likely. Such effects do not appear to involve cognitive processes. Critics therefore find it inappropriate to describe these signals as carrying information (Owings and Morton 1997). The discussion between informational and manipulationist accounts of animal communication continues (e.g. Seyfarth *et al.* 2010).[2]

Notes

1 Here I follow Strawson's (1964) exposition.
2 I am greatly indebted to Dorit Bar-On, Casper Hansen, Simon Hutegger, Balint Kekedi, and Stephan Torre for their excellent comments. Any remaining flaws are mine.

References

Avramides, A. (1989) *Meaning and Mind: An Examination of a Gricean Account of Language,* Cambridge, MA: Bradford Books.

Bach, K. & Harnish, R. M. (1979) *Linguistic Communication and Speech Acts,* Cambridge, MA: MIT Press.

Bar-On, D. (2013a) "Expressive Communication and Continuity Skepticism," *Journal of Philosophy* 110: 293–330.

Bar-On, D. (2013b) "Origins of Meaning: Must We 'Go Gricean'?" *Mind and Language* 28: 342–75.

Bennett, J. (1976) *Linguistic Behaviour,* Cambridge: Cambridge University Press.

Bradbury, J. W. & Vehrencamp, S. L. (2011) *Principles of Animal Communication,* Sunderland, MA: Sinauer Associates.

Brandom, R. (2009) *Reason in Philosophy: Animating Ideas,* Cambridge, MA: Harvard University Press.

Cappelen, H. & Lepore, E. (2006) "Shared Content," in E. Lepore & B. Smith (eds.), *Oxford Handbook of Philosophy of Language,* Oxford: Oxford University Press,

Carston, R. (2002) *Thoughts and Utterances: The Pragmatics of Explicit Communication,* Oxford: Blackwell.

Cheney, D. L. & Seyfarth, R. M. (2007) *Baboon Metaphysics,* Chicago, IL: University of Chicago Press.

Christiansen, M. & Kirby, S. (2003) *Language Evolution,* Oxford: Oxford University Press.

Davidson, D. (2001) *Subjective, Intersubjective, Objective,* New York: Oxford University Press.

Dawkins, R. & Krebs, J. R. (1978) "Animal Signals: Information or Manipulation?" in J. R. Krebs & N. B. Davies (eds.), *Behavioural Ecology: An Evolutionary Approach,* Oxford: Blackwell, pp. 282–309.

Dennett, D. C. (1983) "Intentional Systems in Cognitive Ethology: The 'Panglossian Paradigm' defended," *The Behavioral and Brain Sciences* 6: 343–90.

Fitch, W. T. (2010) *The Evolution of Language,* Cambridge: Cambridge University Press.

Green, M. (2007) *Self-expression,* Oxford: Oxford University Press.

Grice, P. (1957) "Meaning," *The Philosophical Review* 66: 377–88.

Halliday, T. (1983) "Information and Communication," in T. Halliday & P. J. B. Slater (eds.), *Animal Behaviour, Vol. 2: Communication,* Oxford: Blackwell, pp. 43–81.

Hauser, M. D., Chomsky, N. & Fitch, W. T. (2002) "The Faculty of Language: What Is It, Who Has It, and How Did It Evolve?" *Science* 298: 1569–79.

Huttegger, S. H. (2007) "Evolution and the Explanation of Meaning," *Philosophy of Science* 74: 1–27.

Lewis, D. (1969) *Convention: A Philosophical Study,* Cambridge, MA: Harvard University Press.

Maynard Smith, J. & Harper, D. (2003) *Animal Signals,* Oxford: Oxford University Press.

McDowell, J. (1980) "Meaning, Communication, and Knowledge," in Z. van Straaten (ed.), *Philosophical Subjects: Essays Presented to P. F. Strawson,* New York: Oxford University Press, pp. 117–39.

Millikan, R. G. (2004) *The Varieties of Meaning,* Cambridge, MA: MIT Press.

Munz, T. (2005) "The Bee Battles: Karl von Frisch, Adrian Wenner and the Honey Bee Dance Language Controversy," *Journal of the History of Biology* 38: 535–70.

Owings, D. H. & Morton, E. S. (1997) "The Role of Information and Communication: An Assessment/ Management Approach," in D. H. Owings, M. D. Beecher & N. S. Thompson (eds.), *Communication. Perspectives in Ecology, Vol. 12,* New York: Plenum Press, pp. 359–90.

Rendall, D., Owren, M. J. & Ryan, M. J. (2009) "What Do Animal Signals Mean?" *Animal Behaviour* 78: 233–40.

Saussure, F. de (1916 [1983]) *Course in General Linguistics,* Eds. Charles Bally and Albert Sechehaye, London: Duckworth.

Seyfarth, R. M. & Cheney, D. L. (2003) "Signalers and Receivers in Animal Communication," *Annual Review of Psychology* 54: 145–73.

Seyfarth, R. M., Cheney, D. L., Bergman, T., Fischer, J., Zuberbühler, K. & Hammerschmidt, K. (2010) "The Central Importance of Information in Studies of Animal Communication," *Animal Behaviour* 80: 3–8.

Skyrms, B. (2010) *Signals: Evolution, Learning, and Information,* Oxford: Oxford University Press.

Sperber, D. & Wilson, D. (1995) *Relevance: Communication and Cognition,* Oxford: Blackwell.

Stegmann, U. E. (2013) "A Primer on Information and Influence in Animal Communication," in U. E. Stegmann (ed.), *Animal Communication Theory: Information and Influence,* Cambridge: Cambridge University Press, pp. 1–39.

Stegmann, U. E. (2015) "Prospects for Probabilistic Theories of Natural Information," *Erkenntnis,* 80: 869-93

Strawson, P. F. (1964) "Intention and Convention in Speech Acts," *Philosophical Review* 73: 439–60.

Wheeler, B. C., Searcy, W. A., Christiansen, M. H., Corballis, M. C., Fischer, J., Gruter, C. *et al.* (2011) "Communication," in R. Menzel & J. Fischer (eds.), *Animal Thinking: Contemporary Issues in Comparative Cognition,* Cambridge, MA: MIT Press, pp. 187–205.

PART IV

Human and semantic aspects

26

INFORMATION AND COGNITION

Fred Adams

Introduction

What is the relation between information and cognition? It is common to accept that there is a connection between information and knowledge (Adams, 2004). In order to know that Paris is on the river Seine, one needs to find that out. Finding out is having someone tell, reading in a book, finding on the internet that it is so. Hence, finding out is acquiring the information that Paris is on the river Seine. Knowing an empirical fact about the world requires information from the world about such facts. This is not in doubt (Dretske, 1981, 1983).[1]

So knowledge requires information, but do thoughts and other cognitive states themselves require information? Not, perhaps, once one has the capacity to think them, but in their origin do thoughts and other cognitive states require information? I will maintain that the answer is yes and set out to explain the difference between information and cognition.[2]

What is more, can cognition occur further down the biological scale than in just humans or higher animals? Can it descend to the level of plants or, perhaps, bacteria? After all, they too exploit information and change their behavior on the basis of information detection.

In this chapter I shall try to answer these questions and explain the relation between information and cognition. I shall show that a crucial step along the way to the answer to some of these questions is understanding the informational origin of concepts (cognitive states with meaning).

Information is necessary but not sufficient for cognition

Information is necessary for cognition because cognitive states are intentional states: they are representational and have aboutness.[3] A belief, a desire, an intention are prime examples of cognitive states. They are about the world. A belief that the world is getting warmer is about the world getting warmer. A desire for world peace is about the world being peaceful. And an intention to help one's fellow man is about helping one's fellow man.

It is sometimes said that cognition is for action.[4] So it is, but to be for action it must represent either the way the world is or the way it is not (in so far as one represents the way one wants the world to be). Hence, cognitive states are representational and have aboutness.

Intentional states (cognitive states) inherit their aboutness from their informational origins. The representations that are their constituents are formed on the basis of information they carry (were designed to carry). Information itself is intentional in the sense that it has representational aboutness. The information that *a is F* is about *a* and its *being F*. Information that the planet is warming is about the planet and its increasing average temperature (its warming). Anything which carries this information is something that has at least some degree of aboutness.[5]

Here is a quick but easy way to understand aboutness. Consider a thermometer. Thermometers register temperature. There is a law-like co-variation between the reading on the thermometer and the amount of heat in the thing being measured. So if one is taking a child's temperature, there is a correlation between the thermometer reading and the child's body temperature. Since there is a law-like co-variation in these two values, the one (reading on thermometer) can be used to learn about the other (child's body temperature) precisely because the first is *about* the second.

Indeed, for any cognitive state to be about Fs (for any actual kinds F), there must be an explanation of how that cognitive state comes to be about Fs. The best explanation we have is that the cognitive state was built using information about actual Fs. If so, the cognitive state that comes to mean F, has information about actual Fs in its origin.[6] I will say more below about the difference between being informationally about Fs and something's meaning that something is F. My view is that cognition requires states that rise to the level of meaning and above the level of carrying information only, as I shall explain (Adams & Beighley, 2013).

While information is necessary for cognition, for the reasons mentioned, it is not sufficient for cognition. When events happen in the universe their occurrence leaves a trace, a signature of their presence. That trace contains information about the events. This means that throughout the universe, information is within its very fabric. Indeed, recently the signature of the big bang origin of the expansion of the universe was detected. The events that contain and convey this information have existed and reverberated since the big bang itself (Moskowitz, 2014).

If information were sufficient for cognition, the universe itself would be a vast, immense, thinking thing. One well-known philosopher, Spinoza (Spinoza, 1985, but first published in 1677), believed something very close to this. Spinoza rejected the dualistic thinking of his predecessor Descartes. If one does not believe in an immaterial mind or God, but still believes in mind and God, then the universe itself must take on some of the roles traditionally ascribed to immaterial things. For Spinoza, God is the universe. And for Spinoza, the matter of the universe is the mind (God's mind and ours). Indeed, for Spinoza mind/matter were two aspects of the same reality. So, in the end, his view was a kind of Pantheism (everything participates in God) and Panpsychism (everything participates in mind) and Pancognitivism (everything participates in cognition). The mind was everywhere and spread throughout the fabric of the universe – since God's mind is the mental aspect of the physical world.[7]

Today, there are few followers of Spinoza's views. If it were easy to believe that information alone were sufficient for cognition, there would be many who could accept something like the Pancognitivism of Spinoza. But instead, the most common view of cognition is that it requires more than just the generation of information that comes with the occurrence of physical events. Cognition requires certain kinds of work to be done on that information, certain kinds of transformational processing to be applied before genuinely cognitive states come to be (Dretske, 1987). I'll say more about this below.

Cognition is more than information plus sensorimotor movement

There are scientists and philosophers who think that cognition (at least a kind of "basic" or "primitive" cognition) requires only information-driven movement. They sometimes call this "sensorimotor" activity directed by information. It is primarily claimed that bacteria exhibit cognition of this kind, though it is sometimes also attributed to plants (Garzón, 2007; Calvo Garzón & Keijzer, 2011).

What kinds of activity do these scientists and philosophers have in mind? Largely it is activity such as chemotaxis in bacteria (their ability to tumble toward foods and away from toxins based on information gradients in the environment). In some cases, bacteria are said to "learn" (Ben-Jacob, 2009; Shapiro, 2007). Lyon & Keijzer (2007) point out that bacteria change what they do in the future based upon what they did in the past and are thereby attributed the property of "memory." They also emphasize that bacteria utilize the ability to differentiate incoming information to guide and alter their behavior to preserve their wellbeing under changing conditions.

Why do they think this activity is cognitive? For a few reasons. First, the explanation of this behavior does indeed require the exploitation of information by the organisms. A mere mechanical or chemical or genetic explanation alone will not enable science to explain the behavior of the organisms (Shapiro, 2007). What the organisms do depends in part on their sensing information about environmental conditions and responding to environmental variation. Shapiro (2007) points out that *E-coli* have the capacity to detect the difference between glucose and lactose and turn on or off the systems internal to them that chemically process the different substances. What is more, the mechanism by which they do this can be represented as computational steps.

> The information from all these sensors feeds into a computational network that includes the *lac* operon regulatory signals so that the cell can compute the following non-trivial Boolean proposition: "IF lactose present AND glucose NOT present AND cell can synthesize active LacZ and LacY, THEN transcribe *lacZYA* from *lacP*."
>
> *(Shapiro, 2007)*

This kind of explanation rises above the level of physics alone, chemistry alone, and biology alone. It does so because it involves reference to information. So the obvious question is what is the next level of explanation going upward from biology? The next science up is typically psychology and cognition involves a type of psychological state/process that exploits information. So it is quite understandable why scientists and philosophers may believe that it is cognition that is exhibited by bacteria (or plants). Shapiro (2007) points out that this activity has led some researchers (Adler, 1966) to draw comparisons between how information is processed within bacteria and how it is processed within the human brain. In what follows, I will give my reasons for denying that it genuinely is cognition – though I admit it is behavior driven by the exploitation of information.

Cognition

So what is so special about cognition (Adams & Garrison, 2013)? Why is cognition *not* just information or information-driven behavioral change of the form found in bacteria or plants? First, let's remember that if being a conduit of information were sufficient for cognition, the whole universe would think. Despite a few proponents of this view, it seems highly implausible to most. Why? Consider a mercury thermometer. When used to take a child's temperature, it contains information about the body temperature of the child. The level of mercury rises or falls in perfect variation with the rise or fall in body temperature of the child. But the thermometer does not have any cognitive states, despite being a perfect carrier of information about the child's temperature.

What is more, even if we harness a conduit of information to a system that controls behavior, that wouldn't turn the system into a cognitive system. For example, there is a thermometer in one's heating or cooling system. That mechanism measures actual room temperature and compares it to the owner's desired temperature setting and then turns the furnace (air conditioner) on or off according to whether there is or is not a match between actual and desired temperature.

Another such system is the garage door sensor system that detects whether something is under the door. It will not allow the door to close, if something is in the way (saving lives of small children).

Lastly, in the human body there are temperature regulation systems, blood sugar regulation systems, and heart rate monitoring systems. All of these regulate bodily systems by utilizing information and controlling bodily mechanisms in light of that information. For example, in the brain there is structure in the hypothalamus that measures the ratio of sodium to calcium ions in the local fluid. This ratio is nomically correlated with body temperature (so it is a kind of thermometer). An increase in, say, calcium (and body temperature) causes an increase in transmitter substance and increase in synaptic release in the region, causing vasodilation, postural change, etc. When calcium ratio reverses (body temperature goes down), one finds the opposite reaction, vasoconstriction, shivering, posturing to preserve heat (Jones *et.al.*, 1981).

Even though all of these are cases of information-driven movement or change, none of them counts as cognition within cognitive systems. Neither heating engineers, garage door installers, nor neuroscientists consider these systems as candidates for study by departments of cognitive psychology, and for good reasons that I shall now attempt to articulate.

What can cognitive creatures do that the thermometer cannot do? Actually, there is a vast array of things. The child's mother can represent the child's temperature *as the child's temperature*. The thermometer cannot. It has no representation for the child at all. True: it is representing the temperature *of the child*. However, there is nothing on the thermometer or its reading that tells one that. Only the user knows this, not the thermometer. It slavishly represents the temperature with no care whatsoever about whose temperature it is. What is more, it has no representation for *what temperature is*. It has no concepts or understanding, as opposed to the child's mother. Of course, the child's mother had to learn these concepts during her lifetime and, importantly, her concepts were derived from information about the child (who he is) and about temperature (what it is). But the important point is that her cognitive processes *did work*[8] with the information upon which her concepts were built. Her cognitive states did not merely record the bodily temperature of the child or she would be a mere human thermometer and not a cognitive system capable of forming beliefs and thoughts about the child and his temperature.

Not only can she do this, but she can form representations about whether the child's current temperature is the same as it was an hour ago or whether it has gone up or down or stayed the same. The thermometer cannot. The thermometer is *locked in the present*. It can deliver information about what the child's temperature is *now*, but not what it was or whether it is the same or different now from the past. It has no mechanism for storing representations and dating them or comparing them to prior representations of the temperature.

While it may sound surprising to tout this as an advantage, the mom can *get it wrong*. She can misread the thermometer and believe that the child's temperature has gone down when it has not. The thermometer cannot misread the temperature. It is *nomically tied to the truth*. Normally, we would think this is a good thing and the thermometer is better off than the mom. But if we think further about this we will see otherwise.

The thermometer is locked in the present. It accurately co-varies with the temperature it contacts. So even if the child wants to trick the mom and holds the thermometer up to the light bulb when mom is out of the room, the thermometer accurately reads the temperature given off by the light bulb (it doesn't misread the child's temperature). The mom may not know this and again, she gets it wrong in thinking the child has a fever (when he just wants to stay home from school).

The mom can think about the present or maybe the future. She can plan what to do next (take the child to the doctor, re-take the temperature). She can plan far into the future (what to do later in the day, later in the week, later in life). Mere conduits of information can do none of these things. They tell us only what is happening in the *here and now*.

If the thermometer is representing the child's temperature and temperature is mean molecular kinetic energy, then the thermometer is representing the mean molecular kinetic energy of the molecules in the child's body (mouth). But the mom may know nothing about this. She is thinking only about the child's temperature. This is sometimes called "intensionality."[9] That is, a cognitive systems can represent something *a being F* and not *a being G* even if whatever is F is G (by law of nature). A mere conduit of information cannot separate out these pieces of information. Similarly, if we take a's temp and a=b, then we take b's temp. But we may not know that a=b. That is, for cognitive systems it is very important *how* something is being represented in the system – sometimes called the "vehicle" of the representation (Fodor, 1990).

Even if "a" and "b" refer to the very same person, the vehicles "a" and "b" may be different. Consider: Lois Lane knows Superman flies (*a flies*). But she does not know Clark Kent flies (*b flies*), because she does not know Superman=Clark Kent. So she doesn't use the same cognitive vehicles (in this case names) each time she thinks about this single person. Cognitive systems are more finely discriminating in *how they represent* than mere conduits of information. A surveillance camera video of Superman flying is a video of Clark Kent flying. The video is a non-cognitive record of the information captured at the scene.

Why pick these features to be the mark of cognition? Why not pick some of the things the plant scientists think make plants cognitive systems or the things bacteriologists think make bacteria cognitive systems?[10] The main reason is that the term "cognition" was introduced into the language to talk about the processes that lead to human knowledge.[11] Human knowledge involves thoughts and beliefs and reasons. These states all have the properties that I have suggested distinguish mere conduits of information from cognitive systems. So that is why I've picked this set of features to distinguish mere information processing systems from genuinely cognitive systems.

Informational origins of cognition

If we are correct so far, cognition is different from mere information processing. Computers, cell phones, plants, bacteria, and many regulatory systems of the body process information and control behavior based upon that information. Cognitive systems are different in that they utilize representational vehicles (symbols, concepts) that represent or have meaning. If there is a connection between information and cognition it is in the process by which those cognitive symbols derive their meaning from their informational origins (Skyrms, 2010). Now there are several different accounts of how this is done and I cannot go over all of them here.[12] Instead, I shall outline one account that I think captures the essential features of the connection between information and cognition. This is inspired by the work of Dretske (1987), Adams, (2003a).

As we noted earlier, a sign or signal which genuinely carries information that something is the case, cannot be false (Dretske, 1981). It cannot because information is carried by the law-like connection between properties in nature. If it is a law that fire (F) causes smoke (G), then the F – >G law cannot be broken. There is no smokeless fire, and when there is fire there is smoke. So in the forest, smoke indicates fire and carries information that there is fire because of this necessary connection. It cannot be false that smoke indicates fire (Floridi, 2005).

Oh, this is not to say that someone cannot introduce fake smoke or smoke from another source (perhaps to make a movie), but this introduces an outside source of equivocation.[13] In normal forests, the only way smoke gets there is due to fire. The animals in the forest and the human fire spotters up in their lookout towers exploit smoke as a source of information about the existence of fire.

Now given that smoke which carries information about fire cannot be false and that humans can say or think that there is smoke (but be mistaken), there clearly is an important difference between smoke and "smoke." The occurrence of the first can't be a false indicator of smoke, while the latter as a word or its corresponding thought in the mind of a believer, can be falsely tokened. I can falsely believe there is smoke (and consequently think there is fire), when there is none. Nonetheless, "smoke" can be used to mean smoke. And "fire" can be used to mean fire. And most likely the origin of these words and the thoughts that produce them, have information about what smoke is and about what fire is in their origin.

So here is the mystery. How can something which cannot be false, like smoke in a forest indicating the existence of fire, be the cognitive origin of the concept of smoke or the word "smoke," both of which can be falsely tokened? The answer must be that in going from something which carries the information that there is smoke to something which means that there is smoke, the guarantee that a symbol or sign carries information (cannot be false) becomes lost. Concepts as they occur in thoughts or are expressed in words are not guaranteed to be true or to carry information that they were designed to carry. When a sign that carries information that *a is F* is converted into a symbol that has meaning *that something is F* derived from that informational origin, something is lost. What is lost is the guarantee that the symbol, when tokened, will be true – will carry the information that the signal upon which it was formed had to carry (*that a is F*).[14]

So how does this happen? Let me change the example slightly. Suppose we want to know how a prairie dog comes to acquire the concept of a hawk (an overhead threat). The hawk's shadow on the ground carries information of its presence overhead. The shadow cannot be false. In the wild regions inhabited by prairie dogs, only hawks cast such large shadows. So the prairie dog's seeing the shadow also carries the information that there is a hawk overhead.

So far so good, but as before this is only a story about information cast by the hawk's shadow and carried by the prairie dog's visual system. How is this converted into a concept? Since the threat of predation is so real the prairie dog must become sensitive to the presence of hawks. It must develop a dedicated detector of hawks and upon such detection, must take evasive action. The most notable retreat is to dive into its den for safety.

Suppose there is a part of the prairie dog's brain that becomes this dedicated detector of hawks. And suppose this neural assembly becomes neurally recruited to cause evasive behavior when triggered. In this case, information that a hawk is overhead triggers this detection system, and when triggered the detector causes the prairie dog to dive into its hole for safety. That is, the neural state which has the biological function of being a detector of the dangerous hawk predator, comes to have the job of causing evasive behavior *because it is triggered by information of the presence of hawks.* So this neural assembly becomes the prairie dog's *hawk detector.* The reason it becomes a dedicated detector is because in virtue of its doing its job, the prairie dog survives. It gets away when there is a hawk overhead. Its job is to tell the prairie dog to run because there is a hawk. Hence, when it is tokened, what it is saying to the prairie dog is that there is a hawk. Therefore, its causal role, its function becomes set by its successful performance of its role over several real life occasions (Dretske, 1987, Chapter 4).

Now let's fast forward. Suppose it has been months or years since the prairie dog learned to spot and evade hawks by their shadows. Its hawk-detection mechanism is firmly in place and well-functioning. Now suppose that one day a child flies a kite in the area. This is the first time this happens. The kite projects a large moving shadow upon the ground from above the prairie dog. The prairie dog sees it and runs into its hole.

What has happened? Now that the detector mechanism is set with the purpose of detecting hawks via their shadows upon the ground, seeing the shadow upon the ground triggers this neural assembly. What this says to the prairie dog is that there is a hawk overhead. The prairie dog runs into its hole for safety. As it turns out on this occasion, this is a false positive. It wasn't a hawk. But the prairie dog thought that it was a hawk. It thought that it was because it couldn't tell the difference from the shadow. The shadow triggered the neural assembly whose job was to tell the prairie dog when there was a hawk present and then to cause evasive behavior. Since this very assembly is firing, what must be going through the mind of the prairie dog is that its symbol for hawk is firing and it thereby thinks there is a hawk. It is able to do this because this symbol has acquired the meaning (the function of indicating) hawk. In this case, it *means hawk* even though it does not carry the *information that there is a hawk present.* But it still means *hawk* and not kite, because, though triggered by the shadow of a kite this time, it was trained on information about actual hawks. It was recruited to become the prairie dog's concept of *hawk* (not kite).[15]

Now of course this is only one case, but the story generalizes. When the prairie dog or for that matter a human being, develops a *concept F*, it is done by recruiting neural resources for building dedicated *detectors of Fs.* These are built when these neural symbols come to *cause significant behavior because they indicate Fs.* And when the explanation of this causing is that the symbol is a dedicated *detector of Fs,* then the symbol becomes the individual's *concept of Fs* (and comes to *mean* to the individual *that there is an F*).

Now we see that something that *means F* will have its informational origin in its development on the basis of having the *cognitive function of detecting Fs by means of information that something is F.* Once formed with function and meaning fixed, then, and only then, the symbol can be tokened and *mean F* even if the tokening is *false* (even *if nothing present is in fact F*). So things with meaning (thoughts, concepts, words) can shed their informational (truth) guarantee. Their tokening no longer guarantees that they carry the information upon which they were built and the information they were designed to carry. The price of going from informational origin to meaning is that information may be *no longer guaranteed.* As I said earlier, this is indeed a loss, but a small price to pay for the freedom to be able to think about things that are not present.

In the human mind, meaning generates a cognitive freedom that mere information processors do not enjoy. We can think about what happened in the past. We can dream about what may happen in the future. And we can generate fictions that will never happen.[16]

Now returning to the earlier example, smoke in the forest cannot be falsely tokened, so it does not have a semantic content. It is a natural sign and thereby carries information but not meaning in the relevant sense. "Smoke" however does have meaning. You can think that you smell smoke and wonder where it is coming from, even if there is no smoke. This is a case of mistaken belief and a case where your thoughts do not carry information that there is indeed smoke. The connection between information (with its truth guarantee) and meaning (without this guarantee) has been cut.

Cognitive systems process information and generate symbols with meaning. Non-cognitive systems do not.[17] They remain forever locked in the present, processing information but not meaning. This is why the kinds of systems we discussed earlier that have their behavior driven by information from their environment are still not cognitive systems. Just having behavior under the control or direction of information is not sufficient for a system to be a cognitive system. To be a cognitive system is to process information to the level of semantic meaning. Such systems have symbolic structures with informational origins, yes, but they are not mere information processors. They are cognitive processors because they do things with that information that actually generates a loss of the informational guarantee that mere information processors enjoy. However, as I said, cognitive processors enjoy other advantages that more than make up for this loss.

Conclusion

In this chapter I have suggested that there is an informational origin to all concepts and meaning and have attempted to explain how that might happen. I have explained the informational origin of concepts and meaning and the difference between information and cognition.

I have explained why cognition is not merely information-driven behavioral change. Cognitive processing does work on incoming information that transforms that information and loses its guarantee of truth, but also frees the thinker to think about the past, future, and even fictional states.

I have explained why organisms such as plants and bacteria, though utilizing information in the regulation of their behavior do not qualify as cognitive systems. It is because the format of their representations do not rise to the level of symbols (thought vehicles) that attain the properties required for being conceptual structures.

Notes

1   Dretske (1981) was among the first to connect the mathematical theory of information (Shannon and Weaver, 1949) with the theory of empirical, propositional knowledge. For a nice overview of information see Floridi, L. (2005) Information. In Carl Mitcham (ed.) *Encyclopedia of Science, Technology, and Ethics (ESTE)*. Macmillan.
2   As we shall see below, one important difference is that information itself cannot be false, but thoughts and beliefs can be. This important difference has been crucial in developing a naturalized semantics, that is a theory of meaning that utilizes purely natural causes and relations (Dretske, 1981, 1987 & Fodor, 1990, Floridi, 2005).
3   "Aboutness" is a term often used in the same context as the term "intentionality." They are both referring to the representational property of mental (cognitive) states. This is the directedness of representations. Just as a photo of you is *about you* because it is *of you*, similarly a thought *about Obama* is about him because in a sense it too is *of him*. Exactly how thoughts, beliefs, and other cognitive states have this intentionality or aboutness will be explain below.
4   This is a claim made by those who believe in embodied cognition (See Semin & Smith, 2008, Shapiro, 2011).
5   I'll say more later about this degree of aboutness.
6   Here insert one's favorite view of naturalized semantics. I'm partial to that of Dretske (1981, 1987), but Fodor's (1990) is also a strong contender.
7   While it has now fallen out of favor, several philosophers have flirted with a "double-aspect" view of mind and matter, including Spinoza (1985), Roy Wood Sellars (1907, 1923, 1938), Wilfrid Sellars (1971), and at one time even Bertrand Russell (1921, 1954).

8   See Dretske, 1987 for an account of "doing work" when transforming information into concept or beliefs.

9   See Jacob (2014).

10 Lyon & Keijzer (2007) would complain that I'm stacking the deck against the plants and bacteria by picking features of cognition typical of humans and higher animals.

11 I conjecture that cognition is a natural kind and that the term "cognition" was introduced into the language to rigidly designate that kind – that is to pick out the same kind in all possible worlds (Kripke, 1980, though original lectures 1973).

12 Elsewhere, I have attempted to go through the most prominent ones. See Adams, (2003a, 2003b), Adams & Aizawa (2010).

13 The smoke would still carry information, but there would be equivocation on the informational channel because smoke now indicates fire or human tinkering.

14 To see how this story goes for animal cognition and human language, see (Adams & Beighley, 2013).

15 One might say that the prairie dog's concept is *hawk or kite* not just *hawk*. But this is not correct. The explanation of why the prairie dog ran into its hole when its concept was formed was not because a kite was overhead. Kites present no threat to prairie dogs, but hawks do.

16 See my (Adams *et al.*, 1997) for an account of the semantics of fiction.

17 For more on the difference between cognitive systems and mere information processing systems see (Adams & Garrison, 2013, and Adams & Beighley, 2013, and Skyrms, 2010).

Further readings and further issues

Skepticism and non-empirical knowledge

Empirical knowledge that Obama is president requires the information that Obama is president. On most accounts of information, a signal carries the information that p only if, given the signal that p, the probability that p is 1(Dretske, 1981; Adams, 2004). Two questions arise. First, how likely is it that the world ever cooperates sufficiently for us to receive a signal that generates this conditional probability of 1? In fact, knowledge skeptics would maintain that it never happens. We have true beliefs, and therefore survive, but know almost nothing. If not often, then empirical knowledge is much less common than we might think (if the theory connecting knowledge and information is true). Second, what about logical or mathematical knowledge? The probability of a logical truth is always 1 and virtually any signal is such that the conditional probability of the truth on the signal is 1. What is more, since always and necessarily true, logical truths do not generate information by becoming true – unlike Obama's becoming president, which does generate information. So, how do we know logical truths? It seems not by acquiring news (information) of their truth. See Kitcher (1984).

Biological scale and cognition

Is cognition something that happens only in animals? Just as there have been some scientists that think there can be cognitive processes in bacteria, there are also some who think cognition occurs in plants. For claims of support for cognition in plants see (Garzón, 2007; Calvo Garzón & Keijzer, 2011). For arguments on the other side see (Adams & Garrison, 2013).

Empty terms

We said that thoughts (concepts) get to be about things in virtue of their informational origins. A thought about Obama gets to be about him because he is in the causal history of the thought. But what about thoughts that seem to be about things that do not exist and which use names or terms that have no referent. How does one's thought about Sherlock Holmes get to be about Holmes, when there is no Holmes, or about Zeus, if there is no Zeus? How words or thoughts get to be about non-existent entities and how names without referents have meaning is one of the very interesting problems to be solved in philosophy of mind and language (see Adams, 2011, Adams & Stecker 1994 Adams *et al.*, 1997).

Embodied cognition

Most theories of cognition place it in the brain and specifically after perception and before motor areas. A new perspective on cognition says it takes place wholly across the perceptual and motor areas of the brain and is not "sandwiched" in between perception and motor areas. See Semin & Smith (2008) and Shapiro (2011) for more on this new approach to cognition. For some further evaluation of embodied cognition, see Adams (2010) and Weiskopf & Adams (2015).

Extended cognition

In addition to those who think information-driven behavioral change constitutes a kind of cognition, there are those who think an informational loop that may even extend beyond the boundaries of body and brain may constitute a cognitive process. So when you rotate a jigsaw puzzle piece to see if it fits into a spot in the puzzle, this rotation would count as a cognitive process on this view. Interestingly, if true, this would mean cognition extends beyond the boundaries of body and brain into the world. For more on the view and its defense see Clark & Chalmers (1998), Clark (2008), Menary (2010) and Rowlands (2010). For opposition see Adams & Aizawa (2008), and Rupert (2009).

Misrepresentation

I've tried to explain in this chapter how meaning arises and falsity is possible. The explanation of how this is possible was hard won in the naturalized-semantics literature. For an historical overview, see Fodor's "Semantics Wisconsin-Style" in (Fodor, 1990), and my (2003a, b).

References

Adams, F. (2003a). "The Informational Turn in Philosophy," *Minds and Machines*, 13, 471–501.
Adams, F. (2003b). "Thoughts and their Contents: Naturalized Semantics." In Warfield, T. & Stich, S. (eds.), *The Blackwell Guide to Philosophy of Mind*, Oxford: Blackwell, 143–171.
Adams, F. (2004). "Knowledge." In Floridi, L. (ed.), *The Blackwell Guide to the Philosophy of Information and Computing*, Oxford: Blackwell, 228–236.
Adams, F. (2010). "Embodied Cognition" in *Phenomenology and the Cognitive Sciences*, 9 (4) 619–628.
Adams, F. (2011). "Sweet Nothings: The Semantics, Pragmatics, and Ontology of Fiction" in Franck Lihoreau (ed.), *Truth in Fiction*, Frankfurt: Ontos Verlag publisher, pp. 119–135.
Adams, F. & Aizawa, K. (2008). *The Bounds of Cognition*. Oxford: Wiley-Blackwell.
Adams, F. & Aizawa, K. (2010). "Causal Theories of Mental Content," *Stanford Encyclopedia of Philosophy* http://plato.stanford.edu/entries/content-causal/.
Adams F. & Beighley, S. (2013). "Information, Meaning, and Animal Communication," in Ulrich Stegmann (ed.), *Animal Communication Theory: Information and Influence*, Cambridge: Cambridge University Press, pp. 399–418.
Adams, F., Fuller, G. & Stecker, R. (1997). "The Semantics of Fictional Names," *Pacific Philosophical Quarterly*, 78, 128–148.
Adams, F. & Garrison, R. (2013). "The Mark of the Cognitive," *Minds & Machines*, 23, 339–352.

Adams, F. & Stecker, R. (1994). "Vacuous Singular Terms," *Mind & Language*, 9, 387–401.

Adler, J. (1966). "Chemotaxis in bacteria," *Science*, 153, 108–716.

Ben-Jacob, E. (2009). "Learning from Bacteria about Natural Information Processing," *New York Academy of Sciences*, 1178, 78–90.

Calvo Garzón, P. & Keijzer, F.A. (2011). "Plants: Adaptive Behavior, Root Brains and Minimal Cognition," *Adaptive Behavior,* 19(3), 155–171.

Clark, A. (2008). *Supersizing the Mind: Embodiment, Action, and Cognitive Extension.* Oxford: Oxford University Press.

Clark, A. & Chalmers, D. (1998). "The Extended Mind," *Analysis*, 58, 7–19.

Dretske, F. (1981). *Knowledge and the Flow of Information.* Cambridge, MA: MIT/Bradford.

Dretske, F. (1983). "Precis of Knowledge and the Flow of Information," *Behaviorial and Brain Sciences*, 6, 55–63.

Dretske, F. (1987). *Explaining Behavior.* Cambridge, MA: MIT/Bradford.

Floridi, L. (2005) Information. In Carl Mitcham (ed.) *Encyclopedia of Science, Technology, and Ethics (ESTE).* Macmillan.

Fodor, J. (1990). *A Theory of Content and Other Essays.* Cambridge, MA: MIT/Bradford.

Garzón, F. (2007) "The Quest for Cognition in Plant Neurobiology," *Plant Signal Behavior*, 2(4), 208–211.

Jacob, P. (2014). "Intentionality," *Stanford Encyclopedia of Philosophy.* http://plato.stanford.edu/entries/information/

Jones, D.L., Veale, W.L. & Cooper, K.E. (1981). "Alterations in Body Temperature Elicited by Intrahypothalamic Administration of Tetrodotoxin, Ouabain and A23187 Ionophone in Conscious Cat," *Brain Research Bulletin*, 5, 75–80.

Kitcher, P. (1984). *The Nature of Mathematical Knowledge.* Oxford: Oxford University Press.

Kripke, S. (1980). *Naming and Necessity.* Cambridge, MA: Harvard University Press.

Lyon, P. & Keijzer, F. (2007). "The Human Stain-Why Cognitivism Can't Tell Us What Cognition is and What it Does." In B. Wallace *et al.* (eds.), *The Mind, The Body, and the World: Psychology after Cognitivism?* Exeter: Imprint Academic, pp. 132–165.

Menary, R. (2010). *The Extended Mind.* Cambridge, MA: MIT/Bradford.

Moskowitz, S. (2014). "Gravitational Waves from Big Bang Detected," *Scientific American* March 17.

Rowlands, M. (2010). *The New Science of the Mind: From Extended Mind to Embodied Phenomenology.* Cambridge, MA: MIT/Bradford.

Rupert, R. (2009). *Cognitive Systems and the Extended Mind.* Oxford: Oxford University Press.

Russell, B. (1921). *The Analysis of Mind.* London: George Allen & Unwin, Ltd.

Russell, B. (1954). *The Analysis of Matter.* New York: Dover Publications.

Sellars, R. W. (1907). "A Fourth Progression in the Relation of Mind and Body," *Psychological Review*, N.S., 315–328.

Sellars, R.W. (1923). "The Double-Knowledge Approach to the Mind-Body Problem," *Aristotelian Society Proceedings,* N.S., 23, 55–70.

Sellars, R.W. (1938). "An Analytical Approach to the Mind-Body Problem," *Philosophical Review*, 47, 461–487.

Sellars, W. (1971). "The Double-Knowledge Approach To The Mind-Body Problem." *New Scholastics*, 45, 269–289.

Semin, G. & Smith, E. (2008). *Embodied Grounding: Social, Cognitive, Affective, and Neuroscientific Approaches.* Cambridge: Cambridge University Press.

Shannon, C. & Weaver, W. (1949). *The Mathematical Theory of Communication.* Urbana, Il.: University of Illinois Press.

Shapiro, L. (2011). *Embodied Cognition.* New York: Routledge.

Shapiro, J. (2007). "Bacteria are Small but Not Stupid: Cognition, Natural Genetic Engineering and Sociobacteriology," *Studies in History and History and Philosophy of Biological and Biomedical Sciences*, 38, 807–819.

Skyrms, B. (2010). *Signals: Evolution, Learning, and Information.* Oxford: Oxford University Press.

Spinoza, B. (1985): *Ethics,* in Edwin Curley, translator, *The Collected Writings of Spinoza*, vol. 1. Princeton, PA: Princeton University Press.

Weiskopf, D. & Adams, F. (2015). *Introduction to the Philosophy of Psychology.* Cambridge: Cambridge University Press.

27

MIS- AND DIS-
INFORMATION

Don Fallis

Information is a powerful tool. It allows us to cure diseases. It allows us to send rockets into space. More generally, it allows us to carry out a whole variety of joint projects of immense value. Work in philosophy can help us to understand and improve this process. According to Luciano Floridi (2011: 15), the *philosophy of information* focuses on "how information should be adequately created, processed, managed, and used."

But as Floridi (1996: 509) also emphasizes, we should also be concerned with when "the process of information is defective." Kay Mathiesen (2014) provides a useful classification of the various things that can go wrong. Sometimes the problem is that the information that we need *does not exist*. It may have been destroyed (as with the Watergate tapes) or it may not have been collected in the first place. Sometimes the information exists, but we *cannot get access* to it. It may have been censored by our government. It may be too expensive for us to purchase, or we may simply lack the tools and/or skills to find it. Sometimes we can access the information, but it is of *insufficient quality* to serve our purposes. It may not be legible. It may not be comprehensible. It may not be up-to-date. It may not have the precision that we need, or it may actually be misleading. This chapter focuses on this final issue of inaccurate and misleading information.

Whenever an information process is defective, it can have profound epistemological and practical consequences. If we are unable to access high quality information, we may fail to acquire knowledge that it would be useful for us to have. But *misinformation* and *disinformation* can actually put us into an even worse epistemic state than we started from. Moreover, the acquisition of false beliefs can potentially cause serious financial and physical harm. For instance, errors in databases have cost companies and consumers millions of dollars (see English 1999: 7–10). Misinformation about the risks of vaccination has cost lives (see Poland and Jacobson 2011). Indeed, disinformation about the existence of weapons of mass destruction has arguably led to an unnecessary and "disastrous war" (see Carson 2010: 212–21).

In addition to being a pressing practical problem of the Information Age, misinformation and disinformation raise important *epistemological* and *ethical* questions. How can we acquire knowledge from the information that others provide if it might be inaccurate and misleading (cf. Hume 1977; Fallis 2004)? Also, is the intentional dissemination of inaccurate and misleading information ever morally justified (cf. Kant 1959; Bok 1978)? In order to answer such questions, we need to understand what misinformation and disinformation are (cf. Carson 2010: 13).

Philosophers have proposed several analyses of both of these concepts. That is, they have tried to identify a concise set of necessary and sufficient conditions that correctly determines whether or not something falls under the concept in question. This chapter provides a survey of these analyses of misinformation and disinformation. In addition, it discusses the main problems that each of these analyses face.

When philosophers raise worries about conceptual analyses, it usually takes the form of proposed counter-examples. The most serious proposed counter-examples purport to show that an analysis is too broad. For instance, Edmund Gettier (1963) famously argued against the *justified true belief* analysis of knowledge by giving examples of justified true beliefs that we would definitely not want to classify as knowledge. Likewise, an analysis of misinformation (or disinformation) might be criticized on the grounds that it includes cases that should not be classified as misinformation (or disinformation). It is also problematic though if an analysis is too narrow. For instance, an analysis of misinformation (or disinformation) might be criticized on the grounds that it excludes cases that should be classified as misinformation (or disinformation).

This chapter ends with a brief discussion of the epistemology and ethics of misinformation and disinformation.

Misinformation

Misinformation comes in a many different varieties. The headline of *The Chicago Tribune* on November 3, 1948, which reported that "Dewey Defeats Truman," is an example of misinformation that results from an *honest mistake*. Websites on treating fever in children sometimes recommend that parents administer aspirin, despite the fact that it could lead to a dangerous disorder known as Reye's syndrome (see Impicciatore *et al.* 1997: 1876). This is (probably) an example of misinformation that results from *ignorance*. Even when politicians believe what they say about an issue, such as climate change, they often believe it because it fits with what they already believe rather than because the evidence supports it. Thus, they can be a source of misinformation that results from *unconscious bias* (see Edelman 2001: 5–8). Finally, the shepherd boy's cry, "There is a wolf chasing my sheep!" is an example of misinformation that results from *intentional deception*. He intended to mislead the villagers about the presence of a wolf so that they would come running. This sort of misinformation is commonly referred to as *disinformation*. In other words, disinformation is the species of misinformation that is *intended* to mislead people.[1]

All of these types of misinformation have the potential to *mislead* people. That is, they can cause false beliefs. But what exactly makes something misinformation?

Misinformation as false information

Christopher Fox (1983: 201) makes the plausible suggestion that misinformation is simply *information* that is *false* (cf. Floridi 2011: 260). But what exactly does this analysis amount to?

Many different analyses of *information* have been proposed (see Fox 1983: 39–74; Floridi 2010; Floridi 2011: 81–82). Fortunately, a discussion of misinformation does not require that we settle on a specific analysis of information. It does require, however, the assumption that information has *semantic content* (see Scarantino and Piccinini 2010: 324; Floridi 2011: 80).[2] Basically, information has to be something that *represents* some part of the world as being a certain way. For instance, the text "The cat is on the mat" represents the cat as being on the mat. A piece of information is true if it represents the world as being a way that it is, and it is false (i.e., it is misinformation on Fox's analysis) if it represents the world as being a way that it is not.[3] For instance, "The cat is on the mat" is true if the cat *is* on the mat and false if the cat is not on the mat.

The main problem that has been raised for this analysis is actually not a counter-example. Despite its intuitive appeal, some philosophers (e.g., Dretske 1983: 57; Floridi 2011: 93–104) suggest that Fox's analysis is simply incoherent. They claim that there is no such thing as *false information* (that it is a contradiction in terms). As Fred Dretske (1983: 57) puts it, "false information, misinformation, and (grimace!) disinformation are not varieties of information – any more than a decoy duck is a kind of duck." According to these philosophers, something can only count as information if it is *true*. Fred Dretske (1981: 46) writes that

> information is, after all, a valuable commodity. We spend billions on its collection, storage, and retrieval. People are tortured in attempts to extract it from them. Thousands of lives depend on whether the enemy has it. Given all the fuss, it would be surprising indeed if information had nothing to do with truth.

Even if information must be true, however, we can still give an analysis of misinformation that is in the same spirit as Fox's analysis. Namely, as Floridi (2011: 260) suggests, we might say that misinformation is "semantic content that is false."

Alternatively though, we might stick with Fox's analysis by adopting a broader notion of information. While the term 'information' is sometimes used in a sense that implies truth, it is also commonly used in a sense that does not (see Fox 1983: 157; Fetzer 2004a; Scarantino and Piccinini 2010). Andrea Scarantino and Gualtiero Piccinini (2010: 323–26) point out that computer scientists and cognitive scientists use the term information in a way that does not require that it be true. Similarly, when information scientists say that a library is full of information, they do not mean to be referring to just that subset of the collection that happens to be true.

For the sake of simplicity of expression, this chapter adopts the broad notion of information such that information can be false. But even setting aside the controversial question of whether or not information must be true, Fox's analysis faces several potential counter-examples. First, there are two respects in which it seems to be too broad. That is, it is not clear that all instances of false information count as misinformation.

As Graham Oddie (2014) points out, different pieces of false information can be closer to or further from the truth. Consider the following two claims:

The distance from New York City to Los Angeles is 2,500 miles.
The distance from New York City to Los Angeles is 25,000 miles.

Both claims overestimate the actual distance between the two cities.[4] Thus, they are both false. In most contexts though, we would only want to count the second claim as misinformation. The first claim only overestimates the distance by fifty miles or so. Thus, it is sufficiently close to the truth for most practical purposes.

In addition to counting such simplified information as misinformation, Fox's analysis counts many jokes and sarcastic comments as misinformation. For instance, the headline of the satirical newspaper *The Onion* on June 30th, 2008, which reported that "Al Gore Places Infant Son in Rocket to Escape Dying Planet," is certainly false. Even so, it is not misinformation. It is just a joke and is not likely to mislead people.[5]

Second, there are two respects in which Fox's analysis seems to be too narrow. That is, it is not clear that all misinformation is false.

As noted above, a few websites on treating fever in children actually advise parents to administer aspirin. But several websites simply fail to warn parents not to administer aspirin (see Impicciatore *et al.* 1997: 1876). Even if all of the information that is actually posted on such a website is perfectly true, the website as a whole still seems to be an example of misinformation. There is the implication that all of the important stuff about treating fever that you should know is being presented.[6] As a result, incomplete information can be as misleading (and as dangerous) as false information (see Fallis 2004: 468).

In addition to failing to count incomplete information as misinformation, Fox's analysis may fail to count inaccurate and misleading images as misinformation. Images as well as propositions can have semantic content (see Chen and Floridi 2013). For instance, a drawing can represent the cat as being on the mat. Also, a map can represent one island as being much larger than another island. Moreover, such images can be misleading. Despite how it is portrayed, the cat might not actually be on the mat. Also, the island might not be nearly as large as it is depicted to be (see Monmonier 1991: 45–46). However, it is not clear that such images are false *period* and, thus, would count as misinformation on Fox's analysis.

While propositional information (such as "The cat is on the mat") is always either true or false, it makes more sense to say that visual information is simply more or less accurate (cf. Floridi 2010: 50). For instance, a map might misrepresent the relative sizes of certain geographical features to a greater or lesser degree. Also, a map might get the relative sizes right, but get the relative locations wrong, or vice versa.

We do say that a conjunction is false even if just one of its conjuncts is false. Similarly, we might say that a map is false if there is any way in which it represents the world as being a way that it is not. This move would allow Fox to count inaccurate and misleading images as misinformation. But it would also create another respect in which his analysis is too broad. Maps often include small inaccuracies that are intended to enhance comprehensibility. For instance, if roads were really drawn to scale, they would be too small to see (see Monmonier 1991: 30). In a similar vein, subway maps frequently sacrifice "geometric accuracy" in order to more effectively convey the information that riders need (see Monmonier 1991: 34–35). As with the numerical example above, despite the small misrepresentations, such simplified information is not misinformation.

Misinformation as inaccurate information

Peter Hernon (1995: 134) suggests that misinformation is information that is *inaccurate*. This analysis is in the same spirit as Fox's analysis. In fact, it subsumes Fox's analysis because false information is a type of inaccurate information. However, Hernon's analysis avoids some of the problems with Fox's analysis.[7]

First, whereas incomplete information can be perfectly true, there is an important sense in which incompleteness can be a type of inaccuracy. For instance, a website that fails to warn parents not to administer aspirin diverges significantly from the truth about treating fever in children. Thus, unlike Fox's analysis, Hernon's analysis can count such a website as misinformation.

Even so, Hernon's analysis may still fail to count some cases of incomplete information as misinformation. Incompleteness need not always be a type of inaccuracy. For instance, when pursuers – who did not recognize him – asked Saint Athanasius, "Where is the traitor Athanasius?," he replied, "Not far away." Even though Athanasius's statement succeeded in misleading his pursuers about his identity (precisely as it was intended to do), Athanasius's statement was perfectly accurate. Yet it still seems like an example of misinformation.[8]

Second, unlike Fox's analysis, Hernon's analysis clearly applies to visual information as well as propositional information. As it stands though, Hernon's analysis still counts simplified information, such as a geographically inaccurate subway map, as misinformation. However, since inaccuracy is something that comes in degrees, Hernon's analysis might easily be modified to include a threshold of inaccuracy that misinformation must meet. It could be some set level of inaccuracy (e.g., 5 percent, 10 percent, or 25 percent). Or it could be a level of inaccuracy determined by the purpose for which the information is intended to be used. Either way, very few maps will count as misinformation because, despite their small inaccuracies (intentional or otherwise), most maps fail to exceed this threshold.[9]

But whatever threshold we adopt, Hernon's analysis still seems to be too broad. For instance, the headline in *The Onion* about Al Gore is certainly inaccurate in the extreme, but (as noted above) it is not misinformation.

Misinformation as misleading information

Brian Skyrms (2010: 80) suggests that misinformation is "misleading information." That is, it is information that has the propensity to cause false beliefs. According to Skyrms, what makes something misinformation is not a purely semantic property (such as being false or inaccurate). Rather, what makes something misinformation is its likely effect on someone's epistemic state (viz., causing her to have a false belief).

Skyrms's analysis has the advantage of focusing on the property of misinformation that is most troubling. After all, inaccurate information is not a big deal as long as we are able to recognize it for what it is and avoid being misled by it. Moreover, Skyrms's analysis avoids some of the problems with the preceding analyses. For instance, since visual information as well as propositional information can certainly be misleading, it clearly applies to drawings and maps. Also, since Skyrms's analysis does not require falsity or inaccuracy, it counts incomplete information that is misleading as misinformation even if it is perfectly true.

As it stands though, Skyrms's analysis arguably counts jokes and simplified information as misinformation. Jokes and simplified information are certainly not particularly misleading. But that does not mean that no one will ever be misled. There are going to be rare cases where people do not get the joke or where they take some simplified information too literally. For instance, a significant number of people (including a few serious journalists) have actually been fooled by the satirical stories published in *The Onion* (see Fallon 2012). Similarly, a novice subway rider might mistakenly assume that the map of the London Underground is drawn to scale. Thus, just as we needed to set a threshold for inaccuracy in Hernon's analysis, we need to set a threshold for misleadingness in Skyrms's analysis. In other words, we need to specify *how likely* it must be that a piece of information will cause false beliefs in order for it to count as misinformation.[10]

But whatever threshold we adopt, Skyrms's analysis faces another difficulty. Whether a piece of information meets that threshold may depend on who receives the information. For instance, a piece of information that is likely to mislead Dr. John Watson may be unlikely to mislead Sherlock Holmes, Esq. Thus, if we want to analyze misinformation in terms of misleadingness as Skyrms suggests, we also need to specify *who* a piece of information must be likely to mislead.

One obvious suggestion is that something is misinformation *for a particular person* if it is likely to mislead that person. However, this introduces a large degree of contextual dependence into the analysis of misinformation. For instance, there may very well be children, and other highly gullible individuals, for whom the headlines in *The Onion* are misinformation. Also, if misinformation is person-relative in this way, it will sometimes be possible to change the ontological status of a piece of information simply by altering the person who receives it. For instance, a person might gather sufficient evidence on a topic, or she might develop sufficient critical thinking skills, that she is unlikely to be misled by information that previously would have been very likely to mislead her. Since this information no longer has a propensity to cause her to acquire false beliefs, it no longer counts as misinformation for this person.

In order to avoid this sort of contextual dependence, we might utilize a "reasonable person" standard, along the lines of the Federal Trade Commission's definition of deceptive advertising (see Fallis 2009: §4.5; Carson 2010: 187). That is, we might say that a piece of information is misinformation *period* if it is likely to mislead a reasonable person.[11] On this modification of Skyrms's analysis, the headlines in *The Onion* are not misinformation even if a few extremely credulous individuals are regularly taken in.[12] Also, prototypical instances of misinformation are still misinformation even if they would never fool Sherlock Holmes. In a similar vein, iocane powder is still poison even though the Dread Pirate Roberts has "spent the last few years building up an immunity."

Finally, even with this further modification, since Skyrms's analysis of misinformation does not require it to be false or inaccurate, there may be a respect in which it is too narrow. For instance, suppose that everyone is well aware that island A is about the same size as island B. In that case, no one is likely to be misled by a map that depicts it as being much larger. If such a map is not intended as a joke (i.e., if it is seriously intended to represent the way that the world is, but fails to do so), we might consider it to be misinformation despite its not being at all misleading.

Disinformation

Most philosophers have focused on the one specific type of misinformation known as *disinformation*. Other types of misinformation can sometimes be just as dangerous as disinformation (e.g., those websites that advise parents to administer aspirin to children with fever). But in the same way that acts of terrorism tend to be more troubling than natural disasters, disinformation is a particularly problematic type of misinformation because it comes from someone who is actively engaged in an attempt to mislead (see Piper 2002: 8–9; Fetzer 2004b). Moreover, in addition to directly causing harm, disinformation can harm people indirectly by eroding trust and thereby inhibiting our ability to effectively share information with each other.

Disinformation is commonly associated with government or military activity. As George Carlin quipped, "the government doesn't lie, it engages in disinformation." A standard example is *Operation Bodyguard*, a World War II disinformation campaign intended to hide the planned location of the D-Day invasion. Among other deceits, the Allies sent out fake radio transmissions and created fraudulent military reports in a successful attempt to convince the Germans that a large force in East Anglia was ready to attack Calais rather than Normandy (see Farquhar 2005: 72).[13]

However, many non-governmental organizations, such as political campaigns and advertisers, also disseminate intentionally misleading information. In fact, single individuals are often the source of disinformation. For instance, individual reporters, such as Jayson Blair of the *New York Times* and Janet Cooke of the *Washington Post*, have made up news stories that have misled their readers (see Farquhar 2005: 25–29). Also, there are several high-profile cases of purported memoirs that turned out to be fiction, such as James Frey's *A Million Little Pieces*.

Disinformation is often distributed very widely (to anyone with a newspaper subscription, to anyone with a television, to anyone with internet access, etc.). This is typically the case with government propaganda and deceptive advertising. But disinformation can also be targeted at specific people or organizations. This is humorously illustrated in a cartoon by Jeff Danziger (of the *Los Angeles Times*) that shows a couple working on their taxes. The caption is "Mr. and Mrs. John Doe (not their real names) hard at work in their own little Office of Strategic Disinformation." Such disinformation is presumably aimed directly at the Internal Revenue Service.

In addition, while the intended victim of the deception is usually a person or a group of people, disinformation can also be targeted at a machine. For instance, as Clifford Lynch (2001: 13–14) points out, managers of websites sometimes try to fool the automated "crawlers" sent out by search engines to index the internet. Suppose that you have just started selling a product that competes with another product *Y*. When an automated crawler asks for your webpage to add to its index, you might send it a copy of the webpage for product *Y*. That way, when someone uses the search engine to search for product *Y*, the search engine will return a link to your webpage.

Like misinformation in general, all of these types of disinformation have the potential to mislead people (or machines). With disinformation, however, it is *no accident* that people are misled. But what exactly makes something disinformation?

Disinformation as lies

James Fetzer (2004b: 231) makes the plausible suggestion that disinformation "should be viewed more or less on a par with acts of lying. Indeed, the parallel with lying appears to be fairly precise." In other words, disinformation is a statement that the speaker believes to be false and that is intended to mislead.

However, Fetzer's analysis faces several potential counter-examples. First, there are two respects in which it seems to be too broad. That is, it is not clear that all lies count as disinformation. Someone who intends to spread disinformation with a lie might not succeed in doing so. Even though she believes that what she says is false, it might actually (unbeknownst to her) be true (see Mahon 2008: §1.2). While such *accidental truths* are lies, they are not disinformation because they do not have the potential to mislead anyone.[14]

In addition to counting accidental truths as disinformation, Fetzer's analysis counts *implausible lies* as disinformation. Even if she says something that actually is false, someone who intends to spread disinformation still might not succeed in doing so. For instance, even though they are (unrealistically) intended to be misleading, lies that no one will believe are not disinformation because they do not have the propensity to cause false beliefs.

Second, there are two respects in which Fetzer's analysis seems to be too narrow. That is, it is not clear that all instances of disinformation are lies. Lies are linguistic expressions, such as "A wolf is chasing my sheep!" (see Mahon 2008: §1.1). However, doctored photographs and falsified maps are also common instances of disinformation (see Monmonier 1991: 115–18; Farid 2009: 98). It is no accident when people are misled by such *visual disinformation*, because that is precisely what the source of the information intended.

In addition to failing to count intentionally misleading images as disinformation, Fetzer's analysis fails to count *half truths* as disinformation. Although prototypical instances of disinformation are false (and believed by the source to be false), disinformation (just like misinformation) can sometimes be true. As Thomas Carson (2010: 57–58) explains, "half-truths are true statements or sets of true statements that selectively emphasize facts that tend to support a particular interpretation or assessment of an issue and selectively ignore or minimize other relevant facts that tend to support contrary assessments." Athanasius's truthful statement to his pursuers is an example of disinformation of this sort. In addition, politicians often use *spin* to mislead the public without saying anything false (see Manson 2012). Like prototypical instances of disinformation, such *true disinformation* is intentionally misleading.[15]

Disinformation as inaccurate information that is intended to mislead

Floridi (2011: 260) suggests that disinformation is "misinformation purposefully conveyed to mislead the receiver into believing that it is information."[16] Recall that Floridi thinks that information is accurate semantic content whereas misinformation is inaccurate semantic content. So, if we adopt the broad notion of information (such that information can be inaccurate) when we state Floridi's analysis, the idea is simply that disinformation is inaccurate information that the source intends to mislead the recipient. This analysis is in the same spirit as Fetzer's analysis. However, Floridi's analysis avoids some of the problems with Fetzer's analysis.

First, since Floridi requires that disinformation be inaccurate, accidental truths do not count as disinformation. Second, since Floridi's analysis applies to visual information as well as propositional information, intentionally misleading images count as disinformation.

Even so, Floridi's analysis still seems to be too broad. An implausible lie is inaccurate information that the source intends to mislead the recipient. Thus, it counts as disinformation on Floridi's analysis. But as noted above, an implausible lie does not have the propensity to cause false beliefs. Also, Floridi's analysis still seems to be too narrow. A half truth is not inaccurate information. Thus, it does not count as disinformation on Floridi's analysis.

In fact, there is another respect in which Floridi's analysis may be too narrow. Although disinformation is always misleading (i.e., it always has the propensity to cause false beliefs), it is not always intended to mislead. For instance, inaccurate information has been intentionally placed on the internet for purposes of education and research (see Hernon 1995; Piper 2002: 19). A fake website advertising a town in Minnesota as a tropical paradise was created to teach people how to identify inaccurate information on the internet. In such cases, while the educators and researchers certainly foresee that people might be misled by their inaccurate information, they do not intend that anybody actually be misled. Even so, such *side effect disinformation* probably should count as disinformation.[17] Just as with prototypical instances of disinformation, it is no accident when people are misled. Although the educators and researchers do not intend to mislead anyone, they do intend their inaccurate information to be misleading. For instance, a fake website would not be a very effective tool for teaching people how to identify inaccurate information on the internet if it was clear to everyone that it was a fake.[18]

Disinformation as misleading information that is intended to be misleading

Don Fallis (2009: §5) suggests that disinformation is "misleading information that is intended to be (or at least foreseen to be) misleading." This analysis avoids many of the problems with Fetzer's and Floridi's analyses. First, since Fallis explicitly requires that disinformation be misleading, accidental truths and implausible lies do not count as disinformation. Second, since Fallis does not require that disinformation be inaccurate, true disinformation counts as disinformation. Third, Fallis does not require that disinformation be intended to mislead. It is sufficient that it be intended to be misleading. Thus, side effect disinformation counts as disinformation on Fallis's analysis.

Even so, Fallis's analysis faces several potential counter-examples. First, there is one respect in which it seems to be too broad. Strictly speaking, Fallis does not even require that disinformation be intended to be misleading. It is sufficient that it be *foreseen* to be misleading. As a result, Fallis's analysis incorrectly counts some subtle forms of humor as disinformation. For instance, as the editors of *The Onion* are no doubt aware, their articles have the propensity to cause false beliefs in some (highly gullible) readers. However, since the editors do not intend these articles to be misleading to these people, it is an accident if anyone is misled.

However, Fallis's analysis can easily be modified so that it does not count such satire as disinformation. We can simply leave off the "foreseen to be misleading" clause and say that disinformation is misleading information that is intended to be misleading.

Second, there are a couple of respects in which Fallis's analysis seems to be too narrow. Someone can clearly spread disinformation even if she does not intend what she says to be misleading. For instance, a press secretary might innocently pass along disinformation on behalf of her boss. But in that sort of case, there is someone (namely, the boss) who does intend that people be misled. So, this sort of case does count as disinformation on Fallis's analysis. However, as I discuss in the following section, there are yet other cases that do indicate that Fallis's analysis is too narrow.

Adaptive disinformation

All three of the analyses of disinformation discussed so far require that the source of the information intend that it be misleading. Indeed, that is how disinformation was characterized at the outset of this chapter. However, even if the source of a piece of information does not intend that it be misleading, it may be no accident that it *is* misleading.

Many species of animals give fake alarm calls (see Skyrms 2010: 73–75). When animals give alarm calls, there is usually a predator in the vicinity. However, about 10 to 15 percent of the time, animals give alarm calls even when there is no imminent threat. In such cases, the call causes other animals of the same species to run away and leave food behind which the caller can then eat.

There is some evidence that primates understand that other primates can have false beliefs (see Fitzpatrick 2009). Thus, it could be that primates do intend to mislead conspecifics into believing that a predator is nearby with their fake alarm calls. However, when less sophisticated animals who lack this understanding, such as birds and squirrels, give fake alarm calls, they do not intend their calls to be misleading. Even so, these animals (or at least their genes) systematically benefit from giving such deceptive signals.[19] In other words, there is a mechanism that reinforces the dissemination of this sort of misleading information. Namely, the caller gets a free meal. Thus, like prototypical instances of disinformation, such *adaptive disinformation* is not misleading by accident.

If the three preceding analyses (Fetzer's, Floridi's, and Fallis's) simply failed to count the deceptive signals of animals as disinformation, it might not be a serious objection. After all, it is not clear that alarm calls have semantic content and, thus, count as information. However, humans can also disseminate adaptive disinformation. For instance, many of the people who disseminate conspiracy theories (e.g., that the President was not born in the United States or that the United States government was behind the 9/11 terrorist attacks) believe that what they are saying is true. They do not intend what they say to be misleading. Even so, just as with prototypical instances of disinformation, these false claims can mislead people and it is no accident that people are misled. There is a mechanism that reinforces the dissemination of these false claims. By promoting these false claims, certain websites and media outlets are able to attract more readers and viewers who find these claims convincing.[20]

Disinformation as misleading information that systematically benefits the source

Recent work in biology on deceptive signaling in animals suggests another possible analysis of the concept of disinformation. According to Skyrms (2010: 80), "if misinformation is sent systematically and benefits the sender at the expense of the receiver, we will not shrink from following the biological literature in calling it *deception*." Although Skyrms and the biologists that he cites use the term "deceptive signal" rather than the term "disinformation," they are trying to capture essentially the same concept. Thus, we might say that disinformation is misleading information that systematically benefits the source at the expense of the recipient. This analysis avoids the main problem with the three analyses that have been discussed so far. Although people who disseminate conspiracy theories may not intend to mislead others, they do systematically benefit from others being misled. Thus, adaptive disinformation counts as disinformation on Skyrms's analysis.

Even so, Skyrms's analysis seems to be too narrow. Most of the time, disinformation imposes a cost on the recipient, as when the villagers waste their time running to the shepherd boy's aid. However, disinformation need not always impose a cost on the recipient. In fact, it is sometimes intended to benefit the recipient. For instance, when a friend asks you how he or she looks, you might very well say, "You look great!" in order to spare his or her feelings, even if it is not true. Admittedly, such *altruistic disinformation* does not pose the same risk of harm to the recipient that prototypical instances of disinformation do. But like prototypical instances, altruistic disinformation can be intentionally misleading.

Skyrms's analysis can easily be modified though so that it counts altruistic disinformation as disinformation. We can simply leave off the "at the expense of the recipient" clause and say that disinformation is misleading information that systematically benefits the source.[21]

However, Skyrms's analysis still seems to be too narrow because it rules out the possibility of disinformation that does not benefit the source. Most of the time, disinformation does systematically benefit the source. However, it need not always do so. For instance, in order to avoid embarrassment, people often lie to their doctors about their diet, about how much they exercise, or about what medications they are taking (see Reddy 2013). If their doctors are misled, it can lead to incorrect treatment recommendations that can harm the patient. Admittedly, this particular example of *detrimental disinformation* may not pose the same risk of harm to the recipient that prototypical instances of disinformation do. But as with prototypical instances, it is no accident that people are misled by such disinformation.

A disjunctive analysis of disinformation

An analysis of disinformation in terms of an intention to be misleading (or an intention to mislead) seems to be too narrow. Also, an analysis in terms of a systematic benefit to the source seems to be too narrow. But it might be possible to come up with an adequate analysis of disinformation by combining the two. That is, it might be suggested that disinformation is misleading information is that is intended to be misleading *or* that systematically benefits the source.

Such an analysis avoids all of the problems raised for the preceding analyses of disinformation. For instance, it counts visual disinformation, true disinformation, side effect disinformation, adaptive disinformation, and detrimental disinformation as disinformation. Also, it does not count accidental truths or implausible lies as disinformation.

Such an analysis of disinformation has one major flaw though. It is *disjunctive*. If an analysis requires two independent criteria, it suggests that we are really dealing with two separate phenomena rather than just one (see Kingsbury and McKeown-Green 2009: 578–81).

Fallis (2014), however, suggests that there is something that unifies all of the cases of disinformation discussed above. He claims that disinformation is misleading information that has the *function* of misleading someone. It is just that a piece of information can acquire this function in at least two different ways. For instance, in the case of detrimental disinformation, it has this function because someone *intended* it to have this function. By contrast, in the case of altruistic disinformation, it has this function because someone *systematically benefits* from its having this function.

However, it is not clear that this move really keeps the analysis of disinformation from being disjunctive. People certainly treat the design functions of artifacts (such as chairs) and the etiological functions of biological organisms (such as hearts) as being two species of the same genus (see Krohs and Kroes 2009). But it is a difficult task (and one yet to be completed) to give a unified account of functions that subsumes one type of function under the other (see, e.g., Vermaas and Houkes 2003).

The epistemology and ethics of mis- and dis-information

Much of our knowledge about the world comes from information that we receive from other people (see Hume 1977: 74). If a significant amount of this information is misleading, we may easily acquire false beliefs instead of knowledge. Moreover, we may (out of an excess of caution) fail to acquire true beliefs that we might have acquired. Thus, the existence of misinformation and disinformation is an important problem for the *epistemology of testimony*.

One response to this problem is to give people better tools for identifying inaccurate and incomplete information so that they will be less likely to be misled. For instance, David Hume (1977: 75) recommends that

> we entertain a suspicion concerning any matter of fact, when the witnesses contradict each other; when they are but few, or of a doubtful character; when they have an interest in what they affirm; when they deliver their testimony with hesitation, or on the contrary, with too violent asseverations.

In other words, when evaluating a piece of testimony, we are advised to consider things like the authority of the source and the degree to which other sources corroborate what she says. Along the same lines as Hume, researchers in information science have attempted to identify features of websites that are indicative of accurate and inaccurate information on the internet (see Fallis 2004: 472–73).

Unfortunately, information science research on indicators of accuracy and inaccuracy often fails to differentiate among the various different types of misinformation. This is a serious oversight as the clues that suggest that someone is lying are unlikely to be the same clues that suggest that she just does not know what she is talking about. Conceptual analysis in this area can help to fill this lacuna. For instance, since disinformation is very closely related to lying, existing research on lie detection can potentially be applied to disinformation detection. Such research often focuses on physiological indicators of deception, such as perspiration and high pulse rate (see Vrij 2008). However, research is also being done to identify indicators of deception in both text (see Newman *et al.* 2003) and images (see Farid 2009: 100–06).

But making people better evaluators of information quality is not the only way to respond to the problem of misinformation and disinformation. As Mathiesen (2014) points out with respect to low quality information in general, we can take steps on the production side as well as on the receiver side. For instance, we can address the *comprehensibility* of information by creating information that is easier to read as well as by creating better readers. Similarly, we can produce information that is easier to verify as well as train people to be better verifiers. For instance, providers of high quality information can incorporate "robust" indicators of accuracy in much the same way that the United States Treasury utilizes security features that make is easier for people to determine that currency is genuine (see Fallis 2004: 474–80).

In addition to making information more *verifiable*, we can simply try to reduce the amount of misinformation and disinformation that is out there. One obvious strategy is to restrict access to information that is inaccurate and incomplete. However, as John Stuart Mill (1978: 15–52) famously pointed out, such censorship is epistemically problematic since it can just as easily keep people from accessing and/or recognizing accurate information. Thus, a better strategy is to give people incentives to disseminate information that *is* accurate and complete (see English 1999: 401–19). Toward this end, work in philosophy can potentially help us to devise policies that will deter people from disseminating misinformation and disinformation. For instance, a few philosophers (e.g., Sober 1994: 71–92; Skyrms 2010: 73–82) have developed formal models of the creation and spread of disinformation.

Finally, as noted at the outset, when people are misled by inaccurate and misleading information, it can sometimes have dire practical (as well as epistemic) consequences. So, it can be important to understand the moral wrongness involved in the dissemination of the various forms of misinformation. For instance, even though they do not intend to mislead anyone, the authors of websites that advise parents to administer aspirin to children with fever (or even just fail to warn them not to) are probably guilty of negligence. But of course, information that *is* intentionally misleading is particularly problematic from a moral perspective.

Although disinformation is not exactly the same as a lie, much of what philosophers (e.g., Bok 1978; Carson 2010) have written about the ethics of lying almost certainly applies to the ethics of disinformation as well. It is *prima facie* wrong to disseminate disinformation (cf. Bok 1978: 50). But *pace* Kant (1959), there are some circumstances in which it is morally permissible. For instance, the Allies were presumably justified in using disinformation to prevent Nazi world domination. Of course, we have to keep in mind that people who spread disinformation may easily overestimate the likelihood that they are in such circumstances (cf. Bok 1978: 26).

Notes

1 Misinformation and disinformation are sometimes treated as mutually exclusive categories. For instance, Peter Hernon (1995: 134) says that "inaccurate information might result from either a deliberate attempt to deceive or mislead (disinformation), or an honest mistake (misinformation)." However, it is more common to treat disinformation as a subcategory of misinformation as this chapter does (see Skyrms 2010: 80; Floridi 2011: 260).
2 Not all analyses of information assume that it is something that is true or false (see Floridi 2010: 44–45).
3 This way of describing things is suggestive of a *correspondence* theory of truth. But just as many different analyses of information have been proposed, many different theories of truth have been proposed (see Floridi 2011: 184). Nothing in this chapter requires that we settle on a specific theory.
4 They overestimate the distance even further if we have in mind the straight-line distance through the planet rather than the distance along the surface.
5 While articles in *The Onion* are not intended to mislead anyone, it should be noted that some jokes (e.g., April Fools' Day jokes) are intended to mislead, at least for a short time. Such jokes arguably are misinformation.
6 Of course, such websites would be false information if they explicitly stated that "this website includes all of the important stuff about treating fever that you should know."

7   Although Floridi characterizes misinformation as "semantic content that is false," his analysis of misinformation is probably closer to Hernon's than to Fox's. Floridi (2010: 50) suggests that "we speak of veridical rather [than] true data," and, like accuracy, veridicality comes in degrees.

8   Of course, Hernon might stand his ground here and insist that Athanasius's statement is not misinformation because it is not inaccurate.

9   It might even be suggested that simplified information it is not inaccurate at all. It just has a low level of *precision* (see Hughes and Hase 2010: 3) or it is at a high *level of abstraction* (see Floridi 2011: 46–79).

10   It is probably not necessary to give a precise numerical value. In a similar vein, epistemologists rarely specify the exact degree of justification that is required for a belief to count as knowledge. Most simply say that "very strong justification" is required (see Feldman 2003: 21).

11   Even with the reasonable person standard, it would still be possible (at least in principle) to change the ontological status of a piece of information. But it would be much more difficult to make the necessary alteration to an entire population than to make it to a single individual.

12   The famous editorial published in the *New York Sun* in 1897, which said, "Yes, Virginia, there is a Santa Claus," was not likely to mislead a reasonable adult. But it might have been likely to mislead a reasonable child under eight years of age. So, even if we adopt a "reasonable person" standard, we still might want to say that whether or not something counts as misinformation is relative to the group.

13   Not everything that is created in order to mislead someone counts as disinformation. For instance, in addition to sending out fake radio transmissions and creating fraudulent military reports, the Allies built tanks and airplanes out of rubber and canvas to give the false impression that a huge force was preparing to attack Calais (see Farquhar 2005: 73). These fake tanks and airplanes are not examples of disinformation because they are simply material objects rather than something that has semantic content.

14   Like lying, disinformation is not a "success" term. It may not actually mislead the person who receives it. But it would be strange to count something as disinformation if it does not at least have the propensity to mislead.

15   The two categories of disinformation that Fetzer's analysis excludes can sometimes overlap. For instance, a television commercial that pitted *Black Flag Roach Killer* against another leading brand misled viewers about the effectiveness of *Black Flag* without saying or showing anything that was literally false. According to Carson (2010: 187), "the demonstration used roaches that had been bred to be resistant to the type of poison used by the competitor."

16   Floridi had previously proposed two other analyses of disinformation. Floridi (1996: 509) originally claimed that "disinformation arises whenever the process of information is defective." However, this would incorrectly count honest mistakes, such as the headline in *The Chicago Tribune*, as disinformation. Floridi (2010: 50) later claimed that "if the source of misinformation is aware of its nature … one speaks of disinformation." However, this would incorrectly count jokes, such as the headline in *The Onion*, as disinformation. The editors of *The Onion* were well aware that the story about Al Gore was inaccurate.

17   Even though they are not intended to mislead, such websites arguably are lies. Thus, they count as disinformation on Fetzer's analysis.

18   Floridi (2012: 306–07) claims that it is not a problem that his analysis excludes true disinformation and side effect disinformation. He wants to suggest that these are "peculiar cases" of only philosophical interest. However, true disinformation and side effect disinformation are fairly common, and potentially dangerous, real-world phenomena.

19   Birds and squirrels probably just learn to associate (a) making a certain vocalization and (b) conspecifics running away and leaving food behind. Other species, such as fireflies, have *evolved* to send deceptive signals.

20   There is also a mechanism that reinforces the dissemination of the false claims made in *The Onion*. However, in this case, more readers are attracted to the website just because they find these claims amusing.

21   Skyrms (2010: 76) himself notes that his analysis might be modified in this way. He just failed to see that this sort of modification was actually necessary.

Related topics

Semantic Information, The Decisional Value of Information, The Epistemic Value of Information.

References

Bok, S. (1978) *Lying*, New York: Random House.
Carson, T. L. (2010) *Lying and Deception*, Oxford: Oxford University Press.
Chen, M. and L. Floridi. (2013) "An Analysis of Information Visualisation," *Synthese* 190: 3421–3438.
Dretske, F. I. (1981) *Knowledge and the Flow of Information*, Cambridge, MA: MIT Press.
Dretske, F. I. (1983) "Précis of *Knowledge and the Flow of Information*," *Behavioral and Brain Sciences* 6:55–90.
Edelman, M. (2001) *The Politics of Misinformation*, Cambridge: Cambridge University Press.
English, L. P. (1999) *Improving Data Warehouse and Business Information Quality*, New York: Wiley.
Fallis, D. (2004) "On Verifying the Accuracy of Information: Philosophical Perspectives," *Library Trends* 52:463–87.
Fallis, D. (2009) "A Conceptual Analysis of Disinformation," *iConference Proceedings*, http://hdl.handle.net/2142/15205
Fallis, D. (2014) "A Functional Analysis of Disinformation," *iConference Proceedings*, http://hdl.handle.net/2142/47258
Fallon, K. (2012) "Fooled by 'The Onion': 9 Most Embarrassing Fails," *Daily Beast*, http://www.thedailybeast.com/articles/2012/09/29/fooled-by-the-onion-8-most-embarrassing-fails.html
Farid, H. (2009) "Digital Doctoring: Can We Trust Photographs?" in *Deception*, B. Harrington (ed.), Stanford, MA: Stanford University Press, pp. 95–108.
Farquhar, M. (2005) *A Treasury of Deception*, New York: Penguin.
Feldman, R. (2003) *Epistemology*, Upper Saddle River, NJ: Prentice Hall.
Fetzer, J. H. (2004a) "Information: Does It Have to Be True?" *Minds and Machines* 14:223–29.
Fetzer, J. H. (2004b) "Disinformation: The Use of False Information," *Minds and Machines* 14:231–40.
Fitzpatrick, S. (2009) "The Primate Mindreading Controversy: A Case Study in Simplicity and Methodology in Animal Psychology," in *The Philosophy of Animal Minds*, R. Lurz (ed.), Cambridge: Cambridge University Press, pp. 258–77.
Floridi, L. (1996) "Brave.Net.World: The Internet as a Disinformation Superhighway?" *Electronic Library* 14:509–14.
Floridi, L. (2010) *Information – A Very Short Introduction*, Oxford: Oxford University Press.
Floridi, L. (2011) *The Philosophy of Information*, Oxford: Oxford University Press.
Floridi, L. (2012) "Steps Forward in the Philosophy of Information," *Etica & Politica* 14:304–10.
Fox, C. J. (1983) *Information and Misinformation*, Westport, CT: Greenwood Press.
Gettier, E. L. (1963) "Is Justified True Belief Knowledge?," *Analysis* 23:121–23.
Hernon, P. (1995) "Disinformation and Misinformation through the Internet: Findings of an Exploratory Study," *Government Information Quarterly* 12:133–39.
Hughes, I. and Hase, T. (2010) *Measurements and their Uncertainties*, Oxford: Oxford University Press.
Hume, D. (1977) *An Enquiry Concerning Human Understanding*, Indianapolis, IN: Hackett.
Impicciatore, P., Pandolfini, C., Casella, N. and Bonati, M. (1997) "Reliability of Health Information for the Public on the World Wide Web: Systematic Survey of Advice on Managing Fever in Children at Home," *British Medical Journal* 314:1875–79.
Kant, I. (1959) *Foundations of the Metaphysics of Morals*, New York: Macmillan.
Kingsbury, J. and J. McKeown-Green. (2009) "Definitions: Does Disjunction Mean Dysfunction?" *Journal of Philosophy* 106:568–85.
Krohs, U. and P. Kroes (eds.). (2009) *Functions in Biological and Artificial Worlds*, Cambridge: MIT Press.
Lynch, C. A. (2001) "When Documents Deceive: Trust and Provenance as New Factors for Information Retrieval in a Tangled Web," *Journal of the American Society for Information Science and Technology* 52:12–17.
Mahon, J. E. (2008) "The Definition of Lying and Deception," *Stanford Encyclopedia of Philosophy*, http://plato.stanford.edu/entries/lying-definition/
Manson, N. C. (2012) "Making Sense of Spin," *Journal of Applied Philosophy* 29:200–13.

Mathiesen, K. (2014) "Facets of Access: A Conceptual and Standard Threats Analysis," *iConference Proceedings*, http://hdl.handle.net/2142/47410

Mill, J. S. (1978) *On Liberty*, Indianapolis, IN: Hackett.

Monmonier, M. (1991) *How to Lie With Maps*, Chicago, IL: University of Chicago Press.

Newman, M. L., J. W. Pennebaker, D. S. Berry, and J. M. Richards. (2003) "Lying Words: Predicting Deception from Linguistic Styles," *Personality and Social Psychology Bulletin* 29:665–75.

Oddie, G. (2014) "Truthlikeness," *Stanford Encyclopedia of Philosophy*, http://plato.stanford.edu/entries/truthlikeness/

Piper, P. S. (2002) "Web Hoaxes, Counterfeit Sites, and Other Spurious Information on the Internet," in *Web of Deception*, A. P. Mintz (ed.), Medford, NJ: Information Today, pp. 1–22.

Poland, G. A. and Jacobson, R. M. (2011) "The Age-Old Struggle against the Antivaccinationists," *New England Journal of Medicine* 364:97–99.

Reddy, S. (2013) "'I Don't Smoke, Doc'," and Other Patient Lies," *Wall Street Journal*, http://online.wsj.com/article/SB10001424127887323478004578306510461212692.html

Scarantino, A. and Piccinini, G. (2010) "Information without Truth," *Metaphilosophy* 41:313–30.

Skyrms, B. (2010) *Signals*, New York: Oxford University Press.

Sober, E. (1994) *From a Biological Point of View*, Cambridge: Cambridge University Press.

Vermaas, P. E. and Houkes, W. (2003) "Ascribing Functions to Technical Artefacts: A Challenge to Etiological Accounts of Functions," *British Journal for the Philosophy of Science* 54:261–89.

Vrij, A. (2008) *Detecting Lies and Deceit*, Chichester: John Wiley & Sons, Ltd.

28

INFORMATION-THEORETIC PHILOSOPHY OF MIND

Jason Winning and William Bechtel

Introduction

The branch of philosophy known as "philosophy of mind," at its core, is concerned with two closely related questions: What sort of thing is a mind or mental state? And how are these related to the non-mental? We know some of the characteristic activities of minds: thinking, remembering, dreaming, imagining, etc. We consider certain types of things to be *mental*, i.e., to exist only in minds, as mental "states" or properties, or "mental contents": thoughts, memories, desires, emotions, and what philosophers refer to as "qualia" (that aspect of an experience that one refers to by the phrase "what it is like to undergo it"). We also consider certain kinds of things to be non-mental, such as rocks, tables, and rain drops. These do not have minds, do not constitute minds, and cannot exist in minds as mental states or properties. Minds, and the states they can undergo, are *mental*; things that cannot be minds and cannot be undergone by minds are *non-mental*.

But is there a third category of thing, that can exist either inside or outside of minds? Consider the question of how *communication* is possible between minds. Warren Weaver, one of the pioneers of mathematical communication theory, defined communication in mental terms as "all of the procedures by which one mind may affect another" (1949: 2). At least in some instances, communication might be described as a process whereby the contents of mental states (such as thoughts or hopes) can be *sent* from one mind to another. In order for this to occur, there must be some *medium* by which the contents are conveyed – by which the mental contents are able to be sent between minds; naturalistic philosophers do not believe that a semantic content can merely float in space-time by itself, or that the contents of mental states can jump immediately from one mind to another without crossing some type of non-mental medium. These "contents," of course, are not strictly speaking *mental* contents when they are being conveyed outside of a mind; instead of residing in a mind, they reside within (or as it is usually put, are "carried by" or "tokened by") non-mental *vehicles*. 'Vehicle' is a term used by Dennett (1969) to refer to any given manifestation of a content; the vehicle makes it possible for the content to be tokened (instantiated) at a given place and time. Such vehicles might include black ink on a page, or patterns of electricity running along a wire. We also have a word to refer to such tokenized contents while they are being conveyed from place to place, or even when they are being stored or processed outside of minds: *information*. Information is here being understood broadly, as that which has a vehicle and a content.

A further prefatory terminological clarification is in order. The concepts of informational *content* and *vehicle* are also closely related to the concept of *representation*. Sometimes authors use the term 'representation' to refer to the relation that holds between *any* vehicle and its content. Others restrict its use to the relation holding for a particular category of these, and still others use it to refer to either the content or the vehicle standing in such a relationship. The following remarks by Dretske are pertinent here:

> There are representational vehicles – the objects, events, or conditions that represent – and representational contents – the conditions or situations the vehicle represents as being so. In speaking about representations, then, we must be clear whether we are talking about content or vehicle, about what is represented or the representation itself. It makes a big difference. In the case of mental representations, the vehicle (a belief or an experience) is in the head. Content – what is believed and experienced – is (typically) not. … When I speak of representations I shall always mean representational vehicle.
>
> *(2003: 68)*

There is a large debate about the nature of the *representation* relation and how it is (conceptually or otherwise) related to content. Here, we wish to largely sidestep this debate; we will simply follow Dretske in using 'representation' as synonymous with 'representational vehicle' and we will consider representations to be one species of vehicle, possibly among others.

We also wish to sidestep the internalism/externalism debate about mental content. The issue of whether some mental content is "outside the head" is independent of the vehicle/content distinction. Even if mental contents are themselves mind-external, or if they are fixed by mind-external facts, we can still make sense of those contents being communicated to another mind, or of the mental vehicles in another mind taking up that same content. Either way, such a process may involve this content being encoded and transmitted by means of mind-external informational vehicles.

Communication, control, and computation

Karl Pribram has claimed that information is a notion that is "neutral to the mind/brain dichotomy" (1986: 507). As such, it can be a powerful bridge principle in philosophy of mind's quest to answer the questions about the identity of the mental and the relation between the mental and the non-mental. But it is a bridge that has only become available in the last century or so as a result of the development of technologies for sending, generating, processing, storing, and consuming information. These advancements created the practical need, in the mid-twentieth century, for scientific theories of communication (e.g., Shannon 1948), control (e.g., Wiener 1948), and computation (e.g., Turing 1936).

Communication

With the advent of the telegraph and telephone as technologies for transmitting messages, questions arose as to the requirements for reliable transmission. Pioneers in the field of mathematical communication theory such as Harry Nyquist, R. V. Hartley, and Claude Shannon realized the need for exact measurement of information transmission capacity, regardless of the specific technology involved. In doing so they abstracted away from the semantic interpretation of the messages themselves and introduced the crucial conceptual distinction between semantic meaning (sometimes referred to as "semantic information;" see Chapter 6) and the statistically quantifiable reduction of uncertainty that is achieved in a given communication process. By isolating the latter, important mathematical results from thermodynamics and statistical mechanics could be applied directly to problems faced by communications engineers.[1]

Shannon's (1948) mathematical communication theory (which many authors simply refer to as *information theory*; see Chapter 4) was very influential on scientists and philosophers, including those mentioned in the following sections. In particular, it helped convince them that informational processes are as much at home in a purely naturalistic theory as any physical phenomena. It is no surprise that the most influential philosophical treatment of information, Dretske's 1981, discussed in a later section, draws heavily from Shannon's work.

Control

An important use of information is to enable one system to control another system. A basic but highly potent form of control is negative feedback, whereby the activity of a system is corrected in light of information received back by the system about the results of the activity. For example, as you move towards a target you acquire information about the discrepancy between your current location and the target and use that to correct your motion. The potency of negative feedback was independently recognized in engineering and in biology. A particularly prominent mechanical engineering example was James Watt's invention in the 1780s of the centrifugal governor (Figure 28.1) to control the speed of a steam engine. When the flywheel turned too fast, centrifugal force would cause the angle arms attached to

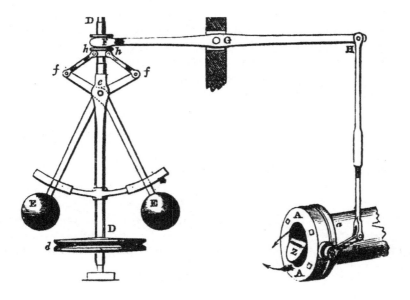

Figure 28.1 Watt's centrifugal governor for a steam engine

Source: Reproduced from J. Farey, *A Treatise on the Steam Engine: Historical, Practical, and Descriptive* (London: Longman, Rees, Orme, Brown, and Green, 1827)

a spindle to extend up and out and, via a linkage mechanism, close the valve. When it moved too slowly, the arms would drop and cause the valve to open.

In biology, Claude Bernard, in attempting to answer the challenge of vitalists who thought that only a non-physical force could explain the ability of organisms to resist destruction by physical processes, introduced the idea that organisms maintain the constancy of their internal environment by responding to conditions that disrupt them, a process Walter Cannon termed *homeostasis*. Drawing upon his own use of negative feedback in designing targeting systems for weapons, as well as Cannon's application of negative feedback in explaining how animals maintain homeostasis, Norbert Wiener (1948) elevated the principle of negative feedback to a general design principle for achieving control in both biology and engineering. He coined the term *cybernetics* to describe this framework and inspired an interdisciplinary movement involving mathematicians, engineers, neurophysiologists, and psychologists, among others, devoted to understanding the control of activities through negative feedback.

Computation

The term *computation* originally applied to the activity of humans in computing sums by applying rules to symbols written on a page. Given the tediousness of the activity, there has been a long history of humans attempting to automate the process. An important milestone was Charles Babbage's design of the difference engine to compute polynomial functions, and the analytical engine, which could be programmed by punched cards to execute any computation. Babbage did not succeed in building either of these devices. Alan Turing (1936) proposed an extremely simple machine that could be configured to compute any function. It consists of an indefinitely long tape on which a string of symbols (e.g., 0s and 1s) are written and a read/write device that can move along the tape while reading from it or writing to it. The read/write device can enter into a finite number of states and has rules specifying what to do when, in a given state, it reads a particular symbol from the tape. A *Turing machine* (as it came to be called; see Chapters 7 and 10) is not practical for actual computing, but in the decade after Turing's theoretical work he and several others created the first electronic computers. John von Neumann developed the architecture that has become standard in contemporary computers and developed a means of encoding programs (representations) that specify operations to be performed on other representations.

Cognitive science and the cognitive revolution in psychology

In recognition of the generality of their application to domains other than the mind, we have introduced the concepts of communication, control, and computation without reference to how they were applied to the mind. But for many pioneers developing these concepts, understanding the mind was an important goal. It is important to emphasize that characterizing what goes on in the mind as comparable to what goes on in communication between people, employing processes like those that had been developed for the control of physical systems and computation in physical machines, was a major conceptual development. This was facilitated by the fact that information was not itself characterized in terms of the physical medium in which it was implemented. The recognition of the import of these ideas for philosophy of mind was mediated by developments in the empirical science of psychology and the developing interdisciplinary cluster that eventually became known as cognitive science.

Empirical inquiries into both brain and mind developed in the late nineteenth and early twentieth centuries independently of the information-theoretical perspective.

Pioneering research in the brain sciences involved the discovery that neurons are distinct cells that conduct electrical signals and deployed techniques such as lesioning and microstimulation to link brain regions with behavioral activities. Psychology developed as a distinct discipline employing a variety of different approaches to study of the mind – act psychology (Brentano), functional psychology (James), structuralist psychology (Wundt, Titchener), cultural-historical psychology (Vygotsky, Luria), Gestalt psychology (Köhler), and genetic epistemology (Piaget). In part due to the lack of a clear framework for objectively characterizing activity in the mind, in North America these various fledgling approaches to psychology were overtaken by John Watson and other behaviorists who sought to make the new discipline appropriately empirical by bypassing the mind altogether and focusing on behavior. It might be said that, in rejecting the project of going inside the mind, behaviorism impeded the development of an information-theoretic understanding of mind. But William Aspray suggests that, in another respect, behaviorism actually fostered the development:

> Behaviorist psychology, by concentrating on behavior and not consciousness, helped to break down the distinction between the mental behavior of humans and the information processing of lower animals and machines. This step assisted the acceptance of a unified theory of information processors, whether in humans or machines.
>
> *(1985: 128)*

Physiological psychologists were among the first to draw upon information-theoretical ideas of computation and control. Neurophysiologist Warren McCulloch began a collaboration with Walter Pitts, a self-trained logician, that began by showing how idealized neurons could, when appropriately networked, implement all the connectives of sentential logic, and by extension could be viewed as carrying out any operation of which a Turing machine was capable (McCulloch and Pitts 1943). In subsequent work they moved beyond viewing brain activity as implementing sentential logic, and focused on statistical properties of networks that would allow them to recognize related stimuli as the same. They also began to relate their networks to the architecture of specific brain regions, a project that was soon taken up by other researchers such as David Marr.

Psychophysics, which addressed questions such as the relation between the magnitude of a stimulus and the psychological experience of the stimulus, was another field of psychology that was not dominated by behaviorism in North America and it was in Stevens' psychophysics laboratory at Harvard that George Miller invoked information theory in his dissertation research on radio jamming. To present his classified research to a wider audience, he shifted the focus to how noise affects the intelligibility of speech and asking why some messages are more robust to noise (a phenomenon Shannon [1948] himself went on to explicate in terms of the redundancy between parts of a message). Initially Miller tried to situate his work within the context of behaviorism using the label 'statistical behavioristics,' but he quickly moved beyond the bounds of behaviorism and began to speak of cognition. His work remained influenced by information theory and one of his most cited papers (Miller 1956) was an investigation of the capacity limits affecting cognitive performance (e.g., limits to the information that can be stored in short-term memory). In a landmark book he, together with Karl Pribram and Eugene Galanter (1960), addressed purposive action and developed a computational conception of how agents could execute plans through a process of comparing a representation of the current state with that of a goal and implementing operations until no differences remained between the representations.

Miller was not alone in applying information-theoretic perspectives to understanding the mind. Donald Broadbent, for example, investigated how people are able to focus their attention on a particular conversation, but quickly shift to tracking a different conversation if they hear their own name. Broadbent invoked the notions of information channels and filtering to explain such phenomena. By the late 1960s the range of research approaches applying information-theoretic ideas to understanding the mind reached a sufficient threshold that a new name was coined for this form of psychology – *cognitive psychology*. Ulric Neisser, in the book that gave this name to the new field, summarizes the importance of information to it:

> There were cognitive theorists long before the advent of the computer. Bartlett, whose influence on my own thinking will become obvious in later chapters, is a case in point. But, in the eyes of many psychologists, a theory which dealt with cognitive transformations, memory schemata, and the like was not about anything. One could understand theories that dealt with overt movements, or with physiology; one could even understand (and deplore) theories which dealt with the content of consciousness; but what kind of a thing is a schema? If memory consists of transformations, what is transformed? So long as cognitive psychology literally did not know what it was talking about, there was always a danger that it was talking about nothing at all. This is no longer a serious risk. Information is what is transformed, and the structured pattern of its transformations is what we want to understand.
>
> *(1967: 8)*

Appropriately, an alternative name for the field is *information-processing psychology*.

Psychology and neuroscience were not the only disciplines that began to employ information-theoretic ideas to explain mental phenomena in the 1950s. Linguistics, like psychology, had been dominated by behaviorism, but linguists such as Zellig Harris soon took up the challenge of characterizing the vast range of syntactic forms available in language that they confronted. To bring coherence to the range of forms, a framework was introduced in which the different syntactic forms were arrived at by applying formal operations to symbol strings. Harris, for example, hypothesized transformations of kernel sentences to account for passive and active versions of a sentence. This approach was further developed by Harris' student Noam Chomsky, who not only developed a number of transformational grammars in the attempt to account for the forms possible in actual languages, but also demonstrated that such grammars required computational power equivalent to a Turing machine.

During this period as well some pioneers in the new field of computer science began to explore whether an appropriately configured computer could be intelligent and established the subfield of artificial intelligence (see Chapters 10 and 11). Especially noteworthy was Newell and Simon's (1956) program Logic Theorist, which constructed proofs, some of them novel, of theorems from *Principia Mathematica*. In subsequent decades these researchers focused on developing a general approach to problem solving and created a programming architecture known as a *production system* that was particularly useful for implementing programs designed to mimic human intelligence (Newell and Simon 1972). The representations used in production systems are modeled on propositions in language and the approach is generally referred to as *symbolic* AI. Other theorists found propositional representations to be too inflexible to account for cognitive abilities and developed larger-scale knowledge structures known as *schemas* or *scripts*, or broke altogether from symbolic approaches and pursued a more neutrally inspired architecture in which the fundamental activity is not application of rules but recognition of patterns through parallel constraint satisfaction.

Although the name *cognitive science* would not be introduced until the 1970s, these efforts in linguistics, psychology, artificial intelligence, and neuroscience provided the foundation for what became a highly productive interdisciplinary endeavor.[2] As the applications of information-theoretic approaches were being developed in these various disciplines, philosophers, especially Hillary Putnam and Jerry Fodor, drew upon them in articulating a new philosophical stance on the nature of mind (for an overview, see Bechtel 1988). In the early twentieth century, dualism and identity theory seemed to be the only live options for characterizing mind: mental states either involved a non-material substance or were identical to material states such as brain processes. To capture the ways the new cognitive disciplines invoked informational states and operations on them, Putnam and Fodor introduced what came to be known as *functionalism*, according to which mental states are states in an information-processing system that might be realized in different physical processes (and thus, are not identical with any of them). The theorists to whom we turn in the next section all worked within this functionalist perspective.

Information enters philosophy of mind

As it was brought into philosophy of mind, the notion of information became intertwined with other concepts that already had a long history of use by philosophers. First, information is closely related to another concept that has enjoyed prominence in philosophical discussions since the time of the Ancient Greeks: *knowledge*. Second, the notions of mental *contents*, mental *representations*, and *ideas* had been central to philosophy of mind since the seventeenth century (see Allen 2013 for an overview). Third, the notion of information has become highly relevant to the problem of *intentionality*, which was given its modern formulation by nineteenth-century philosopher Franz Brentano. Fourth, at the beginning of the twentieth century Frege articulated his highly influential distinction between *sense and reference* that provided an account of meaning in non-mental terms. The task of integrating the notion of information arising from scientific fields with these preexisting philosophical notions has proved to be far from trivial.

We turn first to the problem of intentionality. Brentano had claimed that intentionality was the mark of the mental – mental states are *about* other states, including ones that do not exist. Because it might lack a *relatum*, Brentano characterized intentionality not as a true relation but as *relation-like*. Some philosophers turned to information theory for suggestions: if the mind processes information, then perhaps that could explain the content of mental states. However, as we noted above, Shannon's formal treatment of communication did not address *how* communicated messages carried information; he simply treated it as a basic fact that "frequently the messages have meaning; that is they refer to or are correlated according to some system with certain physical or conceptual entities" (1948: 379). Shannon himself reserved the term *information* for the reduction of uncertainty that was crucial for his analysis of communication.

The two senses of *information*, however, were often conflated. The use of information-bearing states or representations in psychological and AI theories suggests that these accounts can explain the semantic sense of information. In a particularly influential paper, John Searle (1980) argued that such attempts confound the crucial distinction between intrinsic and derived intentionality: any meaning or aboutness that a message, state in a computer, signal running across a wire, etc. can have is dependent on the minded beings that give a message meaning or respond to it. Searle emphasized that the same applies to symbol strings in a computer – they are dependent for their meaning on the programmer. Trying to ground the aboutness of mental states in semantic information, goes Searle's argument, is putting the cart before the horse: the aboutness of information is itself grounded in those mental states. Not all philosophers have accepted Searle's contention that intentionality must be dependent on minds. The theories we discuss next can be looked at as attempts to respond to this line of argument by advancing accounts of the intrinsic aboutness of information in non-mental terms.[3]

Dretske

Perhaps because Shannon's specialized usage of the term 'information' – i.e., to refer to the amount of reduction of uncertainty about the occurrence of potential events that may be afforded by a signal – had become widespread by the 1950s, many philosophers who have been concerned with accounting for intentionality have tended to use the terms 'content' and 'representation' with much greater frequency. Dretske (1981), however, advanced an account, built on the foundation of Shannon's sense of reducing uncertainty, of semantic content. Important for understanding the relation between Dretske's theory and Shannon's is that instead of using 'information' to mean something distinct from content, as Shannon did, Dretske used 'information' to mean something distinct from representation. This was a distinction between kinds of vehicles: information carriers (he also used the term 'indicators') versus representations.

Instead of treating a cognitive agent as the sender of a message, he treated objects or events in the world as the sender and the cognitive agent as the receiver (Adams 2003: 472). Hence, he treated communication as a causal process but instead of thinking of the effect as a message that carries the same information as the cause (drawing from Grice's earlier notion of *natural meaning*) Dretske viewed the effect as carrying information *about* the cause. Being an epistemologist, the account was also well-suited to his goal of accounting for knowledge: on his view, knowledge was the result of the flow of information from the world into the knowing subject (Dretske 1981). This set the basic framework of Dretske's account, but he recognized several ways in which causation by itself was insufficient to account for cognitive states with specific contents. First, causes carry information about more things than what is usually taken to be the semantic content of the effect – for example, a cause carries information about all the intermediate steps in a causal chain. Dretske proposes to explicate this in terms of the direction of causal dependencies: "S gives primary representation to property B (relative to property g) = S's representation of something's being g depends on the informational relationship between B and g, but not vice versa" (1981: 160).[4]

Moreover, messages should be able to be mistakenly tokened without affecting their semantic content. Dretske (1981) appeals to the process of acquisition to explain this – as the causal linkage between sensory stimulus and the message internal to the cognitive agent develops, the internal message can be generated without the sensory stimulus. He later abandoned this view, however, in favor of a teleological view of representations as those content vehicles whose *function* it is to carry information about what is represented (Dretske 1988; a version of this view was advocated earlier by Millikan 1984; see also Chapter 22). Dretske does not believe that his appeal to function prevents his theory from achieving his goal of grounding aboutness "in an objective, mind- (and language-) independent notion of information" (2009: 381):

> What is important for the purposes of information-theoretic semantics is that there be a set of circumstances, or perhaps a kind of history, that, independent of human interests, grounds descriptions of animals and their parts as ill, sick, broken, damaged, injured, diseased, defective, flawed, infected, contaminated, or malfunctioning. If the truth of these descriptions is independent of our interests and purposes, then there is a way natural systems are supposed to be, or supposed to behave, that is independent of how we conceive them.
>
> *(Dretske 2009: 387)*

The most common criticism of Dretske's theory poses what is known as the "disjunction problem." In a case of misrepresentation, a content vehicle A, whose function it is to indicate B, instead indicates C (by being caused by state of affairs C instead of state of affairs B). If A-tokens occasionally carry information C, then in virtue of what is it true that the function of A is to indicate condition B, rather than the disjunctive condition B-or-C? Dretske's theory must be able to give an answer to this that does not itself rely on human purposes and intentions in order to account for misrepresentation. A large literature has been devoted to this problem; see a recent discussion of it in Dretske (2009: 387–9).

MacKay

Other information-based approaches to semantic content began not with the mathematical theory of communication but with the cyberneticists' conception of negative feedback as enabling physical systems to be goal-directed by taking in information about the effects of their actions in determining new actions. Donald MacKay characterizes information as "that which alters" an agent's "total state of readiness for adaptive or goal-directed activity" (1969: 60).[5] This approach, as further developed in the work of Dennett, treats information not quite as mind-independent but as in fact dependent on the (implicit or explicit) goals of the animal:

> since a stimulus, as a physical event, can have no intrinsic significance but only what accrues to it in virtue of the brain's discrimination, the problem-ridden picture of a stimulus being *recognized by* an animal, meaning something *to* the animal, prior to the animal's determining what to do about the stimulus, is a conceptual mistake.
> *(Dennett 1969: 75–6)*

MacKay argues that a message is only *significant* or *meaningful* insofar as receipt of the message would alter the *conditional readiness* of action. Behavior plays a key role in his account of intentionality, but he is clear about how his account is to be distinguished from behaviorism: "What has been affected by your understanding of [a] message is not necessarily what you do – as some behaviourists have suggested – but rather what you would be ready to do if given (relevant) circumstances arose" (1969: 22). The idea here is that mindedness, information, and goal-directedness are interdependent naturalistic phenomena. It is a physical fact about the animal that it has certain needs and certain capacities for acting to meet these needs, and is therefore motivated to act in certain ways under certain conditions. In virtue of such facts, stimuli become relevant to determining how to behave in virtue of information they carry about the effects of such behavior, and thereby acquire significance. For MacKay, this foundational significance ultimately underwrites the aboutness of information, and the aboutness of mental states, as a whole.

Sayre

In contrast to Dretske and MacKay, Kenneth Sayre proposes a process in which Shannon's quantitative sense of information is turned into semantic information. He uses the term 'info(t)' for the "technical" sense of information that Shannon's theory focused on, i.e., that of reduction of uncertainty. 'Info(s),' on the other hand, denotes a signal that bears not merely a statistical significance but a genuine semantic content. His project is to show how info(t) can be transformed into info(s) and Sayre focuses on the visual system to show how this is done. An organism may use info(t) in order to get around and engage in adaptive behavior on a limited basis, but much more adaptive behavior is possible with info(s), that is, when a state of the system has as its *content* the perceptual object.

Central to Sayre's approach is his characterization of organisms in which info(s) states arise. He characterizes organisms as adapting to changes in their environment, either through evolution or learning, but more fundamentally, needing to do this because ultimately they are *organized systems* that must resist dissipation into their environment. In thermodynamic terms introduced by Schrödinger, living organisms are low entropy systems relative to their environment, and to maintain themselves as such, they must extract energy from their environment. Sayre quotes Schrödinger in describing "a living organism as a device 'for sucking orderliness from its environment'" which Schrödinger characterized as negative entropy (1967: 79, quoted in Sayre 1986: 128). In order to perform this crucial activity, organisms need not only a way of incorporating energy from outside themselves but also identifying sources of energy. They do this by receiving info(t) from distal objects at their senses.

The sensory processing system then generates info(s) as it selectively reduces info(t), extracting and retaining only info(t) about a distal object O that is relevant to the actions the organism takes with respect to O. It is by "locking onto" the dynamically changing info(t) that is relevant to responding behaviorally to object O, and so *tracking* O, that the organism generates info(s) that is about O. Looked at in this way, perception is not just a passive process of aligning internal states of the organism with external stimuli, but a process that organisms use to *focus on* objects in their environment with which they need to interact appropriately if they are to continue to live. At some points Sayre speaks of a "perceptual-behavioral control loop," where the behavioral component initiates actions with respect to the object in the environment about which the perceptual system carried info(t). It is through such loops that the info(t) states become info(s) states – they become states the organism uses to engage with the external object. What underlies this transformation is that organisms are active systems that can alter processes such as perception so as to provide the appropriate info(t) for engaging in successful actions in the world. As we will see below, this approach foreshadowed to some extent the later approach of Neo-Gibsonians such as Chemero, who have embraced non-representational information-processing accounts of perception.

The many facets of information in philosophy of mind

Informational theories of intentionality were vigorously debated through the 1990s but interest in the problem has waned since then. Although not couched in information-theoretic terms, recent philosophical discussions of intentionality and vehicles have significant implications for information-theoretic accounts. Accordingly, we discuss some more recent developments in philosophy of mind and their relevance to the topic of information.

The topic of the nature of intentionality/aboutness has itself grown to be very large and contentious, and has recently been the focus of in-depth investigation (e.g., Crane 2013; Yablo 2014). One important upshot is the recognition that there are a number of kinds of aboutness; this implies that for purposes of philosophy of mind, there is a corresponding sense of 'information content' for each of these kinds. For example, "A carries information about B" might mean that A refers to B (i.e., by indicating that B is present), or that B enters into the meaning of A (for example, A might be a story about B, a fictional or even a logically contradictory object). The former case invokes an extensional type of aboutness, the latter an intensional type. Information content can therefore be broken down into intensional and extensional content.

As an illustration of further ways to divide aboutness, consider Martin Davies' distinction between "subdoxastic aboutness" and other kinds of aboutness:

Subdoxastic aboutness is distinct from attitude aboutness since, like experiential aboutness, it is a kind of non-conceptualised content. (Indeed, it is between those two kinds of non-conceptualised content that Evans (1982: 158) distinguishes in terms of serving 'as the input to a thinking, concept-applying, and reasoning system'.) Subdoxastic aboutness is distinct from linguistic aboutness since it is not derived. Subdoxastic aboutness is also distinct from indicator aboutness, since it allows for the possibility of misrepresentation. We can say, for example, that a state of the auditory processing system represents the presence of a sound coming from the left even though there is not in fact any sound coming from the left. And finally, subdoxastic aboutness is quite unlike experiential aboutness – the fourth variety of aboutness – since it is not tied to consciousness.

(1995: 16)

One lesson to draw from this is that it may be an oversimplification to talk as if there is a single notion of "semantic information" (or info(s) in Sayre's terminology).

A second point that is emerging from recent work in philosophy of mind and cognitive science involves the notion of a content *vehicle*. Philosophers have pointed out that vehicles also come in more than one kind. Dennett (1983) for example proposed that information may be manifested non-representationally in simple storage formats – "brute storage" in his words – which do not allow any kind of information processing during storage (only retrieval). Note that the question of what types of vehicles may exist is orthogonal to the question of what types of contents might exist.

This issue has come to the fore in recent debates about perception. Earlier proponents of ecological approaches such as James Gibson had argued against information-processing accounts of processes such as visual perception by maintaining that information needed for action (what he termed *affordances*) already existed in the light. Organisms merely need to pick up this information; they do not need to process it. What marks the approach of Neo-Gibsonians such as Chemero (2009) is that it embraces Gibson's non-representational direct realism, while acknowledging the importance of information processing. For Chemero there is no contradiction here because information processing in direct perception does not require representations in the mind, a point he also expresses by saying it does not require "computation" or "mental gymnastics":

Action changes the information available to an animal's perceptual systems, and sometimes the action actually generates information. Thus there is a sense in which perception-action as studied by radical embodied cognitive scientists involves information processing, but it is a variety of information processing that does not involve mental gymnastics.

(2009: 127)

Discussions about information often assume that all informational content is declarative. Another contribution of recent theorizing questions this. Not all messages communicated between people are assertions: they can also be imperative or interrogative, for example. Belnap (1990) has argued that the semantics of imperative and interrogative sentences cannot be analyzed in terms of assertoric content, and that truth or falsity would not be applicable to such sentences. Further, Belnap along with a number of other philosophers has proposed many-valued logics. These developments, as well as parallel advances in analog and non-binary digital computation, point to the need for richer accounts of semantic information.

Finally, for a piece of information to exist, a content token must become, as it were, *attached* to a vehicle token; they become informationally bound to one another. What are the necessary and sufficient conditions for this attachment to occur? Multiple answers are possible since there are many *schemes* under which such attachment might occur. A might mean B merely by arbitrary stipulation (as in games or stories), it might mean B by means of being linked causally to B in the right way (as in Dretske's indication relation), or it might mean B by being historically linked in the right way (as in Millikan's biosemantics). There is the possibility of natively endowed content, or (as a Kantian might be inclined to say) content imposed by a constitutive faculty of the mind. Each of these might be referred to as a distinct *content tokening scheme*: an ordering principle that determines which contents get tokened or "attached" to which vehicles and under what conditions.[6] The issue of tokening schemes is importantly different from understanding the nature of content itself, a point that has also been made by Rick Grush: "a theory of content, by contrast, need not concern itself with how or why contents are carried by this or that vehicle – rather, it is concerned with what contents are" (1998). Providing a reductionistic account of what it is for A to be *about* B in one of Davies' senses, for example, would not be the same thing as providing a reductionistic account of the potential schemes for tokening such contents.

Final reflections

This brief review reveals that philosophers of mind have adopted multiple perspectives on information. To make progress, future philosophical discussions of information need to acknowledge the multi-faceted nature of information and differentiate at least five dimensions (Table 28.1). If an account treats a physically real thing as a piece of information, it must address at least three questions: What is the intensional content? What is the vehicle? And what is the content tokening scheme? Depending on the type of information, it may need to address two further questions: What is its truth value? And what does it refer to in the

Table 28.1 Five dimensions along which ways of counting something as "information" may vary

Facet of information	Examples
Type of intensional content	Conceptual/non-conceptual, linguistic, experiential, propositional, imagistic, symbolic/non-symbolic, analog/digital
Type of vehicle	Representation (understood various ways), affordance, mere carrier, brute storage
Content tokening scheme	Causal covariation; statistical; biosemantics; teleosemantics; conceptual role semantics; Kantian categorical imposition; convention/stipulation; gestalt structuring; natural vs non-natural
Potential truth/satisfaction values	None; true only; true or false; satisfaction (understood various ways); other possibilities
Type of extensional content	Actual objects; possible objects; rigidly-designated objects; real patterns; facts; relations; events; property instances; tropes; states of affairs; abstracta

world (i.e., what is its extensional content)? As our brief review of philosophical approaches makes clear, not only are there multiple answers to each question, there are multiple *categories* of answers for each question. Continued cross-pollination between philosophy of mind and information-related fields will require both to acknowledge the interrelatedness and multi-dimensionality of information-related notions.

Notes

1 See Aspray (1985) for more details on these conceptual developments.
2 For a historical account of the development of cognitive science, see Bechtel *et al.* (1998). Boden (2008) examines the various roles the notion of information has played in cognitive science. See also Chapter 26, this volume.
3 The "symbol grounding problem," discussed in Chapter 11, is a species of the more general problem of explaining the intentionality of informational states in non-mental terms. The "symbol grounding problem," in particular, is focused on *symbolic* states such as those found in a computer, and those invoked in, e.g., Fodor's "computational theory of mind."
4 Adams (2003: 491) notes the similarity of Dretske's explanation to Fodor's account of asymmetric dependence between a cognitive structure and what it means, but in Fodor's account, the key connection is secured by the existence of a law connecting the referent with the message.
5 Here MacKay's view bears a resemblance to Floridi's (2011, p. 164) "action-based semantics."
6 Grush (2002) uses the term 'content assignation scheme'.

References

Adams, F. (2003) "The Informational Turn in Philosophy," *Mind and Machines* 13: 471–501.
Allen, K. (2013) "Ideas," in P. R. Anstey (ed.), *Oxford Handbook of British Philosophy in the Seventeenth Century*, Oxford: Oxford University Press, pp. 329–48.
Aspray, W. (1985) "The Scientific Conceptualization of Information: A Survey," *Annals of the History of Computing* 7(2): 117–40.
Bechtel, W. (1988) *Philosophy of Mind: An Overview for Cognitive Science*, Hillsdale, NJ: Erlbaum.
Bechtel, W., Graham, G., and Abrahamsen, A. (1998) "The Life of Cognitive Science," in W. Bechtel and G. Graham (eds.), *A Companion to Cognitive Science*, Oxford: Blackwell, pp. 2–102.
Belnap, N. (1990) "Declaratives Are Not Enough," *Philosophical Studies* 59(1): 1–30.
Boden, M. (2008) "Information, Computation, and Cognitive Science," in P. Adriaans and J. van Benthem (eds.), *Handbook of the Philosophy of Science. Volume 8: Philosophy of Information*, Amsterdam: North Holland, pp. 749–69.
Chemero, A. (2009) *Radical Embodied Cognitive Science*, Cambridge, MA: MIT Press.
Crane, T. (2013) *The Objects of Thought*, Oxford: Oxford University Press.
Davies, M. (1995) "Consciousness and the Varieties of Aboutness," in C. Macdonald and G. Macdonald (eds.), *Philosophy of Psychology: Debates on Psychological Explanation*, Oxford: Blackwell, pp. 356–92.
Dennett, D. (1969) *Content and Consciousness*, London: Routledge.
Dennett, D. (1983) "Styles of Mental Representation," *Proceedings of the Aristotelian Society* 83: 213–26.
Dretske, F. (1981) *Knowledge and the Flow of Information*, Cambridge, MA: MIT Press.
Dretske, F. (1988) *Explaining Behavior: Reasons in a World of Causes*, Cambridge, MA: MIT Press.
Dretske, F. (2003) "Experience as Representation," *Philosophical Issues* 13(1): 67–82.
Dretske, F. (2009) "Information-Theoretic Semantics," in B. P. McLaughlin, A. Beckermann, and S. Walter (eds.), *Oxford Handbook of Philosophy of Mind*, Oxford: Oxford University Press, pp. 381–92.
Floridi, L. (2011). *The Philosophy of Information*, Oxford: Oxford University Press.
Grush, R. (1998) "Skill and Spatial Content," *Electronic Journal of Analytic Philosophy* 6(6).
Grush, R. (2002) "The Semantic Challenge to Computational Neuroscience," in P. K. Machamer, R. Grush, and P. McLaughlin (eds.), *Theory and Method in the Neurosciences*, Pittsburgh, PA: University of Pittsburgh Press, pp. 155–72.
MacKay, D. M. (1969) *Information, Mechanism, and Meaning*, Cambridge, MA: MIT Press.
McCulloch, W. S. and Pitts, W. (1943) "A Logical Calculus of the Ideas Immanent in Nervous Activity," *Bulletin of Mathematical Biophysics* 5: 115–33.

Miller, G. A. (1956) "The Magical Number Seven, Plus or Minus Two: Some Limits On Our Capacity for Processing Information," *Psychological Review* 63: 81–97.

Miller, G. A., Galanter, E., and Pribram, K. (1960) *Plans and the Structure of Behavior*, New York: Holt.

Millikan, R. (1984) *Language, Thought, and Other Biological Categories*, Cambridge, MA: MIT Press.

Neisser, U. (1967) *Cognitive Psychology*, Englewood Cliffs, NJ: Prentice-Hall.

Newell, A. and Simon, H. A. (1956) "The Logic Theory Machine: A Complex Information Processing System," *IRE Transactions on Information Theory* 2(3): 61–79.

Newell, A. and Simon, H. A. (1972) *Human Problem Solving*, Englewood Cliffs, NJ: Prentice Hall.

Pribram, K. (1986) "The Cognitive Revolution and Mind/Brain Issues," *American Psychologist* 41(5): 507–20.

Sayre, K. (1986) "Intentionality and Information Processing: An Alternative Model for Cognitive Science," *Behavioral and Brain Sciences* 9: 121–60.

Schrödinger, E. (1967) *What is Life?* Cambridge: Cambridge University Press.

Searle, J. R. (1980) "Minds, Brains, and Programs," *Behavioral and Brain Sciences* 3: 417–57.

Shannon, C. E. (1948) "A Mathematical Theory of Communication," *The Bell System Technical Journal* 27: 379–423, 623–56.

Turing, A. (1936) "On Computable Numbers, With an Application to the *Entscheidungsproblem*," *Proceedings of the London Mathematical Society* Series 2, 42: 230–65.

Weaver, W. (1949) "Recent Contributions to the Mathematical Theory of Communication," in C. E. Shannon and W. Weaver, *The Mathematical Theory of Communication*, Urbana, IL: University of Illinois Press, pp. 1–28.

Wiener, N. (1948) *Cybernetics: Or Control and Communication in the Animal and the Machine*, Cambridge, MA: MIT Press.

Yablo, S. (2014) *Aboutness*, Princeton, NJ: Princeton University Press.

29

THE MORAL VALUE OF INFORMATION AND INFORMATION ETHICS

Mariarosaria Taddeo

Introduction

The expression 'information societies' may not sound new to the reader, it refers to societies whose economic, political, and cultural welfare depends on the elaboration, communication, and manipulation of information. During the past three decades, the media and the press, academic articles, and even everyday discussions have increasingly focused on the informational, technology-driven turn that characterizes this historical moment, in which widely disseminated and radical changes affect both individuals and societies at the same time. Such changes generate new questions and problems ranging from individual well-being and the management of societies to the regulation of design and deployment of technological artefacts, as well as the definition of "good" and "evil" and our understanding and perception of reality itself.

In an influential paper, Moor (Moor 1985) described the changes that the information revolution was prompting and the need for conceptual analyses to address them properly. In his words: "although a problem ... may seem clear initially, a little reflection reveals a *conceptual muddle*. What is needed in such cases is an analysis which provides a coherent *conceptual framework within which to formulate a policy for action*" (Moor 1985: 266; emphasis mine). Three decades later, with contemporary societies turning into information societies, the policy vacuum, and the conceptual muddle underpinning it have become pressing issues to be solved. Understanding and regulating privacy and anonymity, as well as security in the information age offer some examples of the crucial issues that need to be addressed. At the same time, the information revolution is reshaping our understanding of fundamental concepts such as those of identity (Ess 2012), harm/evil (Floridi and Sanders 2001), warfare and state power (Taddeo 2012a), along with the way we act and perceive ourselves and reality (Floridi 2014).

In this chapter I shall focus on the contribution offered by information ethics (IE) to address the changes prompted by the information revolution. I will first describe the moral dimension of information and the implications of the information revolution when observed from an ethical level of abstraction (LoA) (see Chapter 7). This will be the task of the second section. I will then briefly turn my attention to the debate in computer ethics (CE) concerning the nature of the ethical problems related to the dissemination of ICTs, in the third section and its sub-section. In the fourth and fifth sections I will introduce

Floridi's framework for IE as an innovative approach devoted to addressing the ethical problems related to the information revolution. In the first sub-section of the fifth section, I will consider some of the most common criticisms moved to this framework. Finally, the sixth section will conclude the chapter.

The moral value of information

In considering what the moral dimension of information is, one may focus on the relation between moral responsibility and information, as the former cannot be ascribed to an agent for her moral choices if she did not have the relevant information when making her decision. Holding, or ignoring, a bit of information may affect the entire decision-making process; think about how the destiny of both Romeo and Juliet would have been different, had Romeo held the relevant information about Juliet's poison. In this case information would be (i) the epistemic source of a moral action. *Availability, accessibility,* and *accuracy* of information are all crucial issues when focusing on (i), they have been widely discussed in CE: consider the problems related to the ethics of informational resources, their trustworthiness (Turilli *et al.* 2010), and the value of access to information in contemporary societies (van den Hoven and Rooksby 2001; Mathiesen 2012).

Information can also be (ii) the result of a moral decision as remarked in Cavalier (2005). Consider, for example, Alice intentionally distributing false messages to protect her friends. Information warfare (Libicki 1996; Floridi and Taddeo 2014), understood as the dissemination of information (propaganda) among the enemy's civil population so to promote rebellion, offers an example of (ii) (see Chapter 27). Ethical problems pertaining to accountability, liability, and deception arise in this case, as well as issues concerning the sharing and circulation of information, for example problems related to peer-to-peer (P2P) (Taddeo and Vaccaro 2011) and protection of intellectual rights. Advertising, spamming, and viral messages also are instances of (ii).

When we think of actions whose implications affect the informational environment, it becomes evident that information can also be (iii) the target of a moral action. Cyber-attacks offer a good example. Consider the case of distributed denial of service (DDOS)[1] attacks; even when they have specific targets they may still affect the entire set of communication going on in a specific region of the cyber-sphere, in doing so they disrupt the informational environment. (iii) refers to the cases in which the informational environment (more about this in the fourth section) is the receiver of Alice's actions.

Points (i)–(iii) indicate different ways in which moral value can be ascribed to information. However, there is a more fundamental moral dimension of information to be considered. Such a dimension is related to the information revolution and the changes that it has prompted. At first sight, the changes engendered by the breakthroughs in ICTs seem to affect only the way in which we conduct our private and social lives. Smartphones and social networks offer two evident examples. Nonetheless, a more careful analysis shows new and deeper levels of transformation involving the very way in which human beings perceive themselves and the environment. The information revolution now goes hand in hand with a conceptual revolution, which is reshaping our understanding of the world, our metaphysics, anthropology, and ethics.

This is not an unprecedented phenomenon. Following Freud's interpretation of scientific revolutions (Freud 1917), Floridi argues that throughout history, scientific and technological discoveries have contributed in a determining way to the redefinition of our understanding of ourselves and of the universe (Floridi 2014). More specifically, Freud identified three scientific revolutions that, in the course of human history, have also prompted conceptual revolutions: the Copernican revolution, which brought us to acknowledge that human beings are not at the center of the universe; the Darwinian revolution, which showed that human beings are part of the animal kingdom; and the Freudian revolution, which for the first time unveiled that the human mind is far from being transparent to itself. The information revolution is the latest of this kind and Turing is its father. Floridi refers to it as to the *fourth revolution*, to indicate the reshaping of the human nature and the reassessment of the place of human beings in the universe brought about by the informational turn.

By interpreting the information revolution as a conceptual revolution we recognize that the design, development, and implementation of new technological artefacts is part of a bigger process which prompts radical transformations of the intrinsic nature, or ontology, of the environment in which we live, of the agents and objects existing therein. *Re-ontologization* (Floridi 2007) is the word used to describe such a process. It refers to an increase of the informational space as well as to the transformation from analogue to digital data that occurs in the environment. However, the re-ontologization process also highlights the informational nature that is common to all existing entities and to the interactions occurring among them as well as to the environment in which they exist (see Chapter 18).

The re-ontologization process should not be mistaken for a futuristic vision. It is happening before our eyes, and individuals living in information societies experience it on a daily basis. The *blurring* of the boundary between the cyber-sphere and the physical environment offers one of the most common instances of such a process. It has been noted and analyzed by social scientists (Price 2002) and psychologists (Hasebrink 2008), as well as by philosophers (Coole *et al.* 2010; Taddeo 2012b; Floridi 2013; Taddeo 2014b; Floridi and Taddeo 2014). The blurring has widened the range of what we consider "real," of the ultimate nature of reality. The existence of an entity is no longer identified with its physical, in the Newtonian sense, presence. Reality has come to include intangible entities and environments along with physical ones, and existence is no longer related to tangibility as much as to *interactability* (Floridi 2013). Think for example at the way in which Alice and her grandfather Bob enjoy their music: Bob may still own a collection of his favorite LP records in vinyl, while Alice simply logs into her favorite streaming service (she does not even have the files on her computers); books, movies, pictures all serve as good examples of the re-ontolgization process.

In this scenario, also the intrinsic nature of human beings – *inforgs* – and of the environment – the *infosphere* – that they inhabit is being redefined. The former should not be mistaken for the sci-fi stereotype description of a human being – cyborg – nor should it be mistaken for an individual data shadow, or digital alter ego, typically one's online profile or avatar. Rather, inforgs are the product of the re-ontologizing process, when this involves human beings who, by living in the age of the information revolution and conducting their existence in a synchronized, delocalized, correlated reality (Floridi 2006), discover their intrinsically informational nature.

The term "infosphere" has two interpretations: environmental and metaphysical. The environmental understanding identifies the infosphere with the environment along with all existing things, be they digital or analogue, physical or non-physical, and the relations occurring among them, and also the relations between them and the environment. One may recall the LoAs (see Chapter 7), and consider the infosphere as the environment, along with all the entities populating it as well as their relations, observed from an informational LoA. It is worthwhile noticing at this point that the infosphere should not be confused with the cyber-sphere, for the latter is just a portion of the former. Metaphysically, the infosphere refers to the whole realm of reality, the Being, and rests on the assumption of an informational ontology (see Chapter 18) (Floridi 2008a). In this case, the infosphere is the totality of what exists once its informational nature is unveiled.

Ethical problems related to the moral dimension of information, both in the sense of (i)–(iii) and in the one related to the re-ontologization process, are at the center of the debate concerning CE and IE, though the two differ in the visions underpinning their analysis of these problems.

From cybernetics and computer ethics to information ethics

CE and IE have their origins in the 1940s and 1950s in the work of Wiener, who introduced the term "cybernetics" (Wiener 1965) to refer to an interdisciplinary research field dedicated to the study of information feedback both in natural and artificial systems and who, for the first time, focused on the potential impact of ICTs on humankind and society. Famously he stressed: "long before Nagasaki and the public awareness of the atomic bomb, it had occurred to me that we were here in the presence of another social potentiality of unheard-of importance for good and for evil," (Wiener 1948: 27–28). The ethical concern raised by Wiener remained marginal and largely ignored for more than a decade, before it was brought to the fore again between the 1960s and the 1970s, when CE emerged as a new field of study.[2]

IE and CE are tightly related. As we shall see in the rest of this section, IE as an ethical theory offers the conceptual foundations needed by CE as a research field. To clarify this point, a step back is required. Since the mid-1980s, CE has been characterized by a debate over the novelty and uniqueness of the problems with which it is concerned. The so-called *uniqueness debate* (Tavani 2002).

The answers to these questions vary depending on one's view of the problems at stake. Some have regarded these problems as "new versions of standard moral problems and moral dilemmas, exacerbating the old problems, and forcing us to apply ordinary moral norms in uncharted realm" (Johnson 1999). Scholars such as Johnson and Miller (Johnson and Miller 2008) for example do not deem radical, or totally novel, the changes brought about by the information revolution and consider CE to be a research field focusing on specific issues related to the management of information (see points (i)–(iii) in the second section above). For those agreeing with this position, CE endorses a decision-oriented approach and is devoted to offering applicable solutions on a case-by-case basis. This approach has led to addressing specific problems, develops *ad hoc* solutions, and in doing so it focuses on one moral dimension of information at the time; the reader may recall the three moral dimensions of information described in the second section. Criticisms have been made of this approach. For example, Floridi (2013) argues that it has supported the development of CE as a *micro-ethics*. The ethical analyses of ICT-related problems are micro-ethical insofar as the focus is on a smaller problem space than the one that may be addressed by considering all three dimensions of information together (see Figure 29.1).

CE as a micro-ethics is questioned by those scholars who see in the ethical problems pertaining to the development and deployment of ICTs not simply a new version of old ethical conundrums but radically new issues engendered by the specific nature of computers and ICTs (Moor 1985; Mason 1986; Maner 1996; Floridi 2013). In this respect, the analysis proposed by Moor (1985) pioneered this way of considering ICT-related ethical problems. Moor's article stressed for the first time that computing machines were universal tools that can ideally perform any operation as long as this is defined in terms of input, output and logical operators, and that this would lead to unprecedented changes, which would cause difficulties in the management and regulation of the use of such technologies, i.e. the policy vacuum, which posed the need for innovative conceptual analyses. In Moor's words

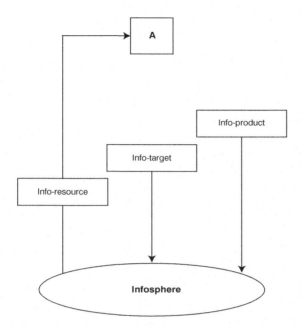

Figure 29.1 The three moral dimensions of information (Floridi 2013: 20)

one difficulty is that along with the policy vacuum there is often a conceptual vacuum. Although a problem in CE may seem clear initially, a little reflection reveals a conceptual muddle. What it needed in such cases is an analysis that provides a coherent conceptual framework within which to formulate a policy for action.

(Moor 1985: 269)

IE rests on this side of the debate and proposes an innovative approach concerned with the scope of the enquiry and the conceptual foundation of CE. Let me begin with the scope of enquiry, I shall deal with the conceptual foundation of CE in the fourth section. IE is presented as a *macro-ethics*: a theoretical, domain-independent, applicable ethics that is concerned with all the moral dimensions of information identified in the second section. In doing so, IE shifts the approach, for it does not focus on information-related problems, e.g. information warfare, privacy, or transparency; rather it analyses the moral scenario *informationally*, that is, it endorses an informational LoA by considering the entities under scrutiny also in relation to their informational environment.

This position rests on an analysis of the shortcomings of CE as a micro-ethics, two of which are noteworthy. Ethical problems addressed by CE may pertain to one or the other moral dimension of information; however clear-cut distinctions are mostly unlikely. Consider for example censorship, which may affect one both as a producer and as a user of information, or testimony. Alice's testimony can be regarded as a product (ii), which then becomes a source of moral decision (in the sense of (i)) when communicated to Bob. The second drawback refers to those problems that cannot really be placed in any of the dimensions of information highlighted in the second section, for they emerge from the interactions among the agents and the environment – pervasive surveillance and cyber-warfare being two notable examples.

A few approaches have been proposed during the past decades to broaden the scope of CE frameworks so to address the need for a macro-CE. The next section focuses on one such a framework proposed in van den Hoven and Rooksby (2001).

Information as a primary good

van den Hoven's and Rooksby's analysis relies on Rawls' theory of distributive justice (Rawls 1999). It rests on an understanding of information as a necessary condition for the well-being of both individuals and societies and proposes two ethical principles ensuring a fair distribution of information among the members of society.

Before analyzing in more detail van den Hoven's and Rooksby's framework, let me briefly introduce some key aspects of Rawls' theory. Rawls' theory offers two principles to shape the design of the basic institutions of a fair society. The principles are such that they would be accepted in the "Original Position," that is a hypothetical scenario, in which rational and mutually disinterested parties acting behind the "veil of ignorance" – i.e. unaware of their social situation, interests, and needs – decide the principles that ought to guide society. The proposed principles are as follows, the first principle being more fundamental than the second one:

- first principle: each person is to have an equal right to a fully adequate scheme of equal basic liberties compatible with a similar system of liberties for all [the liberty principle].
- second principle: social and economic inequalities are to satisfy two conditions. First, they must be attached to offices and positions open to all under conditions of fair equality of opportunity [the opportunity principle]; and, second, they must be to the greatest benefit of the least advantaged members of society [the difference principle] (Rawls 1999: 53).

Rights and liberties are distributed following the first principle, while the second principle focuses on the distribution of opportunities and social primary goods. Primary goods are those goods that are deemed necessary for individual well-being, for they are required by any human agent to make rational decisions and plan his/her life. As Rawls put it "primary goods are singled out by asking which things are generally necessary as social conditions and all-purpose means to enable persons to pursue their determinate conceptions of the good and to develop and exercise their two moral powers" (Rawls 1999: 307). Rawls specifies four categories of primary goods, namely: rights and liberties, opportunities, income and wealth, and the social bases of self-respect.

van den Hoven's and Rooksby's analysis distinguishes between information as true semantic content and informative objects, such as for examples books, websites, and newspapers. While the former cannot be distributed, for its acquisition depends on the effort of the individual agents, the latter are all considered a resource that can indeed be dispensed among the members of societies, just like wealth for example. Hence, the proposed framework focuses on the *access* to informative objects as to a primary good.

More specifically, access to informative objects shows three features that allow it to qualify as a primary good according to Rawls' theory. These are: having access to informative objects is generally desirable and a better condition than being denied access to informative objects, this holds true irrespective of the specific goal one may have; it is desirable to have more access to informative objects; access to informative objects would be useful to an agent whatever her plans for life are.

van den Hoven's and Rooksby's analysis proposes two principles for the distribution of access to informative objects in societies. While the first principle poses access to informative objects as a basic liberty, the second one ensures fair opportunities to exercise information liberties.

1 the freedom to acquire information relevant to rational life-planning qualifies as a basic liberty under the first principle of justice; and
2 opportunities to acquire information are like opportunities for education and health care, afforded under the opportunity principle.

The proposed principles and approach are meant to offer a broad perspective to address ethical issues related to information, including problems such as the digital divide and the trustworthiness of information resources. This framework also offers one of the first attempts to develop a macro-ethical approach to CE. Indeed, it broadens the focus of the analysis moving from ICT-related issues to *information*-related problems and their impact on society at large. Nonetheless, the proposed analysis is still very much centered on the value of information as a resource (in the sense of (i) specified in section 2) to be able to properly address the ethical problems concerning the overall moral value of information and, hence, to expand the scope of enquiry of CE.

At the same time, by relying on Rawls' distributive justice to address information-related problems, the framework embraces Johnson's position about the non-unique nature of such problems. Like Johnson's argument, also this framework is then amenable to the objection of failing to addressing the novelty and the radical changes brought about by the information revolution. As Floridi puts it:

> although the novelty of CE is not so dramatic as to require the development of an utterly new, separate and unrelated discipline, it certainly shows some limits of traditional approaches to the ethical discourse, and encourages a fruitful modification in our metatheoretical perspective.
>
> *(Floridi 2013: 97)*

The analysis of Floridi's framework for IE will be our next task.

The innovative approach of IE

Floridi's framework for IE rests on three conceptual moves, which make its contribution to the analysis of ethical issues related to ICTs more innovative than the ones described so far. These are:

a from an action-oriented ethics to an ethics of *care*;
b from agents to patients;
c from an anthropocentric and biocentric approach to an *ontocentric* approach.

The three moves differentiate quite radically IE from *standard* macro-ethical theories, i.e. consequentialism, deontologism, and virtue ethics, all endorsing an anthropocentric approach. Standard macro-ethical theories, in particular consequentialism and deontologism, focus on actions as the center of their analyses. As such they are also *relational*, insofar as an action establishes a relation between the agent and the receiver of the action. Both consequentialism and deontologism do not focus so much on Alice and Bob as the source and the receiver of the action as much as they do on the nature of the actions and the choice Alice makes. These ethical theories ask the question "What ought I to do?" and are standard macro-ethics, as they have an anthropocentric bias.

IE moves away from this approach and asks quite a different question: "What ought to be respected or improved?" In doing so it shifts the focus from Alice's actions and choices to the *respect/care* that is due to Bob. IE inherits the concept of care from medical and environmental ethics: the agent has the moral duty to care for the receiver of her actions and an action is morally good only when it rests on the care for the patient's sake. The first move prepares the ground for the second one, from agent to patient.

The focus on the patient is also grounded in the approach common to medical and environmental ethics and rests on the view that any form of life has some, although minimal, moral interest and as such deserves respect. The resulting well-being of the patient of a given action is both the measure of the moral standing of the action and the criterion guiding Alice's actions and choices.

The patient, the receiver of the action, is at the center of the ethical discourse, whereas the agent moves to the edge. In doing so, IE widens the scope of moral prescriptions, for rational, informed agents are no longer the only referents in assessing a moral scenario. This leads us to the last move, which sees IE endorsing an ontocentric approach.

(c) is the most complex of the three moves, but it is also the one that allows IE to provide an innovative and sophisticated framework for addressing ethical issues pertaining to ICTs. With this move, information goes from being an epistemic requirement for any morally responsible actions (see (i) in the second section) to being the primary focus (in the sense of (b)) of any moral action.

IE endorses a non-anthropocentric approach for the ethical analysis. It attributes a moral value to all existing entities (both physical and non-physical) by applying the principle of ontological equality, "[which] means that any form of reality ... simply for the fact of being what it is, enjoys a minimal, initial, *overrideable*, equal right to exist and develop in a way which is appropriate to its nature" (Floridi 2006: 28). The principle is grounded in an information-based ontology, according to which all existing things can be considered from an informational standpoint and are understood as informational entities, all sharing the same informational nature. At first glance, an artefact, a computer, a book or the Colosseum seem to enjoy only an instrumental value. This is because one endorses an anthropocentric LoA; in other words, one considers these objects as a user, a reader, or as a tourist. In all these cases the moral value of the observed entity depends on the agent interacting with it and on her purpose in doing so. The claim put forward by IE is that these LoAs are not adequate to support an effective analysis of the moral scenario that the information revolution has brought to the fore.

The anthropocentric, or even the biocentric, LoA prevents us from considering properly the nature and the role of ICT artefacts in the reality in which we live. The argument is that all existing things have an informational nature which is shared across the entire spectrum of reality – from abstract to physical and tangible entities, from rocks and books to robots and human beings – and that all entities enjoy some *minimal initial* moral value *qua informational* entities.

IE argues that universal moral analyses can be developed by focusing on the common nature of all existing things and by defining good and evil with respect to such a nature. The focus of ethical analysis is thereby shifted, since the initial moral value of an entity does not depend on the observer (the reader may recall move (a)), but is defined in absolute terms and depends on the (informational) nature of the entities.

Following the principle of ontological equality, *minimal and overrideable rights* to exist and flourish belong to all existing things and not just to human or living things. The Colosseum,

Jane Austen's writings, a human being and computer software all share *initial* rights, as they are all informational entities. A clarification is now in order. IE endorses a minimalist approach; it considers informational nature as the minimal common denominator among all existing things. However, this minimalist approach should not be mistaken for reductionism, as IE does not claim that the informational one is the unique LoA from which moral discourse is, or should be, addressed. Rather, it maintains that the informational LoA provides a *minimal starting point*, which can then be enriched by considering other moral perspectives (I shall return to this point in the first sub-section of the fifth section). Having clarified the conceptual groundings of IE, we can now focus on the normative prescriptions of this ethical framework.

Informational evil and informational good

"*IE adopts a LoA at which Being and the infosphere are co-referential*" (Floridi 2013: 65; emphasis mine). The reader may recall that the first sub-section of the second section referred to this way of understanding the infosphere as to the metaphysical one, the definitions of informational evil and informational good follow from such an understanding.

Floridi refers to informational evil as to *metaphysical entropy*. The choice of this term was admittedly confusing (Floridi 2013), because it would bring about the concept of physical entropy or entropy as defined by Shannon, which are both not relevant when it comes to IE. Metaphysical entropy has a very specific meaning, for it refers to any form of destruction of information and as such of Being. It indicates the opposite of semantic and ontic information (see Chapter 6), as such metaphysical entropy refers to the decay, the corruption, of content of the infosphere and of the entities inhabiting it, and hence it is a form of impoverishment of Being. Insofar as Being is co-referential to the infosphere, metaphysical entropy is analogous to the metaphysical concept of *nothingness*. Corrupting a file or damaging a piece of art, violating someone's privacy and killing a living being are all examples of metaphysical entropy.

Informational good, as the opposite of the metaphysical entropy, is any form of flourishing of informational entities and of the infosphere. IE endorses an environmental approach, which rests on moves (a) and (b) described in the fourth section. The ultimate patient, whose well-being ought to be at the center of the moral concern of any agent, is the informational environment. This is a key point of IE, which can be also traced in authors such as Adeney and Weckert (1997); Rowlands (2000) and Woodbury (2003).

The environmental connotation of IE explains the centrality of the infosphere. For, according to IE, the enrichment, extension and improvement (without any corresponding ontological loss) including its reshaping and the implementation of new realities in the infosphere is the ultimate good. The reader may recall that the infosphere has both an environmental and a metaphysical meaning. In defining IE as an environmental ethics devoted to supporting the flourishing of the infosphere, one also refers to the ontological commitment of IE toward the flourishing of Being (the opposite of metaphysical entropy).

The environmental focus also places IE in the tradition of non-standard macro-ethics, which endorse a non-anthropocentric approach, like bioethics and land ethics, and in doing so aim at enlarging the boundaries of moral discourse to include non-living entities such as water, air and soil. IE implements this approach and takes it to the extreme by adopting a universal ontology, which excludes nothing from its moral prescription. As such, IE offers four universal ethical principles to identify right and wrong and the moral duties of an agent. These are:

0   entropy ought not to be caused in the infosphere (null law);
1   entropy ought to be prevented in the infosphere;
2   entropy ought to be removed from the infosphere;
3   the flourishing of informational entities as well as of the whole infosphere ought to be promoted by preserving, cultivating and enriching their properties.

The four principles clarify, in very broad terms, what it means to be a responsible and caring agent in the infosphere. They are listed in decreasing order of importance. Breaking rule number 3 is less despicable than breaking rule number 2. Breaking rule number 0, the null law, is the worst an informational agent can do, so the blame is the highest. Accordingly, an action is unconditionally praiseworthy only if it never generates any entropy in the course of its implementation; and the best moral action is the one that succeeds in satisfying all four principles at the same time.

Most of the actions that we judge morally good do not satisfy such strict criteria, for they achieve only a balanced positive moral value; that is, although their performance causes a certain amount of entropy, we acknowledge that the infosphere is in a better state on the whole after their occurrence.

Criticisms to IE

Having introduced the main aspects of IE, I shall now devote my attention to considering three of the most common objections moved against IE and which concern:

1   the intrinsic moral value of *all* (informational) ethics;
2   the reductionism of IE;
3   the applicability of IE.

The first objection questions the possibility of ascribing intrinsic moral worthiness to all informational entities *qua informational entities* (Brey 2008; Floridi 2008b; Vaccaro 2008). The objection rests on the common-sense approach, which easily recognizes as instrumental rather than as intrinsic the value of non-living entities. From this assumption, the criticism moves to stress that it is untenable to address a moral scenario in which all entities share the same moral worthiness. The objection would be correct had it not overlooked the fact that according to IE, entities have *different degrees* of moral value and as such they are entitled to different degrees of moral respect. Such a respect ranges from the minimal, overridable, disinterested and appreciative care due to a stone to the absolute, high-level respect due to a human being. IE does not claim that all entities have the same moral value and hence deserve the same level of moral care. Rather, it claims that since all entities share an informational nature, all entities should be ascribed some *initial, minimal* moral worthiness, which makes all entities participate in the moral scenario. In this way IE develops a comprehensive (universal) moral discourse able to take into account the stance of different moral entities, from artificial and human agents to intangible objects and the de-physicalized environment – all of which, while central in the world as we know it after the information revolution, are not satisfactorily accommodated by other standard macro-ethics (see the third section).

The objection confuses IE commitment to the inclusiveness of the moral discourse with an attempt to create a flat moral scenario where all entities play the same role. In this sense, the criticism betrays a deep misunderstanding of the goals of IE, for it misses both the universality of its approach and the value that IE attaches to diversity and plurality. Ascribing moral value to all entities allows specifically for including them in the moral discourse but it does not lead to ignore their differences.

The second objection also focuses on the informational nature of the considered entities (Stahl 2008; Floridi 2008b). In particular, it criticizes IE for being reductionist in that it reduces all entities to their informational nature and as such overlooks other aspects of patients, agents and of the environment. The starting point of the objection is indeed correct; human beings, but also the environment, and the entities existing within it, are not just information. The criticism, however, is misguided, for it confuses the method of LoAs, which shapes IE's approach, with reductionism and forgets about the pluralism that characterized this method of analysis (see Chapter 7). IE does not claim that everything is *just* information, the claim is rather that if we endorse an informational LoA, then we will be able to find a common, fundamental aspect to all existing things. To use a metaphor: the objection states that if one looks at the world using a black-and-white camera, then one will believe that the world is in black and white and will overlook all the other colors. However, this is not the claim of IE, whose position is rather that by using a black-and-white camera one discovers patterns that are common to all the observed things. This does not imply that the reality is in black and white, nor does it forbid the use of color cameras. There may be situations where the latter are more appropriate. However, having practiced with a black-and-white camera, one may be able to recognize common aspects characterizing different scenarios and hence be able to unveil new fundamental futures. Abandoning the metaphor, IE endorses an informational LoA because this permits the development of an inclusive moral discourse by unveiling the informational nature of reality. This is not to reduce the universe to information, but to highlight a common substrate on which the differences of the entities inhabiting it can then be further appreciated. Ascribing moral value to informational entities provides only a *minimalist starting point*, which is overridable when moral concerns formulated by other macro-ethical analyses require a more fine-grained LoA.

The answer to the second objection may prompt the third criticism, which is concerned with the relevance and the applicability of IE. The question posed in this case is twofold and has to do with the observation that everyday life and ordinary moral decisions often face overriding moral concerns. If this is the case, then IE seems irrelevant, for it does not specify the level of moral worthiness of different entities. Furthermore, if not irrelevant, it is too metaphysical, too theoretical, to ever be of any help in addressing pragmatic cases and ethical conundrums. Let us address one side of the problem at the time.

The relevancy of IE is not questioned by the possible conflicts with other ethical theories. This objection surmises that different ethical theories necessary conflict one with each other, but this is not always the case. In many cases ethical theories can actually be complementary and mutually beneficial; business and environmental ethics, bio- and medical ethics offer interesting examples in this case. Furthermore, the reader may recall that IE is devoted to addressing a specific problem space, the one opened by the dissemination of ICTs and the fourth revolution, that other macro-ethics do not satisfactorily tackle. IE focuses on the new problems posed by an information-dependent, dephysicalized, digitalized society and environment, and calls for a new ethics to educate not just designers and developers and users, but also individuals living in the information society, in order to live, respect and foster the informational environment. The relevance of IE becomes evident, along with the novelty of its approach, when considering the specificity of the problems that it addresses. The possibility of conflicting and being overriden by other ethical theories shrinks dramatically when the uniqueness of the problem space that IE addresses is considered.

One may still argue that IE remains too theoretical to be useful in tackling any ethical problems that information societies may face. The reader may recall that in the second section the absence of a theoretical framework and the tendency to develop case-by-case analyses were mentioned as two of the weakening aspects of CE. IE has the goal to clarify the conceptual muddle underpinning the policy vacuum that Moor (1985) described, and as such, applicability is one of its goals. Since IE has been proposed, several innovative analyses have been developed to address complex pragmatic cases, proving IE not just applicable but also effective (Burk 2008; Turilli and Floridi 2009; Turilli *et al.* 2011; Turilli *et al.* 2010; Taddeo and Vaccaro 2011; Floridi and Taddeo 2014; Taddeo 2014a).

It is also worth recalling that the metaphysical roots of IE and its theoretical approach provide a solid grounding of the theory, which if anything makes it more refined, not less effective. Because of such grounding, IE can afford to provide universal principles that offer the conceptual foundation for developing a web of consistent ethical analyses. The theoretical infrastructure of IE allows for constructing an ethical framework to help design, shape and live in the informational environment rather than a series of *ad hoc* analyses developed on a case-by-case basis.

Conclusion

The chapter has offered an overview of the key concepts related to the moral value of information and to crucial aspect of CE and IE. Its goals were to introduce the reader to the ethical problems that contemporary societies face after the information revolution, to describe the on-going debate about such problems along to the most significant aspects of IE and its contribution to CE as a research field. Of the many features characterizing this ethical theory, three are pivotal:

1 the metaphysical grounding;
2 the macro-ethics scope;
3 the environmental approach.

The metaphysical foundation anchors the ontocentric principle on a solid ground, for it shows that the informational nature is indeed common to all existing things and as such, moral value, albeit minimal, needs to be recognized by all entities sharing this nature: the whole realm of reality. Such moral value is not ascribed because of an entity's role in the environment; according to IE, moral worthiness comes with the very existence of an entity. It is the *degree* of such worthiness that requires further assessment and which can vary.

The ontocentric principle substantiates the universality of IE, which is what allows it to satisfactorily address the issues posed by the information revolution. For IE, as a non-standard macro-ethics, is free from the anthropocentric bias and proves to be a universal ethics. It focuses on the most minimal aspect, the very existence, of entities in order to define the range of the moral discourse.

The environmental focus follows from IE's non-standard approach, for it identifies the infosphere, and not a specific set of entities, for example human beings or artificial agents, as the patient to which the ultimate respect and care are due. In doing so, IE puts a burden on the shoulders of human agents, making them responsible inhabitants and designers of the informational environment with the moral duties to protect and foster its flourishing. Hence IE unveils the Demiurge's responsibility of human agents in caring, designing, and managing the environment. In this sense, IE is an ethics of stewardship, the ultimate form of cybernetics.

Notes

1 A description of DDOS attack can be found here: http://en.wikipedia.org/wiki/Denial-of-service_attack
2 A historical overview of the development of CE and IE falls outside the scope of this chapter, the reader may find interesting in this respect to consult Bynum (2008).

References

Adeney, Douglas, J. Weckert. 1997. *Computer and Information Ethics*. Westport, CT: Praeger.
Brey, Philip, 2008. "Do We Have Moral Duties towards Information Objects?" *Ethics and Information Technology* 10 (2–3): 109–14. doi:10.1007/s10676-008-9170-x.
Burk, Dan L., 2008. "Information Ethics and the Law of Data Representations." *Ethics and Information Technology* 10 (2–3): 135–47. doi:10.1007/s10676-008-9161-y.
Bynum, Terrell, W. 2008. "Milestones in the History of Information and Computer Ethics." In *The Handbook of Information and Computer Ethics*, edited by Kenneth Einar Himma, 25–48. John Wiley & Sons, Inc. http://onlinelibrary.wiley.com/doi/10.1002/9780470281819.ch2/summary.
Cavalier, Robert J., ed. 2005. *The Impact of the Internet on Our Moral Lives*. Albany, NY: State University of New York Press.
Coole, Diana, S. Frost, J. Bennett, P. Cheah, M. A. Orlie, and E. Grosz. 2010. *New Materialisms: Ontology, Agency, and Politics*. Durham, NC: Duke University Press.
Ess, Charles, 2012. "At the Intersections Between Internet Studies and Philosophy: 'Who Am I Online?'" *Philosophy & Technology* 25 (3): 275–84.
Floridi, Luciano, 2006. "Information Ethics, Its Nature and Scope." *SIGCAS Comput. Soc.* 36 (3): 21–36. doi:10.1145/1195716.1195719.
Floridi, Luciano, 2007. "A Look into the Future Impact of ICT on Our Lives." *The Information Society* 23 (1): 59–64. doi:10.1080/01972240601059094.
Floridi, Luciano, 2008a. "A Defence of Informational Structural Realism." *Synthese* 161 (2): 219–53. doi:10.1007/s11229-007-9163-z.
Floridi, Luciano, 2008b. "Information Ethics: A Reappraisal." *Ethics and Information Technology* 10 (2–3): 189–204. doi:10.1007/s10676-008-9176-4.
Floridi, Luciano, 2013. *Ethics of Information*. Oxford and New York: Oxford University Press.
Floridi, Luciano, 2014. *The Fourth Revolution – How the Infosphere Is Reshaping Human Reality*. Oxford: Oxford University Press.
Floridi, Luciano and J. Sanders. 2001. "Artificial Evil and the Foundation of Computer Ethics." *Ethics and Information Technology* 3 (1): 55–66.
Floridi, Luciano and M. Taddeo, eds. 2014. *The Ethics of Information Warfare*. New York: Springer.
Freud, Sigmund, n.d. *A Difficulty in the Path of Psycho Analysis*. Vol. XVII(1917–19): 135–44. The Standard Edition of the Complete Psychological Works of Sigmund Freud. 1955.
Hasebrink, Uwe, 2008. *Comparing Children's Online Opportunities and Risks across Europe: Cross-National Comparisons for EU Kids Online : [European Research on Cultural, Contextual and Risk Issues in Children's Safe Use of the Internet and New Media (2006–2009)]*. [London]: EU Kids Online. http://www.eukidsonline.net/.
Johnson, Deborah G. 1999. "Sorting Out the Uniqueness of Computer-Ethical Issues." http://www.openstarts.units.it/dspace/handle/10077/5541.
Johnson, Deborah G. and Keith W. Miller. 2008. "Un-Making Artificial Moral Agents." *Ethics and Information Technology* 10 (2–3): 123–33. doi:10.1007/s10676-008-9174-6.
Libicki, Michael, 1996. *What Is Information Warfare?* Washington: National Defense University Press.
Maner, Walter, 1996. "Unique Ethical Problems in Information Technology." *Science and Engineering Ethics* 2 (2): 137–54. doi:10.1007/BF02583549.
Mason, Richard O. 1986. "Four Ethical Issues of the Information Age." *MIS Q.* 10 (1): 5–12. doi:10.2307/248873.
Mathiesen, Kay, 2012. "What Is Information Ethics?" SSRN Scholarly Paper ID 2081302. Rochester, NY: Social Science Research Network. http://papers.ssrn.com/abstract=2081302.
Moor, James H. 1985. "What Is Computer Ethics?" *Metaphilosophy* 16 (4): 266–75. doi:10.1111/j.1467-9973.1985.tb00173.x.

Price, Monroe E. 2002. *Media and Sovereignty: The Global Information Revolution and Its Challenge to State Power*. Cambridge, MA: MIT Press.

Rawls, John, 1999. *A Theory of Justice*. Rev. ed. Cambridge, MA: Belknap Press of Harvard University Press.

Rowlands, Mark, 2000. *The Environmental Crisis: Understanding the Value of Nature*. New York: Palgrave Macmillan.

Stahl, Bernd Carsten. 2008. "Discourses on Information Ethics: The Claim to Universality." *Ethics and Information Technology* 10 (2–3): 97–108. doi:10.1007/s10676-008-9171-9.

Taddeo, Mariarosaria, 2012a. "Information Warfare: A Philosophical Perspective." *Philosophy and Technology* 25 (1): 105–20.

Taddeo, Mariarosaria, 2012b. "Information Warfare: A Philosophical Perspective." *Philosophy and Technology* 25 (1): 105–20.

Taddeo, Mariarosaria, 2014a. "Just Information Warfare." *Topoi*, April, 1–12. doi:10.1007/s11245-014-9245-8.

Taddeo, Mariarosaria, 2014b. "The Struggle Between Liberties and Authorities in the Information Age." *Science and Engineering Ethics*, September, 1–14. doi:10.1007/s11948-014-9586-0.

Taddeo, Mariarosaria, A. Vaccaro. 2011. "Analyzing Peer-to-Peer Technology Using Information Ethics." *The Information Society* 27 (2): 105–12. doi:10.1080/01972243.2011.548698.

Tavani, Herman T. 2002. "The Uniqueness Debate in Computer Ethics: What Exactly Is at Issue, and Why Does It Matter?" *Ethics and Inf. Technol.* 4 (1): 37–54. doi:10.1023/A:1015283808882.

Turilli, Matteo, and L. Floridi. 2009. "The Ethics of Information Transparency." *Ethics and Information Technology* 11 (2): 105–12. doi:10.1007/s10676-009-9187-9.

Turilli, Matteo, A. Vaccaro, and Mariarosaria Taddeo. 2011. "Internet Neutrality: Ethical Issues in the Internet Environment." *Philosophy & Technology* 25 (2): 133–51. doi:10.1007/s13347-011-0039-2.

Turilli, Matteo, A. Vaccaro, and M. Taddeo. 2010. "The Case of on-Line Trust." *Knowledge, Technology & Policy* 23.3–4 (3–4, Special issue on Trust in Technology): 333–45.

Vaccaro, Antonino, 2008. "Information Ethics as a Macroethics: Perspectives for Further Research." *APA Newsletter on Philosophy and Computers* 7 (2): 16–17.

van den Hoven, Jeroen, E. Rooksby. 2001. "Distributive Justice and the Value of Information: A (Broadly) Rawlsian Approach." In *Information Technology and Moral Philosophy*, edited by Jeroen van den Hoven and John Weckert, 376–96. Cambridge: Cambridge University Press. http://ebooks.cambridge.org/ref/id/CBO9780511498725A025.

Wiener, Norbert, 1965. *Cybernetics, Second Edition: Or the Control and Communication in the Animal and the Machine*. Second edition. New York: MIT Press.

Woodbury, Marsha, 2003. *Computer and Information Ethics*. Champaign, IL: Stipes Pub LLC.

30

ART AND THE
INFORMATION SOCIETY

Katherine Thomson-Jones

Introduction

Without assuming any particular account of information, there is a basic sense in which information societies have existed as long as human beings have lived together and relied on data exchange. At the same time, there is another sense in which the information society is a very recent phenomenon. As a theoretical notion, the "information society" was introduced by economists in the 1970s to refer to a new, post-industrial phase of development marked by the growth of the service sector and the introduction of digital communications technology (Crawford 1983). The arrival of the personal computer in the 1980s and the rise of the Internet in the 1990s gave this notion even greater significance. The massive proliferation of networked digital devices allows for the processing and distribution of information at an unprecedented rate and without the limitations traditionally imposed by geographical distance or by degradation during copying and storage. A contemporary "digital citizen" has access to and is typically inundated with far more information than they could ever hope to assimilate. With the help of computer-automated tools, we learn to filter and sort the information we receive digitally and online. These tools contribute to the technological infrastructure supporting the contemporary information society, comprised of both hardware and software and associated with server farms, satellite networks, personal computers, cell phones, and digital sound- and image-recording devices. In turn, information and communication technologies, or ICT, are supported by the information and computational sciences, ICS. As Luciano Floridi explains, "The most developed post-industrial societies live by information, and ICS-ICT is what keeps them constantly oxygenated" (Floridi 2002: 127).

This chapter investigates the role of art and the artist in the contemporary information society. How are artists creatively exploiting, responding to, or in some cases resisting digital communications technology, and how is this changing the way we understand and engage with the arts? In taking up this multi-faceted question, our focus shall be on new art forms made possible by digital technology and the most distinctive features of the digital medium as an artistic medium. The theoretical motivation for this focus is the complexity of the relation between the inherent replicability of digital representation and interactivity in the arts, where interactivity is understood in terms of the prescribed generation of multiple display types for an artwork by the work's users. Digital replicability is the feature of the digital that we must understand in order to recognize the basic creative limits and possibilities of digital art. Interactivity is the feature of artworks most frequently cited as having acquired new significance and potential in the digital age. At first glance, there appears to be a strict incompatibility between digital replicability and interactivity in the case of works comprising digital images. This is because digital images are characterized by having a transmissible display, which requires a single, fixed display type, without the possibility of multiple display types generated by user-interaction. Despite this seeming incompatibility, there are plenty of examples of successful works of networked, interactive art incorporating digital imagery. The ever-expanding and polymorphous category of net art is arguably the category of art most distinctive of the digital age. As well as an enormous variety of visual and audio-visual forms, it includes experimental online literature, social media performance art, conceptual browser art, and works drawing on software and computer gaming conventions. Works by leading net artists are collected, curated, and critiqued in the mainstream art world – for example, the Whitney Museum owns a large collection of net art and commissions new works through its Art Port (http://whitney.org/Exhibitions/Artport/). Interactive works of net art, it can be argued, dodge the strict incompatibility of digital transmissibility and interactivity by rapidly alternating their reliance on the two features. The result is a class of works that are particularly emblematic of the contemporary information age, presenting a new kind of challenge to the place of art in society, and feeding a powerful anxiety about the loss of art to information. Although the force of this anxiety needs to be acknowledged and understood, ultimately it needs to be resisted. There is good reason for thinking that art in the age of information and in the age of digital networks can retain or even extend its distinct role and significance in our lives.

In discussions of digital art practice, it is common to distinguish between (i) the use of various digital tools to make artworks in traditional or familiar art forms, such as sculpture, painting and drawing, collage, photography, and cinema; and, (ii) the use of digital tools to make artworks in new and distinctly digital art forms, such as net art, software art, digital installation, and virtual reality art. When a work is in a distinctly digital art form, it can also be said to be in "the digital medium." According to digital art curator Christiane Paul, this implies that the work "exclusively uses the digital platform from production to presentation, and that it exhibits and explores that platform's inherent possibilities" (Paul 2008: 67). Despite ongoing controversy about the coherence of media distinctions in the digital age, the digital medium is frequently attributed characteristic features that set it apart from traditional media. Paul describes the digital medium as "interactive, participatory, dynamic, and customizable," and claims that, while interactivity of various kinds is found in many art forms, there are nevertheless "complex possibilities of remote and immediate intervention" that are "unique to the digital medium" (Paul 2008: 67).

There is a tendency to place great emphasis on the notion of interactivity in discussions of the way digital technologies change the production and experience of art. But interactivity of even the strongest kind can be found in decidedly non-digital art contexts. Experimental theater productions that invite interventions from the audience are strongly interactive. Arguably, John Cage's *4'33"* is a strongly interactive musical work, if it can be said that the audience's creation and allowance of background noise is part of what is prescribed to create a performance of the work.[1] That there are such non-digital cases of strongly interactive art is important to note. Equally important to note, however, is their relatively esoteric nature. In the digital art world, by contrast, strong interactivity is common, almost expected, and indeed a standard feature for certain digital art forms such as video games. In the traditional art world, strong interactivity is uncommon, confined to the experimental. Whether this is necessarily so or simply a contingent feature of a particular, historically-determined art world, is hard to say – perhaps there could be or has been a culture whose standard or dominant form of theater, say, is interactive, or perhaps theater can only be theater if its standard features include non-interactivity. In any case, strong interactivity has an unprecedented role in the contemporary art world, and this has everything to do with the powers of the digital computer as an artistic tool. Digital computer processing allows for extremely rapid and reliable replication and dissemination of information such that an artwork's audience can, in a controlled manner, affect that work's structure and appearance instantaneously, remotely, reversibly, and without having to have any skills in, say, drawing or musical performance. Media theorists have been quick to identify the new prominence of interactivity in the digital age. But as Aaron Smuts (2009) points out, in their discussions of the significance of interactivity, most theorists fail to provide an adequate definition, one that picks out just those artworks that are in some sense more fundamentally interactive than all those artworks requiring active engagement. Before we confront this definitional problem, however, it is helpful to review the nature of digital representation. This is because it is the inherent replicability or transmissibility of the digital that explains the rise of interactivity in the digital art world.

The nature of the digital: transmissibility

On Nelson Goodman's classical account of digital representation (1968), the digital is the finitely differentiated. This condition describes the way in which sets of syntactic and semantic types are related to one another, where those types are sets of possible objects that count as token representations. The condition of syntactic differentiation is met when the differences between classes of token representations are limited such that it is possible for users of the system always to tell that a token belongs to at most one class. The condition of semantic differentiation is met when the extension of each type, or the class of referents corresponding to a class of token representations, differs in limited ways from the extension of any other type; so that users of the system can always tell that a referent belongs to at most one extension.

In general terms, finite differentiation amounts to the possibility of our determining exactly to which type a token belongs, and when that token refers, to the additional possibility of exact (though not necessarily precise) measurement. With differentiation comes the possibility of perfect replication and preservation, since a perfect copy of a token belonging to a certain type is just another instance of that type. When differentiation is satisfied it is simply because we can tell exactly when we have an instance of a certain type. Perfect replication as multiple instantiation is by far the most frequently noted feature of the digital – and not just in relation to digital systems that rely on computer processing. Hence the observation that Shakespeare's sonnets can be endlessly and multiply instantiated without risk of physical deterioration. This is because the sonnets are determined by a sequence of letters and the different letters – or rather, their instantiations – are meant to be easy for us to tell apart regardless of font size, color, or the occasional smudge and squiggle. The limits placed on what makes a difference for a particular mark counting as an inscription of a particular letter are such that we can be sure when we do or don't have an instance of one of Shakespeare's sonnets.

With computer processing, digital replicability reaches a whole new level. Consider an artwork like *I am we_interactive image* (April 2012–present) by the German artist, Wolf Nkole Helzle (http://interactive-image.org/en/). For this work, Internet users contribute images from their daily lives to an ever-changing mosaic image that is displayed online. (Time-slice instances of the work are also screened and printed for display in galleries.) At any point in the evolution of the mosaic image, the work can be viewed on the screen of any properly functioning, networked computer. We have multiple instances of the same image with no original. Even though the artist is in control of the Internet platform created specifically for the work, he does not thereby possess an original of the work from which copies are made for mass consumption. All Internet users, including the artist, view the same image, or rather, interchangeable instances of the same image.

The unlimited instantiability of the digital image is ensured by the binary coding of sufficient properties to ensure recognition of the image. Digital images are stored as pixel grids, two-dimensional arrays of integers that record light intensities at the points of a grid imposed on the picture plane. The value of any pixel represents the average light intensity across a tiny, square portion of the source image, rounded to the nearest integer within a finite range. Once the process of "quantization" has yielded a two-dimensional array of integers, the raster grid or bitmap is stored as binary code in computer memory. Binary code is paradigmatically digital and qualifies, on Goodman's account, as a finitely differentiated scheme: any instance of one of the two types in the scheme can be determined to belong to at most one type. 1s and 0s are easy for us to keep apart, just as it is easy for a computer to register the difference between the on and off settings of its internal switches, the millions of transistors etched onto silicon in its circuit boards. In binary code there are no in-between states that could confuse the determination of type membership and there is no possibility of a token belonging to both types. Once a quantized image has been coded, it can be transmitted electronically and interpreted by various devices to produce displays and printed images. Prior to transmission and presentation, however, the coded image can be easily and endlessly manipulated – all this involves, after all, is the exchange of particular 1s and 0s in the code sequence. Given their physical design, computers can process binary code at a tremendous rate such that a task like image manipulation is executed seamlessly, rapidly, and with no risk of degradation to the image. The most important point is that, by storing light intensity values in binary code, and despite the continuity of objective color values, there is no possibility of confusion for the purposes of instantiating the image.

Helzle's work, *I am we_interactive image*, needs the strict reliability of a digital code to ensure multiple instantiability. Dominic Lopes calls this feature of a digital image the transmissibility of its display. An artwork's "display," in Lopes' terms, is a "structure that results from the artist's creativity and that we apprehend in order to grasp a work's meaning and aesthetic qualities" (Lopes 2010: 4). Different kinds of artworks have very different kinds of display: grasping the meaning and aesthetic qualities of a musical work requires listening to a sequence of sounds, whereas grasping the meaning and aesthetic qualities of a painting requires looking at a colored two-dimensional surface. In the visual arts, Lopes marks a distinction between traditional images and digital images in terms of whether or not the works in question have a transmissible display. Traditional images like paintings are physical objects identical with their displays. Traditional print images and photographs can be shown in more than one place at a time but in a way that is still limited in relation to a physical object – either the matrix used to make printed impressions or the photographic negative. By contrast, a digital image generated from a computer file can be displayed on any number of different computer screens at the same time. Differences in the precise color calibration, resolution, and format of different computer screens need not matter for the re-instantiation of the same image.

Although different prints of the same analog photograph can also vary in tonality and contrast, Lopes points out that the display of an analog photograph is not transmissible (Lopes 2010: 5). Yet there can be multiple instances of the same analog photograph. The question thus arises as to what the difference is between the kind of multiple instantiability possessed by analog photographs and that possessed by digital displays. The difference has to do with the unlimited nature of transmissibility in the case of digital images. The image file preserves sufficient information for image recognition in a finitely differentiated format, and therefore guarantees perfect copies. There can be no degradation; there is no material source for the copying and therefore no risk of degradation of that source, or of corruption in the process of copying from that source. Of course this is assuming that the image file remains uncorrupted; as long as we retain the original code sequence for the image, any instances of the image generated from the code sequence will be interchangeable rather than intergenerational, and theoretically unlimited in number. Of course the same is true of notated musical works and literary works. These works also have transmissible displays. Lopes' point about digital displays is therefore only interesting as a point about a new class of images – the first kind of visual art with transmissibility, made possible by digital technology for high-resolution digital sampling. It is striking that, whereas musical and literary works have always had transmissible displays, images have only come to be able to have them in the contemporary information society, specifically with the development of computer technologies for the digital sampling, quantization, and coding of light intensities.

Digital interactivity

In the case of Helzle's *I am we_interactive image*, only by having a transmissible display can the work employ interactivity as it does – people everywhere and anywhere recording their daily lives in images and contributing those images to the project. Not all strongly interactive artworks have transmissible displays and not every artwork with a transmissible display is strongly interactive. But artworks that are both strongly interactive and have transmissible displays are distinctive of the contemporary information society with its reliance on digital technology. If we are looking for a workable definition of interactive art, the best available is in fact Lopes':

> A work of art is interactive just in case it prescribes that the actions of its users help generate its display.

> *(2010: 36)*

On this definition, a sculpture that we have to move around to view or a movie whose narrative we have to fill in imaginatively do not count as interactive. Our active engagement with these works does not constitute the generation of the work's display, whether the plastic form of the sculpture or the audio-visual array of the movie. When reading a novel, even if I choose to skip chapters or read them out of order, the fact that I can do this does not make the novel an interactive work on Lopes' definition. My actions are not the kind that are prescribed by the work to generate its display. A hypertext novel, on the other hand, that requires users to click on text describing particular narrative events in order to create a sequence for those events, would fit Lopes' definition. A video game requires an even greater amount of user input – via different kinds of console control – in order to determine the look, sound, and feel, as well as the narrative, strategic, and dramatic progression, of a particular playing of the game. Indeed, without ongoing input from a user, the playing of the video game simply stalls – the user is responsible for a great deal of detail in the appearance and development of the playing, but also just its occurring at all and having any kind of structure (as a particular playing of the game). Similarly for works of computer art like *I am we_interactive image*: Helzle's creation and maintenance of the specialized Internet platform for the work could be said to constitute or express a prescription for particular kinds of action on the part of Internet users: to upload photographs from their daily lives that become part of the work's mosaic display.

As Dominic Preston (2014) has pointed out, Lopes' definition for interactive art masks an ambiguity between (1) different users' actions generating different displays for a work and, (2) different users' actions contributing to the generation of progressive changes in a single display for the work. In the latter case, the display is the same, at any one moment, for all users. Over time, the display changes based on the contributions of users. In the former case, different users create their own displays as they, for example, independently play a video game. A second, related ambiguity concerns what it is for a work to have multiple displays. For the purpose of their appreciation, it is significant that videogames can have multiple displays with different aesthetic and structural properties. But for the sake of the transmissibility of digital images, it is essential that the multiple displays of a digital photograph are identical.

To overcome these ambiguities, Preston suggests we distinguish between display and display type, or between the sets of possible structural and aesthetic properties for an artwork and their instantiation (Preston 2014: 271). Digital photographs can have multiple displays but only one display type. By contrast, interactive artworks have multiple display types over one or many displays. Interactive works with many displays are what Lopes calls repeatable works – videogames are the prime example. Works with a single display fit Lopes' description of non-repeatable installation works: *Telegarden* (1995), for example, allows Internet users to view, plant, and take care of a small garden using a robotic arm. But this kind of case must be distinguished from another kind that is not obviously accommodated by Preston's distinction. In fact, our primary example seems to be of this kind: Helzle's *I am we_interactive image* does not seem to fit under either description of interactive art, in terms of multiple display types and multiple displays, or in terms of multiple display types and a single display. The work is not repeatable in the way that videogames are – individual users who access the work online cannot "go back to the beginning" for a private, self-directed re-instantiation of the work, and at any moment in time we are all limited in our access to the same display of the work. At the same time, the work is not like the non-repeatable Telegarden for which the display consists in the relevant features of the growing garden (and the robotic arm), whether the garden is seen live or remotely on a computer screen. Helzle's work has no installation component; it is a work of net art, and so how it looks on users' computer screens is just how the work is. In the same way that digital photographs can have multiple displays because they can be multiply instantiated on screen and in print, so *I am we_interactive image* has multiple displays. The multiple instantiability of digital photographs is a primary instance of what Lopes calls the transmissibility of the display for digital images. Such transmissibility clearly depends on a work having a single, fixed display type that can then be reliably instantiated. On the other hand, Preston indicates that interactivity requires the possibility of multiple display types. In the case of works like *I am we_interactive image*, their interactivity requires the possibility of multiple display types but they also incorporate digital images, which rely on the transmissibility of the digital display to ensure that all users have the same access to the work at any moment in time.

Works of net art, particularly ones that incorporate imagery, thus present an interesting test case for the artistic possibilities of the digital: they simultaneously exploit the transmissibility of the digital display and the affordances for interactivity provided by high-speed, networked computer processing. This can create productive tensions: *I am we_interactive image* relies on digital transmissibility in order to ensure simultaneous, shared access to the work, but strictly speaking, transmissibility is incompatible with interactivity because it requires instantiation of a single display type. The possibility of the work's interactivity only comes with the progressive modification of the display type in response to users' contributions. In other words, Preston's interactivity condition of multiple display types is satisfied progressively rather than concurrently, and with multiple displays for progressively distinct display types.

Although we have relied on the distinction between videogames having multiple concurrent display types and multiple displays, and works like *I am we_interactive image* having multiple progressive display types and multiple displays, in fact this distinction overlooks an important category of videogames that rely on progressive display-type variation. There are many online videogames that are designed to be played together by all the Internet users who subscribe and create characters for a particular game. Among the MMOGs, or Massively Multiplayer Online Games, the most famous example is *World of Warcraft*, which currently has several million subscribers. Many such works rely on the transmissibility of the digital display – they rely on all their users only having access to the same display at any given time. In addition, they meet the conditions for interactivity with the prescription that players progressively generate the work's display type, or generate multiple display types over the course of the game.

Digital art and society

Of course one might question whether *World of Warcraft* and other MMOGs satisfy the conditions for interactivity given that these are conditions for interactivity in art. Although this chapter has proceeded under the assumption that at least some videogames are art, it is certainly not obvious that all videogames, or videogames *qua* videogames count as art. Fortunately, however, impressive efforts have recently been made to defend the general art status of video games (see, for example, Baker 2012; Lopes 2010; Smuts 2005; Tavinor 2009). In light of these efforts, and in light of the influence of both MMOGs and networked digital art, it might be argued that the kind of art most distinctive of the information age breaks down traditional art world boundaries to an unprecedented degree or in an unprecedented way. Another recent art form thought to break down these boundaries is street art, and the comparison between street art and networked digital art is an instructive one.

Street art is often understood in relation to public art: while both kinds of art may physically occupy the street, or the same public, urban space, works in the latter category are sponsored, supported, and funded by government agencies, and may or may not have the approval of those who inhabit the space. Works in the former category, by contrast, are "of the people, by the people, and for the people," reflecting the values of the community. Important works of street art include the oversized portraits of the disenfranchised and forgotten victims of poverty, violence and war that French artist JR plasters across crowded public spaces; Mademoiselle Maurice's delicate works of mass origami that suddenly appear on city walls and pavements; and, Banksy's bitingly witty works of political graffiti. One author encourages us to think of street art as "essentially aconsensual – that is, made on property without the consent of the property owner" (Anon. forthcoming). Another author argues that street art uses the street in a distinctive way, as "an artistic resource," so that the use of the street becomes internal to the meaning of the work (Riggle 2010). These features of street art indicate the ways in which the art form seeks to challenge the traditional institutional structures of the art world. Street art *qua* street art cannot be shown in a traditional art gallery or museum. It cannot be commissioned, nor can it be traded in the mainstream art market. Correspondingly, access to street art cannot be limited to those who go to museums and galleries; it confronts everyone as they pass through public spaces.

Now think about networked, interactive artworks. Like works of street art, these works are outside traditional museums or galleries. Unlike works of street art, this does not mean they are in some other, fixed location (even temporarily); their displays can be accessed at any location. Of course the same is true of any kind of traditional art that is non-site-specific, including traditional paintings and sculptures. But traditional forms of visual art that are non-site-specific are also highly amenable to presentation in traditional museums and galleries. By contrast, net art cannot be contained or limited in its presentation to a traditional museum or gallery. What street art accomplishes by being specific to the street – namely, escape from the museum – interactive net art accomplishes by being virtual, specific to nowhere in particular and thus potentially anywhere. Works of net art are works that come to the user. With works of this kind, art has not just come out of the museum and into public, common spaces; art has entered our private spaces, our living rooms and bedrooms. One might reply that this is also nothing new: art has been doing this for as long as we have been able to hang pictures on our walls, read novels, listen to records, and watch TV in our homes. But the difference with interactive net art, insofar as it is partly a visual art form, is twofold: for the first time (i) we can all have simultaneous access to the same (original) image; and, (ii) we can instantaneously and collectively modify that image (or image sequence).

Having escaped the museum, entered our homes, and then engaged us in collaboratively modifying its displays, interactive net art might seem to herald new possibilities for political and social engagement. We are currently witnessing all the ways in which the use of smart phones, the Internet, and social media applications are changing the organization of political protests and the founding of social movements. These same tools are attractive to artists with a desire to reach an audience beyond the traditional museum – perhaps a younger audience, a more culturally diverse one, or simply one comprised of geographically disparate members. Once the desired audience is reached, interactive engagement with a work of net art could become a pre-requisite for or an ingredient in the kind of involvement required for political and social change. Shu Lea Cheang's *Brandon* was launched as a website at the Guggenheim Museum in 1998 and is considered a pioneering work in "cyberfeminism"[2] The work is based on the story of transgendered Nebraska teen, Brandon Teena, who was raped and murdered in 1993 when he was discovered to be anatomically female (Teena's story also became the subject of the film *Boys Don't Cry*). Cheang's work uses hyperlinked images and live chat to encourage an exploration of different gender roles and critical reflection on the politics of gender. In virtue of its interactivity, the work aims to provide a highly personal and richly experiential understanding of the difficulties faced by transgendered people, the kind of understanding most likely to lead to real-world action and solidarity.

Even if one is pessimistic about the ways in which engagement with net art can lead to social and political action, one might still be optimistic about our increased exposure to the arts through digital technology. We can access and interact creatively with works of visual art wherever we have access to a networked computer screen – including such portable devices as smartphones and tablets. We can also more easily access copies of traditional works of visual art and musical recordings, through high-quality online catalogs and virtual museum tours. We can watch movies on the same networked computer screens through which we can access other kinds of digital art. Yet despite all these new digital possibilities for access, there are those who consider the information age to be an age of decline in true engagement with the arts. There are two main arguments given in support of this view. One concerns the idea that, in virtue of digital technology, art has been reduced to yet more information, of which we already have far too much to be able to absorb. The other argument concerns the idea that networked digital art cannot support rewarding aesthetic experiences, given its transitory nature and its embeddedness in an online world that is primarily mercenary and non-artistic.

The first argument, popular among media and film theorists (e.g., Doane 2007), usually takes the form of an analysis of the "post-medium condition" of the contemporary arts. With the use of computer processing in the production and presentation of art, the image-, sound-, and symbolic-values of artworks are translated into a common binary code for rapid, automated electronic processing and transmission. This phenomenon of "digital convergence" whereby computer processing circumvents the material distinctions between traditional media, is then thought to have serious implications for the way we appreciate art. Traditionally, the terms of appreciation for an art form are set in relation to features of the medium. This is because the materials and practices that comprise an artistic medium present an artist with distinctive creative challenges and possibilities. We then appreciate an artwork as manifesting an artist's response to these challenges and possibilities. Digital convergence, it is suggested, cancels out the terms for the traditional appreciation of art: image, sound, and text are processed in the same way by a computer and so the distinctive challenges of working with each medium are lost. Appreciation can no longer be grounded in awareness of these challenges and can no longer register the different ways artists try to meet these challenges.

Despite its critical influence and rhetorical power, this argument is unconvincing. Most importantly, the media theorists' inference from translatability to medium-free art simply does not hold. That we could set about "translating" the imagery of *Citizen Kane* into a symphony does not mean that the original artwork lacks a medium; it is a movie, after all, and thus in the medium of moving images. The symphonic translation of *Citizen Kane* is not the same work as the 1941 movie by Orson Welles. The latter work necessarily has a visual display, the former a sonic display. This reminds us that, in deciding whether there is a digital medium, we must not reduce the medium to the artist's materials or limit the constitutive materials of a medium to physical materials (see Davies 2003). The case of literature shows that neither the materials of an art form, nor their modes of manipulation, need be physical. The medium of literature is neither paper and ink nor abstract lexical symbols, but letters and words used in certain ways. There are, of course, many different ways of physically storing and transmitting literary works, including by the printed page, in audio recordings, and by memory (human or computer). But from the fact that *The Tale of Two Cities* can be preserved in many different formats, it does not follow that this novel is any less decisively a novel and, as such, in the medium of literature.

Just as with a literary work, the preservation and transmission of digital works in different formats depends on the use of a common code, but a binary numeric code rather than a lexical one. If words and their literary uses constitute the medium of literature, then binary code and its artistic uses constitute the medium of digital art. The digital medium understood in this way can play a standard role in artistic appreciation. Thus digital art curators like Christiane Paul can set out to classify the ways any artwork using digital technologies as an artistic medium "exhibits and explores [the digital] platform's inherent possibilities" (2008: 67). The kind of interactivity that we have been discussing might well be one of those "possibilities," since it is only in virtue of networked computer processing that remote, instantaneous and collaborative image-making becomes feasible.

The second argument against an expanded role for art in the information age concerns whether digital art, and particularly highly ephemeral and fragmentary works of interactive net art, can support rewarding aesthetic experiences. In relation to interactive works that necessarily allow users to create multiple display types, it might be thought that no single user is able to be in a position to appreciate the work as a whole. Moreover, for all but the most dedicated, long-term users of such works, their appreciation will be based on a tiny fraction of the work – say, on one of all the possible display types that can be generated, either concurrently or progressively, for the work. But this worry may be overblown, particularly in light of the fact that many networked interactive artworks are designed for repeated and ongoing engagement. Thus Helzle's *I am we_interactive* image requires its users to create online accounts to facilitate ongoing, daily posting of images. Videogames encourage multiple playings, most basically by keeping a record of a user's performance from one playing to the next, but also by offering users a great range of choices regarding ways in which to navigate a complex virtual world or complete an ever-changing set of tasks. Even in a single playing, however, a user can evaluate the work as a whole based on its ability to generate the particular display of her playing. In turn, the experience provided by the work in a single playing can give the user a sense of other unexperienced possibilities. As Preston explains, when he plays *The Walking Dead*, he can appreciate his own display but also some of the points in the game at which he could have acted differently and thereby generated a significantly different display (2014: 276).

Whatever we might say about the complex appreciation of videogames, however, there remains a more general and fundamental version of the second argument on which interactive art is seen as fundamentally opposed to the aesthetic and to the true function of art. The thought is that when art audiences are comprised of mere "users" and "players," and online artworks jostle for our attention alongside commercial goods, gossip, and propaganda, art is unlikely to be profoundly moving or provide transcendent experiences of beauty. The best response to this objection may well be the mustering of powerful counter-examples: videogames whose worlds contain scenes of breathtaking beauty; political net art that demands emotionally-charged interactions; and, hyperlinked multi-media works that delight with their formal complexity. At the same time, we must see this objection as part of a more general isolationist tendency in the history of theorizing about the arts, a tendency that has already been widely and successfully resisted. This is the tendency to treat art as a pure and isolated phenomenon, distinct from the products of everyday activity, and to treat aesthetic experience as necessarily excluding personal, practical, moral, and bodily concerns. Against this tendency, a host of different arguments have been made for the continuity of art with the everyday, and for the multi-faceted nature of aesthetic experience. In light of these arguments, there is no reason, in principle, why aesthetic subjects cannot also be "users" and "players," and no reason why the experience of interactive net art cannot be both an experience of the flow of information and an experience of the aesthetic.

Notes

1 *4'33"* is a musical work with three movements composed in 1952 by John Cage. The work is composed for any instruments or combination of instruments, and its score instructs performers not to play their instruments for the entire duration of the piece. The title refers to the length of the work's first performance (four minutes and thirty three seconds).
2 See http://www.guggenheim.org/new-york/collections/collection-online/artwork/15337

Further reading

B. Gaut, *A Philosophy of Cinematic Art* (Cambridge: Cambridge University Press, 2010) includes careful analysis of the impact of digital technologies on the art of moving images, understood broadly to include videogames. The philosophical literature on the nature of the digital is surprisingly limited, but two important early responses to Nelson Goodman's classical account are J. Haugeland, "Analog and Analog" (*Philosophical Topics* 12 (1981):

213–26); and, D. Lewis, "Analog and Digital" (*Noûs* 5.3 (1971): 321–7). Drawing on this literature, a new debate has emerged about the allographic status of digital images: J. D'Cruz and P. D. Magnus, "Are Digital Images Allographic?" (*Journal of Aesthetics and Art Criticism* 72.4 (2014): 417–27); and, J. Zeimbekis, "Digital Pictures, Sampling, and Vagueness: The Ontology of Digital Pictures" (*Journal of Aesthetics and Art Criticism* 70.1 (2012): 43–53). D. M. Lopes, *A Philosophy of Computer Art* (London, New York: Routledge, 2010) is the first book-length philosophical treatment of computer art, which argues that computers provide a new medium for art. A. L. Thomasson, "Ontological Innovation in Art" (*Journal of Aesthetics and Art Criticism* 68.2 (2010): 119–30) uses the case of net art to defend the role of the artist in determining the status of the artwork. For an introduction to the emerging subfield of the philosophy of digital art, see my own entry in the *Stanford Encyclopedia of Philosophy*: http://plato.stanford.edu/entries/digital-art/.

References

Anonymous (forthcoming) "Street Art," *British Journal of Aesthetics*.

Baker, A. (2012) "Videogames as Representational Art," *Postgraduate Journal of Aesthetics* 9.2: 28–39.

Crawford, S. (1983) "The Origin and Development of a Concept: The Information Society," *Bulletin of the Medical Library Assoc*. 71.4: 380–5.

Davies, D. (2003) "Medium," in J. Levinson (ed.) *The Oxford Handbook of Aesthetics*, Oxford: Oxford University Press.

Doane, M. A. (2007) "Indexicality: Trace and Sign: Introduction," *Differences: A Journal of Feminist Cultural Studies,* 18.1: 1–6.

Goodman, N. (1968) *Languages of Art: An Approach to a Theory of Symbols*, Indianapolis, IN: Bobbs-Merrill.

Floridi, L. (2002) "What is the Philosophy of Information?" *Metaphilosophy* 33.1/2: 123–45.

Lopes, M. D. (2010) *A Philosophy of Computer Art*, London, New York: Routledge.

Paul, C. (2008) *Digital Art*, 2nd ed., London and New York: Thames & Hudson.

Preston, D. (2014) "Some Ontology of Interactive Art," *Philosophy and Technology* 27: 267–78.

Riggle, N. (2010) "Street Art: The Transfiguration of the Commonplace," *Journal of Aesthetics and Art Criticism*, 68.3: 243–57.

Smuts, A. (2005) "Are Videogames Art?" *Contemporary Aesthetics* 3.

Smuts, A. (2009) "What is Interactivity?" *Journal of Aesthetic Education* 43.1: 53–73.

Tavinor, G. (2009) *The Art of Videogames*, Oxford: Wiley-Blackwell.

"Tele-Garden Info". Ars Electronica Center. Archived from the original on 1997-04-11. Retrieved 2016–04-28.

31

THE INTERPRETATIVE
VALUE OF
INFORMATION

Jan Kyrre Berg Friis

Information is everywhere. Information can be mediated by the dashboard of your car, or revealed to you by reading a text, looking at a poster, seeing a film – or by interpreting fMRI scans or statistics. All are human phenomena infused with meanings understandable by a driver or a film buff, a radiologist or a mathematician. Information can be environmental – like the degrees on a thermometer, or it may come to you in the form of an alarming sound of breaking glass above our head. Information can be mediated quantitatively or qualitatively; the information may be precise, factual. Factual information is either true or untrue. If it is true it yields correct or coherent understanding. If it is untrue we are *disinformed*, or we might have been *unintentionally* misinformed (Floridi, 2009:15). Hermeneutics deals with all kinds of *intentional* information. This chapter will discuss whether hermeneutics is a *method* or an *event* or both conjoined by taking a closer look at the hermeneutics of Schleiermacher, Dilthey, Heidegger, and Gadamer. Lastly, we will take a look at some of the more recent critique directed at philosophical hermeneutics.

What is hermeneutics?

Hermeneutics has always been concerned with the *unveiling* or *decoding* of meaning in texts, religion, law, behavior, and other objects of intentionality originating from the creative practices of humanity. Nevertheless, modern philosophical hermeneutics is today rather far from the original formats of the past. Our present situation in philosophical hermeneutics is, according to Heidegger, due to a transformation of the scientific consciousness in the nineteenth century, when the age-old idealistic systems collapsed. This transformation affected all sciences, not only philosophy (Heidegger, 1992b:13). During the second half of the nineteenth century, an attempt was made to grant the particular sciences their own independency and to secure for philosophy a varied relation to these sciences. Heidegger is here pointing at the reaction against positivistic and empiricist philosophies hailing the research methods of natural science, i.e. physics, as the universal method to be applied by all scientists in all of the sciences, even in philosophy and the humanities. Philosophical reflection was at that time (1840–1960), according to Heidegger, "an arid and crude materialism (…) the *world view of natural science*" (Heidegger, 1992b:14).

Originally hermeneutics became a term given to a specific way of reading texts during the sixteenth century. In particular, it was an attempt to establish a specific interpretative method of biblical scriptures and other texts from antiquity. The original method was a set of rules to be followed in order to secure an understanding of the true content of the scriptures. This is done by using the hermeneutical circle. In classical hermeneutics the circle consisted of the part of the meaning and the whole of the meaning – the significance of the text's parts is determined by the totality of the text as such, likewise the totality of meaning of the text is determined by the meaning extracted from its parts. Interpretation of a text is to run through the hermeneutical circle until one has an understanding of the text in its entirety, which is without internal contradictions (Dahlager and Fredslund, 2011: 159). The truth of an interpretation of a text is maximized when all the parts of the text fit with the overall understanding of the text.

Part of the transformation of philosophy and science, which Heidegger mentions above, was partly due to the writings of Friedrich Schleiermacher (1768–1834), Wilhelm Dilthey (1833–1911), but also a more recent philosopher like Emilio Betti (1890–1968). It has had much to say about hermeneutics as a scientific method in its own right. Schleiermacher and Dilthey viewed singular texts as part of a larger authorship, and authorship as an intrinsic part of the author's life as a human being and a citizen, a life which again is part of a society. Society is part of an epoch, and the epoch is part of world history. In the minds of Schleiermacher, Dilthey, and Betti, hermeneutics should be a strict rational and analytical procedure of interpretation, a method that could be applied by researchers within the humanities and social sciences. Dilthey wanted to secure a place for hermeneutics at the same validity level as the methods applied by the exact sciences – more accurately, he wanted to secure a logical, epistemological, and methodological foundation for the human sciences (Grondin, 2005).

It was with Schleiermacher and Dilthey that the hermeneutical problem became a problem of *science*. It is a problem because hermeneutics, as a scientific method, must be concerned with the vast number of different sources of inputs influencing the interpreter during the interpretation. More specifically, it is a problem because all interpretation takes place within a language, a tradition, a world view and/or a living current of thought, all of which displays some kind of adherence to the ideas inherent in these particular contexts (Ricoeur, 1974: 5). This demands of all interpretation of information a broader definition of experience than presently found within the quantitative natural sciences, because one has to combine psychological abilities like empathy with a broader experience gathered during one's own lifetime together with scholarly knowledge. The psychological perspective is brought in to explain that to understand is for one self to be transported into another life or psyche – the method, based on logic and epistemology, was to arrest any presumptions about interpretation as merely a relativistic and subjective endeavor, and that typically is conducted by persons without the rigorous training provided by the exact sciences.

With Schleiermacher and Dilthey, hermeneutics enjoyed a normative and regulatory function for the interpretation of various forms of written information. Specific hermeneutics were developed for each of the academic disciplines: theology and the interpretation of canonical texts (*hermeneutica sacra*), law (*hermenutica juris*), and classical texts (*hermeneutica profana*). The rule that became regulatory for retrieving these various kinds of information was that parts of the text should be understood on the background of the whole of the text, and again, the whole of the text, and its intent, could only be understood by interpreting its parts. The new element, in order to fully grasp the information or meaning conveyed by the text, is that one should also bring in an understanding of the genre, and to investigate the other works and life of the author (Grondin, 2005).

Heidegger notes that there existed an opinion about the hermeneutics of Dilthey that was superficial. Heidegger was himself profoundly influenced by Dilthey's work and in a defense of the cultural influences on humanity and its understandings, Heidegger writes that the superficiality "(…) is that of a scholar distinguishing between the exact sciences and humanities giving history and psychology distinctive rules, merging the two and thus ending up in a relativistic 'philosophy of life'. Superficially this sketch is correct, but the substance eludes it" (Heidegger, 1992a: 450). Heidegger further explains the function of Dilthey's interpretative process, i.e. hermeneutical circle, as: the way of "trying things out," which is founded in an elemental restlessness and is as such, perhaps, an inextricable aspect of human nature. The goal of humanity, at least in Heidegger's optics, is to understand *life*. Dilthey focused his research on the distinction between humanities and the exact sciences, and also on the history of science, but of great interest to the understanding of the mind of the interpreter, it also became necessary to focus on human psychology. Researching the theory of science, history and psychological hermeneutics, Dilthey found that they permeate and intersect each other throughout the interpretation process. "Everything centers in psychology," Heidegger writes, "in which 'life' is to be understood in the historical context of its development and its effects, and understood as the *way* in which man *is*" (Heidegger, 1992a: 450). This is an understanding that only surfaces during interpretation and it is a method to understand whatever mediates human meaning. Dilthey was forced one-sidedly into the work on a theory of science instead of a further investigation of the psychology pertaining to the act of understanding. Heidegger quotes Dilthey's good friend, count Yorck, who writes that "It gets firmly laid down that the consideration of the Self is the primary means of knowing, and that the primary procedure of knowing is analysis" (Heidegger, 1992a: 451).

What is information in relation to hermeneutics?

There are at least four different hermeneutical trends towards information (Coyne, 1995; Butler, 1998: 286). In Coyne's view there are four perspectives, the conservative, pragmatic, critical and the radical. Among the conservatives we find Emilio Betti and Eric Hirsch who claim that hermeneutics should uncover the original meanings as intended by the author. These meanings are not defined by history or context; the interpretations are corresponding truths and objective. A second trend is the hermeneutics of Heidegger and Gadamer. Coyne includes Wittgenstein in this approach. This trend is defined by its pragmatism and meanings are something that is constructed. Interpretation means getting involved in the norms of the community – meaning is therefore found within historical contexts of the interpreter and the interpreted. The critical approach is represented by thinkers such as Habermas and Karl-Otto Apel. Paradigms of knowledge within societies are challenged – the purpose of interpretation is to emancipate from repressive power asymmetries. Finally there is Derrida and his deconstructionist approach, which can be applied to understand the play of societies in which knowledge is revealed and concealed "through the play of difference and contradiction" (Butler, 1998: 286).

To supplement the four trends within hermeneutics, Grondin writes that conservatives like Betti and Hirsch pursued the foundational work began by Dilthey in order to establish a methodology for all human sciences (Grondin, 2005:1–3). Betti was critical of Gadamer's seeming rejection of hermeneutics as a methodological paradigm, that is to say, Betti could not accept the relativism in Gadamer's claim of following one's own prejudices, stating that it is nothing but a perversion of the very idea of hermeneutics (Grondin, 2005: 3). Likewise, Hirsch rejected the relativistic idea that interpretations can only be offered from a perspective situated in the present. However, contrary to Betti and Hirsch, Habermas hailed Gadamer's position, stating that knowledge is always guided by *interest* – and that hermeneutics is a method of disclosing these interests (Grondin, 2005: 3). Nevertheless, Habermas was critical of Gadamer's reliance on tradition and the importance of authority in understanding – which Habermas found to be too relativistic.

When all that is said, Gadamer's and Heidegger's positions seem to be the preferred hermeneutical approach, for instance within information systems thinking. Butler writes, "There is a marked trend within the field of IS to gravitate towards a phenomenological hermeneutic perspective informed by the philosophies of Heidegger and Gadamer" (Butler, 1998: 287; see also Lee, 1993, 1994; Myers, 1995; Butler and Fitzgerald, 1997a, b). The essence of interpretation, seen in Heidegger and Gadamer, and with relevance for information systems, rests on how to define information. Now, the important question here is of course the interpretative value of information. Hopefully it will become clear that, in order to achieve any insight into the nature of information, one must begin with the most basic theory of interpretation, meaning and understanding available, namely hermeneutics. At the very root of understanding meaning or information lays interpretation.

Interpretation, meaning, and understanding are three *necessary* concepts in hermeneutics and of relevance to any notion of information. Information mediated by technology, or created by a writer or a composer, or any *sender* mediating human intentionality is potentially meaningful, and is as such itself based on interpretation. Any *receiver* has to interpret in order make the received information his own, that is, we have to make sense of it – understanding means we are grasping and getting hold of its meaning. In other words, information is communicated to others by means of signs, language, and symbols and the receiver interprets in order to unlock the information mediated by the symbols or signs, when interpreted or unlocked, the receiver understands and the information is meaningful to him. But as Introna remarks, the information mediated to us can resist our attempts to interpret – it may provoke a struggle in us to overcome cultural or any other contextual distance contained in the information, we are thus struggling against the estrangement of meaning itself, or the values upon which the information is based (Introna, 1993).

Interpretation is not only applied on intentions, behavior, art, or texts. Interpretation is also applied in situations where individuals are trying to understand *natural* objects – that is, non-intentional objects that can be accessed empirically. Just take the tasks of a heart surgeon. First of all, if we consider a student of literature, the prejudice of the student contains information concerning genre, details of the authors' life and work. The surgeon's prejudices, on the other hand, are towards technicalities concerning surgical procedure and anatomy. Moreover, the surgeon also has to interpret quite different mediated information during a very short time.[1] The surgeon is in his procedure of handling the ongoing situation applying a flurry of embodied interpretative skills, which tacitly are influencing his ability to react accordingly. In other words, his understanding of the situation is evolving through an oscillating process of trial and error, not to mention the interpersonal discourse.

Each step in the process of treatment includes the involvement of several persons discussing and offering their understanding of the situational interpretation. They discuss their viewpoints; decide on actions, and trying out likely solutions. There is always some difference of opinion – people do interpret situations differently since they never share exactly the same prejudices. However, all happens within a shared specialist community, which dissolves communicative misunderstanding and where superior experience determines the decision-making. The significance of each other's interpretation is discussed seriously – even if the timeframe is limited, the goal of achieving a solution of how to act is a common determination. This creates a firm ground based on experience and know-how on which the better solution shines through during the discourse.

Hence, there are no pre-given solutions. Each surgical intervention demands a new interpretative process – of testing prejudices and embodied skills up against the situation at hand. Each time a surgeon performs a similar surgical intervention, it will be on a new patient, and again she will have to correct her prejudices, until she suddenly understand what to do next. *Understanding* is in itself an *event*. Every time a surgeon interprets a new patient, she applies the same surgical procedure in a slightly new way, every time the process of interpretation has to be made anew and every time the result – her understanding – is an experience yielding new particularities to her insights and embodied skills about anatomy and surgical technique.

Understanding as an *event*

Hermeneutics is an epistemology. It is a theory of knowledge, and of the involvement of human cognition in the process. Hermeneutics goes beyond the traditional epistemologies that are concerned with valid rational methodological procedures. Heidegger and Gadamer emphasize that there is an intimate connection between life and thinking – this intimacy defines understanding as a fundamental phenomenon of human existence. Two important insights to hermeneutics are therefore that understanding is both a method of interpreting texts, images, and other sorts of information; and also that the fruit of our present understanding has its roots in the past.

Hermeneutics is not solely about method – in an important way it is about human cognition. In the continental philosophical tradition – especially in the German and Scandinavian countries, cognition (*Erkenntnis*) forms together with a formal methodological theory of knowledge what is commonly known as epistemology (*Erkenntnislehre*). Cognition concerns the processes of perception and the act of *thinking* in various stages of conscious awareness. Particular to hermeneutics is the cognitive-epistemological processes of perception and tacit and analytical interpretations, and how these processes suddenly appear as understanding (*Erkenntnisvermögen*). Hermeneutics is therefore about an inherent interpreting ability immanent in perceptions. In other words, hermeneutics as cognition concerns how the inherent interpreting perception-based ability interacts with embodied learning, skills acquired through practice, experiences, temporality, evolution-based instincts, culture, tradition and family, thus constituting what Heidegger, Gadamer and Ricoeur called the *historicity* of human understanding – or *prejudices*, if an ongoing methodological analysis is taking place. According to Gadamer, we should put our *historicity* into methodical use: "It is always a past that allows us to say, 'I have understood'" (Gadamer, 1976: 58).

The interpretative process leading to understanding is circular, hence the term *hermeneutic circle*: our understanding is gradually developing through our pre-judgments about what is going on and our empirical observations of the external event itself. Our pre-judgments are changing when we confront these with the empirical reality we confront them with – as a result our understanding of the event develops. We interpret what baffles us by trying out our developing presuppositions. In other words, the event-specific element is that understanding itself is an internal or cognitive event. We are always, to use Heidegger's expression, thrown into situations consisting of certain possibilities. That we are thrown into situations means that these situations are not of our own choosing. It is here that our historicity (past) or facticity (factual or relatively recentness) is grounded. Facticity defines our limits – how much we are able to understand, plan and control. These are the formal conditions of understanding. What does this imply?

Gadamer writes: "(…) my real concern was and is philosophic: not what we do or what we ought to do, but what *happens* to us over and above our wanting and doing" (Gadamer, 2007: xvi). The main issue for science is to go beyond subjectivity and find a way to the external object-world as it is in itself. The hermeneutical tradition of Heidegger and Gadamer does not need to escape subjectivity – it is quite the contrary. The humanities, or hermeneutics, do not produce objective knowledge. It does not deal with a world that is in-it-self or existing independent of human beliefs, cognitions or perceptions. Heidegger's *Dasein* is *already in the world*: *Dasein* is in its entirety a consequence of the world. It is as Dasein – as persons belonging to the world with everything that entails – we can understand the world. This world is therefore *not* external to us, rather it is *our* world and as such it constitutes a necessary precondition of understanding per se. By being immersed in the world, or as Heidegger terms it, "thrown into the world," we are questioning everything in our immediacy – people, events, concepts, beliefs, practices.

According to Heidegger and Gadamer, it is the *historical* character, which underlies all present and future understanding. We are placing ourselves within a process of a tradition shaped by history, in other words, by the thinking of people through time influencing the tradition, in which past and present are constantly fused. To understand this fully, it is important to keep two of Gadamer's concepts in mind: the "fusion of horizons" and that of "historically effective consciousness." When past and present are fused we are talking about tradition – new thinking arises from the influence of ideas and theories of the past. It is therefore important that we thematize the role of tradition in our understanding.

In his *Hermeneutics and the Human Sciences*, Ricoeur most interestingly describes the effective historical consciousness as a "massive and global fact whereby consciousness even before its awakening as such, belongs to and depends on that which affects it" (Ricoeur, 1981: 74). History, culture, and tradition shape our environment, and are parts of our social, professional, and family life. We encounter our history and culture everywhere in our locality. We read philosophy, literature, and history; we go to movies, the theater, and to concerts; we talk to people – some even have a deep impact on how we think. Take science. Through history science has changed many times over – its ways of understanding changes with it, that is, how we should go about in order to understand (epistemology) and what we actually understand (ontology) – and never have our epistemologies and ontologies changed so many times and so fast as during the last two hundred years. One explanation for these changes could be that interpretations are transformative. Interpretation transforms that which is being interpreted according to interests in actual scientific tradition and culture, but also according to the individual's own tacit mindset. In modern hermeneutics we simply do not have representations of an objective reality as it is "in itself," and that consists of representations that are "independent" of the perceiver. Culture and social life is an inextricable part of modern science – perhaps not a very welcome part when it comes to natural sciences but absolutely necessary when it comes down to hermeneutics. To put it differently, through language we share our interpretations of events, texts, images and ideas. The commonality of understanding is generated through the intersubjective medium of language, according to Gadamer (Gadamer, 2007: 427). Gadamer also uses the term "translation" to describe interpretation; to interpret is to translate. Understanding the information means that we have managed to translate and transform the meanings inherent in the language of the author into our own way of expressing the information. Thus we are fusing horizons, the receiver and the sender's. What *I* understand by way of my own interpretation is the essential – as such my particular understanding of the information will always transcend the intended meaning of the author – but that does not say that our notions don't match – language, tradition, and culture guarantee some degree of fusion of meaning.

However, as hermeneutists we cannot venture deeper into the origins of the *event* of understanding itself. Exactly what elements in culture, history, tradition, social relations, which are influencing our interpretations, we do not know. We may have inklings to certain preferences or interests guiding our actions, as Habermas would have termed it. When that is said, we could ask: Something must constitute the historicity or background informing the interpreter. What constitutes this background? What sort of "data" do we find within the so called "effective historical consciousness"? What is the selection mechanism that is applied in identifying the data? Perhaps there is a clue in Gadamer's statement that hermeneutics is "not what we do, not what we should do, but on the contrary what happens to us beyond what we consciously want and do" (Gadamer, 2007: 474). Gadamer could here be saying that we, as hermeneutists, should also be instigating research on the genetics of phenomenal or perceptual gestalts – where tacit interpretation originates and of which understanding springs.

Unfortunately, hermeneutists does not have the means to do this – all investigation into the processes of interpretation takes an abrupt halt at the doorstep to whatever lies on the other side of consciousness. Phenomenal experience does not allow us to transcend the indirectness of phenomenal experiences, thus we can never view phenomena in their perceptually given originality.

Critique of philosophical hermeneutics

There are several critiques of Gadamer's project; most of the critique is directed towards what is taken to be a relativism of knowledge. Some of his critiques are hermeneutists – the majority, however, belong to the analytical schools of philosophy. This last group has found it necessary to substitute hermeneutics – as an understanding generating method with the hypothetico-deductive method of the natural sciences. Professors Føllesdal and Mantzavinos are proponents of this view.

Among Gadamer's critiques from within hermeneutics, Hirsch declared his opposition to the idea that interpretations always are colored by the present. By following the method any interpreter should focus his efforts on the task of extracting the meaning of the text, the meaning that was intended by the author. This is the true role of hermeneutics. Habermas did not agree with Hirsch. There is no way we can get to know the original meaning of the author because we are, as researchers, and like the rest of humanity, guided by our interests. Interests guide knowledge and tie our understanding and interpretation to the present. Habermas disagreed with Gadamer about the role of tradition and authority in interpretation (Grondin, 2005:4).

From a quite different tradition we find a complete different approach, which is a critique directed not at any one hermeneutist specifically but at the hermeneutic tradition as it is presented by authors like Heidegger, Gadamer, and Habermas. Dagfinn Føllesdal has suggested that "the hermeneutic method is the hypothetico-deductive method applied to meaningful material (i.e. to texts, works of art, actions, etc.)" (Føllesdal, 1979: 320). Føllesdal's critique is directed at Habermas and others "who restrict the hypothetico-deductive method to natural science (...)." (Føllesdal, 1979: 320). Føllesdal's focus here is on method, not on understanding as an event. The event contains many rationally uncontrollable elements since the *perceiving* of an object of interpretation *precedes* conscious awareness and therefore these influences are not rational, i.e. cannot be controlled by the logic of a clear and conscious mind. Føllesdal is concerned about the *rationality* of the method (Føllesdal, 1979: 333). The "relativism" of the individuals' historicity and tradition and how these influences color the interpretative outcome can only be transcended by method, and this is best done by the application of decision theory. Føllesdal writes: "(…) we have no reason to think that a person's behavior springs from causes that are not reasons or from unconscious motives; we shall assume that he acts as a rational agent in the sense of decision theory. This means that he goes through a two-step procedure. First he considers the alternatives which he believes to be possible in the situation at hand. Thereafter he chooses from among these alternatives one which in view of his values and beliefs concerning probabilities maximizes his expected utility" (Føllesdal, 1979: 333).

Following the above statement, it is reasonable to state that Føllesdal wants to replace hermeneutics with the hypothetical-deductive method of the natural sciences – with the help of decision theory. To understand and to interpret is then a rational affair with no unknowns and the hermeneutical circle is replaced by the gradual testing of test implications or empirical consequences following logically from the proposed hypothesis. The interpreter's only concern to uphold a rational procedure is to follow a few rules of thumb: consistency at a time, consistency over time, concern for the future, and interaction between agents. In other words, to have a rational interpretation of a person's actions, we require that "(…) a rational individual who is placed between a number of alternatives to be realized at time *t*, *makes* his choice according to transitive preferences at *t*." And, in order to understand, we also expect a person's preferences to be consistent over time. This means not, says Føllesdal, that a person never changes his preferences; we would like to understand *why* he changes them. Rationality demands that preferences are guided not only by present *desires* (Føllesdal's own word), but by his concerns of his own future. Then, lastly, there is the category about other persons and interactions between these persons. We have beliefs about other persons. Føllesdal suggest using game theory to understand these interactions: "(…) no satisfactory study of man can take place without game theory" (1979: 335).

The diverging philosophical traditions, here represented by the opposition between Gadamer on the one hand and Føllesdal on the other, become clear. Gadamer pursues the processes leading up to the understanding itself, often unconscious and beyond rational control, as part of the sudden event of understanding something. Føllesdal wants to apply decision theory and game theory in addition to the hypothetical-deductive method, to avoid using hermeneutics altogether – he is preoccupied with establishing a notion of understanding as something rational and based in logical procedure or method – Føllesdal is certainly not willing to let hermeneutists like Gadamer have the last word on the topic.

A more recent voice is Mantzavinos (2005). In his book, Mantzavinos has chosen to deal with the positions of Dilthey, Heidegger, and Gadamer. Especially these three are main "sources of inspiration for the hermeneutical wave that is flooding the French- and English-speaking worlds" (Mantzavinos, 2005: x). Mantzavinos, like Føllesdal, rejects hermeneutics as a viable way of pursuing understanding. Mantzavinos also share Føllesdal's view that one should apply the hypothetico-deductive method. There are nuances between Mantzavinos and Føllesdal. Føllesdal has stated that both traditions carry important insights into the nature of knowledge. Mantzavinos argues for a total eradication of hermeneutics as a philosophical pursuit worth doing. In the words of Mantzavinos:

> the philosophical hermeneutics so predominant in the German-speaking world is afflicted with many grave deficiencies and contains little of use. In particular, the hermeneutic views of Heidegger and Gadamer offer no satisfactory solutions – either to the problem of text interpretation or to any other problems. Heidegger's philosophy, developed with impressively formulated, excessive claims, in principle offers nothing more than a series of trivialities that are practically devoid of

information. Gadamer's conception, although more closely connected with the traditional hermeneutic questions, possesses a very low problem-solving capacity: The transcendental vocabulary and the claim to the universality of the approach are not sufficiently substantiated, and they offer neither a correct analysis of the process of understanding nor a useful methodological guide for interpretative praxis.

(Mantzavinos, 2005: 155)

These words highlight perfectly the ongoing controversy between the two traditions. The analytical tradition is post-positivistic, upholding a notion of a unity of scientific method across scientific disciplines. The continental tradition is anti-positivistic in the sense that it is unthinkable that the humanistic sciences should apply the methods of the natural sciences. The continental side has embraced the notion of "rationality" within the seemingly irrational. Hence, philosophical hermeneutics have an easy conscience rejecting the idea that understanding can be achieved through the serenity of logical reasoning alone.

Note

1   The term "mediated" is here used to signify the information given to the receiver indirectly, in the surgeon's case by different types of technology, i.e. ECG, stethoscope, scans.

References

Butler, T. "Towards a hermeneutic method for interpretive research in information systems." *Journal of Information Technology* (1998) 13, 285–300.

Butler, T. and Fitzgerald, B. 1997a. "An empirical model of the information systems development process," in *Training and Education of Methodology Practitioners and Researchers, BCS Conference Series,* Jaratna, N., Fitzgerald, B., Wood-Harper, T. and Larrasquet, J-M. (eds.), London: Springer-Verlag.

Butler, T. and Fitzgerald, B. 1997b. "A case study of user participation in the information systems process," in *Proceedings of the 18th International Conference on Information Systems*, McClean, E.R. and Welke, R.J. (eds.), Atlanta, GA, pp. 411–26.

Coyne, R.M. 1995. *Designing Information Technology in the Postmodern Age: From Method to Metaphor.* Cambridge, MA: MIT Press.

Dahlager and Fredslund. 2011. "Hermeneutisk analyse – forståelse og forforståelse." In Valgårda, S. og Koch, L. (eds.). *Forskningsmetoder i folkesundhedsvidenskab.* Munksgaard Denmark.

Floridi, L. 2009. "Philosophical conceptions of information," in G. Sommaruga (ed.) *Formal Theories of Information*, LNCS 5363, pp. 13–53,

Føllesdal, D. 1979. "Hermeneutics and the hypothetico-deductive method." *Dialectica* 3(3–4).

Gadamer, H-G. 1976. *Philosophical Hermeneutics.* Trans. D. E. Linge. Berkeley and Los Angeles, CA: University of California Press.

Gadamer, H-G. 2007. *Sandhed og metode* ("Wahrheit und Metode" – Danish version). Trans Arne Jørgensen. Academica.

Grondin, J. 2005. "Hermeneutics." *New Dictionary of the History of Ideas.*

Heidegger, M. 1992a. *Being and Time.* Trans. John Macquarrie and Edward Robinson. Oxford: Blackwell.

Heidegger, M. 1992b. *History of the Concept of Time: Prolegomena.* Bloomington, IN: Indiana University Press.

Introna, L.D. 1993. "Information: a hermeneutic perspective." *Proceedings of the First European Conference on Information Systems, ECIS,* Henley-on-Thames.

Lee, A.S. 1993. "Electronic mail as medium for rich communication: an empirical investigation using hermeneutic interpretation," in *Proceedings of the Fourteenth International Conference on Information Systems*, J.I. DeGross, R.P. Bostrum, and D. Robey (eds.), Orlando, FL, pp. 13–21.

Lee, A.S. 1994. "The hermeneutic circle as a source of emergent richness in the managerial use of electronic mail," in the *Proceedings of the Fifteenth International Conference on Information Systems*, J.I. DeGross, S.L. Huff and M.C. Munro (eds.), Vancouver, BC, pp. 129–40.

Mantzavinos, C. 2005. *Naturalistic Hermeneutics*. Cambridge: Cambridge University Press.

Myers, M.D. "Dialectical hermeneutics: a theoretical framework for the implementation of information system." *Information Systems Journal*, 5(1): 51–70. 1995.

Ricoeur, P. 1974. *The Conflict of Interpretations*. Chicago, IL: Northwestern University Press

Ricoeur, P. 1981. *Hermeneutics and the Human Sciences*. Ed. and transl. J. B. Thompson. Cambridge: Cambridge University Press..

32

THE PHILOSOPHY
OF LAW IN AN
INFORMATION SOCIETY

Ugo Pagallo and Massimo Durante

Introduction

Today's information revolution is affecting our understanding about the world and about ourselves: we are interconnected informational organisms that share with biological entities and engineered artefacts 'a global environment ultimately made of information', that is, what Luciano Floridi calls 'the infosphere' (Floridi 2014). A crucial feature of this new environment is illustrated by how the information revolution is transforming principles and concepts of the law, much as the approach of experts to legal information. Consider how technological innovation continuously forces lawmakers to intervene, by adding norms for the regulation of new circumstances and new crimes, such as computer crimes (e.g. identity theft). Likewise, reflect on traditional rights such as copyright and privacy, both turned into a matter of access to, and control and protection of, information in digital environments. Accordingly, the law could be regarded today as that crucial part of the infosphere in which the rights and duties of the individual – as much as the sovereign powers of nation states, or matters of deliberation, representation, accountability, etc. – can be conveniently understood as 'ultimately made of information'.

The identification of the law with (some sort of) information is not an original finding of our times. A classical text like Thomas Hobbes' *Leviathan* makes this point clear. In Chapter 26, 'Of Civil Laws', in which the aim is to define what 'men are therefore bound to observe, because they are members, not of this or that Commonwealth in particular, but of a Commonwealth', Hobbes defines the law as 'a command, and a command consisteth in declaration or manifestation of the will of him that commandeth' (Hobbes ed. 1999). Because of this signalling function, the law appears as a set of rules or instructions for the determination of every legal subject of the system that must be expressed 'by voice, writing, or some other sufficient argument of the same'. Moreover, in the opinion of Hobbes, 'nor is it enough the law be written and published, but also that there be manifest signs that it proceedeth from the will of the sovereign ... There is therefore requisite, not only a declaration of the law, but also sufficient signs of the author and authority' (op. cit.).

Over the past century, Hobbes has been deemed as the father of modern legal and political thought, and, all in all, there are good reasons to follow this historiographical tradition (Bobbio 1993). Still, the way in which Hobbes grasps the connection between law and information, that is, the legal pronouncements of the sovereign as the only source of the system, does not mean that further ways to address this connection are unreasonable. An alternative representation is obviously given by the tradition of natural law, which does not represent the law as a simple matter of commands and obedience, but rather represents it in accordance with an examination of being *qua* being; that is, its essence. Leaving aside the multiple variants of the natural law tradition, which will be mentioned in the second section, the difference between these schools and modern legal positivism can be clarified with the words of Hobbes. Going back to Chapter 26 of *Leviathan*, 'the law of nature and the civil law contain each other and are of equal extent. For the laws of nature, which consist in equity, justice, gratitude, and other moral virtues on these depending, in the condition of mere nature … are not properly laws, but qualities that dispose men to peace and to obedience' (Hobbes ed. 1999).

However, another way to present the connection between law and information does exist, and has to do with sociological approaches to the legal phenomenon, that is, as a matter of knowledge and concepts that frame the representation and function of a given system, and that inform us about the different states of reality. This perspective can coexist with a Hobbesian approach to the law, contrary to what occurs with the alternative between natural law and positivism. Consider one of the most prominent legal scholars from the 1900s, Hans Kelsen, and his definition of the law as a means for social control via a set of rules enforced through the threat of physical sanctions: 'if A, then B' (Kelsen 1949). The formula shows what should be, rather than what is, i.e. punitive sanctions (B) that have to follow terms and conditions of legal accountability (A), rather than effects (B) that follow natural causes (A). Although Kelsen rejected any examination of being *qua* being (from which to deduce the norms of the law) he was open to work on how legal systems actually function. Whilst in the case of Kelsen, his reference was Max Weber's Chapter 7 of the masterpiece *Economy and Society* (Weber ed. 2005), the crucial epistemological point, according to Kelsen, was to keep a firm distinction, or even separation, between what should be and what is in legal terms, namely, between jurisprudence or, in Kelsenian terms, general theory of law, and legal sociology.

In light of this canonical framework, let us go back to our previous remarks on how the information revolution affects the tenets of the law. Even when stressing the endurance of the legal and political thought tradition, it does not follow that the peculiarities of the information era can be ignored. On the one hand, Kelsen's idea of the law as a set of rules enforced through the threat of physical sanctions is currently challenged by such cases as spamming, phishing, digital frauds, or cyber attacks. For example, despite strengthening criminal legislation like the *CAN-SPAM Act* passed by the US Congress in 2003, no threat of sanctions seems to limit spamming. On the other hand, cases that scholars address as a part of their everyday work in the fields of information technology (IT) law, such as data protection, computer crimes, or digital copyright, show how the flow of information on the internet tends to blur conventional boundaries of national legal systems. A twofold tenet of the rule of law is imperilled because the new realities of the information society have not only increased the difficulty of law enforcement in the infosphere, but they often lead to the illegitimate condition where states claim to regulate unilaterally extraterritorial conduct by imposing norms on individuals who have no say in the decisions affecting them. This trend is confirmed by the aim of both lawmakers and private companies to increasingly tackle the challenges of the information era through the means of design, code, and IT architecture, that is, by embedding legal safeguards into information technology. In addition to traditional techniques to solve issues of jurisdiction, international conflicts of law, or diverging interpretations of statutes, we have to take into account the new challenges of technological normativity and legal enforcement by design.

In order to assess continuities and breakthroughs of the law in an information society, this chapter is divided into five sections. The second section sets the proper level of abstraction (see Chapter 7) so as to examine the legal phenomenon in terms of information: drawing on the work of Luciano Floridi, we focus on the connection between information and reality. The third section then dwells on three approaches to legal information 'as' reality, 'for' reality, and 'about' reality, which sum up the multiple and even opposite ways in which positivism, realism, constitutionalism, institutionalism, or the natural law tradition aim to grasp the essence of the legal phenomenon. This level of abstraction is furthered in the fourth section, where we address the complex and even unpredictable ways in which technological developments may affect the law and how the latter aims to shape the evolution of technology, favouring certain choices over others. These dynamics are further analysed in the fifth section, by considering the design of norms and institutions in the information era and how such design may affect both the requirements and functions of the law, namely, what the law is supposed to be (requirements), and what it is called to do (functions). The chapter concludes by insisting that while the law as information is an old idea, ours is a brave new world after all.

Law, information, and reality

By focusing on the law in terms of information, we face a twofold difficulty. On one side, the multiple variations of positivism (both inclusive and exclusive), realism, institutionalism, or the different traditions of natural law, make apparent how much controversy exists about what the law is, or should be. On the other side, information is a heavily debated notion of its own, as already shown by the disagreement of Norbert Wiener and Claude Shannon as to how to understand that concept. For this reason, the first step will be to focus on the notion of information, drawing on the work of Luciano Floridi and what he calls a 'general definition of information' (Floridi 2009). Once this general definition is clarified, the next step will be to present the different families of legal philosophy in terms of information.

By information, we understand that which is made of data, namely, that which is made of lack of uniformity in the real world if, and only if, such data are additionally "well formed" and "meaningful" (Floridi 2009: 21). Along with different types of data, such as analogue, binary, and digital data, there are moreover multiple kinds of information. From a methodological viewpoint, it is thus necessary to set the proper level of abstraction for our analysis, i.e. to set the interface that makes possible an analysis of the legal system in terms of information. The general idea is to define a set of features representing the observables and variables of the analysis, the result of which provides a model for the field under exam (Durante 2011: 190-194; Pagallo 2013: 28-29). The methodological approach of this chapter can be represented by a figure on the interface of the model, its observables and variables (see Figure 32.1).

Significantly, Floridi has adopted different interfaces so as to discern multiple types of information: for instance, in Floridi (2009), attention is drawn to the basic distinction between environmental information and semantic information. The former indicates 'the possibility that data might be meaningful independently of an intelligent producer/informer' (op. cit., 32). Think of the series of concentric rings visible in the wood of a cut tree trunk, which allows us to estimate the age of that tree. In the case of semantic information, the latter has to do with the content of the information, which can be further defined as instructional or factual. Instructional information can be environmental or semantic, and is meant to (contribute to) bring about something. As to the notion of factual information, semantic content refers to the states of the world and is 'the most common way in which information

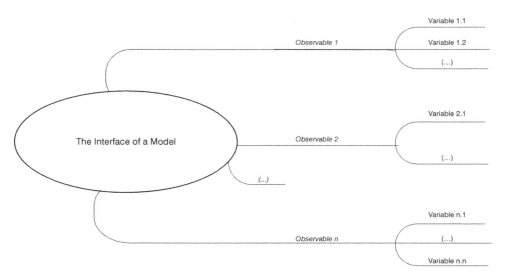

Figure 32.1 Levels of abstraction of a model

is understood and also one of the most important, since information as true semantic content is a necessary condition for knowledge' (Floridi 2009: 36).

In another work, we find a slightly different distinction, tripartite rather than bipartite, which clearly overlaps with Floridi's previous model: indeed, 'information can be viewed from three perspectives: information as reality (for example, as patterns of physical signals, which are neither true nor false), also known as ecological information; information about reality (semantic information, alethically qualifiable); and information for reality (instruction, like genetic information)' (Floridi 2004: 560).

Since the aim of the adopted level of abstraction is to identify the set of relevant features representing the observables and variables of the investigation, i.e. the analysis of the law in terms of information, let us proceed with the latter tripartite division. In light of the manifold ways in which the legal phenomenon has been understood throughout the centuries, this approach pinpoints three fundamental approaches to our subject matter, that is, legal information 'as' reality, 'about' reality, and 'for' reality. This interface with its observables is illustrated by Figure 32.2.

The next section explores how this approach relates to the different schools of jurisprudence and some of its relevant variables. The fourth section then examines the ways in which the interface fleshes out some crucial challenges of the law in an information society.

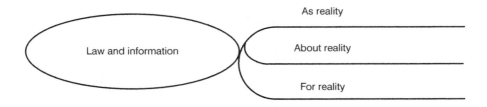

Figure 32.2 A tripartite legal interface for an information society

Three roads to legal information

The first observable of Figure 32.2, namely, legal information 'as' reality, specifies what all the variables of natural law have in common – whether referring to the ancient school of Socrates, Plato, and Aristotle; the Christian tradition of the Middle Ages (e.g., Thomas Aquinas); down to the modern theorizations of natural law and the state of nature, as in Locke and Kant, for example. Despite the differences between these stances, what they share is the idea that the law can be found in the nature of individuals, of the world, of things, i.e. the German 'Natur der Sache', or Nature as such, discussed in Kant's 1795 essay on the 'perpetual peace' (Kant ed. 1996). This perspective has become popular in the field of evolutionary psychology, according to which basic human concepts are wired in our brains, thus grounding cultural evolution. In this context, however, we should pay attention to the theses of Friedrich Hayek on spontaneous orders, *kosmos*, and the law as an emergent property of social interaction: 'man did not adopt new rules of conduct because he was intelligent. He became intelligent by submitting to new rules of conduct' (Hayek 1991: 163). We return to this variable of the natural law tradition in the next section.

The second observable of Figure 32.2, that is, legal information 'about' reality, is elucidated by work on legal sociology. In addition to Max Weber's research, mentioned in the introduction to this chapter, suffice it to mention some variants of legal realism, such as the American (as opposed to the Scandinavian) legal realism, according to which the law is a sort of forecast of what the courts will do in fact (Holmes ed. 1963). Although this approach is mostly popular in the common law area, it does fit many instances of the civil law tradition. After all, people ask for legal information about reality every time they visit a lawyer's office or a clerk to the justices. Moreover, since they are dealing with information as semantic content, which is alethically qualifiable, what people hope is that such lawyer, clerk, or attorney, will speak the truth.

The final observable in Figure 32.2 is the most common and even important in the legal domain: the law conceived as a set of rules or instructions for the determination of other informational objects, i.e. legal information 'for' reality. This is the common ground not only for every kind of positivism, normativism, or imperativism, but also for some aspects of constitutionalism, institutionalism, and the natural law tradition. Going back to Kelsen's aforementioned formula 'if A, then B', this means that the law competes with further forms of regulation, such as the social norms of Hayek's *kosmos*, the economic forces of the market, or the constraints of technological design: 'what distinguishes the legal order from all other social orders is the fact that it regulates human behaviour by means of a specific technique' (Kelsen 1949: 26). In light of today's information revolution, it follows that, once such technique regulates other techniques and, moreover, the process of technological innovation, we can accordingly conceive the law as a meta-technology (Pagallo 2013: 147–152). Much as with Hayek's ideas on *kosmos* and spontaneous orders, this standpoint will be furthered in the next section.

The distinction between legal information 'as' reality, 'about' reality, and 'for' reality does not suggest that we should conceive these three conceptions as worlds apart. Some undisputed champions of the law as information for reality, such as Hobbes and Kelsen, clarify why the different levels of analysis in Figure 32.2 interact. In Chapter 21 of *Leviathan*, Hobbes admits that 'the obligation of subjects to the sovereign is understood to last as long, and no longer, than the power lasteth by which he is able to protect them' (Hobbes ed. 1999). Therefore, scholars have to pay attention to the level of legal information 'about' reality, namely, whether the law is actually effective, in order to ground the obligation of the subjects and whether the command of a sovereign as legal information 'for' reality makes sense. A similar connection between these levels of legal information reappears in Kelsen's *General Theory of Law*: 'a norm is considered to be legally valid … on the condition that it belongs to a system of norms, to an order which, on the whole, is efficacious' (Kelsen 1949: 42).

In order to explain why the subjects obey the sovereign's commands, advocates of legal information for reality need some kind of anthropology. As to the philosophy of Hobbes, scholars have stressed time and again how the attempt to make the political obligation of the social covenant legitimate ends up in a sort of naturalistic fallacy, since Hobbes grounds the moral principles of his doctrine on a number of empirical propositions about human nature (e.g. Hampton 1990: 205). In the case of Kelsen, his theory of the basic norm as a legal assumption, which is required to make the validity of the norms intelligible, prevents such naturalistic fallacy on the basis of a moral formalism: 'You shall obey to the constitution' (Kelsen 1949). Of course, further accounts of the connection between legal information for reality and legal information as reality exist, e.g. John Finnis' naturalism or Lon Fuller's proceduralism. Yet, in light of the manifold ways in which scholars have grasped the nature of the law throughout the centuries, the time is ripe to examine how the information revolution is changing this traditional framework.

The interplay between law and technology

We mentioned some of the ways in which the information revolution is affecting current legal systems, as shown by the problems encountered by the law when dealing with matters of enforcement in the infosphere, or the claim of states to regulate unilaterally extraterritorial conduct by imposing norms on individuals who have no role in the decisions affecting them. Further aspects of this impact concern each of the levels of the analysis on legal information and reality illustrated in Figure 32.2. By considering these aspects, the aim here is to make clear what is new with the law in an information society.

First, regarding the observable of legal information 'as' reality and, especially, Hayek's ideas on *kosmos*, natural law, and spontaneous orders, the information revolution has fostered several fields of human interaction, in which only the unintentional dynamics of social intelligence, rather than the master plan of legislators and policy makers, seem to achieve satisfactory results. This is the opinion of several scholars in IT law today, who either conceive the internet as a 'self-governing realm of individual liberty, beyond the reach of government control' (Solum 2009: 56); or insist on how most online communities have, or rapidly develop, their own social norms (Murray 2007; Schultz 2007; Reed 2012, etc.). Whilst this trend clearly affects the level of legal information 'for' reality with the overlap between different forms of regulation, that is, between social norms and official law making, such competition confirms what was mentioned in the previous section: the different features of legal information 'as' reality, 'about' reality, and 'for' reality should not be understood as unconnected aspects of the legal phenomenon.

Second, regarding the observable of legal information 'about' reality, it is a matter of fact that the possibility of choice between different, or even alternative, sets of rules, which was mostly available only to multinational corporations before the internet era, has been democratised. This trend often goes hand in hand with the norms of transnational law and the agency of non-state, or private (as opposed to public) actors, as new sources of the system. Although scholars frequently equate the hard rules of the law, that is, legal information 'for' reality, with the effectiveness of national legal systems, so that the norms of transnational law and, for that matter, of international law would be less and less binding, this is not necessary so. Consider the network of internet governance and how several of the effective binding rules have their source in the field of transnational law and the forces of the market (*lex mercatoria*). This is confirmed by the set of rules regulating the eBay trading system (Goldsmith and Wu 2006: 130–145), and the powers of the Internet Corporation for the Assignment of Names and Numbers (ICANN). The fact that sovereign states have attempted to divest ICANN of its authority over the past years does not only mean that rearrangements in the system of the legal sources are intertwined with redistributions of power (Durante 2012: 24–25). Furthermore, in accordance with a realistic approach to the law, these rearrangements suggest that the more the tenets of legal information 'for' reality are in flux, the more one should focus on legal information 'about' reality.

Finally, we have to complement our previous remarks on the observable of legal information 'for' reality, in terms of complexity. This viewpoint brings us back to the work of Hayek. In the first volume of his *Law, Legislation and Liberty* he writes that 'one of our main contentions will be that very complex orders, comprising more particular facts than any brain could ascertain or manipulate, can be brought about only through forces inducing the formation of spontaneous orders' (Hayek 1982: 38). A key feature of today's information revolution concerns how the latter affects the whole organization and environment of current legal systems. Such growing complexity is one of the main reasons why national law-making activism has increasingly been short of breath over the past decades, and why constitutional powers of national governments have been joined – and even replaced – by the network of competences and institutions summarized by the idea of governance (Pagallo 2014). The more an issue impacts on the whole infrastructure of the system, the more complex such an issue is; but, the more complex an issue is, the less traditional notions of legal and political thought can tackle such complexity in terms of physical sanctions, national jurisdiction, or self-referential rule of law.

In addition, the complexity of the subject matter that national lawmakers aim to govern has, at times, recommended the adoption of soft law tools of governance, such as codes of conduct and forms of self-regulation, along with further 'nonbinding norms … that often carry powerful normative and persuasive value' (Halliday and Osinsky 2006: 449). *Pace* Hobbes's remarks in Chapter 25 of *Leviathan*, the soft tools of the law concern the content, rather than the source of the norm: 'Command is where a man saith, 'Do this', or 'Do not this', without expecting other reason than the will of him that says it … Counsel is where a man saith, 'Do this', or 'Do not this', and deduceth his reasons from the benefit that arriveth by it to him to whom he saith it' (Hobbes ed. 1999). Matters of convenience, prestige, image, or utility may suggest following the 'counsel' of such soft law authorities and still, their normative power often hinges on the belief that such rules are appropriate to govern people's interaction. This confirms our previous remarks on the social dynamics of the internet and the behaviour of online communities; for members of such communities subject themselves, through their choice, to the rule of the authority that delivers the opinion, insofar as they deem it suitable.

From insisting on the multiple ways in which the information revolution, the dynamics of spontaneous orders, the forces of the market as sources of transnational law, or the governance of complex systems have challenged canonical tenets of the law, that is, legal information 'for' reality, it does not follow that such canonical tenets on the regulatory aims of the law have simply vanished or disappeared. Rather, what we previously dubbed as the aim of the law as 'meta-technology' has been repositioned or realigned. The traditional hard tools of the law, such as statutes and codes supported by the threat of physical sanctions, have increasingly been complemented with more sophisticated forms of enforcement via the mechanisms of design, codes, and architecture. This is the bread and butter of work on the regulatory aspects of technology in such fields as universal usability, informed consent, crime control, social justice, or design-based instruments for implementing social policies (Pagallo 2012). From the viewpoint of the law as a meta-technology that competes with other forms of regulation (such as the social norms of Hayek's *kosmos*) – much as do the forces of the market – we thus assume a bidirectional tension, or interplay, between law and technology. Instead of a one-way movement of social evolution from technology to law, a key component of the legal challenges in an information society concerns the other way around, that is, how the regulatory tools of technology can be exploited by embedding normative constraints into the design of spaces (environmental design), or of objects (product design), or of messages (communication design), so as to comply with the rules of current legal frameworks.

The picture of what is new with the law in an information society has then to be complemented in light of the act of working out the shape and functioning of ICT interfaces, self-enforcing technologies, default settings, etc. The next section explores this new scenario in terms of the law, information, and design.

Law, information, and design

Much as with 'law' and 'information', 'design' is a complex notion of its own. Drawing on the work of the English poet and designer Norman Potter (2002), we mentioned the distinction between the design of spaces, products, and messages. In *The Design with Intent Method* (2010), it is noteworthy that Lockton, Harrison and Stanton describe 101 ways in which products can influence the behaviour of their users. In addition, we should distinguish between the subjects in which design is embedded, and three underlying mechanisms or 'modalities of design' (Yeung 2007). Besides places and spaces, products and processes, we can indeed design biological organisms; witness the genetically modified plants and animals (GMOs) in our agricultural systems, or the current debate on humans, post-humans, and cyborgs. As to the modalities of design, the aim of designers can either be to encourage a change in social behaviour, or to decrease the impact of harm-generating conducts, or even to prevent their occurrence. As an illustration of the first kind of design mechanism, consider the installation of speed bumps in roads as a means to reduce the velocity of cars. As an example of the second modality of design, consider the introduction of airbags to reduce the impact of harm-generating conducts. As an instance of total prevention, it is enough to mention current projects on 'smart cars', which are able to stop or to limit their own speed according to the driver's state of health and the inputs of the surrounding environment (Pagallo 2011).

In this context, dealing with the realignment of legal information 'for' reality, let us focus on this latter design mechanism. There are two reasons that recommend this level of abstraction. First, the aim to embed legal safeguards into places and spaces, products and interfaces of social interaction so as to prevent the occurrence of harm-generating behaviour, alters the traditional view of the law as a set of rules or instructions for the determination of the subjects in the legal system, that is, the Kelsenian formula 'if A, then B'. The automation of the law through the use of self-enforcing technologies, such as systems for filtering electronic communications, digital rights management (DRM), and some versions of the principle of 'privacy by design', should in fact be understood in accordance with effects (B) that would automatically follow technical instructions (A), rather than sanctions (B) that should follow terms and conditions of legal accountability (A), i.e. that which is, rather than that which should be. Because legal interaction has increasingly turned into a matter of access, control, and protection over information in digital environments, the risk is that individual behaviour can unilaterally be determined on the basis of automated techniques, rather than by individual choices on levels of access and control over information: 'the controls over access to content will not be controls that are ratified by courts; the controls over access to content will be controls that are coded by programmers' (Lessig 2004: 152).

Second, we have to take into account the institutional repercussions of this design mechanism. Leaving aside China's 'Great Firewall' and the systems of filters and re-routers, detours and dead-ends, which aim to keep internet users on the state-approved online path, the repressive side of this design policy has shown up in Western democracies as well. Some countries, like France or South Korea, have endorsed the so-called 'three strikes' doctrine, as a part of the graduated system that ends up with disconnection of the user after three warnings of alleged copyright infringement. In December 2010, the EU Commission similarly proposed the adoption of a system of filters in order to control the flow of information on the internet (SEC-2010-1589 final). On March 2012, the Court of Appeals in London ignored the rulings of the EU Court of Justice in *Scarlet Extended* (C-70/10) and *Netlog* (C-360/10), supporting the system for filtering electronic communications in order to identify and block the transfer of files infringing copyright, set up by the UK Digital Economy Act (DEA) from 2010 (CI/2011/1437, n. 82). However, along with the aim of preventing the occurrence of alleged harm-generating behaviour through the use of self-enforcing technologies and internet filtering systems, there is a more subtle side to this design policy, namely, *pace* (Kant ed. 1996), the aim of some lawmakers to protect citizens even against themselves.

This threat of paternalism, after all, has materialized with some EU data protection provisions and certain bizarre decisions of the European institutions (Enzensberger 2011; Pagallo and Durante 2014). Although the purpose is to guard people's wellbeing against all harm, what imperils a basic tenet of the rule of law, such as the autonomy of the individual, has to do with the automation of the law as such. Once the normative side of the law as legal information 'for' reality is transferred from the traditional 'ought to' of the law to what actually is, a modelling of individual conduct follows as a result, collapsing 'the public understanding of law with its application eliminating a useful interface between the law's terms and its application' (Zittrain 2007: 152). In the phrasing of Kant's *Theory and Practice*, the institutional fallout of such mechanisms is a 'paternalistic government', for 'the subjects, as minors, cannot decide what is truly beneficial or detrimental to them, but are obliged to wait passively for the head of state', or the programmers, 'to judge how they ought to be happy' (Kant ed. 1996).

However, there is still the other side of the coin, namely, the difficulty of achieving such total control through design. Although on 23 January 2014 the Chinese Great Firewall locked down for eight hours, knocking out such local giants as Baidu and Sina.com,[1] the problems are not only technical. Of course, it would be important that lawmakers, interpreted as game designers, fully understand that 'the only truly secure system is one that is powered off, cast in a block of concrete and sealed in a lead-lined room with armed guards – and even then I have my doubts' (Garfinkel and Spafford 1997). In addition, doubts cast by 'a rich body of scholarship concerning the theory and practice of "traditional" rule-based regulation bear witness of the impossibility of designing regulatory standards in the form of legal rules that will hit their target with perfect accuracy' (Yeung 2007: 106). The difficulty of achieving a total control through design suggests a more basic fact; that such use of the regulatory tools of technology does not operate in a social vacuum and, furthermore, is influenced by other forms of regulation, such as the social norms of Hayek's *kosmos*, or the economic forces of the market, upon which we have insisted in this chapter. Rather than a one-way flow of social evolution through the design of self-enforcing technologies, filtering systems, and the like, we should grasp the legal challenges in an information society as a complex game in which the three levels of analysis expounded in this chapter, namely legal information 'as' reality (e.g. transnational spontaneous orders), 'about' reality (e.g. private actors and the market as a regulatory source of the system), and 'for' reality (e.g. the upgraded normative side of the law by design), interact. We turn now to this chapter's conclusions.

Conclusions

The law can be conceived today as that crucial part of the infosphere in which matters of deliberation, representation, and accountability, much as the rights and duties of individuals, or the sovereign powers of nation states, can be conveniently understood as ultimately made of information; namely experienced at the proper level of abstraction as coherent sets of information. Accordingly, we have represented the law in terms of legal information by drawing on Floridi's tripartite notion of information 'as' reality, 'about' reality, and 'for' reality (see Figure 32.2). This approach is particularly fruitful, since a unitary informational viewpoint casts light on four crucial points of today's state-of-the-legal-art:

i   The different schools of jurisprudence can be properly represented in terms of legal information as, about, or for, reality. As stressed in the third section of this chapter, think of the natural law tradition in terms of legal information 'as' reality, of different types of positivism as legal information 'for' reality, etc.;

ii As a form of access, control, and protection over information in digital environments, canonical tenets of the law are challenged by the information revolution. Since this chapter's introduction and again, in the fourth section, attention has been drawn to the shortcomings of the traditional idea of the law as a set of rules, or commands, enforced through the threat of physical sanctions;

iii The interplay between law and information technologies makes clear some trends of the law in an information society. As discussed in the fourth section, such trends concern either the level of legal information 'as' reality (e.g. new forms of *kosmos* and the emergence of spontaneous orders on the internet); legal information 'about' reality (e.g. the evolution of the law vis-à-vis new transnational sources of the law in cyberspace); or, of legal information 'for' reality (e.g. how the regulatory tools of the law comprise new forms of soft law that depend on the content, rather than the source, of the legal rule);

iv The interplay between law and information technologies should not be thought of as a one-way movement of social evolution from technology to law. The fifth section has indeed insisted on the other way around, namely on how the regulatory tools of technology can be exploited by embedding normative constraints into spaces and places, products and messages, so as to comply with the rules of current legal frameworks.

Although these levels of analysis are connected, the latter scenario of technological normativity, i.e. the enforcement of norms through technology, appears by far the more urgent and critical. As a reaction to the shortcomings of canonical tenets of the law (i.e. the level of analysis (ii)), such forms of enforcement via design, codes, or architecture, do not only impact on the evolution of the law in an information society (i.e. the level of analysis (iii)). The design of norms and institutions through technology also affects what the law is supposed to be, and what the law is called to do (i.e. the level of analysis (i)), by impinging on some pillars of the rule of law, such as the autonomy of the individuals, the adoption of rules through political representatives, and the application of norms by independent courts. Today's debate on the redesign of legal institutions and norms through the means of technological normativity (i.e. the level of analysis (iv)), is thus likely to become the main subject of the philosophy of law in an information society and to retain the attention of experts of legal information for quite some time. What is at stake here concerns both the requirements and functions of the law, after all.

Note

1 Experts suspect Great Firewall in the crash of the web in China, *International New York Times*, 24 January 2014, p. 13.

References

Bobbio, Norberto (1993) *Thomas Hobbes and the Natural Law Tradition*, transl. by D. Gobetti. Chicago, IL: University of Chicago Press.

Durante, Massimo (2011) Normativity, Constructionism, and Constraining Affordances, *Ethics & Politics*, 13(2): 180–200.

Durante, Massimo (2012) E-democracy as the Frame of Networked Public Discourse: Information, Consensus and Complexity. In: P. Mindus, A. Greppi and M. Cuono, *Legitimacy 2.0. E-democracy and Public Opinion in the Digital Age*. vol. Paper Series, 25th IVR World Congress: Law, Science and Technology (1–28) Frankfurt-am-Main: Goethe University Press.

Enzensberger, Hans Magnus (2011) *Brussels, the Gentle Monster*. London: Seagull.

Floridi, Luciano (2004) Open Problems in the Philosophy of Information, *Metaphilosophy*, 35.4, 554–582.

Floridi, Luciano (2009) *A Very Short Introduction to Information*. Oxford: Oxford University Press.

Floridi, Luciano (2014) *The Fourth Revolution*. Oxford: Oxford University Press.

Garfinkel, Simson and Gene Spafford (1997) *Web Security and Commerce*. Sebastopol, CA: O'Reilly.

Goldsmith, Jack and Tim Wu (2006) *Who Controls the Internet: Illusions of a Borderless World*. New York: Oxford University Press.

Halliday, Terence C. and Pavel Osinsky (2006) Globalization of Law, *Annual Review of Sociology*, 32: 447–70.

Hampton, Jean (1990) *Hobbes and the Social Contract Tradition*. Cambridge: Cambridge University Press.

Hayek, Friedrich A. (1982) *Law, Legislation and Liberty*. Vol. 1: *Rules and Order*. Chicago: University of Chicago Press.

Hayek, Friedrich A. (1991) *Law, Legislation and Liberty*. Vol. 3: *The Political Order of a Free People*. Chicago, IL: University of Chicago Press.

Hobbes, Thomas (1999) *Leviathan*, R. Tuck (Ed.). Cambridge: Cambridge University Press.

Holmes, Oliver W. Jr. (1963), *The Common Law*, M. DeWolfe Howe (Ed.). Boston, MA: Little, Brown.

Kant, Immanuel (1996) *Practical Philosophy*, transl. by Mary Gregor. Cambridge: Cambridge University Press.

Kelsen, Hans (1949) *General Theory of the Law and the State*, transl. by A. Wedberg. Cambridge, MA: Harvard University Press.

Lessig, Lawrence (2004) *Free Culture: The Nature and Future of Creativity*. New York: Penguin Press.

Lockton, Dan, Harrison, David J., and Neville A. Stanton (2010) The Design with Intent Method: A Design Tool for Influencing User Behaviour, *Applied Ergonomics*, 41(3): 382–392.

Murray, Andrew D. (2007) *The Regulation of Cyberspace: Control in the Online Environment*. New York: Routledge-Cavendish.

Pagallo, Ugo (2011) Designing Data Protection Safeguards Ethically, *Information*, 2(2): 247–265.

Pagallo, Ugo (2012) Cracking down on Autonomy: Three Challenges to Design in IT Law, *Ethics and Information Technology*, 14(4): 319–328.

Pagallo, Ugo (2013) *The Laws of Robots: Crimes, Contracts, and Torts*. Dordrecht: Springer.

Pagallo, Ugo (2014) Good Onlife Governance: On Law, Spontaneous Orders, and Design, in *The Onlife Manifesto: Being Human in a Hyperconnected Era*, L. Floridi (Ed.). Dordrecht: Springer.

Pagallo, Ugo and Massimo Durante (2014) Legal Memories and the Right to Be Forgotten. In *Protection of Information and the Right to Privacy – A New Equilibrium?* (17–30), L. Floridi (Ed.), Dordrecht: Springer.

Potter, Norman (2002), *What is a Designer*. London: Hyphen Press.

Reed, Chris (2012) *Making Laws for Cyberspace*. Oxford: Oxford University Press.

Schultz, Thomas (2007) Private Legal Systems: What Cyberspace Might Teach Legal Theorists, *Yale Journal of Law and Technology*, 10: 151–193.

Solum, Lawrence B. (2009) Models of Internet Governance, in *Internet Governance: Infrastructure and Institutions* (48–91), L. A. Bygrave and J. Bing (Eds.). Oxford: Oxford University Press.

Weber, Max (2005) *Economy and Society*, transl. by Ch. Camic *et al.* Stanford, CA: Stanford University Press.

Yeung, Karen (2007) Towards an Understanding of Regulation by Design. In *Regulating Technologies: Legal Futures, Regulatory Frames and Technological Fixes* (79–108), R. Brownsword and K. Yeung (Eds.), London: Hart.

Zittrain, Jonathan (2007) Perfect Enforcement on Tomorrow's Internet. In *Regulating Technologies: Legal Futures, Regulatory Frames and Technological Fixes* (125–156), R. Brownsword and K. Yeung (Eds.), London: Hart.

33

THE SPIRITUAL VALUE OF INFORMATION

George Medley

Introduction

Given the increasing importance of information within our world, our increasing awareness of incidents of naturally occurring information, and the long standing impact of religious experience within our global community, we ignore the relationship between religion and information at our own peril. To be sure, up to this point the interaction between Philosophy of Religion or Theology and Philosophy of Information has been explored almost entirely within the Western Christian tradition, and, for the most part, this chapter will be no exception, but this may be attributed to the fact that the overwhelming majority of written work explicitly concerning Philosophy of Information (PI) has been done by Western scholars operating in cultures with an historical Christian heritage.

Additionally, there is a certain amount of dread that arises in some individuals upon hearing that PI may be approached from a philosophy of religion (or worse a theological) perspective. The immediate thought is that the work will devolve into contentious support for "Intelligent Design" (ID), or something of that sort. While the current ID debate will certainly bear mention, it is not, by any means, the only topic of concern for those engaged in the philosophy of religion. Indeed, as this chapter will note early on, many of the assumptions inherent in the ID movement display a gross misrepresentation of information theory and its ability to prove (or disprove) certain axioms within biology.

Instead, this chapter provides an overview of a variety of issues within the philosophy of religion related to PI. The chapter begins with a discussion of two of the misuses of information theory in relation to religion, in particular focusing on ID. Following that the chapter will examine some of the first forays into PI made by philosophers of religion and theologians. Next, the chapter will examine possible avenues for expanding religious interaction with PI beyond Western Christian thought before examining areas of possible future research. The chapter is not concerned, primarily, with ethics, as this has been addressed in Chapter 30, nor is the chapter concerned with using information merely as a valid justification for belief in God. Rather, the chapter establishes that while PI has informed religious discussions in important ways, it has not satisfactorily answered the fundamental religious question of God's existence, and much of the key interaction between PI and philosophy of religion has itself been introductory. So there remains extensive opportunity for further interaction between PI and philosophy of religion.

The problem with intelligent design

By far the most ubiquitous use of information in a religious context is in reference to the ID movement, especially in its current form as championed by Michael Behe, and to a greater extent by William Dembski (Lennox 2007: 180; for summaries of each one's views see Behe 1996; Dembski 2002). This connection may have occurred earlier, particularly in the works of young earth creationists such as Bill Davis and A. E. Wilder-Smith, who used the term initially in the context of Young Earth Creationism (YEC), the view that the earth is between 5,000 and 15,000 years old. Yet its current usage, especially as employed by Dembski, does not require a commitment to YEC. Dembski himself accepts the standard geological dating of the earth (Davis and Kenyon 1989). It is with the current use of the term ID, as employed by Dembski, that we concern ourselves now. Given the prominence of ID, the rest of this section will focus on the misuse of information within ID. At the same time, misapplication of information theory in the field of evolutionary theory of religion has also been prevalent. This topic will be addressed in the next section.

ID fits well within a discussion of religion and information because the concern of the ID movement is polemical, not scientific. Proponents of ID not only assume that Darwinian evolution, as espoused by mainstream biology, is inaccurate, but that it is diametrically opposed to their religious worldview. In fact, the *only* possible conclusion of ID is that the universe gives evidence to the work of God as the direct, interventionist creator. Dembski illustrates this with his conclusion that "no intelligent agent who is strictly physical" can meet the criteria of a designer as he has defined it, despite earlier claims that extra-terrestrials could fit the bill just as easily as God (Dembski 1998b, 1998a). Thus it becomes clear that ID is not as concerned with science as it is with making a religious point: that the universe in general, and life on earth in particular, was designed and created by God either in cooperation with, or, more likely, independent of evolutionary processes.

Where evolution is employed it is downplayed to the extent that "micro-evolution," or evolution within a species, is understandable as an independent, natural process, but that "macro-evolution," or evolution between species or genus or family groups and beyond requires the intervention of some "intelligent designer" (Behe 1996). Indeed, the rhetoric of the ID movement is at least as concerned with discrediting classical Darwinian theory, though with comparatively little to say about contemporary neo-Darwinian evolution, as it is with promoting ID. While Behe's anti-evolutionary argument has been thoroughly discredited, his position is not as directly related to PI as Dembski's. Dembski, whose first graduate degree was in mathematics, gained notoriety following the publication of the thesis for his second doctorate, in philosophy, entitled *The Design Inference: Eliminating Chance through Small Probabilities* in the Cambridge Studies in Probability, Induction and Decision Theory series (1998a).

In *The Design Inference*, Dembski claims to be able to eliminate chance when improbable events "fit the right sort of pattern" (1998a: xi). In other words, for Dembski, a "design inference" can be drawn when an event of small probability also has "specification" (4–5). From this, Dembski concludes that, by applying his "explanatory filter," he can examine any event to differentiate between those that are both highly improbable and either specific but regular, irregular but non-specific, or irregular and specific. The latter group proves, for Dembski, the existence of an omnipotent designer (Dembski 1998a: 36–37, 63, 118–119). As might be expected by such grand claims from mathematical analysis, Dembski's work is highly problematic.

First, it should be noted that if Dembski's "explanatory filter" were applied uniformly, then his work accomplishes exactly what it purports to do: it eliminates chance (1998a: 36–37). For Dembski, if one were to flip a coin 100 times on three separate occasions and each time it landed heads, it would *require* a weighted coin, or something else to that effect. This is different, of course, from saying that it would simply be *highly likely* that there was a weighted coin, and herein lies the problem. There is simply no room for chance according to Dembski, even in an infinite universe. An infinite number of monkeys typing on an infinite number of typewriters for all of eternity could never produce the collected works of Shakespeare unless one of them had learned to read and was provided with a copy, if we follow Dembski's "explanatory filter" as rigidly as he proposes. It is easy to prove a point when you've stacked the deck so heavily.

Further, Dembski not only assumes that specified and irregular events contain information, which he neglects to account for as context specific, he also assumes that information necessarily requires that the information was designed (1998a: 113–118). While it is true that the term "information" is still used with various meanings within biology (see Chapter 23), there are nevertheless limits to this use, and the same wide range of uses does not pertain to either philosophy or mathematics (Allen and Houser 1992; Floridi 2005: 351). In its most basic sense, information is simply data and meaning (Floridi 2010: 65; Floridi 2005: 352–353; Checkland and Scholes 1990: 303). It may even be granted that certain physical objects have a source that is non-material in nature, and that this source is information (Floridi 2005: 357–358). While this non-material description of information might lead one to conjecture about the involvement of a non-physical being, i.e. God, it cannot be assumed that there is an agency behind information necessarily. This, however, is precisely what Dembski argues (1998a: 62–65). Yet, we have strong reason to believe that information of the sort Dembski describes can occur without recourse to a designing agent; it is frequently the case that information can be transmitted without any intentional agency. For instance, let us consider the flow of a river. By examining various parts of the river, the way wildlife interacts with the river, the makeup of the river, its turns, the valleys through which it travels, we can gain quite a bit of information about the river itself and the pertinent historic, geological, botanical, and zoological information related to this flow. This significant information is extrapolated from the data of the river by agents; however, we are not to assume that the river *intended* to transfer this information.

Perhaps the argument for Dembski is that only information that conforms to his definitions of specification and improbability fits the criteria. However, it could also be the case that one is gleaning misinformation, or misinterpreting the data to yield non-information. After all, this is the premise behind a tarot card reading, or ancient Chinese divination. Each unique "reading" event is highly improbable and, to the interpreter, very specific, as well as irregular. Thus, from reading bones or cards the diviner or reader is able to gain what he or she believes to be information. Yet we do not assume that they have correctly interpreted data. Both have succumbed to an anthropic bias. After all, it is natural for people to see patterns and messages in all sorts of things. This does not mean we are correct in this interpretation. Clearly there is some objective data here, and that data yields some information, but what sort of information it yields (the makeup of the bones and the impact of fire upon them, for instance) may be open for debate. So, we might say that Dembski has begged the question: he has assumed a designer for what he considers particular type of information so that he may prove a designer behind what he considers a particular type of information, without providing convincing evidence that his interpretation of the data is the correct one.

Another of Dembski's errors is that he has assumed that evolutionary biology explains the current biological complexity and diversity with an appeal only to chance and time. Instead there are a number of mechanisms that reduces the improbability of specific events. The first is Natural Selection, which provides a sort of natural agency. It is not the case that any and all genetic mutations have an equal chance of continuing on and reproducing, as Dembski accepts in his spurious calculations (1998c). Rather, those species that have an environmental advantage are more likely to reproduce and successfully raise more offspring, thus passing on the relevant genetic code. This allows for specificity and irregularity within a relatively short period of time once Natural Selection is understood as the organizing principle it is.

Perhaps a larger piece of evidence, which Dembski fails to address, is the self-constructing and self-regulating nature of proteins, which serve to further eliminate improbability. From what we have learned concerning proteins, there is a limited number of ways in which they will fold together, and proteins will, by their very nature, seek out the most efficient way to do so (López-Moratalla and Cerezo 2011). Peter Bak's concept of a "self-organized system" makes the strong case that, given the existence of the world as it is, it will necessarily give rise to life in a way that naturally increases in complexity (Bak 1997). Thus there is no need for a designer. The question of life becomes an ontological one, not a scientific, mathematical or informational question: we might ask "why is there life," from a philosophical perspective, as with Heidegger's famous "why is there something rather than nothing," but this is clearly beyond the bounds of biological investigation.

Given these two mechanisms, Natural Selection and the self-regulating nature of proteins, it becomes clear that not only is it possible for life to evolve into its current complexity without recourse to a designer, but that once life begins, it is very probable that it will continue to develop and evolve in complexity irrespective of the presence of some designer. So while a designer is not necessarily excluded, this becomes a very obvious case of a "God of the gaps" argument. Further, while it may be the case that information is involved in the biological processes, it is not necessarily the case that this information requires agency behind it, as Dembski assumed *a priori*. A cell may transmit biological information via DNA replication, but this cell does not necessarily have some grand design behind that transmission. Thus we can see that ID, at least as concerns PI, is a non-starter.

In fact, if we examine the history of Western philosophy, we will see that, despite the inclusion of various equations, which have a spurious connection to reality, and different terminology, Dembski's argument is no different from that of William Paley, which is itself a reconceptualization of the Aquinian and Aristotelian arguments for the existence of a god. Immanuel Kant notably argued that one cannot move from the synthetic evidence of the observable universe to the speculative claim that God exists. Rather, at least as concerns design of the universe or other similar arguments for the existence of God (i.e. from ethics), one may only presuppose a Supreme Creator and our minds will then cause us to see evidence for this Creator in our world (Kant 1919: 508–514; 631ff.).

Evolutionary theory of religion

A second misapplication of information theory comes from the opposite end of the philosophical/theological spectrum: evolutionary theory of religion (ETR). The overarching goal of ETR is not, *prima facie*, incompatible with most core religious doctrines. The intent of ETR is to offer an evolutionary explanation for the development of religion. In other words, is there some evolutionary advantage to religion that accounts for its prevalence? Nothing would prevent the religious from then claiming that any advantage caused by religious belief is something ordained by God, as this is a claim outside the bounds of science. A conflict arises when researchers in ETR draw conclusions that discount the viability of religion, or the possibility that one or more religious beliefs may be correct irrespective of the evolutionary advantage they give.

As noted by Nathaniel Barrett, the majority of the history of ETR has been grounded within computational evolutionary psychology (Barrett 2010). Computational evolutionary psychology tends to understand the human brain as a processor that takes in data, tries to make sense of it as information, and responds accordingly (see Chapter 29). Our brains process information in a particular way that has, or has had, an evolutionary advantage, or else this processing element would not be present. However, and this is critical, the evolutionary advantage that a particular way of processing information may have given may no longer serve any real purpose (Tooby and Cosmides 2005: 18).

For ETR and the religious, then, the conflict becomes clear. ETR postulates that religion is a response to some environmental bit of information or stimulus that, through a relevant action, gave some survival advantage. For instance, having a certain terror of the dark is advantageous to our early ancestors, for it allowed them to be vigilant at night and tuned to the noises they heard, so that they would be able to avoid nocturnal predators. In many religions there is a negative connotation with the dark, and several even describe demons as associated with darkness or the unseen. The implication, then, is that those sorts of individuals who tended to be more religious were, in general, less curious and more cautious, and therefore more likely to avoid being eaten by a predator. Today, however, there is no need to be wary of predators within our walled homes and cities and behind locked doors, therefore there is no need for this religious sensibility and we should, instead, encourage curiosity and abandon religion which restricts it.

This sort of example is frequently given in precisely this manner: a "just so" story, with no data to confirm or disconfirm it (Ryle 2005). Evolutionary psychology is so speculative that virtually all of its conclusions have been severely criticized. In particular, as concerns religious proclivities, the appeal to the way in which humans process information has assumed a certain kind of information, to which we may only ever speculate, and, as Barrett notes, ignores the important element of context, particularly for the social and "lived" aspect of religions for how information is received and processed (Barrett 2010: 585). In other words, ETR has, until very recently, ignored the impact that community may have upon the way the religious interact with the world and process that information. Nothing is mentioned, either, of the possibility that a genuine historical encounter with a divine may have occurred. The trouble, of course, is that such an encounter cannot be verified, nor is it particularly scientific, and thus this may be excused for ETR.

Further, ETR, reliant as it is upon evolutionary psychology, assumes a computational view of the mind, wherein the mind is merely an information processor and its computation, or thought, could adequately be expressed as any other information processor: as an algorithm (Churchland *et al.* 1993: 48). While one may be able to conceive of many, even most, functions of the mind as able to be expressed mathematically in this fashion, it still remains to be seen whether all functions of the mind may be expressed in this way. In particular, ETR assumes that religious thought, or proclivity to religious thought, must also be reduced to an algorithm. Whether this sort of reductionism is even possible or not, though, it certainly does not encourage congenial interaction between philosophy of religion and ETR.

Still, a more serious problem for ETR rests upon what may be a fundamental misunderstanding of information related to the environment. As Barrett notes, ETR, and most forms of evolutionary psychology, assume information is context independent. That is, information can be gained from the environment alone. However, this is obviously not the case. Data, it may be argued, is objective in any given environment, but the way in which that data is received, the meaning it is given, or the information related to the environment, is heavily context dependent. This difficulty, as well as others related to computational evolutionary psychology in particular, has begun to shift the discussion of ETR. Barrett suggests that ETR does not have a computational base at all, in which case it begins to be less relevant to PI than it would have been otherwise (Barrett 2010: 603–609).

In light of this, and the conclusion drawn at the end of the previous section, it seems that the use of information simply cannot address (either positively or negatively) the existence or non-existence of God. However, this does not mean that PI is irrelevant to the philosophy of religion. Given that most religious communities do not view God as wholly removed from the *cosmos* after its formation, as did eighteenth and nineteenth century Deists, but understand God to be active within the world, Niels Henrik Gregerson suggests that the best manner to approach philosophy of religion from the perspective of information is either to engage in an "explanatory approach" – wherein the idea of a designed cosmos is interpreted in light of philosophical theology to explain how God intervenes effectively within the universe – or to "presuppose" that God, via the *logos,* is at work, and reconcile how the natural world expresses that reality (2002: 80–81). Given that Gregerson devotes the rest of his paper to the second option, and that this chapter is a philosophically grounded work, we will turn now to the former.

Information and philosophical theology

While "philosophical theology" as a term has been subject to varied usage, a suitable definition for it is philosophy done within a particular theological tradition, broadly understood. Thus, rather than attempt to answer questions of the existence of God, which, as has been demonstrated, is well outside the reach of PI, it assumes certain baseline aspects and works within them. By far, the majority of literature within philosophical theology has occurred within the Western Christian tradition, and its interaction with information is no exception. This section will briefly engage the developments of two theologians with information theory before noting the deficiencies inherent in their approaches and offering a third means of examining PI within philosophical theology.

Arthur Peacocke and John Polkinghorne link information with the Christian concept of the *logos*. The *logos*, in Christian theology is, of course, associated with the second person of the Trinity, the Son, who existed as the *logos* prior to the incarnation and continues to exist as the *logos* though also as the resurrected Christ within Christian theology. The alignment of the *logos* with information is, perhaps, the most appropriate way to engage PI with philosophical theology because the first century understanding of *logos* and the modern understanding of information are virtually synonymous (Puddefoot 1996a, 301–20). While Saunders is not entirely correct in his assertion that Polkinghorne is the only theologian to engage with chaos theory, Polkinghorne's integration of it with information is, nevertheless, particularly interesting (Saunders 2002: 174).

Polkinghorne begins his discussion of information by drawing on the idea of God's omnipresence, which, while not named as one of the basic characteristics of God in philosophy of religion, is nevertheless widely accepted, particularly among conservative and evangelical Christians. Polkinghorne claims that God's omnipresence means that there is precisely no distance between God and all of creation. Polkinghorne further describes that, for chaos theory, a small change in entropy over a small distance within a system can lead to massive changes throughout the system, the so-called "butterfly effect."

Although current quantum mechanics accounts for changes across a distance of zero, chaos theory does not. Polkinghorne theorizes that changes caused by God across a distance of zero could have immense, potentially infinite, effects. Polkinghorne then describes the action of God, the *logos*, as a single "input of pure information" without entropy (1991, 40–45). This allows for an indirect, "top-down" causation that still leaves room for undefined change, though within certain limits defined by the input of information. The factor of contingency is important for Polkinghorne who expresses a strong desire to maintain human freedom, important for both ethical and theological reasons. For instance, human freedom is required to maintain culpability, the idea that we are morally responsible for our actions. Theologically this is important because, while most religions accept the reality of sin or some equivalent analog, they cannot entertain the possibility that God, who is generally considered morally perfect, is responsible for the existence of sin (i.e. humans must be free to sin).

In contrast to this somewhat indirect approach, Peacocke offers a more direct approach. For Peacocke, God, as *logos*, acts as a divine "communicator of information" continuously throughout history, instead of just at one particular point as in Polkinghorne's model. This fits with the Christian doctrine of *creatio continua*, or the idea that God sustains creation through his regular and active faithfulness to the created world. Peacocke does not indicate whether he is operating under the paradigm of chaos theory or quantum mechanics, but his use fits either theory. Peacocke, like Polkinghorne, argues that his description of the interaction between information and the created world by God also allows for individual human freedom (1979, 103–05). The metaphor Peacocke uses to describe the interaction between God and the created world, in particular humanity, is of a composer and individual musicians. While the composer, analogous to God, writes the notes, he leaves space for embellishments, tonal differences, artistic expression, and other such freedoms on the part of musicians, his creation (107).

Despite their claims to the contrary, both Polkinghorne's and Peacocke's integration of information into theology lapse into either Deism, which Polkinghorne explicitly states he wishes to avoid, or determinism, for Peacocke. Christian theologians, in general, seek to avoid Deism, the belief that God created the universe, but does not intervene in it since creation, instead allowing it to run in a manner akin to a watchmaker winding up a watch. A major reason for the rejection of Deism is that it runs counter to the very notion of an incarnation and resurrection of God, *the* core doctrines for most Christians. While certain denominations may dispense with the notion of an interventionist God, that is a God who exerts a causal influence in our day-to-day lives, such as through the answering of prayer, most will still require some form of incarnation or resurrection, which necessitate the involvement of God in human history beyond the initial creative act. Again, while it is possible to point to those denominations that dispense with the idea of "miracle" generally and adopt a more humanist approach to the person of Jesus, these are not commitments that either Polkinghorne or Peacocke are ready to abandon.

Furthermore, a purely deistic approach would require the abandonment of human freedom, and with it moral culpability because it assumes that the universe continues on its causal path as a result of the initial act of creation and not through the doctrine of *creatio continua*, the continuous creation or God's act of sustaining his created world. This has to do, in part, with the nature of contingency, and in part with the nature of causation. Deism assumes that each cause necessarily leads to another, and thus the universe is sustained by physical laws that, in effect, amount to a deterministic universe. In order to avoid determinism, from a religious perspective one must argue for a contingent universe that is not governed by causal laws in this fashion, but are sustained by the faithfulness of God to that creation. Simply put, Deism requires a deterministic universe, while an interventionist picture of God does not.

For Polkinghorne, it seems rather clear that his approach, self-described as "top-down," lapses into the Deism he sought to avoid. Polkinghorne's only defense, given preemptively, against the criticism of Deism is to state that theologians are too quick to label theories deistic (1991: 46). Noting that theologians are cautious with regard to Deism, though, does not change the fact that Polkinghorne's use of information theory amounts to Deism. It is difficult to see how it could not be Deism when God, as *logos*, inserts pure information into the world and, with the exception of the later incarnation of the *logos*, wherein the *logos* bears no resemblance to his creative self, performs no other interaction with the *cosmos*, leaving the universe to operate according to a causally directed path. It may not technically be Deism, but its deistic tendencies make it functionally indistinguishable in many respects.

A "bottom-up" approach may have prevented this issue, but Polkinghorne indicates that he believes this would lapse into a form of panentheism. A "bottom-up" approach to causation in the universe requires a contingent, and therefore non-deistic response, because it means that God works from within creation and in cooperation with it, rather than directly guiding it (see below). Of course, this may lead to issues with God's sovereignty, such that it could mean that God does not necessarily achieve the goals he wants since his causal actions are one among many causal actions and thus is input into a broader system. However, this problem is slightly mitigated when one considers that God is conceived of as infinite, in respect to time, presence, and substance, and so it is possible for him to guide the system toward the ends and goals he desires should it be necessary.

What is potentially problematic, at least from Polkinghorne's perspective, is the problem of panentheism, which is the concept of theism, related to but distinct from pantheism, that blurs the line between created thing and creator such that, in its naïve form, all of the physical universe is contained within God, but God is more than the universe, whereas pantheism suggests that God simply *is* the physical universe. There are myriad definitions of pan*en*theism, some of which attempt to sustain a measure of distinction between God and the physical universe. For Polkinghorne, however, panentheism necessarily blurs all distinction and thus denies the sovereignty and transcendence of God. Yet there is no reason to suspect this is the case other than the fact that we are told, by critics of panentheism, that this is so. While it does call into question the doctrine of the immutability of God, the doctrine that God does not change in any way, this idea itself has long been linked with Deism and determinism (Torrance 2005: 8). Not only this, during the twentieth century, in response to a variety of developments from process theology to relativity physics to the Holocaust, the concepts of immutability and impassibility, the doctrine that God does not feel anything and is seen as an extension of impassibility, have been largely abandoned (Bauckham 1984). This is not to say it has been completely abandoned, and certainly among certain reformed and Eastern Orthodox denominations the ideas of immutability remains strong. However, even here, as in other doctrinal commitments, the doctrine has often been modified to remain in accordance with written creeds and councils, while allowing some nuance that does not require absolute adherence (e.g. God does not change in his essential character of faithfulness and love, though he may change in the sense that he is saddened or made glad).

For Peacocke, his application of information cannot avoid the determinism he claims to deny. If God is continually injecting information into a system, and God is omnipotent, no real freedom can be had. This is not the freedom of an orchestral musician in relation to a composer; this is the composer acting as director and all instrumentalists in a one-man band, or a prisoner who is told she or he is free to look at whichever wall she or he wishes. Peacocke was unaware, in his application of PI, that even the chance changes to a system that occur within quantum or chaos theory are not entirely casual, particularly when these are the result of a change in the information input into that system. Later research has demonstrated that information infused reactions in chaos theory models is highly deterministic (Wildman and Russell 1996: 49–92). Given this, it seems that both Polkinghorne's and Peacocke's applications of PI necessarily lead to determinism. There may be another way for philosophers of religion to engage PI while still avoiding determinism.

In Wolfhart Pannenberg's theology, the primary engagement with scientific thought is in reference to field theory. Nevertheless, his work is germane to the present chapter because, on two occasions when he gives an extended treatment of the theological implications of field theory, he also advocates that field theory can find its strongest application within theology only when applied in tandem with information theory (Pannenberg 1981: 75, 1994: 109). Pannenberg's use of field theory and the possible way forward for a "field theory of information" as he terms it cannot be covered by this chapter (see Medley 2013), but one particular aspect of his use of information is particularly helpful and deserves to be outlined.

In contrast to Polkinghorne and Peacocke, who both argue for "top-down" causation, Pannenberg is unique in his push for a "bottom-up" causation. God, for Pannenberg, does not impact the world from outside it, but from within it, so much so that he "has made himself dependent upon the course of history" rather than being the master of it (Pannenberg 1988: 329). Also unique to Pannenberg's approach, though not elaborated by him, is his insistence that the *logos* is not identical to information, as in most treatments of the subject, but one who has access to, and uses all information. The coupling of PI with philosophical theology, then, is done as an extension of God's omniscience, which seems entirely natural, and not as an ontological application.

While a "bottom-up" approach to divine causation, particularly one as extreme as Pannenberg's, may allow for a complete integration of PI within philosophical theology, it may jeopardize certain formulations of the doctrine of divine foreknowledge, though if formulated carefully in light of the doctrines of the Trinity and eternity, this may be preserved in some form. Perhaps more troubling, at least to Pannenberg and Polkingorne, is that it might almost certainly lead to panentheism, though Pannenberg denies that it does actually cross into panentheism (1994: 111–112). The extent to which Pannenberg is successful in avoiding panentheism is debatable, though panentheism is not, as discussed above, necessarily counter to orthodoxy.

It seems, then, that at this point we are left with three options when discussing the spiritual value of information. The first option is that PI and religion are simply incompatible, which is the least attractive of the three. The second is that the "top-down" approaches to divine causality must be reconceptualized if there is to be any fruitful dialogue between religion and PI. The third, and perhaps most attractive option, is to assume a "bottom-up" approach to divine causality and unite this with PI. In the third approach, God must be understood to operate from *within* the universe rather than act *upon* the universe. While this third option is one area where there is strong potential for further research, it is by no means the only one.

Next steps

Outside of the gross misuse of information theory highlighted at the beginning of the chapter, there has been comparatively little interaction between PI and philosophical theology. Despite this, there are clearly areas where additional research can occur. These areas include interaction with other, non-Christian religions, addressing issues of transhumanism, artificial intelligence, and its relation to religion, and even questions of religious epistemology.

Although most interactions between PI and religion have been within the realm of Christianity, this is not the only area of potential impact. While some attempt has been made to relate PI directly to religions other than Christianity, this has largely been done in the context of "information ethics" (Floridi 2008: 193), which was addressed in Chapter 30, and is not necessarily religious in context. Still, it seems that a good starting point would be to examine the wisdom traditions of other religions.

In Judaism, there is a strong wisdom tradition, and while some Jewish sects may conflate wisdom exclusively with the "fear of the LORD,"[1] there is clearly another tradition of wisdom as an intellectual virtue, extending at least as far back to the written portions of the *TaNaKh* (Hebrew Bible) concerning Solomon, and the *Míshlê* (Proverbs) frequently reference wisdom personified as a woman who gives insight to others. In Islam, wisdom is also an important concept, though its use in Islam is not as frequent as in Judaism nor is it as developed as the Christian expression of the *logos*. Confucianism and most forms of Hinduism also have strong elements of wisdom and it may be beneficial to draw connections to PI here as well. Where it becomes less clear is with most forms of Buddhism that understand wisdom negatively, as the emptying of the mind. It may not be possible to connect PI as directly with these religious contexts. Whether this can be done successfully remains to be seen. Yet, PI is not limited in its interaction with religion to specific religious contexts.

One area of rapidly growing interest in philosophy of religion, among other fields, is the nature of transhumanism. While still relatively new, if the claims of proponents of transhumanism, which is founded upon informational and technological principles, are true this has serious religious implications. It may be that the driving motivation behind transhumanism is due to a loss of religious sensibility. In other words, the loss of the concept of an afterlife or something beyond the physical world leads to a crisis in modern humanity where they must find another avenue to respond to the "longing for transcendence," that has been otherwise lost (Eppinette 2007, 192). Many of the questions raised by transhumanism are also tied with the place of AI, or Artificial Intelligence, since transhumanism is predicated upon some concept of "posthumanism" that necessitates a tie to advanced AI, particularly the "singularity," where AI becomes so advanced it begins to be self-learning, advancing its knowledge exponentially (Bostrom 2003, n.p.). While current "transhumanists," those who advocate for transhumanism, do not necessarily demand that the singularity of AI occur prior to "posthumanism," the next evolutionary step toward which transhumanism is in transition (World Transhumanist Association 2015, n.p.), most of their ideas still require a serious reconsideration of AI in relation to personhood before transhumanism or posthumanism could become reality and widely adopted (Jersild 2009: 97–99). Given that this is the case, we do well to briefly consider the role of AI in this discussion.

The main issue for discussing AI, or transhumanism for that matter, in a religious context is in light of a theological or a philosophical anthropology. The Vatican has, for instance, directly addressed whether non-human biological organisms, such as intelligent extraterrestrial beings, can be thought of as having a soul that is redeemable, a concept that could well translate to most other religious traditions, but no religious groups has extended a similar official statement to the realm of AI and transhumanism/posthumanism, with some even issuing statements against this thought (Zaimov 2014, n.p.; Madrid Declaration on Science and Life).

Yet, for Ian Barbour, if there is a conflict it is not a question of mere reductionism, as in some conceptions of ETR above, for much of current work in "symbolic AI tries to explain all cognition in terms of information, but it is not necessarily physicalist or reductionist because information is not reducible to the laws of physics" (Barbour 2002: 84). While it is true that information, being neither matter nor energy, is not bound to the laws of space-time in the same way other observable facts are, it is a bit disingenuous to argue that reducing cognition to the symbolic logic utilized by AI does not amount to a form of reductionism. John Searle somewhat famously responded to this question in his "Chinese Room" thought experiment, which he helpfully summarizes elsewhere by noting that AI can only process syntax. While syntax is a useful component of cognition, to truly "think" and thus to be truly human, semantics is required which will remain beyond the grasp of AI (Searle 1984: 39–41). Of course, Searle's response is far from controversial, and there have been numerous counter arguments to it (see, for instance, Boden 1988: 238–251; Rosenthal 1991: 525, among others).

Perhaps more pertinent to this discussion are Puddefoot's comments that "to be regarded as something approaching the human ... it would need to be finite, aware of its finitude, and condemned one day to die" (1996b: 92). While, on the one hand, this draws in questions as to whether it is possible to conceive of life after death, heaven, a Samsara cycle that includes rebirth, if one is immortal (or an immortal intelligence), Puddefoot's comments point to a more fundamental question of anthropology. Drawing on Herder, Heidegger and others, most philosophical anthropologies, at least as concerns those in the continental tradition, consider finiteness, specifically as it concerns limited time, to be a requisite for humanity. Even here, though, we cannot completely preclude identities identified as AI or "posthuman," for the universe itself is not eternal. Granted the scale of time is exponentially larger than we may be able to speak of sensibly given our current awareness of our own self-finitude, it does not mean that there is no awareness of the finitude, and eventual end, to the universe itself.

In other words we might seriously wonder whether the evangelical Christian could declare that "Jesus died for robots" or that a "posthuman" might consider himself to be a Hindu. Deeper seeded questions arise with respect to our relation to the divine, but even if we allow that AI and posthumanism of the sort that is normally discussed is entirely possible, it does not necessitate that either category constitutes a being that is immortal. While not matter or energy, information that is conscious in this way is still connected to either matter or energy, or at the very least requires a context that includes matter and energy as we know it, and as such the religious question is not entirely abandoned, though it may change in some respects.

Finally, one additional area worth mentioning, one in which there also been very little direct research, is religious epistemology. While religious epistemology as its own topic deserves extensive treatment, it is sufficient for this chapter to note that religious epistemology is concerned with whether a belief in God or a set of particular beliefs about God can be justified, or needs to be justified. Current debates tend to focus on Alvin Plantinga's reformed epistemology, which examines the possibility of "groundless beliefs," arguing that certain types of beliefs, including religious ones, need no justification. For Plantinga, reformed epistemology is a coopting of John Calvin's *Sensus Divinitatus*, which was Calvin's response to the non-universality of Christian belief. Calvin argued that certain people were simply born with a unique sense of God and God's presence, similar to other senses, that cannot be properly explained to those lacking it. Similarly Plantinga argues that religious beliefs, and possibly other beliefs, are also "properly basic" and need no justification, only to be demonstrated as rationally held (see Plantinga 1967 and 2000). As such it is a rejection of evidentialist and inference-based epistemologies that require justification for belief. Since Plantinga is more concerned with determining the "reasonable-ness" of belief, assuming it is already held, and less concerned with giving an evidentialist or inference-based approach to religious belief, his work may have little connection with PI. But this is not the only avenue with respect to religious epistemology.

In the early part of this chapter, we saw that PI cannot directly respond to the question of God's existence, yet it may play a role, together with the broader work on PI and epistemology discussed in Chapter 27, to contribute to a new discussion on religious epistemology. In particular we might consider pairing Wittgenstein's "language games" within a religious context to communicate a religious syntax to outsiders given the appropriate information. If information is guided by context, and Wittgenstein's discussion of the "rules" of language games are similarly guided by context, we might perhaps understand the syntactical hoops that one religious community utilizes to describe a religious experience (see Schönbaumsfeld 2015: 72).

This might find application in the modification of evidentialism provided by John Henry Newman, who argues that religious evidentialism should be held to a similar standard that other decisions are made. If one is justified in choosing to bring an umbrella, for instance, one might be justified for deciding in favor of God if the criteria for belief are similar, although the scale is much different (Newman 1898: 250–276). While this is a bit of an oversimplification, it gets to the heart of the matter: absolute proof is not deemed the standard in non-religious decisions as being justified or not, so there is little reason it should be the standard for religious decisions. However, the evidence for or against a religious decision is often private to the individual. If it were possible to translate the informational content of the religious syntax in a blending of Wittgenstein and PI, under the criteria for religious epistemology from Newman, a profitable dialogue concerning religious belief and epistemology might be possible. Again, this is an area that needs further investigation.

Conclusion

Despite the misapplication of information theory to religious concerns has been common, particularly with the ID movement and, to a lesser extent, with evolutionary theory of religion, there have been some strong initial forays exploring the connection between PI and religion. Polkinghorne and Peacocke may not have accomplished exactly what they wished to accomplish with their use of information theory within philosophical theology, but their works have shown some potential for further developments, particularly with respect to transhumanism, artificial intelligence, religious epistemology, and speaking of PI in non-Western or non-Christian, but still religious, contexts. Considering that PI is relatively recent in its formulation as a discrete subject of philosophical inquiry, there may be numerous other problems within the philosophy of religion where the application of PI may prove fruitful.

Note

1   Readers will notice the intentional use of the four capital letters for the English translation of Hebrew name for God. This is somewhat standard practice for translating the sacred name of God in a Jewish context; the name is not generally pronounced, and is comprised of four consonants, collectively referred to as the *Tetragrammaton*. The use of the English word "lord" is selected because of the Hebrew word (transliterated "*Adonai*") that corresponds to the vowel pointing in the Masoretic text of the Hebrew and pronounced in the place of the personal name for God.

References

Allen, C. and M. Hauser. (1992) "Communication and Cognition: Is Information the Connection?" *PSA* 2: pp. 81–91.

Bak, P. (1997) *How Nature Works: The Science of Self-Organized Criticality*, Oxford: Oxford University Press.

Barbour, I. (2002) *Nature, Human Nature, and God Minneapolis*, MN: Fortress Press.

Barrett, N. (2010) "Toward an Alternative Evolutionary Theory of Religion: Looking Past Computational Evolutionary Psychology to a Wider Field of Possibilities." *JAAR*. 78: pp. 583–621.

Baukham, R. (1984) "'Only the Suffering God Can Help': Divine Passibility in Modern Theology." *Themelios* 9:3, 6–12.

Behe, M. (1996) *Darwin's Black Box: The Biochemical Challenge to Evolution*, New York: Free Press, 1996.

Boden, M. (1988) *Computer Models of the Mind*, Cambridge: Cambridge University Press.

Bostrom, N. (2003) "Transhumanism FAQ: A General Introduction," World Transhumanist Association. Available online (only) http://www.transhumanism.org/resources/faw/html (accessed September 1, 2005). URL no longer active, all content has been shifted and substantially modified and updated to humanityplus.org URL.

Checkland, P. and J. Scholes. (1990) *Soft Systems Methodology in Action*. Hoboken, NJ: Wiley.

Churchland, P. C. Koch, and T. Sejnowski. (1993) "What is Computational Neuroscience?" in E. Schwartz (ed.), *Computational Neuroscience*, Cambridge, MA: MIT Press, pp. 46–55.

Davis, W. and D. Kenyon. (1989) C. Thaxton (ed.), *Of Pandas and People: The Central Question of Biological Origins*, Dallas, TX: The Foundation for Thought and Ethics.

Dembski, W. (1998a) The Design Inference: Eliminating Chance through Small Probabilities, *Cambridge Studies in Probability, Induction and Decision Theory*, Cambridge: Cambridge University Press.

Dembski, W. (August 10, 1998b) "The Act of Creation: Bridging Transcendence and Immanence," Center for Science and Culture, Seattle, WA: Discovery Institute. Available online http://www.discovery.org/a/119 Accessed 08/01/2014.

Dembski, W. (1998c) "Intelligent Design as a Theory of Information." Available online http://www.arn.org/docs/dembski/wd_idtheory.htm Accessed 09/10/14.

Dembski, W. (2002) *No Free Lunch: Why Specified Complexity Cannot Be Purchased without Intelligence*, Lanham, MD: Rowman and Littlefield.

Eppinette, M. (2007). "Human 2.0: Transhumanism as a cultural trend." *Everyday Theology: How to read Cultural Texts and Interpret Trends*. Grand Rapids, MI: Baker Academic, 191-207.

Floridi, L. (2005) "Is Semantic Information Meaningful Data?" *Philosophy and Phenomenological Research* 70: pp. 351–370.

Floridi, L. (2008) "Information Ethics: A reappraisal." *Ethics and Information Technology* 10: pp. 189–204.

Floridi, L. (2010) "Information, Possible Worlds, and the Cooptation of Scepticism," *Synthese* 175: pp. 63–88.

Gregerson, N. H. (2002) "Beyond the Balance, Theology in a Self-Organizing World," in N. H. Gregerson and U. Görman (eds.), *Design and Disorder: Perspectives from Science and Theology*, London: T&T Clark, pp. 53–92.

Jersild, P. (2009) *The Nature of Our Humanity: A Christian Response to Evolution and Biotechnology*, Minneapolis, MN: Fortress Press.

Kant, I. (1919) *Critique of Pure Reason*, transl. by F. M. Müller, 2nd ed., New York: The Macmillan Company.

Lennox, J. (2007) "Intelligent Design: Some Critical Reflections on the Current Debate," in R. Stewart (ed.), *Intelligent Design*, Minneapolis, MN: Fortress Press, pp. 179–195.

López-Moratalla, N. and M. Cerezo (2011) "The Self-Construction of a Living Organism," in G. Terzis and R. Arp (eds.), *Information and Living Systems: Philosophical and Scientific Perspectives*, Cambridge, MA: MIT Press, pp. 177–204.

Madrid Declaration on Science and Life. Issued in cooperation with the World Federation of the Catholic Medical Association. Available online http://www.fiamc.org/bioethics/madrid-declaration-on-science-life/ Accessed 18 May 2015.

Medley, III, G. (2013) "The Inspiration of God and Wolfhart Pannenberg's 'Field Theory of Information'," *Zygon: Journal of Science and Religion*, 48: pp. 93–106.

Newman, J. H. (1898) *Fifteen Sermons Preached before Oxford University*, London: Longmans.

Pannenberg, W. (1981) "Theological Questions to Scientists," *Zygon: Journal of Science and Religion*, 16: pp. 65–77.

Pannenberg, W. (1988) *Systematic Theology, Vol. 1*, translated by G. W. Bromiley, Edinburgh: T&T Clark.

Pannenberg, W. (1994) *Systematic Theology, Vol. 2*, translated by G. W. Bromiley, Edinburgh: T&T Clark.

Peacocke, A. (1979) *Creation and the World of Science*, Oxford: Clarendon Press.

Plantinga, A. (1967) *God and Other Minds: A Study of the Rational Justification of Belief in God*. Ithaca, NY: Cornell University Press.

Plantinga, A. (2000) *Warranted Christian Belief*, Oxford: Oxford University Press.

Polkinghorne, J. (1991) *Reason and Reality*, Philadelphia, PA: Trinity International Press.

Puddefoot, J. (1996a). "Information Theory, Biology, and Christology," in W. Richardson and W. Wildman (eds), *Religion and Science: History, Method, Dialogue*, New York: Routledge, pp. 301–20.

Puddefoot, J. (1996b) *God and the Mind Machine: Computers, Artificial Intelligence, and the Human Soul*, London: SPCK.

Rosenthal, D. (1991) *The Nature of Mind*, Oxford and New York: Oxford University Press.

Ryle, A. (2005) "The Relevance of Evolutionary Psychology for Psychotherapy," *The British Journal of Psychotherapy* 21: pp. 375–388.

Saunders, N. (2002) *Divine Action and Modern Science*, Cambridge: Cambridge University Press.

Searle, J. (1984) *Minds, Brain and Science*, Cambridge, MA: Harvard University Press.

Schönbaumsfeld, G. (2015) "Wittgensteinian Approaches to Religion," in G. Oppy (ed.), *The Routledge Handbook of Contemporary Philosophy of Religion*, Abingdon: Routledge, pp. 63–73.

Tooby, J. and L. Cosmides (2005) "Conceptual Foundations of Evolutionary Psychology," in D. Buss (ed.), *The Handbook of Evolutionary Psychology*, Hoboken, NJ: John Wiley & Sons, Inc., pp. 5–67.

Torrance, T. F. (2005) *Divine and Contingent Order*, Edinburgh: T & T Clark.

Wildman, W. and R. J. Russell. (1996). "Chaos: A Mathematical Introduction with Philosophical Reflections," in R. J. Russell, N. Murphy, and A. Peacocke (eds.), *Chaos and Complexity: Scientific Perspectives on Divine Action*, Notre Dame, IN: University of Notre Dame Press, pp. 49–92.

World Transhumanist Association (2015) No Author "FAQs" Available online http://humanityplus.org/philosophy/transhumanist-faq (Accessed 18 May 2015).

Zaimov, S. (2014) "Pope Francis Talks about Aliens; Says He Would Welcome Martians to Receive Baptism." Available online http://www.christianpost.com/news/pope-francis-talks-about-aliens-says-he-would-welcome-martians-to-receive-baptism-119630/ (Accessed 18 May 2015).

INDEX

Page numbers followed by *n* indicate note numbers.

Printed in Great Britain
by Amazon

42252106R00249